Canadian Social Welfare

FIFTH EDITION

GENERAL EDITORS

Joanne C. Turner
Professor Emerita, Renison College, University of Waterloo

Francis J. Turner
Professor Emeritus, Wilfrid Laurier University

PEARSON

Toronto

Library and Archives Canada Cataloguing in Publication

Canadian social welfare / general editors, Joanne C.
Turner, Francis J. Turner. — 5th ed.

Includes bibliographical references and index.
ISBN 0-205-42863-0

1. Public welfare—Canada. 2. Social service—Canada.
3. Canada—Social policy. I. Turner, Joanne C., 1934–
II. Turner, Francis J. (Francis Joseph), 1929–

HV105.C28 2005   361.971   C2004-905630-1

ISBN 0-205-42863-0

Vice President, Editorial Director: Michael J. Young
Acquisitions Editor: Patty Riediger
Sponsoring Editor: Carolin Sweig
Executive Marketing Manager: Judith Allen
Associate Editor: Paula Drużga
Production Editors: Martin Tooke, Kevin Leung
Proofreader: Laurel Sparrow
Production Coordinator: Janis Raisen
Page Layout: Heidi Palfrey
Cover Design: Lisa Lapointe
Cover Image: Luc Beziat (Gettyimages)

3 4 5   09 08 07 06

Printed and bound in the USA.

Contents

Foreword

This fifth edition of *Canadian Social Welfare* provides a much-needed framework for an overdue national dialogue and a rethink.

Following World War II, our social safety net evolved more our less in sync with Mary Wollstonecraft's vision that what we "need is not more charity, but more justice." As Canadians, we've tended to be self-congratulatory about the superiority of our system over that of our U.S. neighbours, while ignoring the more progressive and comprehensive social welfare systems of many European countries. This was reinforced, in my case, by a year's social work graduate study in New England in the late sixties, followed by another, working in the barely existent social welfare "system" in Texas. If ever justified, any basis for Canadian smugness evaporated in the 1990s with the federal assaults on public funding, public programs, and public entitlement.

No clear Canadian consensus exists, but the evidence is strong that our citizens are generally more compassionate, more generous, and more concerned about enhancing our social welfare system and our social solidarity, than are most politicians of the day.

Citizens and politicians alike will benefit from Joanne and Frank Turner's introduction to Canadian social welfare, which chronicles our history, and formulates our challenges. Wide ranging perspectives from the level of the individual through to global family, shared by 42 policy analysts and practitioners, will enrich the debates about where Canada goes from here. Let's get started.

Alexa McDonough M.P.

Preface

Developing this volume through its now fifth edition continues to be a most interesting odyssey for us. As we mentioned in the preface to the first edition, in 1980, our original purpose in preparing this text was to serve three audiences: the beginning student in social welfare, the committed volunteer, and the inquiring citizen who wishes to know more about the field. It is clear now that the work has emerged over the years as more of a textbook for students than as a resource for the other two groups of readers. This fact, of course, has shaped it in such a way that ensures it meets the needs of students at both the university and the college levels.

As the book targets more and more the students across the land our academic colleagues perceive its usefulness very differently. Those of us who have spent a large part of our lives in the academic world of our profession know that a text rarely answers all of our individual needs and wants in the various courses we teach. Nearly always we have our own suggestions about how to improve a book. Our publishers are aware of this, and for each edition have conducted a survey across Canada seeking suggestions for those changes and improvements. The suggestions are not always consistent one with the other or with our shared perspectives. However, as editors, we have considered each submitted to us carefully. Individually and together all of them have influenced the modifications we introduce into each edition, including this, the fifth one.

Similarly, those who speak for the profession in its many facets across Canada have themselves changed, as reflected in *Canadian Social Welfare*. All the chapters' authors bring to their topics different perspectives on the phenomenon of social welfare we are discussing. Thus as the authors who write the various chapters have changed, so too do the perspectives they present.

Of the first edition's original 25 authors, excluding the two editors, only seven contribute to this most recent edition's 33 chapters; these numbers contrast with the 26 authors and chapters of that first edition. Some of the authors not included in the fifth edition have passed on and others, for various reasons, have elected not to write. As the field has developed, too, new authorities and spokespersons have emerged for various areas of social welfare practice.

The book also reflects developments within the social welfare system. As the content of the chapters is modified, as some topics are dropped and others added, what remains reflects the current reality, frequently cited in the text, that social welfare in Canada is a dynamic field in which the changes are multi-faceted and multi-influenced. So the need for new editions of texts like this one shall be ongoing.

Lastly, the content of this edition reflects a kind of quality peculiar to Canada and all of us who live here. We refer to Canada's unique place in the world. Every day, all of us as citizens, regardless of our interests and expertise, recognize this quality, that even though we exist as an individual, autonomous, and separate nation, we acknowledge our role in the global economy. We both influence and are influenced by the complexities of world developments. In the previous edition, our awareness of this dichotomy led us to add a chapter by Dr. Glenn Drover on Canada's place in terms of globalization. Dr. Drover updates this topic in this edition. In fact, this subject is addressed repeatedly and updated in several chapters of this edition.

Virtually all the chapters have been updated or rewritten. As well, we have added another new chapter, written by Dr. Dan Andreae, on legislative control and social work.

Some things, however, have not changed since the 2001 edition. The book continues to recognize, understand, and expand on the importance of sturdy safety nets of social welfare in all countries, regardless of the ideology and political structures influencing them. The book demonstrates the growing understanding that Canadian social welfare is a unique structure in the ways that it differs from its counterparts in other countries in both its strengths and weaknesses. As we continue to study social welfare as it develops around the world, as indeed we must, we want to remember that our system is unique and should be understood on its own terms.

We conclude on the same theme on which we ended in the preface of the fourth edition. One of the defining facts of Canada is its bilingual structure, a framework that in so many essential ways has shaped the image of modern Canadian social welfare. The argument that a book such as this, especially a textbook in the field, should exist in both languages is self-evident. However, as the text nears its twenty-fifth anniversary, a full quarter of a century since its initial publication, it has not been possible to reach this goal—yet.

As we continue our journey into the new millennium, we do so in the awareness that Canadian social welfare will continue to evolve. Those responsible for its ongoing development must continue to study it, debate it, and explicate it.

Acknowledgments

As the process continues of preparing further editions of this text, the writing of an acknowledgment paragraph, the final phase of the task, becomes increasingly difficult. Of course one is grateful to the colleagues who have participated and responded politely and supportively to the ongoing reminders and nudgings regarding the realities of deadlines. Their work and input are naturally the essence of the piece. In particular we are appreciative of the assistance of Carlos Pereira, our research assistant, who contributed greatly to the logistics and organization of the work flow.

Although much more in the background than with earlier editions, our family are ever present, ever curious, and ever supportive. One very different facet of which we are very conscious in this edition is the place of technology. Of course technology is the new reality of publishing. The various aspects of these constant and increasingly necessary communication resources have both facilitated and sped up the process of information exchange. We have all reached the point where we now expect responses to queries and requests not in a few days but rather in a few minutes. However, as in earlier editions, Canada Post still plays a crucial role. The quantity of hard copy correspondence has decreased, yet the number of trips to the local postal station for one or the other of us has not. As deadlines drew near, too, we still received material late in the day by hand to the front door or through the mail slot. In particular we are grateful to the students across the country who have found this work useful and whose questions and concerns have contributed to identifying needed areas for updating as the months and years go by.

To all, we are grateful!

J. C. Turner
F. J. Turner
May 2004

Supplements

Canadian Social Welfare, Fifth Edition, will be supplemented by a **Test Item File** and **PowerPoint Slides**.

Both supplements can be downloaded by instructors from a password-protected location on Pearson Education Canada's online catalogue (**vig.pearsoned.ca**). Simply search for the text, then click on "Instructor" under "Resources" in the lefthand menu. Contact your local sales representative for further information.

Contributors

Dr. Dan Andreae is a professor at the University of Waterloo, Renison College, and also at the University of Guelph/Humber, where he was recently selected as a professor of the year. Dr. Andreae has been the executive director of agencies including an organization that provides national eating-disorders information at Toronto hospitals and also was the first executive director of the Alzheimer Society for Metropolitan Toronto. He is the longest serving president of the Ontario Association of Social Workers (OASW), from 1993 to 2000, where he successfully led a campaign to achieve statutory regulation. Dr. Andreae has received numerous awards for his contributions, including CASW Social Worker of the Year, Wilfrid Laurier University Alumnus of the Year, and the Governor General's Commemorative Medal.

Dr. Ken Barter is a professor in the School of Social Work, Memorial University of Newfoundland. From September 1998 to April 2004 he held the chair of Child Protection. His years of experience in public child welfare, combined with his academic research, support his belief that services to children and families must be reconceived if public child welfare systems are to respond to the many challenges of contemporary society.

Mel Basbaum is a private practitioner in Hamilton, Ontario. He was formerly director of social work at the Chedoke Hospital and McMaster University Medical Centre and assistant clinical professor at McMaster University, Department of Psychiatry. He is a board member on several voluntary agencies that serve the disabled.

Dr. Francois H. Bilodeau was involved in the planning, implementation, and evaluation of French-language social services for more than 30 years, through his full-time professional activities as a clinical supervisor, program manager, university professor, and private consultant. Now retired, he is focusing his love of nature on environmental projects.

Rose Blackmore received her MSW from the University of Toronto and the advanced diploma in Social Work from Columbia University. She held practice and administrative positions with the Ontario Ministry of Community, Family and Social Services in vocational rehabilitation and staff development. She joined the Faculty of Social Work at Wilfrid Laurier University, Waterloo, Ontario, in 1970 where she taught in the clinical stream. Currently she is involved in a variety of community agencies in the Kitchener-Waterloo area, including the Mid-Western Branch of the Ontario Association of Social Workers.

Catherine Brothers received her MSW from Waterloo Lutheran University and has been practising social work for more than 35 years in a range of social work settings. Currently, she is the executive director of the Catholic Family Counselling Centre in Kitchener, Ontario, a major provider of Employee Assistance Programs. For more than 20 years she was a sessional lecturer in Family Studies at the University of Guelph. She has also served on a range of hospital, association, service club, and, social service boards of directors.

John Brothers received his MSW from Waterloo Lutheran University and his MBA from the same institution, which had become Wilfrid Laurier University by that time. John is a psychogeriatric specialist at Cambridge Memorial Hospital, Ontario. He has extensive clinical practice experience in Employee Assistance Programs, as well as in adult and forensic psychiatry. He has also served on the Ontario Review Board and the National Parole Board and has taught at the University of Guelph and Wilfrid Laurier University in Ontario.

Dr. Carole Pigler Christensen is a professor and a former director of the University of British Columbia's School of Social Work. She chaired the Task Force on Multicultural and Multiracial Issues in Social Work Education of the Canadian Association of Schools of Social

Work. This led to accreditation standards that take these issues into account. She initiated and serves as program director of the Vancouver-based Multicultural Family Centre, and she has published extensively in multicultural and anti-racist social work, the focus of her research, practice, and teaching for many years.

Melanie Cohen earned her BSW from York University. Her professional interests are clinical practice in the area of psychosocial adjustments, child welfare, and social policy. She actively volunteers with a group of psychiatrically disabled people.

John Cossom is Professor Emeritus, School of Social Work at the University of Victoria. He has also taught at Regina Saskatchewan, and at Waterloo and Wilfrid Laurier universities in Ontario. He practised in child welfare, family services, and corrections.

Dr. Roger Delaney is a professor of Social Work at Lakehead University, Thunder Bay. He has co-written *Canadian Social Policy: An Introduction* as well as co-edited five books on northern and rural social work. His main interests are social work/welfare philosophy and ethics, social policy and social welfare, rural and northern social work, poverty, organizational and community development, family violence, child welfare, and young offenders.

Yvon Dugas has an MSW from the University of Ottawa and has completed more than 30 years of social work practice. Beginning in the field of addictions, he went on to devote seven years to the planning and development of French-language services and spent 16 years as a professor in the French-language social work program at La cité collégiale in Ottawa.

Dr. Glenn Drover is an adjunct professor of the Maritime School of Social Work at Dalhousie University in Nova Scotia and the School of Social Work at Carleton University in Ottawa. Since his retirement he continues to teach for Dalhousie (on-line) and conducts research on social welfare issues. He previously taught at the City University of Hong Kong, the University of British Columbia, and McGill University. He has recently co-edited two books on globalization and its impact on social welfare: *The Privatization of Mandatory Private Income Protection* (2004) and *Regionalism and Subregionalism in East Asia* (2001). He pursues research interests mainly in social policy, social development, and social welfare theory.

Donald G. Evans is a former assistant deputy minister of Policing Services, Ministry of the Solicitor General (Ontario). He lectures in penology and policing at Woodsworth College, University of Toronto. He is president of the Canadian Training Institute in Toronto and a past president of the International Community Corrections Association and of the American Probation and Parole Association. He contributes a regular column to *Corrections Today*, published by the American Correctional Association.

Dr. Patricia M. Evans is an associate professor at Carleton University, Ottawa. Her writing and research focus on gender and the welfare state, with particular attention to income security issues. She co-edited *Women's Caring* (1998) and *Women and the Canadian Welfare State* (1997), and co-authored *Walking on Eggshells: Abused Women's Experiences of Ontario's Welfare System*, the first Canadian study to examine the impact of welfare reforms on women who are leaving abuse.

Kerri-Ann Fitzgerald, MSW, RSW, currently practises as a social worker in the Centre for Student Development at McMaster University in Hamilton. She provides counselling support to students with mental health, chronic medical, and hearing disabilities. She also works as a research assistant, focusing her current research on grandparenting and caregiving in long-term-care facilities.

Dr. James Gladstone is an associate professor in the School of Social Work at McMaster University. He has concentrated his research on grandparenting, the relationships of elderly couples, people's relocation to long-term care, and the relationship between formal and informal caregivers. He also conducts a private clinical practice with individuals, couples, and families.

Matthew Goodman is the principal consultant of Goodman & Associates, a consultancy firm that specializes in strategic planning, project management and implementation, community consultation, and evaluation in health and social services. He also sits on the boards of Affiliated Services for Children and Youth and Under the Willows.

Dr. John R. Graham is a professor of social work and the Murray Fraser professor of community economic development at the University of Calgary. He has published extensively on international social work, Canadian social policy, and social welfare history. He recently co-wrote *Canadian Social Policy: An Introduction* (2003, 2d edition) and co-edited *Multicultural Social Work in Canada* (2003).

Professor Sheila Hardy, Anishnaabe-Kwe from northern Ontario, is an associate professor in the Native Bachelor of Social Work program. There she teaches courses in Aboriginal research methodologies and community organizing and is currently editor for the next *Native Social Work Journal*. She has also held positions of coordinator and field/admissions coordinator for the program. She focuses her doctoral work on Aboriginal trauma, historical witness, and Aboriginal pedagogy.

Dr. Dorothy Chave Herberg, PhD, retired after teaching courses between 1973 and 1996 in the multicultural provision of social and other human services at the School of Social Work, York University, Toronto. Her widely used book, *Frameworks for Cultural and Racial Diversity*, was published in 1993.

Dr. Edward N. Herberg, PhD, retired from teaching sociology—mainly on ethnoracial communities in Canada and social inequality—at the University of Toronto from 1973 to 1999. He also taught social policy between 1974 and 1994 at the School of Social Work, York University, Toronto. His book *Ethnic Groups in Canada: Adaptations and Transformations* was published in 1989. The second edition, renamed *Ethno-Racial Communities in Canada: Adaptations and Transformations*, is forthcoming.

Dr. Rose Marie Jaco is Professor Emerita at the School of Social Work at King's College, University of Western Ontario. She is keenly interested in the delivery of social services and health care and the impact of the delivery method on clients' well-being. Dr. Jaco has served as a board member for several agencies over the years and strongly supports partnerships and collaboration among the various sectors of social welfare. She continues to teach and has a private practice in counselling and therapy.

Gayle Gilchrist James, MSW (University of Toronto), RSW (Alberta), has been an associate professor at the University of Calgary Faculty of Social Work since 1975. She has served as president of both the Alberta and the Canadian Associations of Social Workers, and was president of the International Federation of Social Workers for two terms, the first Canadian president of a provincial, national and international social work association. She is a former chair of the National Council of Welfare, a former board member of the Canadian Council of Social Development, and served for many years on the board of the Canadian Research Institute for Law and the Family.

Teri Kay, MSW, RSW is the director of Family and Community Service at Jewish Family & Child Service in Toronto. She is also a board member of Family Service Ontario and an accreditor and member of the accrediting committee of that body.

Dr. Dennis Kimberley, PhD, RSW, DAC, received his MSW from McGill University and his PhD from the University of Toronto. His practice has largely included addictions, mental health, child abuse and exploitation, sexual deviation and sex offending, and parents' capacity. He was a director with the Addiction Research Foundation of Ontario, 1968–1977 (now the Centre for Addiction and Mental Health). As executive director of the Canadian Association of Schools of Social Work from 1977 to 1985, he contributed to education policy, accreditation, and curriculum design. Since 1985 he has been a professor at the School of Social Work at Memorial University in Newfoundland and Labrador. He has been asked to conduct consulting, training, and board work provincially, nationally and internationally, and he has also represented Canada in many international arenas.

Dr. Brigitte Kitchen is an associate professor of Social Work at York University, Toronto. She is active in the community and has chaired the Centre for Social Justice and PEACH (Promoting Economic and Community Health). From 1990 to 1993, she was a commissioner of the Ontario Fair Tax Commission. She has written many articles on the issues of social policies affecting the living standards and quality of life of families that are raising children.

Dr. Ross A. Klein teaches research methods at the School of Social Work, Memorial University in Newfoundland. He has conducted research in a variety of areas, including child abuse prevention, women and addictions, and community-based treatment for chronic psychiatric patients. His work on employability enhancement has led to the development of innovative programs for the transition from social assistance to work. Currently he focuses his research on children in care. He has also written three books about the cruise ship industry.

Dr. Roland Lecomte is a retired full professor and founding director of the School of Social Work at the University of Ottawa. He is the founding director of the new Gerontology program at that same university. He has written and co-written several publications on social work education and evaluative research. His recent work concentrates on epistemological issues in the development of knowledge and identity in social work. The Canadian Association of Schools of Social Work awarded him an honorary life membership for his outstanding contributions to social work education.

Dr. Grant Macdonald received his doctorate from the Faculty of Social Work, University of Toronto, in 1982. He is currently an associate professor at the School of Social Work, York University, Toronto, where he teaches research methodology at the graduate and undergraduate levels. Two research areas he is currently pursuing are the impact of SARS on social work practice and an evaluation of a program for youth who are suspended or expelled as a result of Ontario's "Zero Tolerance Policy" in schools.

Dr. Frank McGilly, who obtained his PhD from the University of Pittsburgh, retired in 1997 from the McGill University School of Social Work after many years' service as professor and director. He is the author of *An Introduction to Canada's Public Social Services* (2d edition, 1998).

Dr. Anne-Marie Mawhiney is dean of the Faculty of Professional Schools and professor of social work at Laurentian University in Sudbury, Ontario. She is a former director of the school and of the Institute for Northern Ontario Research and Development.

Dr. Ramesh Mishra is a Professor Emeritus at the School of Social Work, York University, Toronto. His interests are in comparative social policy and the political economy of social welfare. His books include *The Welfare State in Capitalist Society* (1990), *Globalization and the Welfare State* (1999), and, as co-editor, *Modernizing the Korean Welfare State* (2004).

Louise Osmond, MSW, RSW, received her BSW and MSW from Memorial University in Newfoundland. She has worked in children's rehabilitation and social work in schools and has been in private practice since 1993. She has also taught child abuse assessment and intervention and has presented papers nationally and internationally. Her areas of expertise include sexualized and traumatized children; sibling incest; sex offending and sexual deviation; victims of domestic violence and sexual assault; assessment and treatment of trauma; treatment of addicted and dual disordered persons; and treatment-integrated foster care.

Dr. Barbara Decker Pierce is an assistant professor in the School of Social Work at King's College of the University of Western Ontario. Before entering academia she worked in program design and delivery for Ontario's Ministry of Community and Social Services. She focuses her research on organizational issues in the human service sector, specifically leadership and organizational structure. She is also particularly interested in research as it applies to evidence-based service delivery.

Dr. William Rowe is a professor and the director of the School of Social Work at the University of South Florida. He holds appointments in the College of Public Health, the AIDS Education and Training Center, and the Moffitt Cancer Center. He is formerly director of the Centre for Applied Family Studies and director of the Schools of Social Work at McGill University in Montreal and Memorial University in Newfoundland. He has worked extensively in social work education, child welfare, corrections, health, and HIV. He has edited and authored more than 100 scholarly and professional books, articles, monographs, and research papers on a variety of topics and currently serves on the editorial board of a number of academic and professional journals. He also edited *Canadian Social Work* for five years. He has led the development of social work programs in the Middle East, the Persian Gulf, and Indonesia.

Jack Spence retired from the position of executive director for Family Services of Peel (Ontario) in 1997. Before that he had been the director of the Family Services Branch for the Ontario Ministry of Community and Social Services for five years and prior to that was an assistant professor in the Faculty of Social Work at Waterloo Lutheran University for three years. He served on the boards for Family Service Ontario and Family Service Canada, including terms as president of both. He has an MSW from UBC and a diploma in Advanced Social Work from the University of Toronto.

Patricia Taylor is a Professor Emerita from the University of Windsor's School of Social Work. During her 29 years of teaching, she concentrated her special interests on policy and practice issues for social work in health care. She has published and presented many academic papers in Great Britain, the United States, and Canada on this subject. She has also served on many boards, including the Ontario Hospital Association's social work section and Families First (previously Family Service America) as well as the Kellogg Health Care Fellowship program. She has published extensively on health care issues in Canada and abroad. Her present research and writing focus is women's health care.

Dr. Francis Turner is a Professor Emeritus and former dean of the Faculty of Social Work at Wilfrid Laurier University, Waterloo, Ontario. He has written and edited several books on theory and practice, including *Social Work Practice: A Canadian Perspective*, 2d edition, and *Social Work Treatment: Interlocking Theoretical Perspectives*, 4th edition. He is also editor of the soon-to-be-published *Canadian Encyclopedia of Social Work*. He earned his Master's degree from the University of Ottawa and his doctorate from Columbia University, New York.

Dr. Joanne Turner is a Professor Emerita and former director of Social Work, Renison College, University of Waterloo, Ontario. She has extensive experience in clinical practice, teaching, supervision, research, and policy initiatives. She served as past chair of the Ontario College of Certified Social Workers and currently serves on the executive of the Ontario College of Social Workers and Social Service Workers.

Dr. Susan Watt is a professor in the School of Social Work and acting associate dean of Social Sciences at McMaster University, Hamilton, Ontario. Her work focuses on the effects of policy on practice and of practice on the delivery of services, with special attention on issues of availability, access, and funding. Most recently, she has specialized on these issues in relation to health care utilization by mothers and their newborn infants. With an interdisciplinary team, she has published widely in this area.

Dr. Michael Kim Zapf is a professor with the Faculty of Social Work at the University of Calgary where he has served as associate dean, acting dean, and head of the BSW Access Division. Following years of practice in the Yukon Territory, he taught in and researched issues of rural and remote practice, geography, and social work education. He has presented work on remote social work practice across Canada and the United States (including Hawaii) as well as Australia, Denmark, Finland, and Sweden.

chapter one

Canadian Social Welfare: A Shared Inheritance

Francis J. Turner

INTRODUCTION

This book is based on the premise that every citizen of Canada, whether newly arrived or descended from families living here for generations or even millennia, is a social welfare recipient. Each one of us, from the Prime Minister to a developmentally handicapped, single, older woman, at different times in our lives directly benefits from one or more provincial or federal programs of assistance. They are a part of the complex structure of Canadian social welfare. Also, as more social services are provided through structures other than governmental ones, many of us are or will become the recipients of such services.

Further, every citizen, including the Prime Minister and the developmentally handicapped single, older woman, contributes to the financing of the social welfare network. We do so indirectly through the complex municipal, provincial, and federal systems of taxation and the wage deductions that finance this structure. To an increasing extent, too, many citizens also contribute directly through voluntary donations to the myriad of causes we are asked to support, whether giving a loonie to a street person or a large annual donation to the Red Cross.

Because this system of social welfare is complex and expensive, because it touches all of us, and because it faces considerable critical challenges, it is important that we as responsible citizens seek to understand it and its place in our lives.

Our goal, then, is to present an overview and analysis of that essential component of Canadian society—"social welfare." Differing viewpoints about the advantages and disadvantages of various forms of social welfare have always existed. However, owing to a number of changing political and ideological factors, especially in North America, social welfare has been particularly singled out as an alleged major cause of society's economic problems. Hence it is now the target for much public, political, and journalistic criticism. Since we are all "on welfare" now or will be at some time in our lives, we must not view this subject as a we–they situation as many proclaim it to be but as a part of the reality of modern living.

Most of us are aware of at least some aspects of this component in the Canadian social fabric. Many, however, do not understand its pervasiveness, complexity, and importance. An over-selective and overly narrow view can lead to misunderstandings that, in turn, can become distortions and insensitive or negative views about social welfare and its importance for us and our country. Because of its complexity and the many different views of how this system should be structured, financed, and delivered, it is far from a perfect or complete system. It is, in fact, like any complex societal reality. The system undergoes constant review and change, as the world changes, as attitudes change, as our economy changes, as social needs change, and as the country changes to adapt to the realities of our dynamic world.

DEFINITION

Let us begin with a discussion of what we mean by social welfare. "Social welfare" is a generic term. It encompasses the complex network of legislation, policies, programs, institutions, professions, resources, and services that exist in all societies to try to ensure that individuals and groups have access to a range of goods and services they need. They require these to achieve their full human potential and to do so in a manner they can accept while showing due regard for the rights of others.

Policies, methods, programs, goals, structures, and the extent of social welfare vary from country to country, and indeed within countries. Thus, to understand a particular social welfare system, we need to understand something of the society in which it has developed, especially its values, attitudes, and history.

In looking at Canada, we need to look at the wide and frequently diverging attitudes and values about helping each other that have existed over the years and exist today in different segments of our society. Because of these differences, the social welfare system that has emerged is not homogeneous but uneven in its structure, impact, adequacy, and equitableness. Yet it is still a system of at least moderate effectiveness overall.

SOME ATTITUDES AND PERSPECTIVES

The differing views and attitudes about the structure and extent of a social welfare system for Canada emerge from the broad spectrum of values in Canada. These values touch on concepts of self-sufficiency, individual and group responsibilities to others, and the perceived social roles and responsibilities of communities, families, churches, business, and government in our lives. Our values also differ according to ideological, political, and professional positions about collective duties and responsibilities to individuals and groups. Whatever their origins, these values in turn shape the kinds, structures, and extent of policies and services that our country has developed and supported. These factors will be discussed more thoroughly in subsequent chapters; we will touch on a few here to set the scene for what is to follow.

For many Canadians, this commitment to help each other arises from a theological perspective of humanity and the exigencies of the virtue of charity in the word's proper theological sense. Indeed, one still hears people refer to some aspects of social welfare as charity, and some social agencies and institutions include "charity" in their names—for example, the Catholic Charities. Those persons deemed to be blessed in possessions and talents by divine providence are seen as having a responsibility to help those less fortunate than they. Those considered privileged do so directly by sharing goods or supporting groups and organizations that provide such help.

In Canada, many of the first organized systems of social service were begun and continue to be operated by religious groups of all denominations. Over the decades such services have shifted from being funded completely by donations to full public funding. Currently public funds are being withdrawn from many such services, and voluntary funding has become far more important again.

Many others in our society often view the concept of social welfare as co-terminus with the word "charity," in the pejorative sense of that word. Throughout our history there has been a strong and long-standing work-oriented ethic that frowns on the idea of some people's having access to the goods and services of that society without "working" for them or "deserving" them. A few years ago the term "welfare bum" was used to describe people blamed for "taking" from society through available benefits rather than contributing to it through "employment." Underlying this term is the notion that some aspects of the social welfare system foster a disincentive to work. Although the recession of the early 1990s helped modify this idea when many long-time members of the workforce suddenly found themselves unemployed and needing assistance, the perception remains very strong.

In recent years some politicians have strongly fostered this view of a disincentive as a justification for cutting back on various benefits. They have proclaimed the virtues of "work for welfare." This perception of alleged large-scale abuse of the social welfare system is frequently heralded as a primary cause of our economic problems even though the evidence strongly shows that very few people prefer public assistance to meaningful employment and very few abuse the benefits they receive. At this point in our history, most people recognize that in a society as complex as ours, many situations can arise in which individuals and groups require others' help. The differences arise when one asks why we should help each other. Whom should we help? In what circumstances should we help? And for some, whom should we *not* help?

Others advocate that the responsibility to provide social services arises from a particular philosophy. They argue that, as intelligent members of the human race, each of us has a social responsibility to ensure that all people have access to what they need to achieve their full human potential. It is this belief in a common societal-group responsibility that motivates individuals and groups to lobby for, sponsor, and support a vast range of philanthropic endeavours across our country. In addition to providing these services, such a point of view promotes advocating and lobbying for more just, effective, and universal social policies and programs at all levels of society. We can deduce another aspect of this philosophical approach to social welfare in the value position that each citizen has a right to society's assistance and, when needed, access to its resources simply because he or she is a citizen. The concept of individual citizen rights and duties has developed over centuries of thought and debate and varies within, and between, various political systems. Canada is a part of the tradition that supports the concept of individual worth based on a concept of social justice; every person can expect—indeed has a right to—society's assistance in many critical areas of life.

Individuals differ in deciding what rights are included in such an entitlement. Few Canadians would deny our individual rights to education, and most would support the right of all to a minimum level of health care; interestingly, there is less commitment to a right to the resources a person needs to maintain an adequate standard of living. Because of these areas of uncertainty and because rights continue to evolve, arguments have been put forward for the need to enshrine a charter of human rights more clearly in our constitution.

For many Canadians our rights and duties to each other in meeting social welfare needs extends to people in other parts of the world as well who may be in need of help that we can provide. There is much less consensus within the country on this issue. Nevertheless, Canada to date has an excellent track record in aiding the people of other countries in particular circumstances.

Another approach to social welfare argues that whether we have a right to such services or not, it is sound economic practice for every country to have a system that ensures distribution of that country's resources and services to everyone. Some argue that, because of the complexities and uncertainties of economic structures

within and between countries, mechanisms should be in place to ensure that resources are distributed to everyone in a minimum package of goods and services; these resources then permit each individual to lead a growth-oriented life and the system fosters a smooth-running national and international economy.

Most countries of the world support the concept of redistributing resources between and within countries to some extent. However, the ways the concept is applied and interpreted vary dramatically from country to country and between governments within countries. Even in Canada, there are wide disagreements about the degree and nature of the desired or necessary involvement of outside bodies and agents in people's lives. Unfortunately, the debates surrounding such issues are frequently translated into either–or positions rather than addressed as a continuum.

Also, from an economic perspective, others hold that it makes good economic and business sense to enable all people to participate in the commerce of a country and to help them to use their individual potentials by contributing to their countries. Such a position avoids asking who should and should not be helped and focuses instead on the public and economic benefits of a fully functioning and participating citizenry.

Finally, some believe but rarely express openly the idea that a strong, fairly administered social welfare system functions as a measure of social control and hence should be supported and encouraged. Without a well-structured social welfare system of adequate public assistance, medical care, unemployment insurance, pensions, etc., the argument runs, persons in need will become upset, angry, and liable to commit violent acts and even foment revolution. Thus good political policy ensures that the basic needs of a population are met to ensure peace, order, and maintenance of the status quo.

Because of this latter view, some people perceive social workers and others who work in the social welfare structure as agents of social control—even their own colleagues. It is said that their task is to maintain the current order of things and to avoid changing it. Such a position suggests that other needed systemic changes are less likely to be addressed as long the basic needs of citizens are met.

TYPES OF NEED

We can find all of the above arguments in support of a strong social welfare structure in Canada today. Of course they translate into large differences of opinion as to what services and policies we need as a society and which we should discard, modify, or create. Few of these perceptions of social welfare mentioned above are new. They have all produced different impacts on our social network at various times.

From the early days of European settlement in Canada, society has strongly emphasized hard work, responsibility for oneself, and avoiding dependency on others except in times of special need or disaster. Various groups of immigrants and refugees who have come to this country have held equally strong positions that foster a sense of communal aid and commitment to mutual assistance.

Also, even before the first waves of European immigrants arrived, complex and effective systems of mutual aid existed among the various groups of the First Nations peoples. Discussions of social welfare have long overlooked these. Only in recent years have these systems finally been rediscovered and resumed a place of respect and importance in our understanding of our country's social development.

Through the various approaches to social welfare runs a strong moralistic tradition that holds that there are two kinds of persons in need in society, those who deserved or deserve help and those who were and are undeserving of help. This distinction has been expressed in many different ways. It was most clearly enshrined in the Elizabethan Poor Laws of Britain with the terms the "Deserving Poor" and the "Undeserving Poor."

The "Deserving" were those persons and groups who, through no fault of their own, through birth, accident, or disaster, were unable to care for themselves either temporarily or permanently. Since they were deemed not responsible for their state of need, society considered its care of them fitting, indeed morally demanded. Through one of its subsystems, such as the parish or the poorhouse, society provided assistance to them.

The "Undeserving" were those, who, in the opinion of persons of influence, were in need through their own faults or failings. Such persons were lazy, irresponsible, improvident, or immoral, and thus evil members of society. Accordingly, they had no claim on society's assistance. (The idea that persons could be in need as a result of flaws in the social or economic system that excludes them from access to adequate resources was often and still is totally discounted.)

Such persons were to be helped, but only as a moral imperative, and with the conviction that they were an unfair drain on society's resources. Any help would only contribute further to their supposed indolence. Society was to provide such help grudgingly, to make appeals for it as unattractive and punitive as possible. The assistance was also to be kept to an absolute minimum.

An episode in the nineteenth-century novelist Charles Dickens's *A Christmas*

Carol exemplifies this attitude. Two business men who are parish visitors approach the wealthy miser Ebenezer Scrooge to ask him for a charitable contribution. Scrooge responds by suggesting that the workhouse and the treadmill are much better solutions to poverty than almsgiving.

This concept still runs strongly through Canadian society, although today we refer to such programs as "workfare." In this alleged dichotomy it has never been clear who is to decide and on what grounds the criteria for membership in either of these two groups.

This idea that only two classes of persons need society's assistance persists today. In public and private discussions about social welfare, many strongly believe that large numbers of those who receive particular forms of social assistance, especially money, should be denied such help. These individuals or societal groups deem these people undeserving because of any number of facts about their ways of life. As in Gilbert and Sullivan's operetta *Mikado*, many people have their "Little Lists" of those others who should be excluded from society, and there is little consensus among such lists.

This reluctance to give money directly to persons in need through means other than employment has deep and complicated roots in Canadian society. Although many other benefits that society provides are considered acceptable and indeed rights, the same idea does not pertain to the provision of money. For example, it is quite astonishing how little concern is voiced about the billions of dollars in public funds funnelled annually into the health care system for people with illnesses caused by smoking; yet people raise a loud hue and cry about providing adequate, ongoing cash assistance to families who are out of work because of company mismanagement and closings. Some people would deride the suggestion that a wealthy person who receives costly smoking-related cancer health care should be forced to rake leaves in front of city hall to pay off her debt to society as left-wing rhetoric. But to insist that an abandoned single mother do the same in return for her totally inadequate public assistance cheque is seen as sound economics, effective public policy, and a lesson in good living—for the mother, that is.

THE UNIVERSALITY OF NEED

However, it would be a mistake to overemphasize this notion of the undeserving. For the most part this attitude has shifted to a concern that our system should be fair and adequate to all, allowing that some people may occasionally abuse that system, and that these problems should be addressed as they arise. Unfortunately, the media have publicized widely gross exaggerations of the amount of such abuse.

As mentioned earlier, studies in various countries have shown that the amount of this misuse of public assistance is very small. In fact, this misuse probably costs much less than paying the investigators who are hired to find and punish the transgressors. Indeed, the definition of what constitutes abuse is itself often unfair and at times even an abuse in itself. Over and over again the data show that people would prefer not to have to rely on the social welfare network that provides them with money. Evidence shows that the problems reside in the economic system, not in the individuals. Society is learning that arbitrarily categorizing the deserving and nondeserving is simplistic. It is even irrelevant in the face of our country's need for a comprehensive system of social welfare to reduce the impacts of today's complex and unpredictable economic system.

As a country we are learning that virtually everyone is in some type of personal or resource need at some time in their lives. Unfortunately, some persons face such needs all of their lives. The underlying reasons for these needs may be complicated and related to the system, having little or nothing to do with the moral integrity or perceived lack of it in the needy person or group. We are becoming more knowledgeable about the systemic causes of poverty, the effects of heredity and psychosocial history, the enduring scars of childhood deprivation, abuse, and neglect, the crushing impacts of some environments, the long-term debilitation of various injuries and illnesses, the dramatic crises caused by political and economic events, and the devastating unpredictability of natural disasters; at the same time, we are also accepting the fact that no one can be self-sufficient all the time. All of us are vulnerable some of the time. Whatever our ideological positions, it behooves us and our societies to ensure that the services and resources we all need are made available to all.

Three events in the first half of this century and one more recent have helped Canadians appreciate the universality of potential need: World Wars I and II, the Great Depression of the 1930s, and the economic recessions of the 1990s. In each instance many hundreds of thousands of previously self-sufficient Canadians suddenly found they were unable to sustain themselves without assistance owing to events totally beyond their control.

At the end of World War I thousands of veterans returned home with a wide range of disabilities. They and their families required services related to health, finance, rehabilitation, and day-to-day living. Refugees from the countries most affected by the war shared similar needs. The same situation was repeated following World War II, and even today many of these veterans and their families still need, and receive, a range of services that permits them to function in self-fulfilling ways.

During the Depression of the 1930s Canada once again found itself dealing with many thousands of once self-sufficient people who were suddenly unable to provide for themselves and their families. One of this book's authors remembers well as a young boy in the summers of the 1930s men regularly visiting our back door to ask his mother for something to eat. Most of them were veterans travelling back and forth across the country in a relentless search for work in a collapsed economy.

These nationwide events of earlier decades taught Canada a great deal about system-caused vulnerability and the economic advantages of universal social welfare services and policies. Out of this recognition grew a very strong, reasonably effective, and much-envied social welfare network for all of Canada. Yet we forget the past easily; early in the 1990s this society faced a recession almost as serious as the Depression of the 1930s. We saw companies, even entire industries long considered stable, dramatically cutting their employees and putting many people out of work, including very senior employees who had considered themselves employed for life. Pensions, unemployment insurance, family benefits, and company benefits enabled many thousands of families to ride out this period in a manner very different from the days of the 1930s. Since then such resources have allowed many to almost forget this recession in contrast to the many Canadians who still bear psychic scars from the Depression.

But during the 1990s we also learned of serious gaps in our social welfare system. In a very short time many people moved from positions of affluence and satisfaction to sudden need for the most basic of social services.

We were also reminded forcibly how such economic fluctuations affect the poor of a country the most. Many of the existing programs often do not help the most needy. It remains a shock, embarrassment, and puzzle to most Canadians that, when Canada is now viewed as one of the most affluent countries in the world, virtually every city has had to set up its own food banks, hostels for the homeless on our streets, and shelters for women and children fleeing domestic assault.

We are living in a time in which we support public policies that have drastically cut back on needed services while decrying that our affluent country has children living in abject poverty, families standing in line for basic foodstuffs, people begging on our streets in order to survive, and women fleeing from life-threatening situations. We can justify this situation easily by blaming the victims to avoid our collective need to assume responsibility. The spectres of the "deserving" and "undeserving" still hover!

We have not yet found fully adequate answers to these challenges to our society However, perhaps we are not yet aware as a society of system-caused individual vulnerability. Nor do we recognize our mutual interdependence within Canada and beyond our borders, through world events as we in Canada influence them and they affect us. We are learning more and more how seemingly unrelated situations frequently affect one another. A technological development in one part of the world can cause a dramatic drop in the value of a particular metal and put whole communities in Canada out of work. An industrial accident many kilometres away can devastate the tourist industry of a large part of the country. Emissions from an industrial site can harm the aquatic life in a lake that provides a livelihood for a band of First Nations people. These exam-

ples all demonstrate a growing understanding of the need for a strong social welfare network.

But how best should such a social network be constituted? Because of the diversity of opinions about the hows and whys of social welfare, the complexity of our governmental system, and the various political, historical, sociological, and economic factors cited above, our social welfare evolves and advances in a complex, slow, multifaceted, and frequently uneven manner.

For example, in 1948 the Canadian government instituted a long-discussed and frequently opposed system of family allowances. This social welfare program provided money to every Canadian family with children under the age of 16. Important in individual people's lives, the system also marked an historic milestone in the development of a universal program that made every Canadian family a welfare recipient. Eventually, after much debate, this legislation was enacted although the bases of the support varied.

Some saw this program as a not-too-subtle scheme to increase Canada's post-war population; hence its popular nickname of "baby bonus." Others viewed it as the majority party's attempt to win support of segments of the population in which large families were the norm. Many others saw it as an element in developing a universal safety net to help prevent the terrible suffering of the Depression if one ever happened again. I can well remember the excitement and gratitude of my parents the day the first Family Allowance cheque arrived in our home.

Still others argued that the program was a means of redistributing money to help stimulate the country's economy; with more money in each household the country could sell more stoves, refrigerators, and vacuum cleaners and other consumer products. Some saw the scheme as another covert way that the government could ensure domestic peace in a troubled world.

Finally, many others saw the program as an essential form of support to which all families had a right as citizens.

Each of these positions, and others, affected the legislation's final form and the various alterations made following its implementation. As important as this legislation was in its day, it has now been repealed. A different form of child credits has since been substituted and is viewed as a tax-saving measure that still answers need. Today selective programs are considered better than universal ones.

Another more contemporary example— one set at the neighbourhood rather than the national level—also reflects how this complexity of perception can and does influence the implementation of policy through services. In this era of de-institutionalization, a community group may identify the need for a neighbourhood-based residence for developmentally challenged young adults. The goal is to permit them to live a more normal community life than they could within an institution.

Presuming that there is community support for this idea, something that cannot always be assumed, people could support this suggestion for very different reasons. Because of the uncertainty of this support, those involved in the project would need to take all those views into account to ensure the project's success.

Some might see the project as a way of bringing public funds into the community through much needed building contracts and jobs. Others might support it as a way of demonstrating the need for additional services for community-based projects. To still others, it might seem to show that young people with disabilities can function well outside institutions. Others might simply want to give a group of citizens an opportunity to develop better living skills and greater self-sufficiency. And another group might argue for the project as a matter of human rights, believing that every citizen has a right to a place in the community.

At all levels of social welfare we find a range of perspectives comparative to those discussed here. Out of this amalgam of viewpoints emerge the compromises required for consensus. Once a policy is implemented, the same range of opinions will determine the way a new idea or project is received and supported or resisted.

Other important realities continue to shape the development of our social welfare system. Ours is a country of great geographic and meteorological differences, complex cultural relationships, diverse ethnic patterns, and a highly uneven geographic distribution of people and resources. Different groups and individuals have varying basic needs, depending on a broad spectrum of cultural, economic, lifestyle, and geographic factors. This is one of the challenges to overly categorized universal programs. For example, some people consider a cellular telephone an instrument of convenience and a luxury; for others it is an essential means of contact with the outside world and a necessity. A snowmobile is a recreation toy for many Canadians while for others it represents the difference between life and death during a harsh winter. With our great variety of ethnic groups, what might be an acceptable and welcome "Meals on Wheels" service for one family may be totally inappropriate for another.

UNDERSTANDING CANADIAN SOCIAL WELFARE

So, the concept and structure of social welfare in our country are not simple. Within the Canadian mosaic, social welfare struggles to bring together differences in perception and attitude, varying views of needs and responsibilities, and a range of historic, cultural, and geographic factors. The ongoing dialogue has produced a structure comprising legislation, services, institutions, programs, persons, policies, resources, professionals, volunteers, formal agencies, funding bodies, research institutes, lobbying bodies, policy centres, foundations, and informal self-help groups.

As mentioned at the beginning of this chapter, every Canadian is aware of some aspects of Canada's social welfare network through such highly visible programs as Employment Insurance, Old Age Pensions, general welfare assistance, and various child welfare services. Most Canadians are unaware of the extent and complexity of the system. These programs are supported by taxes. Many other components also form part of the tax structure. The federal and provincial transfers of funds, support of various training programs, disability allowances, and workers' compensation are also parts of our social welfare system, even though all these programs make up major items in federal, provincial, and municipal budgets.

Besides these tax-supported programs, many others are financed through voluntary giving. Most of us know of some of them through the annual fundraising drive of the United Way in our cities. The United Way in turn supports a network of locally based special services.

Canada boasts a rich array of foundations as well that fund many agencies or special projects within agencies. A significant amount of this funding helps support research centres that continually evaluate the impact of various social services and test new strategies and programs.

Finally, there remains one other aspect of the Canadian social welfare structure. This is the less formal but very important network of mutual aid that has long existed in our country. From this source, help of many kinds is made available to many groups and individuals, on either an ongoing basis or a special-needs basis. The voluntary component of social welfare is a vital and frequently overlooked means by which Canadian society demonstrates a powerful level of concern for all citizens.

The following chapters will address these various components of our welfare system more fully. Readers will want to familiarize themselves with some of the terminology that will be used.

Social services is the term often applied as a synonym for social welfare. In its precise meaning, however, social services are the network of the formal settings by which a broad range of specific services are provided to individuals, families, and groups. It defines the organizational component of social welfare underlying specific programs. These include such well-known services as child-welfare agencies, municipal public-assistance departments and family counselling centres, mental health centres, and social planning councils. The number of such individual services in large cities is vast, as evidenced by the size of local agency directories; often these contain several hundred different service types and settings.

Social services reflect the *social policies* of the agency's sponsoring body, be it government or private. Social policies form the philosophical and/or ideological base that directs the goals and objectives of the various groups, whether professional, religious, government, or community. They reflect the *mission statements* of particular bodies and vary widely in this large nation. For example, a federal social policy may aim to provide medical insurance for all citizens and an adequate standard of living for the elderly, abolish child poverty, or promote equality of opportunity for developmentally challenged people. On a different level a local agency may serve a particular group in a community, such as battered women, street people, or AIDS victims in that geographic area.

Social work is a term frequently applied in discussions of this aspect of Canadian society. This is the formal title for the principal, but not the only, profession in the social welfare system. As will be discussed in a later chapter, social work as a profession pursues the enhancement, restoration, or modification of the psychosocial functioning of individuals, groups, families, or communities, or of the systems with which individuals interact.

One further term used in this context is *the welfare state*. The term emerged following World War II when it was first used to describe countries strong committed to a highly developed and integrated system of social welfare programs. Post-war Great Britain and the Scandinavian countries are most frequently identified as welfare states. As more countries have come to recognize comprehensive social welfare structures as an economic necessity, the term has become less useful in defining specific countries. It is now primarily a political term, sometimes used pejoratively, to reflect the priority a country accords social welfare.

Social security is a term similar to "the welfare state." The United States was the first jurisdiction to describe this important development in its legislation, which established a basic comprehensive pension plan for all employed Americans. The plan still exists, and every American who has ever been employed has a "social security number," similar to the Canadian "Social Insurance Number." As an integral component of American social welfare, the program has assumed a much broader application that transcends national borders. People frequently use the term today to denote the stated goal of most systems—to provide a lifelong network of services and resources.

The concept of a "social contract" originates in the writings of the eighteenth-century philosopher Jean-Jacques Rousseau (1712–1778). It too has been absorbed into the lexicon of Canadian social welfare. Recently, provincial governments have used it to describe the partnership that lays out the mutual responsibilities of individuals and their governments. On its side, the government agrees to upgrade and maintain a social network to ensure the availability of resources to meet its citizens' complex psychosocial needs at various stages of their lives; it also commits itself to meet a range of exigencies.

CONCLUSION

We began this chapter with the premise that we are all involved in the social welfare system, both as supporters and recipients. We are all in and on welfare! As responsible citizens in a democratic country, we assume we have a responsibility to understand this important part of our lives and our society. We have this responsibility whether our goal is to become social workers, social service workers, members of other, related professions, better informed recipients of social services, volunteers, advocates for social change, or just fully participating members of our society.

We do not accept that social welfare institutions, policies, and services should be taken for granted. We demand accountability from those segments of society that exist to assist us in our individual lives. Social welfare is an important societal system that affects us all. This means we have a responsibility to understand its structure and functioning. This book contributes to our understanding of this essential feature in Canadian life.

REFERENCES

Armitage, A. 1988. *Social welfare in Canada: Ideals, realities and future paths*. 2d ed. Toronto: McClelland and Stewart.

Turner, Francis J. (Ed.). 2002. *Social work practice: A Canadian perspective*. 2d ed.

Woodruffe, K. 1968. *From charity to social work*. London: Routledge and Kegan Paul; Toronto: Prentice Hall, Allyn and Bacon.

chapter two

The Philosophical and Value Base of Canadian Social Welfare

Roger Delaney

The test of nonalienating work is not that it is always easy or fun, but that it makes sense to us. It makes us feel connected to others, and to a larger ethical or spiritual purpose.

Michael Lerner, 1997, p. 249

INTRODUCTION

As Turner notes in Chapter 1, widely divergent views on the nature of social welfare exist within each society, and between different societies. These views are based on competing perspectives and values, each with its own definition of human nature, society, and the relationship of people and society. In many ways, social welfare becomes each society's definition "of the good and the desirable which in turn are embedded in societal values" (Frederico 1984, 20).

As the twentieth century progressed, Canada's governments began to take a greater role in social welfare, and social programs began to expand. However, the positive gains achieved by the Canadian social welfare system from the 1940s to the 1970s were slowly eroded during the 1980s and the 1990s.

One major factor in the decline of Canada's social programs and its concomitant decrease in its citizens' physical and emotional resources is the "globalization" social movement. Driven by multinational companies and neo-conservative governments, free trade agreements are eroding the ability of governments to govern and to control the economic forces within their own territories (Clarke 1997). Included with these free trade agreements sanctioned by neo-conservative and right-wing liberal governments is also a sinister and malevolent effort to destroy the Canadian social welfare system.

"Their [neo-conservatives'/free trade advocates'] remarkably successful demonization of the public sector has turned much of the citizenry against their own [sic] mechanisms. Many of us have been enrolled in the cause of interests that have no particular concern for the citizen's welfare, our welfare. Instead, the citizen is reduced to the status of a subject at the throne of the marketplace" (Saul 1995).

This new thrust, known as corporatism, is entering the lifeblood of social programs and is being driven by a desire to alter the very culture of Canadian social welfare. Because social programs depend on the government or the public for funding, governments' social and economic policies have the power to determine not only the nature of services, but also, equally importantly, how these services will be delivered.

"Well, corporatism with its market- and technology-led delusions is profoundly tied to a mechanistic view of the human race. This is not an ideology with any interest in or commitment to the shape of society or the individual as citizen. It is fixed upon a rush to use machinery inanimate or human while these are still at full value; before they suffer any depreciation" (Saul 1995, 162).

With a powerful rhetoric (language), propaganda (self-serving information), and dialect (use of corporate language), corporatism is trying to gain global control of the economy and ascendency of that economy over social policy (Saul 1995). Moreover, because of the international infiltration by the multinational companies and other economic interest groups, it is very difficult to find the "enemy" with whom to be angry. How does a citizen confront what is global? Moreover, the ideas driving the neo-conservative agenda are not new ideas at all; they have been hotly debated for centuries. What is new is the advancement of technology and communications, which have permitted globalization access to the entire world.

This chapter examines the philosophical base that underlies different views Canadians have about social welfare. Philosophy is the search for wisdom and truth based on an understanding of the rational principles on which our notions of reality are founded. In our modern era, we use applied philosophy to help people understand the meaning of the concepts we use when describing our social welfare values (Plant 1974). All social welfare programs are based on societal approval. This approval in turn represents society's dominant values—the intrinsic worth of the individual, the responsibility of society for the welfare of its members, and what constitutes individuals' and society's shared responsibility for the common good. Therefore, depending on how each society defines these beliefs, distinct variations will exist in each society's social welfare programs.

THE NATURE OF SOCIETY

In Canada, we strive for a pluralist society: that is, a society that benefits from the many world views that contribute to our societal definition of the common good. We value bilingualism, multiculturalism, and a multi-party political system, among other elements of our national life.

Two major issues that arise from pluralism have particular implications for social welfare. First, pluralism encourages competition for political dominance among these different world views. Depending on which view dominates, the social welfare system in Canada looks very different. Second, some of these world views do not accept that social welfare should even exist as a social institution. In fact, some people do not accept pluralism as a valued social goal. The current constitutional debate in Canada and the creation of new political parties that would dismantle existing structures that support pluralism are examples of these different priorities.

While much of Canadian philosophy does not directly address the issue of social welfare, distinct philosophical views influence our thinking about the nature of society. The *accommodationist perspective* asserts that all theories contain part of the truth within them. The philosopher is the one to seek the common ground in all theories in order to find closer approximations of truth (Rabb 1989; Armour and Trott 1981).

From the accommodationist perspective evolved the *polycentric perspective*. This supports pluralism by arguing that the common-ground approach leaves out those features of a world view that differ from it, so this view limits what could be considered truth. The *polycentric perspective* argues that radically different world views reveal not only something about culture and language but also about reality itself and the ways different people come to know it. Therefore, each world view reveals something about the total picture, which can never be fully known. We can achieve an accurate picture of reality only by attempting to accommodate and reconcile as many world views as possible (McPherson and Rabb 1993). This perspective supports social work's emphasis on maintaining the individuality, dignity, and freedom of choice of all people through self-determination.

Another major philosophical perspective is *communitarianism*, which places an intrinsic and instrumental value on both the community and the individual (Cragg 1986; Grant 1959). In *Canadian Identity*, Robin Mathews defined communitarians as "the seekers of means to anchor values in human worth" (Mathews 1988, 32). In communitarianism, individual rights arise from community rights; thus the community rights can override individual rights. The same right that the community has to survive translates into limited consideration given to the rights of individuals to benefit from that community or indeed to the distribution of power, status, privilege, or resource allocation within that community. Therefore, the poor or individuals having difficulty in functioning socially could very well be seen as detrimental to the community's well-being. Social workers tend to resist this perspective and support the worth and dignity of the individual.

Ramsay Cook, a Canadian historian, provides further insight into the Canadian perspective on social welfare with his concept of *regeneration*. He suggests that the crisis of faith that affected Canadian Protestants in the late nineteenth century resulted from the social impact of early industrialization and that it subsequently required that society dramatically change its focus. This change shifted the meaning of regeneration from a spiritual rebirth that individuals experienced to a "rebirth" through social salvation. This drastic change in thinking gave rise to the Social Gospel Movement and the Liberalism Movement from which many of our current attitudes about Canadian social welfare derive today.

These different perspectives on Canadian philosophical thought support Rein's (1974) perspective that social policy is the product of competing values and their associated world view. Therefore, the social policies that govern the social welfare system can result from one value perspective's gaining dominance over all others. Similarly, political parties, when they win majority government status, may very well follow their own value-based agendas regardless of their impact on society.

THE NATURE OF HUMAN VALUES

Since the term "values" is important in our understanding the philosophical base of Canadian social welfare, we must take care to understand just what values are. Milton Rokeach (1973, 5) defines a value as an enduring belief that "a specific mode of conduct or end state of existence is personally or socially preferable to an opposite mode of conduct or end state of existence." All individuals have beliefs about what is true about themselves, about the meaning of life, about God, about appropriate behaviour, and about other people, other cultures, and other societies. The social work profession espouses a social welfare system in which all members of its society come together to determine social policies. For example, citizen participation is a means by which members from different groups in society experience each other and integrate their different beliefs. Universal social welfare programs prevent one group from being identified as different (isolated) from other groups.

According to Rokeach, there are three types of beliefs. *Descriptive* or *existential beliefs* define what is true and what is false. For example, I might believe that my notion of God is the only true definition and so reject all other notions of God as false. I might also believe that all people are born good and reject the notion that any people are born evil.

Evaluative beliefs define what is good and what is bad. Again, I might believe that pleasure is good and reject the notion that pleasure is bad. I might believe that doing good things for people makes them lazy and dependent and reject the notion that doing good things for them is good.

Finally, *prescriptive beliefs* define what means or ends of action we judge desirable or undesirable. In this case, I might believe that hitting anyone is an undesirable act or that being cruel is appropriate in the work world but not at home. Obviously, when there is congruence between these three types of beliefs, then the bonds between them are stronger, which increases that system of beliefs' resistance to change. For example, if I believe that every individual is responsible for his or her own success, then achieving my own success makes me feel good about myself and, at the same time, I need not worry about what I had to do to become successful.

This discussion suggests that human beings have a complex system of values and beliefs. Together, these give each person a unique world view. However, in today's society, there is often such an abundance of information that the world, once comprehensible, seems increasingly complex and confusing. To handle this information overload, people often feel compelled to clarify and simplify the world by applying their own world views in accepting or rejecting new information. Harvey (1967) defines this way of organizing our experiences, our knowledge, and our values in order to comprehend the world around us as a conceptual system.

Conceptual systems help explain why so many Canadians continue to believe that many people who receive social assistance are really just being lazy or trying to cheat the public. This mistrust continues to exist despite the evidence from social science research, and from several public inquiries, that shows this is not what is really happening (Macarov 1995, 1978). These data suggest that individuals can translate elements of their values in order to comply with a dominant social value system. For example, Judeo-Christian believers can translate "Thou shalt not kill" and the aspiration of unconditional love to allow them to kill when certain conditions are met, such as in self-defence and for national security.

Erich Fromm (1955, 13) casts more light on this phenomenon. He posits his notion of the pathology of normalcy, which suggests that a "collective value when held by the majority becomes the normative basis for determining appropriate social actions." In essence, this means that no matter how pathological a behaviour is, as long as the majority believe it is not pathological, those people will behave as if this behaviour is normal. This helps explain why people continue to discipline their children (and each other) with violence, for example, despite the abundance of literature that indicates that violence is a dehumanizing and ineffective problem-solving tool and, in fact, an act of oppression and power.

DIVERSE PERSPECTIVES AND VALUES

This section of the chapter began with a statement that there are diverse perspectives and values on the nature of social welfare. These competing perspectives are based on values that support various views on what human beings are and what responsibility society and its members have for each other. In addition, each individual possesses a unique world view to which he or she adapts an array of individual values. When the majority of a society shares a world view, it becomes the dominant and prescriptive norm. The following section will explore and define these competing values as they relate to social welfare.

COMPETING VALUES ON THE NATURE OF SOCIAL WELFARE

Many social welfare theorists apply the residual and institutional perspectives to social welfare to delineate the differences between a restrictive and a supportive approach to social welfare as a social institution (Wilensky and Lebeaux 1958). This chapter is concerned with the values and theories that underlie these approaches. One of the major goals of social welfare advocates (and of the social work profession) is to establish a societal environment that promotes and enhances the human potential of all members of that society, each in accordance with his or her own potential.

Institutional Perspective

The institutional concept views social welfare as a necessary social institution that essentially meets the needs of people in industrial societies. To explain these needs we can consider that human beings are required to perform a vast array of life tasks that are both developmental (life-cycle tasks) and instrumental (skill-acquisition tasks). To accomplish these, humans require resources that are material, emotional, and spiritual. If a person faces a discrepancy between the life tasks he needs to perform and the appropriate array of resources that would allow him to do so, then that person will find his ability to perform personal and social tasks proportionately limited. Society's members are interdependent, and thus value-sharing resources are means to ensure that all can equally and uniquely contribute to the common good.

In other words, if each member of a society is constantly improving her social functioning, then this improvement, in turn, benefits all other members of that society. Advocates of social welfare tend to support the notions of mutual aid, social justice, equality, altruism, common human needs, socialized individualism, and humanization. We will discuss these concepts later in this chapter.

Residual Perspective

The residual perspective essentially sees social welfare as a limited and temporary societal response to human problems that affect families or the marketplace when normal functioning fails. Opponents of social welfare argue that each person or family is responsible for its own growth and will acquire the resources necessary to maximize that growth, if the person or family values such growth. Therefore, what each individual or family acquires by its own merit, gained by hard work and personal/financial risks, is justifiably that party's property. From this perspective, human freedom becomes essentially non-societal interference, and the social hierarchy establishes itself by superior talent and/or the superior ability to acquire resources.

This perspective supports this notion of independence through the belief that if people can survive and even surmount the challenges of surviving in a society, then the whole of society will benefit by having those stronger individuals. Those who become dependent, then, are the weaker elements of a society and weaken the society as a whole. Those who oppose social welfare tend to support the corporatism, globalization, earned access, possessive individualism, existentialism, utilitarianism, the Protestant work ethic, laissez-faire economics, mistrust, social Darwinism, and the Malthusian Theory of Population.

THE CONCEPT OF HUMAN NATURE

Perhaps one of the most difficult and unanswerable questions that confronts humanity is "What is a human being?" Social welfare tries to address this eternal problem by focusing on the notion of human nature itself rather than debating definitions of human. Some common beliefs about human nature support the view that social welfare is a social institution:

- Humans are rational, emotive, and social beings (Aristotle, Aquinas, Kant).

- Humans are in a constant state of "becoming"; not only can humans transcend physical nature, but also they share an ontological vocation to become more fully human (Kierkegaard, Marx, Teilhard de Chardin, Freire).

- This human potential for development responds to and affects the physical and social environments; the environment influences the human potential for development and the human potential for development influences the environment.

- The basis for understanding this reciprocity with the physical environment is commonality; the physical environment is the common place to sustain all of the world's life forms. A further balance exists that allows all life forms to co-exist in an interdependent state.

- The basis for understanding our reciprocity with the social environment is mutuality; humans cannot fulfil their potential if that fulfillment restricts or denies any other human being's opportunity to fulfill her potential. In this sense, equality is the shared journey of all humans to fulfill their potential to become more fully human, and mutuality is the fundamental predisposition for survival and developmental co-existence.

• The end state of human potential is a transformed human state that every human being can achieve. It is characterized by such terms as love, knowledge, harmony, peace, and beauty (Fromm, Rousseau).

As Frankl (1969, 18–19) notes, "Man transcends himself either toward another human being or toward meaning. Love, I would say, is that which enables him to grasp the other human being in his very uniqueness. Conscience is that capacity which empowers him to seize the meaning of a situation in its very uniqueness, and in the final analysis meaning is something unique."

Social welfare advocates tend to operationalize these propositions in terms of society's obligation to provide people with the "means" and "opportunities" in an environment that supports every person's right to develop. Conversely, social welfare advocates tend to criticize social arrangements and conditions that promote the potential development of one set of people at the expense of another set of people (elitism), that suggest that one set of people has greater human potential than another set (through gender or racial inequality), or that deny that one or more sets of people have human potential (through oppression or slavery).

These beliefs also suggest that our observations in the real world (*experiential reality*) are subject to interpretation. Our interpretation draws on the array of values, knowledge, and experience that constitutes each person's world view about what is true, what is good, and what are appropriate actions (*conceptual system*). We share these interpretations with those whose opinions we deem valuable, producing an *agreement reality* that allows each of us to interpret an external event or behaviour according to the symbolic meaning the

event or behaviour has in relation to our individual conceptual system (*symbolic interactionalism*). When a large number of people share this agreement reality, that common interpretation becomes self-reinforcing; each member who agrees with it supports the continuation of that agreement with all other members (Babbie 1986, 1977).

This collective association of agreements, then, defines truth. It also shapes and defines how the social arrangement between people (social structure) should look according to those people who are part of the symbolic interactionalism. Because these agreements simplify reality by denying that other truths could co-exist, they also reduce personal and social anxiety by stabilizing the environment and limiting the scope for change (Schon 1971; Fromm 1955). Frankl (1969) states that we find this association of agreement realities in such entities as social values, social mores, and political ideologies. As this association of agreement realities consists of shared individual agreement realities, it itself becomes a unique perception of reality, or *gestalt*—one that is consistent with, but different from, any one member's individual agreement reality.

In an ideal pluralist society, agreement realities from a *polycentric perspective* would be open systems that constantly accept, interpret, and adapt information the society gains from other agreement realities. They would therefore be in a constant state of flux and reorganization (Hegel 1907). In a society where one dominant agreement reality defines the social order, the agreement reality is a closed system; it values the stability held through law and order. When this dominant agreement reality reflects the view of a minority group but is politically imposed upon the majority, it produces a state of oppression. The minority prescribe to the majority an agreement reality that imposes one group's choice upon another, transforming the consciousness of the majority group into one that conforms with that of the minority group (Freire 1985, 1969). Accordingly, social welfare advocates are very concerned with the ways power, privilege, status, and wealth are distributed within society and tend to promote "power-with" strategies of "openness, trust, vulnerability, creativity, risk, emotional expression, honesty, giving before receiving" (Bishop 1994, 46).

VIEWS OF SOCIAL WELFARE

Those who oppose social welfare tend to view human nature as essentially evil or neutral (Kluckholn and Strodbeck 1961). They believe that humans are motivated essentially by desires for power, happiness (pleasure/pain), and security. The *economic view* of social welfare is based on the principles of *utilitarianism, laissez-faire economics*, and *possessive individualism* (MacPherson 1962; Bentham 1967; Smith 1937).

Figure 2.1 presents a visual arrangement of beliefs that support and oppose social welfare and the resulting societal views that are compatible with each set of beliefs. In other words, one would expect that people who express beliefs that support social welfare would also support Commonality, Mutuality, and Equality and those expressing beliefs that oppose social welfare would also support societal arrangements that tolerate Elitism, Class, Gender, & Racial Inequality, and Oppression & Slavery. However, the degree to which one espouses these beliefs also reflects the degree to which these societal views are held.

Adam Smith (1937) believed that no one should be allowed to interfere in any way with the free operation of supply and demand, self-interest, and competition. He used the term *laissez-faire* to describe a "hands-off" approach to the marketplace. In essence, supply and demand will regulate the marketplace and determine the incomes of those who produce the goods. Thus, efficiency and effectiveness, free from any government influence, would determine economic survival based on the producers' ability to meet the demands of the market.

MacPherson (1962) uses the term *possessive individualism* to describe the consequences of an economic view of people. Because people essentially are responsible for themselves based on their own capacities, they are not responsible for society as a whole nor for any of its members. Human freedom is seen as independent from the wills of other people, except those whom one agrees to befriend, based on self-interest. Each person, therefore, owns him- or herself and thus enjoys all the freedoms associated with ownership, including a laissez-faire approach to social freedom.

Utilitarianism was the first set of principles that gave rise to the concept of "the economic human." In this view (Bentham 1967), all questions regarding society must be reduced to questions regarding individuals, all questions regarding individuals must be reduced to questions regarding their happiness, and all questions regarding happiness must be reduced to questions regarding measurable pain and pleasure (*felicific calculus*).

For example, if we are considering a particular social or economic policy, we must examine it according to whether it will increase (pleasure) or decrease (pain) the happiness (or self-identified well-being) of individuals. Only those changes that measurably bring more pleasure than pain to the majority of people should be approved by government. Since all humans are basically lazy and selfish, according to philosophy, the only way we can motivate

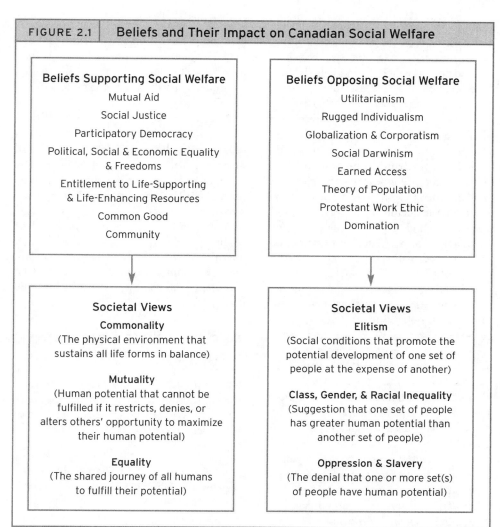

FIGURE 2.1 | **Beliefs and Their Impact on Canadian Social Welfare**

Beliefs Supporting Social Welfare

Mutual Aid

Social Justice

Participatory Democracy

Political, Social & Economic Equality
& Freedoms

Entitlement to Life-Supporting
& Life-Enhancing Resources

Common Good

Community

Beliefs Opposing Social Welfare

Utilitarianism

Rugged Individualism

Globalization & Corporatism

Social Darwinism

Earned Access

Theory of Population

Protestant Work Ethic

Domination

Societal Views

Commonality
(The physical environment that
sustains all life forms in balance)

Mutuality
(Human potential that cannot be
fulfilled if it restricts, denies, or
alters others' opportunity to maximize
their human potential)

Equality
(The shared journey of all humans
to fulfill their potential)

Societal Views

Elitism
(Social conditions that promote the
potential development of one set of
people at the expense of another)

Class, Gender, & Racial Inequality
(Suggestion that one set of people
has greater human potential than
another set of people)

Oppression & Slavery
(The denial that one or more set(s)
of people have human potential)

people is to allow them to have as much pleasure as they can earn. Government should therefore act in the least intrusive way possible in the affairs of business and personal property of people, including their spouses and children.

John Stuart Mill's (1806–1873) notion of *individualism* countered this notion of utilitarianism. Mill's theory emphasized the reality and importance of human liberty and spontaneity and interpreted pleasure not in terms of the greatest amount possi-

ble, but in the attainment of the highest pleasures humans could achieve. To Mill, the mature human being is free to determine the meaning of experience in her or his own way, rather than to try to imitate others. Each human being is unique and therefore capable of making a unique and creative contribution to society as a whole.

In the modern economic view human beings are economic beings who work for economic gain and whose behaviour is economically determined. *Individualism* has come to be associated with independence and looking solely after oneself (*rugged individualism*). This is the "dog-eat-dog" view society in which the individuals' best-developed talents increase their personal advantages. Other members of society are opponents attempting to gain control over social power and resources. Winning and surviving on one's own merits are highly valued. Dependent people are seen as morally inferior and less worthy than independent people. Material possessions become an indicator of social power, privilege, status, and worth. People are valued for what they own and not for who they are; "to have" becomes a primary motivation for human existence (*possessive individualism*). Fromm (1967) identified the outcome of these beliefs as the creation of *homo consumens*, the human being whose primary purpose in society is to consume goods; therefore, being a consumer of goods is perceived as an attribute of human nature.

Two views that support the neutral view of human beings are *social biology* and *technological determinism*. The first suggests that human behaviour is instinctual and endemic to the human species. A human's potential is predetermined genetically, and people act according to these genetic predispositions (Lorenz 1968). The technological determinists argue that, over time, human society will reach such a disastrous state that knowledge and technology alone will solve the world crisis (Mishra 1981).

Jacques Ellul (1964) sees a world driven only by knowledge and technology as one in which modern people are sterile and living in hopeless and endless irrelevance. Both of these views succumb to the *is–ought fallacy*: although both describe what exists (is), this description in itself does not limit what could be (ought). For example, social biology correctly identifies that all humans have genetic maps that unfold over their lifespans (truth that exists). However, to imply that these maps determine human potential denies that any other human factors can influence human development, such as human spirituality, conscience, and self-actualization.

Opponents of social welfare accept a "power-over" mentality, which Bishop (1994, 36) describes as "a world of systems designed to keep people in unjust and unequal positions [which] is held in place by several interrelated expressions of 'power-over': political power, economic power, physical force, and ideological power."

Both advocates and opponents of social welfare disagree on what human nature is and also on the relationship between human beings and society (the environmental context within which people live) as well.

PERSPECTIVES ON HUMAN BEINGS IN SOCIETY

One approach to understanding the relationship between society and its people can be summarized by considering the following statements:

- "Society is what people make it." Every member of society has the power to shape society in accordance with her own belief about what society should look like.

- "It is society's well-being, not the individual's well-being, that is important." Therefore, each member of society must be prepared to sacrifice his own self-interest if and when it benefits society as a whole to do so.

- "Society's well-being and the individual's well-being are mutually interdependent." Therefore, what benefits society also benefits its members and what benefits its members also benefits society. Conversely, what diminishes society diminishes its members and what diminishes its members diminishes society.

Within the realm of these statements the different concepts of human nature come into play. Social welfare advocates tend to accept the last statement as true, and social welfare opponents tend to accept the first two statements as true. Each perspective is based on a set of beliefs about people in society, and these beliefs shape the thinking of both advocates and opponents of social welfare.

The following is a summary of the sets of beliefs and major theoretical perspectives that support each of these perspectives. The student of social welfare should understand that these sets of beliefs do not influence a perspective individually but collectively. However, how much each belief contributes to one's perspective depends on the value one puts on it. One belief can certainly have more influence on one's thinking than another. This helps explain why there are not only differences in perspectives between advocates and opponents of social welfare but also among advocates and opponents of social welfare. Nor are these two categories of beliefs mutually exclusive; a person who promotes social welfare might accept one or more of the sets of beliefs that some social welfare opponents do, and vice versa.

Canadian advocates of social welfare generally support the following principles and beliefs about people in society:

- Mutual aid is the very essence of human relationships as well as the basis for individual and societal existence (Macarov 1978). This view supports Kropotkin's (1925) conclusion that the species that have survived evolution have not been those that could dominate or destroy others but those most able to cooperate with one another.
- A system of social justice that ensures each individual maximum freedom to the extent that an individual's pursuit of

freedoms does not impinge on, restrict, or deny another individual's pursuit of freedoms must prevail (Rawls 1973).

- Democracy, whether participatory or representative, is a preferred social arrangement. However, all citizens must have equal rights and opportunities so they can participate in social decisions or elect representatives to do so on their behalf.
- Political, social, and economic equality must govern all aspects of society. Equality and freedom are fundamental human rights and necessary prerequisites for humanization (Freire 1994, 1968; Teilhard de Chardin 1955). These include the right of all citizens to work and to be equitably reimbursed for that work.
- Society is obliged to ensure that all citizens have sufficient life-sustaining and life-enhancing resources to perform their life tasks (Gil 1992).
- All citizens are socially responsible for maximizing their own potentials and respecting the similar striving of other citizens. Thus each citizen has a dual moral responsibility to help other citizens reach their goals and to help society to reach its goals (Siporin 1975).
- The common good as a major social goal is concerned with the well-being of the community, which includes the integrity and preservation of its basic institutions, practices, core values, and human growth and development. Social workers with a common-good perspective tend to focus on individual well-being, community intervention, organizational change, legislative lobbying, and other forms of social work intervention (Reamer 1993).

Opponents of social welfare tend to espouse the following set of beliefs:

- Self-help, economic freedoms, and social liberty are the prerequisites for all societal arrangements. Except in exceptional circumstances, society must not interfere in the private or business life of its citizens (Armitage 1996; Mencher 1967).

- Access to society's resources must be earned and society must never limit this access or the amount of material resources individual talents, risks, and success gain. Competition for limited resources acts as a stimulant to citizens to maximize their growth and human potential.

- The Theory of Population as articulated by Thomas Malthus (1766–1834) still applies in our world today. Malthus stated that human populations grow geometrically (2, 4, 8, 16, 32...) whereas food production grows only arithmetically (1, 2, 3, 4...). Therefore, because people need food to survive and human sexual passion (especially among the poor) will not decrease, eventually population must outstrip food resources (Dismal Theorem). Increasing the food supply arithmetically and therefore improving health and survival temporarily will only lead to more people being born, thus increasing the number of those who will eventually die of starvation (Utterly Dismal Theorem). Irresponsible people who have more children than they can afford to feed, then, should not be protected by the state, and the poor should practise moral restraint (Macarov 1978).

- The Protestant work ethic is the principle underlying and shaping social responsibility. First articulated by Martin Luther (1483–1546), work was viewed as a vocation—that is, a calling to do God's work in all things. John Calvin (1509–1564) extended the work ethic to define work as a divine vocation, and therefore work in the marketplace is a religious experience. As such, the material rewards from work are less important than the act of working. For many endorsing this work ethic, material success became proof of God's personal favour. One's failure to succeed demonstrated personal immorality or moral inferiority. The concept of the deserving and the undeserving stems from the work ethic (Macarov 1995; Nisbet 1932).

- Since all citizens must take personal responsibility for their own behaviour and life choices, society is responsible only for assisting these individuals to return to the marketplace where they can earn back their pride and self-esteem.

- Society has the right to protect itself from those who would seem to radically change it or from those who illegally seek to benefit from it.

- Charity (philanthropy) is an individual choice a citizen makes or that the state makes on behalf of its citizens. In other words, society values humanitarian acts over state responsibility.

While these sets of beliefs are not inclusive, they do orient the value systems of advocates and opponents and their view of people within society.

These sets of beliefs form the basis from which Canadians determine the cause of a particular social problem and the steps required to resolve the problem. For example, the marked rise in unemployment and social assistance that the economic recession in the first half of the 1990s created was viewed by some (advocates) as caused by the North American Free Trade Agreement (Canada/United States) and the Goods and Services Tax. They claimed that this accord unjustly affected Canadians whose jobs or income were vulnerable to these political decisions. This group saw the solution in the political arena and the resolution in the restoration of employment and economic security to those adversely affected. Others (opponents) saw the same situation as a lesson for Canada about the way our social programs and unionized labour force had eroded Canada's economic competitiveness with other countries. For this group, the solution was to dismantle universal programs and redirect social benefits to those most in need; they prescribed that society suffer through the difficult period until the economy recovered.

Advocates tend to favour political and collectivist resolutions to social problems. The advocate believes that society is responsible for ensuring that all citizens have the means to meet common human needs, particularly at physiological and safety and security levels. Opponents tend to favour a functionalist and individual approach, which suggests that the existing society is the best there is, and that only incremental adjustments are necessary when problems arise.

A further issue arises from these sets of beliefs about people in society: some people claim that they reflect the English Canadian experience. French Canada, on the other hand, has been greatly influenced by other factors—existentialism, Roman Catholicism, social freedoms, and the belief in the family as a distinct unit. These influential factors also shape how French Canadians view social problems and their resolutions. One obvious resolution for the people of Quebec would be to design social programs that are compatible with that province's value systems. However, social welfare advocates with a *polycentric perspective* would hope that Quebec would resolve its social problems not through isolationism but would contribute to developing Canada's world view on social programs. The same argument would apply to other members of Canada's multicultural communities.

CONCLUSION

Modern Canadian thinking is being influenced by globalization, and also by postmodernism. According to this latter theory, meta-theories and professionalism are

"oppressive function(s) in society, perpetuating the capitalist/liberal social order to the advantage of the few over the many" (McKay 1999, 13). Postmodernists call for new mechanisms to allow the voices of the many to be heard and demand "the acknowledgement and celebration of diversity in cultures, sexualities, abilities, ages, and other human characteristics" (Leonard 1997, xiii).

For some social workers, postmodernism constitutes a call "to integrate a social justice orientation into everyday practice" (Gil 1998, 126) and to take political action (Carniol 1987). For other social workers, it is a call to return to neighbourhood and community (McKnight 1995), where we can replace the deconstruction of oppressive community narratives with one that incorporates many voices and many meanings. These would take into account those that are discordant or unpleasant, and that can awaken people to an alternative and more hopeful view of their communities.

Key here for the social workers who are trying to understand the community's ways of interpreting its own history is their ability to hear multiple layers of stories, even conflicting stories, of the same event, without silencing or suppressing discordant voices. Social workers can understand the full meaning of an event only when they take the time to really listen to the forgotten stories and the marginalized voices (Delaney, Brownlee, and Sellick 1999). Harmonizing social work values and postmodern thinking challenges social work to "ground its interventive practices in a clearly articulated, revitalized expression of identity and purpose" (McKay 1999, 20).

This chapter presents the competing values that exist in Canada regarding beliefs about the intrinsic worth of the individual, society's responsibility for its members, and the responsibility of those members for the common good. It is imperative that those people advocating social welfare as a vital and necessary social institution possess a clear and concise understanding of these values. Such clarity allows them to interpret more precisely various efforts at social change and enable the systematic analysis of current events and their potential impact on the social and personal well-being of Canada's citizens. A fundamental governing principle for both social welfare advocates and the social work profession is the belief that all human beings have potential and that this potential is best nurtured in an environmental context governed by mutuality and respect.

REFERENCES

Armitage, A. 1996. *Social welfare in Canada revisited.* 3d. edn. Don Mills, ON: Oxford University Press.

Armour, L., & Trott, E. 1981. *The faces of reason: An essay on philosophy and culture in English Canada, 1850–1950.* Waterloo, ON: Wilfrid Laurier Press.

Babbie, E. 1986. *Observing ourselves: Essays in social research.* Belmont, CA.: Wadsworth.

Babbie, E. 1977. *Society by agreement.* Belmont, CA.: Wadsworth.

Bentham, J. 1967. *A fragment of government and an introduction to the principles of morals and legislation.* Oxford: Basil Blackwell.

Bishop, A. 1994. *Becoming an ally: Breaking the cycle of oppression.* Halifax: Fernwood.

Carniol, B. 1987. *Case critical: The dilemma of social work in Canada.* Toronto: Between the Lines.

Clarke, Tony 1997. *Silent coup.* Toronto: CCPA and James Lorimer.

Cragg, W. 1986. Two concepts of community or moral theory and Canadian culture. *Dialogue. XXV.* 31–52.

Delaney, R., Brownlee, K., & Sellick, M. 1999. Communities. In R. Delaney, K. Brownlee, & M. Sellick (Eds.), *Social work with rural and northern communities* (pp. 1–13). Thunder Bay: Lakehead University Centre for Northern Studies.

Douglas, J. (Ed.). 1970. *Freedom and tyranny: Social problems in a technological society.* New York: Alfred A. Knopf.

Ellul, J. 1964. *The technological society.* New York: Alfred A. Knopf.

Federico, R. 1984. *The social welfare institution.* 4th edn. Toronto: D. C. Heath and Company.

Frankl, V. 1969. *The will to meaning.* Scarborough, ON: Plume.

Freire, P. 1968. *Pedagogy of the oppressed.* New York: Seabury Press.

Freire, P. 1985. *The politics of education: Culture, power and liberation.* South Hadley, MA: Bergin and Garvey.

Freire, P. 1994. *Pedagogy of hope.* New York: Continuum.

Fromm, E. 1955. *The sane society.* Greenwich: Fawcett.

Fromm, E. 1967. The psychological aspects of the guaranteed income. In R. Theobald (Ed.), *The guaranteed income* (pp. 183–193). Garden City, NY: Anchor.

Gil, D. 1992. *Unravelling social policy.* Rev. 5th edn. Rochester: Schenkman Books.

Gil, D. 1998. *Confronting injustice and oppression: Concepts and strategies for social workers.* New York: Columbia University Press.

Grant, G. P. 1959. *Philosophy in the mass age.* Toronto: Copp Clark.

Harvey, O. J. 1967. Conceptual systems and attitude change. In C. Sherif & M. Sherif (Eds.), *Attitude, ego involvement, and change.* New York: Wiley.

Hegel, G. W. 1907. *Theologische Jugendschriften* Nohl, Ed. Tubingen: Mohr.

Kluckhohn, F., & Strodbeck, F. 1961. *Variation in value orientations.* Evanston, IL: Row Peterson.

Kropotkin, P. 1925. *Mutual aid: A factor of evolution.* New York: Alfred A. Knopf.

Leonard, P. 1997. *Postmodern welfare: Reconstructing an emancipatory project.* London: Sage.

Lerner, M. 1997. *The politics of meaning: Restoring hope and possibility in an age of cynicism.* Don Mills, ON: Addison-Wesley.

Lorenz, K. 1968. *On aggression.* London: Methuen.

Macarov, D. 1978. *The design of social welfare.* Toronto: Holt, Rinehart, and Winston.

Macarov, D. 1995. *Social welfare: Structure and practice.* Thousand Oaks, CA.: Sage.

McKay, S. 1999. Postmodernism, social well-being, and the mainstream/progressive debate. In F. Turner (Ed.), *Social work practice: A Canadian perspective* (pp. 10–22). Scarborough, ON: Prentice Hall/Allyn and Bacon Canada.

McKnight, J. 1995. *The careless society.* New York: Basic.

MacPherson, C. B. 1962. *The political theory of possessive individualism.* Oxford: Clarendon Press.

McPherson, D., & Rabb, J. D. 1993. *Indian from the inside: A study in ethnometaphysics.* Occasional Paper 14. Thunder Bay: Lakehead University Centre for Northern Studies.

Mathews, R. 1988. *Canadian identity.* Ottawa: Steel Rail Publishing.

Mencher, S. 1967. *Poor law to poverty program.* Pittsburgh: University of Pittsburgh Press.

Mishra, R. 1981. *Society and social policy.* 2d edn. London: Macmillan.

Mullaly, B. 1993. *Structural social work: Ideology, theory and practice.* Toronto: McClelland & Stewart.

Nisbet, R. 1932. *The contribution of religion to social work.* New York: Columbia University Press.

Plant, R. 1974. *Community and ideology: An essay in applied social philosophy.* London: Routledge and Kegan Paul.

Rabb, J. D. 1989. The polycentric perspective: A Canadian alternative to Rorty. *Dialogue, XXVIII.* 107–115.

Rawls, J. 1973. *A theory of justice.* London: Oxford University Press.

Reamer, F. 1993. *The philosophical foundations of social work.* New York: Columbia University Press.

Rein, M. September 1974. Social policy analysis as the interpretation of beliefs. *Journal of the American Institute of Planners.* 297–298.

Rokeach, M. 1973. *The nature of human values.* New York: Free Press.

Saul, J. R. 1995. *The unconscious civilization.* Concord, ON: Anansi.

Schon, D. 1971. *Beyond the stable state.* Toronto: George McLeod Limited.

Siporin, M. 1975. *Introduction to social work practice.* New York: Macmillan.

Smith, A. 1937. *The wealth of nations.* New York: Modern Library.

Teilhard de Chardin, P. 1955. *The phenomenon of man.* New York: Harper and Brothers.

Wilensky, H., & Lebeaux, C. 1958. *Industrial society and social welfare.* New York: Russell Sage Foundation.

chapter three

The Knowledge Base of Canadian Social Welfare

Frank McGilly

Things should be made as simple as possible, but not any simpler.

Attributed to Albert Einstein

This chapter deals exclusively with social welfare. Aspects of social work will be left to other contributors.

Social welfare is an inclusive domain. If "social welfare" means "the welfare of society," then its knowledge base is virtually everything that has to do with social life. To make purposeful thought possible, however, we must impose some boundaries.

"Social welfare" might be limited to certain explicit policies and programs of governments: those related to income transfers to individuals and/or families; some insurances, notably those against contingencies that cause loss of income; and assistance with housing. Some regulatory functions might be included, such as the regulation of workplace conditions, food safety, and environmental protection. It might well be assumed that all activities of government ought to aim at improving the welfare of society. Still, for our purposes, it makes sense to exclude even such functions as transportation and public works, despite their direct impact on people's welfare. More debatable would be the exclusion of education and the administration of justice, but they require such special resources and skills as to be fields of their own. Excluding the provision of health services is even more debatable, if only because poverty and insecurity of income, the irreducible core matters of "social welfare," are obviously linked to poor health. Some parts of any defining boundary must be seen as permeable.

Social welfare is invariably characterized as interdisciplinary. Martin Rein lists history, politics, philosophy, sociology, economics, and psychology as contributing disciplines.[1] The student of social welfare cannot master all those disciplines; proposed here is an outline of the necessary knowledge base founded upon four systematically related levels of content: facts, practice, theory, and values. This approach differs from the study of any of the aforementioned social sciences to the extent that welfare is essentially a field of practice while the sciences are not; the values at play in welfare are broader and must be made more explicit than those of the social sciences (though no one would suggest that social scientists ignore value issues).

FOUR LEVELS OF CONTENT

The lines between the four levels of content—facts, practice, theory, values—are not firm. Theories should rationally be founded on facts, but one of the functions of theory is to tell us which facts are relevant. Practice is guided by theory, but it is also taken as a test of theory, and facts often emerge during the course of social welfare practice that challenge received theories.

The Level of Facts

Certain kinds of data tell us about the level of well-being in society, particularly about shortcomings in the level of welfare, or of welfare among certain segments of the population—income levels, provision for income security, nutrition, health. It is inevitable that indicators of well- or ill-being in these areas incorporate value

judgments, but such judgments are not necessarily arbitrary or culture-bound; few value structures lead their adherents to deny that having enough food is better than having too little.

To be sure, many important dimensions of welfare are difficult to define in terms that all would accept. Poverty is one example. A definition, and therefore a measurement, of poverty agreeable to the Fraser Institute would likely outrage the National Anti-Poverty Organization, but at least their respective definitions can be understood.

It is not necessary to beg the question as to which facts really count. The knowledge base proposed here equips students to question their sense of what is important, and to modify it as their understanding evolves.

The Level of Practice

Social welfare is a *doing* subject. The facts are worth knowing and the understandings worth thinking about only in relation to efforts to improve matters. We need, therefore, to attend to those things that are done to enhance welfare—programs of many kinds and their outcomes, both successes and failures. This seemingly bland assertion comes freighted with the demanding implication that social welfare is concerned as much with means as with ends. This can be a hard lesson; good intentions are not enough.

The Level of Theory

Giving shape to the known facts—that is, those facts taken as known at a given time—is the function of theory. Theory looks for relationships between bits of information; it tries to explain why things are the way they are, and perhaps to hazard predictions of outcomes should conditions change in certain ways. Whereas statements of fact may be determined to be true or false, theoretical propositions are not so much "right" or "wrong" as more or less consistent with the observed evidence and with each other. The delicate relationship between theory and facts, already referred to, is taken up below.

The Level of Values

Finally, the study of social welfare is value-driven. One claims to have good intentions. Very well: what is good? Says Martin Bulmer, "The policy researcher differs from the discipline-based social scientist in seeking to influence policy and achieve changes as well as to understand basic causes."[2] Of course social scientists may have policy preferences and may work to achieve them, but that is not their function as social scientists. Social welfare, for its part, is essentially normative as well as cognitive. Its knowledge base must include, therefore, a critical awareness of the competing and conflicting value structures that have shaped welfare objectives and policies. This may be the most difficult part of the task: to explore, as part of what one studies, value structures other than one's own.

Means, as well as ends, must be criticized from the point of view of values.

The next task is to depict in more detail the four levels of the knowledge base—facts, theory, practice, values—recognizing that they interact. In fact, the reciprocal interplay among them is the most important point here.

THE FACTS

People and Society

As noted, virtually all that society does is, in some degree, related to welfare. Many public issues may be difficult to distinguish from the domain of welfare, even though they do not spring to mind as core welfare concerns: subsidization of public transportation, for example.[3] As a first approximation to a definition of the field, and of the particularly relevant facts, we may stipulate that social welfare essentially consists of efforts to address social conditions that inflict or threaten material deprivation or harm.

We recognize social problems on the basis of data on such things as income distribution and income security, employment and unemployment, health conditions (life expectancy, infant mortality, prevalence of illnesses, malnutrition), and behaviours considered self-destructive and/or anti-social (addictions and substance abuse, child neglect, inadequate education). In virtually all of these matters, except birth and death, both definition and observation are more or less difficult. What exactly are we looking for? How do we look for it?

Much of the data of social welfare, and of social welfare activity, deal more with individual symptoms than with underlying social causes—a familiar complaint. As Aristotle says in the most-quoted proposition of social science, man is a social animal. All serious human problems have a significant social component, but it can be difficult to see past the individual's hardship to its social roots. To focus thus on problems and hardships may seem to limit social welfare to the deplored residual function of repairing harm and to deny it the institutional function of preventing evil and promoting good. (References to this residual–institutional axis echo throughout social policy discourse.[4]) Still, a beginning focus on problems hardly rules out efforts to avoid them; on the contrary, one can hardly prescribe for prevention until one knows what one wants to prevent.

Acknowledging, then, that the selection of the relevant facts is unavoidably problematic, what are some examples of the data basic to social welfare?

The People: Numbers, Age, Gender, Etc.

The ultimate foundation of the knowledge base of welfare is knowledge of the people who make up society. How many people are there? Are their numbers increasing, stable, or declining—nationally, regionally, locally? What is the age composition of the population? Is it changing? Assuming the existence of families and/or households (the definitions of which may be contentious), how large are the family/household units? Are they growing smaller or larger? How are they made up—women, men, children?

The answers to these questions are at the root of social policy concerns. It has long been known, for example, that Canada's population is aging. In all industrial countries, the long-term trend is for the average age to increase, through a combination of longer lifespans and a decline in the birth rate. (Currently there is concern in the wealthiest countries that obesity may actually reduce the average lifespan.) Population aging poses real challenges, but poor countries, with a lot of famine, disease and high birth rates, have young populations; presumably most would prefer the problems of population aging.

The material support of older people is, consequently, a front-burner issue in Canada. Our response is affected by prevailing social conventions such as those governing retirement, including voluntary and involuntary early retirement, workforce participation of the sexes, typical age of entry into the workforce, responsibilities for child-rearing, etc.

All of these factors have changed more or less, some more slowly than others. Unless based on correct age-specific information, any opinion on this subject is useless.

Equally relevant are the different age profiles of women and men. Everybody knows that women live longer than men, on the average, though the gap appears to be narrowing. Less obvious are the compound implications of (1) the increase in both the *numbers* and the *proportion* of elderly people and (2) the ratio of females to males, well over 1:1 at age 60, higher at every successive age. What problems are created by this age-linked preponderance of females? The social theorist, brooding on these facts, will ask, are the problems due to peculiar artifacts of our society, like our historic pattern of female paid employment? Or would there be problems even if women had not been at a lifetime income-earning disadvantage? What to do depends on the answers.

Just as important are demographic developments throughout the age range. The baby boom of the 1950s and 1960s led to the succession of pressing social issues of the last generation: shortages of family housing, demand for schools, demand for higher education, persistently higher-than-usual youth unemployment, signs of alienation among young adults, now the pressures on "the sandwich generation," and so on.[5] For 50 years our social policy has been driven by the progress of the baby boomers through their life cycle, with more to come. Population trends will always thus govern social policy—not always with foresight, even when known in advance.

The study of social welfare begins, then, with knowledge about the elementary stuff of society, the people. The Census of Canada is the bedrock of our knowledge base, fortunately a well-designed, reliable one.

Material Well-Being

It may be argued that well-being is inadequately measured by dollar income, but income provides the best measure of the material possibilities open to an individual, family, or group.

How are annual incomes distributed, from high to low? Knowing this distribution, a judgment may be made as to what is a high or low income; on that basis, we know the numbers of low-, middle-, and high-income recipients, as individuals and as households. The most commonly cited indicator of well-being, by far, is income, but *wealth* is just as important—how much one has, as distinct from how much one receives over a period. Here again, the census is the primary source, though reporting difficulties cause some gaps in the data, especially on wealth.

The distributions of income and wealth are the prime indicators of the extent of material welfare and deprivation. Knowing how high the average or median family income is, for example, we know what constitutes an income substantially lower. Accurate knowledge corrects against frequent misconceptions, understatements, and exaggerations concerning poverty and inequality. If we do not know these data, we cannot sensibly discuss problems of income distribution, let alone develop measures to alleviate them.

We also need to know how incomes are received. Most income is received through work. Almost all work income is earned through employment—in other words, working for an employer. What kinds of work, what kinds of jobs, what kinds of employers? The knowledge base includes discernible trends in employment and in employment compensation. Many employees receive some kinds of non-cash compensation—health insurance, pension contributions, extended vacations. Some employees' incomes are so significantly supplemented by so-called fringe benefits that commentators on compensation have begun to speak of the decline in the importance of salaries, though not, it must be said, at lower income levels. A surprisingly large share of our society's total allocation of resources to welfare is distributed in this way. And it is recognized that inequality in access to fringe benefits is much greater than inequality in dollar incomes.

As employment is the main source of income, unemployment is one of the principal causes of income deficiency and of poverty. Adequate knowledge of the complexities of employment in late industrial society is essential to any understanding of unemployment. (We leave aside the psychic and social benefits of work and the converse damages of unemployment, important as they are.) In discussing unemployment, we may begin with the official unemployment rate, but we must know more than that, and not only because that familiar statistic does not claim to account for all Canadians out of work.

Rates like the unemployment rate are normally seen as "facts," but it is necessary to understand the various rates that are commonly circulated. The unemployment rate is a carefully defined quotient: the number of people unemployed, carefully defined, divided by the number of people in the "active workforce," also carefully defined, expressed as a percentage. Many who are not employed will not be numbered among the unemployed. Do we include people over 65, receiving pensions, possibly ample pensions, not working but looking for a job? Or the potential earner of a second income in a family, willing to work though not in need of the income? "Need" does not enter into consideration in any way. It would complicate the counting to include "need" in the definition; for one thing, many employed people might well be deemed to be in need. Do we count as unemployed a single mother, living on public assistance, who would take a job instantly if it offered a reasonably secure improvement on her present situation? Or jobless people who have grown so discouraged that they have stopped looking energetically?

This most elementary of facts, the number of unemployed people, will vary with our answers to these questions. Those who refer to the rate of unemployment without knowing exactly how it is derived know only vaguely what they are talking about. The same is true of all rates—poverty, mortality, birth, crime.

Which industries regularly have high numbers of unemployed workers, and which do not? We cannot simply say, "Let's have less of the one and more of the other." Yet knowledge of the different experience of different industries is a first step towards policy. How does the prevalence of unemployment vary in different parts of Canada? Again, we cannot simply say, "Workers in region A should move to region B," though of course many do. Knowing the facts, should we give similar, ostensibly equal, treatment to workers in all regions? The history of (controversial) regional differences in Employment Insurance benefits illustrates the difficulty of coping with such facts.

Unemployment is only one of many welfare-related economic problems. Similar knowledge is required concerning low income. What levels of income do we consider "low"? A judgment call is required; once it is made, and clearly explained, important questions may be asked. How many people have low incomes? What kinds of people—young, old, educated, uneducated, able-bodied, handicapped? Where are they located—in big cities, small towns, rural areas, east, centre, west? Are they "low-income" for short spells or for generations? How do women fare compared to men? The welfare of women is a serious issue, only recently getting the attention John Stuart Mill gave it more than 130 years ago.[6]

Public Finance

Welfare programs take up anywhere from a quarter to a half of the public expenditures of industrial countries, including the United States, a country that is too hastily labelled as hostile to all such public intervention. Such programs (see "Practice in Social Welfare," p. 37) are clearly part of our subject, even though surprisingly little of the money disbursed goes to the poor or the nearly poor. It is as important to know where the money comes from as to know where it goes. Some grasp of public finance is basic knowledge for the student of welfare—in Canada, now more than ever, as the federal government's system of budgetary management has become, of itself, a major influence in social policy.[7]

Public finance has long been a central instrument of public policy. The visible face of social policy, namely explicit welfare measures like Public Assistance, Old Age Security, family tax credits, and the like, is only part of the machinery by which governments try overtly to enhance the general welfare as they see it. A much larger part works through fiscal policy—manipulation of the balance between government revenue and expenditure. (The theory underlying modern fiscal policy is a legacy of the economist John Maynard Keynes (1883–1946), though his authority is not as commanding as it once was.) Whether or not fiscal policy works as advertised, its effect on material welfare is enormous.

Moreover, revenue administration is not just a matter of collecting enough money to pay the nation's bills, in the current year or later (by borrowing). Different decisions will mean different burdens and benefits for different people. In order to follow, let alone influence, the relevant debates, one must have a grasp of the available revenue options.

What to tax? What to exempt? There are equally relevant, equally complicated issues surrounding public spending. The choices made affect the final distribution of real income more than all the explicit income transfer and income security programs put together.

Income distribution, the labour market, and public finance are the leading economic topics in the knowledge base of social welfare. Not every student's knowledge base will include in-depth understanding of these topics, but in each of the relevant areas, a range of questions like those raised above should be asked. What every student should possess is knowledge of the kinds of facts that are relevant, and not just those facts brought forward to support a point of view.

The Cohesive Factors in Society

Since human beings are social animals, social welfare must take into account the interaction of the individual with the institutions of society. The isolated person is at risk. This interaction will do much to determine the material and the moral well-being and health of individuals, their identities, their personal autonomy, the realization of their capacity for growth, and the well-being of their communities. Here again, one's perceptions of what *is* in social life must not be clouded by one's notions of what *ought to be*. Different societies are held together by some different and some similar things. What are these constituent institutions of society?

Family It is said of virtually every society that the family is its basic unit. The meaning of "family," however, varies. In some societies, "family" means married parents and their children, with other generations and lateral relatives on the periph-

ery. In others, extended family ties are so strong that, with respect to a given child, an outsider might be unable to tell who in a given group are its "real" (biological) parents and who are other relatives, and the members of the group might not think it was particularly important. In Canada, the meaning of "family" is evolving. We speak of blended families, lone-parent (usually lone-mother) families, same-sex-couple families. Judicial decisions at the provincial and federal levels in 2003 allowed for the possible recognition of the marriage of persons of the same sex.

Many policies related to welfare, from taxable status to entitlement to benefits, have hinged on family status. The conventional stereotype of the family made up of an income-earning father, a housekeeping mother, and the children of this couple has not wholly reflected reality in Canada for a long time, if it ever did; this can be confirmed by consulting past censuses. Of interest are the range and prevalence of different family structures in Canada, the sizes of families, the variations between different ethnic and religious groups, etc. Just as a concern with unemployment leads us into the economics of the labour market, observation of contemporary family structures will lead us into the sociology of the family for theoretical understanding, but it is the information that comes first, the sociology that is derivative.

Other institutions are powerful: tribes, religious groups, and abstract institutions such as taboos and rites. The network of relationships around work has become increasingly important, as both men and women now typically pursue work careers. This is illustrated by the way the workplace has become a favoured setting for movies and television series. Religion has always been tremendously influential, even when secular currents are as strong as they are today. The ways that people respond to the challenges of welfare may be influenced, even governed, by religious adherence. Religions may be universalist or exclusive, active or contemplative, human-centred or other-worldly. Consider the impact of the "ultramontane" ("beyond this world") movement among Catholics in Quebec in the nineteenth century, and that of the down-to-earth work of Father Georges-Henri Levesque in Quebec in the twentieth, or of the "Social Gospel" movement in some Protestant groups in Canada from the 1920s to the 1940s.[8]

The relevance of ethnicity and culture is greater today than ever, as Canada becomes more and more pluralist as a society. Canada has been a multicultural society for a long time; even before the massive European immigration between 1880 and 1910, our ethnic mix belied somewhat the prevailing notion of two founding peoples. Now, outside Quebec, only the smallest provinces are dominated by one ethnic group, the British, and even that statistical domination depends on making "British" a single ethnic category, something that the English, Scottish, Irish, and Welsh might not willingly concede.

We shall not attempt an inventory of the institutions and processes that associate individuals with meaningful groups, thereby holding society together. Possibly the most important common characteristic in the lives of many whose welfare is problematic is the weakness of their bonds with society: they are left without meaningful connections. Some things that hold people together may also drive them apart. Notoriously, the bonds that some people rely on give rise to prejudice in the eyes of others and tend to marginalize them.

The Facts of History

In social affairs, history is the closest thing we have to a test laboratory. Experiments virtually do not exist in the world of social policy. Certainly, we can try things out and evaluate the outcomes, but the effects of social programs are too long term, too diffuse, too entangled in the complexities of life ever to be captured in a controlled experiment, though evaluators do their best to find technical surrogates for experimental conditions. A so-called experiment with a program that yields results over a five-year period cannot tell us with confidence what will happen over the next five, let alone the next 25, years. History will not do for us what the controlled experiment purports to do: establish reliable if–then relationships, which may point the way to cause-and-effect relationships. History can hint at the conditions conducive to and those hostile to the achievement of a desired outcome and at the complications that accompany attempts at change. From the record of mixed successes, failures, and surprises, students must draw what lessons they can, for there are few other lessons to be had.

When one reads history, one also reads the historian. The way authors see their subject will influence the emphasis they give to the different facts their research discloses, which includes leaving some out. The student ought therefore to bring a measure of skepticism to any one reading. What history, then, has a claim on one's attention?

Canada: Public and Private Responsibilities A Canadian must know how our present pattern of the public–private sharing of welfare responsibilities evolved. Support of the needy was not consensually established as a core function of the state until after the Great Depression and World War II. Previously, Canada had relied heavily on the private sector—religious and philanthropic good works. Left to the state was responsibility for those whom private largesse could not reach or whose difficulties were unambiguously recognized as consequences of the social system, chiefly "needy mothers," orphans, and widows without means. To be sure, there was a measure of state financial support for some private charitable endeavours.

Just a few years after the end of World War II in 1945, the situation was substantially the other way round. In Canada there are now only scattered instances of private programs providing income support. The private sector still shares in meeting some material needs such as shelter and food. Services of other kinds, such as counselling, provided under religious and philanthropic auspices, continue to have their place.

As noted above, the private sector now bears a considerable part of the total social welfare burden through the evolution of employment (pensions, supplementary health care, parental leave); only a small part of this support goes to the relief of the poor, most of whom have, at best, tenuous connections with employment. In programs ancillary to public assistance, such as work training and rehabilitation, the private sector, both profit-seeking and non-profit, plays a substantial role. We are in the midst of the Canadian variant of a vogue for the privatization of welfare-related services that is endemic throughout the industrialized world. The balance between private and public continues to shift back and forth, and accordingly the history of that balance remains relevant.

Provincial–Federal Sharing of Responsibilities

Since Canada is emphatically a federal country, the historical development of the sharing of responsibilities among levels of government is important. What is to be done by the provinces and what by the federal government, and why, are live, heated questions, nowhere more so than in the field of social welfare.[9]

The relevant clauses in the Constitution Act (until 1982 the British North America Act) are Section 91, enumerating the powers of the federal Parliament, Section 92, enumerating those of the provincial legislatures, and Section 94A, concerning old age pensions. Section 92 has been interpreted as giving jurisdiction over health and welfare to the provinces. The terms of the Constitution concerning federal and provincial powers have undergone only a few changes, all related to social welfare— an amendment permitting the federal Parliament to legislate unemployment insurance and later amendments concerning old age pensions. Also important has been Section 106, which simply allows the Parliament to authorize spending "for the public service"; translated into the so-called spending power, this seemingly innocuous phrase has made possible important federal–provincial financial arrangements leading up to the Canada Health Transfer and the Canada Social Transfer of 2004.

Other Countries

In the experience of other countries, certain episodes are especially interesting: in the United States, the Progressive Era (roughly 1880–1920), the New Deal (1932–1940), the "War on Poverty" (1964–circa 1970), and the subsequent retrenchment, still proceeding; in Great Britain, the era of Liberal social reform (1905–1914), and the period when the Welfare State took hold (from the publication of the Beveridge Report in 1942, at a low point in World War II, to about 1960), with a backward glance at the history of the Poor Law of 1834 and its predecessor, the Elizabethan Poor Law; in Germany, the paternalistic measures undertaken under Otto von Bismarck, first chancellor of the German Empire from 1871 to 1890; and the widely copied Swedish and other Scandinavian programs of the twentieth century. More recent British and American developments, deplored by most advocates for comprehensive social policy, should not be ignored.[10]

From such foreign histories Canadian students can learn, first, what others have done, faced with situations broadly similar to our own: industrialization and its sequels, the rise of capitalism, some form of democracy in most cases, some common religious traditions, and so on. The first countries to be struck by a major social change have some excuse for being taken by surprise; others should profit from others' earlier experiences.

Second, given that situations may be comparable, we can analyze the similarities to and the differences from the Canadian context to sharpen our assessment of what might work here.

Third, the histories of welfare in other countries reinforce the student's sophistication about the springs of any particular action. Why was it done? What were the apparent motives of its initiators and supporters? Who opposed? Why? What went well? What went wrong?

PRACTICE IN SOCIAL WELFARE

Practice in social welfare amounts really to the implementation and administration of social programs; in our time these have been mostly publicly financed. True, in the early twenty-first century there appears to be a widespread swing to greater private responsibility, but almost all private programs require a mandate based ultimately on some legislation. They rely on subsidies or tax relief, to obtain which they must meet legislative or regulatory standards, and they are regulated in their conduct. Between the moment that advocates for a cause identify a problem and the time a program is launched to deal with it,

many hands contribute to that program's design, promotion, and execution. It will be shaped in part even by those who oppose it. It will be constructed so as to satisfy a number of interests, as well as to meet the particular problem it ostensibly addresses. As Bismarck is supposed to have said, a law is like a sausage: even if you like it, you don't want to know everything that went into it. Yet even if untainted by any compromises, a single program is unlikely to meet all the demands of a social problem that is, as all are, multifaceted—the more so since the creation of the program itself adds a new facet, a new clientele, and possibly a new bureaucracy (true in both the private sector and the public). The program becomes part of the playing board, affecting the behaviour of all the players: for example, employers, workers, and provincial welfare departments react differently to unemployment because of the federal Employment Insurance program.

The essential components of a welfare program are:

- the authorizing legislation (if it is a public program) or the status and mandate of the responsible organization (if it is a private program);
- the services and benefits provided;
- the categories of people covered, and the conditions under which they become eligible for benefits (to define *eligible* is also to define *non-eligible*);
- the means by which it is financed. The principal financing options are general taxation, special contributions (usually tied to work income), and charges for services (not common in public welfare), and in the case of private programs, philanthropy, service charges, and government grants; and
- the nature of the body responsible for administration. The principal options in

the public realm are regular government departments, directly responsible to the government of the day, and appointed "boards" or "commissions" with mandates according them some defined degree of autonomy from government.

These features are interrelated. Public assistance, whose benefits are based on need, can hardly be financed other than by taxation; if benefits are scaled to earnings, as in insurance-type programs like Workers' Compensation, Employment Insurance, and the Canada and Quebec Pension Plans, it makes sense that contributions by and on behalf of the persons covered also be scaled to earnings. If financed by taxation, for which the government of the day is politically accountable, it is appropriate that the program be administered by a politically accountable government department. If contributions are collected from potential beneficiaries, and if benefits are distributed on a contractual insurance basis subject to the occurrence of a contingency like a work accident or job loss, it is appropriate that the program be administered by a body at some remove from the political preferences of the current government.

In real life, nothing stays simple. Mixed financing and administrative arrangements have at times been found appropriate. For 50 years, Unemployment Insurance, as it was known until 1996, whose benefits were earnings-related, was financed partly out of general taxation; the administration of the current program, Employment Insurance, is closely tied to the federal Human Resources and Skills Development Canada (HRSDC).

In coming into execution, a program is subject to threats from at least two quarters. First, to satisfy some interests whose support is considered necessary, it may acquire features that deflect resources towards needs or wants other than those of the core problem it supposedly attacks: Unemployment insurance tries to meet needs that are essentially extraneous to unemployment as such, such as maternity leaves and interregional income redistribution.[11] Second, it probably will not meet all the demands flowing from the core problem. If welfare is narrowly defined as concerned with material provision, private welfare programs are now common chiefly in providing food, clothing, and shelter. More broadly, private programs are important in providing information, advice, self-help, and advocacy, and, usually through contractual arrangements with government, in training in job skills and life skills and in community development.[12] Voluntary organizations vary widely in the links between financial supporters, mandates (sometimes narrow), administrators, and beneficiaries (at times defined in somewhat exclusive terms). Private agencies are relatively unfettered by the bureaucratic structures that political accountability imposes on government agencies, but they are subject to significant constraints of their own. When partially supported by public funds, as when executing contracts with government for delivery of a service, private agencies may acquire some quasi-governmental characteristics.

THEORY

Theory is not exactly knowledge at all; it is an attempt to discern relationships between facts. Items with no perceived relationships will be considered irrelevant; they will not be systematically observed as "data." As long as an accepted framework of relationships remains convincing, changes in theory will be slow. Repeated observations that challenge theory will ultimately bring about its modification— as Abraham Kaplan says of theory, "The possibility of failure is intrinsic to its effort"—but theorists are slow to abandon a way of thinking that seems to work.[13]

Theory influences the means of observation; if you think you know which facts are relevant, you will look for ways to observe those facts. In the end, however, no one would deny that theory should follow, not govern, the evidence. Leonard Marsh, a pioneering Canadian scholar of social welfare, profoundly influenced social policy in the 1940s and after by arguing not that the leaders of the time did not care about poverty, unemployment, and ill health, but that the established ways of looking at them were misleading; when reality was more truly recorded, the theory of how society works would have to be renewed.[14]

Three examples of theoretical issues basic to the field of social welfare illustrate issues related to individualism–collectivism, voluntarism–determinism, and subjectivity–objectivity. Though these terms are somewhat abstract, responses to them have concrete impacts on welfare practice.

The Individualist–Collectivist Axis

Positions on the way society functions can be plotted on a continuum ranging from those that explain everything, or almost everything, in terms of the behaviour of the individual (entrepreneur, worker, parent, child, political leader) to those that explain everything in terms of collectivities (class, nation, religious or ethnic group, sex).

Among collectivist theories, much the most influential in the literature and in modern history have been those that analyze society in terms of class. The concept of class gives some coherence to the way decisions are made and goods and evils distributed in society.

One finds such coherence in theories. The central figure here is Karl Marx (1818–1883), for whom class was determined by one's relationship to the means of production, either as owner or servant, but one may derive much insight from the concept of class without coming to Marxist conclusions.

Some find that any general propositions about class must be so covered over with qualifications and exceptions as to throw insufficient light upon reality. Race, alternatively, may explain much of what happens. (Caution: many scholars challenge the validity of the concept of "race.") More recently, feminist analyses have put gender at the centre: they suggest that what happens socially to someone depends more on that person's gender than on any other characteristic.

No student of society ignores the impact of collective factors on the lives of individuals. At the time of writing, however, liberal individualist theories have the wind in their sails in the Western world. The individualist theoretical argument asserts that when all the collective influences have been accounted for, they do not explain observed experience as well as do individual capacities, motivations, and choices. (The issue for theory is whether individual or collective perspectives better explain reality, not which *should* dominate ethically or politically. The link between theory and values is explored below.)

Part of the reason for the current individualist vogue may be a general feeling that the proof of the pudding is in the eating. Political regimes founded on a collectivist view of society have done poorly in the last half century. Even in the well-established Scandinavian welfare states and in the European democracies, there has been an intellectual reaction against the (inevitably) imperfect success of various social programs; state-run old age pensions, for example, have become a hot political issue. The individualist wave is no doubt based more on dissatisfaction with program performance than upon a profound popular preference for one *theory* over another, but even in the theoretical literature the individualist swing has been strong.[15]

The Voluntarist–Determinist Axis

Debates over the opposing claims of free will and predetermination loom large in the history of Western thought. What part of the individual's behaviour is freely chosen, what part determined by forces beyond his or her control?

Whether clearly articulated or not, one's theory about what makes society tick will influence one's choice of remedies to repair damage or of preventives to avoid evil. Proponents of a voluntarist theory will favour programs that rely on individual motivation—to get a job, to keep the family together, to practise safe sex, to kick the habit, while those with determinist views will emphasize social supports for the beleaguered individual—income supports without work tests, financial support for traditional family functions, free needle exchanges for drug addicts at risk of AIDS, and certain controls over behaviour. Determinists will not deny that the individual enjoys some measure of autonomy—they may indeed insist that they aim to maximize such autonomy as is possible; they will, however, also insist that such autonomy is fundamentally hedged by environmental factors, which must be controlled.

The Objectivity–Subjectivity Axis

The reciprocity between theory and data has been noted: analysis of observed data ultimately refutes or tends to confirm a theoretical proposition, but the theory itself tells us which data to look for and how to analyze them.

The technical problem of the separation of the observer from the data being observed is illustrated by the well-known "Hawthorne effect," first clearly described in reports of studies conducted by Harvard social psychologists in the 1920s in the Western Electric Company plant in Hawthorne, Massachusetts. They concluded that the behaviour of human subjects was influenced by being observed—so one cannot be sure of their behaviour if not observed. Social science discourse is replete with discussions of this problem and with attempts to circumvent it. What degree of objectivity is feasible in the observation of human behaviour? In other words, is it possible for one observer to report on behaviour exactly as another would? Once one suspects such objectivity is problematic, even with ingenious methodological safeguards in place, one's confidence in the research upon which theory and practice are based will be shaken. (The problem is recognized in the physical sciences, too. Observation of sub-atomic particles requires a concentration of energy upon them: hence the well-known "uncertainty principle," according to which we cannot know precisely both the location of a particle and the direction and speed of its motion. In one of the most curious coincidences in intellectual history, the uncertainty principle was enunciated by the physicist Werner Heisenberg [1901–1976] at much the same time that the Hawthorne effect was enunciated by the Harvard social scientists.)[16]

The technical problem of the objective recording of human behaviour, exemplified by the Hawthorne effect, is aggravated by problems created by the biases of the observer. To a degree, we are inclined to see, report, and conclude what we prefer to see, report, and conclude. One somewhat extreme response is to declare that preconceptions and biases are too profound to be overcome; in a sense, we do not really want objectivity, even if we fool ourselves into believing that we are trying to achieve it. From there, it is an easy leap to a radically relativist stance from which one says, "Truth varies with the observer; the best one can do is what one thinks, or feels, is right." Acting on such a basis, totalitarians of various stripes have had considerable success, and have inflicted considerable damage, in our time.

An alternative response is to be all the more careful about one's research methods and all the more aware of their limitations. Admittedly, objectivity is elusive, but it can be usefully approximated. It is precisely because of the risk of bias that we bother with the apparatus of research methodology. The responsible course is seen to be to try to purify observation, not to abandon the enterprise.

Expositors of theory do not cluster around the extreme poles of an alignment such as "voluntarist–determinist" or "objective–subjective"; they distribute themselves between the poles. Students owe themselves an acquaintance with a sampling of the major theoretical points of view. Ramesh Mishra and the British team of V. George and P. Wilding present such samples along a kind of left-to-right dial. Such reviews are no substitute for reading the major contributions first hand: for example, read Marx, not only commentators on Marx—certainly not only his detractors. A pluralist bias would suggest three reasons why students should confront a range of theories, especially those with which they are inclined to disagree:

- to understand them, since the fact that reasonable people adhere to them, and act on them, makes them relevant;
- to guard against presentations of theoretical viewpoints by writers unsympathetic to them; and
- to test continually the validity of whatever theoretical view one holds oneself. The worst that can happen is that one might reconsider.

THEORY AND VALUES DISTINGUISHED

A brief digression is in order. Theory helps us to see reality clearly. Values guide us in deciding what is good. A person's style of thinking and his or her criteria of good and bad are likely to be consistent with each other, but not so that the one can be predicted precisely from the other.

The link between theory and values can be exemplified by exploring the individualist–collectivist axis. The individualist–collectivist theoretical array may seem to run parallel to the range of value positions from those that derive all values from the individual (freedom, self-expression, reward for success) to those that base all judgments on effects upon the collectivity (equality, solidarity, security). But a person who centres all values on the individual may still logically think, albeit with regret, that the individual is not the crucial factor in what happens in society. There is a school of socialist thinkers who insist that the individual embodies the highest value, over the group, the class, and the state;[17] others assign the highest value to the "community," the non-hierarchic "natural" grouping within which individuals best pursue their needs and aspirations. Philosophical socialists of these stripes might not have had as much impact on events as political socialists who have given pre-eminence to the state, but their collectivist theory and their individualist values are entirely coherent.

Similarly, apologists for the liberal society, from Adam Smith to the Hayeks and Novicks of our era, stoutly insist that the whole of society—poorer as well as richer—is best served both materially and morally by maximizing the freedom of the individual; but the broad liberal tradition includes many leading thinkers (Smith himself, J. S. Mill, T. H. Green, John Maynard Keynes, John Rawls) who give

much weight to the theoretical significance, for purposes of analysis, of various
groups within society, and few who minimize it. Smith wrote, "The difference of
natural talents in different men is, in reality, much less than we are aware of…. The
difference… between a philosopher and a
common street porter… seems to arise not
so much from nature, as from habit, custom and education"—social factors all.[18]

The extensive "Don't blame the victim" literature of the last five decades is an
example of individual values combined
with collective analysis. It says two things:

- in addressing social problems the individual is the measure of value: the member
  of a racial minority, the AIDS sufferer,
  the single mother, the addict;
- the anti-social behaviour of many individuals (feeble attachment to work,
  family instability, addiction, even much
  criminality) is best explained theoretically
  not through individual weakness but
  through social disadvantage.[19]

VALUES: THE MOST FUNDAMENTAL OF FUNDAMENTALS

Everyone who participates in debates and
campaigns around social welfare does so
from a value base. Naturally we take our
basic values too much for granted to be
fully conscious of them at all times; life
would be difficult indeed if we had to re-
examine our values in depth every time
we did something significant. But
because values govern the way people
think about and act upon problems, students must understand values, their own
and those of others.

In real life, values such as freedom or
dominance, fairness or greed, are
expressed not singly but as complex value
packages. The knowledge base of values

relevant to welfare might be approached by
studying the value systems of representatives of contending schools: individualists
and collectivists, state socialists, communitarian socialists, freedom-first liberals,
traditional conservatives.

There is a tendency to oversimplify
discussion by presenting value differences
in terms of polar opposites: racism versus
tolerance, oppression versus freedom, and
so on. In practice value differences usually
present themselves as mixtures. The
unthinking prejudices of nice "ordinary"
Canadians, expressed in everyday speech
and behaviour, probably cause as much
pain among the poor and disadvantaged as
outright selfishness and racism. And students will find much practical convergence
among individualists and collectivists, as
noted above, although their respective rhetoric may obscure the convergence. A current example is the debate over free trade,
attacked with equal vehemence by
entrenched corporations and by anti-
corporation leftists.

The Criticism of Values

To say that some preference is "a value
judgment" seems often to be taken as virtually terminating discussion. But value
systems are too important not to be scrutinized. They can be criticized for their
internal consistency, or for the way they
work out in practice, as in the assessment
of socialism's, or communism's, success in
meeting its own criteria in the former
Soviet Union, or the lukewarm liberal
assessment of the economic and moral performance of capitalism in the United
States. Value criteria must be applied to
means as well as ends.

We must not deceive ourselves:
believers can resist a lot of unwelcome
evidence. A militant for the cause of an
oppressed group may be dismayed to see

his cause looked at coolly. A believer in one interpretation of social solidarity may dismiss criticism of the effect of universal income transfers on poverty, however robust the criticism, but students cannot adopt such uncritical attitudes. "When objective facts threaten the orderly framework which assigns meaning to events, we tend to repudiate the facts rather than abandon the framework."[20]

A Tentative Outline of Value Systems

To represent welfare value positions on a simple left-to-right alignment, as is often attempted, is inadequate.[21] The left end must find places for both the communitarian socialist and the centralizing communist, the right end for both the libertarian and the believer in powerful, authoritarian governments—the fascist, if you will. Both couples are incompatible. It is more realistic to add to the left–right dimension a second dimension representing the value put on authority, ranging from the maximum of decentralization and individual freedom to the maximum of control, the latter propounded by totalitarians of both left and right.

No discussion of values in Canadian society can ignore those derived from the major religious traditions. Direct religious administration of welfare services—homes for the destitute and for the elderly, special hospitals, "soup kitchens," etc.—is still important, but less so than before World War II; our willingness to deliver certain services, even when it may be founded upon religious conviction, now emerges most strongly in support for social policy.

THE MATERIAL WORLD

The last component of the proposed knowledge base is perhaps a novel one, namely a measure of understanding of natural science. In *The Two Cultures* (1959), C. P. Snow deplored the gulf that has developed between those educated in the natural sciences and those who identify with the humanities and social sciences. The gulf poses a danger. The threat of nuclear destruction and our experience with man-made environmental damage has made us fearful of irresponsibly used science. Similar dangers lie in wait for scientifically misguided social policy. Advancing science and its offspring, technology, if not *the* crucial variables in social change, do create possibilities and set limits.

Three currently prominent examples are (1) the shifts in industrialized countries from "manufacturing" to "service" and information industries, resulting in radical changes in the nature of employment, (2) the technologies of population control, assisted birth, enhanced fertility, contraception, abortion, and scientific advances in genetics, gender roles, and sexual orientation, and (3) the lengthening of the lifespan, owing to improvements in hygiene and nutrition, to the control of childhood diseases and infectious diseases and to improvements in health-related technologies. All call for social policy responses; if these are based on a faulty understanding of the relevant science, they will fail.

The recipe is not to study a little physics, biology, and chemistry. What matters is a general understanding of the processes by which science is conducted. Of course the science itself becomes too rarefied for the non-specialist, like this writer; fortunately the human and social implications of scientific activity attract the attention of writers who address themselves to the general public, like Jeremy Bernstein and the late Isaac Asimov and Stephen Jay Gould.

CONCLUSION

Social welfare is a broad field of action, and therefore a broad field of study. Its breadth is mitigated by three considerations:

- Among fields of policy, there is considerable overlap in the knowledge required; the values and theories relevant to health policy apply in some measure to income security, etc. The spiky questions may poke out from the overlap, but that is what theory is for—to identify the important questions.

- The welfare specialist may certainly become competent in a related discipline, but she or he need not try to become at once an economist, sociologist, political scientist, or psychologist. To take advantage of sociologists' insights in order to criticize programs affecting the family, one need only understand the context in which sociologists conduct their inquiries and present findings.

- Social welfare is a *doing* endeavour. Without knowledge and thought, action will lead to disaster, yet action is always at the centre. Action takes place in the midst of change; action itself provokes further change. The target is always moving; even the best policies and programs can never be perfect.

The work of social welfare and the study of social welfare are never done. The knowledge base is not a base on which to rest, but a base from which to move.

NOTES

1. Martin Rein, *Social Policy: Issues of Choice and Change* (Harmondsworth: Penguin Books, 1976), p. 3.

2. Martin Bulmer, Kenneth G. Banting, et al., *Social Science and Social Policy* (London: Allen & Unwin, 1986), p. 221.

3. Robert Pinker, *Social Theory and Social Policy* (London: Heinemann, 1970), pp. 120–21.

4. See, for example, Dennis Guest, *The Emergence of Social Welfare in Canada* (Vancouver: University of British Columbia Press, 1997).

5. David K. Foot with Daniel Stoffman, *Boom, Bust & Echo* (Toronto: Macfarlane Walter & Ross, 1996).

6. John Stuart Mill, *Principles of Political Economy*, Book 2, Ch. XIV, and Book 4, Ch. VII.

7. Ken Battle and Sherri Torjman, *How Finance Reformed Social Policy* (Ottawa: Caledon Institute, 1995); Ken Battle, *Constitutional Reform by Stealth* (Ottawa: Caledon Institute, 1995).

8. Richard Allen, *The Social Passion: Religion and Social Reform in Canada, 1914-29* (Toronto: University of Toronto Press, 1973); Frank McGilly, "Ideology and Public Assistance: The Use and Abuse of a Slippery Concept," in *Ideology, Development and Welfare: Canadian Perspectives*, ed. William Kirwin (Toronto: Canadian Scholars' Press, 1991).

9. Keith G. Banting, *The Welfare State and Canadian Federalism* (Kingston and Montreal: McGill-Queen's University Press, 1982); Alvin Finkel, "Origins of the Welfare State in Canada," in Leo Panitch, ed., *The Canadian State: Political Economy and Political Power* (Toronto: University of Toronto Press, 1977); Dennis Guest, *The Emergence of Social Security in Canada,* op. cit.; Frank McGilly, *An Introduction to Canada's Public Social Services* (Toronto: Oxford University Press, 1998), pp. 15–26. For materials concerning Quebec's special role in this evolution, see Serge Mongeau, *L'evolution de l'assistance au Québec* (1967) and McGilly, in *Ideology, Development and Welfare,* op. cit. In "Transformation: Canadian Social Policy Since 1985," *Social Policy and Administration*, vol. 32, no. 4

(December 1998), Ken Battle reviews far-reaching recent shifts in responsibilities from the federal government to the provinces. See also Chapter 4 of this book.

10. Among general works, see Karl Polanyi, *The Great Transformation* (Boston: Beacon, 1957); Gaston Rimlinger, *Welfare Policy and Industrialization in Europe, America and Russia* (New York: Wiley, 1971); Gosta Esping-Andersen, *Politics Against Markets: The Social Democratic Road to Power* (Princeton, NJ: Princeton University Press, 1985). Recent developments in several countries, including Canada, are concisely reviewed in IIAS Working Group on Social Security Systems, *Transformations in Social Security Systems* (Brussels: International Institute of Administrative Sciences, 1997). For more critical reviews, see Robert E. Goodin, Bruce Headey, Ruud Muffels, and Hen-Jank Dirven, *The Real Worlds of Welfare Capitalism* (Cambridge: Cambridge University Press, 2000); Esping-Andersen, ed., *Welfare States in Transition* (London: Sage, 1996); Ramesh Mishra, *The Welfare State in Capitalist Society: Policies of Retrenchment in Europe, North America and Australia* (Toronto: University of Toronto Press, 1990); Neil Gilbert, *Transformation of the Welfare State: The Silent Surrender of Public Responsibility* (New York: Oxford University Press, 2002).

11. Richard Splane, "Social Policy-Making in the Government of Canada," in Shankar Yelaja, ed., *Canadian Social Policy* (rev. ed.) (Waterloo: Wilfrid Laurier University Press, 1987), pp. 258–59.

12. Sherri Torjman, *Community-Based Poverty Reduction* (Ottawa: Caledon Institute, 1998), and *Reintegrating the Unemployed Through Customized Training* (Ottawa: Caledon Institute, 1999).

13. Abraham Kaplan, *The Conduct of Inquiry* (New York: Columbia University Press, 1964), pp. 294–326.

14. Leonard Marsh, *Social Security for Canada* (Toronto: University of Toronto Press, 1975, 1947); *Health and Unemployment* (Toronto: published for McGill University by Oxford University Press, 1938).

15. Esping-Anderson, ed., *Welfare States in Transition*, op. cit.; Neil Gilbert, *Transformation of the Welfare State*, op. cit.

16. On the Hawthorne effect, see Elton Mayo, *The Human Problems of an Industrial Civilization* (Boston: Harvard, 1933). Heisenberg's first paper on the uncertainty principle appeared in 1927, while the Hawthorne research was under way. He was awarded the Nobel Prize for physics in 1932. On the avoidance of observer influence, see Eugene Webb, Donald Campbell, Richard D. Schwarz, and Lee Sechrest, *Unobtrusive Measures: Non-Reactive Research in the Social Sciences* (Chicago: Rand McNally, 1966).

17. For example, Abba Lerner, *The Economics of Control: Principles of Welfare Economics* (New York: Macmillan, 1944).

18. Adam Smith, *The Wealth of Nations*, Book I, Chapter 2.

19. William Ryan, *Blaming the Victim* (New York: Vintage, 1976).

20. Rein, *Social Science and Social Policy*, pp. 250–51.

21. See V. George and P. Wilding, *Ideology and Social Welfare* (London: Routledge and Kegan Paul, 1975); A. W. Djao, *Inequality and Social Policy: The Sociology and Welfare* (Toronto: Wiley, 1983); Mishra, *Society and Social Policy*, op. cit.; Andrew Armitage, *Social Welfare in Canada Revisited: Facing up to the Future* (Toronto: Oxford University Press, 1996).

chapter four

The Political Bases of Canadian Social Welfare

Ramesh Mishra

INTRODUCTION

Social welfare is a vast enterprise, made up of short publicly mandated programs and services such as education, medical care, income security, housing, and personal social services that meet basic needs. It is underwritten by the government and involves major decisions about taxing and spending. It absorbs more than one fifth of the national income, employs hundreds of thousands of people, and involves a good deal of regulation and the organization and delivery of services. Not surprisingly, social welfare raises many questions of policy such as: How far should government be involved in providing programs and services? What services should be provided and to whom? How should they be funded and delivered?

These are controversial issues that cannot be settled outside politics. No neutral, scientific study exists that can, for example, tell us that a public system of retirement pensions is preferable to, say, private pension plans, Registered Retirement Savings Plans, and the like. No doubt research, investigation, and systematic studies can tell us about the merits and demerits of different kinds of pension systems. But in the end we have to make a choice between various alternatives. And this is a matter of judgment. There is no basis for an automatic consensus over these issues.

The history of social welfare in Canada and elsewhere shows that people hold different views about the nature of social problems and how they should be tackled. Such views have to do with the beliefs and values of different groups of people as well as with the distribution of power and influence in society, such as who decides and whose values and preferences count. In any case, whether we value freedom ("Canadians should have the right to spend their own money to buy private health care") over equality ("All Canadians should have equal opportunity to receive adequate health care") or property rights rather than social justice matters a great deal; so does our notion of government's proper role in the economic and social life of the community; so does our idea of what may or may not work.

In Western democracies the political system permits free expression of values, beliefs, and interests ("political and ideological pluralism"). These different values and interests are, in the main, aggregated by political parties that compete for our support in their quest for office. Parties differ in their political and social agendas, and of course social welfare is expressed politically in this most obvious form. But more than political ideology as it operates through electoral and party politics shapes social welfare.

Political pluralism also means that different interests—business, labour, professions, advocacy groups—organize into associations and social movements that interact with government on a host of social policy issues. A key player in the development of social welfare is government bureaucracy or the administrative staff—an important behind-the-scenes presence that is very influential. There is also the nation's Constitution, which conditions the nature and scope of government action. Canadians hardly need reminding about controversies centred on the division

of powers between federal and provincial levels of government that have bedevilled the development of social programs. In sum: ideologies and beliefs, elections and party politics, constitutional arrangements, pressure groups, and government bureaucracy are among the major political factors that influence the nature and development of social welfare.

In this chapter we shall say little about globalization and the economic context of social welfare, issues that are discussed elsewhere in this book. Their importance, which must kept in mind, lies in the way they limit the nature of pluralism and constrain choice. For example, globalization restricts political choice as governments come under pressure to follow policies that key players in the global economy favour, such as multinational corporations and bond markets (Barlow and Campbell 1997; Mishra 1999).

IDEOLOGIES OF SOCIAL WELFARE AND POLITICAL PARTIES

Ideologies of welfare may be described as more or less coherent systems of belief about the nature of social problems and their solutions. Ideologies suggest—indeed prescribe—certain courses of action. They derive from broader political philosophies, such as conservatism or liberalism, to which political parties generally subscribe (George and Wilding 1994).

At least four distinct approaches to welfare based on such political philosophies can be identified: conservative, liberal, social-democratic, and socialist. Perspectives such as feminism, antiracism, and environmentalism cut across these ideologies. Table 4.1 presents a schematic view of the latter in relation to social welfare.

TABLE 4.1	Political Ideology and Social Welfare	
	Basic beliefs and attitudes	Approach to social welfare
Conservatism	19th-century version paternalistic and collectivist ("One-nation Toryism"). 20th-century version individualistic and libertarian. Faith in laissez-faire and market economy with emphasis on personal responsibility. Economic and social, including gender, inequality seen as normal and inevitable. Belief in traditional family values and gender relations. Neo-conservatism or "neo-liberalism" a stronger version of these beliefs.	State role in welfare to be minimal. Selective rather than universal social programs. Support for private and voluntary action for meeting needs.
Liberalism	19th-century version individualistic and libertarian. Belief in economic and social laissez-faire. 20th-century version recognizes the weakness of laissez-faire and the need for state regulation of economic and social life. Concern with equity and equality of opportunity for all in a free society.	Described as "reluctant collectivist." State welfare necessary but should be limited to a basic minimum. Private and voluntary forms of social protection should complement and enhance state welfare.
Social Democracy	Collectivist and egalitarian. Unregulated market economy seen as unstable, inefficient, and unjust. Support for state regulation of the economy. In favour of greater economic and social, including gender role, equality.	Favours a full-employment welfare state with universal social programs of a high standard. Strong support for social rights. In favour of progressive taxation and income redistribution.
Socialism	Communitarian and highly egalitarian. Favours common ownership of productive resources. Considers equality and solidarity as the basis of social life.	Right to work/basic income. Universal and generous social provision. Democratic and participatory management.

Of these ideologies conservatism, liberalism, and social democracy have direct relevance for Canadian politics. Major national parties, namely the Conservative (formerly Progressive Conservative), Liberal, and New Democratic may respectively be seen as representing these three ideologies. Of the two new federal parties formed since the 1980s, Reform stood for a populist and more radical version of conservatism ("neo-conservative") but merged with the Progressive Conservatives in 2003 to form the Conservative Party. Bloc Québécois, a party of Quebec nationalism and sovereignty, lacks a distinctive ideological orientation.

However, the social welfare policy that these parties espouse, not to say pursue, when in office, does more than simply reflect their ideologies. Indeed, it often appears that parties, no matter what their political stripe or rhetoric, follow broadly similar policies when in office. Undoubtedly there is some truth in this view. Quite apart from the economic constraints mentioned earlier, governments have to consider a wide range of interests and issues, which limits their courses of action.

In any case, the two federal governing parties, namely the Liberals and the Conservatives, tend to be more pragmatic than ideological in their approach. More recent trends suggest a further erosion of ideological differences as governments of all persuasions, working in the context of a global market economy and the ascendancy of neo-conservative beliefs, tend to follow pro-market and pro-business policies.

Nonetheless, political parties do try to shape policies in the image of their own values and beliefs. For example, it was a social democratic (the Co-operative Commonwealth Federation—later the New Democratic Party) government in Saskatchewan that, in the 1950s, took the bold step of implementing a medicare program for the first time in a North American jurisdiction (Taylor 1978, Chs. 2, 5). In the 1980s the Mulroney (Progressive Conservative) government's attempt to renegotiate the basic principles of Canadian social welfare and its piecemeal but systematic retrenchment of social programs exemplifies the connection between ideology and social welfare. At the provincial level, the Conservative governments of Ralph Klein in Alberta and Mike Harris in Ontario offer prominent examples of a neo-conservative policy of whittling down social protection while providing tax breaks for businesses and the well-off. At the other end of the political spectrum, the long reign (1932–1976) of the social democrats in Sweden had a great deal to do with the development of a full-employment welfare state in that country (Mishra 1990). In short, although in recent years there has been a rightward shift in social policy, party politics and political ideologies do matter.

Ideology apart, it is possible to identify in many countries a set of mainstream values and priorities around which there is a good deal of national consensus. The durability and pervasiveness of a consensus around core values make it possible to speak of a national tradition or approach. Public opinion polls, for example, show that such a broad consensus exists in Canada. A Royal Commission, which investigated the state of the Canadian economy in the mid-1980s, found "solid" support among Canadians for basic social programs. Public preferences in social welfare were based on an "uneasy amalgam of collectivist and individualist values" that had changed little over the years (Royal Commission 1985, 579). More recent studies find similar attitudes (Peters 1995; Graves 2000).

The importance of broad national consensus surrounding a set of values and priorities lies in the way in which it sets the limits within which the politics of social policy is played out, irrespective of the party in power and its ideology. Thus, in 1984 Brian Mulroney's Progressive Conservatives campaigned on a platform that promised not only to maintain social programs but also declared the principle of universality was a "sacred trust." Clearly electoral considerations required that the party not be seen as going against the prevailing Canadian consensus in favour of universal programs.

On the other hand, the national consensus is not written in stone. One function of political ideology, as translated into policy by the governing party, is to shift the prevailing consensus in its own favour, preferably on a long-term basis. Moreover, we have to remember that public opinion or national consensus need not prevent a political party from pursuing its own agenda once it is voted into office.

Again, the case of the Mulroney government is instructive. It shows how much of the conservative agenda can be realized without conducting a frontal assault on the principle of universality in social welfare. A wide range of arguments—"the deficit must be reduced," "we can't afford social spending"—and techniques—de-indexing of benefits, changing the formula of federal transfers to provinces—is available that can move social welfare policy gradually and unobtrusively in a neo-conservative direction (Gray 1990; Pierson 1994).

If the parties of the right face "democratic" constraints—stemming from public opinion and attitudes, election promises, and the like—parties of the left often face "capitalist" constraints—now stemming from an increasingly global market economy—in their attempts to pursue ideological objectives. Social democratic governments, for example, have to take into account the wishes of the business community since the economy depends largely on private enterprise for investment and job creation. A climate favourable for business, however, may require policies very different from those supported by social-democratic values and beliefs, of strengthening social rights, for example. Indeed, much of the art and craft of social democracy consist in reconciling the demands of a popular agenda with those of a capitalist market economy. The government of the New Democratic Party's Bob Rae in Ontario (1990–1995), for example, faced these challenges in an acute form (Walkom 1994).

Evidence from Canada and around the world suggests that policy constraints on parties of the centre and the left have increased as a result of globalization. While politicians' protestations, such as "there is no alternative" or "global investors demand it," cannot be taken at face value, the right turn in social welfare policy in Western countries cannot be understood without reference to the strengthening of neo-conservative ideology associated with economic globalization (Teeple 1995). The social policy of the federal Liberal government (1993–1997), with its drastic reduction in transfer payments to the provinces and massive cutbacks to the unemployment insurance program, is a case in point. The Democratic presidency of Bill Clinton in the United States and the Labour government of Tony Blair in the United Kingdom are other examples of a right shift in social policy. These developments raise the question of whether and to what extent elections and party governments can make a difference to social policy. On the other hand, the continuing commitment of many European countries to maintaining high standards of social protection suggests that, despite these constraints, governments do have a choice and that politics do matter (Sykes et al. 2001).

FEDERALISM AND SOCIAL WELFARE

The constitution of a country lays down the ground rules of how it is to be governed. The party in power has to work within the framework of that constitution. This includes the division of powers and responsibilities between different levels of government. Since social welfare policy is about government action concerning basic needs, the powers of government are of obvious relevance.

In Canada, the constitutional ground rules were laid down by the British North America (BNA) Act of 1867, now incorporated into the Constitution Act of 1982. Despite various amendments and the patriation of the Constitution in 1982, this basic framework has remained unchanged. The combined effect of Sections 91 and 92 of the BNA Act has been to infer that the provinces (and territories) have all the general powers in the field of social welfare not included in the specific list of federal powers. In other words, the federal presence in social welfare is what requires justification. Apart from specific subject matters enumerated as falling within federal jurisdiction—such as matters concerning First Nations peoples—the federal right to intervene in matters of social welfare also derives from general powers such as those for making laws for the "peace, order and good government" of Canada and for taxing and spending (Banting 1987, 48).

The development of a modern industrial society in Canada created the need for social programs and services, and the government was called upon to play a bigger role. The division of rights and responsibilities between different levels of government, as it related to social welfare programs, emerged as a critical issue. In the twentieth century and especially since World War II, the dynamics of federalism and social welfare have centred around "nation-building" on the one hand and "province-building" on the other. The imperatives of nation-building have led the federal governments to legislate social policy for Canada as a nation-state. The provinces in turn have often seen this as an encroachment on a field of activity that properly belongs to them. The first major challenge to federal authority came in 1937 when the Supreme Court judged the Federal Employment and Social Insurance Act unconstitutional. The federal right to set up an unemployment insurance program had to be established in 1940 through a constitutional amendment. On the other hand, Family Allowances, the first cash grant available to all Canadians, were instituted in 1944 under the federal government's general spending powers.

Even a cursory glance at the history of the Canadian welfare state shows that major attempts to develop or change social welfare policy at the national level have been accompanied by a constitutional wrangle implicating federal and provincial governments. The welfare state that emerged in the post–World War II period has been described as "bifurcated," or split, in that federal programs are prominent in income security, while the provinces dominate in the field of health, education, and welfare (Banting 1987, 58). The Canada Pension Plan, the Child Tax Benefit, Old Age Security, (un)Employment Insurance: these are federal programs. Workers' Compensation, on the other hand, is a provincial program with no federal participation. Other major programs such as medicare, post-secondary education, and many of the social services, including social assistance (welfare), are administered and delivered by the provinces but the costs have been shared, until recently, by the federal and provincial governments (see below). Indeed joint-funding, or the mechanism of cost-sharing, has been an important vehicle for federal initiative and presence in social welfare, which, under the Constitution, remains essentially a provincial responsibility (Banting 1987).

Federal involvement in the area of social welfare has been justified on a number of grounds (Armitage 1996, 136). They all derive from the fact that Canada is not simply a congeries of provinces and territories or regions but also a nation. Fostering the sense of a national community, then, has been one of the main reasons for federal involvement. Programs of income security, health, and welfare based on an agreed national standard contribute to a sense of belonging to one nation, an important consideration given Canada's sparse population and vast geography. The second and a related objective has been that of promoting a measure of equitable distribution of income across the nation. Canada's provinces and regions vary a good deal in their command of economic resources. National programs of income security and transfer payments to the provinces help to redistribute income across regions as well as income groups. A third reason for national programs is to ensure portability of benefits across the country and thus facilitate geographical mobility. A fourth reason is that social expenditure, especially on income security, is closely related to broader economic and fiscal policy of the country, which remains a national responsibility. A fifth and perhaps less explicit reason for federal participation in social welfare is that social programs, especially those that confer direct monetary benefits, are a constant reminder of the benign presence of the federal government, a government that might otherwise seem remote from people's lives and day-to-day concerns.

Be that as it may, a complex network of social welfare programs has developed in Canada under federal, provincial–territorial, or joint auspices. And whatever the rationale for federal intrusion in the field of social welfare policy, it is an intrusion that the provinces resent, especially the richer ones. Indeed, much of the history of Canadian social welfare can be seen as a continuous bargaining relationship between the two levels of government. Quebec has been a major catalyst in this process. As French Canada, it has sought greater provincial autonomy in order to preserve and develop its distinctive character in ways most suited to its majority franco-phone population. The autonomy the provinces have enjoyed has sometimes given rise to provincial initiatives that the federal government has later followed. Saskatchewan's pioneering role in developing medicare is the outstanding example.

In the 1980s Canada's constitutional development took a new direction. In 1982 a Charter of Rights and Freedoms was entrenched in the Constitution. In 1987 an agreement known as the Meech Lake Accord, among other things, sought to accommodate Quebec's quest for a special status in the federation. This agreement, however, failed to become law and was followed by yet another constitutional agreement known as the Charlottetown Accord. It too failed when a majority of Canadians gave it thumbs-down in a special referendum in 1992. These Accords included provisions and clauses relevant to social welfare.

The Constitution Act of 1982 made little difference to the division of powers between federal and provincial governments. It affirmed the principle of equalization payments to the poorer provinces by the federal government and also strengthened provincial control over natural resources.

The relevance of the Charter of Rights and Freedoms for social welfare is only indirect. It is not a "social" charter as it does not include economic or social rights. Nonetheless, in upholding the right to equal treatment, its equality clause, Section 15(1), offers all Canadians protection against unfair discrimination. For example, under this clause, lone fathers won the right to receive welfare on the same basis as lone mothers (Banting 1987, 204). Another example of an enhanced judicial role in social welfare is the Supreme Court's ruling that upholds the rights of gay and lesbian couples (Malcolmson and Myers 2002, 105). Moreover, most provinces have enacted laws that prohibit discrimination against lesbians and gay men (Graham et al. 2000, 77–78, 119).

Since the failure of the Meech Lake and the Charlottetown accords, no further attempts have been made to enact constitutional reforms. Meanwhile, a de facto devolution of power to the provinces, in train since the late 1980s, has weakened the federal role in social welfare significantly. It has come about largely through a substantial reduction in federal funding for the cost-shared programs of medical care, post-secondary education, and social assistance. The Conservative government began the process in the late 1980s through seemingly technical devices such as the partial de-indexing of transfer payments to the provinces and the introduction of a ceiling on social assistance payments made to rich provinces. Although the structure of cost-sharing itself was left intact, the federal share of costs plummeted, leaving the provinces increasingly to fend for themselves.

The Liberals, returned to power in 1993, made massive cuts to federal funding and also set the seal on federal withdrawal by formally ending cost-sharing arrangements. In 1996 a new block grant to provinces known as the Canada Health and Social Transfer (CHST) replaced Established Programs Financing and the Canada Assistance Plan under which medicare, post-secondary education, and social assistance and welfare services were funded (Prince 1999, 176–79). Under the CHST, provinces are free to use federal money as they see fit. Although the basic principles of the Canada Health Act remain in place and to that extent provinces are held accountable, in other respects they have a free hand. Social assistance programs, for example, stand with nearly no conditions except that the provinces cannot impose residency requirements for eligibility to assistance. Under the Canada Assistance Plan, for example, need alone was the criterion for receiving assistance. This is no longer the case. The provinces are now free to develop schemes of "workfare" as a condition for social assistance (Armitage 1996, 81). These developments, most commenta-

tors agree, have diminished significantly Ottawa's influence on provincial social programs and have weakened the prospect of maintaining national commitment and standards in social welfare. The Social Union Framework Agreement of 1999 seeks to regularize federal–provincial relations in social welfare, including provincial accountability, while ceding substantial autonomy to the provinces and territories (Dyck 2002, 264–65).

The importance of a strong federal presence in social welfare becomes clear when we compare Canada with the United States. Canadian social welfare programs have been and still remain a good deal more uniform and redistributive across the country (Banting 1995; Hurtig 2002, 221). The recent trend towards decentralized federalism definitely puts some of these past achievements at risk (Dyck 2002, 265). Apart from Canadian politics and history, global trends—economic as well as ideological—also favour privatization and offloading responsibility to lower levels of government. Yet people's sense of belonging to a national community and their expectations of equal opportunity and access to services also persist. The challenge for Canadian federalism is to acknowledge and reconcile these conflicting tendencies and to adapt creatively to change.

PRESSURE GROUPS AND SOCIAL WELFARE

Pressure groups are associations of people with common interests who seek to influence public policy. In liberal democracies the right to form associations is a basic one and we find a bewildering array of associations ranging from very large or powerful national organizations to small local ones.

Pressure groups can be classified in a variety of ways (Pross 1992). For our purposes, one significant distinction separates the interest group from the promotional or advocacy group. Interest groups seek to advance their members' interests. Labour unions, professional organizations, trade and business associations, and ratepayers' associations are fairly typical examples. Advocacy groups or public interest groups, on the other hand, espouse a cause, such as civil liberties, environmental protection, or reproductive rights, or they advocate on behalf of a particular group of people—for example, the poor, the homeless, the disabled. The difference between interest groups and advocacy groups is essentially analytical. In reality these groups may overlap and a single organization might combine the roles of advocacy and protection of members' interests.

Pressure groups may share common values and interests with certain political parties but they act independently. Irrespective of the party in power these groups try to influence government decisions in their favour.

How far do they succeed in this? There are four major pressure groups relevant to social welfare policy: business, labour, professional, and advocacy groups. But not all groups and associations have the same brief for influencing policy or the same clout. The Canadian Manufacturers' Association, the Canadian Council of Chief Executives (formerly the Business Council on National Issues or BCNI), the Canadian Labour Congress, the Canadian Council on Social Development: these are national organizations that represent interests on a very wide policy front. Others, such as the National Anti-Poverty Organization or the Canadian Medical Association, are more specialized in their areas of concern or members' interests. Besides national organizations many provincial or more localized interest associations focus their attention on provincial or municipal governments. Established interest organizations devote a great deal of lob-

bying activity at the level of ministries and departments, which develop regular consultative relations with these groups. The idea of a "policy community" seeks to capture the ongoing interaction among the major interests or stakeholders in a particular policy field, such as non-profit housing, mental health, or child protection.

Pressure groups vary enormously in the resources at their disposal and consequently in their lobbying capacity. Well-funded organizations can afford permanent staff, conduct research of high quality, keep track of legislation and establish alternative sources of information—all of which contribute to successful lobbying. On the whole, producer interests, such as those of professionals and public sector workers, tend to be better organized and more influential than consumer/client groups or general public interests. Business, labour, and professional associations tend to be better financed, more cohesive, and better organized compared with most advocacy groups (Hadow 1990).

Business interests in particular tend to be highly influential. This influence is not merely a matter of effective lobbying. A privately owned market economy relies on business to produce goods and services and to create jobs. The nation's standard of living depends on the success of business. The wishes and claims of business therefore receive top priority. The mass media, too, tend to favour the business perspective. Business generally espouses what we have described earlier as a conservative or in present-day terminology a neo-conservative or "neo-liberal" approach to welfare. Business calls for reducing public-sector provisions and promotes privatization. It calls for economic and social deregulation and lower taxes, especially for business and high-income earners. However, although business opposes public spending on social welfare, it apparently feels no compunction about appropriating public funds. Governments channel substantial funds, directly or indirectly, to business. Subsidies and allowances, tax write-offs and deferrals, tax credits, and the like add up to a vast, albeit hidden, welfare state that receives far less public attention than governments and their spending on social welfare (McBride and Shields 1997, 55–56; Cameron and Finn 1996). Indeed, it would be pointless to deny that a strong built-in bias exists in a capitalist society in favour of business. Government agendas may thus be set in accordance with business demands. For example, reducing government deficits may receive a high priority, which often means high unemployment and cutbacks on public spending.

From about the late 1970s on, business has sought to influence social policy more openly and directly. For example, the BCNI (Business Council for National Issues), an organization with members drawn from the largest corporations in the country, targeted social spending in particular for drastic reduction. It campaigned persistently against the principle of universality (Barlow and Campbell 1995, 47–50; Hurtig 2002). Cutting back on unemployment insurance has been another persistent demand. Right-wing think-tanks such as the Fraser Institute in Vancouver have also sought to influence social policy in a strongly neo-conservative direction. Clearly, business's demands have met with a great deal of success in recent years (Hurtig 2002, 129–140).

At the national level, the Canadian Council on Social Development (CCSD) is among the more prominent organizations that lobby on behalf of the social welfare constituency. The National Council of Welfare, an advisory council set up by the federal Department of Health and Welfare in 1970, is another advocate for social welfare. Its well-researched reports, reasoned

criticisms, and thoughtful recommendations exert primarily a moral and educational influence on policy. Although social welfare lobbies can point to some tangible results, their influence is often felt indirectly, as through their efforts to rally public support and educate the public on social welfare issues.

No doubt organizations such as the CCSD and the Caledon Institute of Social Policy do a good deal of research, consultation, and the like on social welfare matters and can claim to expertise and detailed knowledge about them. But at the end of the day the government may choose to ignore the social welfare lobby as far as big decisions on social policy and social spending are concerned (Hadow 1990). The Social Security Review of 1994 is a case in point. The reform agenda, meant to modernize Canadian income-security programs, was virtually hijacked by the financial wing of the government. Its major priorities were the reduction of deficit by scaling down social spending, and shrinking the unemployment insurance program, which was seen as creating disincentives to mobility and entry into low-paying jobs (Barlow and Campbell 1995, Ch. 7).

As we pointed out earlier, the global economy has given business additional leverage. Corporations can choose to invest abroad if they do not like government policies at home. The social welfare constituency has no such weapon at its disposal. Moreover, business—in common with other producer interests, only more so—can finance its organization and lobbying activity from private sources. By contrast, organizations such as the CCSD, in common with many others in the social welfare sector, tend to rely rather heavily on government funding (Hadow 1990). The result is that with general retrenchment in government spending, their funding also gets reduced. The CCSD, for instance, has had its funding reduced substantially in recent years. The National Action Committee on the Status of Women, a strong advocate for women's welfare, has suffered the same fate (Cardozo 1996). Thus social welfare advocacy groups may become less effective at the very moment that their voices most need to be heard. In any case, many voluntary organizations dependent on government funding and support face a potential conflict of interest in trying to influence "the policy and program choices of government" (Dobell and Mansbridge 1986, 40). Moreover, many non-governmental organizations are not very knowledgeable about the machinery of government and how best to influence it (Dobell and Mansbridge 1986, 25). The role of labour organizations such as the Canadian Labour Congress, the Canadian Union of Public Employees, and the like as lobbies for social welfare policy is not well documented. On the whole they have called for public sector programs, adequate unemployment insurance, and government responsibility for maintaining employment. They often stand in the front line in opposing service cutbacks and privatization, not least in defence of their members' interests.

Somewhat different from pressure groups are the social movements. They tend to be more loosely organized and to use more open, publicly oriented methods of action, such as marches and demonstrations. Feminist, environmentalist, antiracist, and aboriginal movements as well as single-issue coalitions, concerning poverty or health care, for example, are some typical examples. Recent decades have seen a burgeoning of social movements and citizen action groups—from Mothers Against Drunk Driving to The Council of Canadians—concerned with a variety of interests and causes. Social movements can make a sizeable impact on social policy partly because of the wide publicity and media attention they receive.

Social movements and pressure groups are not necessarily mutually exclusive. The distinction between them is primarily analytical. In practice they may overlap. For example, pressure groups might get together to form a single-issue coalition and use methods typical of social movements—for example, the Ontario Health Coalition. It is perhaps best to see these as two distinct *strategies* of influencing policy rather than as two distinct types of *organization*.

Canadian pressure groups are said to be less influential than their counterparts south of the border. The Canadian policy-making process offers less access to lobbies. The cabinet system of government and tight party discipline makes for more centralized decision-making. Moreover, given the delicate nature of intergovernmental relations, policy issues are often decided through behind-the-scenes, closed-door negotiations. However, the policy-making process has opened up more and become more consultative in Canada over the last two decades and governments are more willing to listen to citizens' concerns (Rice and Prince 2000, 30–32).

THE BUREAUCRACY

Although the part played by government officials, especially those in higher ranks, in policy-making is less visible than that of politicians and pressure groups, it is nonetheless very substantial. Nominally the bureaucracy is a neutral agent. It is there to *execute* policy, not to make it. In practice, the bureaucracy is centrally involved in policy-making.

The reasons for this are logical. First, government departments and ministries are the repositories of a vast amount of knowledge about particular policy areas. Ministers come and go while the departmental bureaucracy remains permanently in place. A stable administrative base, and the expertise and detailed knowledge that go with it, gives the bureaucracy a great deal of leverage. Incumbent politicians have to rely on the information and advice of senior bureaucrats about what is feasible and what is not. As informal policy advisers, senior officials such as the deputy minister or the assistant deputy minister wield a good deal of influence. They bring to bear to the process their own interests and viewpoints, which may differ considerably from those of the minister.

Second, the bureaucracy has direct and continuous contact with the consumers of public services and professionals and others who run them. Pressure groups often make their representations to departmental officials. The bureaucracy thus acts as an intermediary between the minister and the public receiving or delivering the service. It acts as a filter in the process of communication linking these two levels and providing feedback to each. This is a strategic role.

Third, policy initiatives come not only from the ministers or cabinet. They also originate in the bureaucracy, which can take the lead in developing policy proposals. Richard Splane, for example, has described the work of "reforming bureaucrats" of the early post–World War II decades who actively shaped policy in the Department of Health and Welfare (Splane 1987, 258–59). The reform bureaucrat seems to have been a phenomenon peculiar to the early post-war years. More generally, however, departmental officials are closely involved in the preparation of new legislation—in the drafting of bills and cabinet documents and taking care of many other details. Ministers are busy people and they

naturally delegate a great deal of responsibility to their deputy ministers and other senior officials. One way or another, then, a great deal of discretionary power accrues to the bureaucracy.

Last but by no means least, the bureaucracy's job is to *implement* legislation—to translate policy into concrete programs, procedures, and organizations. To a large extent, the effectiveness of a policy depends on its implementation. Here again the bureaucracy has a great deal of discretion. It frames the guidelines and interprets and oversees their application on an ongoing basis. It deals with the various interest groups and others involved in the process and decides many significant details of policy. The departmental budget, which sets the priorities in terms of resource allocation, is also based on its officials' information and advice. It is no secret that Canadian federalism gives the executive arm of the government—ministers and their senior officials—a great deal of leverage in decision-making, to the detriment of Parliament and backbenchers.

As mentioned earlier, the delicate nature of the relations between the federal and provincial governments and the interlocking nature of financial and administrative arrangements between the two levels of government mean that a great deal of bargaining and negotiations take place behind closed doors. These sessions often involve the respective ministers and their senior officials. Divided jurisdiction and interdependence also mean that the senior levels of federal and provincial bureaucracy must cooperate closely in ironing out various problems and in formulating viable procedures and systems. This collaboration too enhances the role of the bureaucracy in policy-making. Not unexpectedly, the bureaucracy is a principal target for lobbying by pressure groups.

CONCLUSION

We argue that the nature of social welfare of a country cannot be understood apart from its political institutions and processes. The major influences we identify and explore in relation to Canadian social welfare are political parties and their ideology, the constitutional division of power between the federal and provincial governments, pressure groups, and government bureaucracy. We note that the increasing globalization of economies has strengthened the influence of corporate business interests and weakened the influence of domestic politics and party ideology on social policy.

Undoubtedly one outstanding feature of Canadian social politics is its brand of federalism and its continuing significance for social welfare policy. Yet this does not mean that the other influences we identify are necessarily less important. The student of social welfare needs to explore selectively the literature on the politics of social welfare while paying particular attention to the way the various determinants interact with another to produce policy outcomes.

REFERENCES

Armitage, A. 1996. *Social welfare in Canada revisited.* Don Mills, ON: Oxford University Press.

Banting, K. 1987. *The welfare state and Canadian federalism.* Kingston and Montreal: McGill-Queen's University Press.

Banting, K. 1995. The welfare state as statecraft: Territorial politics and Canadian social policy. In S. Leibfried & P. Pierson (Eds.), *European social policy.* Washington, D.C.: Brookings Institution.

Barlow, M., & Campbell, B. 1995. *Straight through the heart: How the Liberals abandoned the just society.* Toronto: HarperCollins.

Cameron, D., & Finn, E. 1996. *Ten deficit myths.* Ottawa: Centre for Policy Alternatives.

Cameron, D., & Watkins, M. 1993. *Canada under free trade.* Toronto: James Lorimer.

Cardozo. A. 1996. Lion taming: Downsizing the opponents of downsizing. In G. Swimer (Ed.), *How Ottawa spends, 1996–97.* Ottawa: Carleton University Press, 303–336.

Dobell, A. R., & Mansbridge, S. H. 1986. *The social policy process in Canada.* Montreal: Institute for Research on Public Policy.

Dyck, R. 2002. *Canadian politics (*Concise 2d ed.). Scarborough, ON: Nelson.

George, V., & Wilding, P. 1994. *Welfare and ideology.* Hemel Hempstead, UK: Harvester Wheatsheaf.

Graham, J. R., et al. 2000. *Canadian social policy.* Scarborough, ON: Prentice-Hall Canada.

Graves, F. 1999. Rethinking government as if people mattered. In L. A. Pal (Ed.), *How Ottawa spends, 1999–2000.* Don Mills, ON: Oxford University Press.

Gray, G. 1990. Social policy by stealth, *Policy Options, 11.2.* 17–29.

Hadow, R. 1990. The poverty policy community in Canada's liberal welfare state. In W. Coleman & G. Skogstad (Eds.), *Policy communities and public policy in Canada.* Mississauga, ON: Copp Clark Pitman, 212–237.

Hurtig, M. 2002. *The vanishing country.* Toronto: McClelland & Stewart.

McBride, S., & Shields, J. 1997. *Dismantling a nation: The transition to corporate rule in Canada.* Halifax: Fernwood Publishing.

Malcolmson, P., & Myers, R. 2002. *The Canadian regime.* Peterborough, ON: Broadview Press.

Mishra, R. 1990. *The welfare state in capitalist society*. Toronto: University of Toronto Press.

Mishra, R. 1999. *Globalization and the welfare state*, Aldershot, UK: Edward Elgar.

Peters, S. 1995. *Exploring Canadian values: A synthesis report*. Ottawa: Canadian Policy Research Networks.

Prince, M. J. 1999. From health and welfare to stealth and farewell: Federal social policy, 1980–2000. In L. A. Pal (Ed.), *How Ottawa spends, 1999–2000*. Don Mills, ON: Oxford University Press.

Pross, A. P. 1992. *Group politics and public policy*. Don Mills, ON: Oxford University Press.

Rice, J. J., & Prince, M. J. 2000. *Changing politics of Canadian social policy*. Toronto: University of Toronto Press.

Royal Commission on the Economic Union and Development Prospects for Canada. 1985. *Report*. Vol. Two. Ottawa: Supply and Services Canada.

Splane, R. 1987. Social policy-making in the Government of Canada. Parts 1 and 2. In S. A. Yelaja (Ed.), *Canadian social policy*. Waterloo, ON: Wilfrid Laurier University Press. 224–265.

Sykes, R., et al. (Eds.). 2001. *Globalization and European welfare states*. Houndmill, Basingstoke, UK: Palgrave.

Taylor, M. G. 1978. *Health insurance and Canadian public policy*. Montreal: McGill-Queen's University Press.

Teeple, G. 1995. *Globalization and the decline of social reform*. Toronto: Garamond Press.

Walkom, T. 1994. *Rae days*. Toronto: Key Porter Books.

chapter five

The Geographic Base of Canadian Social Welfare

Michael Kim Zapf

Space and time are always and everywhere social. Society is always and everywhere spatial and temporal. Easy enough concepts, perhaps, but the implications are only now being thought through.

Nigel Thrift, 1997, p. 401

INTRODUCTION

What does it mean to suggest that a geographic base underlies Canadian social welfare? The idea appears to be a relatively recent addition to the literature. The first two editions of *Canadian Social Welfare* (Turner and Turner 1986, 1981) identified a philosophical base, a knowledge base, a historical base, and a base in the sense of individual pioneers in the field. The third edition (1995) then added

a political base. Armitage's *Social Welfare in Canada Revisited* (1996) presented a foundation that included features of industrialism and affluence, politics, economics, and societal values. Chappell's *Social Welfare in Canadian Society* (1997) confirmed the conventional list of foundation influences. None of these explorations of Canadian social welfare accorded geography the status of a base. It was not until the fourth edition of *Canadian Social Welfare* (Turner and Turner 2001) that geography was recognized as a base for social welfare in Canada.

I am not suggesting that geography has been ignored completely in discussions of social welfare in Canada. I have written elsewhere of the importance of geographic factors as part of Canadian social work (Zapf 2002). The first three editions of *Canadian Social Welfare* did contain material on demographics, location, isolation, climate, and physical characteristics in chapters entitled "Canadian Realities" (Woodsworth 1981, 1986; Watt 1995), but these discussions appeared as part of the context rather than the base of Canadian social welfare.

Far from a trivial distinction, this distinction between a base and a context is crucial to understanding the potential impact of geography as an influence on social welfare in this country. According to the *Oxford Dictionary*, context can be "the circumstances that form the setting for an event, statement, or idea"; a base is defined as "a foundation, support, or starting point... a main element or ingredient to which others are added" (Soanes, 2000). The difference between a core element (base) and a background or milieu (context) is key to understanding geography's importance to the Canadian social welfare system.

To consider geography as simply a context for Canadian social welfare is to explore how features such as topography, climate, population distribution, and transportation routes affect the practical design and delivery of social welfare services. To consider geography as a base, on the other hand, is to explore the importance of geographic concepts and issues for the theoretical foundation of Canadian social welfare. That is the aim of this chapter.

A second matter of terminology requires clarification at the outset. Throughout the following discussion, I refer to "social work" rather than "social welfare" when making comparisons with geography. Turner (2001, 10) describes social work as "the formal title for the principal, but not the only, profession in the social welfare system." Associated with this professional status is the recognition of social work as a specific discipline within adult education institutions. Primarily professionals trained in the discipline of social work design and deliver Canadian social welfare. Key elements of geography and social work—focus, activities, concepts—can be compared more easily when both are viewed as established academic disciplines.

Pile (1997, 430) made a useful distinction between *peopled places* and *placed people*. Using this terminology as a framework, I have gathered examples of parallel activities in geography and social work as both seek to understand the complex relationships between person and environment. I present evidence of convergence between the two disciplines that support a vision of the person–environment connection that some indigenous or traditional knowledge systems may already express. Geography has been strangely absent from the acknowledged foundations of social work in this country and elsewhere, but the future could well see these related disciplines merge in a new vision of Canadian social welfare for the twenty-first century.

PERSON/ENVIRONMENT AND SOCIAL WORK: PLACED PEOPLE

A perspective of person-in-situation or person-in-environment, borrowed from ecology, has been a popular starting point in the discussions of Canadian social work for the past two decades. I find a common but subtle and generally unacknowledged pattern in the presentation of this metaphor. A clear and early example can be seen in this excerpt from Yelaja's (1985, 29) discussion of the dominant concepts that influence Canadian social work: "The use of the ecology metaphor accentuates the reciprocal relationships between the individual and the environment and the continuous adaptation of both person and environment to each other.... Within the ecological perspective, human growth and development constantly change in relation to the social environment—and the social environment changes in response to the human factors."

What happened here? Within one paragraph, "the environment" has become "the social environment"!

This pattern appears frequently in the Canadian literature. Heinonen and Spearman (2001, 201) highlight the importance in social work of "a fit between the person and her or his environment so that both mutually experience benefits and growth," but this fit is explained only as occurring through "social exchanges." McKay (2002, 21) also asserts that "social work's identifying characteristic is its dual focus on person and environment," then comments on the importance for mainstream practitioners "of attempting to change the social environment." Hick (2002, 16) agrees that the person-in-environment perspective distinguishes social work from other helping professions, and then states that "these environments extend beyond the immediate family and include interactions with friends, neighbourhoods, schools, religious groups, laws and legislation, other agencies or organizations, places of employment and the economic system." These accounts appear to exclude the physical environment from the person-in-environment focus.

In his examination of the many theories that comprise the foundation for Canadian social work practice, Turner (2002, 50) asserts that the "uniting thrust" of Canadian practice is "the person-in-situation," whereas the foundation for the profession is "knowledge of the human person in interaction with societal systems" (p. 46).

This unacknowledged narrowing of environment to its social components has also been evident for some time in American social work literature. In a special volume devoted to clarifying conceptual frameworks, the National Association of Social Workers (1981) declares that "social workers focus on person-and-environment in interaction," but they define the purpose of social work "to promote or restore a mutually beneficial interaction between individuals and society in order to improve the quality of life for everyone" (p. 6). Johnson (1988, 31) presents an overview of the historical development of the person-in-environment concept in the United States, concluding that "to empower individuals to change their environment is a noble cause, but the generalist social worker must also be willing to help change the social environment in other ways when this course is more appropriate." (Within a single sentence, the environment once again has become the social environment.)

Compton and Galaway (1999, 4) declare the focus of "social work intervention is directed to the interaction between individuals and their environments," then on the same page assert that social work "intervenes or mediates between people and their social environments." Hancock (1997, 7) declares the cornerstone of social work theory as "always viewing the person and situation as a single entity," then defines "situation" as a social environment that includes family, workplace, and the broader community. Hepworth, Rooney, and Larsen (1997, 12–13) similarly state that "social work's focus is on the person in a situation" and they identify the corresponding knowledge base as one that includes "theories about the range of social systems in which individuals live."

The limiting of environment to social environment appears to be entrenched in social work literature, and a perspective that continues in the most recent sources.

Zastrow's (2004) conceptualization of person-in-environment comprises only interactions between the person and various social systems. Miley, O'Melia, and DuBois (2004, 9) present the dual focus of social work as "releasing human power" to help individuals reach their full potential and "releasing social power" to create change at the societal level. Hull Jr. and Kirst-Ashman (2004, 9) explain that "a person-in-environment focus sees people as constantly interacting with various systems around them" while continuing in the next sentence to list only social systems—"family, friends, work, social services, politics, religion, goods and services, and educational systems."

I am reminded of the comedian George Carlin (1990) who laments that, sometime in his lifetime without notification or permission, several major changes have taken place: "toilet paper" has become "bathroom tissue," "dumps" has become "landfills," and "the poor" have become "economically disadvantaged." Sometime during my social work career, it seems "the environment" became "the social environment" without formal notification, permission, or even rationale.

In the literature, I do find sporadic glimpses of an expanded notion of the physical environment beyond the social systems. Unfortunately, broad concepts of environment appear only as teasers in intriguing introductions before they quickly fall victim to concentrations on the social environment alone. For example, the *Social Work Dictionary* (Barker, 1999, 156) includes the natural world in its broad definition of environment as "all the influences, conditions, and natural surroundings that affect the growth and development of living things," yet the only other entries in the entire volume remotely connected to the physical environment comprise fewer than 20 lines devoted to rural social work issues.

Following a similar pattern, Lehmann and Coady (2001, 72) define the environment as "any aspect of the physical, social, and cultural environment, and what is most important will vary with individuals, time, and geography." For some unexplained reason, the diagram of their ecological perspective captures social and cultural contexts while completely ignoring the physical environment.

Some authors include the physical environment and relegate it to a lesser status. Rothery (2002, 243) reaffirms that Canadian social work "has always been informed by frameworks that focus on people and their environments," then describes how an ecological perspective emphasizes "the adequacy of the many relationships that link individuals and families to their social (and physical) environments." The physical environment is acknowledged here, but as a parenthetical subordinate to the social environment. Sheafor, Horejsi, and Horejsi (2000, 8) offer an expanded definition of the environment as "that multitude of physical and social structures, forces, and processes that affect humans and all other life forms," but proceed to distinguish between a person's "immediate environment" (social supports and systems) and a person's "distant environment" (drinking water, breathable air, arable soil, adequate shelter). The "distant environment" is then described as beyond the scope of social work because problems are "less evident and more difficult to change." I find this a peculiar rationale for dismissing so many serious environmental concerns closely connected with human activities, potential, and social justice.

Miley, O'Melia, and DuBois (2004, 257) refer specifically to the physical environment as "the final piece to consider in assessing human systems," and they immediately limit this promising perspective to secondary issues, such as adequate lighting, decent ventilation, and availability of private space. So they limit the physical environment to manufactured living conditions. Social work's interest becomes the "intentional design of space to promote social change" (p. 352), which relegates the physical environment to the background where it can be manipulated and controlled easily.

Even following the declared focus on person-in-environment, both practice and education in social work have tended to concentrate on the personal side of the duality at the expense of the environmental side (McKay 2002; Zapf 2002). The literature identifies a number of disciplines that have contributed directly to the social work knowledge base: psychology, sociology, anthropology, economics, education, history, political science, psychiatry, physiology, and biology (Chappell 1997; Heinonen and Spearman 2001; Johnson 1998; Zastrow 2004). All emphasize the individual and/or society over the natural world. Turner (2002, 50) identifies "close to thirty different theoretical bodies that drive practice," yet, again, almost all focus exclusively on individuals, or relationships and exchanges between people.

Social work has long been satisfied with a simple categorization of environments into urban, rural, and, more recently, remote (Collier 1993; Zapf 2001, 2002). Our knowledge base for Canadian social welfare appears to provide many more categories for understanding people than environments. One partial explanation may be found in David Suzuki's (1999, 45) observation that "most people now live in the human-created environment of big cities where it's easy to believe the illusion that we have escaped our biological dependence on the natural world." Well over 80 percent of the Canadian population now lives in metropolitan centres or adjacent areas scattered across vast rural

regions of this country (Mendelson and Bollman 1998; Wood 2002).

Returning to the terminology introduced earlier by Pile (1997), we could say that social work's development of the person/environment interaction has shifted social work's focus to *placed people*. The individual person or group has been the subject, the main concern, while the environment has been presented as mere modifier or context.

PERSON/ENVIRONMENT AND GEOGRAPHY: PEOPLED PLACES

Some geography literature reveals the same unintentional sleight of hand found in social work. In the introduction to a special UNESCO publication on the state of the art in geography, Mabogunje (1996, 443) says that the discipline has been defined as "the study of human–environment interaction." Then he describes a focus on "the fascinating but ever-changing relations between human beings and the physical environment." The "environment" here has become the "physical environment." (Having made my point about the language, I must be fair to Mabogunje and acknowledge that he is clearly aware of the artificial distinctions between physical and human geography. He does argue for "a concentration instead on the interrelations between the two sub-fields." In this respect, geography may be further ahead than social work in recognizing the tendency to limit its vision through assumptions from its past as a discipline.)

Geography was presented to me in my early schooling as a discrete subject. I recall some attempts to combine geography and history under the heading of social studies, but in high school there were grades assigned for geography alone, so naturally it took on the status of a distinct discipline in my mind. Not only distinct but boring. I recall academic geography as a series of long lists to commit to memory—capital cities, annual precipitation, landforms, economic products—plus the dreaded tests that required us to place names on intimidatingly blank maps. I was a victim of what Taaffe, Gauthier, and O'Kelly (1996, 3) identify as "the popular stereotype that geography is a discipline steadfastly devoted to long factual inventories and rote memorization." I lived in a state of "geographic illiteracy" (de Blij and Murphy, 2003, 6), with no real understanding of why particular settlement patterns developed as they did or how regions interacted and affected one another.

I also accepted without question certain assumptions about the geography presented to me. I can recall vividly the coloured map of Canada displayed prominently on the wall of every grade school classroom. I understood this as the reality of my country. There we were, brightly coloured but without neighbours on three sides. To our north, east, and west, all I could see was a thin strip of ocean giving way to the bare wall. Only to the south, the bottom of the map, did I see a neighbour. My country was firmly anchored to the mainland United States. No one told me then that this was only one of many possible perspectives. This, I was told, was Canada.

After many years as a northern social work practitioner and educator, I now see that grade school map for what it was. Looking at a different projection map with the North Pole at the centre, I can easily see our neighbours in Siberia, Scandinavia, Greenland, Iceland, and Alaska. I begin to get a sense of the common issues we face relating to the Arctic Ocean, the pollution, indigenous peoples, development, and resource management. Indeed, Canadians have been criticized for failing to recog-

nize that we are a northern people (Zaslow 1971; Hamelin 1988). I suspect the perspective and assumptions promoted by that grade school map have a lot to do with this.

Modern geography is a discipline that has been described as "synthesizing or integrative" (Taaffe, Gauthier, and O'Kelly 1996, 41): it "uniquely straddles the divide between the social and the physical (natural) sciences" (de Blij and Muller 1994, 40). Current geographic frameworks focus on physical geography—landforms, coastlines, climates, soils, vegetation, animals—as well as on human geography (spatial patterns of human activities). Yeung (1997, 102) observes that "the subject matter of geography is changing. ... The new geography has less to do with location, commodity flows, geopolitics, and traditional international trade, but has everything to do with human and cultural resources, information flows, knowledge infrastructure, technology, and amenities." As an academic discipline, this new geography could be interpreted as an exploration of the interactions between human behaviour and the surface of the Earth. Geography's "disciplinary interests, while seriously preoccupied with the Earth's environment, are also closely related to the mainstream concerns of the social sciences" (Mabogunje 1996, 447).

Norton (2002, 2) identifies three interrelated themes that guide an approach to human geography: *Humans and Land* (alterations to the physical environment; meanings created between people and places); *Regional Studies* (using variables to divide the Earth's surface; patterns created over time in particular areas); and *Spatial Analysis* (explaining locations; why things are located where they are). Others have identified a number of subcategories or particular fields of analysis.

Political geography, for example, is "the study of the interaction of geographical area and political process" (Association of American Geographers quoted in Glassner 1996, 11). Demographic geography examines population distributions and features such as density, dispersion, and pattern (de Blij and Muller 1994; Fellmann, Getis, and Getis, 1997). Economic geography looks at "the spatial organization of economic systems" (Dicken and Lloyd 1990, 7). Cultural geography explores the ways that the members of a society "organize the portion of the earth that is theirs" (de Blij and Muller 1994, 20) with a focus on "where cultural ideas and practices developed, how and where they diffused, and how they affect landscape, human perception, and human–environment relations" (de Blij and Murphy 2003, 20). Regional geography studies parts of the world defined by distinctive features, physical or human, resulting "in an understanding of human society, its physical geographical under pinnings, and a sense of place" (Bone 2002, 38). Phenomenological geography searches for the meanings places have for people as they perceive and subjectively experience their environments (Relph 1976). And new applications or specialized fields of analysis are developing all the time. One of these would be medical geography or "the study of health in geographic context" (de Blij and Murphy 2003, 461), which involves mapping disease patterns—source areas, routes of diffusion, regional victimization.

The developing approaches in human geography constitute evidence of a continuing effort to integrate our understanding of human behaviour and interaction with classical physical geography. Daniels (1997, 364) refers to a "geography without man" as "at once intellectually deficient and morally blind." Norton (2002, 28) concurs that contemporary human geography may be developing as "a social science, but one with special and valuable ties to physical sci-

ences." While the discipline may be asserting a "unity between physical and human geography," Norton (2002) cautions, however, that there is not much real evidence of this unity among geographers who still tend to perceive two separate and distinct components. To return once again to the terminology of Pile (1997), it could be said that geography's historical development of the person/environment interaction has led to a priority imposed on *peopled places*. The location or setting is the primary given, with human activity the modifier.

SOCIAL WORK AND GEOGRAPHY: CONVERGENCE

I am continually astonished at the lack of formal interaction between the two disciplines. When I attend and present at gatherings of geographers, I am usually the only social worker present. I see no geographers at our social work conferences, nor do I find much evidence of joint scholarly activity or publications. How surprising, given the parallel nature of our endeavours!

The preceding discussion identifies similar perspectives at the cores of the disciplines of social work and geography, a simultaneous consideration of person and environment. Both disciplines profess an interest in this person–environment interaction, yet historically they have approached this issue from different perspectives. Is there any evidence of a convergence, a coming together of *placed peoples* and *peopled places*?

Norton (2002) observes that "human geography is grounded in such academic disciplines as history, economics, anthropology, sociology, psychology, and political studies." As reported earlier, the same list has been identified as underlying the social work literature. Given that both disciplines recognize this virtually identical interdisciplinary base of knowledge, I find it strange that neither has acknowledged the other formally as a major contributor or partner.

Certainly there are indications of parallel work in the two disciplines. The ecosystems concept is fundamental in human geography (Norton 2002) as well as in social work (Germain and Gitterman 1980; Rothery 2002). Golledge (1996, 475) describes how geographic theories "have covered scales from micro-behavioural to global and are exploring both qualitative and quantitative models"; could there be a clearer statement of social work's micro–macro focus and our current research models? Thrift's (1997, 389) vision of a geography of social action that is "bent towards theoretical and emancipatory aims" coincides with the notion of empowerment practice advocated in the social work literature (Miley, O'Melia, and DuBois 2004; Shera and Wells 1999). Issues of damage to the physical environment are beginning to appear in the comprehensive definitions of social justice on a global scale (Wilson and Whitmore, 2000, 54).

Feminist geography argues the case for links between the oppression of women and the domination of nature, links connected historically to the patriarchal view of nature as feminine and culture as masculine (Nesmith and Radcliffe 1997); feminist social work challenges societal issues of gender exploitation and oppression, practices rooted in social policies, attitudes, and institutions developed from a patriarchal perspective (Heinonen and Spearman 2001; Valentich 1996).

Grand theories in geography, on the other hand, have been criticized because they "provide no handle for dealing with such diverse issues of the moment as gender, the disadvantages of ethnic minorities, the disabled, the mentally ill, the aged,

children, and so on" (Mabogunje, 1996, 445). The ecological perspective in mainstream social work has also been criticized for stressing balance and goodness-of-fit, notions that can disguise underlying social inequalities, oppression, and exclusion (Carniol 2000; Mullaly 2002). Smith (1997, 15) observes that geographers are often uncomfortable with abstract and unrealistic grand theories and are "more in tune with the messy reality of actual human behaviour." In social work deMontigny (1995, 220) mirrors this dissatisfaction with his plea that we build a new progressive practice rooted "not in the clear blue heavens built on abstraction but in the muddied grounds of day-to-day life."

In his exploration of the evolving nature of the helping relationship over time, Collier (1993) charts the evolution of many societies from a foraging phase through an agricultural economy, and finally to industrialism. He describes first the egalitarian members of groups connected as kin supporting each other, followed by the charity functions assumed by the church and landowners, then finishes his analysis with the paid professional helpers of industrial society. Collier finds evidence of increased social inequality as a society moves through these phases, as the helping role shifts from communal responsibility to paid specialists employed by government services "designed to force a rapid transfer to industrialization" (p. 18). A very similar analysis appears in the geography literature, where Roberts (1996, 493) examines patterns of "human-induced transformation of the natural world." He begins with HFGs (hunter-fisher-gatherer peoples), then proceeds through an agricultural phase, then imperialism, and concludes with industrial society. Using the same chronology as Collier, Roberts highlights severe environmental degradation in the shift from renewable to non-renewable resources designed to meet the energy needs of industrial society.

Given the common focus on person/environment and all of this parallel activity, one might reasonably wonder what suppports the separation of social work and human geography. How is a distinction between *placed people* and *peopled places* maintained in practice? One possible answer may be found in the very wording itself. Declaring a focus on person/environment still involves assuming two components—the *person* and the *environment*—connected yet conceived and perceived as separate elements. Each component can be emphasized to the detriment of the other, as we have seen. What might happen if there were essentially no separation between them? The traditional knowledge systems of many indigenous peoples do not make any such distinction between person and environment.

PERSON/ENVIRONMENT AND TRADITIONAL KNOWLEDGE

The government of the Northwest Territories formally defines traditional knowledge as "knowledge and values which have been acquired through experience, observation, and from the land or from spiritual teachings, and handed down from one generation to another" (Wenzel 1999, 113). Sahtouris (1992, 4) explains that this way of knowing "includes biology, geology, astronomy, navigation, meteorology, botany, medicine/pharmacology, psychology, agricultural engineering, plant genetics, ecology, social and political sciences [and] is based on thousands of years of observations and experiments in living nature.... It is not a science that stands apart from nature to look at it objectively; it does not eliminate the sacred, but integrates it. It

fosters dialogue between humans and the rest of nature."

At first glance, traditional knowledge may appear to be similar to social work and geography in connecting human experience with that of the natural world. Turner (2002) and Chappell (1997) both include First Nations theory as part of the knowledge base for contemporary social work in Canada, for example. I have argued elsewhere, however, that any assumption of traditional knowledge as just another theory base disguises a fundamental difference in world view (Zapf 1999). Morrissette, McKenzie, and Morrissette (1993, 93) articulate the essence of this difference: "While Aboriginal people do not embrace a single philosophy, there are fundamental differences between the dominant Euro-Canadian and traditional Aboriginal societies, and these have their roots in differing perceptions of one's relationship with the universe and the Creator."

Western disciplines such as social work and geography, with their focus on person–environment interaction, can be seen as problematic from the perspective of traditional knowledge because the person and the environment are still understood as two separate (although interacting) entities. In contrast to this notion, the foundation metaphor of traditional knowledge has been characterized as a perspective of *"I am I and the Environment,"* a phrase first attributed to Ortega y Gasset (1985) and later elaborated by Stairs and Wenzel (1992, 8–9), who contrasted indigenous *"world-image* identity" with Western *"self-image* concepts." Stairs (1992, 120) distinguishes between Western *"egocentric"* identity patterns and Inuit *"ecocentric"* patterns "involving connections within and between the human, animal, and material worlds." Goehring (1993, 55) contrasts

Eurocentric notions such as "land is an economic resource like any other" and "land belongs to us" with the indigenous versions of "land is the source of life" and "we belong to the land." From his exploration of regional identity in Lapland, Suopajarvi (1998, 3) similarly concludes that "I'm not in the place but the place is in me." Referring specifically to the helping professions, Hart (1996, 63) explains the contrast this way: "Western models of healing separate and detach individuals from their social, physical and spiritual environments, isolating 'patients' for treatment purposes and then re-introducing them into the world. Traditional healers are concerned with balancing emotional, physical, mental, spiritual, aspects of people, the environment, and the spirit world."

Colorado (1993, 93) attributes the "great imbalance" between Western and indigenous peoples to "linear thought which emphasizes separation and hierarchy... [and shapes] the mind so powerfully that Western-thinking people often confuse linearity with reality." Such a predilection for separation and hierarchy in Western thought helps explain how social work and geography have remained separate academic disciplines, each highlighting a different perceived aspect of the person–environment relationship. Maybe this is how we continue to miss the essential unity of *placed people* and *peopled places*.

Colorado (1991, 21) has emphasized the centrality of spirituality and natural energies within traditional knowledge in her explanation that "native scientists, through their rituals and songs, etc. are working all the time with energies—the energies of the earth—in a way which is just as precise as the ways western scientists work." Peat (1994, 265–267) also explores this notion of natural energy and connects it closely to a geographic sense of place: "Unlike Western science, the impor-

tance of the landscape, and specific places in it, is a characteristic of all Indigenous science....Within Indigenous science there is an association of spirit or energy with particular places, and it is important to visit these places and carry out ceremonies there.... This idea of the significance of place and the energies associated with it is common to Indigenous sciences all over the world.... Western science does not appear to have a corresponding concept."

With reference to the Western Apache, Basso (1996, 146) elaborates on the interconnectedness of place, spirit, and self: "As Apache men and women set about drinking from places—as they acquire knowledge of their natural surroundings, commit it to permanent memory, and apply it productively to the workings of their minds—they show by their actions that their surroundings live in them. Like their ancestors before them, they display by word and deed that beyond the visible reality of place lies a moral reality which they themselves have come to embody. And whether or not they finally succeed in becoming fully wise, it is this interior landscape—this landscape of the moral imagination—that most deeply influences their vital sense of place, and also, I believe, their unshakable sense of self... selfhood and placehood are completely intertwined."

While there is little evidence in the literature that either social work or geography has ventured very far into this realm of spiritual energy, I find some small indications. In their explication of the major terminology necessary to understand the ecological perspective in social work, Hull Jr. and Kirst-Ashman (2004, 10) define energy as "the natural power of active involvement between people and their environments." From a geographic perspective, Jackson (1994, 90) observes a loss of spirit in the Western world view of the man–nature relationship. He concludes that the natural landscape is no longer sacred but has become a potentially dangerous source of energy that "has to be filtered, diluted, made to conform to federal standards of health and safety." While not a full acceptance of a spiritual component of place, the notion of a "geographical imagination" that is creative, inspirational, and also recognizes the relevance of space and place to the diversity of human activity could be a step in that direction (Harvey 1973; Norton 2002).

When the person and the environment are understood as one entity, the connections between them become more than social interaction or landscape modification; they are profound expressions of the same whole and assume a dimension of energy or spirit.

DIRECTIONS

What can be concluded from this exploration of geography and social work? To return to the question posed at the outset of this chapter, should geography be acknowledged with the other listed disciplines as a major contributor to the theoretical base of Canadian social welfare? This discussion leads to a view of geography as more a living cousin than an ancestor of social work. Rather than offering a static base of knowledge as a building block, human geography is a dynamic discipline with activities and potential that closely parallel current social work. The two disciplines appear as two sides of the same coin; each engages person-and-environment interaction from its own particular historical perspective. We should see geography as a partner rather than a building block for social work, yet we have a curious history of ignoring each other's efforts. Larger forces may now be pointing us towards convergence.

Social welfare has been defined as "a generic term that encompasses the complex network of legislation, policies, programs, institutions, professions, resources, and services that exist in all societies to seek to ensure that individuals and groups will have access to the range of goods and services necessary to achieve their full human potential in a manner acceptable to them with due regard to the rights of others" (Turner 2001, 2). Canada is a huge country with a small ribbon of population concentrated along its southern border. Much of the country is wilderness with tiny communities scattered over vast regions. These simple facts of physical and demographic geography have powerfully influenced the development of social welfare.

Most of the legislation and policy that define our social welfare system have been designed in urban centres in the south. Professional social workers, trained in these same centres, deliver programs and services through institutions based in urban locations and world views. Can we expect the resulting "range of goods and services" to be appropriate for persons trying "to achieve their human full potential" in regions outside urban southern Canada? If "full human potential" involves some balance or connection with the social and physical environment, then the vision of that potential would differ a great deal between an outport fishing village in Newfoundland, a mining town in Northern Ontario, a trapping community in the Yukon, and a Haida village on the West Coast.

Social welfare's "due regard to the rights of others" may have to be expanded to include a regard for the rights of the environment, an attitude of respect and stewardship rather than exploitation, an understanding that "full human potential" must exist beyond individual achievement. Full potentials for individuals, societies, and environments are not separate goals; they are expressions of the same desirable healthy state. Norton (2002) argues that degradation of the physical environment and the creation of social inequalities both result from industrial society's belief that progress is based on maximizing production through its domination of nature. Suzuki (1999, 45) issues this challenge for integration: "I believe there is no dichotomy between environmental and social needs. Hungry people will not care if their actions endanger an edible species or an important habitat. Unemployment, injustice or insecurity lead to desperation and the need to survive at all costs. To protect an environment for future generations, we have to build a society on a foundation of clean air, water, soil and energy and rich biodiversity to fulfil our biological needs; we have to ensure full employment, justice and security for all communities to serve our social needs; and we have to retain sacred places, a sense of belonging and connectedness with nature and a knowledge that there are cosmic forces beyond our comprehension or control, to satisfy our spiritual requirements."

To describe such an interconnected world, Gould (1996, 449) offers the intriguing metaphor of a "braided stream, with its waters constantly flowing from one channel to another." This image suggests that Western academic disciplines, such as geography and social work, attempt to divert the waters into well-defined channels that can be manipulated and managed. As academics, we tend to work exclusively in our own channels, largely unaware of parallel efforts in other channels. Those in the social work channel have developed knowledge of *placed people* and are reaching for a fuller understanding of the environment. Those in the geography channel have developed knowledge of *peopled places* and are reaching for a more fully human geography. Both may be on the verge of incorporating a lost sense of spirituality that reintroduces a unity of person and environment. We could have much to learn from each other and from other traditions of knowledge. As Gould (1996, 459) concludes, "In a very deep sense, nothing is unconnected in today's world, which is perhaps why it is important not to channel braided streams, but to let them mix their currents and find their own respective ways."

REFERENCES

Armitage, A. 1996. *Social welfare in Canada revisited*. Don Mills, ON: Oxford University Press.

Barker, R. L. (Ed.). 1999. *The social work dictionary*. 4th edn. Washington, D.C.: National Association of Social Workers Press.

Basso, K. H. 1996. *Wisdom sits in places: Landscape and language among the Western Apache*. Albuquerque: University of New Mexico Press.

Bone, R. M. 2002. *The regional geography of Canada*. 2d edn.. Don Mills, ON: Oxford University Press.

Carlin, G. 1990. Euphemisms. *Parental Advisory: Explicit Lyrics*. Cassette Recording No. 79 15934. Scarborough, ON: Atlantic Recording Corporation and WEA Music of Canada.

Carniol, B. 2000. *Case critical: Challenging social services in Canada*. 4th edn. Toronto: Between the Lines.

Chappell, R. 1997. *Social welfare in Canadian society*. Scarborough, ON: ITP Nelson.

Collier, K. 1993. *Social work with rural peoples: Theory and practice*. 2d edn. Vancouver: New Star Books.

Colorado, P. 1991. A meeting between brothers—indigenous science. Interview with J. Carroll. *Beshara, 13*. 20–27.

Colorado, P. 1993. Coherence: A process of social work education with aboriginal students. In K. Feehan & D. Hannis (Eds.), *From strength to strength: Social work education and aboriginal people* (pp. 79–94). Edmonton: Grant MacEwan Community College.

Compton, B. R., & Galaway, B. 1999. *Social work processes.* 6th edn. Pacific Grove, WA: Brooks/Cole.

Daniels, S. 1997. Arguments for a humanistic geography. In T. Barnes & D. Gregory (Eds.), *Reading human geography: The poetics and politics of inquiry* (pp. 364–376). London: Arnold.

de Blij, H. J., & Muller, P. O. 1994. *Geography: Realms, regions, and concepts.* 7th edn. New York: John Wiley and Sons.

de Blij, H. J., & Murphy. A. B. 2003. *Human geography: Culture, society, and space.* 7th edn. New York: John Wiley and Sons.

DeMontigny, G. A. J. 1995. *Social working: An ethnography of front-line practice.* Toronto: University of Toronto Press.

Dicken, P., & Lloyd, P. E.. 1990. *Location in space: Theoretical perspectives in economic geography.* 3d edn. New York: HarperCollins.

Fellmann, J., Getis, A., & Getis, J. 1997. *Human geography: Landscapes of human activities.* 5th edn. Madison, WI: Brown and Benchmark Publishers.

Germain, C. B., & Gitterman, A. 1980. *The life model of social work practice.* New York: Columbia University Press.

Glassner, M. I. 1996. *Political geography.* 2d edn. New York: John Wiley and Sons.

Goehring, B. 1993. *Indigenous peoples of the world: An introduction to their past, present, and future.* Saskatoon, SK: Purich Publishing.

Golledge, R. G. 1996. Geographical theories. *International Social Science Journal, 150* (Special Issue on Geography: State of the Art I—The Environmental Dimension). 461–476.

Gould, P. 1996. Space, time and the human being. *International Social Science Journal, 150* (Special Issue on Geography: State of the Art I—The Environmental Dimension). 449–460.

Hamelin, L. E. 1988. *The Canadian North and its conceptual referents.* Ottawa: Canadian Studies Directorate, Department of the Secretary of State of Canada.

Hancock, M. R. 1997. *Principles of social work practice: A generic practice approach.* New York: Haworth.

Hart, M. A. 1996. Sharing circles: utilizing traditional practice methods for teaching, helping, and supporting. In S. O'Meara & D. A. West (Eds.), *From our eyes: Learning from indigenous peoples* (pp. 59–72). Toronto: Garamond Press.

Harvey, D. W. 1973. *Social justice and the city.* London: Arnold.

Heinonen, T., & Spearman, L. 2001. *Social work practice: Problem-solving and beyond.* Toronto: Irwin Publishing.

Hepworth, D. H., Rooney, R. H., & Larsen, J. A. 1997. *Direct social work practice: Theory and skills* (5th ed.).. Pacific Grove, WA: Brooks/Cole.

Hick, S. 2002. *Social work in Canada: An introduction.* Toronto: Thompson Educational Publishing.

Hull, Jr., G. H., & Kirst-Ashman, K. K. 2004. *The generalist model of human services practice.* Pacific Grove, WA: Brooks/Cole.

Jackson, J. B. 1994. *A sense of place, a sense of time.* New Haven: Yale University Press.

Johnson, L. C. 1998. *Social work practice: A generalist approach.* 6th edn. Boston: Allyn & Bacon.

Lehmann, P., & Coady, N. (Eds.). 2001. *Theoretical perspectives for direct social work practice: A generalist-eclectic approach.* New York: Springer.

Mabogunje, A. L. 1996. Introduction. *International Social Science Journal, 150* (Special Issue on Geography: State of the Art I—The Environmental Dimension). 443–447.

McKay, S. 2002. Postmodernism, social well-being, and the mainstream/progressive debate. In F. J. Turner (Ed.), *Social work practice: A Canadian perspective.* 2d edn. (pp. 20–32). Toronto: Pearson Education Canada.

Mendelson, R., & Bollman, R. D. 1998. Rural and small town population is growing in the 1990s. In R. D. Bollman (Ed.), *Rural and Small Town Canada Analysis Bulletin, 1.1.* 1–11.

Miley, K. K., O'Melia, M., & DuBois, B. L.. 2004. *Generalist social work practice: An empowering approach.* 4th edn. Boston: Pearson Educational Publishing.

Morrissette, V., McKenzie, B., & Morrissette, L. 1993. Towards an aboriginal model of social work practice: Cultural knowledge and traditional practices. *Canadian Social Work Review, 10.1.,* 91–108.

Mullaly, R. 2002. *Challenging oppression: A critical social work approach.* Don Mills, ON: Oxford University Press.

National Association of Social Workers. 1981. Conceptual frameworks II. *Social Work, 26.1.* 6–75.

Nesmith, C., & Radcliffe, S. A. 1997. (Re)mapping Mother Earth: A geographical perspective on environmental feminisms. In T. Barnes & D. Gregory (Eds.), *Reading human geography: The poetics and politics of inquiry* (pp. 195–210). London: Arnold.

Norton, W. 2002. *Human geography.* 4th edn. Don Mills, ON: Oxford University Press.

Ortega y Gasset, J. 1985. *Meditations on hunting.* New York: Scribners.

Peat, F. D. 1994. *Lighting the seventh fire: The spiritual ways, healing, and science of the Native American.* New York: Birch Lane Press.

Pile, S. 1997. Human agency and human geography revisited: A critique of "new models" of the self. In T. Barnes & D. Gregory (Eds.), *Reading human geography: The poetics and politics of inquiry* (pp. 407–434). London: Arnold.

Relph, E. 1976. *Place and placelessness.* London: Pion.

Roberts, N. 1996. The human transformation of the earth's surface. *International Social Science Journal, 150* (Special Issue on Geography: State of the Art I—The Environmental Dimension). 493–510.

Rothery, M. 2002. The resources of intervention. In F. J. Turner (Ed.), *Social work practice: A Canadian perspective.* 2d edn. (pp. 241–254). Toronto: Pearson Education Canada.

Sahtouris, E. 1992. The survival path: cooperation between indigenous and industrial humanity. *Proceedings of the United Nations Policy Meeting on Indigenous Peoples.* Santiago, Chile. Available at **www.ratical.com/LifeWeb/Articles/survival.html**

Sheafor, B. W., Horejsi, C. R., & Horejsi, G. A.. 2000. *Techniques and guidelines for social work practice.* 5th edn. Needham Heights, MA: Allyn & Bacon.

Shera, W., & Wells, L. (Eds.). 1999. *Empowerment practice: Developing richer conceptual foundations.* Toronto: Canadian Scholars' Press.

Smith, D. M. 1997. Market forces, cultural factors and locational processes. *International Social Science Journal, 151* (Special Issue on Geography: State of the Art II–Societal Processes and Geographic Space). 11–22.

Soanes, C. (Ed.). 2000. *The Oxford compact English dictionary.* 2d edn. Oxford: Oxford University Press.

Stairs, A. 1992. Self-image, world-image: Speculations on identity from experiences with Inuit. *Ethos, 20(1),* 116–126.

Stairs, A., & Wenzel, G. 1992. "I am I and the environment": Inuit hunting, community, and identity. *Journal of Indigenous Studies, 3.1.* 1–12.

Suopajarvi, L. 1998. *Regional identity in Finnish Lapland.* Paper presented at the Third International Congress of Arctic Social Sciences, Copenhagen, Denmark.

Suzuki, D. T. 1999, June 14. Saving the Earth. (Essays on the Millenium series). *Maclean's, 112.24.* 42–45.

Taaffe, E. J., Gauthier, H. L. & O'Kelly, M. E.. 1996. *Geography of transportation.* Upper Saddle River, NJ: Prentice-Hall.

Thrift, N. 1997. On the determination of social action in space and time. In T. Barnes & D. Gregory (Eds.), *Reading human geography: The poetics and politics of inquiry* (pp. 376–407). London: Arnold.

Turner, F. J. 2001. Canadian social welfare. In J. C. Turner & F. J. Turner (Eds.), *Canadian social welfare.* 4th edn. (pp. 1–11). Toronto: Pearson Education Canada.

Turner, F. J. 2002. The theoretical base of practice. In F. J. Turner (Ed.), *Social work practice: A Canadian perspective* (2d ed., pp. 46–56). Toronto: Pearson Education Canada.

Turner, J. C., & Turner, F. J. (Eds.). 1981, 1986. *Canadian social welfare.* 1st & 2d edns. Don Mills, ON: Collier Macmillan Canada.

Turner, J. C., & Turner, F. J.. (Eds.). 1995. *Canadian social welfare.* 3d edn. Scarborough, ON: Allyn and Bacon Canada.

Turner, J. C., & Turner, F. J.. (Eds.). 2001. *Canadian social welfare.* 4th edn. Toronto: Pearson Education Canada.

Valentich, M. 1996. Feminist Theory and Social Work Practice. In F. Turner (Ed.), *Social work treatment* (4th ed.). New York: Free Press.

Watt, S. 1995. Canadian realities. In J. C. Turner & F. J. Turner (Eds.), *Canadian social welfare.* 3d edn. (pp. 120–129). Scarborough, ON: Allyn and Bacon Canada.

Wenzel, G. W. 1999. Traditional ecological knowledge and Inuit: Reflections on tek research and ethics. *Arctic 52(2)*, 113–124.

Wilson, M. G., & Whitmore, E. 2000. *Seeds of fire: Social development in an era of globalism.* Halifax: Fernwood; and Ottawa: Canadian Consortium for International Social Development.

Wood, J. (Ed.) 2002. *Canada: A portrait.* 57th edn. Ottawa: Minister of Industry.

Woodsworth, D. 1981. Canadian realities. In J. C. Turner & F. J. Turner (Eds.), *Canadian social welfare* (pp. 59–72). Don Mills, ON: Collier Macmillan Canada.

Woodsworth, D. 1986. Canadian realities. In J. C. Turner & F. J. Turner (Eds.), *Canadian social welfare* (2d ed., pp. 61–76). Don Mills, ON: Collier Macmillan Canada.

Yelaja, S.A. 1985. Concepts of social work practice. In S. A. Yelaja (Ed.), *An introduction to social work practice in Canada.* Scarborough, ON: Prentice-Hall Canada.

Yeung, Y. 1997. Geography in the age of megacities. *International Social Science Journal, 151* (Special Issue on Geography: State of the Art II—Societal Processes and Geographic Space). 91–104.

Zapf, M. K. 2002. Geography and Canadian social work practice. In F. J. Turner, *Social work practice: A Canadian perspective.* 2d edn. pp. 69–83). Toronto: Pearson Education Canada.

Zapf, M. K. 1999. Location and knowledge-building: Exploring the fit of western social work with traditional knowledge. *Native Social Work Journal, 2.1.* 139–153.

Zapf, M. K. 2001. Notions of rurality. *Rural social work, 6(3)*, 12-27.

Zaslow, M. 1971. *The opening of the Canadian North, 1870–1914.* Toronto: McClelland and Stewart.

Zastrow, C. 2004. *Introduction to social work and social welfare: Empowering people.* 8th edn. Belmont: Brooks/Cole-Thomson Learning.

chapter six

The Historical Base of Canadian Social Welfare

Joanne C. Turner

History, of course, has much to teach us about present society and perhaps most of all about human complexities. We can and thankfully sometimes do learn from both the successes and failures of history. The most profitable lessons often come out of the frustrations of failure.

Over the centuries, all societies have had to come to terms with social problems, especially poverty and disease, through charity or alms-giving.[1] To understand contemporary Canadian social welfare, we must know something of these earlier events. In Canada the development of social welfare has been influenced by a range of factors. However, the early principal shaping influences come from developments in Western Europe, as does much of our culture.

To set the stage for our discussion, let us review the advantages and disadvantages of the feudal system, which began in Western Europe as early as the fifth century and flourished until the fourteenth century. This system was a form of land tenure based on a lord's delegation of property to a subordinate servant or serf to cultivate. This agricultural agreement provided "a social, political, military and economic structure to the society of that time."[2] Among many negative aspects of this arrangement was the fact that the serfs did not own the land but worked it for their lords. On the positive side, the system did meet most of the serfs' basic needs. It provided a home, food, fuel, community, some independence, and usually someone to take care of them when they were unable to work because of sickness, accident, or old age. Often care was provided by the lord's household or by the local parish. Of course, the serfs paid a price for this security in lack of freedom, for they were bound to serve their lords in whatever way the latter saw fit, sometimes as soldiers though more often as farmers. Serfs were also forbidden to leave their villages without permission, and such permission was hard to obtain.

Under the feudal system, then, life for the serfs offered limited stability. The decline of the system resulted in the dislocation of the labourers from the land, which brought them more freedom but less security. Ever since the breakdown of the feudal system, individuals, groups, and governments have been trying to create a system of social welfare that gives people both freedom and security. To date, no attempt has been entirely successful.

BRITISH ROOTS

For centuries, the Christian church bore the major responsibility for the organization of charity in Western society. The state supported, or at least tolerated, that arrangement. The tradition changed dramatically in England in response to the onset of the bubonic plague, which wiped out two-thirds of the English population within two years (1348–1349). The resulting shortage of labour and the simultaneous rise in wages compelled Edward III to issue the Statute of Labourers of 1349. The law required able-bodied labourers to accept employment from any masters willing to hire them, and it forbade them to leave their parishes. Furthermore, citizens were prohibited from giving alms to able-bodied beggars. Evidently the law was intended to prevent begging and to force the serfs to stay on the land.

In the sixteenth century, Henry VIII broke with the Pope and the Roman Catholic church. This schism further weakened the church's tradition of caring for the poor for, in closing monasteries and confiscating their properties and wealth, Henry made it almost impossible for the church to continue as the principal reliever of economic distress. This lent urgency to a long process, begun in 1349, in which the state slowly and reluctantly assumed responsibility for those who could not care for themselves. In the end, public money collected through taxation was allocated to solving the problem. As Karl de Schweinitz explains it, "The experience of the years between 1349 and 1601 had convinced the rulers of England of the presence of a destitution among the poor that punishment could not abolish and that could be relieved only by the application of public resources to individual need."[3]

This realization led to a long series of measures known as the Poor Laws, many of which were formalized by legislation under Elizabeth I (1533–1603), and eventually over four more centuries through a lengthy series of modifications led to Britain's National Insurance Act and the Beveridge Report of 1943. The latter serves as the basis of the modern system of social security in the United Kingdom today.

Although these historical events are both interesting and enlightening, they are documented in detail elsewhere.[4] This chapter will examine two significant factors with long-term implications for the development of social welfare systems in Britain and then in Canada. These are the principles of less eligibility and the perception of need.

The principle of less eligibility can be traced to the *Report of the Royal Commission for Inquiring into the Administration and Practical Operations of the Poor Laws* in 1834.[5] It laid out that

"The assistance provided for people in need must be such as to cause their condition to be less desirable, less satisfactory,... less eligible than the condition of the lowest-paid labourer who was not in receipt of welfare."[6] This concept arose from the fear that more than minimal assistance would encourage people to seek it rather than to work. This concept still underlies the attitudes of some policy-makers today.

Able-bodied or employable men who wished to obtain relief, along with their wives and children, were obliged to move into workhouses. There the men were housed in one section, women in another, and children in still another. Thus were families were broken up, and all members, including children over the age of 7, were obliged to work in return for their bed and board. It is no wonder that Benjamin Disraeli, the great British prime minister (1868 and 1878–1880), felt compelled to say of this system, "It announces to the world that in England poverty is a crime!"[7]

The practice of relegating those in need to a second-class existence strongly influenced the development of social welfare in Britain, the United States, and Canada. Evidence of this practice will be given in the discussion of early events in Canadian history.

The second principle, perception of need, concerns how people view other people who are in need. There are two ways of looking at need: people are impoverished because of their own personal failures or because of the failures of society and its economic system. The first position suited the individualism fashionable in eighteenth- and nineteenth-century England. As Wilensky and Lebeaux comment, "As doctrine, individualism states that the good of all will best be served if each individual pursues his self-interest with minimal interference."[8]

The concepts of capitalism and a market economy usually coexist with the belief that people are in need because of their own failures. A leading proponent of the concepts of capitalism and a market economy was Adam Smith, an eighteenth-century economist and philosopher from Scotland. His *Wealth of Nations*, published in 1766, is a thorough analysis of the process by which economic wealth is produced and distributed. The work details rent, wages, and profits, the key points of the capitalist system. For our purposes, Smith states most significantly that individuals pursuing their own good work toward achieving the good of all. Any interference by government in business would most certainly be harmful, writes Smith. This philosophy came to be known as laissez-faire and it strongly influenced thinking in Britain about welfare matters in the eighteenth and nineteenth centuries.

Laissez-faire as a concept profoundly influenced Britain, and it provoked some strong opposition as well as support. Leading social reformers of the nineteenth and early twentieth centuries, such as Robert Owen[9] and Beatrice and Sidney Webb, pushed theories of humanitarianism that redefined certain persons as needy owing to circumstances outside their control. Based on this philosophy, the social reformers fought for better wages, housing, and working conditions. They often debated with proponents of laissez-faire.

THE CANADIAN APPROACH

The 1700s

A review of early events in Canada reveals that these ideological differences spread beyond Britain and Europe. Before Confederation, proponents of laissez-faire and the principle of less eligibility often clashed with those who held more humanitarian views of the obligation to their neighbours.

The traditional leader in the arena of social welfare was the church, and the Catholic church in particular continued to pioneer in the lands that would eventually become Canada. Its long experience in Europe in ministering to the suffering, its strong administrative organization, its personnel and wealthy patrons, and its abundant resources equipped the church as an institution to meet the temporal as well as the spiritual needs of the people newly arrived to this land.

Marguerite Bourgeoys founded the Sisters of the Congregation of Notre Dame in New France in the mid-seventeenth century, who taught and cared for the children of New France, especially young girls the mother country sent to the colony. The influence of the religious orders, in particular of these sisters and the Jesuit fathers, spread beyond the boundaries of New France to develop into a vast network of institutions in the new world.

The church humanitarian groups in Quebec in the mid-eighteenth century established centres for poor relief in three urban communities as well, which demonstrates a growing social responsibility on the part of colonial society toward the worthy poor.[10]

Atlantic Canada strongly felt the British philosophy of less eligibility. The government of Nova Scotia adopted the English Poor Laws in 1763, complete with such institutions as public workhouses and orphanages. One public workhouse for both adults and children in that province dealt out whippings, shacklings, starvation, and other punishments for many years to correct the behaviour of its reluctant or vagrant inmates.[11] The Poor Laws also operated in New Brunswick, although not in Prince Edward Island.

When government social-welfare programs began to appear in Upper Canada, they aimed to protect society from undesirables, such as criminals, delinquents, the poor, and the mentally ill. In general, they were intended to reinforce the responsibility of individuals for their own welfare through negative and punitive measures.

Upper Canada led all the territories in the development of child welfare legislation, again reflecting the earlier concept of the worthy and the unworthy poor. An act to provide for the education and support of orphaned children was passed in 1799. This first Canadian child welfare legislation provided that two justices of the peace could bind an orphaned child to an apprenticeship until she or he reached the age of 21.[12] Almost 50 years later, two other acts were passed in Ontario, both concerned with the protection of children whose parents could not provide for them.

The 1800s

In 1867, the British North America Act assigned welfare provisions to the provincial governments. This assignment of responsibility to the provinces greatly influenced the development of a variety of approaches to welfare services across the country. At that time welfare was not seen as a major function of governments. In the early years following Confederation, public welfare fell under the provision of the Poor Law, which was almost wholly the responsibility of the municipalities. Following this British precedent, municipalities found themselves obliged to provide for the poor, while the provincial governments did little beyond operating jails or insane asylums.[13] Toward the end of the nineteenth century, people began to realize that this decision made in 1867 would create many problems for the quickly growing young country.

Between 1867 and 1900, social welfare legislation was enacted more and more frequently as Canada began to appreciate the complexity of need among many societal groups. Most provisions concerned the protection of neglected and delinquent children. Two important events took place in Toronto, owing in large measure to the work of J. J. Kelso, a Toronto journalist who had become concerned about children's welfare. In 1891, the Children's Aid Society of Toronto was organized in recognition of society's responsibility to care for neglected children. And in 1893, the first piece of child welfare legislation was passed in Ontario, An Act for the Prevention of Cruelty to and Better Protection of Children. It was intended to encourage the founding of additional children's aid societies in Ontario. The Act gave the new societies the power to apprehend and bring before a judge any child that the Act classified as neglected. Mr. Kelso was appointed Ontario's first superintendent of neglected and dependent children in 1893.[14] Clearly, needy children were classified as members of the worthy poor. Overall, however, the principles of "laissez-faire" dominated the emergence of a social welfare system for the country. Welfare was not considered an urgent matter and for the most part was left to local governments.

The 1900s

In the early twentieth century, it became obvious that the constitutional decision to allocate responsibility for welfare to the provinces did not fit either the complexities of a modern welfare state or the need for strong central planning in welfare matters. During the 1920s and 1930s, returned World War I veterans and their families pressured the federal government more and more with their staggering needs. Yet under law that level of government did not have the power to assume responsibility for health and welfare matters.

In 1926, Parliament tried to find a way around the Constitution. It passed enabling legislation that allowed the federal government and the provincial government to cost-share the funding provided by the Old Age Pension Act.[15] This set the precedent for legislative initiative for the federal government in the field of social welfare.

In 1932, the federal government set up relief camps for single men under the supervision of the Department of National Defence. Refused assistance by municipal authorities, most men had no alternative but to work in the camps for 20 cents a day. By spring, 1935, 4000 angry, restless camp workers in Vancouver organized a march, although they travelled by freight car, to Ottawa to meet directly with the federal government. The authorities stopped them in Regina and encouraged them to send delegates to Ottawa instead to confer with Prime Minister R. B. Bennett. The applicants achieved nothing at the meeting with Bennett, and when the men attempted to continue their symbolic march the police arrested several truckloads of them. The discontent finally erupted in the Regina Riot of July 1, 1935, in which one man was killed, more than 100 injured, and more 80 people arrested.[16] Confusion, anger, and dismay were found at every level of government, and it was obvious that provincial revenues were no longer adequate to meet society's needs.

By 1933, the effects of the Depression had intensified. Fifteen to 20 percent of the population was dependent on municipal social assistance, and the local municipalities were quickly going bankrupt under the strain. "Twenty-five percent of the normal male working force was unemployed; and most of the young men had not found their first jobs after leaving school."[17]

Out of this turmoil, the government of the day made its first timid attempts at welfare state legislation. In 1935, Bennett's

Conservative government introduced an unemployment insurance scheme, which ignored the provisions of the Constitution. In 1937, it was declared unconstitutional, and the Liberals under Mackenzie King eventually had to reintroduce the measure in 1940 as an Unemployment Insurance bill, which was safely passed with an amendment to the BNA Act.[18]

The Royal Commission on Dominion–Provincial Relations (the Rowell–Sirois Commission) was appointed in 1937 to propose new fiscal agreements and legislation between the federal and provincial governments. Its principal recommendation was that the federal government relieve the provinces of their constitutional responsibility for the unemployed and any debts that had accumulated. The commission also proposed that the federal government in turn be given exclusive rights to levy necessary duties and taxes on personal and corporate incomes.[19]

The outbreak of World War II in 1939 overshadowed the commission's work, and its report was never implemented. The two federal–provincial conferences that followed both collapsed. Kenneth McNaught writes: "To implement the Rowell–Sirois Plan would have required a combination of BNA Act amendments and policy agreements between Ottawa and at least a majority of the provinces. Such agreement was never reached. Throughout the Commission's period of research it was virtually boycotted by the premiers of Ontario, Quebec, and Alberta."[20]

World War II to the 1970s

The war nearly eradicated unemployment, yet world events were moving Canadians closer to accepting that their society needed broad-based social security legislation. The citizen's right to social security was formulated in the Atlantic Charter of 1941, one result of the historic meeting between Winston Churchill and Franklin Delano Roosevelt during World War II. An agreement was also reached that provision must be made in the post-war world to cover those risks and contingencies of family life that lie beyond the capacity of the average person. Further, there was a general agreement that the greatest need in a social security program was adequate provision for the unemployed. The necessity of legislating for particular categories of need, such as permanent pensions for disabled war veterans, was also recognized. For Canada, a country still strongly bound by a traditional approach to social welfare, a laissez-faire philosophy and a belief in the worthy and the unworthy poor, all of these developments represented a dramatic change in thinking.

A greater public recognition of these needs also lent strong endorsement of a report the federal government commissioned on present and anticipated needs in social welfare in the early 1940s. Leonard Marsh, then director of social research at McGill University, prepared *The Report on Social Security for Canada*, which was presented to the House of Commons Special Committee on Social Security in 1943. It has been hailed as a "pivotal document in the development of war and post-war social security programs, the equivalent in Canada of the Beveridge Report in Great Britain."[21]

Marsh and his commission produced a lengthy and complicated document. He began by describing the universal risks against which individuals cannot protect themselves, then outlined a comprehensive scheme of social security that he believed would protect society from those risks. He also proposed a system of social insurance and taxation to pay for the proposed plan.

Two important themes emerge from this historic document. First, it stated that provisions for unemployment are the greatest priority in any social security program for a modern industrial society. Second, universal risks, which apply to all persons, and employment risks, which apply to wage earners only, must be clearly distinguished. The report declares that society must provide for those needs that individuals cannot fill; it rejects the concepts of laissez-faire and of the worthy and unworthy poor and signals a growing recognition that many problems of individuals originate in the economic system, not personal ones.

Marsh's proposals gave impetus to the concept of a national minimum or a guaranteed annual income, which the federal Department of Health and Welfare has been advocating ever since.[22] To date, the provinces, especially Ontario and Alberta, have not supported the idea of a guaranteed annual income.

On January 28, 1944, the *Vancouver Sun* reported that the federal government had promised "a comprehensive scheme of social insurance which will constitute a charter of social security for the whole of Canada." By the following summer, Parliament had enacted legislation to authorize both a national Family Allowance scheme and the establishment of the federal Department of Health and Welfare.

At the Dominion–Provincial Conference of 1945, the federal government submitted proposals to the provinces for developing a comprehensive welfare program, a "rearrangement of fiscal resources, economic policies and health and welfare services."[23] The conference, however, did not succeed in its goals, and Liberal hopes for a complete package deal for health and welfare services were disappointed.

Instead, the federal government proceeded to add piecemeal to welfare services, as quickly as rapidly rising expectations and a developing sense of

social justice allowed. In the first two decades following the war, an impressive, if at times uncoordinated, series of social welfare laws and improved social services was established. Parliament passed at least eight major pieces of social legislation in the 1950s and 1960s,[24] the most significant being the Canada Assistance Plan (CAP) of 1966. This plan brought together and consolidated previous cost-sharing programs, unemployment assistance, blind and disabled persons' assistance, child welfare measures, and administrative costs. It also extended the federal cost-sharing presence in provincial social welfare programs.[25] According to Melchers, "CAP is the largest single source of funding for social services in Canada, accounting for an average of 38.5 percent of provincial spending."[26] Costs were to be shared 50–50 with the provinces.

During the 1970s, the emphasis in social welfare shifted from developing new social welfare programs to an evaluation and reorganization of programs already established. This evaluation process produced the tabling of several White Papers. The first, *Income Security for Canadians*, appeared in 1970. *Unemployment Insurance in the Seventies* and *The Report of the Royal Commission on the Status of Women* were also tabled that year, and in 1973 the federal government published the *Working Paper on Social Security in Canada*.[27] This particular working paper constituted the federal government's contribution to a joint federal–provincial review of the total social security system of the country. It examined what each government had done individually and what the governments had done collectively in the field of social welfare. The federal government made a number of changes in its social welfare programs as a result. Benefits under the Family Allowance program tripled, for example.

In February 1976, the federal and provincial ministers of welfare legislation gathered at a conference to discuss sharing the costs of developing and delivering social services, based on strategies developed during the federal–provincial social security review. Under the proposed legislation, the social services were recognized as a miniature collective force in their own right, or, as Marc Lalonde, then minister of health and welfare, described them, as a linchpin, rather than a residual role.[28] This marked recognition of an important distinction: society would have to build in provisions for social services in certain high-risk areas, such as loss of income owing to accident or high unemployment, rather than hustle to provide these services in the middle of a crisis.

Thirty-three years after the release of Marsh's report, it seemed that social welfare was finally accepted as a necessary institution of Canadian society and would be taken into account in all future planning.

On June 20, 1977, Lalonde introduced a new social services bill in the House of Commons. It was one of the main outcomes of the social security review he had launched in April 1973 and of the negotiations that followed between the federal and the provincial governments. At the time, the new act was described as one that "would allow the federal government to share with the provinces in the cost of a wider range of social services than is possible at present. This includes cost-sharing of the provision, development, extension, and improvement of social services throughout Canada in order to ensure that adequate services are available. These additional services are required to meet the current needs of society which have changed since the previous legislation was implemented."[29]

The government accepted the bill but it was never given final reading. Although two subsequent ministers, Monique Bégin and David Crombie, adopted parts of the proposed legislation, to date no further comprehensive plan has been introduced by the federal government.

Social Policy in the 1980s and 1990s

Since the mid-1980s, with the election of Brian Mulroney and a Progressive Conservative federal government, social policy-making has shifted away from liberalism and toward neo-conservatism. Fundamental values have shifted in ways that, along with the poor economic climate of the early 1990s, have affected social welfare policies and governments' willingness to intervene.

Conservative philosophy holds that employment should naturally flow with the economy and that government intervention in creating full employment only creates more economic problems. As Mishra (1989) writes, "Neo-conservatives believe that unemployment is an unavoidable feature of market economies, a price to be paid for freedom of enterprise and growth."[30]

In addition, neo-conservatives generally believe that welfare dependency is a consequence of people's reluctance to accept low-wage jobs. Indeed, welfare payment levels in Ontario did provide most claimants with an income higher than minimum wage earnings until the early 1990s. On the principle that claimants should not be better off on social assistance than they would be employed, governments devoted attention to devising ways to ensure that assistance to the working poor continued to motivate them to work instead.[31]

Generally, neo-conservatism aims to reduce government spending on social welfare. The move away from universality toward selectivity in social policy development has affected employment, child poverty, health, and education in far-reaching ways.

The following pieces of legislation are examples of this shift in direction.

Bill C-21 Bill C-21 is an Act to Amend the Unemployment Insurance Act and the Employment and Immigration Department and Commission Act. It came into effect in November 1990. According to the Canadian Council on Social Development, "Nineteen-ninety will be remembered as the year Canada discarded universality in two established income programs and terminated its funding of a major income security program—Unemployment Insurance…." The bill altered provisions of the act to conform with the Canadian Charter of Rights and Freedoms. It also ended the federal government's contribution to the fund, ending a 50-year association with the program.[32]

Bill C-69 Bill C-69 (1991) capped the federal contribution to the Canada Assistance Program, which had been a federal–provincial, equally shared program paying for social assistance, child care subsidies, homemaking programs, and child welfare. The program also reduced the federal government's funding for post-secondary education and health care. This cap on transfer payments was applied to the three wealthiest provinces, Ontario, British Columbia, and Alberta.[33]

Withdrawal of federal support for the Canadian safety net changed the original cost-sharing agreement between the federal and provincial governments regarding social assistance and social services. One commentator has claimed that "It is thereby fundamentally changing the CAP in a way inconsistent with its purpose as adopted by the Parliament of Canada."[34]

Bill C-80 In 1993, Bill C-80 set out to amend the Income Tax Act, to enact the Children's Special Allowances Act, amend certain other acts affected by these changes, and repeal the Family Allowances Act.[35] Bill C-80 became effective in January 1993 and was perceived as a landmark that ended the universality of services in Canada.

The Child Tax Benefit proposed in the White Paper and in the 1992 budget was intended to replace family allowances, as well as refundable and non-refundable child tax credits. The poorest families on welfare, then, did not benefit at all. The working poor received a 41 percent increase, lower-middle-income families received a 38 percent increase, those in the upper-middle-income bracket received 7 percent less, and high-income families received the Child Tax Benefit decreased by 17 percent.[36]

The social, political, and economic changes of the 1990s placed a great deal of stress on the social welfare system. As government funding was cut back, new problems emerged that demanded attention. For example, immigration policies increased the need for the greater integration of minorities into Canadian life. According to Bracken and Walmsley, "Ensuring full participation of minorities in Canadian society as well as equal access to and treatment by social service systems are emerging challenges for Canadian social welfare."[37] The family structure was also changing, and higher divorce rates led to a greater number of single-parent families and blended families. There are now more teenaged single parents and fewer teen marriages, thanks to lowered social expectatation that parents marry. In addition, in 1992 one of every five children in Canada was living in poverty.[38] Finally, the stresses of modern-day life led to a myriad of problems, not the least of which that both sexes were absent from work more often between 1977 and 1991.[39]

In 1993, the Liberal government under Jean Chrétien replaced the federal Progressive Conservative government. Ideologically, when the Liberals were elected in 1993 they declared their ongoing commitment to traditional liberal values. These included concern for individual welfare, faith in humanity, and recognition of people's potential to change and grow, the value of equity—which included eliminating discrepancies in the treatment of different groups within Canadian society; a belief in equality—general issues of inequality as well as the ongoing dilemma of child poverty in Canada specifically; the importance of community as a structure and a system in which most Canadians grow up; diversity, the need to recognize and appreciate differences between individuals and groups within society; and, finally, a faith in democracy. In reality this last point translates into the concept that the elected representatives of all parties debate and vote on changes and developments in the policies and laws of a nation and carried out through the political processes of the party in power. Philosophically, the newly elected Liberal government of 1993 still embraced a social welfare system that provided security for all citizens and freedom of lifestyle choice based on personal values and economic opportunity.

Brian Mulroney's legacy is quite another matter. The McDonald Commission of 1985—formally the Royal Commission on the Economic Union and Development Prospects for Canada—had submitted its report, recommending as its third major proposal changes to the Canadian Income Security System. The commission called "for a universal income security program [to replace the guaranteed income supplement, family allowances, child tax credits, married exemptions, child exemptions, federal contributions to social assistance payments, and federal social housing programs]. The central features of the UISP would be a universal minimum guaranteed rate of income, federally funded and administered. Payment of UISP would be reduced with receipt of other income at a rate that would maintain work incentives and integrate with income tax rates. Although the commission made specific proposals for guarantee and tax back rates it also made plain that these features should be flexible."[40]

The commission recommendations suffered the same fate as earlier counterparts had in that none of them was adopted by the Conservative government. One of the major problems the Liberals inherited in 1993 was a social security system that had been partly unravelled by the neoconservative philosophy of the former Conservative government and by the economic recession of the early 1990s.

Social policy scholars (Evans, Armitage) define the social welfare system in 1993 as one seriously damaged by the country's fiscal problems in the industrial recession of 1990 to 1992. The weak economy had reduced government revenues in central Canada and raised social security expenditures. As Dr. Evans notes, "The Canadian experience in targeting child benefits, and the slow death of Family Allowance, indicates the dilemmas of maintaining universal benefits in a climate of fiscal restraint."[41] In addition to these fiscal problems, the new Liberal government took over Canada's tradition of humanitarian social welfare. A significant percentage of its citizens believed universal programs such as health care, Old Age pensions, and the former Family Allowance benefits were their rights, regardless of the country's economic climate.

The fledgling Chrétien government faced a further challenge: the state of the Canada Assistance Plan, as described earlier in the chapter. The Conservatives had slated the plan for demolition and had already surrendered a large share of the federal transfer payments to the provinces. As Armitage recounts, "Lloyd Axworthy, then Minister of Human Resources Development, held a series of consultations on the future of our social security and our safety net and a discussion paper, 'Improving Social Security in Canada,' was developed in 1994. Concurrently, the Minister of Finance, Paul Martin, released a report entitled 'Creating a Healthy Fiscal Climate' and held a series of consultations based on that report. The result of these two consultations and reports was the passing of the Canada Health and Social Transfer Act in 1995, which replaced the Canada Assistance Plan."[42]

The CHST that came into being in the 1997 fiscal year is a block-funding method. It has decreased, then stabilized, transfers for health, post-secondary education, and social assistance.[43] Today this has translated into a major change in federal transfers to the provinces for the programs mentioned above, and it continues to affect relations between the two levels of government.

Implementation of the Canada Health and Social Transfer Act (Bill C-76) redefined the nature of the federal government presence in social welfare. As Chenier notes, "This single funding mechanism replaced both Established Program Financing (EPF) transfers covering health and post-secondary education and Canada Assistance Plan (CAP) transfers covering social assistance and services."[44] This major change gave the provinces greater power in deciding the redistribution of funding to these three key areas.

Its proponents at the time argued that the CHST would allow the provinces more leverage to meet their regional needs; its critics worried that less federal presence in provincial decisions would result in a patchwork of programs across the country.

IDEOLOGICAL PERSPECTIVE

In the twenty-first century the challenge for social democracies such as Canada "consists of being able to reconcile the demands of a popular agenda with those of a capitalist market"[45] In this country over the last 20 years Mishra has pointed out that both ruling parties have demonstrated "a tendency to be more pragmatic than ideological in their approach... and to follow pro-market and pro-business policies." He also cautions that globalization in the economic sector has helped strengthen the influence of corporate business interests and widened "the influence of domestic politics and party ideology on social policy."[46]

As government support and funding shrink, governments are encouraging communities to take on more responsibility to maintain needed social services. In such countries as Canada the voluntary sector has had to step into this breach. Communities committed to maintaining the quality of life people had enjoyed since the 1950s now find themselves relying heavily on the volunteers in every area of the "'non-profit'" sector. While the voluntary sector employs more than one million workers, six and one-half million volunteers working within 180 000 organizations across the country support its unofficial network. In tightknit cities like Oakville, Ontario, volunteers comprise the largest workforce in their communities.

The new model in community development is called "the social economy," which is defined as economic activity with social goals. It represents community partnerships between voluntary and non-voluntary sectors. Such organizations subscribe to such values as sustainable development, equal opportunity for all, the inclusion of disadvantaged people and people with disabilities, and enhancing the civil society.[47] The current Liberal government, which supports such initiatives, has promised financial resources through Canada's small-business program. It is to be hoped that that government will implement all such commitments in the near future.

CHILD WELFARE AND CHILD POVERTY

Canada's child welfare policy and practice have come under intense and very noticeable public scrutiny for the past several years. A disturbing number of Canadian children in the care of a provincial child welfare system have died, and this fact has fuelled the public perception that these services are crumbling. During the past 25 years child welfare practice has shifted away from out-of-home care and toward bringing the services to children in their own homes. As Nico Trocmé noted in 1997, the number of children in care in Ontario dropped from close to 18 000 in the early 1970s to an average of 10 000 in the 1990s. Simultaneously, the same agencies are serving a greater number of families, more than 80 000, the number having risen from slightly fewer than 30 000.[48]

Actually, experienced front-line workers were the first to request more home-based services. They concluded that removing children at risk from their own homes was not itself a solution. Too many of these workers know first-hand of many children who drift through the foster care system from one home to another and end up at age 16 essentially on their own and with few supports. Conversely, there is little evidence to date that the return to home-based services has caused unfore-

seen damage if sufficient support systems are indeed in place. However, during the 1970s and 1980s a number of innovative programs designed to teach parenting and homemaking skills in high-risk neighbourhoods were introduced. Other community initiatives were attempted as well, most with positive results. Then, during the recession of the late 1980s governments made major cuts to child welfare agencies, and many of these new preventive programs were discontinued. These changes, of course, hurt the programs' former clients.

Over the past two decades, however, child welfare experts and forward-thinking agencies across the country have continued to develop innovative new programs and services that offer a greater range of options to meet the very complex and compelling needs of children and their families. Time will tell whether the new child welfare legislation passed recently in Ontario, for example, will continue to allow further development of the best types of intervention. Otherwise, the system faces a return to an earlier time in which a child's removal from home was the social worker's primary intervention. As Trocmé notes, "We must ensure that we do not lose the momentum towards a diverse and community-based child welfare system."[49]

Stuart Alcock conducted an excellent review of the major changes to child welfare in British Columbia, published in 1997, and the province's ongoing efforts to resolve the issue of child protection successfully by means that he described as "being mirrored in Ontario and other provinces across the country."[50]

While neither social scientists, economists, nor politicians deny the negative relationship between poverty and children's healthy development, we still cannot agree on a general definition of poverty for both families and children.

On one side of the debate stands the Fraser Institute, a major representative of neo-conservative thinking. The institute has suggested that "child poverty is really only a problem among those who live in families where incomes are so low that the parents cannot even afford adequate food and shelter."[51] On the other side, people like David Ross of the Canadian Council on Social Development, a proponent of more liberal thinking, reminds us that Canada is not a have-not country. He describes our country as a "socially complex economically advanced and democratic society,"[52] in which adult success requires far more than physical survival; it demands of each person a complex set of social, cultural, and moral norms. People learn these foundations at home within their families. Ross urges us to consider the real consequences of economic hardship.

Social scientists, economists, and informed citizens in general share the worry that our quality of life is declining. As Canadians we value "our level of safety, cohesion, civility, our generally high standard of health, and our economic and cultural prosperity. Few among us would want to create a large underclass of desperate people who are unable to attain and help maintain these societal goals."[53]

Some significant statistical evidence indicates that family income dramatically affects children's well-being. Two large national surveys have published data that show that children's chances of developing to their full potential increase steadily as their families' incomes rise.[54]

It is to be hoped that the federal government's commitment to attack child poverty and support healthy early development (1999) will include provisions to reduce what Ross dubs "the poverty of opportunity." This situation prevents too many of our children from reaching adulthood in possession of the four main ingredients they need to live as successful adults—good health, good social skills, good learning skills, and economically sustainable skills.[55]

Indeed, the Liberal government considered this commitment a major policy initiative for the past five years. Since 2002, with the establishment of the Early Childhood Development Agreement, the federal government has promised $2.2 billion over a five-year period (2001–2006) to the provinces and territories to improve and expand their programs and services in early childhood development. The agreement targets four areas—healthy pregnancy, birth and infancy, parenting, and family support.

The federal budget of 2003 set aside an additional $900 million over five years specifically to improve access to affordable high-quality, regulated early-learning and child-care programs and services in the provinces and territories. Under the agreement, additional funding will be available for early childhood development and early-learning and child-care programs for First Nations children living on reserves.

Within the current funding allocations, early learning and child care under the Canada Social Transfer will amount to $150 million in 2004–2005 and $225 million in 2005–2006, to rise to $350 million annually in 2007–2008.[56] While the debate continues over the amount of funding needed, such substantial fiscal supports should at least reduce the number of children caught in the "poverty of opportunity" cycle that Ross describes above.

In Ontario in October of 2003 a new Ministry of Children's Services was created by the province's new Liberal government. The Child Welfare Program became a core program of this new ministry. Shortly after, a program evaluation was undertaken to "examine Ontario's child welfare system to identify and recommend further improvements in the design, delivery and management of services across the province" (p. 1).[57] The study concluded that "the present child welfare program is not sustainable without modifications to the funding framework, to government policy and to CAS approaches to service delivery."[58]

The evaluation recommends many changes, including integration of services, especially in children's mental health services, and accountability and efficiency and sustainability, to prepare for "the introduction and ongoing management of a multi-years' funding approach in the child welfare sector."[59] The anticipated results of this evaluation and the recommendations to be implemented encompass a wide range of adjustments: improving the overall quality of life for children through evidence-based practice and specific outcomes; increasing the efficient use of public resources through changes in service-delivery patterns and changes to the funding framework. The evaluation also advocates integrating child welfare services better through the array of child and family services with shared outcomes and formal partnerships.[60] Positive outcomes in these areas over the next three years affect social policy development considerably in Canada's child welfare.

At the local level, the design and delivery of child welfare programs have also been revamped, also across the country. In the spring of 2004 the Children's Aid Societies and Violence Against Women agencies unveiled a Collaboration Agreement marking an innovative new joint initiative in the child welfare field in Toronto. The agreement posits that "in order to effectively end violence against women and children, service coordination between VAW and CAS agencies along with a shared understanding of woman abuse and child abuse and neglect is essen-

tial."[61] It outlines monitoring and accountability processes to ensure that both agencies work together at specific points of intersection where the two sectors connect.

THE 1999 BUDGET: TAX RELIEF

The Liberal government revealed its first real response to the poverty issue in its budgets of 1998 and 1999. As early as the 1998 budget, the government announced the elimination of the federal deficit that would allow the government to introduce tax relief. The budget of 1999 built on the measures that made this possible, and together the two budgets provided $16.5 billion in tax relief over three years.

While this sounds like a huge amount, the individual Canadian taxpayer feels little effect. The 1998 budget raised by $500 the amount of income low-income taxpayers could receive tax-free. The 1999 budget increased that amount to $675 and extended it to all taxpayers. As a result of both of these budgets, 600 000 lower-income Canadians were taken off the tax rolls altogether. As well, the 1998 budget began the process of eliminating the 3 percent surtax for taxpayers with incomes up to $50 000 and reducing the surtax for those with incomes of between $50 000 and $65 000. The 1999 budget completed that process by wiping out the 3 percent surtax for all taxpayers. As a result, single taxpayers earning $20 000 or less each year saw their federal income tax shrink by at least 10 percent. Further, families with an annual income of $45 000 or less had their federal income tax reduced by at least 10 percent. Families with two children and an annual income of $30 000 or less paid no federal income tax.

The 1999 federal budget provided additional assistance for families with children through the Canadian Child Tax Benefit (CCTB). This benefit increased total federal support for families by $2 billion, and by July 2000 it had reached an annual level of close to $7 billion. This measure ensures that most taxpayers with children pay less tax than individuals with similar incomes and no children. The 1999 budget committed an additional $300 million to CCTB payments, which increased child benefits to 2 million low- and middle-income families.[62]

The 1999 Budget: Health Care

Finance minister Paul Martin delivered the federal budget in March 1999, and it was widely acclaimed as a good-news budget. Perhaps its most important component was the government's promise to enhance Canadians' quality of life, particularly their health care. In fact, the 1999 budget made health the focus of the largest single investment this Liberal government had ever made. Over a five-year period the provinces and territories would receive an additional $11.5 billion specifically for health care costs. In addition, the government pledged to invest close to $1.4 billion in health information systems research, First Nations and Inuit health services, prevention efforts, and other initiatives to improve the lives and health of Canadians.

Of the $11.5 billion dedicated to health care over the next five years, $8 billion will go to future increases in the Canada Health and Social Transfer Act (CHST), the successor of CAP (Canada Assistance Plan). Over the next three years the provinces will receive $6.5 billion. For the 1999 fiscal year, the budget allocated $3.5 billion as an immediate one-time cash injection into the CHST. The provinces and the territories could draw on these funds in ways that best

suited their most pressing needs in their individual health care systems. A further budget item allocated $240 million over the next two years to carry out the proposal of a national task force that represented the health research community: to develop the Canadian Institute of Health Research (CIHR). The institute would bring together the best researchers from across Canada to study aging, arthritis, women's health, cancer, heart disease, and other subjects. It would constitute a major step toward bringing Canada back into the mainstream of health-related research.[63]

In 2004 health-related issues continue to dominate the concerns of many Canadians, and hence of the federal government. As noted, the government has continued to allocate large amounts of money to the provinces for their health care systems. In the 2003–2004 budget, the federal government allocated a total of $36.8 billion to health care over a five-year period. Priorities cited health research, First Nations, children's programs such as early learning and child care, and a new public health ministry among other areas in this major investment in our health care system.[64]

Also in 2004, Bill C-6, an Act Respecting Assisted Human Reproduction and Related Research, became law. An all-party committee drafted this significant piece of legislation over three years, following a lengthy consultation process with experts in this field. It gives Canada one of the most comprehensive legislative frameworks in the world regarding assisted human reproduction.

Both federal and provincial governments grapple with developing a model of health care that provides access to all citizens in a timely and effective manner, while being financially sustainable now and in future economic climates.[65]

POVERTY AND HOMELESSNESS

The primary source of information for this section comes from the report of the Task Force on Homelessness commissioned by the City of Toronto in 1998 and chaired by Ann Golden. Its contents exemplify the very similar situations that members of the task force learned about during visits to Vancouver, Calgary, Winnipeg, and Montreal.[66]

The task force encountered difficulties with coming up with a common definition of "homelessness" that all its members could accept. This proved a major obstacle as the Toronto group began its work in 1998. Data from an earlier longitudinal study conducted between 1987 and 1996 revealed that 170 000 different persons had been homeless within that period in the city of Toronto; in 1996, 26 000 persons used the available shelters and of that number, 5300, or one in five, were children. This group breaks down further into the chronic users, who constitute about 14 percent of those studied. Chronic users tend to stay in the hostel system for more than a year on average and to move from shelter to shelter. They consume almost 50 percent of the resources available in Toronto. If homelessness for the chronic users could be resolved, it would reduce the demand for scarce resources by almost half. Persons suffering from mental illness, addictions, and substance abuse characterized the chronic group.

A second significant variable that quickly emerged was the link between the causes of homelessness and poverty, at a time in Ontario when the economy was prospering and poverty was increasing. The commission found that the poverty trends coincided with all levels of governments' withdrawal from affordable and subsidized housing programs. The number of rooming houses continued to decline steadily; at the same time, the province reduced by 21.6 percent the social assistance it contributed to many families who depended on it to make their rent payments. Particularly hard hit were single-mother families, and the severity of the housing situation worsened.

"One of the most significant pieces of work done by this Task Force was the identification of systemic problems in our communities which result in homelessness and add to the poverty of individuals," the report states.[67] Three of these problems are worth noting: a housing market that does not supply an adequate amount of affordable housing, a changing job market that leaves people poorly paid or unemployed, and a weakening social safety net that does not provide what the vulnerable groups need to exist day to day. The task force confirmed the cycle of homelessness triggered by eviction, loss of jobs, personal crises, and premature releases from mental health institutions. The report's recommendations pertain not only to Toronto but to urban centres across the country. These include a multi-pronged strategy that would involve all three levels of government. Together they would provide more supportive housing for vulnerable people unable to compete in the normal housing market, more affordable housing for low-income groups, rental assistance to the working poor at risk of losing their current homes, and, finally, improved coordination of all the relevant systems.

HOUSING IN THE TWENTY-FIRST CENTURY

Since publication of the Golden Report in 1998, although housing remains the responsibility of provincial and municipal governments, more and more people are coming to understand the immensity and complexity of the problem across the country. This realization is producing some significant movement at the federal level to assist in this area.

Indications of the beginning of a countrywide trend were evident in November 2001 in Quebec City where federal, provincial, and territorial ministers responsible for housing met to discuss common concerns. Agreements were reached about how federal funding could be transferred to the provinces and territories to help expand affordable housing that respected the provincial responsibility in this area and permitted the funding transfer without creating unnecessary levels of administration.

An ongoing series of agreements on the types and administration of such housing emerged from the same gathering. Suggested policies encompass encouraging residential development to include a designated proportion as affordable housing, modifying the code requirements to lower construction costs, and facilitating the use of secondary suites for both younger and older homeowners to permit them to collect additional income.

Overall the federal government certainly recognizes that safe and affordable housing is critical to the maintenance of family life and that it can be provided in various ways to meet various needs in various parts of Canada. These discussions appear to be leading to a committed effort to view this problem from a national perspective that encourages and facilitates diversity within some agreed-upon national objectives.

IMMIGRATION

Over the decades immigration has played an important role in the history of Canadian social welfare. The structure of our immigration policies has varied over the years, shaped by world events, the perceived needs of the country, and various ideological positions of the policy-makers of the day. The significance of immigration in the new millennium continues.

A federal–provincial meeting of the ministers responsible for immigration in Victoria, British Columbia, early in 2004, best expressed the nation's current policy regarding the importance of attracting skilled and knowledgeable immigrants to Canada: "Immigration is critical to building our economy and society," stated the Honourable Judy Sgro, Minister of Citizenship and Immigration. "We need to ensure that newcomers have every chance to succeed whether they come to Canada as skilled immigrants, to join family members, for business reasons or as refugees fleeing persecution."[68]

Flowing from this statement, the various programs and procedures stress several themes. Among these are increased efforts to provide higher levels of training in Canada's two official languages and a related emphasis on work placements and mentoring opportunities. A significant new focus in this area is group processing for refugees. This means of processing would seek to identify entire refugee populations and resettle them together in the same community, satisfying the human need for safety and encouraging permanence as a step in helping the groups better integrate into Canadian culture.

In the twenty-first century, amid the new realities of terrorism, unrelenting warfare, and a shifting global economy, all levels of government in Canada face challenges to maintain the social welfare system within a healthy economy and environment that provide security and freedom for all Canadians, all based on personal values and economic opportunity.

NOTES

1. Although the early church praised charity and helping one's neighbour, often the state did not. In 800 A.D., under the statutes of Charlemagne, citizens who gave alms to able-bodied beggars were fined. In sixteenth-century Germany, Martin Luther tried to organize relief at a parish level and implored the princes, who refused to take any responsibility for the poor, to forbid begging. In the same century, the Spanish philosopher Juan Luis Vives proposed a program of relief for the poor of the city of Bruges in Flanders, which was not adopted until two and a half centuries later in Hamburg in 1788.

2. *Funk and Wagnalls New Encyclopedia*, vol. 9 (New York, 1973), p. 436.

3. Karl de Schweinitz, *England's Road to Social Security* (New York: Barnes, 1943), p. 29.

4. Ibid. See particularly chapters 1, 3, 4, 7, and 21.

5. Ibid., p. 117.

6. Ibid., p. 124.

7. William F. Monypenny, *The Life and Times of Benjamin Disraeli, Earl of Beaconsfield*, vol. 1 (New York: Macmillan, 1910), p. 374.

8. Harold L. Wilensky and Charles N. Lebeaux, *Industrial Society and Social Welfare* (New York: Free Press, 1968), p. 34.

9. *Columbia Encyclopedia*, 3rd ed. (New York: Columbia University Press, 1963), p. 338.

10. Robert Owen, *A New View of Society* (London, 1813), pp. 9, 23.

11. Donald Bellamy, "Social Welfare in Canada," *Encyclopedia of Social Work* (New York: National Association of Social Workers, 1965), pp. 36–37. For a fuller account of this period, see also Allana G. Reid, "First Poor Relief System of Canada," *Canadian Historical Review* 27.4 (December 1946): 424–31.

12. Bellamy, "Social Welfare in Canada," p. 37.

13. John Melichercik, *The Development of Social Welfare Programmes in Canada: A Chronology of Significant Events at the National and Ontario Levels* (Waterloo, ON: Wilfrid Laurier University Press, 1975), p. 2.

14. Harry M. Cassidy, *Public Health and Welfare Reorganization* (Toronto: Ryerson Press, 1945), p. 7.

15. John Melichercik, *The Development of Social Welfare Programmes*, p. 5.

16. John Melichercik, *Constitutional Factors Affecting the Development of Social Welfare Legislation in Canada* (Waterloo, ON: Wilfrid Laurier University Press, 1975), p. 6.

17. Jack Williams, *The Story of Unions in Canada* (Toronto: Dent, 1975), pp. 148–50.

18. Leonard Marsh, *Report on Social Security for Canada 1943*, (Toronto: University of Toronto Press, 1974), pp. 14, 19.

19. L. Marsh, *Report on Social Security for Canada*, pp. 14–15.

20. Canada, *Report of the Royal Commission on Dominion-Provincial Relations* ("The Rowell–Sirois Report"), 3 vols. (Ottawa: King's Printer, 1939).

21. Kenneth McNaught, *The Pelican History of Canada* (Markham, ON: Penguin, 1969).

22. Michel Bliss, in *Preface* to Marsh, *Report on Social Security for Canada*, p. 9.

23. For some background material regarding the many attempts of the federal Department of Health and Welfare to introduce a guaranteed annual income, see *The Report of the Special Senate Committee on Poverty* (Ottawa, 1971); *The Working Paper on Social Security in Canada* (Ottawa: Department of Health and Welfare, 1973); *Income Security for Canadians* (Ottawa: Department of Health and Welfare, 1970); and the proposed New Social Service Bill (Ottawa: Department of Health and Welfare, 1977).

24. John S. Morgan, "Social Welfare Services," in *Social Purpose for Canada*, ed. Michael Oliver (Toronto: University of Toronto Press, 1961), pp. 138–39.

25. John Melichercik, *The Development of Social Welfare Programmes*, pp. 14–17.

26. Andrew Armitage, *Social Welfare in Canada* (Toronto: McClelland and Stewart, 1975), p. 277.

27. Ronald Melchers, "The Cap on CAP," *Perception* 14.4 (Autumn 1990): 19.

28. Canada, Department of Health and Welfare, *Working Paper on Social Security in Canada* (Ottawa, 1973), pp. 1–3.

29. Notes from an address by Marc Lalonde to the Social Planning Council of Metropolitan Toronto Seminar on "Family Income Security Issues," 1976, p. 16.

30. Health and Welfare Canada, *News Release*, June 20, 1977, p. 2.

31. Ramesh Mishra, "Riding the New Wave: Social Work and the Neo-Conservative Challenge," *International Social Work* 32.3 (July 1989): 174.

32. M. Loney, "Pricing the Poor Back to Work," *Policy Options* 13.10 (December 1992): 21–23.

33. Canadian Council on Social Development, "Constitutional Reform and Social Policy," *Social Development* 1 (Fall 1991).

34. Canadian Council on Social Development, "Constitutional Reform and Social Policy," *Social Development* 1 (Fall 1991).

35. Melchers, "The Cap on CAP," p. 19.

36. House of Commons, *Statutes of Canada*, 1993.

37. Ken Battle, "White Paper Whitewash: The New Child Benefit," *Perception* 16.2 (Spring/Summer 1992): 3.

38. Dennis Bracken and Christopher Walmsley, "The Canadian Welfare State: Implication for the Continuing Education of Canadian Social Workers," *The Social Worker* 60.1 (Spring 1992): 23.

39. Ibid.

40. "Employee Absenteeism Changing, Study Says," *The Globe and Mail,* March 25, 1993, p. B1.

41. Andrew Armitage, *Social Welfare in Canada Revisited: Facing Up to the Future*, 3d ed. (Don Mills, ON: Oxford University Press, 1996), p. 206.

42. Patricia Evans, "Eroding Canadian Social Welfare: The Mulroney Legacy, 1984–1993," *Social Policy and Administration* 28(2) (June 1994): 110.

43. Andrew Armitage, 1996, p. 204.

44. O. Madore and C. Blanchette, *The Canada Health and Social Transfer.* (Ottawa: Government of Canada, 1997).

45. Nancy Chenier, *The CHST: The Debate over Outcomes.* (Ottawa: Parliamentary Library, 1997), p. l.

46. Ramesh Mishra, "The Political Bases of Canadian Social Welfare in Canadian Social Welfare," 5th ed, eds. J. C. Turner and F. J. Turner. Toronto: Pearson Education, Chapter 4, p. 7.

47. Ibid., p. 22.48. Bonnie Brown, *Oakville Report* (Oakville, ON: 2004), pp. 1–4.

49. Nicol Trocmé, "Staying on Track While the Pendulum Swings: Commentary on Canadian Child Welfare Policy Trends," *OASW News Magazine* 24.4 (Winter 1997): p. 13.

50. Ibid., p. 14.

51. *OASW News Magazine* 24.4 (Winter 1997): 18.

52. David P. Ross, "Rethinking Child Poverty." *Insight: An Information Series.* (Ottawa: The Canadian Council on Social Development, 1998), p. 1.

53. Ibid., p. 1.

54. Ibid., p. 2.

55. Ibid.

56. Ibid., p. 4.

57. Department of Finance, Federal Transfer to Provinces, **www.fin.gc.ca**

58. *Child Welfare Programme Evaluation Report* (Toronto: Ontario Ministry of Children's Services, 2003), pp. 1–56.

59. Ibid., p. 2.

60. Ibid., p. 5.

61. Ibid., p. 36.

62. *CAS/UAW Collaboration Agreement for Toronto.* Toronto, April 2004, pp. 29–81.

63. Summarized from the *Liberal Times*, March 1999.

64. Ibid.

65. *Key Highlights: The Liberal Record on Women, 1993–2004* (Ottawa: Liberal Party of Canada).

66. *Bill C-6, An Act Respecting Assisted Human Reproduction and Related Research* (Ottawa, Government of Canada, 2004).

67. Ann Golden. "Speech to the Canadian Club of Toronto" (Toronto, September 28, 1998), pp. 3, 9.

68. Canadian Intergovernmental Conference Secretariat, **www.scics.gc.ca.**

chapter seven

Canadian Realities

Susan Watt

Matthew Goodman

INTRODUCTION

Social policy develops within a variety of contexts, which include physical, economic, political, and social realities. This chapter intends to highlight, in broad strokes, some of the conditions that have promulgated and shaped Canadian social policy.

While we take a discrete approach to each of these realities, we also point out that they affect one another and, perhaps, even produce their own synergies as a result. Each makes its own mark on the definition of what is an important issue, how a social policy develops, how policy is enacted, and how key stakeholders evaluate those actions, as well as the general public.

Finally, readers should remember a central truth: Canada is not a homogeneous country. Much has been written about the search for a Canadian identity. A common fact remains: Canada is a vast, geographically varied, physically challenging, economically mixed, culturally diverse, and politically discrepant federation of people, provinces, and territories, each with its own political and social agenda. These are bound together by history, geography and, to varying degrees, by a commitment to a national vision. It must be left to other scholars to reflect accurately the boundaries of this identity, and the complex, often conflicting relationships between the parties. Historically, the federal and provincial governments have struggled for control with one another, often in the context of constitutional debates. Always these disagreements involve who will pay for and who will control policy content. These struggles continue, and their outcomes will determine the future of Canadian social policy.

PHYSICAL REALITIES

Physical Canada is the second-largest country in the world, covering 10 million square kilometres. The 10 provinces and the three territories range widely over diverse topographic and climatic conditions. The country extends 4634 km from north to south and 5514 km from east to west at its extreme points. Its geography takes in wide regions of prairie, Precambrian mountain ranges, boreal forests, hundreds of thousands of lakes and rivers, and vast expanses of tundra (Statistics Canada, 2004a). Only 11 percent of the whole land mass is populated, with a density of 3.1 persons/square kilometre (Statistics Canada, 2004b).

Lying mostly above the 49th parallel, the Canadian climate varies as much as its topography. The Arctic desert covers much of the northern region while southern border areas are subject often to heavy rain and snow including blizzards and tornadoes. Areas west of the Rocky Mountains have high levels of precipitation and, in the southern reaches, moderate temperature conditions, making them an ideal growing area. By contrast, the northern territories have little commercially arable land yet support a multitude of animals and plant life that has adapted to barren and inhospitable conditions.

The Canadian population of 30.7 million people (Statistics Canada, 2004c), diverse in its origins and initially dependent on immigration rather than reproduction, has at its base an Aboriginal population dispersed throughout the country. By 1900, only 19 percent of the population was Aboriginal, dropping to 6 percent by 1986 and 3 percent in 1996. The 2001 census identifies a population that describes itself as Canadian (30 percent), English (20 percent), French (16 percent), and Scottish (14 percent) (Statistics Canada, 2004d).

Immigration to Canada has been highly controlled and economically driven. Immigrants have come to Canada often on their way to other countries. People of British or French origin had much easier access to immigration; federal quotas restricted those of other backgrounds according to the knowledge and skills the economy needed at any particular time. With the rare, but much publicized, exception of some political refugees, our immigrants have been drawn from relatively wealthy citizens of their mother countries. Even the post–World War II immigration of displaced persons preferred those with high levels of education and personal resources at home and in Canada. Policies that favour family repatriation reinforce this pattern.

The origins of Canadian immigrants over the last 40 years have shifted. Immigration from Britain, Northern, Western, and Southern Europe has declined while immigration from Eastern Europe, Asia, and Africa has increased (Statistics Canada, 2004e). The Immigration and Refugee Protection Act (RSC 2002) reinforces traditional Canadian immigration policy by strengthening family reunification provisions, promoting immigration to meet the country's labour force needs, and supporting the administrative mechanisms of immigration applications and appeals (Banting & Battle, 1994; Forsey, 1994).

Discussion about immigration within Canada, similar to that of other countries, has changed since September 11, 2001, when hijacked planes crashed into the World Trade Center towers in New York City, the Pentagon in Washington, and a field in Somerset County, Pennsylvania. In reaction to these attacks, American policy-makers have imposed stricter border regulations, tightened security measures at airports, and worked to identify and eliminate perceived threats to American security. Canada's support for the US-led anti-terrorist strategies raises questions about its own immigration policies. Canada's challenge will be to balance the potentially competing agendas of sustaining immigration and of responding to US pressure to manage and maintain restrictive security measures.

Canadians are an aging population with a rate of 1.5 live births per female. They are living longer (82.2 years for women, 77.1 years for men) and healthier lives (Statistics Canada, 2004f). Infant mortality rates have dropped in the last 50 years, although they remain disproportionately high among Native peoples (Stout & Kipling, 2002; Health Canada, 2003).

Morbidity (illness) and mortality (death) statistics show that Canadians become sick and die of illnesses associated with aging, such as diabetes, cancer, and heart disease. These pathologies are associated, also, with environmental and lifestyle variables and so they correlate with social circumstances and policy developments. Poverty remains a major determinant of Canadians' health and longevity (Statistics Canada, 2004g).

Canadian history is intimately linked to the history of transportation, and particularly to that of the railroad. Connecting the country by rail in part motivated the original colonies to enter into Confederation as regions sought to be added to a transcontinental railroad system. This would allow them access to markets for their products and manufactured goods. Despite the

development of a sophisticated air transportation system, small communities, farming, and industry have continued to depend on the railroads. Roads connect most communities to the world beyond; the Trans-Canada Highway links the country from east to west. Road-building, repairs, and maintenance in an unforgiving geography and climate have required large, ongoing investment in transportation technology and construction. The mix of interprovincial, intercity, and urban transportation systems influences policy development, both in the resources committed and the effects of transportation on the need for, and use of, services.

Finally, transportation growth has opened the country's natural resources to commercial development—oil, gas, lumber, water, and a variety of minerals such as gold, silver, and uranium. Dependent industries are established on this foundation of rich resources. These tend to be heavy industries, such as steel, gas and oil, and some manufacturing industries, such as furniture and automobiles that need international transportation outlets.

ECONOMIC REALITIES

The Canadian economy plays an important role in shaping social policies. On these resource-based industries—such as mining, pulp and paper–manufacturing, and farming—and service industries Canadians enjoy one of the highest standards of living in the world (Statistics Canada, 2004h).

Canadians' average family income reached $70 814 in 2001; unemployment was 7.4 percent nationally (Statistics Canada, 2004i) with wide regional and seasonal variations. For example, in 2003, unemployment rates ranged from 18 percent in Newfoundland to 4.8 percent in Alberta. Even within provincial boundaries, unemployment shifts greatly from community to community—for example, St. John's, 9.6 percent; Halifax, 5.4 percent; St. John, 7.6 percent; Sherbrooke, 7.2 percent; Montreal, 8.9 percent; Toronto, 6.7 percent; Thunder Bay, 6.2 percent; Ottawa, 6.9 percent; Windsor, 7.2 percent; Winnipeg, 4.1 percent; Saskatoon, 6.9 percent; Calgary, 5.5 percent; Vancouver, 6.1 percent; Victoria, 7.8 percent (Statistics Canada, 2004j).

Tax revenues produce most of the federal government's revenues, which in 2002 amounted to $193.8 billion, almost 60 percent of which derive from income taxes. Expenses for the same period were $187.6 billion, with social service expenditures of $73.8 billion, or almost 40 percent, of the total, an increase from 30 percent in 1997 (Statistics Canada, 2004k).

Provincial and local government revenues, based primarily on income and sales taxes, and on property tax and non-tax sources, respectively, have risen significantly in the same period. Health (27 percent), education (21 percent), and social services (15 percent) constitute the largest provincial expenditures. Local revenues go to education (42 percent), transportation and communication (11 percent), security (9 percent), and environment (8 percent) (Statistics Canada, 2004l). The federal governments transfer monies to the provincial governments, and the provincial governments transfer monies to the local governments for both specific purposes—federal to provincial transfers for health care, provincial to local transfers for education—and under general-purpose agreements—such as the equalization payments to ensure services to less wealthy provinces.

In 2002, Canada's gross domestic product was $1 154 949 million, compared to $828 997 million in 1996 (Statistics Canada, 2004m). This significant increase in GDP reflects growth in both production in the manufacturing sector and in Canadian exports.

Overall, the wealth of the nation and its individuals has increased in both absolute and relative terms in the last 20 years. What is less evident is the disparity, which is lost by averaging figures. Relative poverty remains, especially among traditionally marginalized groups—children, the elderly, Native Canadians, and single-parent and female-headed households. Therefore, the distribution of wealth, rather than its measurement in absolute terms, both drives and determines the Canadian economy.

Intimately linked to these factors and, some would argue, dominating all others, is the United States' economy and its effects on Canada. US owners or investors control major aspects of Canadian manufacturing and resource-based industries. For example, $1.2 billion in trade crosses the Canada–US border every day (Statistics Canada, 2004n)! This interconnectedness has brought Canada the benefits of expanded capital investment, especially in the manufacturing sector. The North American Free Trade Agreement (NAFTA) of 1992, the Open Skies Agreement in 1995, and the planned expansion of a North American Free Trade Zone to encompass Central America as proposed in 2003 (Canada, 2004o) reinforce these links.

This reciprocal contagion may also affect the sphere of social policy. For example, calls for decreased spending on social programs in Canada echo the more conservative and residual view of social policy generally found in the United States. This emphasis on economic policy may come at the price of social policy neglect in Canada. The loss of social programs intended to ensure the well-being of all citizens (medicare, Old Age Security), and the increased demand for needs-based welfare provisions reflect American neo-conservative political perspectives. On the other hand, some Americans look to the

Canadian health system, for example, for comparable, if not structurally similar, models to meet their own social needs. They study ways to lift the burden of financing such a system from private sector corporations (Physicians for a National Health Program, 1994).

POLITICAL REALITIES

Canada is a multi-party, parliamentary democracy. The features of this political model are at least as complex and important as the physical and economic realities that help determine our social policies. Even the founding provisions of the British North America Act of 1867 (BNA Act), are subject to the ongoing interpretations and negotiations of any social relationship.

One political opinion states that Canada is a voluntary union of independent provinces, which delegated their individual authorities to one federal government in exchange for security in the face of a US military threat. This view holds that the provinces may join or secede from the union at will. The opposing opinion is that the BNA Act established an essential, single nation whose provincial governments assigned specific rights and responsibilities to a federal government (Guy, 1995).

Whichever interpretation one supports, the impact on social policy development has been profound (Forsey, 1997; Whittington & Van Loon, 1995). The BNA Act as amended over the decades has designated that basic income programs of Old Age Security, (un)Employment Insurance, and Family Allowance were responsibilities of the federal government. The federal and provincial governments have had to negotiate the introduction of all other programs, as well as their impacts on income taxes and transfer payments. In general, the federal government has held the purse strings for major social programs.

Canada's Charter of Rights and Freedoms (enacted as Schedule B to the Canada Act 1982 (U.K.) 1982, c. 11, which came into force on April 17, 1982) declares individuals' fundamental freedoms and democratic, mobility, legal, and equality rights. The Charter defines those rights and freedoms in which federal standards supersede provincial authority (Canada, 2004p). In January 2004, the Supreme Court of Canada upheld section 43 of the Criminal Code that allows parents to spank their children (Canadian Legal Institute, 2004). While the court did impose limitations and restrictions on parents' spanking, several groups questioned the decision in the hope that a repeal of the law might help eventually strengthen provincial child protection and welfare legislation.

One of the more dramatic and enduring examples of federal influence in provincial social policy has been the development and maintenance of a nationally regulated and provincially operated medical insurance system. The Canada Health Act (1983) used transfer payments to force the provinces to comply with federal standards or face direct dollar losses. Despite serious provincial opposition, the federal government prevailed, stopping many provincial governments from instituting or continuing copayments and deterrent fees to raise additional revenues.

Canada has committed itself over the years to address and repair historical imbalances in its relations with its First Nations people. The governments have demonstrated this resolve in the negotiations and settlements of Native land claims. For example, in August 2003, members of Labrador's Inuit community and representatives from both the provincial and federal governments initialled the first land-claims and self-government agreement in Atlantic Canada. On ratification, the Final Agreement (Canada, 2003) will open up historic new opportunities for the Inuit people, establish new relations with both governments based on new political frameworks that will help guide the future development of these communities. The agreement will enable changes in resources ownership, environmental control, and the development of new self-government structures. The latter will respond to the ongoing complexity of balancing social, historic, environmental, and justice claims. By undertaking negotiated settlements on land claims and self-government, Canada and its First Nations people are in fact developing new, mutual political realities and opportunities.

The politics of Canada have forged a series of legal decisions, intergovernmental compromises, and comprehensive mechanisms for the negotiation of many social and political issues. Effectively, these maintain a moderate, conservative social structure. That structure is rooted in capitalism and a market economy, and it is tempered by a sense of social justice that buffers the individual from the most dramatic impacts of both economic and physical change. This sometimes strange blend of universal and residual social policies is grounded on universal social security and health care policies designed to guarantee all Canadians a social minimum as a right rather than a privilege. The system produced reflects a negotiated blend of neo-conservative, liberal, and socialist party politics.

The social policy agenda—an agenda that will express the traditional and continuing compromises characteristic of Canadian politics—will derive according to current and future political winds determining federal–provincial jurisdictions, resolution mechanisms, and management functions. Doubtless the result will continue to shape our Canadian union.

SOCIAL REALITIES

Having looked at some of the physical, economic, and political factors that shape Canadian social policy, we now turn to the social realities, the intricate fibres of all the perspectives that weave through a nation, and how they have influenced social policy.

Describing Canada's structure as a society is a complex task. Although Canada's population has been compared to a mosaic, it is perhaps more helpful to think of a Canadian kaleidoscope—constantly changing patterns of people, climate, and economic conditions bounded by a constant geography and a unique history.

British colonialism has heavily influenced our history. It has set the stage for concepts of entitlement and social responsibility predicated on the fact that Canada was settled rather than pioneered. Settlement, by government and later commercial interests, created communities with an intrinsic sense of self to which the government and business owed security. This arrangement constituted a primitive social contract that included the government's obligation to provide food, shelter, and medical care to people in return for their willingness as skilled labour to settle and extend the empire and master the inhospitable topography and climate.

Unlike nations forged in revolution, whose identities are moored on an entrenched, singular view, Canada traces its beginnings through evolution, and a search for a national identity. Its origins stand in stark contrast to those of the United States, in which a revolutionary anti-government sentiment, coupled with pioneering, highly individualistic, rights-based beliefs, produced its social framework. Among those qualities are valuing the individual over the group, the group over the state, and the nation over the rest of the world. Americans presume that a massing of individuals, either as an electorate or a military force, resolves conflicts, and they hold the sure conviction that the American way is the better way.

Canadians, on the other hand, have emphasized negotiation and compromise, sometimes at the cost of individual rights. The social policies of Canada manifest a cautious acceptance of a social contract that encourages the ongoing negotiation of rights and responsibilities, of relations among differing cultural and ethnic peoples, and between the citizens and their government.

Even the most divisive of Canadian issues, the relations between French and English Canada, has been the subject of debate and negotiation right from the Plains of Abraham in 1759 and into the corridors of Parliament Hill today. Canadians constantly try to integrate and accommodate rather than assimilate differences. As one example, Canada's constitution promotes union rather than separation of church and state. As a result, Canadians do not face an essentially divisive choice between their individual allegiances to their religions or their political beliefs. Instead they struggle to find a path that permits and respects both ideologies as powerful forces in determining the course of their lives.

This spirit of compromise has not immunized Canada from the negative "isms" of modern society—racism, ageism, sexism, and ethnocentrism. Canada is still susceptible, too, to the global forces that affect the world economy, family structures and roles, poverty, crime, perceptions of authority, and downsizing labour force demands in a technological era. Environmental awareness has generated a sense of urgency that Canada preserve and protect its natural resources and improve the methods by which business extracts economic benefits from the land without endangering the nation's future existence and profitability.

Similarly, technological developments have forced Canadians to re-evaluate their ownership of resources and the impact of international claims on these resources on the lives of individuals and communities as well as the general economy. Canadians have had to come to terms with the fact that renewable resources may not be replenished at a rate equal to the demands made upon them; we have had to strike a new balance of expectations and restraints between economic and social realities.

Technological advances have forced us to review social policies, such as universal health insurance, to re-evaluate the intent and extent of our social contract. In particular, questions have been raised about the allocation of scarce and expensive technological resources in health care, such as diagnostic imaging machinery, neonatal units, and organ transplantation teams. Questions regarding the efficacy of these developments and their use have become a priority for policy development.

As a result of complex and changing social patterns, social policies have been subjected to negotiation and revision. The essential social contract of preserving a social minimum, discussed earlier, has come under attack by those who would argue that Canada can no longer afford the "luxury" of these social commitments in an economic downturn and weakened competitiveness in international markets. Others argue that Canada cannot afford to compromise its social obligations especially at a time when the welfare of its citizens is most threatened, that it is precisely at such a time that the social contract between individuals and the state is most needed. Canada risks losing the very character and spirit of the nation if it does not modify its social contract; it must either entrench or abandon these essential elements or pay attention to its own unique features as a society.

True to tradition and temperament, we will likely negotiate some compromise to ensure individual protections from the most deleterious effects of change while allowing for adaptation to a turbulent economic and political climate. Looking neither to the left nor the right, Canada will probably continue to walk the tightrope that a social democracy walks when built on a competitive market economy that has evolved into a bilingual, multicultural, resource-rich and economically interdependent Western nation.

CONCLUSIONS

Canadian realities serve both as background and as formative influences in the development of social policies. The physical foundation, the economic pulls, the lessons of history, and the happenstances of politics have shaped the intricate, organic state that is present-day Canada. Its social policies reflect the distinctive and the shared, the laudatory and the flawed, the controlling and the benevolent characteristics of the nation. Above all, these policies express a fundamental social contract born of historical necessity, enhanced by economic prosperity, threatened by self-interest, and retained by public demand.

In such a pluralistic democracy, we need to exercise constant vigilance to maintain a balance among our many competing interests and stakeholders. The ultimate test of this composite Canadian reality will be the degree to which federal, provincial, and local social policies can reflect the nation's commitment to equity, to equality, and to social justice.

REFERENCES

Banting, Keith, & Battle, Ken (Eds.). (1994). *A new social vision for Canada?* Kingston: Queen's University Press.

Canada. (August 26, 2003) Indian and Northern Affairs, *News release.* **www.ainc-inac.gc.ca/ nr/prs/m-a2003/2-02367_e.html**

Canada. (January 31, 2004a). *Statistics Canada 2001 census.* **www.statcan.ca/english/Pgdb/ phys01.htm**

Canada. (January 31, 2004b). *Statistics Canada 2001 census.* **www.statcan.ca/english/Pgdb/ demo01.htm**

Canada. (January 31, 2004c). *Statistics Canada 2001 census.* **www.statcan.ca/english/Pgdb/ demo02.htm**

Canada. (January 31, 2004d). *Statistics Canada 2001 census.* **www.statcan.ca/english/Pgdb/ demo28a.htm**

Canada. (January 31, 2004e). *Statistics Canada 2001 census.* **www.statcan.ca/english/Pgdb/ demo25.htm**

Canada. (January 31, 2004f). *Statistics Canada 2001 census.* **www.statcan.ca/english/Pgdb/ demo04a.htm**

Canada. (January 31, 2004g). *Statistics Canada 2001 census.* **www.statcan.ca/Daily/English/ 030925/d030925c.htm**

Canada. (January 31, 2004h). *Statistics Canada 2001 census.* **http://142.206.72.67/03/03_ 000_e.htm**

Canada. (January 31, 2004i). *Statistics Canada 2001 census.* **www.statcan.ca/english/Pgdb/ famili.htm#inc**

Canada. (January 31, 2004j). *Statistics Canada 2001 census.* **www.statcan.ca/english/Pgdb/ lfcmaua.htm**

Canada. (January 31, 2004k). *Statistics Canada 2001 census*. **www.statcan.ca/english/Pgdb/govt49a.htm**

Canada. (January 31, 2004l). *Statistics Canada 2001 census*. **www.statcan.ca/english/Pgdb/govt51a.htm**

Canada. (January 31, 2004m). *Statistics Canada 2001 census*. **www.statcan.ca/english/Pgdb/econ04.htm**

Canada. (January 31, 2004n). *Statistics Canada 2001 census*. **www.dfait-maeci.gc.ca/can-am/menu-en.asp?mid=1&cat=1029**

Canada. (2004o). *Transportation Canada: International policy*. **www.tc.gc.ca/pol/en/policy_menu.htm**

Canada. (2004p). Department of Justice. *The Canadian Charter of Rights and Freedoms*. **http://laws.justice.gc.ca/en/charter/**

Canadian Legal Institute. (January 30, 2004). *Canadian Foundation for Children, Youth and the Law v. Canada (Attorney General)*. 2004 SCC 4 **www.canlii.org/ca/cas/scc/2004/2004scc4.html**

Forsey, Eugene. (1997). *How Canadians govern themselves*. 4th edn. Ottawa: Public Information Office, Library of Parliament.

Guy, James John. (1995). *How we are governed: The basics of Canadian politics and government*. Toronto: Harcourt Brace and Company.

Health Canada. (February 2, 2004). *A statistical profile on the health of First Nations in Canada*. **www.hc-sc.gc.ca/fnihb/sppa/hia/publications/statistical_profile.pdf**

Physicians for a National Health Program. (1994). A better-quality alternative: Single-payer national health system reform. *The Journal of the American Medical Association (JAMA)* (September 14). 274. **www.pnhp.org/publications/a_better_quality_alternative.php?page=all**

Stout, M. D., & Kipling, G. D. (2002). *Aboriginal health*. Sharing the learning: The health transition fund synthesis series. **http://dsppsd.communication.gc.ca/Collection/H13-6-2002-5E.pdf**

Whittington, Michael S., & Van Loon, Richard J. (1995). *Canadian government and politics: Institutions and processes*. Toronto: McGraw-Hill Ryerson.

chapter eight

French Language Services: An Integral Part of Our Bilingual Heritage

François H. Bilodeau

Yvon Dugas

INTRODUCTION

Much has been written about Canada's bilingual heritage. Since Confederation, our English–French duality has provoked its share of tensions and struggles. On the whole, however, Canadians have come to a fragile acceptance of this duality, often based on a sincere and difficult dialogue. Throughout the Pierre Trudeau years, efforts to promote bilingualism across the country were constant and sustained, while nationalism in Quebec was gaining strength. With the support of several provinces that openly favoured bilingualism, especially New Brunswick and Ontario, the federal government passed the Official Languages Act in 1969. Social service agencies then increased their efforts to offer services in both languages.

Our bilingual heritage in the social services did not develop uniformly. Given the complexity and range of issues surrounding French-language services and the program's uneven development across Canada, this chapter will limit its analysis to developments in Ontario and, more specifically, to the Ottawa-Carleton area. The demographic characteristics of the region make it an appropriate choice for study: francophones represent approximately 20 percent of that population and experience more or less the same problems and pressures as francophone groups concentrated elsewhere in Ontario. We believe this is a valid premise even though the Ottawa-Carleton region enjoys more French-language services than other designated areas. (The French Language Services Act, passed in 1986 by the government of Ontario, identifies those areas with significant francophone minority populations.)

Even though the linguistic situation differs from one province to the other, we also believe that this analysis is sufficiently generic to apply to other areas outside Ontario, provided an adequate number of francophones justifies the development of French-language services. Although the formula "where numbers warrant" is flawed in that it limits an otherwise legitimate principle, we will not examine it in this chapter.

We will analyze the following themes as they relate to social services:

- the role of political will in the development of French-language services;
- the strategic use of the ethnocultural identity of the francophone minority to advocate for French-language services;
- consultation with the francophone community;
- the dilemma of legislating minority language rights.

POLITICAL WILL

The percentage of francophones outside Quebec and the degree to which a province's population as a whole may grant official recognition of the French language are directly related. According to Statistics Canada's Census of Population (1996), the Acadian population in New Brunswick accounts for one-third (32.5 percent) of the 738 133 residents of that province— namely, 239 730 persons whose mother tongue is French. Given the voting strength of the Acadian population, it is not surprising that New Brunswick is the only officially bilingual province in Canada.

In Ontario, approximately 479 285 persons describe French as their first language, which is the highest number outside Quebec. Yet, by 1996, the proportion of francophones in Ontario had fallen to only 4.5 percent of the province's 10 million plus. Numerically, therefore, Ontario francophones' real political leverage is rather modest, if not weak. In fact, non-official language groups are rapidly becoming major political entities in Ontario.

As well, anglicization at the current estimated rate of 50 percent among young francophones does not augur well for the future. In the early 1980s, the rate was closer to 30 percent. It is estimated that 40 percent of Franco-Ontarians now speak English at home. Assimilation is particularly high among young adults between the ages of 20 and 35. However, new immigrants have offset this decline over the last few years. According to the Association multiculturelle franco-ontarienne (AMFO), the number of French-speaking persons in Ontario has reached nearly one million when we include the allophone communities that use French as a second language. One must anticipate, therefore, the need to redefine French-speaking communities in Ontario in terms of their diverse linguistic characteristics.

Regarding bilingual services, the Ontario government has always been sensitive to the mood of its voters. Regardless of the party in power, the government has consistently favoured a step-by-step conservative policy involving a minimum of risk. Measures have been introduced one by one to accommodate the political climate and to avoid backlashes. In earlier decades, Association canadienne-française de l'Ontario (ACFO) maintained pressure that translated into exceptional gains in the education sector, and the current restructured French-language school boards.

The government undertook new measures in social services only toward the end of the 1970s. These included the translation of government legislation, the establishment of ministerial offices responsible for francophone affairs, and the simultaneous translation of Legislative Assembly debates. On the pan-Canadian political checkerboard, Ontario felt compelled to show all the other provinces, especially Quebec, that the francophone minority outside Quebec held a legitimate place within the Canadian community.

The French Language Services Act, adopted in November 1986, was the long-awaited culmination of various incremental governmental measures. Did it come 75 years too late? Certainly, the francophone community in Ontario would have been more widespread and better established in the 1990s if primary and secondary schools, social service agencies, health services, and legal services had been established in French during the first part of the twentieth century.

Various analyses suggest different historical explanations for this rampant assimilation. For example, some researchers highlight the impact of a cultural genocide resulting from the colonial mentality of elitist classes that sought to progressively assimilate Franco-Ontarians while exploiting them as a willing labour force. Other studies point out how slowly the social and religious structures of the French-Canadian community in general adapted to the requirements of a modern society. From this point of view, francophones have for too long tended to accept conditions as fate; they believe they have been placed on this Earth for meagre rewards. Negative tensions between the Irish and French-Canadian clergies also compounded francophones' linguistic difficulties. Others point to the typical forces of assimilation affecting a minority, whatever its official status. These forces often result in exogamy and anglicization of the francophone parents in mixed marriages. The children of such marriages often end up using English only instead of retaining their bilingual heritage. To the extent that any of these theories can be upheld, it is reasonable to conclude that otherwise the francophone population of French-Canadian origin in Ontario was expected to exceed one million easily by the 1990s.

USING ETHNOCULTURAL IDENTITY TO ADVOCATE FOR FRENCH LANGUAGE SERVICES

One defines a minority not only in terms of its self-perception but also according to the characteristics the majority perceives. One must also take into account the goodwill and sense of justice and equity expressed by the anglophone majority and not only the demands of the francophone minority in this context. The promotion of social services in French would hardly prosper without the support of anglophone citizens or associations promoting bilingualism, such as Canadian Parents for French. This is a difficult fact for francophones outside Quebec to swallow as they consider themselves Canada's first founding people from Europe. Hence the paradox stands of a minority group whose members speak one of the two official languages and which must design strategies to become recognized beyond its official status—a status all too often recognized in principle rather than in fact.

During the 1970s and 1980s, anglophones were well placed to promote the entitlement of francophones to French-language services. Since important anglophone allies insisted on the need for these services, francophones did not need to resort to begging, or putting themselves forward as a "deserving" minority—both very humiliating—or worry about an anglophone backlash. Their anglophone allies could convince their anglophone peers that the "French fact" would not disappear through assimilation and that francophones require a certain equity at the level of service delivery.

At the time francophones in the Ottawa-Carleton region were using up to 30 percent of social services as a whole, yet they comprised only 20 percent of the total population. This might have embarrassed some francophone leaders. However, it also helped convince the senior managers of agencies of the very real need to provide access to services in French similar to those available in English. When necessary, the point was made that, historically, francophones' rights to services had been thwarted. Some also argued that anglophone clients were better served because the largest agencies, managed traditionally by anglophones, could not fully understand the needs of their francophone community.

One must remember that, during the 1970s, it was almost unthinkable that francophones could manage social service agencies (other than school boards). The only exceptions could be found in regions where francophones made up the majority of the population, especially the united counties of Prescott-Russell east of the Ottawa-Carleton region and the town of Hearst in Northern Ontario.

THE SOCIAL PLANNING COUNCIL OF OTTAWA-CARLETON

In 1976, the board of directors of the Social Planning Council of Ottawa-Carleton approved the establishment of a standing committee of 15 persons. Its

terms of reference focused on language requirements in social service agencies. Called the French Language Requirements Committee, it included well-known active francophones from various settings as well as a small number of prominent anglophones who were proficient in French.

The committee's initial task was to draw up objectives aimed at an "extensive catch-up strategy" for French-language services. And since its mandate dealt with sensitive issues, the committee decided to remove the word "requirements" from its original name to avoid provoking unnecessary resistance to new or better services. It was therefore renamed the French Language Services Committee.

Twenty years ago, the availability of French-language services in the Ottawa-Carleton area was very uneven. Practically no francophone agencies existed. Some services mandated by the Child and Family Services Act, notably those of the Children's Aid Society of Ottawa-Carleton, had to be provided in French. The Catholic Family Services of Ottawa-Carleton was for many years one of the few voluntary agencies with a policy that guaranteed delivery of services in both official languages.

A number of anglophone agencies had attempted, out of professional concern, to provide services in French by hiring a few bilingual employees. The francophone community was sometimes cynical about these agencies, claiming that their efforts were mainly a façade. Other agencies retained their blinkers and soldiered on as though all of the clients in the region came from an anglophone mold. Francophones criticized anglophone agency directors who ignored their very existence. Needless to say, the members of the French Language Services Committee had to function with a great deal of resourcefulness and tact. Of course they wanted to avoid exacerbating linguistic tensions; they also wanted to create a climate of awareness and agreement conducive to improving French-language services. With much effort, the committee successfully avoided polarizing positions and, over the years, it earned substantial credibility from both the anglophone and francophone communities.

The following are some of the committee's achievements:

- the establishment of the first francophone residential facility in Ontario for treating alcohol and drug addiction, funded by both the Ministry of Health and the Ministry of Community and Social Services;
- an extensive study on the future of French-language services for senior citizens in Ottawa-Carleton;
- a detailed report on the shortage of francophone professionals in health and social services in Ontario; and
- the promotion of a graduate studies program in social work at the University of Ottawa, which, as of September 1992, began offering the Master of Social Work program (Maîtrise en service social) in French.

CONSULTING THE FRANCOPHONE COMMUNITY

In order to plan for and develop long-overdue French-language services, it was imperative that policy-makers consult the francophone community to determine its greatest needs. Faced with many gaps in services, limited funds, and sometimes incompatible priorities, the most pressing needs had to be identified without overlooking other medium- and long-term needs. In principle, it is difficult to argue against the benefits of consulting a minority group. But which method of consultation should be chosen? Around which service sectors should the consultation

process revolve? These and other questions require the careful consideration of many factors, especially the political considerations necessary when seeking funding from public sources.

As in all areas of social planning, community consultation requires leadership at several levels. Regardless of the service sectors involved—mental health or services to families, children, or seniors—both government and voluntary agencies require a professional elite to carry out social planning. Compared to anglophones, the francophone elite is numerically smaller and its professional profile is more modest overall. Despite this fact, it is important to draw on existing professional resources to develop a more committed and permanent francophone professional elite.

In June 1987, l'Association canadienne-française de l'Ontario held a forum in Ottawa on French-language social and community services in Ontario. The forum's theme was "Rendons-nous service." Local, provincial, and federal sources fully funded this major event. It was organized specifically to consult francophones from across Ontario. The forum caught the attention of several media. It included speeches by senior public servants, offered conferences by experts and workshops on key subjects for the francophone community. Twenty summary reports were published on the workshop themes, and each report put forward recommendations with action plans. Hopes were high that this important gathering would lead to better things for the francophone community.

Unfortunately, after that brief high pitch of enthusiasm, life resumed its usual course. Though not insensitive to the new hopes of the francophone community, the policy-makers found themselves with little room to manoeuvre in meeting various French-language service needs. The francophone community had no choice but to again be patient in the face of very few signs of immediate action. However, when a consultation focus is sustained, the chances of realizing concrete changes increase because the real obstacles are clearly identified.

It should be noted that the majority of francophone professionals work in anglophone agencies. These bilingual persons live the Canadian duality, risking a gradual loss of their own mother tongue and their cultural identity. They are often geographically dispersed, very busy, and isolated. Few actually become active visible leaders. Fortunately, some do, and their involvement and commitment become very valuable.

Public servants must also lead in consulting with the francophone community. More often than not, this leadership contributes to an objective and impartial vision of the consultation process. A final decision to grant long-term funding usually becomes possible only when sustained leadership has been provided. Either unilingual anglophone senior staff or their bilingual colleagues would have to bear the standard within the public service. Let us repeat: the commitment to provide French-language services should not necessarily be identified with francophones' leading the way. The fact that a senior public servant is francophone does not necessarily imply his or her firm commitment to French-language services.

THE MINISTRY OF COMMUNITY AND SOCIAL SERVICES

In 1979, the former southeast regional office of the Ministry of Community and Social Services requested that the Ottawa Area office distribute to its transfer payment agencies, through a selection process, approximately $600 000 in start-up funds for the development of French-language services.

Since the initiative also applied to three areas outside Ottawa—the united counties of Stormont, Dundas, and Glengarry, the united counties of Prescott-Russell, and the county of Renfrew—the Area Office's senior staff decided to set up a community-based selection committee. The committee's terms of reference were to examine submissions according to specific criteria and to submit recommendations for the allocation of funds. Well-known volunteers from the various geographical areas were appointed through the informal network of francophone or bilingual agencies. The ministry's senior staff was impressed by the committee members' work, which produced a unique perspective of the francophone community's needs. On the basis of this experience, the ministry decided to establish a standing Francophone Advisory Committee, chaired by a ministry representative and comprising six to 10 francophone-community representatives and a few other key ministry staff members. This unique ministry committee met four to six times a year and became a source of pride for all its members during its first few years.

The committee acted in a very useful advisory role between 1980 and 1986 when urgent needs had to be met. Francophones from other regions of Ontario were impressed by the Ottawa Area office's progressive leadership. For example, mental health services for francophone children, at that time the responsibility of Ottawa's only psychiatric hospital, were transferred to a new independent agency—the Centre psycho-social pour enfants et familles d'Ottawa-Carleton—to serve francophone children with emotional problems. The centre today serves the francophone culture and its diverse needs very capably.

The committee established a scholarship fund for francophone staff working in agencies funded by the ministry. A subcommittee determined the selection criteria for awarding the scholarships. Initially set at $10 000, the scholarship fund reached $25 000 in 1987. In 1990, La Société d'études et de conseil ACORD issued a glowing evaluation of the fund. For the fund's recipients, it was appreciated for its symbolic value as much as for its modest financial assistance to students. Unfortunately, the fund ceased in 1994 as the result of widespread cutbacks.

When the French Language Services Act was passed in 1986, the committee was asked to adapt to a new administrative and quasi-judicial structure. In principle, it should have clarified its own role. In June 1987, senior area office and regional ministry staff asked that the committee's membership be expanded to include representatives from the entire Southeast area—namely the Kingston and Peterborough area offices (both non-designated areas), as well as the city of Pembroke and two surrounding townships (designated areas). In the fall of 1988, the committee members felt a need to review its activities as a whole, particularly to clarify the respective roles of community and ministry representatives. Accordingly they devised a nomination procedure for new members with a two-year mandate and, for the first time, elected a community member as chairperson.

Following this restructuring, the committee had its moment of glory in dealing with a very delicate issue, the designation of the Rideau Regional Centre in Smiths Falls, an important residential centre where francophones and anglophones with developmental handicaps had been placed for a number of decades. Under the new French Language Services Act of 1986, the centre was required to establish service units exclusively for the francophone residents and their families. Although the centre had two units with a minimal bilingual capacity already, the committee decided against implementing the plan, considering it

unrealistic to try to provide all of the required specialized services in French in a completely English-speaking area. The committee insisted instead that the ministry implement its long-term community integration plan for persons with developmental handicaps so that the centre's francophones could also be integrated. The recommendation resulted in a long process of community consultation, especially in the Ottawa-Carleton area, which in 1990 led to the creation of a new francophone agency, L'Association pour l'intégration sociale d'Ottawa-Carleton.

In 1990, the committee elected to review its operations further. It hired outside consultants to evaluate the relevance and usefulness of its consultation mechanisms, and the consultants' recommendations were discussed at a full-day study session in January 1991. Everyone present agreed on a cross-sectoral consultation mechanism as essential. And a new mechanism, to be implemented by a subcommittee, was proposed: namely, that small francophone cross-sectoral advisory committees be formed for each geographic region the Ottawa Area office covered, each instructed to promote meaningful dialogue with the area office. With the ministry's assistance, these small groups would hold annual meetings to report on various issues relating to French-language services.

Within this context of ongoing restructuring and in recognizing the need to maximize the efficiency of its own service delivery system, the Ottawa Area office decided to pause and rethink its options. The group wanted to consider other consultation strategies. The French Language Services Act does not impose consultations nor does it suggest any wide-ranging structural solutions. Up to that point, the consultation models followed since the early 1980s had concentrated across various sectors. Given its progress over 12 years, the area office saw one major obstacle remaining to the long-term development of community-based French-language services: the critical mass of francophones who worked primarily in both francophone and bilingual social agencies continued to do so in relative isolation from one another.

In June 1992, the Société d'études et de conseil ACORD submitted a report on French-language social services for children, adolescents, and families in Ottawa-Carleton. The society had consulted the francophone community at various levels—clients, workers, agencies. Because of the acute importance of primary services to children and their families, it delivered a major recommendation, that a coordinating network model be developed for all children's services, in effect regrouping the service units more efficiently. On reviewing the three models, one of which would require a whole new coordinating agency, the area office concluded that each would require more planning input than it considered appropriate at that time.

Guided by the policy direction articulated in the ministry's document *Making Services Work for People*, the committee invited designated francophone and bilingual agencies to form autonomous sector-specific consultation committees for each of the three major programs, children's services, child care services, and services for developmentally handicapped persons.

As autonomous units operating in French, each committee would set its own agenda and set its own priorities. For each program sector, the committees realized benefits in two critical areas—namely, a more effective collaborative use of existing resources for francophones within each sector and, as required, the planning of consultation meetings with ministry officials on critical and specific program issues.

For the area office, this structure would provide a more rational administrative fit with the program-specific role of the program supervisors. It also moved consultation with partner agencies to a more flexible and responsive level of dialogue in dealing with critical service issues. Under the terms of this arrangement, as in any partnership, either party could ask the other for a meeting. In considering community-based participation in its consultations, the area office felt that in this case the agencies involved could undertake that function as needed.

LEGISLATIVE DIFFICULTIES

Though we have no intention of analyzing all 15 sections of Ontario's French Language Services Act, it is important to itemize some of its terms of reference, given its significant repercussions on the development of French-language services. We will examine its application to its two major administrative sectors, government services and provincially funded community services.

To begin, we will identify the major features of the Act. Democratic governments usually impose an absolute minimum of rules governing human behaviour. They prefer to leave languages to evolve naturally rather than through coercive bureaucratic means. But once "language" legislation is passed, its true value rests in its implementation and the degree of commitment backing it. The series of challenges that test a law's implementation go far beyond the basic principles that underlie the actual legislation. One must not be surprised that areas like language and culture are difficult to legislate.

How, then, should language legislation actually be administered? In Ontario, the French Language Services Act applies only to designated geographic areas—municipalities, counties, or townships—as determined by the proportion of francophones living in each area. To be designated, an urban area must have at least 5000 francophones, while non-urban areas must demonstrate thay have at least 10 percent francophones. Twenty-two areas were designated on the basis of these criteria, including Ottawa-Carleton and the surrounding counties of Prescott-Russell, Stormont, Dundas, and Glengarry (the complete list is appended to Bill 8). Consequently, the higher authorities had no administrative responsibilities towards francophones outside the designated areas, other than to be aware of Franco-Ontarians' contribution to the province's history, which was acknowledged in the French Language Services Act.

Another important feature of the Act was its giving provincial ministries up to three years, until November 19, 1989, to develop the services required in the criteria laid out by the Office of Francophone Affairs of Ontario. For their part, the non-profit agencies receiving government funding were encouraged by the respective ministries to undertake the designation process. As in territorial designation, the process called for an agency's administrative commitment to meet quality standards for French-language services. The Act did not set a time limit for the possible designation of agencies. Its implied goal was to negotiate the designation of agency programs within a reasonable period of time.

In either case, senior agency or ministry management was given ample time to develop a whole range of new requirements of its own relating to language within its organization. In other words, since language and culture issues were so sensitive, one had to develop quality French-language services carefully, without provoking senseless and harmful resistance within the work environment. Information sessions for all staff, for example, were essential to create a climate

of trust and to manage changes equitably. Since certain existing positions were to be designated as bilingual or targeted to become bilingual, the process depended on a common vision based on justice and rational management principles.

It also made good sense that the ministries set an example for the community agencies by meeting their own French-language service objectives within the three-year time frame. To promote a partnership approach, the anglophone agencies funded by government could develop their own plans of action and projected time frames. Even in the case of government-mandated services, such as child protection services in children's aid societies, the Act contained no coercive measures to force agencies to designate their programs beyond French-language services they already administered.

For a limited number of unilingual francophone agencies, the designation confirmed symbolically what they were already doing. As for the so-called bilingual agencies, they had to comply with the five designation criteria that the Ontario French Language Services Commission established in 1986. These sought to ensure that French-language services would be of the same quality as those provided in English.

We now examine very briefly each of these criteria and how the Ministry of Community and Social Services interpreted and applied those criteria. By the end of 1998, 39 of the 60 agencies with programs designated by the ministry were located in areas served by the Ottawa Area office.

Permanency and Quality of Services

The ministry considered it necessary to reflect the permanency of services in the agencies' goals and objectives for their service plans and that the quality of those services be measured in terms of established competency standards.

Adequacy of Access of Service

To assess whether services are readily accessible, various factors come into play. These include the proximity of services to the francophone population, the application of language requirements to intake/reception services, bilingual signs, the individual agency's appeal to francophones, and the availability of competent francophone staff, etc.

Effective Representation of Francophones in Agency Administration

The ministry and the agencies concerned had to be prudent in applying this criterion since it could be interpreted in different ways. How does one define a "francophone"? Should this person be known for supporting the cause of the francophone minority? Should he be able to speak French? How does one measure this person's ability to represent her cultural peers adequately? Who can proclaim himself an effective representative on a board of directors? It is difficult to find francophones who are willing to serve as board members with agencies where the English language prevails. All of these questions can be both challenging and problematic.

Francophone Representation at Management Levels

This criterion seeks to ensure that francophone staff participate at the administrative and professional decision-making levels of an agency. Such a requirement may initially pose a threat and be perceived as instigating disorganization. To illustrate this point, a francophone supervisor will normally favour the supervision of social workers and the preparation of reports in French. Similarly, she would also encourage a regrouping of francophone staff in units. So the eventual and constructive application of this particular criterion must be balanced against administrative factors.

Accountability

This criterion formally confirms an agency's commitment to providing services in French. To be accountable, the board of directors must formulate a policy that expresses its intention to pursue designation of its French-language programs. Second, it must develop a service plan to be implemented over two to five years, depending on the agency's size and its objectives. During that period, the agency must consult the francophone community and, as a rule, establish a standing committee on French-language services that reports to the board.

AN EXAMPLE OF IMPLEMENTATION

We will now examine how the Ministry of Community and Social Services implemented the French Language Services Act in its own administrative structure. Like any bureaucracy, the ministry's structure is somewhat unwieldy, and changes occur slowly. To bring about the changes under discussion, each area office was asked to develop an Internal Readiness Plan to gradually integrate French-language services into its structure. The plan had to include:

- guidelines for designated positions
- a quarterly report on the number of designated positions

- the provision of bilingual back-up staff for intake/reception services
- the hiring of bilingual employees
- an evaluation of French-language proficiency of the existing staff
- conditions and eligibility criteria for French-language courses
- the development of information sessions
- a mechanism for handling complaints
- visible signs in both English and French
- an administrative protocol for oral and written communications.

Unless one has worked in a bureaucratic system, it is difficult to imagine how many memos, reports, and committee meetings are needed to implement all the above successfully. The administrative process could be compared to trying to add a fifth wheel of a different size to an existing structure already rolling along on its customary four-wheeled platform.

Like all other Ontario ministries, the Ministry of Community and Social Services has its own way of doing business. English, of course, is the official language of its administration. And given the profound influence of the norms and values of the dominant culture, it is not surprising that the organizational structure confined itself to meeting French-language requirements without devoting much serious attention to the cultural aspects of service delivery. In fact, the French Language Services Act does not refer to the cultural dimensions of service delivery, except in its preamble. Bureaucratic levelling exerts a powerful force in many areas; whatever our profession, the colour of our skin, or the language we speak, the organizational structure within which we work imprints a standard form of behaviour on all employees. It is quite remarkable, therefore, that French-language services were integrated and achieved the level that they did.

A common feature in bureaucratic structures, a complaints mechanism, was set up by the Office of Francophone Affairs. This mechanism set out to assure the general public and the ministry's clients that the government would conduct an inquiry whenever it received a complaint. For the two major Ontario ministries heavily invested in human services, the Ministry of Health and the Ministry of Community and Social Services, the possibility of shortfalls that could produce complaints about their French-language services was very real. Hence, the mere existence of a complaints mechanism demonstrated the government's earnest intention to provide quality French-language services. If those services were not provided, a client could lodge a formal complaint.

For instance, if a receptionist did not greet a francophone in French—saying "Bonjour" being the minimum requirement of the reception desk in providing French-language services—then a client could make a formal complaint. However, because clients become dependent on the "hand that feeds them," it is not surprising to note that the number of formal complaints has been small. Besides, many francophone clients have long formed the habit of speaking in English and few would consider complaining about it. The bilingual signs at reception desks, which state that services are provided in French and English, are particularly important for those persons who demand services in French. However, despite the best efforts of management and other staff, there will be days when French-language services will be less available than those in English at one level or another of the organization. In fact, section 7 of the French Language Services Act suggests that one should not expect perfection, as long as all reasonable efforts and steps have been taken within the given circumstances.

SUBJECTIVE LINGUISTIC/CULTURAL FACTORS

The following examines some subjective factors to be considered when implementing a language policy. Bearing in mind that sensitive linguistic/cultural issues tend to be kept under cover in organizations, it is nonetheless imperative to determine employees' level of comfort or discomfort concerning the official status of the "second" official language. Though it appears entirely legitimate to provide quality services in both languages, the emotional reactions to the matter of French-language services vary from one employee to the next.

As everyone's cultural background is different, any attempt to legislate linguistic and cultural behaviour is risky. Cultural background is largely responsible for the way each of us constructs our own social reality. Culturally based attitudes and values constitute the makeup of the social universe of each of us, confirming our social identity. Unquestionably, linguistic and cultural traits become key identifiers that distinguish one individual's world from that of other cultural groups.

At another level, Canadian multiculturalism is affecting persons of Canadian origin more and more. When aware of linguistic and cultural differences, we can either extend our own horizons to accept other cultural realities or develop opposite reactions, such as embarrassment, mistrust, hostility, or, in extreme cases, xenophobia. On the other hand, a person who acquires bicultural and bilingual aptitudes during youth can move easily from one cultural world to another. The capacity to enter a cultural universe other than one's own while maintaining one's personal cultural identity is a valuable asset. One is able to transfer significant social symbols from one linguistic context to another.

THE OTTAWA AREA OFFICE OF THE MINISTRY OF THE COMMUNITY AND SOCIAL SERVICES

We now examine how a new language policy was implemented in Ontario. Our analysis continues to focus on the subjective reality, in this case that of the employees of the Ottawa Area office of the Ministry of Community and Social Services. Before official implementation of the French Language Services Act in November 1989, 52 percent of the 215 employees of the Ottawa Area office spoke both English and French, and bilingual signs had been posted for several years. With the new legislation, the bilingual staff hoped that their language skills would receive more recognition.

As the Act came into force, the designation of approximately 37 percent of all the positions in the Ottawa Area office as "bilingual" spelled out more clearly the roles and duties of staff in ensuring French-language services to clients. By 1998, designated positions reached a plateau of 48 percent—165 out of 340 positions. Also, with recent developments in high-tech communications, features identifying the language of preference facilitated linguistic lines of communication for both English-speaking and French-speaking callers.

The ministry had to reassure unilingual anglophone employees who held targeted positions that would eventually be designated bilingual. It developed guidelines indicating, among other things, that if a unilingual employee occupied such a position, that position would not be designated as long as that unilingual employee retained it. In the meantime, other solutions were developed for those positions. Information sessions were organized to explain to all staff the scope of the French Language Services Act. These sessions were essential in creating understanding and goodwill. Within this atmosphere of trust, each administrative unit could deal with any resistance, misunderstanding, or fear. It was important that each service unit develop an effective management mechanism to deal with problems as they arose and prepare an annual report for the executive committee of the Ottawa Area Office.

The integration of French-language services in the organizational structure also demonstrated that the smaller the service unit, the better it could create a "family" atmosphere, and the more smoothly the language requirements would be implemented day to day. A smaller unit was more flexible and not bound by a tight definition of roles. Its esprit de corps gave it more manoeuvrability in finding solutions without complicating matters; in such units, managers could relate to an individual's cultural/familial experiences. Inevitably, large bureaucratic units have more difficulty in creating an environment that takes into account their employees' cultural/familial experiences.

Language training is another factor conducive to the personal acceptance of French-language services. During the period 1986–1989 when interest in French-language services was very high, an impressive number of anglophone employees took the French sessions the ministry offered at the rate of two two-hour courses per week (most within working hours). Though modest compared to the federal program, the area office program supported more than 50 anglophone employees in measuring their skills, as well as limitations, for learning a second language. Those employees more proficient in

French had the opportunity to take an annual one-week immersion course.

The majority of those enrolled abandoned the language program after a few years. Only a small number of them reached the advanced level of proficiency, but all who registered for the courses gained at least some appreciation of the French language and culture. Since one of the main objectives was to improve the quality of French-language services, the Ottawa Area office wisely concluded that hiring bilingual staff was by far a less costly and more effective solution.

Francophone employees had the opportunity to have their French-language proficiency evaluated. But few appreciated the advantages of this because the ministry did not demand the same requirements of unilingual anglophone employees to have *their* English language proficiency evaluated. This is understandable since this evaluation, even if voluntary, could have been perceived as a form of discrimination. It illustrates how a language policy can indirectly hinder the development of the most qualified human resources a group needs to ensure its successful implementation. However, bilingual employees reacted more positively when the Ottawa Area office decided in 1990 to provide them with practical work tools in French—a language dictionary, one for synonyms and antonyms, a manual on the usage of French in work settings, etc. The tools were appreciated although, ironically, the majority of bilingual employees used written French rarely since all the services units had translation services available, and some standardized bilingual form letters were provided.

CONCLUSION

As a prelude to our conclusion, we observe that the blueprint for province-wide social service–delivery systems is currently undergoing major structural changes. The devolution of specific services to municipalities raises some concerns because municipalities in designated regions are exempt from the French Language Services Act. While cost-sharing measures are already being implemented under the new legislation, some of the service delivery functions appear destined to remain with the ministry for some time yet. Noted exceptions are the service delivery of child care programs and the combined services of the former Family Benefits and General Welfare Assistance programs. However, the ministry has been proactive in initiating agreements with municipalities by which designated service requirements would be respected in the event of the full devolution of a program.

As we enter this new millennium, the Franco-Ontarian community will be sensitive not only to the structural impact of the devolution of services to municipalities but also to the critical impact of population growth and distribution as these factors affect support for bilingualism and biculturalism. Two promising areas should be noted—the growing number of young adult anglophones entering society who enrolled in French immersion at the primary school level and the new Canadians who use French as a second language. As well, technological innovations such as the internet will continue to expand opportunities for the ongoing development of Franco-Ontarians' cultural identity.

Without losing sight of the Franco-Ontarian minority's remarkable ability to survive, some will conclude that the development of French-language services in the Ottawa-Carleton region has progressed beyond cherished hopes. Others affirm the need to work relentlessly toward acquiring homogeneous French-language services. Depending on one's point of view, the period of militancy may be considered

over in light of the important gains achieved, or, on the contrary, the need for advocacy may be seen as greater than ever.

From a brief historical vantage point, we show that a number of important struggles have been won. Yet the issue of French-language services is far from resolved. The chessboard is littered with various strategies based on different personal, political, and organizational interests. We believe these interests would be better consolidated; otherwise the professional isolation and dispersed energy of an always insufficient number of committed francophones will remain a stumbling block to the development of French-language social services. Albeit there is strength in numbers, the human resources, although well intentioned, are limited. In Ontario we now have a critical mass of persons aware of both the need and the ideal surrounding French-language services, but they must continue to seek ways to mobilize themselves for collective action without relying unduly on public funds.

Certainly, we must be pleased with the real progress of the structural changes designed to ensure the permanency of French-language services in Ontario. During these years of progress, those persons involved in the day-to-day administrative implementation of French-language policies and service plans can now understand the complexity of the new issues better, such as emerging services for multicultural groups and new ways to promote bilingual services.

We cannot overemphasize the need to take steps to bring about the creation of French-language services managed by francophones within a broad context of collaboration with anglophone colleagues and other multicultural groups. This is where the future of French-language social services in Ontario lies.

chapter nine

Aboriginal Peoples in Canada

Anne-Marie Mawhiney

Sheila Hardy

First Nations have never given up their right to exist as individual First Nations and to be self-governing peoples within Canada. They have never agreed to be subjugated and do not want to be subjugated by the government of Canada. The individual First Nations do not want to be assimilated into any other society and culture, Aboriginal or non-Aboriginal. They demand that their rights to exist freely as distinct self-governing peoples within Canada be fully recognized and respected by all other people.

Assembly of First Nations, 1988

INTRODUCTION

Many Canadians remain perplexed about Aboriginal peoples' demands for recognition of their inherent rights of self-government and self-determination. For many Canadians, part of the problem is a lack of knowledge about the historical, socio-political, and economic context for these assertions. Government policies have had far-reaching and negative consequences for the welfare of Aboriginal peoples in Canada, so it is particularly important that social workers understand the historical context for the development of culturally appropriate social services provided to Aboriginal communities. It is for this reason that this chapter is included in a book on Canadian social welfare.

Before examining the history of relations between Aboriginal peoples and the government of Canada, it may be helpful to include some background information about Aboriginal peoples. The term "Aboriginal peoples" refers to organic political and cultural entities that originate from the first peoples of North America (Royal Commission on Aboriginal Peoples 1997). Here "Aboriginal peoples" is used as a term that encompasses all Aboriginal people in Canada, including status and non-status Indians, Métis, and Inuit.

Great diversity exists among Aboriginal peoples and is reflected in the many languages, cultures, traditions, and philosophical beliefs. For example, the Assembly of First Nations, a national political organization, represents 592 000 people from 633 First Nations across Canada. The Inuit Tapirisat of Canada represents 30 000 Arctic Inuit (Foster 1982).

Inuit are those Aboriginal peoples who live in the far northern regions of Canada; they are distinct, culturally and legally, from First Nations peoples and the Métis. In 1939, the Supreme Court of Canada determined that the federal government was responsible for the Inuit but they were not legally Indians (Brizinski 1989). By early 1999, however, some Inuit communities were beginning to challenge the court decision and were seeking First Nations status.

Métis people are those of mixed Aboriginal and non-Aboriginal heritage (Brizinski 1989).

After generations of fighting for constitutional recognition, the Constitution Act of 1982 acknowledged existing Aboriginal and treaty rights of Canada's Aboriginal peoples under Section 35. This section provides that "35 (1) The existing aboriginal and treaty rights of the aboriginal peoples of Canada are hereby recognized and affirmed. (2) In this Act, 'aboriginal peoples of Canada' includes the Indian, Inuit and Métis peoples of Canada." However, only in September 2003 did the Supreme Court recognize the distinctiveness of the Métis Nation. The Powley decision recognizes and protects Métis people's existing Aboriginal rights.

Each Aboriginal group has its own distinct culture and tradition. For example, there are 11 separate Aboriginal Language groups and 53 distinct Aboriginal languages spoken in Canada (Foster 1982).

Living conditions in Aboriginal communities have been compared with those of people living in Third World countries. Studies undertaken over the last 30 years (Hawthorn 1967; Social Conditions 1982; Assembly of First Nations 1988; RCAP 1997) have shown time and again that the social and health indicators of Aboriginal peoples in Canada fall far below those of Canadians in mainstream society. First Nations people are admitted to hospital at more than twice the rate of the national population; the infant mortality rates among First Nations people are 60 percent higher than the national rate; Aboriginal people have a life expectancy 10 years shorter than the national average; and the death rate of First Nations is two to four times that of other Canadians (Assembly of First Nations 1988). These grim statistics highlight the correlation between health and living conditions: First Nations people's average income is half to two-thirds of the national average, and their unemployment rate ranges from 35 percent to 90 percent (Royal Commission on Aboriginal Peoples 1997; Assembly of First Nations 1988).

Until now, a piecemeal, Band-Aid approach has been taken to address the social and health conditions among Aboriginal peoples. These statistics tell a compelling story. First Nations people in Canada live in difficult and impoverished conditions unimaginable to the average person in Canada. Virtually all Aboriginal people experience these realities and know very well the impact of poor economic and social conditions on themselves, on family members, and on their communities.

The horrific living conditions of Aboriginal peoples in Canada are difficult for many people to acknowledge. Yet it is impossible to ignore the structural inequities that Aboriginal peoples experience, as individuals and as communities. The conflicts between Aboriginal peoples and the federal and provincial governments are best understood by connecting the realities of everyday experiences of Aboriginal communities with the social policies and programs instituted by Euro-Westerners since the early days of contact.

HISTORICAL BACKGROUND

To understand the relations between Aboriginal nations and Euro-Westerners, we look at traditional lifestyles before their contact with Europeans, during early contact and the formation of Canada in the nineteenth century to the circumstances of the 1990s. We are concerned here with the ways that Aboriginals' relationships with various groups of non-Aboriginal peoples have affected the well-being of generations of their peoples living within and outside their nations. We also examine the ways that Aboriginal peoples have preserved, or in some cases reclaimed, the traditional values and lifestyles they practised in support of their well-being for centuries before contact.[1]

Pre-Contact and Early Contact

Aboriginal traditional lifestyles were complex and differed from one community to the next. A complete description of traditional lifestyles would far exceed the scope of this chapter. However, a brief sketch of the social structures of some Aboriginal peoples may help to explain the political, economic, and social clashes that followed this contact.

Each Aboriginal community has its own unique social structure, traditions, culture, language, and ways of living, thinking, and viewing the world. The following describes some Anishnabe Nations near Lake Huron. Even within this geographic area, their traditions differ from one location to another; this discussion of their experiences will also serve as useful background for the rest of the chapter.[2]

Before contact, the Anishnabe peoples operated on the basis of community welfare; they placed the best interests of the community or group far ahead of the interests of individuals. Their priority was the survival of the group. Young children were taught to cooperate for the benefit of the community rather than focus on their individual interests. Through role modelling and various other socialization techniques, they learned the importance of "wisdom, love, respect, bravery, honesty, humility, and truth" (Odjig-White 1992).

Before European contact, Anishnabe people lived with social and economic equality between the sexes. The social structure of the community was egalitarian; all members were equal, and no individual, with the exception of the elders—who were revered—stood apart as special or above anyone else. All members received their fair and equal shares of any goods. The people's survival depended on a balance of labour between women and men, who contributed equally to the community and whose work was equally important. Women cared for the children, gathered and prepared food supplies, and provided shelter and clothing. Men harvested game and ensured the safety and security of the community. Elders were largely responsible for ensuring that the children learned the people's values, beliefs, and ways of life.

In contrast, European social structures were based on individualism and independence. Gender roles were based on a patriarchal model. When they set out to colonize various regions throughout the world, the Europeans brought with them a belief in their superiority as a race and culture. They based their ethnocentric views on an assumption that in all things they were the best, the most able, and the most civilized.

To the Europeans, Christianity was fundamental to civilization, so converting Aboriginal people to Christianity became the newcomers' first attempt to make over the Aboriginal peoples the missionaries encountered. It was generally believed by the colonizers that if these conversions could be accomplished, the Aboriginal peoples might eventually be integrated into European civilized society and perhaps even become worthy citizens (Frideres 1983). Of course, conversion required that Aboriginal peoples reject their own spiritual beliefs and practices and accept Christian philosophical and moral principles.

Well aware that economic self-sufficiency did not serve their own commercial interests, the newcomers set out to convince original inhabitants to give up their valued items and practices in exchange for "better" things and "better" ways. The fur traders in North America learned to promote and exploit Aboriginal peoples in order to obtain goods and services valuable to them. Through their economic relations with European traders, Aboriginal peoples became less and less self-sufficient. Economic relations between the two civilizations, combined with changes in spiritual practices, had a tremendous impact on Aboriginal values, on family and community relations, and on their traditional ways of meeting human needs.

The Europeans did recognize they had much to learn from Aboriginal peoples about surviving in North America, yet they were, for the most part, blind to the wisdom of Aboriginal values and practices. It

did not occur to them that Aboriginal cultures had created their own fully integrated systems for ensuring the physical, mental, emotional, and spiritual well-being of all community members.

For a time, conciliation and diplomacy characterized the Europeans' treatment of Aboriginal peoples. The latter proved valuable partners in the fur trade and later, when that trade began to decline, formidable allies in the French–British struggle for supremacy in North America. Neither the French nor the British recognized the sovereign powers of Aboriginal nations. Furthermore, since the land the Aboriginal peoples occupied was perceived as belonging to the French or British crowns, neither of the latter was willing to legally recognize Aboriginal land rights. However, to the extent that it served their purposes, Euro-Canadian governments were prepared to enter into nation-to-nation relations with Aboriginal groups.

French Aboriginal policy aimed to assimilate the Aboriginal peoples (Tobias 1983). This goal had nothing to do with mutual assimilation, whereby each group would take on some of the characteristics of the other. Instead, the French set out to achieve one-sided assimilation—making "them" like "us." They wanted to convert the Aboriginal peoples into servants of the Christian God and the French king through convincing them to accept the values and practices of Roman Catholicism and French economic interests as well as the language, the laws, and the political authority of France.

As we move beyond the period of early contact, we see that the problems that characterized relations between Europeans and Aboriginal peoples were compounded when the state, to protect colonial interests, began to impose its authority forcibly on Aboriginal nations. In the nineteenth century, policy-makers and legislators took up the task of assimilation, establishing patterns of disruption with new and greater significance.

From Self-Government to State Control

The Royal Proclamation of 1763 was the first significant legislation in Canada that concerned Aboriginal peoples. The proclamation re-established friendly relations with some Aboriginal groups who had been dissatisfied with their earlier contacts with Euro-Christian missionaries by recognizing Aboriginal land rights (Nazar unpublished) and ensuring Aboriginal control of their own lands. Under the proclamation, and until 1857, tribal councils still made decisions about their own people.

Self-government was starting to erode as the government of the United Canadas assumed more responsibility for decisions about Aboriginal peoples. In 1857, the British government passed the Gradual Civilization Act, which proposed moving smaller groups of Aboriginal peoples onto reserves. The legislation provoked a serious crisis. Tribal councils, seeing its danger, rejected it. They demonstrated this rejection in a variety of ways: some councils removed their children from schools, others refused to participate in surveys and the census, and others stopped providing financial support for schools (Milloy 1983). The Crown responded by centralizing responsibility for Aboriginal peoples within the United Canadas.

Enfranchisement—from the French word *franchiser*, to cloak—was one of the means used to promote assimilation from 1857 into the early twentieth century. To become Canadian citizens, and thereby to acquire certain rights such as voting, property ownership, and advanced education, Aboriginal peoples had to prove their readiness to be absorbed into Euro-Canadian society. To become a citizen of Canada, an Aboriginal person was required to demonstrate an adequate level of "civilization" as defined from the European perspective.

A rigorous means test was applied to determine this. It included the candidate's demonstration that he or she was able "to read and write either in the French or English languages, was free of debt, and of good moral character" (Tobias 1977). This criterion, as Tobias suggests, was paradoxical in that many Euro-Canadians who were illiterate and in debt were unable to meet the same standard of civilization. Nevertheless, Euro-Western leaders rationalized the double standard out of a belief that Aboriginal peoples were inherently inferior and needed civilizing.

From a present-day perspective, these assumptions are obviously racist. In the late nineteenth century, however, all parts of Euro-Western society endorsed them. As a result, Europeans accepted the double standard as an appropriate way of dealing with Aboriginal peoples.

The Indian Act of 1876

Shortly after the British North America Act (BNA Act) (1867) came into effect, several pieces of legislation were passed that resulted in the Indian Act of 1876. The legislation eroded Aboriginal peoples' control over their own lives in several ways. The BNA Act established the Canadian federal government and gave it jurisdiction over Indian affairs. At that point, federal control officially replaced Indian self-government. The Indian Act of 1876 established the Canadian government's complete control over the cultural, social, economic, and political activities of those persons defined in the Act as Indian. And in doing so, the government redefined who was Indian; the Act defined the criteria:

- any male person of Indian blood reputed to belong to a particular band
- any child of such person, or
- any woman who is or was lawfully married to such a person (Venne 1981, 24)

By 1876 the government definition was limited to male persons, their children, and their spouses. Obviously, these changes reflected increasing restrictions on who the government would define legally as an Indian person and, consequently, on who would be eligible to receive health, education, and social services, as well as tax exemptions available to Indians living in the reserve communities, which were negotiated during the treaties in exchange for land for European settlers.

In the post-Confederation period education and Christianity were the key methods for assimilating Aboriginal peoples. In the late nineteenth and early twentieth centuries, Aboriginal children were physically disconnected and removed from their families and communities for extraordinarily long periods, in some instances for their entire elementary school years, and placed in residential schools to instill proper work habits in them. This measure was consistent with the civilization mission humanitarians established for poor children in Europe during the same period. Aboriginal children attended schools that taught them no more than rudimentary skills, and emphasized the Euro-Western values of hard work. Taught by religious clerics, the children were forbidden to speak their home languages and subjected to racist curriculum delivered through force and domination (AFN 1994; Mecredi & Turpel 1993; Miller 1997; Milloy 1999; RCAP 1996). Documented emotional, mental, spiritual, and physical abuse, including sexual abuse (AFN 1994; Reed 1999), during the residential school era has had profound and long-lasting effects for

Aboriginal individuals, their families, and their communities.

Some Aboriginal leaders resisted the government policy that required that their children attend residential schools. It took government threats of military intervention and starvation to force the leaders to send their children to school (Kellough 1980). As a consequence of this separation from their communities, many children lost access to their elders and hence to their traditions and values. By the 1950s, Aboriginal peoples were thus "caught between two cultures" (Shkilnyk 1985, 81), and alcoholism, suicide, and violence in reserve communities began to replace many traditional ways of life.

In 1951, the Indian Act was amended again. Throughout the twentieth century, several amendments were made to the Act in an attempt to increase the federal government's control over status Indians. With the amendments in 1951, provincial laws applied to status Indians under section 87. As a consequence, Indian children were encouraged to attend provincial schools, and provincial child welfare policies were enforced in reserve communities. The 1951 revisions also changed the legal definition of "Indian": "Indian means a person who pursuant to this Act is registered as an Indian or is entitled to be registered as an Indian" (Venne 1981, 315).

With these amendments, the provinces started to wield their new authority over First Nations in the area of child welfare. Aboriginal children were removed from their homes and placed in Euro-American foster and adoptive homes, and decisions about which children would be placed in Euro-American homes were based on Euro-Western, middle-class standards of child care. The traditional child-rearing practices of Aboriginal families were not considered appropriate. In addition, the many years of oppression of the Aboriginal peoples—through the residential schools, for example—meant that some had not developed appropriate parenting skills, according to the ways of either culture. Policy-makers decided that adoption by Euro-American families was the best way to assimilate Aboriginal children into mainstream society. As a result, the children were again separated from their families and cultures, and many were sent to the United States, Europe, and other parts of Canada.

Removing large numbers of Aboriginal children from their culture by provincial legislation—in some communities as many as 77 percent of the children were removed (Johnson 1983)—strongly affected the First Nations. Certain communities lost a whole generation of their children. The families' and communities' trauma resulting from this loss has begun to be understood only recently by Euro-Canadian policy-makers and social workers (RCAP 1997).

Adopted children also suffered trauma; they found themselves surrounded by dominant values and ideas reflected in schools, health care facilities, social service systems, the media, their peers, and by Christian denominations. Values and ideas esteemed in their own cultures were not introduced or reinforced, and many of the children did not fully fit in with the Euro-Canadian society. They often experienced discrimination and racism. Many children suffered serious deprivation and abuse at the hands of their adoptive families; others felt they did not fit into either their own culture or their adopted culture.

The 1951 amendments to the Indian Act occurred as our Euro-Canadian society's views shifted as a result of the events of World War II. The world's horror at Nazi Germany's policies of genocide produced a condemnation of racist practices in democratic societies—including Canada. Social equality, justice, and humanitarianism

became important concepts. At the same time, treaty and status Indians and other Aboriginal groups were becoming more vocal about their special rights to education, health, and social services. They also argued for the right to work, for adequate housing, and for equitable treatment within Canada.

The federal government suggested improvements in the terrible living conditions of Aboriginal peoples, probably motivated in part by the active participation in the war effort by thousands of Aboriginal people (Tobias 1983). As well, the government was shifting its laissez-faire approach to social programs to that of a welfare state. This shift in government function supported the ideological concepts of equality and humanitarianism. As the provinces developed social policy measures for dependent groups within their Euro-Western populations, they found the gaps between the slightly more generous provincial benefits for those people and the less generous federal benefits for status Indians more difficult to justify (Getty and Lussier 1983).

The White Paper of 1969

The Hawthorn Report (1967), a study of social and economic conditions on reserves, revealed the large divide between the ideal of social equality and the deplorable circumstances in which Canada's status Indians were living. It was obvious that the ways the federal authorities had addressed issues related to Aboriginal peoples had had negative results. Alternative approaches to improving social and economic conditions were needed. In 1969, the government responded to this challenge with its *Statement of the Government of Canada on Indian Policy*, also known as The White Paper.

Before writing their statement, government officials consulted various Aboriginal groups across Canada in meetings held between July 1968 and May 1969. The process raised expectations among status Indians and other Aboriginal groups that the government was considering their priorities in formulating its policy changes relating to them. The priorities Aboriginal groups cited included recognition of their special rights as the original inhabitants in Canada and land-claim settlements to redress their historical grievances, particularly about agreements that had been made with the Crown during treaty negotiations. Equally important, they wanted to participate directly and meaningfully in developing and implementing the policies that would affect their own future. However, the White Paper released in June 1969 proved the government's consultative process had been a façade and had not influenced the intentions of Euro-Western policy-makers (Chiefs of Alberta 1970).

Prime Minister Pierre Trudeau held strong views about Quebec's place in federalism and he rejected special status for Franco-Québécois during the early 1970s. These issues also had a significant impact on the framework for this policy on Aboriginal peoples across Canada. Trudeau rejected consideration of special status for any group. Rather, he emphasized individualism, freedom, and competition—all trademarks of modern liberal ideology—not only for individuals but also for cultural groups (Weaver 1981). The White Paper policy was intended to create an equal society for all; Aboriginal people would not enjoy any special relationship with the federal government or any special status as original peoples of this land. In effect this policy made the white settler society the new rightful and equal owners of the country. In response to the White Paper, Aboriginal people mounted a concerted effort to resist the continued colonial oppression, regain control over their lives,

and maintain their status as the original peoples of Canada (Erasmus 1989; NIB 1972).

Because the recommendations in the White Paper removed their entitlements to land and services, the chiefs of Alberta, in a document called *Citizens Plus*, asserted their collective cultural rights. They considered themselves legally and culturally separated and distinct from Euro-Canadians. In contrast to a policy of integration, status Indians were advocating cultural pluralism and a goal of eventual self-sufficiency that would free them from their political and economic dependence on the Canadian state. They could also maintain their own traditions and social practices.

The message the chiefs delivered in *Citizen Plus* was clear: they were prepared to assume responsibility for the welfare of their own peoples. The institutions to handle this responsibility, they said, would be based on self-determination rather than on integration.

On the contrary, the White Paper suggested that the institutions providing services to status Indian peoples should remain under Euro-Canadian control and should be shifted from federal to provincial jurisdiction. This transfer of jurisdiction implied the integration of status Indians and would effectively eliminate the federal government's fiduciary responsibility to them.

During the late 1970s, Aboriginal peoples came to see the repatriation of Canada's Constitution as a critical issue. They feared that the proposed Charter of Rights and Freedoms, which was to be included in the amended Constitution, would override their rights. Various Aboriginal groups, including status and non-status Indians, Métis, and Inuit, insisted on participating in the process of constitutional reform (Hawkes 1985). When the Supreme Court of Canada prevented unilateral repatriation of the Constitution in 1981, Aboriginal leaders lobbied to ensure that Section 25—which recognizes existing Aboriginal and treaty rights—would be included in the charter. They wanted a guarantee that the equality rights of Section 15 would not challenge their rights. Since the Royal Proclamation of 1763 and various land-claims settlements, the Constitution had confirmed protection of all Aboriginal or treaty rights.

Aboriginal groups further pressed to have Section 35 of the Constitution entrenched. That section recognized the treaty and Aboriginal rights of Indian, Inuit, and Métis peoples, regardless of gender (Constitution Act 1982). The identification and definition of the specific rights were left to a series of first ministers' conferences that ended in 1987 without accomplishing the task. Aboriginal peoples' insistence that the concept of self-government be included in the definition remained a major point of contention.

Until Aboriginal rights are identified and defined, the Constitution's protection of those rights remains ambiguous and weak. On the other hand, because of the Aboriginal peoples' powerful pressure on the issues of self-government and their rights, the federal government has not successfully formulated and imposed any unilateral modifications to Indian policy since 1982; the government needs the agreement of the Aboriginal peoples before implementing any new policy.

From the release of the White Paper in 1969 to the early 1980s, status Indians and other Aboriginal groups demanded more control over decisions that affected them. During the mid-1970s (1974 until 1978), the National Indian Brotherhood and the Joint National Brotherhood Cabinet Committee strengthened status Indians' political ability to influence decisions. At the same time, the demand presented in *Citizens Plus*— that the government consult with status Indians before formulating

policy—transformed into demands for self-government with the repatriation of the Constitution in 1982 and the implications of Section 35 for all Aboriginal peoples (Gibbins 1986).

Repatriating the Constitution had serious ramifications for Aboriginal rights and self-government. To understand these questions from the Aboriginal perspective, the House of Commons established a committee—chaired by Keith Penner—to review these and related questions. The committee consisted of members of Parliament from the three major political parties in constituencies with significant numbers of Aboriginal people. They were therefore viewed as having some knowledge of the issues as the First Nations perceived them (Tennant 1985). In addition to the MPs, three national Aboriginal organizations, the Assembly of First Nations, the Native Council of Canada, and the Native Women's Association, were all invited to work with the committee as ex officio members.

The committee released its *Report of the Special Committee*, also known as the Penner Report, in 1983. It came out in support of special and distinct status for the Indian First Nations. The committee also recommended that self-government be entrenched in the Constitution (Penner et al. 1983). Instead of recommending details for any new legislation, the committee proposed general principles to allow all parties to reach consensus with enough flexibility to accommodate different arrangements for each specific First Nation. The committee proposed that Aboriginal and treaty rights be taken into account in any new legislation to conform to constitutional standards.

The government responded to the Penner Report by advocating increased powers for First Nations. However, the Liberals specified that decisions defining the new powers should be controlled by, and subject to the approval of, the federal government. In other words, a limited level of self-government was proposed. In contrast, Aboriginal peoples saw self-government as control over all decisions that affected their lives. They would require the federal government to relinquish its control, particularly in the areas of health, social services, education, and economic development. The government, accordingly, accepted the principle of self-government in very broad terms, as it was later to do in the constitutional conferences; however, the federal government would continue to control the services for Aboriginal peoples. By the mid-1980s, Euro-Canadian policy-makers' ideas about Aboriginal peoples had started to favour ideas of special status and self-government, a shift away from the liberal notion of social equality.

But then events in the 1990s would overshadow the actions of the various governments.

The 1991 Royal Commission on Aboriginal Peoples

The Royal Commission on Aboriginal Peoples was established in August 1991, by an Order in Council of Parliament. In part it was an answer to the Oka Crisis of the previous summer. The commission's mandate is outlined in the following passage: "The Commission of Inquiry should investigate the evolution of the relationship among aboriginal peoples (Indian, Inuit, and Métis), the Canadian government, and Canadian society as a whole. It should propose specific solutions, rooted in domestic and international experience, to the problems which have plagued those relationships and which confront aboriginal peoples today. The Commission should examine all issues which it deems to be

relevant to any or all of the aboriginal peoples of Canada..." (RCAP 1997, 2).

The commission consulted extensively with Aboriginal peoples and recorded a large number of Aboriginal testimonials and traditional teachings to help shape their final recommendations. RCAP's publications are voluminous and should be required reading for all social work and other students as they convey a comprehensive understanding of relations between Aboriginal peoples and the Canadian government. The publications point out the differences in ways of thinking and living between Aboriginal and non-Aboriginal groups. They also recount the oppression and dominance of Aboriginals by Euro-Canadians and trace the drastic ramifications for Aboriginal peoples. The RCAP proposes that the Canadian government return to its original nation-to-nation relationship with Aboriginal governments and spells out the ways the transition to this new relationship might best be accomplished. The principles of this renewed relationship would be mutual recognition, mutual respect, sharing, and mutual responsibility (RCAP 1991). To date, the federal government has endorsed few of these recommendations, with one limited exception. The Minister of Indian Affairs apologized publicly for the treatment of Aboriginal children in residential schools and the allocation of funds for healing these students. The government response to the RCAP was initiated in early 1999 by the Assembly of First Nations, who began a consultation process with Aboriginal leaders and elders on working out the transition process on Aboriginal governance.

Whether the RCAP recommendations will form the basis of a new relationship between Aboriginal governments and the federal government is not yet known. Many Aboriginal peoples are now starting to operate on the basis of the commission's recommendations despite the federal government's slow response to it.

The 1997 Delgamuukw Decision of the Supreme Court of Canada

Another significant event in December 1997, the handing down of the Delgamuukw decision by the Supreme Court of Canada, has offered direct legal support to Aboriginal peoples' demand for a new relationship between them and Canadians. In this decision the justices of the Supreme Court of Canada set down the basis for decision-making regarding the traditional lands of Aboriginal peoples; the locus of decision shifts from Euro-Canadian hegemony in decisions about Aboriginal peoples' lands and other entitlements to one where Aboriginal peoples have more power and control.

The 1997 Supreme Court decision in Delgamuukw lends support to the Aboriginal perspective on their relationship to the government of Canada. Some Aboriginal leaders do take exception to having to accept a Euro-Canadian institution's validation of what Aboriginal leaders have asserted all along: if Euro-Canadian governments would recognize and respect the inherent rights of Aboriginal peoples, then the latter could regain control of their own lives. Aboriginal criticisms of the need for Delgamuukw are fair, in light of governments and resource industries having refused, until now, to recognize Aboriginal rights. Delgamuukw at least requires other parties to take the inherent rights of Aboriginal peoples into account in decisions that affect their lives. Any parties contemplating new resource developments that impinge on Aboriginal lands, whether under land claims or actually held by Aboriginal peoples, must enter into a new contract with those peoples and

involve them in the development process. This marks a fundamental shift in government and business practice.

What is evident from events in the late 1990s—including the 1997 Delgamuukw decision, the establishment of Nunavut in April 1999, and the May 1999 Nisga'a Treaty in British Columbia—is the shifting relations among Aboriginal and Canadian peoples. Whereas in the past federal and provincial governments made binding decisions about Aboriginal peoples and their territories, now Delgamuukw signals that such unilateral decisions by outside governments are no longer possible.

Aboriginal Women

We would be remiss if we did not speak to some of the unique issues of Aboriginal women.[3] Egalitarian relationships structured the roles and responsibilities of the sexes in traditional Aboriginal societies. Aboriginal women participated actively in community decision-making and contributed to overall family and community maintenance and survival. With Euro-Western contact and colonization, patriarchal and racist ideologies led to the subjugation of Aboriginal women. As a result, they found their roles and status in many communities minimized and traditional forms of self-government replaced by male-dominated hierarchial systems (Voyageur 1996). No longer could they participate in decision-making (Alfred 1999; Stevenson 1999).

The Indian Act evinces a clear example of gender discrimination: "The patriarchal provisions of the Indian Act removed Native women from their roles as decision-makers and teachers and robbed them of their voice in community affairs" (Anderson 2000, 70). Until the Act was amended in 1985, Aboriginal women who married non-Indians also lost their

Aboriginal status. This completely denied them as well as their children any legal recognition as members of their home communities. They lost eligibility for any services or programs provided to those with "status" (Stevenson 1999; Russell 2000). However, when Aboriginal men with "status" under the Act married non-Indians, they retained their status. In fact, until 1985, only Indian women who married Indian men gained "status" and for all purposes were regarded as Indians, and so were their children by such marriages. The 1985 amendments to the Indian Act, Bill C-31, restored their status to women and to their children. The amendments also allowed the women who had lost their status to have it reinstated (Stevenson 1999; Russell 2000).

Aboriginal communities have steadfastly resisted the extreme pressures to assimilate and integrate into Euro-Western society and have survived. This resistance finds its source partly in the many aspects of traditional women's roles. As Anderson (2000) points out, "underneath all the oppression and confusion, there has always been a part of them [Aboriginal women] that knew the strength and vitality of being a Native woman. Uncovering this part is an act of recognition, a physical, spiritual and emotional remembering that can link us back to our ancestors and to a time when Native women were uniformly honoured and respected" (Preface, n.p.). Many Aboriginal women still adhere to their traditional responsibilities for maintaining family and culture, ensuring a strong sense of community, and caring for future generations, including the land (Anderson 2000; Voyageur 1996).

IMPLICATIONS FOR SOCIAL WORK

Aboriginal leaders argue convincingly that the deplorable economic and social conditions of their peoples over the generations can be traced back to social policy-makers, social workers, and other agents of the government. They blame the Eurocentric interventions that have eroded Aboriginal cultural traditions and ways of living and thinking. According to those who work with Aboriginal peoples, the high rates of incarceration, suicide, violent death, and physical and sexual abuse can be found in the experiences of several generations of children being placed in the residential schools and then in non-Native foster and adoptive homes. Some Aboriginal communities have watched their values and spiritual base eroded through this lack of continuity from one generation to the next.

As part of an ongoing decolonization process Aboriginal peoples are reclaiming, and reaffirming, their own history, stories, and traditional beliefs. They are declaring their right to educate their own people and to control how their health and social services are provided. They are involved in the education of their own social work professionals in Canadian colleges and universities and are educating non-Natives as well, who can learn from them about helping others.

What are the implications of this history for social work practice as we move further into this millennium? Presumably, Aboriginal peoples' assertions about self-determination and self-government are goals that social workers can support, as these are consistent with the profession's ideological position of respecting self-determination and cultural diversity, advocating against oppression and inequity, and promoting non-discriminatory practice. These are all critical elements in our practice. However, some changes are needed in the ways we practise if we are to act on these ideals.

First, we must acknowledge the extent to which learning in mainstream social work education programs is still predominantly middle-class, patriarchal, and white in its values, traditions, assumptions, and ways of thinking—qualities that are limited in their application to Aboriginal peoples and their communities. Part of addressing these limitations must be building on an understanding of the history and context of Aboriginal and Euro-Canadian relations. We cannot expect existing relationships to improve unless we face up to ongoing colonial systems of practice, racism, and oppression. While we have made some progress in the ways that we educate social workers about gender, race, and class, these issues are still mainly being taught in Canada by Euro-Canadian academics who are, for the most part, teaching Euro-Canadian students. We need to make structural shifts in how we prepare social workers for practice. Indeed, in some Canadian schools these shifts have begun.

In Canada, some Aboriginal human services programs for students from Aboriginal groups and others have been developed, controlled, and taught by Aboriginal faculty members and elders. These programs' curriculum reflects Aboriginal beliefs, values, traditions, and ways of life and breaks down the barriers students in mainstream programs have had to overcome. More of these students stay in the programs, and, most important, the graduates are prepared to work in both Aboriginal communities and in mainstream settings on behalf of their people.

To ensure meaningful participation in Aboriginal human services programs, Aboriginal faculty members need greater representation in schools of social work to influence curriculum development, research, and publications. They need appropriate supports so they can articulate fundamental Aboriginal values, traditions, assumptions, and ways of thinking, upon which to formulate and teach new social work theory and practice to all students. In

this area, Euro-Canadian faculty members should follow rather than lead.

There is another shift in the interactions between Aboriginal and non-Aboriginal students and faculty. Non-Aboriginal students and faculty need to learn other ways of thinking and helping others that are sensitive to Aboriginal realities and ways of living. In some schools Aboriginal professors and students are beginning to guide this process. They are working to pull the concept of cultural diversity out of the abstract, to create an environment in which students and faculty can start to confront their own belief systems. Then they can examine how these beliefs influence their own practice and thus learn other ways of thinking for working across cultures without appropriating those traditions and cultures. This is as difficult, and at times painful, a fine line to walk as it is a crucial one.

This shift in social work education would produce obvious benefits in the education of mainstream students and faculty. It would also have significant benefits for Aboriginal faculty and students. Mainstream students and faculty are learning that self-determination for Aboriginal people means that the same students and faculty will develop their own services and ways of helping their own peoples. When invited to become involved, mainstream social workers should provide the support requested and not interfere otherwise.

Recent shifts in social work education parallel the development of culturally appropriate social services within Aboriginal communities, rural and urban. These services draw on traditional ways of helping guided by community elders. They also operate along the lines of some Western European helping traditions that Aboriginal workers have adapted to fit within their own values and beliefs. Some Aboriginal people who have lost touch with some of their traditions are now learning more about them and seeking advice from their elders on how to bring traditional ceremonies into contemporary life.

The ways of helping promoted in many communities share a community-based approach. While individuals and families are assisted in various healing processes, ways of helping them are integrally linked to their own historical, social, economic, political, and spiritual context. The social work profession also recognizes that we need to make major structural changes to improve the economic and social conditions in which Aboriginal people live.

CONCLUSION

In spite of the various studies and projects undertaken in the last three decades, there still remain two very different perspectives on the nature of the relations among the Aboriginal peoples and the governments of Canada. The Canadian governments, federal and provincial, still hold the view that all Aboriginal peoples are citizens of Canada and subject to all the policies and legislation that these levels of government set, whether or not Aboriginal leaders agree to those policies or even when government decisions are unilateral ones.

Aboriginal leaders see the relationships as those of nation-to-nation which flow from the past treaties between governments: Canada (or the Crown, before Confederation) on the one hand and the various Aboriginal governments on the other. They assert their right to be part of any decision and to have a veto over policies and legislation that affect their peoples (RCAP 1997).

The historical interactions between social workers and Aboriginal peoples have paralleled those at the political level. Social workers working in front-line, research, and policy agencies have operated from ethnocentric and Eurocentric values and belief systems and have imposed these on Aboriginal peoples. In the last decade, the consequences of past interventions by non-Aboriginal social workers have become evident, and some social workers are beginning to support Aboriginal social workers in their mission to establish services and policies consistent with Aboriginal peoples' own values and beliefs.

However, it is difficult for many non-Aboriginal social workers to give up control in setting policies and in working across cultures. Doing so requires that they accept the role of students and create space for Aboriginal social workers to work in their own ways. Just as feminist theory has changed the ways that we as a profession view our own society and the people living in it, so too are the theories and practices advocated by Aboriginal social work educators and practitioners revolutionizing our profession's understanding of race and culture, particularly regarding Aboriginal peoples in Canada. The question for all new social workers is whether they will become allies or barriers to the establishment of Aboriginal services and ways of working.

NOTES

1   For a thorough analysis of this history readers are encouraged to read Volume 1 of the Royal Commission on Aboriginal Peoples, *Looking Forward, Looking Back* (1991).

2   The author acknowledges with gratitude feedback on an earlier version of this chapter by Arthur Solomon, Carol Nadjiwan, and Jennifer Keck.

3.   It is important to note that this does not represent a comprehensive overview of the unique issues and challenges Aboriginal women in Canada experience. The reader is encouraged to seek out additional writings, including the References below.

REFERENCES

Anderson, Kim. 2000. *A recognition of being: Reconstructing native womanhood.* Toronto: Second Story Press.

Brizinski, Peggy. 1989. *Knots on a string: An introduction to native studies in Canada.* Saskatoon: University of Saskatchewan.

Chiefs of Alberta. 1970. *Citizens plus.* Edmonton: The Indian Association of Alberta.

Culhane, Dara. 1998. *The pleasure of the crown.* Vancouver: Talon Press.

Foster, Michael. 1982. *Canada's first language.* Ottawa: Commissioner of Official Languages.

Frideres, James. 1983. *Native people in Canada: Contemporary conflicts.* Scarborough, ON: Prentice-Hall Canada.

Getty, A. L. & Lussier, A. S. 1983. *As long as the sun shines and water flows.* Vancouver: University of British Columbia Press.

Gibbins, Roger. 1986. Canadian Indians and the Canadian constitution: A difficult passage toward an uncertain destination. In J. Rick Ponting (Ed.), *Arduous journey: Canadian Indians and decolonization.* Toronto: McClelland & Stewart.

Government of Canada. 1969. *The statement of the Government of Canada on Indian policy.* Ottawa: Minister of Supply and Services.

Haig-Brown, Celia. 1988. *Resistance and renewal: Surviving the Indian residential school.* Vancouver: Tillacum Library.

Hawkes, David. 1985. *Negotiating aboriginal self-government.* Kingston: Queen's University Institute of Intergovernmental Relations.

Hawthorn, H. B. 1967. *A survey of the contemporary Indians of Canada.* Ottawa: Indian Affairs Branch.

Johnson, Patrick. 1983. *Native children and the child welfare system.* Toronto: James Lorimer and Company.

Kellough, Gail. 1980. From colonialism to imperialism: The experience of Canadian Indians. In John Harp & John R. Hofley (Eds.), *Structured inequality in Canada.* Scarborough: Prentice-Hall Canada.

Knox. R. H. 1982. *Indian conditions: A survey.* Ottawa: Ministry of Indian Affairs and Northern Development.

Milloy, John. 1983. The early Indian Act: Developmental strategy and constitutional change. In Ian A.L. Getty & Antoine S. Lussier (Eds.), *As long as the sun shines and the water flows.* Vancouver: University of British Columbia Press.

National Indian Brotherhood, Assembly of First Nations. 1988. *The MacPherson report on tradition and education: Towards a vision of our future.* Ottawa: Department of Indian Affairs and Northern Development.

Odjig-White, Lena. 1992. *Nishnaabe kinoomasdwin naadmaadwin field manual for SWRK 3605 EN.* Sudbury, ON: Laurentian University Press.

Penner, Keith, et al. 1983. *Report of the special committee on Indian self-government.* Ottawa: House of Commons Issue #40.

Royal Commission on Aboriginal Peoples. 1997. *For seven generations: An information legacy of the Royal Commission on Aboriginal Peoples.* Ottawa: Libraxus.

Royal Commission on Aboriginal Peoples. 1997. *Looking forward, looking back.* Ottawa: Canada Communications Group Publishing.

Russell, Dan. 2000. *A people's dream: Aboriginal self-government in Canada.* Vancouver: UBC Press.

Shkilnyk, Anastasia M. 1985. *A poison stronger than love.* New Haven: Yale University Press.

Stevenson, Winona. 1999. Colonialism and First Nations women in Canada. In Enakshi Dua & Angela Robertson (Eds.), *Scratching the surface: Canadian anti-racist feminist thought.* Toronto: Women's Press.

Tennant, Paul. 1985. Aboriginal rights and the Penner report on Indian self-government. In M. Boldt & A. Long (Eds.), *The quest for justice.* Toronto: University of Toronto Press.

Tobias, John. 1976. Protection, civilization, assimilation: An outline history of Canada's Indian policy. In *The Western Canadian Journal of Anthropology*. 6 (2).

Tobias, John. 1983. Protection, civilization, assimilation: an outline history of Canada's Indian policy. In Ian A.L. Getty & Antoine S. Lussier (Eds.), *As long as the sun shines and the water flows*. Vancouver: University of British Columbia Press.

Venne, Sharon Helen. 1981. *Indian Act and amendments, 1868–1975: An indexed collection*. Saskatchewan: University of Saskatchewan, Native Law Centre.

Voyageur, Cora J. 1996. Contemporary Indian. In David Alan Long & Olive Patricia Dickason (Eds.), *Women in visions of the heart: Canadian Aboriginal issues*. Toronto: Harcourt Brace Canada.

Weaver, Sally. 1981. *Making Canadian Indian policy*. Toronto: University of Toronto Press.

chapter ten

Women and Social Welfare: Exploring the Connections

Patricia M. Evans

The welfare state is not just a set of services, it is also a set of ideas about society, about the family, and—not least important—about women....

E. Wilson, 1977

INTRODUCTION: WOMEN, SOCIAL WELFARE, AND DIVERSITY

As many chapters in this book illustrate, critical perspectives on class, race, and gender have contributed to a sharper awareness that social welfare provisions, while they provide important benefits, often reinforce the inequalities that underlie Canadian society. In this chapter, we consider the interplay between women's position at home and in the economy and the design of social services and social welfare benefits.

A feminist critique of social welfare is not the only critique, but it is an important one. It throws into particular relief women's situation without at the same time taking for granted that their experiences are identical or that gender is necessarily the most important arena of inequality. We examine social welfare through the lens of gender, keeping in mind that there is no "universal" woman; women's experiences differ in a multitude of ways, particularly in terms of race, class, ability, and sexual orientation.

At a time when "structural" and "anti-oppressive" approaches to social work expand the analysis beyond the scope of any one particular lens of inequality (Lundy 2004; Mullaly 2002), feminist perspectives may seem, as Marilyn Callahan (2004, 128) notes, "out of fashion." But women do tend to share in "unpaid family work, low pay, and a small fraction of power in public and private life" (Pascall 1997, 22). Just the specific forms and the scale of the disadvantages will differ sharply. Vickers and Dhruvarajan (2002) suggest four important dimensions of difference in women's experiences: (1) geographic location and location in the global political economy; (2) class and/or caste; (3) communal affiliation, which includes race, faith, language, ethnicity and/or nationality; and (4) personal status—age, marital or reproductive status, sexual orientation, and dis/ability.

A gender perspective is particularly important at a time when social welfare is being transformed to accommodate the "universal and inevitable" forces of global competition and economic restructuring (for further discussion, see the chapter by Dr. Ramesh Mishra in this volume; McKeen and Porter 2003). This transformation concerns more than significant cuts to the social safety net, although, as we shall see, these have been very problematic. It also pertains to changing the nature of social citizenship and the expectations of Canadians toward their government. The market becomes increasingly important, the idea of the "social" is eclipsed, and social welfare is reduced to cut costs and improve "incentives." The "good" citizen becomes the individual who makes no claims on the state (Brodie 1996). Those who do make claims find that not only is there much less available for them, but they are also regarded as "*less deserving* of basic social rights" (emphasis in the original; Little 1999, 60).

Social welfare needs to be examined with a focus that keeps women's experiences in view for several reasons. First, many policies and programs are grounded in problematic assumptions about women's roles and responsibilities. For example, social assistance programs increasingly expect single mothers to be "workers" rather than "mothers" despite the lack of affordable child care and decently paid employment. In Ontario, these changing expectations surrounding single mothers, work, and welfare have helped to render them "less deserving" and to justify a 22 percent cut in their benefits in 1995. In fact benefits have not increased in almost a decade. As a result, those on assistance are struggling to survive on low wages, low assistance levels, or some combination of both. Women and children—and men—are enduring severe hardship because of the inadequacy of welfare rates, including the greater risk that women will not leave abusive husbands or will be more likely to return to them (Ontario Association of Interval and Transition Houses [OAITH] 2003; Mosher, Evans, & Little 2004).

The problems in policies and programs are not confined to the conventionally conceived women's issues such as child care, reproductive rights, pay equity, and violence toward women. As public debates on health care to labour market programs to trade policy make increasingly clear, there are few, if any, gender-neutral policies. One of the outcomes of the 1995 UN Fourth World Conference on Women held in Beijing was the unanimous agreement of 189 countries to assess their policies, programs, and legislation for their impacts on the genders (Rankin & Vickers 2001). Since 1995, federal government departments and agencies have been required to assess their policies and legislation for their impacts on women (including different groups) and on men (Status of Women Canada 1998). While attention to this kind of analysis is important, its implementation at the federal and provincial levels suggests that its full potential is far from being realized (Rankin & Vickers 2001; Teghtsoonian 2000).

A second reason that an examination of social welfare from women's perspective is important is that women dominate both sides of the social work and social welfare "encounter" (Davis & Brook 1985). So gender is significant, although it often disappears in the language we use: "single parents," "family," and "community care." Women are more likely than men to be employed as social workers, child-care workers, visiting homemakers, and to serve as foster parents as well as to work in the community as volunteers. In 1996, women comprised 72 percent of the workers in the social service sector (Canadian Association of the Schools of Social Work 2000). Women are also more likely than men to use social services, although, as Krane (2003) notes, they often make their requests for service on behalf of others, such as their children and elderly parents. The social and legal regulatory functionaries of the state are more likely to scrutinize the "mothering" of women, when it is deemed "inadequate"—poor women, and minority women in particular. In 2002–2003, almost three-quarters of the families involved with the Children's Aid Society of Metropolitan Toronto had incomes that fell below the poverty line, and the majority (52 percent) identified themselves as members of a minority race or culture. Single parents headed half of the families (overwhelmingly single mothers), although they represent only 20 percent of the broader population (Children's Aid Society of Metropolitan Toronto n.d.). However, the implications of gender, racialization, and poverty for who is identifying and monitoring neglect are written out of the official record (Swift 1998, 2001; Callahan 2001).

Women figure prominently in the world of social welfare and social services.

Understanding why this is so reveals the paradoxes and contradictions that shape their relationship to welfare. An exploration of this relationship portrays the particular experience of women, and it also helps to understand the complex nature of social welfare in Canadian society.

This chapter proposes to unravel this relationship—one that is neither simple nor straightforward, one that is fashioned instead in contradiction and paradox. The welfare state simultaneously protects and controls women, although in recent years the protection it has offered has diminished as programs have contracted. Nonetheless, viewing it simply as an instrument of either oppression *or* liberation obscures its complex history while masking its implications for women (Pascall 1997; Evans & Wekerle 1997).

The first part of the chapter identifies the assumptions and structures that underpin the gendered division of labour and connects the concept of caring labour to social welfare. We then examine the contribution that women have made to the modern system of social welfare. The last two sections explore how assumptions about men and women's separate roles and responsibilities are reflected in income support policies and social services.

GENDERED ASSUMPTIONS ABOUT WOMEN'S CARING

The last several decades have witnessed significant changes to Canadian families. A decline in birth rates, longer life expectancies, greater numbers of people cohabitating, more separations and remarriages, and women's growing participation in the labour force have all altered the composition of Canadian families (Baker 2001).

Families in which the father is the sole economic provider and the mother is a full-time caregiver are in the distinct minority today: about one in every four Canadian families with children, according to Statistics Canada (2004). Despite the current economic reality that even two-parent households need two incomes, the nuclear family remains a powerful ideal (Baker & Phipps 1997). Several related assumptions constitute the image of this nuclear and presumed heterosexual family:

- The father is the primary breadwinner and the mother is the primary caregiver, even though both may engage in paid work and unpaid caregiving.
- Women can and should depend on men for financial support.
- Women are available to look after family members without pay and will leave paid employment in order to do so.

Assumptions regarding the gendered division of labour continue to find expression in our social policies and programs, despite the changes that have taken place. As feminist scholarship has shown, this division is not natural, inevitable, or neutral in its impact. Nor are all women affected in the same way. The intersecting forces of capitalism, patriarchy, and neo-colonialism, for example, mean that many black women have a longer and more prominent history of paid employment than white women, while much of this employment has involved caring for non-family members. As Dionne Brand (1999, 90) notes, "These jobs gain 'moral value' as being nurturing and caring when done by white women in their own households. But when done by Black women for wages the same tasks are not valued in the society on any level." The structure of immigration policies has also meant that women are much more likely to enter Canada as dependants of their male partners than as independent immigrants. Still other women can gain entry to Canada only on condition that they leave behind their own

children and come as live-in caregivers to look after other people's children (Arat-Koc 1999; McWatt & Neysmith 1998).

The dynamic interplay between class and gender means that better-off women are able to buffer the consequences of their caregiving by choosing to purchase services, such as child care and help in the household, most often from women who have fewer resources and fewer options. Cutbacks in social welfare programs cause problems for many women. Women's informal and unpaid labour increases to compensate for shrinking services. The public sector has been an important source of employment for women in recent years, but it too has shrunk and is increasingly characterized by temporary, part-time, and contracted work (Townson 2003). The decade from the mid-1980s to the mid-1990s witnessed the disappearance of one-third of the staffed hospital beds across Canada (National Anti-Poverty Organization 1998). As Pat Armstrong (1996, 27) notes, decreased funding for health simply transfers the costs to women who form "the majority of those employed in health care, of those receiving services, and of those providing care in the home."

So women's participation in the work has increased markedly, yet the gendered division of care work remains very evident as women continue to bear the major share of responsibilities for their children and households.[1] Estimates suggest that women provide about 80 percent of society's unpaid informal care of children, the sick, and the elderly in Canada (Neysmith 2002). In 1997, a Status of Women Canada report suggested that the "unequal sharing of dependant care may be the most persistent barrier to gender equality" (cited in Ecumenical Coalition for Economic Justice 1998, 4).

But the impacts of the gendered division of labour extend beyond the household. In the workplace, women face occupational segregation and low pay. Much of their work in the labour market mirrors work in the home and it frequently embodies important components of caregiving and personal service. In 2002, 70 percent of women employed in Canada held occupations related to teaching, health, clerical/administrative work, sales, and services compared to approximately 30 percent of men. In addition, women who are full-time employees earn, on average, 72 percent of men's earnings, and a substantial amount of this gap cannot be explained by such factors as education, experience, and job tenure (Cooke-Reynolds & Zukewich 2004). Women of colour face a racialized as well as gendered labour market and, as a group, have the lowest average employment income (Canadian Association of Social Workers [CASW] 2004; Ghorayshi 2002).

The combined stresses of the workplace and the home have been cited as important factors in women's risk of strokes and heart disease (Picard 1999). As well, the stress of providing care, and its financial consequences, has been associated with the mental health problems of elderly women (Neysmith 2002). The "double shift" theory is borne out by findings that when both parents are employed full-time, mothers perform most of the child care and household chores (Rice & Prince 2000). Unlike men, women's blood pressure levels do not return to normal after they leave their workplaces; they remain elevated well into the evening as a result of their ongoing responsibilities for the care and maintenance of other family members and their households. Class also takes its toll as the double day intensifies; women may need to work longer hours for pay and/or as caregivers to members of their families at home because they cannot afford to purchase services.

The concept of women's caring labour suggests the complex nature of the work women do for others. "Caring" refers to the web of activities they undertake in looking after and tending others that involve physical, mental, and emotional effort. "In our society, much of this work is done by women in varying forms throughout their lives. It is done as mothers, daughters, and wives in the context of individual relationships, in the community as volunteers, through the professions as nurses, social workers, and teachers, and as low-wage workers in hospitals, child-care centres, and home-care services. The persons who receive care are usually those we view as dependent, and include children, people with physical, intellectual, or psychiatric disabilities, and the frail elderly. However, within the family, the cared-for may also include able-bodied men" (Baines, Evans, & Neysmith 1998, 3). This work can be done in the home, in the workplace, and in the community. But wherever it is carried out, the work is highly gendered, typically undervalued, and often invisible (Baines, Evans, & Neysmith 1998). In addition, caring work, whether paid or unpaid, denotes a complicated web of relationships that are "defined in terms of ties or bonds signifying degrees of personal familiarity and obligation" (Thomas 1993, 652).

We must not overlook the structural roots of women's caring work. As Hilary Graham (1983, 25) suggests, caring should not be understood as the outcome of women's psychological disposition, "but as an expression of women's position within a particular kind of society in which the twin forces of capitalism and patriarchy are at work." More than 20 years of analysis from women of colour attest to the presence of a third influential force: the process of neo-colonization. This factor has had profound implications for the nature and the circumstances in which caring work is carried out:

for example, immigrant women are cast as both breadwinners and careers in their paid and unpaid work. As Dua (1999) points out, although the nuclear family also organizes gender relations among women of colour, many also struggle to overcome the historical and contemporary processes that have hampered their ability to participate in nuclear families. The treatment of First Nations people, sponsorship regulations, and programs that recruit women as domestic workers without their families are all ways that Canada has regulated the disruption of certain kinds of families.

The reasons why women are assigned the responsibilities for caring labour, and not men, may be explained through the combination of four primary and interrelated factors:

- the development of capitalism and a waged labour market that values the market's "productive" work and devalues the "unproductive" work performed outside a cash economy;
- the processes of racialized and class-based state policies that have tended to channel most white women into the private realm of unpaid work while women of colour and poor white women are channelled into paid domestic work;
- a tradition of (white) male power and dominance in structures that institutionalize the undervaluing of women's work in the home and in the labour market; and
- the ideology, socialization, and institutional processes that help to transmit these gendered, classed, and racialized norms to make them seem "normal."

Together these factors create a false perception of an overall "dependency" of many women on men and at the same time translate, too frequently, into the reality that many women are economically vulnerable without male partners. Men are indeed involved in caregiving work, and their par-

ticipation is increasing. Yet they are involved to a much lesser extent than women. In 2001, for example, seven of 10 adults who spent 30 or more hours a week caring for children were women. Women also constituted two-thirds of the adults who spent more than 10 hours a week caring for seniors (Statistics Canada, 2001 Census). In addition, evidence suggests that men who provide care are likely to receive more help through formal services than women (Aronson & Neysmith 1997). There is no male equivalent to maternal bonding and mothers, unlike fathers, do not babysit their own children. Women's caring usually passes without notice, unless it falls below expected standards, when it is likely to become subject to considerable scrutiny (Krane 2003; Swift 1998). Caring also forms a significant nexus for women in social welfare. Women are employed as home-helps, hospital workers, and child-care workers, while in their role as family caregivers they frequently depend on these services. Child-care workers, home-helps, foster mothers, and nursing aides can also experience the mixed feelings of obligation, affection, and resentment associated with caring work within the family. An ethic of care has also been important in recruiting women into nursing, social work, and teaching. At the same time, the tension between professionalization and altruism, as we shall see, has also been problematic for them (Baines 1998).

THE WORK OF WOMEN IN SOCIAL WELFARE

As already stated, the gendered nature and impact of women's caring have been an important part of the story of the development of Canadian social welfare, from its early days to the present. Only relatively recently, however, have women's contributions been recognized as more diverse and complex than suggested by the conventional images of white, middle-class Lady Bountifuls who patronizingly dispense their aid to the poor. An expanding body of feminist work is resurrecting important and misunderstood gender issues in the story of social work and social welfare, and it challenges the inaccuracy and inadequacy of this image.

The industrialization and urbanization in Canada toward the end of the nineteenth century introduced a range of new social problems, including urban poverty and slum housing, particularly among women and children. Canadian women made early efforts to respond to these needs on an ad hoc basis, and before long, society began to recognize the need for a more organized and coordinated response. The organizations that developed reflected a range of approaches (see Mitchinson 1987 for a discussion of white middle-class organizations), including the message of the social gospel.

This has been described as a social religion that shifted the focus from individual salvation to social justice (Baines 1998). Women combined this message with maternal feminism, the belief that it was more than legitimate: it was crucial that they transfer their special nurturing qualities to the public sphere. Maternal feminism supported and helped to glorify women's traditional roles without being entirely a conservative response. A study of the early days of the Toronto Child Welfare Council suggests that the women involved were "a mixture of maternal feminism and radicalism that defies any simple definition" (Wills 1992, 34).

Women of colour have also been active in social reform since the early nineteenth century, although these activities have received relatively little attention (Dua 1999). Not surprisingly, their social justice work focused on anti-racism and their early organizing advocated equity in resources and opposed race-segregated schools (Daenzer 1997). Women gathered in "study clubs" to address concerns about the economic and social future of blacks, and they banded together in organizations to provide material help to people in need (Bristow 1993). Women who came to Canada from Asia, Africa, and the Caribbean established their own autonomous organizations, a trend particularly evident from the mid-1970s on. These were characterized by political agendas of social justice that included a right to social services, demands that were honed from the exclusion produced by "the race and gender biases of mainstream institutions" (Agnew 1996, 134).

Following World War I, the drive to professionalize the "mainstream" voluntary organizations mirrored efforts to dissociate the emerging occupation of social work from its maternal feminist roots and to adopt a more scientific, rational approach. In 1914, the University of Toronto opened its doors to the first class enrolled in its Social Services Department; women taught the entirely female student body in the practice areas and men taught what were regarded as the academic courses. The fields of service paralleled the same division along gender lines: women were employed in direct service with individuals and families while men were more likely to work in social planning and social policy (Baines 1998).

Davis and Brook (1985, 9) comment on a similar trend in the historical organization of social work in Britain: "it was important to ensure that women's essential qualities of enthusiasm, sympathy, self-sacrifice, and eye for detail were steadied by the logic, business sense, and distance of men, who would be responsible for overall management. The iconography was of a perfectly matched husband and wife.... He was the head, and she the heart of the enterprise."

The gendered division of labour that structured social welfare and its ally, social work, are hardly surprising. They reflect the divisions in the wider society, divisions that persist to the present day. A study of Ontario's social workers found that men continue to earn significantly more than women and are overrepresented in managerial positions (Kenyon 1997). James Struthers (1987, 126) commented nearly two decades ago that "although the profession has prided itself, historically, on its role as a vehicle for social change, the sexual division of labour within social work mirrors rather than challenges the job ghettoization and power and income disparities which surround women's work in the larger society."

The tension between professionalization, the head, and an ethic of care, the heart, also continues, although not necessarily imbued with the same gender differences that marked the earlier period. Even so, the values of hierarchy, efficiency, and competition that found particular expression as men entered the social work profession are echoed in today's concerns that "managerialism" has tended to objectify clients and increase the distance between social workers and the people they serve (Baines 1998; Wills 1992). A later section of this chapter will explore how the current climate of cutbacks has exacerbated some of these concerns.

WOMEN, POVERTY, AND INCOME SUPPORT

The primary responsibility that women bear for caring for others is critically important to understanding why they, as single mothers and elderly women living on their own, are so much more likely to be poor than men in similar circumstances. We have already seen that women are disadvantaged by the structure of the labour market through its occupational segrega-tion and wage discrimination; they are also individually disadvantaged by constraints on their own employment with their care-giving and household responsibilities.

These factors converge with special force when women are the primary, and often the only, providers for themselves and their families. The reasons why 45 percent of families headed by single mothers had low-incomes in 2001 include the scarcity of decent jobs, lack of affordable and quality child care, low levels of social assistance, and inadequate child support payments by absent fathers. The low pension entitlements that condemn so many elderly women living on their own to poverty sharply highlight the accumulated impact of labour market disadvantages: 46 percent in 2001 compared to 33 percent of their male counterparts (CASW 2004).

Women and men dominate different "tracks" of the income security system. Men have tended to claim a greater share of benefits from social insurance programs, programs based on their employment record as "public citizens." Women, in contrast, have been more likely to benefit as "private citizens" as wives and mothers, drawing on the less generous, and more stigmatized, layer of income security based on demonstration of need, not entitlement. Elderly women, for example, rely more heavily than elderly men on income-tested age-related benefits and men are more likely to benefit from work-related pensions and investments (CASW 2004).

Similarly, women form a larger share of the social assistance caseload and are underrepresented in the unemployment benefits administered under Employment Insurance (EI). For example, women made up 59 percent of adults of the "employables" on the Ontario social assistance caseload in December 2003 (Ministry of Community, Family, and Children's Services 2004). In 2001, however, they had constituted only 37 percent of EI's unemployment beneficiaries (Canadian Labour Congress [CLC] 2003, calculated from p. 7).

Cuts to income support programs in the 1990s were severe and the elimination of the Canada Assistance Plan and introduction of its replacement, the Canada Health and Social Transfer (CHST), exacerbated these effects. The CHST, which has been described as "the worst social policy move in a generation" (Battle & Torjman 1996, 57), combined federal transfers for health, post-secondary education, social assistance, and some social services into one huge and unconditional transfer of funds to the provinces. It dramatically reduced federal responsibility for social programs by eliminating cost-sharing provisions and abandoning national standards. At the same time the federal government significantly reduced its overall financial contribution (Evans 2002). The CHST has hit women particularly hard as they are more likely than men to receive social assistance and to rely on other, previously cost-shared services such as child care, homemaking services for the elderly, and shelters for women fleeing abuse (Day & Brodsky 1998).

In replacing the CHST with the Canada Social Transfer and the Canada Health Transfer on April 1, 2004, the government has not addressed either the lack of national standards or the transparency needed for social expenditures (Canadian Council on Social Development [CCSD] 2004b). Squeezed in the climate that produced the CHST in the first place and directed at a population increasingly seen as "undeserving," social assistance rates are inadequate and deteriorating. In 2002, the benefits for a single mother with one child ranged from 48 percent (Alberta) to 72 percent (Newfoundland and Labrador), expressed as a percentage of the poverty line (National Council of Welfare 2003). A report by the Ontario Association of Interval and Transition Houses (OAITH) (2003) documents women's greater and greater difficulty in attempting to leave abusive situations that result from these woefully inadequate social assistance rates, deteriorating access to affordable housing, and cuts to such services as shelters and legal aid (see also Mosher, Evans, & Little 2004).

Between 1990 and 2001, the proportion of Canada's unemployed who qualified for benefits fell dramatically—from 74 percent to 39 percent—as a result of new restrictions in the eligibility criteria. Changes made to Employment Insurance in 1996 that were supposed to improve the position of "non-standard" workers—predominantly women—have proved particularly damaging to them. The proportion of unemployed women who received benefits dropped from 39 percent to 33 percent between 1996 and 2001 as the proportion of men declined from 45 percent to 44 percent (CLC 2003).

Other changes to EI have been more helpful to women. In 2001, the parental benefits period was extended from 10 to 35 weeks, which, when combined with maternity benefits (15 weeks), provide substitute income for a parent to stay at home with a newborn child for almost a year. The take-up of this benefit, however, still reflects gender and class divisions. While more men are using the parental benefits, mothers claim them overwhelmingly. In 2001, women represented 90 percent of the claimants (calculated from Human Resources Development Canada n.d.). As well, maternity and parental benefits confer advantages on certain groups of women. Before 2001, those most likely to claim benefits included first-time mothers, mothers in higher income families, those with higher rates of pay, those employed full-time, and women working in unionized or government environments (Shillington 2001). As of January 2004, EI also provides a six-week Compassionate

Care Benefit so that those who qualify can receive benefits when they take time off from employment to care for a close family member who is terminally ill.[2]

While parental leave and compassionate care benefits do help in allowing some individuals to care for their relatives, they do not, and are not intended to, tackle the gender division of labour or redress the privileges of relative affluence. They simply provide income to compensate for the caregiving of some individuals. Excluded are the self-employed, those who cannot participate in the labour market at all or enough to meet the EI requirements, and those who qualify but cannot afford the lower income that is the reality of benefits set at 55 percent of a person's earnings to a maximum of $413 a week.

The "patriarchal" model of the family, in which the father/husband is presumed to be the breadwinner, and the mother/wife is assumed to be his dependant was the historic basis for many income support programs (Eichler 1997). Programs and policies have been altered and "degendered," yet important limits on women's economic independence continue. For example, in all provinces except Quebec, a woman who is living with a man is generally not eligible for social assistance in her own right. Even if the man is not the father of her children and has no legal responsibility to support her or her children, it is assumed that he *should* be financially responsible. The Supreme Court is reviewing a challenge to the constitutionality of Ontario's "spouse in the house" regulation, and if it agrees with the lower court's decision, the Supreme Court will find the regulation violates the Charter of Rights and Freedoms (for further discussion, see Mosher, Evans, & Little 2004, 47–49).

Similar assumptions of dependency are also apparent in the tax system. Among the contradictions and anomalies, a tax credit can be claimed for a dependent spouse, who is almost always the female partner. Although some argue that this policy recognizes the contribution of women's unpaid labour in the home, the tax credit disappears when the woman becomes employed, even though her labour in the home continues. In addition, the tax credit is available even if the actual labour has no social value—when the beneficiary is, for example, a healthy adult male.

Many of the gender-specific provisions of the past have been replaced by provisions that are formally gender-neutral. However, these do not necessarily serve women well (Eichler 1997; Evans 1997). Policies that incorporate a gender-blind notion of equality may treat individuals in exactly the same way even as they can still produce unequal outcomes by ignoring the very different contexts and constraints that shape women's and men's lives. For instance, while men's and women's access to the Canada Pension Plan is formally on equal terms, women's disadvantaged position in the labour market means that they received, on average in February 2004, only 58 percent of the benefits that were paid to men (calculated from Social Development Canada 2004). As indicated earlier in the chapter, the employment expectations of social assistance recipients have also been "degendered." Single mothers, once viewed as "mothers," are now defined as "workers" with little consideration given to the obstacles they confront in child care or the availability of jobs (Mosher, Evans, & Little 2004). Family law also reflects expectations about women's economic self-sufficiency that diverge sharply from the realities of their lives (Mossman & Maclean 1997).

What directions should be pursued to address women's poverty and inequities in the income support system? First, we need to work toward policies that recognize "women's complex allegiances and claims, and offer more choice" (Lewis 1986, 97). This will require a more sensitive evaluation of policies' impacts on women's economic autonomy that do not, at the same time, bind them to expectations that are well in advance of the realities of their lives. It is essential to recognize that women are positioned differently and that we cannot pursue gender equity while ignoring the claims of class or race. As one instance, the income-tax deduction for child care expenses, while it recognizes the costs associated with women's paid work, is inequitable because it gives higher-income mothers a significant advantage.

Margrit Eichler (1997) outlines a "social responsibility" model to guide future policies. She assigns the state a much more vigorous role to ensure accessible and affordable child care, an enhanced child benefit to eliminate child poverty, and a state-guaranteed child support program to protect children and mothers in divorce and separation.[3] She also acknowledges that, despite the importance of such changes to Canadians' welfare, her proposals for comprehensive reforms may win little support in the current climate.

The most promising initiatives may lie outside the realm of income policies and in measures that endorse a collective commitment to social care. These efforts should include national and publicly supported child care and home care programs, and the development of workplace policies that respond to the needs of workers with family responsibilities. These important steps would expand responsibilities for care and reduce the costs that women currently bear for their caring labour.

WOMEN'S CARING AND SOCIAL SERVICES

Expectations of women's caring help to shape the way problems are defined, influence the solutions we seek, and therefore delineate the parameters of the services we offer. The care of children, individuals with disabilities, and the frail elderly is first and foremost viewed as "a private concern to be carried out in those places where intimate relations with women are found" (Hanmer & Statham 1988, 64). The Canadian state plays a role that is residual and generally limited to filling only the serious gaps that families are unable to close themselves. Unlike some Scandinavian and European countries where child care and supports for the elderly are available as rights, Canadian services, with the notable exception of Quebec, are premised on assumptions of family responsibility.[4]

In the context of cost-cutting, neo-liberalism, and individualism, the goal of "community" care for the frail elderly and individuals with severe disabilities typically translates into more and more care by family members, mostly women (Aronson & Neysmith 2001). It is estimated, for example, that only 10 percent of the care that elderly people receive is formal services (Aronson 1998). And individuals are finding even these services reduced (Aronson & Neysmith 2001; Morris, Robinson, & Simpson 1999).

Commenting on the pervasive gendered nature of home care, the authors of a study of home care in St. John's and Winnipeg comment, "Not only are most paid and unpaid caregivers women, but more than two thirds of those receiving home care are women" (Morris, Robinson, & Simpson 1999). Gender is also important in interpreting need: when both are employed, sons tend to receive more support services when they care for their elderly parents than daughters do (Guberman 1988).

Expectations regarding women's responsibilities for providing care also shape our definition and response to child welfare. The principle of non-interference, rather than that of social responsibility, dominates. The current discourse surrounding this issue appears to have little to do with a collective commitment to ensure a nurturing environment for all children and much more to do with a narrowly constrained focus of public responsibility on child protection. The gendered nature of child welfare slips out of view despite the fact that mothers are the ones held responsible for failing to protect their children, even when, as in the case of incest, they are not the perpetrators of the abuse (Krane 2003). Although we may use the language of "parents," it is mothers, particularly single mothers struggling on pitifully inadequate incomes, who are so disproportionately represented in child welfare cases. The implications of the connections between poverty, racialization, and gender inequalities lie hidden under a body of literature and behind practices and procedures that too frequently focus on documenting and remedying the mothers' inadequacies. As Karen Swift (2001, 68) comments, "Poverty, bad housing, malnourishment, insecure child care arrangements, poor job possibilities, woman abuse, addictions, health and mental problems are the everyday concerns of child welfare workers. These crucial issues, arising in large part from structural inequalities and sharpened by neoliberal policies, merit virtually no mention in new child welfare policy directions."

While gender links women on both sides of the social welfare encounter, race often divides them. Systemic racism helps to ensure that women of colour are more likely to work in social services as home-helps than to be on the receiving end of these services or to be employed as social workers themselves. Practices may pay little attention to the power differences between workers and clients or to the structural inequalities that impede minority women and men's use of social services (George

2000). A shelter may offer escape from a violent relationship; it provides little or no protection from racism and probably cannot offer a culturally appropriate setting for a minority woman in need. Agencies strapped for cash are using informal community interpreters, for example, rather than professional cultural interpreters (CCSD 2004a).

Spending cutbacks are shrinking many statutory services and placing in peril the very existence of many community-based services. A survey of community-based agencies in Metropolitan Toronto documents a sizeable increase in the number of agency closings. It notes that most agencies faced decreased funding at the very time that demands for their services increased. Cutbacks in future are expected to fall most heavily on services to women, immigrants, refugees, and low-income families (Social Planning Council 1997). Following a 5 percent cut in 1995, the increase in government funding to Ontario's women's shelters between 1999 and 2003 averaged about 5 percent, well below the rising costs of energy, insurance, and other items. During that period, the number of women served grew as well, and most disturbingly the average length of stay increased by more than 50 percent. These facts in turn attest to the greater difficulty of people's finding, among other things, affordable housing (OAITH 2003). Food banks, unknown in Canada before 1981, now appear as institutionalized features of the social welfare landscape.

At a time of shrinking resources, social work services are being rationed more and more according to the criteria of risk and deservingness. The "new managerialism" pressures workers to do more with less and to become increasingly "efficient and effective in rationing their chosen interventions at the same time as demand for their services is rising dramatically" (Dominelli 2004, 3). Social workers often find they are carrying heavier caseloads while the demands for their accountability increase; they must also adhere to recording requirements that are becoming more onerous, legalistic, and often technologically based. (For the dilemmas it raises for practitioners in child welfare and hospital-based settings, see Aronson & Sammon 2000; also Swift 2001 & Callahan 2001.)

In times of cutbacks and neo-liberal attacks on social welfare, the relationships between clients and workers may be even more likely to reproduce and exacerbate gender and other inequities. Social work today concentrates on ensuring that the social welfare relationship is underpinned by non-authoritarian, non-discriminatory, and collaborative values. (For more discussion, see Gil 1998.) The challenge this poses to individual workers is both more elusive and more essential than ever. The expectations of women's caring and the social services available reflect the paradoxes and ambiguities that pervade women's relation to the welfare state. Although the social control aspects of this relationship are emphasized most often, and indeed they are very apparent, this perspective can portray women as passive victims all too easily. This focus neglects the very active role that women themselves have taken in initiating and shaping services on behalf of their children and themselves. They have worked to expand the boundaries of the welfare state, by articulating demands for needed services and by creating their own services—shelters, counselling, and resource centres. Ironically, social welfare today both constricts and extends their options.

CONCLUSION

This chapter begins to unravel women's relationship with social welfare by considering their role in its development. It examines some of the assumptions that structure Canadian social policies and social services and explores their implications for women. The analysis becomes more important as reductions in social service funding take their toll on women, who form the majority of both users and providers.

Analyses of gender have had a longer history of taking class into account, and such studies are now making greater efforts to understand and integrate the processes of racialization. There continues to be a considerable challenge, however, to considering the contradictions, the paradoxes, and the dilemmas that thread through the fabric of women's relation to the welfare state. While this chapter points out the ways that social welfare has, at times, expanded their choices, it also clearly identifies the ways that it limits them.

Restructuring social welfare in ways that do not put women at a disadvantage requires a much more active role on the part of government. The state must share the caring equitably between men, women, and itself. This requires a network of guaranteed services that does not depend on women's, and other family members', acknowledgement of their failures and inadequacies in order to access those services. These only become more urgent as Canada's elderly population increases in number and age, and mothers primarily, and fathers, continue to scramble to secure adequate, accessible, and affordable child care.

The first step in repositioning the relationship between the state and Canadian women's caring is to recognize that individuals comprise families, yet what is good for "the family" may not be equally good, or equitable, for each of its members. This in turn requires "the recognition of women's rights to benefits as *individuals*, as well as the priorization of a *collective* commitment by society to the care of children, the elderly, the frail and the otherwise dependent, in ways which respect their needs and wishes" (Williams 1989, 68). Proposals that simply compensate women for the caring labour they do, without redistributing that work, do not address the problem that women are overwhelmingly the ones who carry out that work. Although some have suggested that the policy problem should be identified as one of men's independence rather than women's dependence (Cass 1994), the most important challenge may be to recognize the interdependence of both sexes.

Women connect to the welfare state in a variety of ways: as clients, as workers, and as a diverse range of individuals who are not all affected the same way by the poli-cies and the programs. Their relationships are full of contradictions and paradoxes.

Social programs can expand women's choices, limit options, engage people in ways that are helpful and in ways that are controlling and unhelpful. Future direc-tions must mean a reformulation of caring that includes a sensitive appraisal of the costs of our current social policies and a much wider scope for services. Concerns of cost-cutting and narrowly conceived notions of efficiency should not eclipse a larger commitment to socially just and non-oppressive programs and services. An approach that is sensitive to gender, in the context of diversity, marks an important step toward this objective.

NOTES

1. The labour force participation of married women with children under the age of 16 increased from 38 percent in 1976 to 72 percent in 2003 (Statistics Canada 2004).

2. These benefits require medical certification that there is a significant risk of death within six months.

3. Eichler also proposes that a small career allowance be paid to those who take care of others with socially recognized dependencies. This proposal is a subject of controversy among feminists (see Evans 1998).

4. In 1997, Quebec embarked on a major child care reform, making it universally available without regard to parental employment; space, however, has been an issue. For a discussion of Quebec and other provinces, see Jenson, Mahon, & Phillips, 2003.

REFERENCES

Agnew, V. 1996. *Resisting discrimination: Women from Asia, Africa, and the Caribbean and the women's movement in Canada.* Toronto: University of Toronto Press.

Arat-Koc, S. 1999. Gender and race in "non-discriminatory" immigration policies in Canada: 1960s to the present. In E. Dua & A. Robertson (Eds.), *Scratching the surface: Canadian anti-racist feminist thought* (pp. 207–233). Toronto: Women's Press.

Armstrong, P. 1996. Privatizing care. In P. Armstrong, H. Armstrong, J. Choiniere, E. Mykhalovskiy, & J. White (Eds.), *Medical alert: New organizations in health care* (pp. 29–54). Toronto: Garamond Press.

Aronson, J. 1998. Dutiful daughters and unde-manding mothers: Constraining images of giving and receiving care in middle and later life. In C. Baines, P. Evans, & S. Neysmith (Eds.), *Women's caring: Feminist perspectives on social welfare* (2d ed.) (pp. 114–138). Don Mills, ON: Oxford University Press.

Aronson, J., & Neysmith, S. 2001. Manufacturing social exclusion in the home care market. *Canadian Public Policy.* 27.2. 151–165.

Aronson, J., & Sammon, S. 2000. Practice amid social service cuts and restructuring: Working with the contradictions of "small victories." *Canadian Social Work Review* 17, 2. 169–187.

Baines, C. 1998. Women's professions and an ethic of care. In C. Baines, P. Evans, & S. Neysmith (Eds.), *Women's caring: Feminist perspectives on social welfare* (2d ed.) (pp. 23–46). Don Mills, ON: Oxford University Press.

Baines, C., Evans, P., & Neysmith, S. 1998. Women's caring: Work expanding, state contracting. In C. Baines, P. Evans, & S. Neysmith (Eds.), *Women's Caring: Feminist perspectives on social welfare* (2d ed.) (pp. 3–22). Don Mills, ON: Oxford University Press.

Baker, M. 2001. *Families, labour and love.* Vancouver: University of British Columbia Press.

Baker, M., & Phipps, S. 1997. Family change and family policies: Canada. In S. Kamerman & A. Kahn (Eds.), *Family change, family policies in Great Britain, Canada, New Zealand and the United States* (pp. 105–106). Oxford: Clarendon Press.

Battle, K., & Torjman, S. 1996. Desperately seeking substance: A commentary on the social security review. In J. Pulkingham & G. Ternowetsky (Eds.), *Remaking Canadian social policy: Social security in the late 1990s* (pp. 52–66). Halifax: Fernwood.

Brand, D. 1999. Black women and work: The impact of racially constructed roles on the sexual division of labour. In E. Dua & A. Robertson (Eds.), *Scratching the surface: Canadian anti-racist feminist thought* (pp. 83–96). Toronto: Women's Press.

Bristow, P. 1993. The hour-a-day study club. In L. Carty (Ed.), *And still we rise: Feminist political mobilizing in contemporary Canada* (pp. 145–172). Toronto: Women's Press.

Brodie, J. 1996. Restructuring and the new citizenship. In I. Bakker (Ed.), *Rethinking restructuring: Gender and change in Canada* (pp. 126–140). Toronto: University of Toronto Press.

Callahan, M. 2001. No: "These tools… do not reduce risk for children" in Debate: Risk assessment in child protection services. *Canadian Social Work Review.* 18.1. 157–162.

Callahan, M. 2004. Chalk and cheese: Feminist thinking and policy-making. In B. Wharf & B. MacKenzie (Eds.), *Connecting policy to practice in the human services* (2d ed.) (pp. 128–140). Don Mills, ON: Oxford.

Canadian Association of the Schools of Social Work. 2000. In *Critical demand; Social work in Canada: Overview of findings and strategic directions.* Ottawa: CASW. Available at **www.socialworkincanada.org**

Canadian Association of Social Workers (CASW). 2004. *Women's income and poverty in Canada revisited.* Ottawa: CASW.

Canadian Council on Social Development (CCSD). 2004a. *Nowhere to turn? Responding to partner violence against immigrant and visible minority women.* Ottawa: CCSD. Available at **www.ccsd.ca/pubs/2004/nowhere/**

Canadian Council on Social Development (CCSD). 2004b. *What kind of Canada? A call for a national debate on the Canada social transfer.* Ottawa: CCSD. Available at **www.ccsd.ca/pr/2004/social_transfer/st.htm**

Canadian Labour Congress (CLC). 2003. *Falling unemployment insurance protection for Canada's unemployed.* March. Retrieved May 3, 2004, from **www.unemployed.ca/Falling%20UI%20Protection%20for%20Canada%27s%20Unemployed.pdf**

Cass, B. 1994. Citizenship, work, and welfare: The dilemma for Australian women. *Social Politics* 1, 1.

Children's Aid Society of Metropolitan Toronto. n.d. *Fact sheet, 2002–2003.* Retrieved April 29, 2004, from **www.casmt.on.ca/Publicationsmainframe.htm**

Cooke-Reynolds, M., & Zukewich, N. Spring 2004. The feminization of work. *Canadian Social Trends.* 24–26. Statistics Canada Cat. No. 11-008.

Daenzer, P. 1997. Challenging diversity: Black women and social welfare. In C. Baines, P. Evans, & S. Neysmith (Eds.), *Women's caring: Feminist perspectives on social welfare* (2d ed.) (pp. 269–290). Don Mills, ON: Oxford University Press.

Davies, L., McMullin, J., & Avison, W., with Cassidy, G. February 2001. *Social policy, gender inequality and poverty*. Ottawa: Status of Women Canada.

Davis, A., & Brook, E. 1985. Women and social work. In E. Brook & A. Davis (Eds.), *Women, the family and social work* (pp. 3–27). London: Tavistock.

Day, S., & Brodsky, G. 1998. *Women and the equality deficit: The impact of restructuring Canada's social programs*. Ottawa: Status of Women Canada.

Dominelli, L. 2004. *Social work: Theory and practice for a changing profession*. Cambridge, UK: Polity Press.

Dua, E. 1999. Beyond diversity: Exploring the ways in which the discourse of race has shaped the institution of the nuclear family. In E. Dua & A. Robertson (Eds.), *Scratching the surface: Canadian anti-racist feminist thought* (pp. 237–259). Toronto: Women's Press.

Ecumenical Coalition for Economic Justice 1998. *Breakthrough for women in Canadian census*. Toronto: ECEJ.

Eichler, M. 1997. *Family shifts: Families, policies, and gender equality*. Don Mills, ON: Oxford University Press.

Evans, P. 2002. Downloading the welfare state, Canadian style. In G. Goldberg & M. Rosenthal (Eds.), *Diminishing welfare: A cross-national study of social provision* (pp. 75–102). Westport, CT: Auburn House.

Evans, P., & Wekerle, G. 1997. The shifting terrain of women's welfare: Theory, discourse, and activism. In P. Evans & G. Wekerle (Eds.), *Women and the Canadian welfare state: Challenges and change* (pp. 3–27). Toronto: University of Toronto Press.

George, U. 2000. Toward anti-racism in social work in the Canadian context. In A. Calliste & G. Dei (Eds.), *Anti-racist feminism: Critical race and gender studies* (pp. 111–122). Halifax: Fernwood.

Ghorayshi, P. 2002. Working Canadian women: Continuity despite change. In V. Dhruvarajan & J. Vickers (Eds.), *Gender, race, and nation* (pp. 123–146). Toronto: University of Toronto Press.

Gil, D. 1998. *Confronting injustice and oppression: Concepts and strategies for social workers*. New York: Columbia University Press.

Graham, H. 1983. Caring: a labour of love. In J. Finch & D. Groves (Eds.), *A labour of love: Women, work and caring* (pp. 13–30). London: Routledge and Kegan Paul.

Guberman, N. 1988. The family, women, and caring: Who cares for the carers? *Resources for Feminist Research*. 17.2. 37–40.

Hanmer, J., & Statham, D. 1988. *Women and social work: Towards a woman-centred practice*. London: Macmillan.

Human Resources Development Canada n.d. *More parents spend critical first year with their children in 2001*. Retrieved on May 11, 2004, from **www.hrdc-drhc.gc.ca/common/news/insur/021106.shtml**

Jenson, J., Mahon, R., & Phillips. S. 2003. No minor matter: The political economy of childcare in Canada. In W. Clement & L. Vosko (Eds.), *Changing Canada: Political economy as transformation*. Montreal and Kingston: McGill-Queen's University Press.

Kenyon, G. 1997. Gender and income among Ontario social workers: The source of disparity. *Canadian Social Work Review*. 14.2. 155–166.

Krane, J. 2003. *What's mother got to do with it? Protecting children from sexual abuse*. Toronto: University of Toronto Press.

Lewis, J. 1986. Feminism and welfare. In J. Mitchell & A. Oakley (Eds.), *What is feminism? A re-examination* (pp. 85–100). New York: Pantheon.

Little, M. Spring 1999. The limits of Canadian democracy: The citizenship rights of poor women, *Canadian Review of Social Policy.* 43. 59–76.

Lundy, C. 2004. *Social work and social justice: A structural approach to practice.* Peterborough: Broadview.

McKeen, W., & Porter, A. 2003. Politics and transformation: Welfare state restructuring in Canada. In W. Clement & L. Vosko (Eds.), *Changing Canada: Political economy as transformation* (pp. 109–134). Montreal and Kingston: McGill-Queen's University Press.

McWatt, S., & Neysmith, S. 1998. Enter the Filipina nanny: An examination of Canada's live-in caregiver policy. In C. Baines, P. Evans, & S. Neysmith (Eds.), *Women's caring: Feminist perspectives on social welfare* (2d. ed.) (pp. 218–232). Don Mills, ON: Oxford University Press.

Ministry of Community, Family and Children's Services 2004. Statistics and Analysis Unit, Ontario Disability Support Program Branch, March 19; calculated from tables provided through e-mail communication.

Mitchinson, W. 1987. Early women's organizations and social reform: Prelude to the welfare state. In A. Moscovitch & J. Albert (Eds.), *The "benevolent" state: The growth of welfare in Canada* (pp. 77–92). Toronto: Garamond Press.

Morris, M., Robinson, J., Simpson, J. November 1999. *The changing nature of home care and its impact on women's vulnerability to poverty.* Ottawa: Status of Women Canada.

Mosher, J., Evans, P., & Little, M. 2004. *Walking on eggshells: Abused women's experiences of Ontario's welfare system.* Final Report of Research Findings from the Woman and Abuse Welfare Research Project. April 5. Available at **www.yorku. ca/yorkweb/special/Welfare_Report_ walking_on_eggshells_final_report.pc**

Mossman, M., & MacLean, M. 1997. Family law and social assistance programs: Rethinking

equality. In P. Evans & G. Wekerle (Eds.), *Women and the Canadian welfare state: Challenges and change* (pp. 117–141). Toronto: University of Toronto Press.

Mullaly, B. 2002. *Challenging oppression: A critical social work approach.* Don Mills, ON: Oxford University Press.

National Anti-Poverty Organization. 1998. *Government expenditure cuts to health care and post-secondary education: Impacts on low-income Canadians.* Ottawa: NAPO.

National Council of Welfare. Spring 2003. *Welfare incomes, 2002.* Ottawa: NCW.

Neysmith, S. 2003. Caring and aging: Exposing the policy issues. In A. Westhues (Ed.), *Canadian social policy: Issues and perspectives* (3d ed.), (pp. 182–199). Waterloo, ON: Wilfrid Laurier Press.

Ontario Association of Interval and Transition Houses (OAITH). 2003. *Choose to change this.* Retrieved November 30, 2003, from **http://dawn.thot.net/oaith.html**

Pascall, G. 1997. *Social policy: A new feminist analysis* (2d ed.). London and New York: Routledge.

Picard, A. 1999. Balancing work and home tasks raising women's blood pressure. *Globe and Mail* (March 29): A6.

Rankin, L. P., & Vickers, J. 2001. *Women's movements and state feminism: Integrating diversity into public policy.* Ottawa: Status of Women Canada.

Rice, J., & Prince, M. 2000. *Changing politics of Canadian social policy.* Toronto: University of Toronto Press.

Shillington, R. 2001. *Access to maternity benefits.* Retrieved on October 20, 2003, from **www.shillington.ca/benefits/Maternity_ Benefits.doc**

Social Development Canada. February 2004. *Statistical bulletin: Canada Pension Plan and Old Age Security.* Retrieved May 12, 2004, from **www.sdc.gc.ca/en/isp/statistics/ pdf/statbulletin0204.pdf**

Social Planning Council of Metropolitan Toronto. 1997. *Profile of a changing world, 1996: Community agency survey*. Toronto: City of Toronto and Social Planning Council of Metropolitan Toronto.

Statistics Canada. 2002. *2001 Census. Population 15 years and over by hours spent looking after children, without pay, provinces and territories*. Retrieved on April 19, 2004, from **www.statcan.ca/english/Pgdb/famil58a.htm** and Population 15 years and over by hours spent providing unpaid care or assistance to seniors, provinces and territories. Retrieved on April 19, 2004, from **www.statcan.ca/english/Pgdb/famil57a.htm**

Statistics Canada. 2004. *Women in Canada: Work chapter updates*. Retrieved on April 19, 2004, from **www.statcan.ca/english/freepub/89F0133XIE/89F0133XIE2003000.pdf**

Status of Women Canada. September 1998. *Gender-based analysis: A guide for policy-making*. Ottawa: Status of Women Canada,.

Struthers, J. 1987. Lord give us men: Women and social work in English Canada, 1918–1953. In A. Moscovitch & J. Albert (Eds.), *The "benevolent" state: The growth of welfare in Canada* (pp. 126–143). Toronto: Garamond Press.

Swift, K. 1998. Contradictions in child welfare: Neglect and responsibility. In P. Evans &

G. Wekerle (Eds.), *Women and the Canadian welfare state: Challenges and change* (pp. 160–187). Toronto: University of Toronto Press.

Swift, K. 2001. The case for opposition: Challenging contemporary child welfare policy directions. *Canadian Review of Social Policy*. 47. 59–76.

Teghtsoonian, K. 2000. Gendering policy analysis in the government of British Columbia: Strategies, possibilities and constraints. *Studies in Political Economy*. 61 (Spring), 105–127.

Thomas, C. 1993. De-constructing concepts of care. *Sociology*. 27.4. 649–669.

Townson, M. March 2003. *Women in nonstandard jobs: The public policy challenge*. Ottawa: Status of Women Canada.

Vickers, J., & Dhruvarajan, V. 2002. Gender, race and nation. In V. Dhruvarajan & J. Vickers (Eds.), *Gender, race, and nation: A global perspective* (pp. 25–63). Toronto: University of Toronto Press.

Williams, F. 1989. *Social policy: A critical introduction*. Cambridge: Polity Press.

Wills, G. 1992. Values of community practice: Legacy of the radical social gospel. *Canadian Social Work Review*. 9, 1, 28–40.

Wilson, E. 1977. *Women and the welfare state*. London: Tavistock/

chapter eleven

Canada's Ethno-Racial Diversity: Policies and Programs in Canadian Social Welfare

Dorothy Chave Herberg

Edward N. Herberg

INTRODUCTION

This chapter surveys the changes in the ethno-racial[1] composition of Canadian society and how this has influenced and will affect our social welfare policies and programs. The chapter has three sections. First, we examine the alteration in ethno-racial mix of Canadians and development of social welfare for minority ethno-racial communities. Then we analyze issues of cultural identity in human-service relationships, especially those that affect the client and the worker. The final section posits models for service delivery and ways that ethno-racial community and mainstream agencies can and should share their expertise to mutually benefit their joint constituencies.

Aboriginal peoples are affected in quite different ways than the ethno-racial communities that immigrated here, first because the inherent human rights of First Nations and the Inuit were all illegally abrogated over the past four hundred years. Now, they are beginning to benefit from the new special relationships with federal and provincial governments and the transformation to various forms of Aboriginal self-governance engendered by successful court challenges, and changes in government policies, especially the lesser reluctance of governments to negotiate land and rights treaties. These issues were addressed in Chapter 9, Aboriginal Peoples in Canada.

POLICIES AND PROGRAMS FOR MINORITY ETHNO-RACIAL COMMUNITIES

The Emergence of Ethno-Racial Community Social Agencies in Canada

The changing ethno-racial composition of the Canadian population, owing mainly to the increase in visible minority immigrants here, has resulted in immense alterations in national, provincial, and municipal social-welfare policies and programs. Between 1900 and 1930, nearly 4.6 million people immigrated to Canada (E. N. Herberg, 60–65], to enter a society only in the adolescence of its industrial development.

Back then, most Canadians were rural residents and socially segregated by race, ethnicity, religion, birthplace, and social class. Social policy of the pre–World War II era was based on family self-sufficiency, and the state was the last resort for aid. Thus, to sustain people who needed aid before the Great Depression, mutual aid or "mutual-benefit" organizations were developed within urban neighbourhoods and especially within immigrant communities. The meagre funds that could be raised went first to maintaining families, and then to English-language courses and job training, so that the immigrants could achieve economic security. After these needs were met, additional funds went to other community services, such as cultural and recreational institutions. Of major importance to the development of these ethno-racial community agencies was the financing by or under the direct aegis of the immigrants' places of worship (Harney, 1978, 1979).

Post-World War II Developments

In contrast, for the more than 4.4 million immigrants who entered Canada between 1951 and 1981, a generation later, Canada's social values had become very different. In 1961 Canada was a post-industrial society, with nearly half its population residing in cities of more than 100 000 people, with tremendous pressure to integrate the new Canadians into the burgeoning workforce.[2] Moreover, the ethno-racial composition of the Canadian population in this period began to change very rapidly, with the new, more objective "Points System" criteria experimentally applied to immigrant selection from 1962 to 1967. The Points System was integral to the colour-blind Immigration Act of 1968, which had replaced the notoriously racist criteria of earlier immigrant selection.

In the 1980s and 1990s, Canada welcomed more than 2.2 million immigrants. That rate has continued into the twenty-first century (Citizenship and Immigration Canada, to 1989; CIC website, 1990 to 2003). Before 1960, visible minorities constituted less than 1 percent of the immigrants to Canada, and only about 13 percent during the 1960s. During the 1970s, though, they amounted to 41 percent of all the immigrants admitted. In 1991 this number had grown so much that nearly three-quarters (71 percent) of Canada's immigrants came from Third World nations—that is, countries with visible minority residents. More than one-third of Canada's immigrants (40 percent) now come from Asian nations: China, Hong Kong (now a province of China), the Indian subcontinent, the Philippines, Vietnam, and other ex-Indochinese nations, and another 35 percent or so visible minority persons come from other countries (CIC website, 2000–2003). In 1961, immigrants comprised about one-sixth of Canada's population; this proportion has been rising slowly but steadily since the late 1980s and today has reached 18 percent. Given the government's policy to maintain high immigration levels, perhaps as high as 1 percent of the total population annually, the number of immigrants among Canadians will continue to increase.

In 1941, the British constituted just less than half of the population. From the end of World War II, Canada has increasingly been a nation of ethno-racial minorities. As recently as 1981, the visible minorities made up only 6 percent of Canadians, the British another 44 percent, and the French 27 percent (E. N. Herberg, 1989, 40–41). By 2001, however, visible-minority Canadians had increased to 14 percent, while single-origin British declined to a mere 9 percent and single-origin French to but 4 percent of all Canadians[3] (Statistics Canada website, January 2003). Slowly over those decades, minority-community ethnocultural agencies,[4] originally founded and funded within each minority's ethno-racial community for its own members, came to be endorsed and subsidized by the United Way, as well as all levels of government. This institutionalization of ethno-racial community service agencies transformed them from an officially ignored, residual resource into an indispensable element in Canada. From that point on, they would require that economic and social benefits be realized from the full use of all Canadian residents' education and skills.

The pressures generated by the vast numbers of immigrants, and their being mostly visible minorities, combined with the enactment and improvement of our human rights legislation. These forces shifted our legal, economic, and social welfare principles to more egalitarian lines. In the 1960s, the provinces and the federal government enacted human rights codes, which assured protection from discrimination on the basis of ethnicity, race, religion, birthplace, and such. Perhaps more important, these codes also mandated commissions to adjudicate complaints of discrimination. Then, on October 8, 1971, Prime Minister Pierre Elliott Trudeau announced in the House of Commons that cultural pluralism—"multiculturalism"—was henceforth to be Canada's official policy.

Constitutional ethno-racial minority rights were realized 11 years later with the inclusion of the Charter of Rights and Freedoms in our new constitution. The charter guarantees cultural, racial, and religious pluralism. It not only prohibits discrimination on these grounds and legitimizes federal and provincial anti-discrimination programs, but it establishes that it must be "interpreted in a manner consistent with the multicultural heritage of Canadians" (*The Charter of Rights and Freedoms: A Guide for Canadians*, 1982, Section 27). These principles were further expanded by the Canadian Multiculturalism Act of 1988, which asserted in part that the government would act "in the elimination of any barrier to full and equitable participation... in social, cultural, economic and political institutions..." (Canada, Multicultural Ministry, 1998).

These developments produced egalitarian shifts in both policy and attitudes between the so-called charter and the country's ethno-racial and religious minorities. Canadians no longer viewed themselves as a nation of disparate groups, isolated by race, culture, and birth, but as a nation whose hallmark now was cultural diversity. Thus, differences from the cultural mores of the "founding" British and French groups no longer constituted legal or moral impediments; rather, they reflected the shift to equality within the "mosaic"—cultural heterogeneity.

Shifts in the composition of ethno-racial social welfare agencies and their services paralleled these developments. Since the beginning of the post–World War II wave of immigrants, ethnic agencies had begun to diversify to meet the most recent newcomers' needs, and also of the pre-war generation of immigrants, as well as their adult, Canadian-born children. With the passage of the Canada Assistance Plan in 1966, these agencies were relieved of their income maintenance role.

At the same time, the changed needs of both older and younger generations within ethno-racial communities stimulated development of new programs to serve needs that had not existed since the 1930s— English- or French-language training, employment orientation, job-skills training for recent immigrants. In addition, family and personal counselling were set up to address several new problems, between the original and more recent immigrants, between immigrant and Canadian-born generations, and between the cultural traditionalists within a minority community and the more egalitarian gender and age roles of post-industrial Canada (Ontario Council of Agencies Serving Immigrants, 1990).

Ethnic community agencies, especially before World War II, clearly were the resource of choice for meeting their members' social needs. Even with the high immigration levels beginning in the 1950s, and especially after the changed immigrant source-countries since the 1970s, ethnic agencies have faced increased demands for almost every kind of social and occupational service. Even the Canadian-born generations in minority communities found it daunting to seek service from ethnic, racial, or religious strangers with little knowledge and often little respect for their cultural traditions. As a result, their own community agencies, which extended respectful empathy for their cultural values, were the first, and often the sole choice for social service. Because so many new immigrant-refugee communities exist in Canada's metropolis, probably even more today than in the 1950s and 1960s, the primacy of the ethnic community agencies continues (Allmen, 1990; Medeiros, 1990). Agencies of the larger, older minority communities that had been operating for decades often stand at the forefront of social service innovation, going

far beyond the ability or interest of the mainstream public or private agencies to cater to the specific needs of ethno-racial and religious minority clients. Indeed, over the past 30 years, many ethnic agencies have extended their services to clients beyond their own groups, to other ethno-racial communities. In part they found themselves responding to fewer demands for services by their own community members. Mainly, however, they recognized the critically pressing need of members of the newer immigrant communities for the services they could provide. The new groups had too few members themselves or/and inadequate resources to develop their own agencies. Also, the ethno-racial community agencies of today have become almost "establishment" entities in their breadth of experience, financing, and personnel, and in their ability to serve minority clients.

Thus, word of mouth and the burgeoning ethnic media informed prospective clients of the great diversity of services available to them, including precisely those the newcomers needed: English-language (or French-language) training, orientation to Canada, skills training and job searching, family and personal counselling, and the like. Since the mid-1990s, too, governments had decreased their funding to ethnic agencies, and this fact gave more impetus to the established agencies to invite the clients of other communities to approach them. They also solicited applications from the members of those communities who were not represented by their own agencies. In the best Canadian fashion of combining pragmatism and altruism, the largest and frequently the oldest and most experienced agencies within long-established communities adapted first to serving members outside their own groups. In addition, they served as advisers to enable the newer communities to establish agencies of their own.

Outside the minority communities, social welfare perspectives and programs had to adapt to both the spirit of the charter and to governments' multicultural mandates. Immigrants from literally all nations were arriving with overt and rapidly growing needs for social welfare services. This pressure also induced leading mainstream agencies to begin to provide services that the ethnic agencies had delivered previously. Soon, both federal and provincial agencies began offering various economic services—language training, occupational skills courses or skills upgrading to Canadian standards, and so on. Often, governments contracted out the delivery of these services to the private sector—frequently by the very ethnocultural community agencies that had inaugurated the services.

SOCIAL WELFARE NEEDS OF REFUGEES

Over the past 40 or so years, refugees have comprised from 6 percent to 24 percent of all immigrants. Since 1980, the period of Canada's heaviest intake of refugees, they have averaged 14 percent of the overall immigrant inflow. They made up their highest percentages in 1980, 1989–1991, and 1993–1994. Yet they comprised the smallest segment of immigrants in the early 1980s and between 1997 and 2002 (Canada Immigration Commission website, 2003).

For refugees, the problems of adjustment and settlement are much more complex and difficult than they are for those other immigrants who are able to plan and prepare for their immigration here. Not only are refugees' arrivals usually preceded by arduous, often dangerous journeys, but their flights are usually precipitated by strife—social, ethnoracial, religious, or political—even war. Many of them have been the victims of horrific torture or atrocities or have witnessed these abuses. These newcomers to Canada require social welfare services of an extraordinary sort. These had not been

developed, even within the ethnic communities, before refugee acceptance became a Canadian priority (Allodi et al., 1986; D. C. Herberg & E. N. Herberg, 1987). Never had Canada admitted so many refugees before the 1970s, especially from the Third World.

Evolution within the Mainstream Agencies

Over the past few decades, only certain mainstream agencies have managed to provide culturally responsive services to their clients from minority communities (E. N. Herberg, 1991). These agencies have transformed their organizational values, processes, and practices to complement, not contradict, their clients' cultures. These services are often those not available within the cultural community, either because the ethnic agency cannot obtain the funding or it is unable to hire and retain the highly trained, experienced staff it needs (E. N. Herberg, 1991; D. C. Herberg & E. N. Herberg, forthcoming).

Mainstream social welfare agencies' perceptions and policies can be insensitive and oppressive to minorities of different races, cultural norms, and experiences. Two barriers in this regard continue to prevent this practice's becoming the norm rather than the exception. First, agency managers and their staffs are not sufficiently knowledgeable to offer culturally responsive services, or to implement the necessary structural, and technological alterations. Nor has this philosophy of operating been clearly communicated to their personnel. Second, too many professional education facilities and agency directors and their staffs are unable or reluctant to force their services to evolve from offering generic services for every client to offering the same service to each client regardless of multicultural diversity and with respect for all cultures and norms.

CULTURAL IDENTITY ISSUES IN THE HELPING RELATIONSHIP

Special critical considerations relating to the life experiences of refugees, regular immigrants, and other ethno-racial minority clients emerge when using the contexting framework to set social welfare policy, practice, and programs for these client groups.

Contexting is a method and process by which the people providing the services acquire knowledge and understanding of the socio-cultural contexts within which their clients live. They can then serve their clients within their own cultural contexts by employing resources in ways that complement, not contradict, those cultural contexts.

Cultural Prescriptions

All immigrants bring to Canada complete repertoires of cultural patterns and behaviours that cover every aspect of their social lives. Depending upon their specific cultural traditions, immigrants also bring varying expectations about their interactions with others here.

High-context peoples or communities are socialized to a set of kin and of relationships in which the expectations that shaped these relationships were laid out completely from birth. Each comes equipped with an implicit understanding of what is expected of each person within that network of relationships. Just as implicit in these people's experiences are the social contexts of other people's behaviour. So this understanding does not have to be explained before each interaction (Hall, 1976).

Definitions and expectations of the self, of family, and of community are transported whole from patterns rooted in each person's home country. Ideas and values about work and play, politics and religion, health and illness, discipline and freedom, success and adversity, rights and obligations, and giving and receiving help are as carefully packed and carried to Canada as are their physical belongings.

For high-context persons, the basis of help and control lies in the extended family. Decisions are made within an established hierarchy, men and women behave according to their gender-segregated roles. They find help in the comprehensive interdependencies within their families. They believe good fortune lies in their paying proper attention to the holistic balance of forces, maintaining a respectful connection to the supernatural in its myriad forms, and devoting careful attention to maintaining the continuity of their past and their future.

In contrast, *low-context* peoples have very few, or just vestiges of, expectations for interactions with their kin and others. Rather, they learn to construct a different social context for each new situation or person. Whereas low-context people quickly seek out professional help for illness and other problems, high-context people turn first to fellow family members and their fully developed network of connections between tradition and their immediate circumstances (see Table 11.1).

CULTURE SHIFT

Many factors contribute to a family's or an individual's decision to leave the home country. In the past, millions felt "pulled" to the better opportunities offered by the New World. Although "push" factors have always existed, in many ways the "push" now seems to predominate. Today environmental, political, economic, and civil instability have motivated huge refugee populations to emigrate from so many places. When people arrive in Canada as refugees, they often have lived for months, even years, in a marginal state while officials decided the validity of their claims to their refugee status.

TABLE 11.1	Values in High- and Low-Context Cultures	
High-Context Values	**versus**	**Low-Context Values**
1. The family unit is central		The individual is central
2. Members are hierarchically ordered		Members are egalitarian
3. Men and women are segregated		Men and women are integrated
4. All are highly interdependent		Independence is paramount
5. The society is religious		Secularism is dominant
6. Traditions are unquestioned		Everything is questioned
7. Time is polychronic		Time is monochronic
8. Approach is holistic		Approach is fragmentary and analytical
9. Communication is oral		Communication is written
10. Place of origin is important		Mobility is essential

Source: D. C. Herberg. 1993. Education for Cultural and Racial Diversity. Toronto: Canadian Scholars' Press, pp. 35–65.

For these and other immigrants, once people have made the decision to leave their home countries—or been forced to leave—the process begins whereby these people become "landed" and they begin their residency in Canada. This process of immigration can involve enormous changes, not just for those immigrating but also for the residents of the host nation, depending on the specifics of the transition. The process produces a "culture shift" for both immigrants and Canadians.

The legal events at the immigrants' time of arrival are very important for Canada as the country of destination. The host country must accept control of taking in the new residents, and the newcomers must qualify for admission as such under specific legislated criteria. While the relative importance placed on the various classes of immigrants changes somewhat, it is likely that, first, refugees will continue to be an important, if not very large, category in the years ahead. Second, in order for Canada to grow as a nation with a native birth rate far below what is required to maintain, let alone increase, our workforce, the country will need a large inflow of people over the foreseeable decades. Among the most important and numerous of immigrant categories is the family class, wherein relatives of Canadian residents are sponsored, to reunite people with their families.

One of the critical social welfare issues related to Canadian immigration is the scores of thousands of people living here who are illegal immigrants. At times professionals have had to deal with requests for services by people who are not legal residents; the social worker must decide how to proceed. In some agencies, policies and procedures are flexible, allowing illegals to obtain service—for example, children are permitted to enrol in school. At other agencies, staff must adhere strictly to requirements—for example, they cannot accept illegals as clients under any circumstances. Many non-governmental organizations bridge this gap by aiding illegals who are unable to obtain even the most necessary service from government offices.

Settlement Period

The period of immigrants' initial adaptation to Canada is called the "settlement period." It is difficult to state any definite time frame for this. For some immigrants, it can be as long as five or six years. Those who have benefited from advanced education and positive experiences in previous moves generally adapt in shorter times. Other parts of Canadian society such as the education and health care systems face enormous policy problems in serving illegal adults and children. Social welfare workers often find themselves embroiled in these dilemmas.

To "settle" in a Canadian community, new immigrants must pass through a few cycles of the seasons. Every sphere of living has a rhythm, and until newcomers experience and understand the many rhythms in their new place of residence, they are likely to feel off balance and unsettled. Disman ([1990]) has described this phenomenon as immigrants having "broken images," not understanding what and how things are done in Canada, and feeling like strangers for sometimes very long periods.

Government-funded programs provide services for newcomers for particular purposes and for varying lengths of time. They may be administered either by private agencies on contract or by government social welfare agencies helping with residence needs such as finding jobs, accessing transportation, translating documents, and using legal services. Moreover, if immigrants/refugees are "illegal," then the settlement issues affecting them will be much more complex, including many sorts of distress, such as fear of detection and apprehension, exploitation by employers, and lack of equal opportunity for both the children and the adults in the family.

The psychosocial process of settlement is often complex and agonizing. Long ago,

Sluzki (1979) developed the concepts of "overcompensation" and "decompensation" to illuminate certain aspects of this process. *Overcompensation* refers to the initial period after a person's arrival, when she experiences great excitement and may ignore or not experience negative feelings about the transition. *Decompensation* refers to the person's feelings of loss, homesickness, and doubts that can later set in. Such doubts can take the form of questions persons in this position ask themselves, such as "Where am I?" "Why did I leave?" "What do I (or we) do now?" and even "Who am I?" These can cause considerable stress and anxiety.

Helping professionals can assure clients going through this phase that their fears will subside—given that their basic needs are provided for—and that they will regain a balance in their feelings. Of course, for refugees who have suffered torture, deprivation, and other severe trauma, the processes of overcompensation and decompensation may not follow a standard course. Instead, as the literature documents, these newcomers may suffer ongoing emotional disturbances and other mental health and social problems (Allodi et al., 1986) These people require very specialized services, available only at a few agencies, and in only the largest cities.

ETHNO-RACIAL IDENTITY OF PROFESSIONALS AND CLIENTS

Social welfare professionals need to understand that people—immigrants as well as the Canadian-born—relate to their own cultures in different ways. Some cling to their traditional values with all their emotional and moral strength. Others abandon many of their original customs and mores, actively rejecting the "old ways." In between are those who gradually acculturate in Canada and learn new ways bit by bit. Some minority communities tolerate changes for males, but are wary of comparable role changes for females. Moreover, most people who perceive and accept their origins in other countries clearly continue to maintain their ethno-racial identities and connections to their specific communities, even if attenuated ones (Driedger, 2003, Chapter 6, 125–136; E. N. Herberg, 1989, Chapters 4–9; Isajiw, 1999, 199–205).

It is crucial, therefore, that professionals gain the skills to gauge their clients' original cultures and their central parameters. Service providers cannot make headway in client relationships when they misunderstand their clients' cultural values, or, worse, trample on them. In a perhaps unrecognized fashion, this inattention to client culture violates the value-primacy of client self-determination in social welfare and several sections of the Charter of Rights and Freedoms.

Social workers and other helping professionals therefore must develop the capability to adapt to client systems as each exists. There is no better preparation for this reality than agencies' training their staff and their own experiences to aid them in developing this self-awareness about their own cultural values and identities.

We have pointed out that client cultures invariably are perceived from the vantage point of the service provider's own culture, even if this process is an unconscious one. Consequently, a vital component of the training and professional discipline required by those working with people from other ethno-racial minority communities is learning to recognize and appreciate their own values, in order to refrain from imposing them on their clients. Only when social welfare professionals have become comfortable with and respectful of their own cultures can they can deliver services to benefit clients of differing cultures.[5]

ETHNO-RACIAL DISCRIMINATION IN CANADIAN SOCIETY

We maintain that many of the current problems and needs of both ethno-racial communities and the mainstream agencies that serve them stem from ethno-racial discrimination. We also contend that it is unintended for the most part. The human rights codes and especially the Charter of Rights and Freedoms and the anti-discrimination legislation emanating from these extinguished the structural discrimination that had existed in Canada since the arrival of the Europeans.

However, two forms of ethno-racial discrimination still exist. *Institutional* discrimination[6]—the presence of discriminatory practices and barriers, intentional or inadvertent in some of society's institutions—persists in many social agencies, preventing clients access to social resources or rewards that are readily available to members of the dominant ethnic group. Because this practice is blatantly illegal, the prevalence of intentional discrimination has declined, but unintended discrimination in agencies continues to be a pernicious affront to the ability of minority clients to obtain equitable services.

Personal discrimination also exists. A staff member plays a crucial "gatekeeping" position in an organization—manager, personnel officer, supervisor or team leader, counsellor, service provider—and through personal prejudices may block minority clients' access to social welfare services available to non-minorities. Personal discrimination is particularly troublesome as it is difficult to detect and to demonstrate and prevent.

For immigrants, being victims of discrimination, perhaps for the first time, can be shocking. The helplessness they feel is exacerbated by their lack of knowledge of the societal values and standards in their new home. Also, people of ethno-racial minorities who have a long history in Canada generally have suffered some forms of long-term discrimination. These Canadians tend to be continually on their guard against the knife edge of prejudice and discrimination. Members of visible minorities feel forced by events into the stance of being ever vigilant, prepared to defend themselves from discrimination in every new encounter with members of other groups. That they fall victim to discrimination in social welfare agencies, the very places they come to for aid, offends the democratic values that Canadians espouse so proudly.

Discrimination is a pervasive and virulent social pestilence that handicaps all who do not share the dominant ethnicity and who cannot do so because of their colour or their minority cultures. Ethnoracial discrimination produces a myriad of social pathologies that must be eliminated with social welfare policies that implement, rather than ignore, the charter and the human rights codes. This is the only way we can guarantee that we reach the goal of ethno-racial equity. Though we and others (such as Herberg & Herberg, 1987) have long remonstrated against such social agency-based discrimination, it still exists.

Ethnic Communities

Practitioners also need to learn about their clients' ethnic communities because those communities serve as resources in language, cultural, and clinical matters. After all, we share the deeper meanings of cultural ceremonies and traditions with our fellow family members or our communities. The term "communities" here refers to the collectivities of people with whom clients feel a cultural connection, based on same ethnicity, geographic origin, race, and/or religion.

At this subtle nexus, certain ideas must be explored regarding social welfare policies and programs for minority ethnoracial communities. The people in these communities and the communities themselves evolve and change in unique ways, depending on their circumstances in their ancestral homes and their current situations in Canada. Of particular importance is the number of the ethnic community's members and the community's size in relation to its surrounding city or region. This information often determines how institutionally complete each particular ethno-racial community is.[7] The establishment of these communities' places of worship, cultural education, economic organizations, including retail stores, recreational and cultural organizations, social welfare and health agencies, media, and governance[8] makes it possible for group members to plan a full development and expansion of their community for the future. Obviously, their ethnic institutions also serve as resources for social welfare agencies.

Furthermore, most members of a minority community, whether immigrant or Canadian-born, are raised in and retain a particular cluster of religious, language, political, and social-class compositions. To outsiders, the central variables of this "ethno-racial community" cannot be perceptible, let alone understood. All that may be obvious is that a certain set of people share a language and perhaps a physical appearance, attend the same "ethnic" event, and so forth. Group members' deeper beliefs, such as the religious creeds they share, their socio-political ideologies, their perceptions about their situation and treatment in Canada, and their expectations for the future are neither familiar to nor can be understood by outsiders.

Moreover, when there are active ethno-racial institutional structures, they can act as a brake to individuals' adaptation. "Old-country ways" and even the ethnocultural forms that were developed in Canada can retain primacy over the push toward assimilation to dominant ethnicity or mainstream norms and mores in Canada. This is especially the case for group members who perceive themselves historically or/and currently as the victims of prejudice and discrimination. Therefore such structural features of minority communities require that social welfare agency staff be specially trained to enable them to provide appropriate services in a culture-respecting fashion.

MODELS OF SERVICE DELIVERY

Partnerships of Ethnic and Mainstream Agencies

Matsuoka and Sorenson (1991) identify four typologies of how social services can be delivered to ethno-racial minorities:

1. generic services (all get the same service for the same need) provided in mainstream agencies

2. ethno-racial community agencies providing to their own group members resources parallel to those of the mainstream generic agencies

3. the multicultural agency, serving a multiplicity of minority ethno-racial clients

4. a "bridging" structure, in which mainstream agencies have a cadre of service providers for their few minority clients

We recommend a fifth model that Matsuoka and Sorenson have not, one that has emerged since the mid-1980s:

5. mainstream agencies and ethno-racial community agencies forging partnerships

that actively seek to serve a multicultural clientele with both kinds of agencies

This last point draws on the special qualifications and expertise of both mainstream and minority sectors to better serve these constituencies (Herberg & Herberg, 1987). Such partnerships need not be restricted to special projects of government services, such as child welfare services involving selected ethno-racial communities. They can extend to routine services available from either mainstream or ethnic agencies. Ethno-racial community agencies have been pleased to meet requests to train mainstream agency staff in the principles and intricacies of serving clients from their own communities. Likewise, mainstream agencies usually welcome the opportunity to act as consultants and trainers to upgrade the skills of service providers in ethnic agencies, who sometimes are undereducated for their jobs.

Implications for Mainstream Agencies

Mainstream agencies generally use generic modes of service. Yet this approach has long been recognized as counterproductive to serve those constituencies whose cultures are neither the dominant British nor French cultures (Welin & Ervin, 1991). *All* mainstream agencies still employing a generic approach to service provision are actually violating both the intents and the words of the Canadian Constitution's Charter of Rights and Freedoms and of the Human Rights Code (HRC) provisions that guarantee equitable access and treatment to ethnic, racial, and religious minorities.

D. C. Herberg (1979, 1982, 1983) spelled out the steps to reverse this ethno-racial discrimination and fully implement the charter, HRCs, and the Multiculturalism

Act more than 20 years ago. The first is to mandate the delivery of ethno-racially sensitive services as official agency policy. Second, agencies should train all their staff members to transform them into "multicultural" service providers, capable of serving a polycultural client mix. This training begins by making individual staff members aware of their own ethno-racial-religious origins, and enabling them to identify and acknowledge their own feelings about their ethnic identities and cultures. This process is followed by one during which staff are given a basic knowledge of and respect and sensitivity to other cultures and races. The goal here is to connect the service providers' own cultural awareness to clinical applications, enabling them to be sensitive to their clients' cultural differences and needs. Their own cultural awareness becomes the starting point for their recognizing the most distinctive elements of others' cultural beliefs and customs (Roy, 1991). The use of translators complements these measures as needed, and so does the hiring of people of various minority backgrounds in the mainstream agencies as service providers themselves.

Thus, rather than contrasting the five models as mutually exclusive, we should consider them as evolving alternatives within Canadian social welfare. They are works in progress that are improving the knowledge base, relevance, and sensitivity with which all kinds of social agencies can better serve their many ethno-racial and religious constituencies.

CONCLUSION

It is obvious that social welfare in Canada must advance beyond the relatively few positive steps that only some mainstream social agencies have taken. Policy-makers and those implementing policy must apply existing knowledge about ethno-racial minority communities and their minority-community social agencies to enhance public and private sector services for those communities. Because the mainstream agencies comprise the vast majority of Canada's social welfare facilities and receive almost all the social welfare funding, with them resides the responsibility for formulating new, proactive strategies and tactics to ensure that all their clients have equal access to services of a high quality from mainstream agency services, as the charter mandates.

Moreover, the unfolding and evolving of patterns over the past 30 and more years demonstrate that immigration levels will continue to be high. In fact, the numbers of newcomers to Canada will even expand, perhaps to as much as an annual rate of 1 percent of the country's population.[9] Social service agencies will always have to evolve with the ever-increasing new immigrants and refugees who arrive here. The minority communities' social agencies will continue to perform at a minimum their extremely significant function for these newcomers and, indeed, for their second- and even third-generation constituencies.

So far as we can determine, no lawsuits claiming discriminatory practices in mainstream agencies—which includes child welfare, income-maintenance, family-service agencies, education, hospitals, and clinics—have yet been filed. There is always the likelihood that this could change. Beyond that threat, human service agencies operate under both ethical and legal obligations to conform stringently to the charter and adhere to other requirements that assure minorities equitable treatment. Mainstream social welfare agencies must transform themselves into fully multicultural facilities, functioning in concert with ethno-racial community agencies. For us, this is the only means to reach that indispensable and inevitable outcome.

NOTES

1. The term "ethno-racial" includes as sources of group identity not just the ancestral ethnic or cultural group and/or the assumed race of one's lineage, but also national origin, and especially religious affiliation. It need not be more than merely observed here that "ethnic" and "religious" sources of group and individual identity overlap considerably (E. N. Herberg, 1989, 145–182).

2. "Integration" is a process with goals and outcomes very different from assimilation of immigrants with a non-British and non-French culture. "Assimilation" means the coerced or voluntary abandonment by members of minority ethnicities of their original cultural heritage. In contrast, integration is the inter-action and participation among people of different ethno-racial origins within the same mainstream institutions—in religion, education, the workplace, the political arena, and so on—without any inferences of assimilatory outcomes (E. N. Herberg, 1989, 8–10).

3. From 1981 to 2001, those reporting multiple-group origins of British plus another non-British origin, or French plus another non-French origin were assigned to that *other* non-British/French origin. This procedure of counting only British or French single-origins contributed to the large percentage declines for the two charter ethnicities between the 1971 pattern and in 1981 through 2001, and to some degree of the increases in minority communities.

4. The preferred term of reference here for social agencies developed entirely within a minority ethnic community is "ethnic" or "ethnocultural" agency. We particularly avoid the oft-used term "ethno-specific," because that term is self-contradictory today, as we show below. Ethnic agencies are contrasted with "mainstream" agencies, those facilities funded by government or public charities, which serve the dominant ethnic group in the community and minority persons assimilated to the dominant culture. Theoretically, however, all the people in their geographic domains make up the constituencies of these latter agencies.

5. For a complete explication of the many issues, variables, and procedures involved in educating professionals to serve an ethnically, racially and religiously diverse clientele, see D. C. Herberg, *Frameworks for Cultural and Racial Diversity*, 1993.

6. Institutional discrimination was termed *systemic* by Rosalie S. Abella in her 1984 ground-breaking *Equality in Employment: A Royal Commission Report*.

7. See Breton, 1964, pp. 193–205, and part of his chapter on "The Ethnic Group as a Political Resource" in Breton, 1990, pp. 196–255; Isajiw, 1999, p. 200; E. N. Herberg, 1989, Chapter 9 on "Institutional Completeness," pp. 208–241.

8. For a full analysis of all institutional sectors of all eight institutional sectors in minority communities—religious, education, economic, social and recreation, media, arts and culture, governance, politics—see E. N. Herberg, 1989, Chapter 9, pp. 219–241.

9. The *first* generation in Canada consists of the immigrant-refugees into this country, and today these people make up 18 percent of all Canadians. Their Canadian-born children are the *second* generation, 17 percent of the total population, and the Canadian-born children of Canadian-born parents are the *third and later* generations—nearly two-thirds, 64 percent, of Canadians.

REFERENCES

Abella, R. S. *Equality in Employment: A Royal Commission Report*. Ottawa: Minister of Supply and Services Canada, 1984.

Allmen, E. "Counselling and Settlement: The Current and Future Role of Mainstream Settlement Services." *Proceedings of the*

Settlement and Integration of New Immigrants Conference. Ed. S. A. Yelaja. Waterloo, ON: Wilfrid Laurier University Press, 1990. 199–221.

Allodi, F., et al. "Community Consultation on Refugee Integration: American Refugees and Survivors of Torture," *Canada's Mental Health* 34.4 (December 1986): 13–15.

Breton, R. "The Ethnic Group as a Political Resource...". In Breton et al., *Ethnic Identity and Equality: Varieties of Experience in a Canadian City*. Toronto: University of Toronto Press, 1990. 224–255.

———. "Institutional Completeness of Ethnic Communities and the Personal Relations of Immigrants." *American Journal of Sociology* 70.2 (September 1964): 193–205.

Canada Immigration Commission (CIC), *Immigration Statistics*, Annual issues to 1989, and CIC website. *Immigration Statistics*, 1990–2003.

Canada Multicultural Ministry. *Multiculturalism: A Policy for All Canadians*, 1998. 7.

The Charter of Rights and Freedoms: A Guide for Canadians. Ottawa: Minister of Supply and Services Canada, 1982.

Disman, M. Executive Summary of *Stranger's Homecoming: A Study of the Experience of Immigration*, n.d. Ph.D. dissertation at the University of Toronto, 1981. 8–11.

———. "The Process of Admission of Immigrants to Canadian Culture and Communities." *Settlement and Integration of New Immigrants to Canada*. Ed. S. A. Yelaja. Waterloo, ON: Wilfrid Laurier University Press, 1990. 54–64.

Driedger, L. *Race and Ethnicity: Finding Identities and Equalities*. Don Mills, ON: Oxford University Press, 2003.

Hall, E. T. *Beyond Culture*. New York: Anchor Books, 1976.

Harney, R. F. "Introduction" and "Records of the Mutual Benefit Society." *Polyphony* 2:1 (1979): 1–3, 5–16.

———. "Religion and Ethnocultural Communities." *Polyphony* 1.2 (Summer 1978): 3–10.

Herberg, D. C. "Development in Social Agencies: Meeting the Unmet Social Service Needs of the Ethnic Population." *Multiculturalism* 3.2 (1979): 9–13.

———. *Frameworks for Cultural and Racial Diversity*. Toronto: Canadian Scholars' Press, 1993.

———. "Issues in Multicultural Child Welfare: Working with Families Originating in Traditional Societies." *Social Work Papers* 17 (Summer 1983): 45–57.

———. "Multiculturalism and Services to Migrant Populations." *The Province of Ontario: Its Social Services*. Toronto: Ontario Social Development Council, 1982. 187–205.

Herberg, D. C., and E. N. Herberg. "Ethnicity, Ethno-Racial Communities and Ethnocultural Services." *Canadian Encyclopedia of Social Work*. Eds. J. C. Turner & F. J. Turner. Forthcoming.

———. "Issues Concerning Agencies Serving Immigrants and Refugees." Submission and requested presentation to the Canadian Task Force on Mental Health Issues Affecting Immigrants and Refugees, Toronto, Ontario, May 6, 1987. (Some parts of this brief were quoted in their Report.)

Herberg, E. N. "Ethnic Families—Yesteryear, Today, Tomorrow: Structures and Policy Implications." *Report of the National Conference on Families*. Ottawa: Government of Canada, 1991. 45–68.

———. *Ethnic Groups in Canada: Adaptations and Transitions*. Scarborough, ON: Nelson Canada, 1989.

Isajiw, W. W. *Understanding Diversity: Ethnicity and Race in the Canadian Context*. Toronto: Thomson Educational Publishing, 1999.

Matsuoka, A., and J. Sorenson. "Ethnic Identity and Social Service Delivery." *Canadian Social Work Review* 8.2 (Summer 1991): 255–268.

Medeiros, J. "Family Services for All." *Achieving Our Potential Together.* Toronto: Ontario Ministry of Community and Social Services, 1990. 12.

Ontario Council of Agencies Serving Immigrants (OCASI). *Special Report on Funding to Metro Immigrant Services Agencies.* Toronto: OCASI, 1990.

Roy, G. "Incomprehensions interculturelles et adjustments de pratique chez les travailleurs sociaux." *Canadian Social Work Review.* 8.2 (Summer 1991): 278–291.

Sluzki, C. E. "Migration and Family Conflicts," *Family Process.* 18.4 (1979): 379–390.

Statistics Canada website. "Ethno-Cultural Profile of Canada: Table 1," January 2003.

Welin, L., and A. M. Ervin. "Refugee Clients and Social Service Agencies: Some Aspects of Cross-Cultural Misunderstandings," in Eds. S. P. Sharma, A. M. Ervin, and D. Meintel, *Immigrants and Refugees in Canada: A National Perspective on Ethnicity, Multiculturalism and Cross-Cultural Adjustment.* Saskatoon and Montreal: University of Saskatchewan and University of Montreal, 1991. 178–195.

chapter twelve

Immigrant Groups
in Canada

Carole Pigler Christensen

INTRODUCTION

Social workers serve clients who are increasingly diverse in terms of their ethnicity, culture, and race. Social work is the sole profession charged with the responsibility of offering services to individuals, groups, families, and communities while taking into account the complex relationships between people and their environment. Ethical practice demands that practitioners be cognizant of the complex social, economic, and political forces that enhance, or limit, clients' life chances and social service needs.

This chapter examines the effects of immigration regulations, formal and informal social policies, human rights, and services and resources on immigrant groups. The impact of these important racial, cultural, and ethnic factors, seldom addressed in the social welfare literature, is considered.

The chapter begins with an overview of the motivations underlying immigration and the major changes in patterns of immigration over time. Also discussed is the status immigrants of European and non-European ancestry assume within the Canadian system of stratification, the major effects of immigration and refugee policies on individuals and population groups, and Canada's responses to various multicultural realities. To illustrate, the experiences of four immigrant groups are briefly examined, noting the extent to which their social welfare needs have been met or impeded by conditions in Canada, and by governmental and voluntary efforts. The chapter ends with a discussion of programs that assist immigrants and identifies the implications for social work in a multicultural and multicultural Canadian society.

WHY DO PEOPLE IMMIGRATE?

Migration has always been practised around the world. In the modern era, people of all origins have left their home countries seeking greater economic opportunities, improved living standards, and greater social, religious, or political freedom and stability. As a relatively new, sparsely populated country, rich in natural resources, Canada has sought to attract immigrants to fill specific needs. Migration can best be understood in terms of *push factors* that cause people to leave a country and *pull factors* that attract immigrants to receiving countries. These factors must be considered in a global context.

During the colonial era, European explorers migrated here in search of land and raw materials to enrich their mother countries. Later, Canada attracted permanent European settlers, as surplus labourers from densely populated cities and depressed rural areas sought opportunities in the "new world." During the peak of this migration, between 1845 and 1924, some 50 million people travelled to North America and South America, the greatest migration in recorded history. Canada's need for unskilled labour again became a pull factor during the post–World War II abundance economy. As Western Europe continued to prosper, migration was tied to war and political upheaval, resulting in displaced persons or refugees.

Currently, great migrations are taking place in Third World post-colonial countries in Asia, Africa, and Latin America, where newly independent countries are caught up in a global system of social and economic stratification. Since the 1960s, pressures have been placed on relatively wealthy postcolonial Western countries such as Canada to accept more immigrants and refugees. Because of population growth and limited opportunities for upward mobility, people in Third World countries are likely to continue to wish to emigrate, as the Europeans did before them, in search of better lives. However, recent changes in Europe's Eastern bloc countries and the dissolution of the former Soviet Union have led to renewed demands from countries experiencing unrest and uncertainty.

Formulation of Immigration Policy

Canada established its Department of Citizenship and Immigration in 1950 and passed its Immigration Act of 1952. Before this time the government had no coherent policy regarding the many categories of people who wished to enter the country, such as independent immigrants, family members of immigrants, refugees. Popular myth suggests that Canada has always had an open-door immigration policy, allowing almost anyone to enter. In fact, immigration policies have been devised regarding national and racial origins of prospective immigrants; Canada's economic conditions and labour needs; international conditions of poverty; political unrest, war, or natural disaster; people in Canada wishing to sponsor relatives; and the anticipated short- and long-term effects of specific immigrant groups on the French and English communities.

In recent years, low fertility rates and an aging population are additional factors affecting government attitudes toward immigration (Canada Employment and Immigration Advisory Council, 1989).

Who Is an Immigrant?

Canada is often referred to as a nation of immigrants. With the exception of the First Nations populations, all Canadians are descendants of immigrants.

The Earliest European Immigrants: The Charter Groups
From 1667 to 1763, French settlers consolidated their control of the political, economic, and religious spheres in New France, as the colony was then called. The economy was based mainly on the fur trade and extracting natural resources. Following the British conquest of 1759, French immigration slowed considerably. By the time of Confederation in 1867, British nationals had become the largest single source of immigration, a status they maintained, albeit in declining proportions, through most of the twentieth century. The British government promoted migration to Canada, often paying people's transportation costs. In the decade immediately following Confederation, 60 percent of the population was British and 35 percent was French. Only the high birth rate, encouraged by the Catholic church, enabled French Canadians to maintain their relatively stable percentage within the population.

A second European immigration phase began around 1880. Land made available in the Prairies attracted those from outside the British Isles and France. At that time only 8 percent of the population was of ethnic origin other than British or French: 70 percent were German and 10 percent were Dutch. As the dominant cultural group outside Quebec, the British assumed control of immigration and major economic, social, and political decisions. They determined which groups to allow into the country, which jobs they could fill, and what social ranking would be accorded them. From the time of Confederation until

1902, fewer than 100 000 immigrants came to Canada annually.

Other European Immigrants
During a third phase of European immigration, between the turn of the century and World War I, more than 200 000 people arrived every year. A record number of immigrants (400 870) arrived in 1913, fleeing poor socio-economic conditions or religious and political persecution. Most settlers who were not British were Scandinavian, Slavic, or Russian and included Mennonites, Hutterites, Ukrainians, Poles, and Doukhobors. Most were poorly educated, with little or no knowledge of English or French. Western Canada became a truly pluralistic society. Language differences led to regional concentrations of these ethnocultural groups.

The fourth immigration phase occurred between World Wars I and II when the Depression greatly reduced the flow. Those allowed to enter were mainly skilled technicians, who settled in urban areas. Restrictions continued for those speaking "enemy" languages and those of other than European ancestry, who were considered difficult or impossible to assimilate owing to their cultural, linguistic, religious, or climatic backgrounds (Bolaria & Li, 1988). A 1923 order-in-council gave "most favoured" immigrant status to those from Britain and the United States, followed by Northern and Western Europeans. Southern, Central, and Eastern Europeans were accepted only if no one else was available for specific employment categories. A "Euro-Canadian" flavour (rather exclusively British and French) prevailed, and newcomers were expected to conform to Anglo-Saxon norms.

The last immigration phase that began after World War II has extended to the present. Numbers again increased, as did the diversity of the immigrants. By 1941, the British had become a statistical minority (44 percent of the population). About half of the unskilled immigrants in the 1950s came from Italy, Portugal, and Greece. A "third force" was emerging, too, composed of immigrants neither British nor French in origin. While each ethnic group comprised less than 5 percent of the population, together they had become a quarter of the total population of Canada.

Immigrants from Outside Europe

Until the 1960s, only whites were considered "suitable" immigrants. This made Canada almost inaccessible to those of other racial backgrounds and prevented immigration from sources outside Europe. Racist ideologies remained that prevailed since the colonial era, based on the principles of Manifest Destiny and Social Darwinism. These ethnocentric theories fostered the belief that Europeans had proven themselves fittest to survive by conquering the "uncivilized" peoples on the North and South American, Asian, and African continents. According to a pseudo-scientific bio-social system conceived by eighteenth- and nineteenth-century Europeans, humankind formed a hierarchy from the "superior" white Europeans to "inferior" yellow, brown, red, and black "races." This belief system was used to implement policies of oppression and extermination to claim the land and to justify the enslavement of First Nations people and blacks. Although the concept of "race" is indeed a social construct—there being but one human species—the ideology of white supremacy played a major role in shaping Canada's immigration policies. It formed the basis of majority–minority relations as we know them today (Christensen, 2003).

In 1947, Prime Minister Mackenzie King illustrated the official attitude toward immigration from continents other than Europe in an overtly racist statement. He noted that Canadians did not wish to alter "the character of our population" in the interests of growth, and that immigration should be selectively restricted to people who could be "advantageously absorbed" into the economy (Ramcharan, 1982). The Immigration Act of 1952 empowered the governor-in-council to prohibit or limit prospective immigrants' admission for reasons of nationality or ethnic group; peculiar customs or modes of life; climatic and socio-economic unsuitability; and probable inability to become readily assimilated or to assume the responsibilities of Canadian citizenship (Hawkins, 1972). The official ranking of preferred immigrants was strikingly similar to the ranking of the "superior" and "inferior" races postulated in Europe two centuries earlier. Only those preferred categories of Europeans could sponsor relatives without difficulty. Third World families were separated, with devastating effects, when only one member managed to immigrate (such as domestic workers). Vestiges of such policies survive today.

The ideology of Britain's Elizabethan Poor Laws formed the basis for early Canadian social welfare legislation. It also planted the seeds for viewing the "able-bodied poor" as "sturdy beggars" who should be forced to work under distasteful conditions (Christensen, 1996). Policies that ignored the plight of immigrant groups experiencing systemic racism reflected this laissez-faire attitude. Instead, these immigrants were blamed for being unwilling to work hard owing to their "cultural attributes." This thinking fostered racial prejudice. Until the mid–twentieth century, discriminatory legislation on the basis of race was introduced periodically to sanction and promote negative attitudes and stereotypes toward racialized groups.

RISING IMMIGRATION FROM THE THIRD WORLD

In response to the contradictions of a racially restrictive immigration policy and Canada's desired reputation as a country fostering equality and human rights, the federal government passed the Immigration Act of 1962. The legislation finally removed obvious restrictions based on race. A Points System was introduced in 1967. Consequently, the number of immigrants from European sources has declined while greater and greater numbers of immigrants have arrived from Third World countries. The Points System encouraged applications from independent immigrants evaluated on the basis of their "probable adjustment" to Canadian life in the short term (such as arranged employment or knowledge of French or English); and factors indicative of an immigrant's positive long-term adjustment without dependence on the government (factors such as relative youth, education and training, and "personal qualities"). For the first time, residents whose origins were other than European could sponsor or nominate close relatives to immigrate as well.

Although hailed as a racially non-discriminatory merit system, critics of the Points System note that certain forms of discrimination remained. The points awarded differ for the independent and the family-reunification classes. Immigration officers exercise considerable discretionary powers in choosing which applicants to evaluate and how to allocate points in terms of "personal potential." Also a disproportionate number of immigration offices are located in predominantly white countries (such as the United States), with few in the Third World (say, India and Africa). Except for the highly educated, the skilled, or the wealthy, who are needed to support the economies of their own Third World countries of origin, white individuals still find it easiest to qualify as independent immigrants.

Because of the points allocated for educational attainment, immigrants arriving since the 1970s have been the most highly educated ever. The education level of immigrants of colour has generally been higher than that of the Canadian-born population (Fleras & Elliott, 2002). The unprecedented rise in the number of Third World immigrants—approximately one-third of the total admitted—between 1967 and 1977 led to protest from many quarters, resulting in the more restrictive Immigration Act of 1978. The annual quota of 100 000 was half the number admitted in 1975, and immigrants could be deported for not supporting the family members they sponsored or if they themselves were considered a security risk. The nominated category was abolished and the Points System made more stringent. Still, European immigration dropped from 90 percent in 1961 to 25 percent from 1981 to 1991. By 1986, more than one million Canadians or permanent residents were born in, or emigrated from, Asia, Africa, South and Central America, and the Caribbean.

RECENT TRENDS

From time to time, Canadian governments hold public hearings to ascertain the national climate toward immigration and, apparently, to alleviate Euro-Canadians' concerns about the number of Third World migrants Canada can "absorb" without threatening the nation's own social cohesiveness and "cultural identity." Other factors that receive national attention include vast backlogs in the processing of immigration applications and refugee claims, and stakeholders' advocation of more sympathetic family-reunification policies and transparency regarding appeals to the

Refugee Board. The conflicting interests of conservative forces (traditionally labour) and those favouring freer immigration have fuelled ongoing debate. Nonetheless, support for growth in immigration has continued, as Canada needs skilled workers and its population ages (Employment and Immigration Canada, 1990). Consequently, discussions of absorbing immigrants who are not white have abated.

Since 2000, more than one-quarter of Canada's new permanent residents have come from China and India, as Table 12.1 shows, with the People's Republic of China the main source country.

The 2001 Census indicated that the proportion of Canada's population born outside the country has reached its highest level in 70 years (*Daily* 2003). Before 1971, most immigrants dispersed throughout the country, but since then, about half of the immigrants to Canada have settled, like the Europeans before them, in Ontario. Of the total number of immigrants arriving in 2002, settlement patterns were Toronto, 49 percent; Montreal, 14 percent; Vancouver, 13 percent (Citizenship and Immigration Canada Facts and Figures, 2002: Immigration Overview, 7). Most visible minorities live in these three urban areas where they are most likely to find employment. Of the three Prairie provinces, Alberta receives the highest proportion of immigrants, 6 percent

TABLE 12.1	Foreign Nationals Accorded Permanent Resident Status by Top 10 Source Countries, 2000–2002								
	2002			2001			2000		
Country	Number	%	Rank	Number	%	Rank	Number	%	Rank
China, People's Republic of	33 231	14.51	1	40 315	16.09	1	36 716	16.15	1
India	28 815	12.58	2	27 848	11.12	2	26 088	11.48	2
Pakistan	14 164	6.18	3	15 341	6.12	3	14 184	6.24	3
Philippines	11 000	4.80	4	12 914	5.16	4	10 088	4.44	4
Iran	7742	3.38	5	5737	2.29	7	5608	2.47	8
Korea, Republic of	7326	3.20	6	9604	3.83	5	7629	3.36	5
Romania	5692	2.48	7	5585	2.23	8	4425	1.95	11
United States	5288	2.31	8	5902	2.36	6	5815	2.56	7
Sri Lanka	4961	2.17	9	5514	2.20	9	5841	2.57	6
United Kingdom	4720	2.06	10	5350	2.14	10	4647	2.04	10
Yugoslavia (former)	1620	0.71	31	2788	1.11	22	4723	2.08	9
Total for top 10 countries only	122 939	53.67		134 110	53.54		121 339	53.39	
Total for other countries	106 152	46.33		116 374	46.46		106 007	46.61	
Total	229 091	100		250 484	100		227 346	100	

Source: Citizenship and Immigration Canada, "Immigration by Top Ten Source Countries (Principal Applicants and Dependants)," *Annual Report to Parliament on Immigration*, 2003. **www.cic.gc.ca/english/pub/facts2002/ immigration/immigration_5.html**, retrieved May 31, 2004. Reproduced with the permission of the Minister of Public Works and Government Services Canada, 2004.

(Citizenship and Immigration Canada, Monitor, Issue 03/02-immigrants.html, p. 1). Out of a total population of 29 639 035, 13.4 percent, or 4 million, are identified as visible minorities (Statistics Canada, 2001a, Census of Population).

MAJORITY AND MINORITY GROUP IMMIGRANT STATUS

Majority Group Immigrant Status

The majority or dominant group must take into account not only numerical considerations but also the dimensions of power, privilege, and prestige. Even when small in numbers, the majority group occupies the highest social, economic, and political positions in a society. This is the group from which the elite are drawn. This group's culture and values are transmitted through society's formal institutions—the schools, the media, and the social welfare agencies. The social welfare needs of this dominant group receive the greatest attention and sanction from official sources.

For example, the British have occupied the majority group position in all provinces except Quebec. Until recently, even in Quebec, they have tended to occupy the highest ranking economic positions in corporate structures. Historically, white immigrants of British descent have automatically become part of the majority group and have moved into society's mainstream institutions. The preferred categories of British, Northwest Europeans, and white Americans have traditionally been encouraged to immigrate freely, followed by Eastern and Southern Europeans. The same has been true for many "white ethnics" who have been absorbed into the dominant group through assimilation, including intermarriage. White skin has for centuries functioned as an informal and invisible kind of

"affirmative action" benefiting majority group immigrants and those so identified. However, some European immigrant groups retain a collective national, ethnic, or religious identity and voluntarily remain somewhat apart from the Anglo or French ideal type—for example, the Hutterites. Canada's bilingual status has meant that immigrants must integrate into the English or French linguistic communities in order to participate fully in the wider society.

Minority Group Immigrant Status

All immigrants not British or French in origin are, by definition, minority Canadians. These immigrants will have entered the country in response to specific pull factors—for example, to fill certain employment categories—and will generally have been assigned an entry status below that of British and French immigrants. These groups are minorities in more than numbers; they are also minorities in terms of the amount of power, prestige, and privilege they enjoy. These immigrants have historical backgrounds and cultures to which Canadian public schools and the media and other formal institutions pay little attention. They are also underrepresented in decision-making bodies. Most important, they are aware of their subordinate status in the social, economic, and political spheres of life.

Some groups occupy minority status in several categories, such as language, religion, or racial origin. However, one category becomes the *master status*, or the most salient feature, in the eyes of the majority group, along a continuum of acceptance or rejection (Kallen, 1982). Perceived racial origin has been the major distinguishing precondition of minority status in Canada, reinforced by common stereotypes and menial positions in the job market

(Satzewich, 1991). The limited number of racial minorities who were initially allowed to enter Canada tended to come as transient labour through Canada's international agreements with poor Third World countries, including the Caribbean, Mexico, and the Philippines. These people were easily exploited (Bolaria & Li, 1988). The degree of any minority group's participation depends on the extent to which the majority group allows them to participate. Racialized minorities have suffered "not occasional insults or prejudice to some of their members, but blatant, prolonged, and persistent discrimination" (Krauter & Davis, 1978, 2).

Minority/Majority Group Relations Today

In his classic work *The Vertical Mosaic*, John Porter indicated that, in 1965, immigrant groups in Canada constituted a ladder-like hierarchy, based on ethnic ranking or stratification and, implicitly, on race (Porter, 1965). At the top were the British and immigrants from Northern and Western Europe; the middle ranks included Eastern and Southern Europeans and a small number of individuals from racial minorities; and at the bottom of the hierarchy in the greatest numbers were racialized minorities and the First Nations.

Recent studies indicate that this general pattern of stratification has persisted, despite individuals' gains in upward mobility in the middle ranks—by Jews, who years ago formed a parallel elite structure, and by the Chinese (especially business-class immigrants) entering Canada with high educational, occupational, and economic standing (Satzewich, 1991). Attacks on pluralism still occur in times of economic and political stress (such as economic restraints, job losses). It has been suggested that "the urge to return to, or to sustain what is left of the vertical mosaic, remains strong in the land" (Tepper, 1997, 65).

Today, *culture* is no longer a major issue for the vast majority of Europeans, whose own cultures are generally accepted in Canada. However, people considered to be of different *races* are still considered less likely to "fit in." Race remains a potent concept in Canadians' everyday perceptions. Many who are not white prefer such terms as "people of colour," or "racialized" minorities (terms used interchangeably in this chapter, according to context) to the uniquely Canadian term "visible minorities," that official government documents employ. The Employment Equity Act defines visible minorities as "persons, other than Aboriginal peoples, who are non-Caucasian in race or non-white in colour" (Daily 2003).

Regulations specify categories: Chinese, South Asians, Blacks, Arabs, West Asians, Filipinos, Southeast Asians, Latin Americans, Japanese, Koreans, and other visible groups, such as Pacific Islanders (Statistics Canada, 2001b). Such labelling could be interpreted as state-initiated racialization, whatever the original intention behind applying these terms; these disparate groups did not choose the term "visible minorities" themselves and they have nothing in common with one another save for their not being white and, therefore, facing discrimination. Racialized groups find meanings are attributed to their identifiable features, giving them special, exotic, or negative significance and justifying their treatment as less deserving "others," with respect to the normal benefits of Canadian society. This rejection on the basis of ethnic or racial characteristics can be social, economic, or cultural (Simmons, p. 30) and is evinced in Canada's political structures and generally in various combinations of these characteristics.

Recent studies show that racism in all areas of daily life—the justice system, employment, housing, education, the media—is alive and well in Canada (Berry, 1991; Fleras & Kuhz, 2001; Henry, Tator,

Mattis & Rees, 2001). Notably, research also indicates that, in some communities, the second generation is accomplishing less than their parents' generation did in terms of education and employment. White Canadians deny the existence of racism, and even some people of colour deny it. Some, especially new immigrants, may not recognize Canadian forms of racism; others may find it too painful to acknowledge.

Displeasure with the growing ethno-racial diversity of the population is expressed by the activities of organized hate groups such as the Heritage Front, skin-heads, and neo-Nazis advocating white supremacy (Laquian & Laquian, 1997, p. 11). Even if having generations of Canadian ancestors, with or without foreign accents, people of colour are regularly asked, "Where are you from, *really*—before coming to Canada?" Such instances of having to prove one's legitimacy as truly Canadian confirms that people of colour continue to be perceived as newcomers, or immigrants indefinitely. Those categorized as similar by virtue of "visibility," and so treated differently, may eventually unite to defend their human rights and to gain a sense of belonging.

The Persistence of Inequality

Canada professes to adhere to equality and multiculturalism, so it is often difficult for students of social welfare to understand why some immigrant groups maintain a minority status over time while others seem to be upwardly mobile and are eventually absorbed into the dominant culture. In fact, some immigrant groups have been barred from equal access and life chances more than others, in their dealings with major social institutions and other decision-makers. Racial minorities have suffered "not occasional insults or prejudice to some of their members, but blatant, prolonged, and persistent discrimination" (Krauter & Davis, 1978).

Majority-group Canadians have employed a number of *techniques of domination and control* that ensure that, once in Canada, immigrant groups are likely to retain their positions in the racially and ethnically stratified system. Table 12.2 demonstrates the degree to which these techniques have been applied to immigrants of European and racial minority backgrounds. Racialized minority immigrants and their descendants have had to face the greatest number of restrictions. Skin colour and other racialized features make them identifiable targets for discriminatory treatment. As noted by Anderson & Frideres (1981), generalizations about assimilation and integration may not necessarily hold for "visible minorities" (p. 106). Moreover, all the individuals within a particular ethnic category do not experience the same degree of discriminatory treatment, either objectively or subjectively. Because of the hierarchy of racism in Canada, some racialized groups more than others find themselves accepted by Euro-Canadians, and find some degree of change possible over time. For example, Japanese Canadians, considered "enemy aliens" during World War II, are now accepted as a "model minority." Domination and control techniques may be expressed in the form of covert institutional racism rather than overt, individual discrimination. Institutional discrimination is rooted in racism that is ingrained in the very fabric of society's systems and perpetuates itself.

Those exposed to a continuous cycle of unequal access suffer the cumulative effects, from birth to old age. Attitude studies suggest that 12 percent to 16 percent of Canadians admit to holding bigoted, intolerant attitudes, but these responses may be skewed by Canadians' desire to give "liberal" responses (Henry, Tator, Matthis, & Rees, 1999, 59). Racism persists because it is part of the value system and the discourse of the dominant culture; supports a capitalist economic system; and provides

TABLE 12.2	European and Non-European Immigrants' Overall Experiences of Techniques of Domination		
Techniques of Domination	British and North/West European Immigrants	East/South European Immigrants	Non-European/ and Non-White Immigrants
1. Immigrant restrictions	Low	Medium	High
2. Persecution and expulsion	Low	Medium	High
3. Land ownership restrictions	None	None	Medium to High
4. Denial of civil liberties	Low	Medium	High
5. Voting restrictions	Low	Low	Medium
6. Arbitrary search and seizure	Low	Low	High
7. Employment and promotion restrictions	Low	Low	High
8. Housing restrictions	None	Low	High
9. Public accommodation restrictions	None	None	High
10. Education restrictions	None	None	Low to High
11. Formally sanctioned negative racial myths and stereotypes	None	Medium	High
12. Mass media restrictions	Low	Low	High
13. Different treatment by financial institutions	None	Low	Medium to High
14. Social welfare/social service restrictions	None	Low	Medium to High

personal, group, and social satisfaction by protecting privileges that few whites acknowledge or would wish to share (Christensen, 1999).

CURRENT IMMIGRATION AND REFUGEE POLICY

Like many Canadians, students of social welfare may not know exactly how immigrants differ from refugees and other types of residents. Yet these distinctions have important meanings in residents' daily lives. Preceded by Bill C-11 in 2001, the current Immigration and Refugee Protection Act (IRPA) came into effect on June 28, 2002, replacing the Act of 1976. The new IRPA was intended to modernize Canada's immigration policy; facilitate the entry of adaptable workers with flexible skills, rather than specific occupations; and provide new security measures preventing the entry of those deemed a threat to the "safety and security" of Canadians (Annual Report to Parliament on Immigration, 2003).

Noteworthy emphasis was placed on safety and security measures—improved screening of prospective refugees and immigrants, and screening at borders and airports—and avoiding abuse of Canada's "generosity through illegal or fraudulent activities." Since the events of September 11, 2001, the Government of Canada has designated $49 million for improved security measures, cooperating closely with the United States. Objectives of Canada's new Anti-Terrorism Act—in which the word "terrorism" is poorly defined—include protecting the Canada–US border from terrorist acts; creating tools to identify, remove, detain, or prosecute, convict, and punish terrorists; and addressing the root causes of such hatred (Citizenship and Immigration Canada, 2001).

Countless people, assumed to fit the profile of terrorists, have been seriously affected by the provisions of the Security Information Act, at airports and ground borders. One of the best known of these is Maher Arar, a Muslim Canadian citizen who questions the culpability of the RCMP in his 2002 deportation to Syria from a United States airport. He suffered 11 months of torture and imprisonment in Syria. Muslims and those presumed to have Arab features, in particular, find themselves at risk today.

The Department of Citizenship and Immigration (CIC) is responsible for policies ensuring that those coming to Canada contribute to its social and economic interests, whether as permanent or temporary residents wishing to work, study, or visit. The department emphasizes the likelihood of individuals' integration. The three categories for permanent residents are (1) economic class (skilled workers, business immigrants, provincial nominees, and live-in caregivers); (2) family (spouses, partners, children under age 22, parents and grandparents of the sponsors); and (3) refugees in need of protection, or asylum (see "Refugees," below). Exceptionally, those who do not meet the usual criteria are accepted on humanitarian, compassionate, or public policy grounds.

As of September 2003, applicants for independent immigrant status are awarded points according to six "selection factors":

(1) Education: 5 to 25 points maximum (from high school to a Master's degree or Ph.D. and at least 13 years of full-time or equivalent study);

(2) Language: 0 (neither official language) to 24 points maximum (for fluency in both English and French);

(3) Experience: 15 to 21 points maximum (for years of work experience);

(4) Age: 10 points maximum (if 21 to 49 years of age) less 2 points for each year older than 49 or younger than 21;

(5) Arranged employment: 10 points maximum (for confirmed job offer);

(6) Adaptability: 3 to 10 points maximum (including point awarded for education level of spouse or common-law/same-sex partner).

An applicant requires a minimum of 67 points to "pass" (Citizenship and Immigration, 2003b).

A non-refundable "right of permanent residence fee" of $975 is charged to the principal applicant and to any accompanying spouses or common law partners, to be paid before Canada will issue an immigration visa in the country of origin. This fee is not required for dependent children, a child to be adopted, or an orphaned family member, or for protected persons, including Convention Refugees. Selection criteria and application fees are subject to change without notice. Those with applications being processed before December 17, 2001, and who had received no selection decisions before the new Act was implemented, were assessed according to the old criteria until January 1, 2003.

Business immigrants are considered particularly important for a strong Canadian economy and are recognized as one of three types: investors with business experience and a net worth of at least CAN$800 000 and investing $400 000 for job creation and economic development; entrepreneurs with a net worth of at least CAN$300 000, who are able to own and manage a business that creates jobs for Canadians or permanent residents; and self-employed persons who demonstrate their intentions to contribute significantly to Canadian culture, athletics, or farm management. Families are included in these immigrant categories.

In 2002, of the 229 091 permanent residents accepted into Canada, 60 percent were economic immigrants and their dependants; 28 percent were categorized as family class; 11 percent were refugees and other protected persons; and 1 percent were labelled "other." As to sex, 51 percent were female and 49 percent were male; however, most economic-class immigrants (73 percent) were men, while most of those entering as live-in caregivers were women (82 percent) (Citizenship and Immigration Canada 2003a, p. 15). The majority of the newcomers (43.3 percent) spoke English, 4.7 percent spoke French, and 6 percent spoke both languages. The remainder spoke neither official language.

Nine provinces and one territory now participate in joint federal–provincial collaborative agreements: Quebec, New Brunswick, Saskatchewan, Manitoba, British Columbia, Newfoundland and Labrador, Prince Edward Island, Yukon, Alberta, and Nova Scotia. Allowing the provinces to select their own immigrants according to economic need makes the coordination of immigration policies and programs easier. The provinces' nominees bypass the federal Points System if they meet health and security requirements (Annual Report to Parliament on Immigration, 2003). The British Columbia and Manitoba agreements include joint responsibilities for settlement and integration services. Under the most comprehensive of these agreements, the Canada–Quebec Accord of 1991, Quebec sets its own annual immigration targets, selects its own immigrants (though not refugees), and provides its own integration services. Most immigrants to Quebec come from French-speaking Third World regions such as the French Caribbean and francophone Africa. Notably, recent amendments to the IRPA note that the federal and the provincial governments aim to work together to secure better recognition of the foreign credentials of permanent residents. A major frustration for immigrants is that, having received high selection points for education, many find only menial jobs are available to them once they arrive in Canada.

In 2004, Canada expects between 220 000 and 245 000 more permanent residents, of whom 60 percent will be economic-class immigrants and their dependants. Similar numbers are targeted for 2005. It is estimated that in 10 years, the labour market will grow exclusively through immigration (Canadian Bar Association, 2002).

Citizenship and Residency

After three years in Canada, landed immigrants may apply for citizenship. In the meantime, they are restricted from voting in federal and provincial elections. Providing they meet the residency requirements, pass citizenship tests, and have no criminal records, they will be granted the full rights and privileges of citizenship. Permanent residents and citizens 18 years or older may sponsor relatives who want to become permanent residents as well as family-class immigrants. The controversial new Citizenship Act of December 7, 1998, imposed Canadian residency and age-related requirements for the second and third generations of children born to Canadian parents abroad, in order to maintain their citizenship. In the case of "obvious error," citizenship officers, and not judges, can make decisions that only the Minister of Immigration can reverse, rather than an appeal board (Sarazin, 1999). Citizenship is clearly considered a privilege, not a right.

In 2001, the first stage of the IRPA, Bill C-11, was tabled in several versions, and greatly criticized during the national consultation process—by, among others, the Canadian Bar Association and Canadian Council for Refugees; aspects of the Act died in the Parliamentary Committee process. However, the current IRPA that was adopted in June 2002 has retained certain controversial regulations of Bill C-11, including those concerning permanent residents.

The requirement that all "permanent residents"—landed immigrants who are not citizens—carry a Permanent Resident Card took effect on January 1, 2004. The card generally expires after five years and a resident who is abroad cannot return without it. Permanent residents must be present in Canada for a cumulative period of two years for every five working years, unless they are working for a Canadian company or accompanying someone doing so.

Critics of the regulation cite the measure as systemic discrimination against business people and senior executives with multinational firms, and those involved in elder care in Asia, separating them from their families. In December 2003 about 100 Chinese immigrants from Toronto and Vancouver brought as-yet-unsettled lawsuits against the Immigration and Citizenship department for $50 000 to $300 000 each in a bid to stop the card requirement. Only flights from African and some Asian countries, including China and Taiwan, require that travellers have this card (*Toronto Sun*, December 22, 2003, p. 7; *Vancouver Sun*, December 22, 2003, pp. 1–2).

Refugees

Social workers often serve refugees, and these workers should be aware of how these newcomers differ from other immigrants. Refugees seek resettlement in foreign countries for reasons other than voluntary immigration. Most have experienced trauma, persecution, and oppression. As a signatory to the United Nations Convention and protocol relating to the status of refugees, Canada has declared its international responsibility to protect "Convention refugees" from being returned to countries where these people fear persecution.

Convention refugees are individuals who, "by reason of a well-founded fear of persecution for reasons of race, religion, nationality, membership in a particular social group or political opinion are outside their country of nationality or habitual residence, and are unable or unwilling by reason of that fear to return to that country" (Citizenship and Immigration Canada, 2003a, 11). Convention refugees are selected abroad and become landed immigrants in Canada, with all related entitlements. Under the Settlement Assistance Program, the government provides support to the refugees for up to one year, which is subject to being repaid. Some refugees have private sponsors—for example, religious organizations—from whom the government may collect social assistance costs should the sponsor not provide its own financial support.

IRPA defines a second category as persons in need of protection in Canada. These "asylum seekers" arrive as visitors, or illegally, and apply for refugee status through the Immigration and Refugee Board. In theory, their claims are to be processed within three working days, but negative decisions often lead to extremely lengthy waiting times for appeals. A "pre-removal assessment" was introduced, said to take into account that risk to a person who might be removed from Canada and returned to a changing political situation in another country. Risk of persecution, torture, cruel and unusual punishment, or risk to life is assessed. If accepted, "protected" refugees, including their family members, may then apply for permanent residence status.

Freedom of movement does not necessarily apply to refugees. They may be questioned, arrested, detained, or deported while awaiting examination at ports of entry or immigration inquiries, or be subject to the execution of removal orders if they are considered security risks or dangers to the Canadian public. Those unable to confirm their identity may also be detained, although they may be unable to obtain passports and other documentation as refugees. A person from a third country, considered "safe" by an immigration officer, may be arbitrarily returned to that country, with little hope of appealing the decision (Canadian Bar Association News, **www.cba.org/CBA/News/2001**).

Desperate refugees threatened with deportation have gone on hunger strikes after being detained for months, without due process or access to legal counsel. Others have sought asylum in churches to avoid deportation when their claims have been rejected and they fear torture or persecution if returned to their countries of origin.

Canada's response has political overtones, depending on the reputation this country may gain, or lose, in the international arena. An estimated 150 million refugees and displaced persons exist worldwide (Citizenship and Immigration Canada, 2001), and Canada may be pressured to demonstrate humanitarian concern. Canada expects to accept 7600 refugees in 2004 (Citizenship and Immigration Canada, 2003a).

Foreign Workers and Temporary Residents

One of IRPA's objectives was to facilitate the movement of foreign workers who play a vital, if unrecognized, role in filling gaps in the Canadian labour market. Generally, they require work permits specifying the prospective jobs, the employers, and the duration of their employment. In 2002, Canada admitted 87 910 workers from the United States and Mexico, the primary source countries since signing the North American Free Trade Agreement (Citizenship and Immigration Canada, 2003a).

Other temporary workers fall under the jurisdiction of special agreements Canada has signed with Third World countries— for example, the Philippines. Participants in the Live-in Caregiver Program (formerly the Domestic Workers Program) must have completed the equivalent of Canadian secondary school education; have six months of full-time training in a field related to that they require for a work permit; speak, read, and understand English or French; and sign a contract with the future employer.

Caregivers can apply for permanent residence after two years and within three years of their arrival (Citizenship and Immigration Canada, 2003a, 37). Critics note that although often well educated, caregivers are also often exploited, working long hours and facing threat or harassment. Given the source countries, the live-in requirement, and the female gender of most participants, many see in this policy racist, classist, and sexist components (Villasin, & Phillips, 1994).

Canada's Seasonal Agricultural Workers Program imports temporary labourers, the large majority of whom come from Mexico and the Caribbean— particularly Jamaica—ensuring that Canada's crops are planted and harvested at the best times. They fall completely outside the regulations and benefits that apply to other Canadian workers.

As tuition rates across Canada rise, temporary foreign students, who pay the highest tuition fees, find their entry into

Canada easier. Those who register in programs with periods of six months or less no longer require study permits.

Critics of the current IRPA fault the Act for lack of transparency of its framework legislation. It leaves operational details to the regulations outside the domain of the House of Commons and thus avoids public scrutiny. It also gives greater powers to immigration officers and the Minister of Immigration; retains race, class, and gender issues, associated family-class versus independent immigrants, implying that families, women, and Third World immigrants may be a burden to Canadian society (Canadian Council for Refugees, 2001).

CANADA'S RESPONSE TO MULTICULTURAL REALITIES

The Multiculturalism Policy

The multiculturalism policy became the federal government's primary response to promoting intergroup and interpersonal harmony in the interests of increasing diversity, not least of all in Quebec. The report of the 1969 Royal Commission on Bilingualism and Biculturalism indicated that those of non-French and non-British heritage felt their contributions to Canada had been ignored (Royal Commission on Bilingualism and Biculturalism, 1970). As a result Prime Minister Pierre Trudeau formulated the 1971 policy of "multiculturalism within a bilingual framework."

Briefly stated, the policy promoted the cultural and racial diversity of Canadian society as a fundamental characteristic of Canadian heritage and identity, This entailed the equitable participation of individuals and communities of all origins in shaping Canadian society; the removal of barriers to such participation and access to

services; and equal treatment and protection under the law.

While acknowledging the contributions of other cultural groups, including Aboriginal peoples, multiculturalism was promoted *within* the framework of the official languages, English and French. The policy called on federal institutions in particular to ensure equal opportunity in employment and advancement. Policies, programs, and statistical data were to support the development of practices that fit with Canada's multicultural reality.

The earliest phase of multiculturalism (1971–1980) emphasized heritage languages and cultural traditions—such as dancing, food, dress, and the "ethnic" press—to preserve ancestral folkways. However, racialized minorities became increasingly concerned with such issues as employment opportunities and access to necessary services. From 1980 through 1988, policies entered a phase of "institutional multiculturalism," prompted by reports that documented pervasive inequality in the hiring and promotion of visible minorities, women, Native peoples, and disabled persons (for example, Abella, 1984, *Equality Now*).

In 1988, the Multiculturalism Act made Canada the first country ever with an official multiculturalism law (Supply and Services Canada, 1988) and a Multiculturalism ministry to promote cultural pluralism and harmonious race relations. Further measures to reduce discrimination were promised. Subsequent employment equity legislation produced some improvement in the private sector for racialized minorities, and only limited progress in the government public services. However, women made considerable progress in both sectors.

A final phase of "instrumental multiculturalism," which capitalizes on the economic benefits of a culturally diverse workforce, began in the 1990s and continues today. This phase emphasizes economic-class investors and entrepreneurs. Under the Department of Canadian Heritage, Multiculturalism and Citizenship focuses more on integrating ethno-racial minorities than on dealing with racism and its societal effects.

Official multiculturalism has come under attack by majority-group Canadians, and some minority groups fear that their being viewed as "special interest groups" may create stratified ethnic enclaves. Euro-Canadian discourse refers to a "backlash," as some white males suggest that employment-equity provisions discriminate against them. Some minority individuals consider multiculturalism a form of social control that co-opts oppressed groups through the rhetoric of equality without actually alleviating structural inequalities. So multiculturalism policies are simultaneously viewed as threatening and enhancing national unity. Governments and the media devote little attention to multicultural issues during elections and constitutional debates, perhaps because the racialized minorities most affected by those policies have yet to organize an effective, united, response.

The Charter of Rights and Freedoms

Section 15 (1) of the charter states, "Every individual is equal before the law and has the right to the equal protection and equal benefit of the law without discrimination and, in particular, without discrimination on the basis of race, national and ethnic origin, colour, religion, sex, age or mental or physical disability." Racialized minorities have criticized the "notwithstanding clause," which states that despite laws protecting targeted groups—that is, women, racial minorities, Aboriginal peoples, and

the disabled—the provinces may choose to opt out of adhering to specific sections of the charter. Provision is made for affirmative action programs for "amelioration of conditions of disadvantage," including race, ethnic origin, colour, and religion, yet to date women from majority-group backgrounds have benefited most from equity clauses and the affirmative action legislation affecting hiring and promotion. The potential long-term effects of racialized minorities' testing the equality clause of the charter, as the Supreme Court interprets it, have yet to be determined.

Although human rights commissions at the federal level and in various provinces have been somewhat effective in combatting discrimination, they are often criticized for being slow to act and for being lacking in public accountability and enforcement provisions. Moreover, governments in power have disbanded some provincial commissions on whim, as has happened both in Ontario and, most recently, in British Columbia under the government of Gordon Campbell.

In 1997, Hedy Fry, then Secretary of State for Multiculturalism and the Status of Women, announced the creation of a charitable organization, the Canadian Race Relations Foundation (CRRF). Its purpose is to document the nature and extent of racism, facilitate the sharing of information on race relations, increase public awareness of the need to eliminate racism and discrimination, develop policies and programs to counteract racism and discrimination, and empower the groups targeted by racism through advocacy, education, and persuasive information (Canadian Race Relations Foundation, 1999). The effectiveness of this organization to influence meaningful and lasting change in the status of racialized minorities has yet to be determined.

A SUMMARY OF THE SOCIAL WELFARE EXPERIENCE OF THREE IMMIGRANT GROUPS

Social workers must be able to recognize the subtle and overt inequalities that various groups have endured historically and which continue to influence majority and minority immigrants' experiences and perceptions of social justice and equality. For purposes of illustration, the past and present social welfare experience of three immigrant groups is highlighted here.

Jewish Immigrants

The first Jewish settlers began to arrive under British rule, when restrictions against non-Catholic settlers were lifted (Weinfeld, Shaffir, & Cotler, 1981). Most of the 107 Jewish settlers listed in the 1831 census were relatively wealthy emigrants from the Thirteen Colonies of what would become the United States. They settled in Montreal with little difficulty. These Sephardic Jews, with ancestry in North Africa, Portugal, and Spain, established the congregation of the Remnants of Israel as early in 1768, through which they offered new immigrants help in adjusting to Canadian socio-economic conditions.

From 1840 to 1900, Jews from Germany, Poland, and the Russian Empire came as colonists, and were listed as more than 2000 residents in the 1889 census, mostly in Ontario and Quebec. These European or Ashkenazi immigrants had experienced poverty and suffering and survived as a closely knit, unified community. As their religious customs differed somewhat from those of the earlier Sephardic congregation, they founded Montreal's Shaar Hashomayim Congregation.

From 1870 to 1914, religious persecution in Russia drove 15 000 immigrants to seek better living standards and religious freedom in Canada. These refugees settled in Winnipeg, having accepted homestead grants or work on the Canadian Pacific Railway. By 1915, Jewish congregations existed in Winnipeg, Calgary, Regina, and Saskatoon, and the community in Canada was 125 000 strong (Tulchinsky, 1992).

Jewish immigration fluctuated according to economic conditions and religious persecution in their countries of origin. During World War I, the number of Jews from Eastern Europe increased; the number decreased during the Depression and rose again during World War II, despite protests in Canada. At the time Jews fell into the "less preferred" immigrant category (Glickman, 1981). The Jewish Immigrant Aid Services (JIAS), established in 1919, formulated a response to Canadian immigration policy, a role that it has continued to play. In 1934, the Canadian Jewish Congress lobbied on behalf of those Jewish refugees hoping to escape the Nazi regime and, despite protest from some quarters, Jewish immigration peaked between 1930 and 1940, when 11 005 were admitted. In the 1950s, these new arrivals were mostly displaced persons from the Hungarian uprising and the Jewish expulsion from Egypt in 1956.

In the late 1950s, the character of Jewish immigration entered a new phase, with the arrival of Israeli and North African Jews. Those from Morocco spoke French, were darker in appearance, and practised different religious rites and customs, which made their integration into the older European Jewish community challenging. During the 1970s, some 35 000 Jews (3500 yearly) immigrated to Canada. Currently the Canadian Jewish population stands at 348 605 (Statistics Canada, 2001), 99 percent of whom live in urban areas. The cities with the highest concentration of Jews are Montreal, Toronto, Winnipeg, Vancouver, and Ottawa.

Practising "acculturation without assimilation" (Shaffir, 1983), the Jewish community is among Canada's most institutionally complete. This means that, in major cities, Jewish organizations cater to the cultural and social welfare needs of their community—with hospitals, Jewish Family Services, and Jewish Vocational Services. Studies conducted over a 20-year period have indicated that, along with the British, Canadian Jews are overrepresented at the highest economic, education, and occupation levels, and they have integrated into the social, economic, and political fabric of the wider society.

Surely, their integration would not have been possible without most Canadians' acceptance and opportunities for population growth and upward mobility. Nevertheless, anti-Semitism exists in forms of covert discrimination, the occasional desecration of gravesites, hate propaganda, and holocaust denial. Issues in the Middle East continue to provide a focus for the community. Many in the community wish to vigorously pursue Nazi war criminals at home and abroad. Such ongoing issues both unify and divide their members, given the varying attitudes toward civil liberties and the emotions surrounding the holocaust.

Black Immigrants

Apparently, few Canadians realize that people of African descent were among the earliest people to come to Canada. This fact of the early black presence destroys the myth that legalized slavery never existed here (Christensen, 1998). Unique among people of colour, the Canadians of African descent had ancestors who suffered the cruel indignities of enslavement under French and British rule for more than 150 years (Winks, 1972). For blacks in Canada, and indeed throughout the Americas, oppression was normalized (even if unconsciously) in the psyches of white people through the legacy of slavery.

In 1628 Oliver de Jeune was the first slave recorded sold in New France. In 1689, the French king Louis XIV legalized slavery, to provide Africans to work in the fisheries, mines, and agriculture in New France, in Montreal, Quebec City, and Trois-Rivières. By 1759, there were some 4000 slaves in New France. The *Code Noire* regulated their lives, enacted to protect whites from slave revolt, theft, and escape. The law against intermarriage was not enforced in Quebec, and when a white man married a slave woman she gained freedom; everywhere else, freedom was gained only through "gift or purchase" (Cartwright, 1851).

Throughout the "founding" of present-day Quebec, New Brunswick, Nova Scotia, and Ontario, blacks were held as slaves until the early nineteenth century (Walker, 1980). They were legal chattels, advertised and sold on livestock markets. Their social welfare needs were ignored. Slaves who repeatedly attempted to escape were diagnosed as suffering from "drapetomani," a mental illness.

During the American Revolution in 1776, British Loyalists brought their 3000 freed slaves to Nova Scotia, their number exceeding that of whites in some areas. Land promised to blacks who had served in segregated armies seldom materialized. Blacks could be whipped, and they were denied food rations during the 1789 famine. In fact, three hangings for theft of food were recorded at the time. Mob violence in Shelburne and Birchtown resulted in the burning of their homes. Hundreds of disillusioned blacks left the colonies of the Canadas for Sierre Leone, Africa, in 1792, and more in 1800, to escape intolerable conditions.

During the War of 1812, ancestors of most of Nova Scotia's present African Canadian population arrived, having deserted their masters in the former American colonies. Debates about the profitability and morality of slavery led to its eventual abolishment, throughout the

British colonies, in 1833. Hundreds of slaves escaped from America to Canada by means of the Underground Railroad, but here too they found themselves denied access to community services, fair wages and union membership, housing, recreational facilities, and restaurants. By 1860, Canada had a population of 60 000 blacks. After the American Civil War, many returned to the United States.

The first official Canadian census, in 1871, recorded 21 496 blacks, the third-largest non-charter group, surpassed only by the Dutch (29 662) and the Germans (202 991). In Nova Scotia, New Brunswick, and Ontario, segregated residential areas, schools, and land ownership restrictions were legislated. Segregated public schools and social services ended only in the 1960s in Nova Scotia (for example, the Home for Coloured Girls) and parts of Ontario. Blacks were also unwelcome in the Prairies. Other than the 3000 Caribbean females allowed in as domestic servants between 1955 and 1965, immigration restrictions kept most blacks out of Canada. Professions such as nursing were closed to black women until the 1950s (Calliste, 1996).

The closest approximation to equality that blacks experienced during the early 1900s was on Vancouver Island. There skilled and literate blacks opened businesses and seemed generally accepted by Victoria's white population although they were restricted from serving on juries. Black pioneers also settled on Saltspring Island.

The next large wave of blacks came in the late 1960s, when racially restrictive immigration regulations were removed (Christensen & Weinfeld, 1993). Most came from the West Indies as skilled labourers (95 percent) and found work with the railway (as porters, for example, the occupation most readily available to them).

Haitians are Canada's newest black immigrants, numbering about 90 000. Most have settled in Montreal (Jean-Baptiste, 1979). Two "black solitudes," the Creole/French-speaking and the English-speaking, now exist. Those Haitians who came in the early 1960s were mostly professionals; for example, 150 were physicians (LaFerriere, 1983). Some 17 000, arriving later (1967–1973), had varied backgrounds. Some came as "visitors" and remained under the general amnesty of 1973; 1500 were deported; and those who remained illegally were exploited in the job market. Currently, these Haitian immigrants are facing prejudice and discrimination familiar to the older English-speaking black community, but with fewer linguistic difficulties.

Blacks have responded to racism and inequality by organizing black churches, self-help movements, political lobby groups, social services, and the black press. This fact broadens the skewed portrayal of blacks in the mainstream media showing them as involved almost exclusively in sports, entertainment, and crime (Fleras & Kuhz, 2001).

Today, about 662 210 blacks live in Canada (Statistics Canada, 2001), a population that is ethnically, culturally, and religiously diverse. They are united in their experience of systemic racism in education (Burrell & Christensen, 1987), employment and promotion (Henry & Ginzberg, 1985), and the justice system (Christensen, 2003). Major human rights and equity issues hinder their well-being and upward mobility, even for those of the well-educated middle class. Owing to racial profiling and police brutality, black males in particular are regularly harassed. Many have been killed, though unarmed. Blacks are now overrepresented in prisons in Ontario (Henry et al., 1999).

Historically, blacks have made significant contributions to Canada, but their racial identity is seldom associated with their achievements (for example, Mathieu d'Acosta translated the Micmac language for the French explorer Samuel de

Champlain in the early 1600s; freed black artisans designed Nova Scotia's historic Citadel; James Douglas, who was bi-racial, served as the first governor of the colony of British Columbia in the 1850s). More recently, black men and women have entered all Canada's professions and hold elected office at both provincial and federal levels. They will undoubtedly continue to press for the enforcement of their human rights and for equity legislation, hoping to soon enjoy full participation and a sense of belonging in Canada.

The Chinese

The Chinese first came to the Canada during the Fraser River gold rush of the 1850s. They wanted to escape the economic hardships caused by imperialist invasions and peasant revolts in China (Li, 198; Nguyen, 1982). Referred to as "the yellow peril," many hoped to return one day to China, and government officials expected them to do so. When they were unable to amass sufficient wealth to return to China, most remained in British Columbia, and were viewed as casual cheap labour.

Another wave of about 17 000 Chinese entered the country to help build the Canadian Pacific Railroad in the mid-1800s. They experienced extreme forms of harassment and oppression from the general public, and also as a result of government policies. Prevented from bringing their wives and children to Canada, Chinese "bachelors" faced social sanctions for "lusting after" white women. When the railroad was completed, an unknown number who were able to afford passage did return to China. Those who remained took any available work they could, including laundry work, clearing forests, gardening, and domestic service, for low wages. Even such employment was perceived as unfair competition by white workers, who formed the Workingman's Protective Association in Victoria, British

Columbia. Chinese workers there were charged a $30 licence fee, and a $500 licence fee was charged for the use of opium. Considered inferior and unsuitable for assimilation, the Chinese were barred from receiving welfare benefits, owning crown lands, employment in public works, owning liquor licences, and by 1875, voting. They formed secret societies and self-help groups, which faced organized opposition from the Anti-Mongolian League, which claimed to be concerned about Chinese morals.

The Alberta public was no kinder, blaming the Chinese for spreading smallpox during the 1892 epidemic. The Royal Canadian Mounted Police often had to respond to violent anti-Chinese outbreaks and threats of lynchings. A Royal Commission on Chinese Immigration in 1884 reported that British Columbia's citizens desired restrictive legislation, to allow the province to be "reserved for people of the European race." Whites instigated a race riot against Chinese people in Vancouver in 1907. Head taxes ranging from $100 to $500 were imposed on all Chinese entering Canada between 1885 and 1903.

Finally, the Chinese Immigration Act of 1923 completely barred the entry of people from China. Until the Act was repealed in 1947, wives could not enter Canada. There were 12 men for every woman, the highest imbalance of all the ethnic groups in the country. The growth of a second generation was delayed, as family members had to live apart most of their lives.

Politicians and the media debated the "Oriental problem" for some hundred years. The unfair treatment of the Chinese continued until well into the twentieth century, severely affecting their social welfare experience. In both World Wars, Chinese men were barred from military service until the country acknowledged the desperate need for more soldiers; Chinese recruits served in segregated units. Elderly Chinese were not admitted to the British Columbia

Provincial Home as late as 1936; until 1947, although they could become physicians, the Chinese were legally barred from many other professions, such as law and dentistry; and in 1948 organized labour was still protesting Chinese immigration at hearings. "Chinatowns" were considered places of ill repute, not tourist attractions (Anderson, 1991).

Still, the Chinese and their institutions managed to survive. The 2001 census indicates that the 1 029 395 Chinese in Canada are among the most highly educated groups and among those with the most people in higher occupation categories, no doubt enhanced by the number of business-class immigrants entering Canada in recent years. Many give generously to Chinese agencies and mainstream institutions, gaining a measure of acceptance in both communities. In major cities, there are Chinese hospitals, old people's homes, language and cultural schools, social services, and an ethnic press. Today's Chinese community is neither homogeneous nor institutionally complete; members' daily needs cannot be totally satisfied independent of the institutions of the wider society. Moreover, ethnic social-welfare institutions serve immigrants from Hong Kong, Taiwan, and Mainland China, and other parts of the world, including Vietnam.

The first wave of ethnic Chinese arrived from Vietnam in 1975, when Canadian attitudes were sympathetic toward refugees created by the Vietnam War. Educated, French- or English-speaking, middle-class, and urban, they integrated successfully, 60 percent settling in the province of Quebec (Employment and Immigration Canada, 1982). The second, and largest, wave of ethnic Chinese from Vietnam arrived between 1979 and 1980, when Canada received some 60 000. These "boat people" represented a broader spectrum of social classes. Most of these refugees spoke neither French nor English and government agents settled them far from Chinese support networks, in, for example, the Yukon and the Northwest Territories. Government programs and private sponsors assisted with relocation efforts.

Although overt forms of prejudice and discrimination against the Chinese have decreased considerably, challenges remain. Resentment of Chinese monster houses, Asian malls, English as a Second Language (ESL) courses in public schools, and Chinese "boat people" hoping to enter Canada illegally (Daggett, 1999) is frequently expressed. Canadian media report gang activity that many Chinese consider exaggerated. Schools and social service agencies are concerned about teenagers left alone while their "astronaut" parents return to Asia on business. Some perceive anti-Asian prejudice that lingers under the surface of civility shown toward the Chinese today (Laquian & Laquian, 1997).

However, these problems exist with mitigating factors as well. The Governor General of Canada, Adrienne Clarkson, is of Chinese ancestry, and Chinese Canadians exercise more political participation. China's international standing as an emerging global force also is a source of pride for this group.

PROVIDING FOR THE SOCIAL WELFARE NEEDS OF IMMIGRANTS

Social welfare provisions that affect services for immigrants must be considered in terms of specific services to immigrants and in the context of Canadian social welfare generally (Christensen, 1999). Upon arrival, immigrants immediately need social welfare supports for information and referrals, housing and, often, for language interpretation or translation. Long term they may need some of the above services, as well as health, recreation, and education for school-aged children or adults who must upgrade their skills or have foreign credentials accepted.

Although a laissez-faire philosophy led Canada's earliest immigrants to fend for themselves with little state intervention, the development of the welfare state has altered attitudes toward immigrant needs. For many of these newcomers, the universal programs provided in Canada, such as medicare, Employment Insurance, and Old Age Pension, go far beyond the provisions they knew in their countries of origin. However, the erosion of government programs in recent years has been detrimental to immigrants, as well as to the general public.

Government Programs

Since 1966, designated federal government departments have been mandated to provide for immigrant workers' reception and basic needs. They have been responsible for assisting with immigrants' long-term social, political, and cultural integration, supplemented by the services of voluntary agencies. However, because of the lack of formal agreements and inadequate budgets and staff, little more than language training and a small grant for voluntary agencies has traditionally been provided.

Under the British North America Act, immigration was a shared jurisdiction, with social welfare the responsibility of the provinces. The provincial and the federal governments have established few mechanisms for ongoing consultation between themselves regarding programs for immigrants and those programs that exist have been inadequate in their research, language training, program funding, and cooperation with the voluntary sector.

This lack of coordinated planning has, historically, left the question of immigrant adjustment in a twilight zone. Despite more federal–provincial agreements concerning immigrants' recruitment and admission,

problems of jurisdiction and joint planning to address their settlement needs remain. Majority-group Canadians seem to feel that immigration may be beneficial in the long term but problematic and costly in the short term, so most provinces have let the federal government assume major responsibility for immigration matters.

The federal government conducted a major review of its role in settlement in 1994. In 1995, the Settlement Renewal initiative announced the government's intention to transfer funds to the provincial and territorial governments for settling immigrants (Sutherland, Summer/Fall 1999, 38); but only two provinces, British Columbia and Manitoba, have signed such agreements to date. Today the greatest responsibility for managing immigrant settlement programs remains with Citizenship and Immigration Canada.

A number of these programs currently exist, carried out in various regions of the country. They provide services in the form of orientation, referral to community services, and counselling, with emphasis on the labour market and adaptation to it. The Immigrant Settlement and Adaptation Program (ISAP) funds organizations to deliver direct, essential services; the HOST program matches new immigrants with Canadians to help them integrate; and the Language Instruction for Newcomers to Canada (LINC) program helps the newcomers with their new language. A Global Case Management System is slowly being implemented (2000–2005) intended to assist business immigrants overseas and inland.

Problems in Government-Sponsored Programs Lack of funding remains the biggest problem in government-sponsored services. Programs are often temporary, inadequate, and not guaranteed for the long term Major structural problems include regional disparity (few services exist in rural areas); disparities in access to government decision-makers, social agencies, and social-welfare bureaucracies among the various ethnic and racial groups (gained through employment opportunities and representation on boards and committees); variations in the length of time that immigrant populations may receive services; and the very nature of the bureaucratic structures through which the services are offered.

Government bureaucracies too often lack the personnel to offer quality services to immigrants from underrepresented backgrounds. Professionally trained social workers constitute a minority of those involved with immigrant selection and adaptation.

Service delivery is further hampered by the immigrant groups' lack of knowledge about lawful rights and services, which leads to underused services; lack of a full range of services available in immigrants' languages; weak coordination in referral services between mainstream agencies and those serving immigrant and ethno-racial populations; and a dearth of qualified staff familiar with the special problems immigrants face, including those that are systemic.

Voluntary Sector and Non-Government Services

The responsibility for immigrant integration is often left to the voluntary sector by default. The several hundred voluntary services across Canada that are involved in immigrant social welfare can be categorized, roughly, as follows:

- sectarian agencies serving, for example, those of Catholic, Baptist, or Jewish faith
- non-sectarian agencies with professional personnel specifically to serve immigrants (for example, Montreal's Service d'accueil aux voyageurs et aux immigrants)
- community organizations and services with professional staff who often serve immigrants in addition to their other

activities (for example, university settlement houses, YMCA/YWCA, YMHA/YWHA)
- committees offering immigrant adaptation as part of their services (for example, the National Black Coalition)
- professionally run organizations helping immigrants of their own ethnic groups (for example, Jewish Immigrant Aid Services)
- organizations that contribute to immigrant welfare by providing public information and education (for example, Toronto's Urban Alliance on Race Relations)
- cultural organizations that promote cohesion in ethnic groups by maintaining traditions
- miscellaneous organizations that have procured temporary, and often precarious, funding to assist with specific needs such as health and well-being (for example, Vancouver's Multicultural Family Centre)

Issues in Voluntary and Non-Government Sectors The extent to which various ethnic and racialized groups have been able to supply the needs of their own members varies greatly. Factors range from their internal resources, cohesiveness, and organization to access to society's economic structure to access to major decision-makers. Similarly, the degree of help mainstream organizations themselves seek is far from uniform, and some groups are greatly underrepresented (Christensen, 1986). Popular stereotypes suggest that some ethnic and racialized groups "take care of their own," whereas important needs of these populations—especially those of women, children, and the elderly—are simply not being met. Dependence on government causes competition among ethnic agencies for scarce dollars, limits the types of programs they can offer to accord with government priorities, and makes long-term planning difficult. Even so, the agencies established by ethno-racial or immigrant communities themselves are often reported as more effective in responding to their members' unique needs than mainstream agencies with better, and more permanent, funding.

IMPLICATIONS: SOCIAL WORK'S ETHICAL RESPONSIBILITY

Historically, schools of social work have not viewed the preparation of their students to work with immigrants and racialized groups as a priority (Christensen, 1996). Given the source countries of Canada's immigrants since the 1960s, any continuation of this state of affairs must be considered unethical and in violation of the codes of ethics of both the national body (Canadian Association of Social Work, 1994) and most provincial associations.

Traditional social work methods have been recognized as often inappropriate at best, and harmful in the worst instances, to immigrants and long-term residents of racialized minority backgrounds (Christensen, 1999). It is now widely acknowledged that practice methods, expectations, and values are geared to white North American middle-class clients, the group from which professional social workers were traditionally drawn (Christensen, 2003, 82).

However, as more people from these minorities enter the profession, the emphasis has changed from the "culturally different" client to the social worker's need to be culturally competent when serving clients of various backgrounds (Fong and Gibbs, 1995). Concerns about practice methods include (1) an intra-psychic, individualistic approach to what causes problems—what is inappropriate for those living in extended families and for those dealing with systemic racism; (2) different treatment offered to racialized groups based on social workers' biases or lack of knowledge—for example, removing children from their parents when the parents are having trouble adapting to life in Canada or assuming male dominance or violence are cultural values; (3) the inappropriate intervention into individual and family situations that actually require advocacy, community development, or structural change methods. Many racialized minority immigrants view such methods as unhelpful and as the means of maintaining the status quo (Christensen, 1990).

Problems and gaps in services arising from the above have been repeatedly noted in the literature, and their negative impact on minority immigrants is well documented (Christensen, 1986; Doyle & Visano, 1987). Studies note, for example, the lack of qualified staff who know and understand immigrant cultures; perceptions of immigrants as "multi-problem" clients and immigrants receiving only short-term help; work overload for ethno-racial minority staff. On top of these problems rest the expectations that the workers be experts on their clients' assumed backgrounds; the disproportionate numbers of children of colour living in care or detention centres; needs for translation and interpretation services; and policies that constrain workers who wish to use culturally appropriate modes of treatment.

The *Crossroads Report*, by the Task Force on Multicultural and Multiracial Issues, (commissioned by the Canadian Association of Schools of Social Work, 1991), documented the perceptions of faculty, students, field instructors, and community groups as to how schools of social work in Canada were faring regarding immigrant and minority groups. The report recognized that all other forms of diversity—such as sexual orientation, gender, disability—are affected by ethnicity and racialization. It called for qualified faculty to teach required courses dealing, in depth, with issues that specifically affect immigrants and racial minority groups. There is still work to be done before we achieve this goal. Social work educators have an ethical responsibility to ensure that their students graduate well prepared for the realities of their multicultural and multiracial clients (Christensen, 1999).

CONCLUSION

More than a decade ago, a Canadian government report recommended that "in order to ensure that immigrants from the Third World and their progeny are not discriminated against," the government institute a more vigorous race relations program with adequate resources, strong leadership, and new initiatives (Canada Employment and Immigration Advisory Council, 1989, 14). Today, rather than the decision-makers providing the leadership, the opposite has come to pass. We are seeing evidence of a backlash against the short-lived race relations and anti-racism programs that government departments have set up and those established by many other organizations in the public and the private sectors. Apparently, many are satisfied that problems of racial discrimination were dealt with sufficiently in short training sessions on this topic over two decades from 1980 to 2000.

Today we perceive a general lack of understanding in Canada's liberal democracy that, given our colonial legacy, eradicating racism is both a personal and a societal journey. We cannot solve these problems with a "quick fix." A Statistics Canada study indicates that, although the education level of immigrants continues to exceed that of those born in Canada, immi-

grant males earned 40 percent less than their Canadian-born counterparts in 2000, double the 17 percent gap that existed in 1980. The wage gap between immigrant and Canadian-born women is also widening, although less dramatically (*Vancouver Sun*, 2003). Certain racialized minority-group immigrants in particular know that they face systemic barriers that may play a role in their downward mobility. In Canadian society, one's quality of life is determined, to a great extent, by monetary resources; a wage earner must purchase (for him- or herself and a family) food, higher education, housing, supplemental costs of medical care, and a way of life, from birth to the senior years, dependent on the degree of economic security one can attain.

Despite these obstacles to full participation, immigrants contribute to Canada in important ways. For one thing, they become taxpayers and consumers, putting far more into the economy than they take out of it in social welfare services. Employable adults contribute to the labour force at no cost to taxpayers for their education. The children of immigrants inevitably become bicultural, contributing to the "Canadian way of life." Last, but surely not least, immigrants contribute positively to the qualities that make Canada an exciting country in which to live.

To the extent that Canada ensures immigrants and their progeny equal opportunities, they will no doubt assume positions in all walks of life. There is now ample evidence to suggest some of the steps to be taken if we are to move toward all groups' equal access and full participation in social welfare:

- Social welfare personnel at all levels must become aware of the effects, however subtle, of ethnocentrism and racism in existing policies and practices on the social welfare of minority immigrants.

- Outreach, information, and education programs must be developed to involve underserved and underrepresented minorities in all aspects of social welfare, from policy and planning to direct service and evaluation. Also, more racialized minorities must enter the profession.
- Mainstream and ethnic agencies must undertake joint efforts to bring minority immigrants' needs before governments and the public (by use of the media, for example) as legitimate and vital concerns that affect the well-being of society as a whole.

- Anti-racism must be integral to every aspect of social welfare policy and practice as we seek to improve the experience of people of colour in the coming decades.

At the beginning of the twenty-first century, social work professionals have an opportunity to lead the way courageously toward a truly egalitarian Canadian society, one in which the human needs of all are fulfilled and people of every background have the opportunities to reach their full potential.

REFERENCES

Abella, R. (1984). *Report of the Commission on Equality in Employment*. Ottawa: Supply and Services Canada.

Anderson, A. B., & Frideres, J. S. (1981). *Ethnicity in Canada: Theoretical perspectives*. Toronto: Butterworths.

Anderson, K. J. (1991). *Vancouver's Chinatown: Racial discourse in Canada, 1875–1980*. Montreal: McGill-Queen's University Press.

Berry, J. W. (1991). Sociopsychological costs and benefits of multiculturalism. Working Paper #24. Ottawa: Economic Council of Canada.

Bolaria, B. S., & Li, P. S. (1988). *Racial oppression in Canada*.(2d ed.). Toronto: Garamond Press.

Burell, L. F., & Christensen, C. P. (1987). Minority students' perceptions of high school: Implications for Canadian school personnel. *Journal of Multicultural Counseling and Development*. 15. 3-15.

Calliste, A. (1996). Anti-racism organizing and resistance in nursing. *CRSA/RCSA*. 33.3, 361-390.

Canada Employment and Immigration Advisory Council. (1989). *Immigration in the 1990s*. Ottawa: Ministry of Supply and Services Canada.

Canadian Association of Schools of Social Work (CASSW). (1991). *Social work education at the crossroads: Report of the Task Force on Multicultural and Multiracial Issues in Social Work Education*. Ottawa: CASSW.

Canadian Association of Social Workers. (1994). *Social Work Code of Ethics*, reprinted in F. Turner & J. Turner (Gen. eds.) (2001), Appendix. *Canadian social welfare* (4th ed.). Ottawa and Toronto: Allyn & Bacon.

Canadian Bar Association (January 2002). *Submission on Immigration and Refugee Protection Regulations, Parts 1 to 17*. Ottawa: National Citizenship and Immigration Law Section, Canadian Bar Association.

Canadian Council for Refugees. (2001). Bill C-11 brief.

Canadian Race Relations Foundation (CRRF). (1999). *CRRF Overview*. 1–2.

Cartwright, S. A. (1851). Report on the diseases and physical peculiarities of the Negro race. In A. C. Caplan, H. T. Engelhardt, & J. J. McCartney (Eds.), *Concepts of health and disease* (pp. 691–715). Boston, MA: Addison Wesley, 1981.

Christensen, C. P. (May 1986). Chinese residents' expectations of mainstream social services: Clues to service underuse? *Intervention*. 74. 41–49.

Christensen, C. P. (1990). Toward a framework for social work education in a multicultural and multiracial Canada. In S. A. Yelaja (Ed.), *The settlement and integration of new immigrants to Canada* (pp. 103–124). Waterloo, ON: Faculty of Social Work, Wilfrid Laurier University & Centre for Social Welfare Services.

Christensen, C. P. (1996). The impact of racism on the education of social service workers. In C. James (Ed.), *Perspectives on racism and the human service sector: A case for change* (pp. 140–151). Toronto: University of Toronto Press.

Christensen, C. P. (1998). Chapter 5, Social welfare and social work in Canada: Aspects of the black experience. In V. D'Oyley & C. James (Eds.), *Re-visioning: Canadian perspectives on the Education of Africans in the Late 20th Century* (pp. 36–57). Concord, ON: Captus Press.

Christensen, C. P. (1999). Multiculturalism, racism and social work: An exploration of issues in the Canadian context. In G. Yong-Li & D. Este (Eds.), *Professional social service delivery in a multicultural world* (pp. 293–310). Toronto: Canadian Scholars Press.

Christensen, C. P. (2003). Canadian society: Social policy and ethno racial diversity. In A. Al-krenawi & G. J. R. Graham (Eds.), *Multicultural social work in Canada: Working with diverse ethno-racial communities* (pp. 70–97). Don Mills, ON: Oxford University Press.

Christensen, C. P., & Weinfeld, M. (1993). The black family in Canada: A preliminary exploration of family patterns and inequality. *Canadian Ethnic Studies.* XXV. 26–44.

Citizenship and Immigration Canada. (1998). *Building on a strong foundation for the 21st century: New directions for immigration and refugee policy and legislation.* Ottawa: Minister of Public Works and Government of Canada.

Citizenship and Immigration Canada. (October 12, 2001). *News Release 01-19: Strengthened immigration measures to counter terrorism.* Ottawa: Government of Canada.

Citizenship and Immigration Canada. (2002). *Facts and figures, 2002: Immigration overview.* Ottawa.

Citizenship and Immigration Canada. (2003a). *Annual report to Parliament 2003.* Ottawa: Minister of Public Works and Government of Canada.

Citizenship and Immigration Canada. (2003b). Point System from **www.cic.gc.ca**

Daggett, L. (October 14, 1999). Chinese migrants: Myths and facts #1. *AMSSA update.* Vancouver: Affiliation of Multicultural & Service Agencies of B.C.

The Daily. (2003). **www.statcan.ca/Daily**

Doyle, R., & Visano, L. (1987). *Access to health and social services for members of diverse cultural and racial groups.* Reports 1 and 2. Toronto: Social Planning Council of Metropolitan Toronto.

Employment and Immigration Canada. (1982). *Indochinese refugees: The Canadian response, 1979 and 1980.* Ottawa: Ministry of Supply and Services Canada.

Employment and Immigration Canada. (1990). *Annual report to Parliament: Immigration plan for 1991–1995.* Ottawa–Hull: Ministry of Supply and Services.

Fleras, A., & Elliott, J. L. (2002). *Unequal relations: An introduction to race, ethnic and aboriginal dynamics in Canada.* Scarborough, ON: Prentice Hall Canada.

Fleras, A., & Kuhz, J. L. (2001). *Media and minorities: Representing diversity in a multicultural Canada.*

Fong, G. W., & Gibbs, J. T. (1995). Facilitating services to multicultural communities in a dominant culture setting: An organizational perspective. *Administration in Social Work,* 19. 1–24.

Glickman, Y. (1981). Political socialization and the social protest of Canadian Jewry: Some historical and contemporary perspectives. In J. Dahlie & T. Fernando (Eds.), *Ethnicity, Power and Politics in Canada* (pp. 123–150). Toronto: Methuen.

Hawkins, F. (1972). *Canada and immigration: Public policy and public concern*. Montreal: McGill-Queen's University Press.

Henry, F., & Ginzberg, E. (1985). *Who gets the work? A test of racial discrimination in employment*. Toronto: Urban Alliance on Race Relations and the Social Planning Council of Metropolitan Toronto.

Henry, F., Tator, C., Mattis, W., & Rees, T. (1999). *The colour of democracy: Racism in Canadian society* (2d ed.). Toronto: Harcourt Brace & Company Canada.

Jean-Baptiste, J. (1979). *Haitians in Canada*. Hull, QC: Ministry of Supply and Services Canada.

Kallen, E. (1982). *Ethnicity and human rights in Canada*. Toronto: Gage.

Krauter, J. F., & Davis, M. (1978). *Minority Canadians: Ethnic groups*. Toronto: Methuen.

LaFerriere, M. (1983). The education of West Indian and Haitian students in schools of Montreal: Issues and prospects. In J. E. Elliott (Ed.), *Two nations, many cultures* (pp. 158–172). Scarborough, Ont.: Prentice-Hall Canada.

Laquian, E., & Laquian, A. (1997). Asian immigration and racism in Canada—A search for policy options. In E. Laquian, A. Laquian, & T. McGee (Eds.), *The silent debate: Asian immigration & racism in Canada* (pp. 3–28). Vancouver: Institute of Asian Research, University of British Columbia.

Li, P. S. (1988). *The Chinese in Canada*. Don Mills, ON: Oxford University Press.

Nguyen, S. D. (1982). The psycho-social adjustment and mental health needs of Southeast Asian refugees. *Psychiatric Journal of the University of Ottawa* 7.1, 6–34.

Porter, J. (1965). *The vertical mosaic*. Toronto: University of Toronto Press.

Ramcharan, S. (1982). *Racism: Non-whites in Canada*. Toronto: Butterworths.

Royal Commission on Bilingualism and Biculturalism. (1970). *The cultural contributions of the other ethnic groups: Report book IV*. Ottawa: Queen's Printer.

Sarazin, D. (Winter 1999). A new citizenship act. *Vis-à-Vis: The Citizenship & Immigration Canada Magazine*. Ottawa: Minister of Public Works & Government Services Canada.

Satzewich, V. (1991). Social stratification: Class and racial inequality. In B. S. Bolaria (Ed.), *Social issues and contradictions in Canadian society*. Toronto: Harcourt Brace Jovanovich, Canada.

Shaffir, W. (1983). Jewish immigration to Canada. In J. E. Elliot (Ed.), *Two nations, many cultures: Ethnic groups in Canada* (pp. 280–291). Scarborough, ON: Prentice-Hall.

Simmons, A.B. (1997) Globalization and backlash racism in the 1990s: The case of Asian immigration. In E. Laquian, A. Laquian, & T. McGee (Eds.), *The silent debate: Asian immigration & racism in Canada* (pp. 29–50). Vancouver: Institute of Asian Research, University of British Columbia.

Statistics Canada. (1996). *1996 Census of Canada*. Ottawa: Ministry of Supply and Services Canada.

Statistics Canada. (2001a). *2001 Census of Population*. Ottawa: Ministry of Supply and Services Canada.

Statistics Canada. (2001b). *Visible minority population: census metropolitan areas*. URL Internet **www.statcan.ca**

Supply and Services Canada. (July 1988*). An act for the preservation and enhancement of multiculturalism in Canada*. Ottawa: House of Commons of Canada.

Sutherland, P. (Summer/Fall 1999). *Vis-à-Vis: The CIC Magazine*. 38. Ottawa: Citizenship and Immigration Canada.

Tepper, E. L. (1997). Multiculturalism and racism: An evaluation In E. Laquian, A. Laquian, & T. McGee (Eds.), *The silent debate: Asian immigration & racism in Canada* (pp. 51–65). Vancouver: Institute of Asian Research, University of British Columbia.

Tulchinsky, G. (1992). *The origins of the Canadian Jewish community.* Toronto: Lester Publishing.

Vancouver Sun. (2003a). Shifts in economy cut earnings of immigrant men. *Vancouver Sun*, "Business" section. Thursday, October 9, 2003. D-4.

Vancouver Sun. (2003b). Ottawa sued over residency cards, *Vancouver Sun*, Monday, December 2, 2003, A1–2.

Villasin, F. O., & Phillips, A. M. (1994). Falling through the cracks: Domestic workers and progressive movements. *Canadian Women's Studies.* 14. 2. 87–90.

Walker, J. (1980). *The history of blacks in Canada: A study guide for teachers and students.* Ottawa: Minister of State for Multiculturalism.

Weinfeld, M., Shaffir, W., & Cotler, I. (1981). *The Canadian Jewish mosaic.* Toronto: John Wiley.

Winks, R. (1972). *The blacks in Canada: A history.* Montreal: McGill-Queen's University Press.

chapter thirteen

Contemporary Issues in Biopsychosocial Functioning

William Rowe

INTRODUCTION

Difficulties in daily living can be divided into three broad areas: issues related to individual persons and families, challenges related to developing, sustaining, and exiting relationships, and pressures stemming from or exacerbated by one's social structure and the environment. Not only do these three general categories relate to one another but they add further levels of complexity to one other. For example, the family shapes more than our understanding of the individual; it exists as a unit active in solving and creating its problems. The structure of the broader society exists on a third level that is active in problem-solving and problem-creating at the local, national, and international levels.

This chapter is divided into nine sections. Issues of self-worth and issues associated with sexuality, aging, and substance abuse are some of the biopsychosocial concerns with which individuals commonly struggle. The sections concerning problems associated with relationships and with living within a family look at how the system as a unit contributes to and solves problems. Finally, the sections on issues in the workplace, difficulties associated with cultural diversity and systemic racism, problems that arise from industrial/environmental and biomedical disasters, and global uncertainty show how all of these challenge biopsychosocial functioning.

The individual's capacity to cope with or adapt to life's problems is influenced primarily by three phenomena. These may be referred to as "nature," "nurture," and "fate." "Nature" in this context refers to a person's biological and neurological endowments. His or her capacity to respond to biopsychosocial problems will be influenced in some situations by his or her inherited physical attributes (size or attractiveness) and mental abilities (developmental delays or exceptional IQ). An individual with a genetically determined learning disability will face a greater challenge in the learning environment and, as a result, may fail to achieve both in school and later in the work environment.

The term "nurture" refers to the rich mix of physical and psychological care or "feeding" that people require in order to develop their full potential. Poor nutrition, for example, can have long-term as well as immediate effects, and inadequate psychological nurturance can greatly affect personality development. A person who is overfed may become obese and the victim of ridicule by peers, whereas a person who grows up in the unstable environment of an alcoholic household may be left with disabling feelings of insecurity and inadequacy.

The term "fate" is used to describe the multitude of situational and serendipitous experiences that people must negotiate or cope with in their lives. These include accidents, sickness, loss, and numerous other calamities. A person who is preparing for marriage could be crippled in a car accident, become sexually dysfunctional, and as a result feel less confident in a relationship. Fate can also provide opportunities that increase a person's capacity to negotiate the world. Falling in with "the right crowd" or meeting an inspirational teacher who takes a special interest are fortuitous events that open doors of opportunity.

The individual's capacity for adaptation is often expressed as a person's level of biopsychosocial functioning. Two people faced with the same life crisis, such as

marital separation, will respond differently. Beyond the levels of social, financial, and emotional supports available in their environments, they will also respond according to the individual personality (passive or independent) and experience (previous divorce in the family) of each. A person who is chronically depressed or physically incapacitated will face additional stress during the crisis, which may increase the likelihood of a maladaptive response.

It is imperative that the social worker not be judgmental about personal traits and capacities (for example, deeming someone lazy or stupid). He or she must be equipped to make an objective and accurate assessment when considering biopsychosocial problems.

People who experience problems in biopsychosocial functioning form the bulk of those referred to clinical social workers for help. Their problems may be mild or severe, acute or chronic, situational or endemic, and most of us will experience these problems to some degree in our lives.

The types of biopsychosocial problems can vary widely, and effective intervention requires a great deal of knowledge and skill. The following sections detail some of the more common ones that challenge social workers and their clients.

ISSUES ASSOCIATED WITH SELF-WORTH, IDENTITY, AND ALIENATION

An individual's sense of self-worth or self-esteem is a fundamental component of her overall personality. Self-worth is established early in life and is influenced heavily by the quality of physical and emotional nurturance available to the developing infant. If a child perceives herself as worthless, she may filter all of life's events through a low-grade depression and never achieve fulfillment in tasks or relationships.

If her early self-perception is grandiose or inflated, she may become narcissistic and find herself constantly disappointed in events and people. A person born with a physical disability may develop self-loathing both by virtue of physical discomfort (pain, clinical poking, and prodding), and social discomfort (fear of rejection by others, inability to participate). Even people who appear otherwise successful and competent to others may be emotionally damaged by criticism or repeated failures as a result of fundamental self-esteem problems.

A person's ability to establish a separate and secure sense of identity is also heavily influenced by the quality of early nurturance the individual experiences. If a toddler is reinforced for autonomous activity and receives positive messages about his unique attributes, he will develop a sense of confidence about his individuality that forms the basis for the establishment of his personal identity.[1] Successive roles and achievements through adolescence and young adulthood further shape the mosaic of his personality.

Without this core sense of self, young people may experience identity crises that can lead to depression, aimlessness, or substance abuse as they try to answer the question "Who am I?"[2] If a person's whole identity is based on one function or job, and that role changes or ceases to be, she may be less able to adapt to such changes than those people whose identities are rooted in more diverse aspects of themselves. An executive displaced following a company reorganization can confront an identity crisis, just as a parent experiencing the "empty nest" syndrome can when her last child leaves home.

Various events can trigger a person's alienation, from himself, from others, or from society in general. The crisis can be both the cause and the effect of poor social functioning. For example, if an infant is raised in an emotionally confusing or anxiety-filled environment, she may retreat from feelings altogether and find that she is out of touch with her "inner" self. Such feelings may be transitory or persistent, circumscribed or pervasive. Alienation from self can be a factor in major mental illnesses such as schizophrenia, or it may underlie a generalized unhappiness or a lack of purpose in life, which is a feature of depression. Even though it is widely accepted that major mental illnesses are associated with biochemical imbalances that require pharmacological management, the psychosocial issues strongly shape recovery and re-adaptation.

Alienation from others can be caused by an individual's inadequate capacity for building or sustaining a relationship. It can also be the result of a series of disastrous or destructive relationship experiences. People in such circumstances may find themselves unable or unwilling to interact with others, which can lead to isolation or loneliness.

People's alienation from society in general can be the result of a "poor fit" between an individual's norms and fundamental beliefs and those of the general population. Sometimes this condition is linked to racial, religious, or cultural differences and sometimes to basic differences in values. In some circumstances, this kind of alienation becomes a factor in the formation of counter-culture youth groups or in antisocial behavior in general.[3] The older members of immigrant families may find assimilation into a new culture more difficult and become withdrawn and depressed. Helping these individuals get involved in ethnically appropriate seniors centres can help them considerably.

Most people experience some problems with self-worth, identity, and alienation as they attempt to navigate life's challenges. A great deal can be done to restore self-esteem and prevent its loss, to support individual identity, and combat alienation in order to improve people's general social function.

ISSUES ASSOCIATED WITH SEXUALITY

Sex and sexuality provide an extraordinary preoccupation in many areas of our society. The media, the entertainment industry, art, religion, and the helping professions all devote a great deal of attention to promoting, repressing, improving, or controlling the expression of sexuality. In addition to its obvious function in procreation, sexuality has become increasingly significant as a dimension of the human personality, expressed in infinite variations that can improve or disturb social functioning.

"Sexual identity" and "gender" are two important concepts. Sexual identity is one of the first things that distinguishes one person from others: are you male or female and to what degree? Gender refers to the roles and behaviours we learn as part of what it means to "be a man" or to "be a woman."[4] The media convey caricatures of the macho male and the feminine female that few people measure up to. Yet falling short of these images can greatly affect the degree of confidence a person has in him- or herself.

Children are clearly differentiated sexually by the age of 3, as much by the external messages they receive as by their own biology or internal perceptions.[5] In extreme cases, people can express problems with sexual identity as transvestitism or transsexualism. Even though the latter can be corrected by transsexual surgery, the post-operative adjustment of people who are gender-dysphoric is fraught with complications. The 1970s and 1980s witnessed increasing tolerance for and, in certain circles, preference for androgyny, which is essentially an individual's ability to accept and display the characteristics of both masculine and feminine personalities. While this trend has provided some degree of refuge or comfort for those who are uncomfortable with rigid sex role stereotypes, sexual identities remain a signifi-cant preoccupation for most teens and young adults. Since the 1990s there appears to be much wider acceptance of the range of sexual characteristics through dress, jewellery, hairstyles, and body art.

Primary sexual orientation—whether homosexual, bisexual, or heterosexual—can cause major adjustment problems for some people. While the influences on a person's sexual orientation remain unclear, it is now recognized that most people experiment with both heterosexual and homosexual partners at some point in their development.

Homosexuality appears to have a hormonal and possibly a genetic basis, while bisexuality appears to be influenced more by cultural norms.[6] Whatever the cause, gay men and women are both marginalized and oppressed in our society, which leads to significant psychological and social difficulties. Given that these individuals must negotiate their developmental milestones in an intolerant environment, it is understandable that statistics show a higher incidence of substance abuse and self-destructive activities for gay teenagers. Support groups for "coming out" and more exposure in mainstream television and films have been helpful. However, gay bashing and hate crimes still take place and they cause irreparable direct and indirect damage.

A third problem associated with sexuality may be referred to as sexual intent. The range of attitudes and approaches to sexual partners appears to exist on a continuum that flows from "peaceable mutuality" to "hostile victimization."[7] This dimension of a person's sexual personality is heavily influenced by her personal introduction to sexual relationships (whether by force, by seduction, or with empathy) and the predominant manner in which relationships in her life are observed (respectful, open, and mutual versus degrading, controlling, and abusive). The issues of rape and sexual assault are much too complex to be examined through the single dimension of sexual intent alone and warrant a full analysis. However, the dimension of sexual intent can greatly influence the degree of satisfaction a person achieves in sexual relations.

The definition of sexual health in general has been expanded to take new dimensions into account in the past decade. Teenagers can find their lives greatly complicated by unwanted pregnancies and sexually transmitted diseases that often result from inadequate sex education or their poor access to birth control. Sexually transmitted diseases such as chlamydia, herpes, and HIV add stresses and pressures that were previously unknown to earlier generations. New problems regarding low sexual desire, erectile dysfunction, and medications' side effects leave many adults feeling sexually frustrated and unfulfilled. The popularization of sexual enhancement drugs such as Viagra introduces new variables as people try to cope with this changing landscape.

Many of the sexual problems described above are intensified by other problems an individual may have in social functioning; some relate to problems with others or with their own self-concepts. It is clear that social workers must have up-to-date knowledge about human sexuality and exhibit a non-judgmental attitude in order to respond to these complex and value-laden issues.

ISSUES ASSOCIATED WITH AGING

With improved nutrition, sanitation, and health care, the life expectancy of Canadians has increased. Consequently, the extent and complexity of the biopsychosocial problems associated with aging have also increased. Aging often coincides with physical and mental decline, with children's leaving home and moving away, the loss of friends and spouses, possible institutionalization, role loss, and isolation. The quality and quantity of a person's older years are significantly affected by nature (inherited physical characteristics), nurture (quality of relationships, nutrition, exercise, use of tobacco), and fate (contracted illness, accidents, poverty). While decline and deterioration are inevitable, many factors influence the quality of life for the aged.

Many people suffer progressive impairments to their senses and the problems these create. They lose muscle tone and find their bodies less flexible, which places certain activities beyond their reach. The progressive deterioration in the brain cells that we now identify as Alzheimer disease causes memory loss, confusion, and personality changes.

Erik Erikson describes the biopsychosocial crisis of "old age" as a period of ego integrity versus despair.[8] Ego integrity is the achievement of a measure of satisfaction with one's life; despair reflects self-castigation or a disdain for one's lack of fulfillment.

Poverty, homelessness, alcoholism, and over-medication intensify the biopsychosocial problems of aging. The media and social work literature have recently identified disturbing patterns of elder mistreatment that greatly worsen the problems of this already vulnerable group. The aged can also fall victim to muggers, con artists, and manipulative relatives.

Biopsychosocial services for the aged have improved, but still may not be as available in rural settings or to non–English- or non–French-speaking immigrants. Some elder-care facilities cannot offer the range of counselling and support services that would make a great difference to the nature and quality of adjustment many elderly people must make to thrive in institutional care.

The restructured health system has resulted in hospital closings, fewer services, and more reliance on home care. It has placed a greater burden on families to care for their aging relatives and has significantly exacerbated the situation for those seniors who live alone or without support.

ISSUES ASSOCIATED WITH SUBSTANCE USE AND ABUSE

People have used mood- and mind-altering substances in varying degrees for centuries. While governments have made numerous attempts to control the use of such substances, the early twentieth century witnessed the actual criminalization of substance users—those who use alcohol, narcotics, or marijuana—as well as suppliers—bootleggers and pushers.[9] Our society has been both ambivalent and ambiguous in its approach to substance abuse, which has produced stark disagreements between generations and social groups about acceptable and unacceptable use.

Clearly, alcohol and drug abuse contribute to numerous social problems, including family violence, impaired driving, poverty, theft, and mental and physical illness. The psychology of addictions is complex, and a great deal remains unknown about causes and cures. Some individuals seem to become addicted to alcohol after their first drink, whereas others develop dependency only after long-term use. Some people turn to drugs to relieve the misery of their emotional or physical environments, while others gradually became dependent on legal prescription drugs such as sedatives or barbiturates.

Whatever a client's circumstances, the social worker must have some understanding of the physiological, neurological, psychological, and social effects of substance use and abuse in order to respond effectively. The substance abuse itself may actually "induce" some biopsychosocial problems. Impaired judgment or the disinhibiting effects of alcohol may be associated with inappropriate sexual behaviour or emotional instability. A person's use of alcohol and cocaine can lead to her poor work performance and can result in severe financial problems. As well, over-medication of the aged and the disorientation and physical problems it causes is a growing concern for health care professionals.[10]

In other circumstances, substance abuse can "rekindle" biopsychosocial problems." For example, a man having difficulties in relating to people may make those difficulties worse through long-term marijuana use, or his latent insecurities and anxieties may surface strongly with amphetamine or cocaine abuse. Undesirable personality traits such as selfishness or overdependence that a person had previously been able to control may manifest themselves and be magnified.

Social workers discover a third set of difficulties when a person compounds her major problems with substance abuse. A person suffering from a major mental illness such as schizophrenia or bipolar illness will have even more difficulty dealing with an addiction. A person suffering from post-traumatic stress syndrome, such as a war veteran or an adult survivor of child sexual abuse, will often find those difficulties compounded by substance abuse and addictions. Children born with fetal alcohol syndrome may have stunted growth and neurological impairment, and an intravenous-drug-using mother may give birth to an HIV-infected baby. The latter situation has tremendous ramifications for the biopsychosocial adjustment of the child.

Runaway teens frequently become disastrously involved in the criminal underworld, as any association with drugs and alcohol brings them into contact with prostitution, theft, and pornography. Recent anti-drug laws with stiff penalties and incarceration for drug users have come into question in part because of these factors. Some jurisdictions are experimenting with harm-reduction approaches such as methadone maintenance and needle exchanges.[11] In 2003 the city of Vancouver took a bold new step; it established the first safe injection site in North America for addicts. While such programs have proved successful in Europe and Asia, it remains to be seen if they will work so close to the US "war on drugs."

ISSUES ASSOCIATED WITH RELATIONSHIPS AND MARRIAGE

Most adults in our society establish and attempt to maintain a two-person bond, a "relationship." Many formalize the bond in marriage and this forms the basis for establishing a family. In Erikson's stages of psychological development, this occurs in the young adulthood phase of intimacy versus isolation.[12]

Teenagers experiment with relationships by "going steady." They express the emotional trials and tribulations of such experiments through the music, art, and literature familiar to us all. A person's capacity for sustaining a good relationship requires numerous individual attributes (openness, honesty, trustworthiness), interpersonal skills (good communication, empathy, understanding), and emotional maturity (capacity to tolerate closeness, distance, disagreement, intimacy).

We develop many of these traits early in life through our relations with our primary caregivers. If our early experiences are inadequate or disturbed, then we may be less capable of negotiating or maintaining mutually satisfactory relationships as adults. For example, if an infant is overly dependent on a primary caregiver and develops a psychological boundary confusion (what is "me" and what is "not me"), she may grow up with unrealistic expectations about relationships in general and

place impossible demands on a partner or be perpetually disappointed in others.

Relationships themselves pass through different phases, whether they are short term or long term. The "attraction and honeymoon" phase, with all its excitement and magical delights, carries with it emotional tumult and tremendous feelings of jealousy and vulnerability.

The relationship may progress to a more realistic but still mutually satisfying phase in which both partners recognize and accept each other's limits and capacities. Or it may decline into unreasonable struggles for power and control. If the partners can achieve a good level of differentiation (a strong sense of identity), their relationship will evolve to a maintenance phase. At that point both partners are secure enough to develop independent as well as shared interests. If they do achieve this stage, the relationship may deteriorate so far that neither person sees any reason to be together or they may feel so much anger and bitterness that the relationship is irreparably damaged.

The dissolution of a marriage often leaves people with significant feelings of individual failure and many emotional wounds that take a great deal of time and support to heal. A troubled relationship is rated as one of the highest levels of stress that a person can experience.[13] It can contribute to physical problems, diminished work effectiveness, and major psychological disturbances.

The high incidence of divorce in our society has lessened the social stigma previously associated with marital breakup, yet individuals who separate often find themselves isolated and overwhelmed by their sudden return to single status. They can find negotiating new relationships often impeded by residual feelings of inadequacy, hurt, and anger from the earlier "failed" relationships. Some people place much higher expectations on their new relationships or believe they have learned from their mistakes, only to discover that their new relationships have to progress through all the same stages as the previous ones and that their own characteristics and behaviours have not changed significantly.

Some people respond to these disappointments by experimenting with non-monogamous relationships. Others engage in a form of "serial monogamy," changing relationships according to their needs and interests. Still others adjust better to living alone, meeting their needs for intimacy through casual or long-term friendships. However people experience relationships, it is clear from the sheer volume of clients' demands—for biopsychosocial counselling, couples' therapy, and groups for newly separated or divorced individuals—that difficulties in relationships and marriage are central to many problems in biopsychosocial functioning.

ISSUES ASSOCIATED WITH LIVING IN A FAMILY

The family, in its many variations, is the basic unit for procreation, for nurturance, and for acculturation in our society. Like other relationships, families develop through identifiable stages, beginning with the coupling phase, through the childbearing and child-rearing phase, the disengagement phase (adolescence), the empty-nest phase, and finally the concluding phase that ends with the death of a spouse. Most families are organized around a set of rules and roles, implicit or explicit, and provide economic and emotional support to the various members.[14] Those rules and roles delineate the boundaries between the various subsystems within the family. For example, a parent may enter a child's bedroom (a weak boundary), but the child may not enter the parent's bedroom (a rigid boundary).

Numerous stressors create hardship for families—poverty, sickness, loss, divorce—but the way a family copes with or adapts to these factors will vary with that family's internal and external resources. A family with weak boundaries may become emotionally dysfunctional following the death of a family member, whereas a family with rigid boundaries may appear emotionless and uncaring under similar circumstances.

Families often invest in the maintenance of myths (we are a supportive, happy family; therefore we cannot tolerate disagreements or anger) or secrets (we do not acknowledge Dad's alcoholism) that make members' communication unclear, indirect, or simply non-existent. Indeed, much of family therapy aims to facilitate open, honest communication and establish clear but flexible boundaries between the various subsystems.

Today's family may be subjected to increasing amounts of stress as other societal systems break down: in the workplace through layoffs, in the church through lack of membership, or in the neighbourhood through greater mobility. The family structure cannot absorb the level of dysfunction these stresses cause.[15] Family dysfunction is seen as either a partial factor or a contributing one in mental health problems for children and adults, It is clearly linked to numerous biopsychosocial ills, including suicide attempts, delinquency, addictions, and eating disorders. Extraordinarily frequent incidents of family violence have been reported over the past two decades, ranging from spouse battering to child abuse and sexual assault.[16] Indeed, the family is the most violent civilian group in our society today.[17] Although such behaviours are not new, they have received more attention and analysis partly because of the efforts of the women's movement to bring these issues to light. The sheer volume of psychological and physical damage that accompanies incidents of family violence lends a new urgency to those programs aimed at protection and prevention.

Additional challenges to families arise from changing demographics. We live in an age of significant increases in single-parent families, families by second marriages, and interracial marriages. In situations in which young families are forced to reside with their parents for economic reasons, normal identity-development tasks and relationship tasks can arise and complicate their lives. Increasingly, middle-aged parents are assuming caregiving roles for their own aging parents, adding to an already overburdened family system.

In response to the above, some social work agencies focus the majority of their resources on family support, family counselling, and family therapy.

ISSUES IN THE WORKPLACE

Numerous biopsychosocial issues are also reflected in the area of work, career, profession, or vocation. One major psychological milestone in a person's development is her achievement of a sense of competence about herself and her abilities. A person's identity is significantly affected by what she does for a living. The work ethic still operates in the majority of people in our society, and work satisfaction goes far in determining individuals' overall well-being.

The influences of nature, nurture, and fate are key to understanding and analyzing biopsychosocial problems in the workplace. A person gifted with the "right" innate characteristics—size, intelligence, confidence, attractiveness—will clearly have an advantage in certain types of work. Those making hiring decisions may feel that the person's characteristics render her more appropriate and possibly more capable for the job. The quality of physical and psychological nurturance the individual receives also will affect his orientation to success and achievement, ability to work independently or in a group, attitudes toward authority figures, or attitudes toward subordinates. Fate greatly influences the opportunities available to people through education, connections, and location. Affirmative action programs have attempted to level the playing field over the past few decades with both positive and negative consequences.

The entire process of career selection and adjustment can raise specific and generalized anxieties that require a therapeutic or supportive response. Once in a job, a person faced with the fear of layoffs and firings often suffers a number of stress-related problems. Alvin Toffler notes that the continual change and demand for expanding knowledge that characterizes the modern workplace can have similar consequences.[18] Many large companies and organizations have begun to appreciate the cost of poor performance and attendance by employees and have arranged for biopsychosocial counselling through employee-assistance programs.

The past decade has witnessed a wholesale adjustment in the workplace. Normally reliable companies have closed or downsized, often putting the most highly employable individuals out of work with little hope of finding other equal or even lesser work. Hard work and loyalty no longer guarantee satisfactory employment and secure pensions. The expression "going postal" has entered our vocabulary as tensions between workers and co-workers or administrators have erupted in extreme violence. Responding to traumatic or catastrophic events in the workplace has become an entire specialty in social work.

An additional concern arises from those situations in which people change their careers in mid-life. While dramatic changes from executive to gardener, or accountant to child-care worker, may be good adjustments for the individual, that person's spouse or family may react negatively to possible changes in status or in demands.

ISSUES ASSOCIATED WITH MARGINALIZATION AND CULTURAL DIVERSITY

Canada is a culturally diverse nation that is seen as relatively tolerant of various ethnic, religious, and social minorities. Clearly there is little legal discrimination in Canada, but for some groups social differentiation is coupled with social inequality, resulting in collective discrimination.[19] Some visible minorities and First Nations peoples fall into this category. For some people, their unique cultural identity is a source of pride and strength, whereas it can intensify feelings of separateness and anomie for others.

When mainstream society effectively marginalizes minorities, the resulting oppression, stigmatization, and victimization lead to greatly increased biopsychosocial problems within those groups. Such groups are overrepresented in statistics concerning corrections, mental health, and poverty. Women, the aged, homosexuals, visible minorities, and disabled persons are often referred to as marginalized groups and commonly suffer devaluation and hostility.

Biopsychosocial problems may not be specific to a particular marginalized group, but a high incidence of adolescent and adult adjustment reactions, depression, suicide, and substance abuse are observable and understandable.

While women form a slight majority in our society, they too are marginalized by their historically subordinate status. This subordination is more pronounced in certain groups. Over the years it has led to increased biopsychosocial problems for women across all strata of society. In their efforts to achieve equality, women have used many of the same strategies the civil rights movement in the United States employed to raise consciousness, form support groups, improve services, and effect policy and legislative change. Better understanding of women's issues has led to more appropriate and accessible health and mental health services, including female-specific counselling, transition houses, and women's centres.

Social workers must be able to identify cultural and minority group competence in order to respond to biopsychosocial issues in context. Where possible, members of minority groups must also be encouraged and supported to enter and obtain professional education.

ISSUES ASSOCIATED WITH GLOBAL AND ENVIRONMENTAL DISASTER

The age of information is upon us, and modern telecommunications has put Canadians in daily contact with "the Global Village."[20] Whether it is war in Eastern Europe, the breakup of the Soviet Empire, or starvation in Africa, people of all ages are directly or indirectly affected by the sights, sounds, and meaning of monumental events. Some have friends and relatives who live in these strife-torn areas; others watch family members go off to war or to provide aid; and others find validation or reinforcement of the helplessness and hopelessness they already feel in response to the information.

While the immediate threat of nuclear holocaust lessened with the end of the Cold War in the 1980s, it quickly resurfaced when India and Pakistan detonated their new nuclear devices. Genocides in

Africa, ethnic cleansing in the Balkans, and wars in Afghanistan and Iraq directly affect some and create generalized anxiety for others. The September 11, 2001, terrorist attacks in New York, Pennsylvania, and Washington, D.C., have destabilized the geopolitical landscape and left us in an increasingly uncertain world.

The very real threat of eco-disaster looms. Canadians see the pollution, see our forests disappear, and feel the economic stress of our declining fishery and other industries. While some respond with activism through organizations like Greenpeace, many quietly despair or simply leave a depressed area in hopes of improving their economic opportunities elsewhere.

The HIV pandemic has also touched many Canadians in one way or another. It has created an inordinate level of angst for the population at large and it has intensified the misery of some already marginalized groups and individuals.

Social workers have had to become more aware of how environmental disasters affect their clients at biopsychosocial levels in order to help instill hope and mitigate the negativism that pervades an existential crisis. Indeed, problems of an existential nature have increased signifi-

cantly in the past decade. People's general disillusionment, fuelled by war, economic instability, and loss of faith in social institutions—government, schools, and the church—has left many questioning the point and meaning of life. Modern social workers must also be philosophers as they help their clients grapple with issues of life, death, freedom, and commitment.[21]

CONCLUSION

Issues in biopsychosocial functioning are many and varied. In fact, social workers pride themselves on their readiness to accept and work with the uniqueness of their clients, both individually and collectively. In light of this, social workers must be ever ready to recognize new and unfolding biopsychosocial concerns. They must also continue to deal with the evolving nature of traditional problems and circumstances. Social workers must accept the influence of nature, nurture, and fate on individuals. This means acknowledging people's capacity to adapt to problems in biopsychosocial functioning while trying to challenge dysfunctional and oppressive social structures and promote equality and social change.

NOTES

1. Margaret S. Mahler, Fred Pine, and Annie Bergmen, *The Psychological Birth of the Human Infant* (New York: Basic Books, 1975).

2. Erik H. Erikson, *Identity: Youth and Crisis* (New York: W.W. Norton, 1968).

3. Robert K. Merton, *Social Theory and Social Structure* (enlarged ed.). (New York: Free Press, 1968).

4. M. Makie, *Constructing Men and Women: Gender Socialization* (Toronto: Holt, Reinhart and Winston, 1987).

5. Henry W. Maier, *Three Theories of Child Development* (New York: Harper and Row, 1969).

6. Bruce King, Cameron Camp, and Ann Downey. *Human Sexuality Today* (Englewood Cliffs, NJ: Prentice Hall, 1991).

7. S. B. Levine, in *Sexuality and Medicine: Conceptual Roots*, Ed. E. E. Shelp, (Dordrecht, Netherlands: Reidel Pub, 1987). 39–54.

8. Erik H. Erikson, *Childhood and Society* (2nd ed.) (New York: W.W. Norton, 1963); Erik H. Erikson, *The Life Cycle Completed: A Review* (New York: W.W. Norton, 1982).

9. Alvin Novik, "Social Attitudes as a Co-Factor in the Etiology of AIDS," paper presented at the Canadian Conference on AIDS, Toronto, 1988.

10. N. Col, E. Fanale, and P. Kronholm, "The Role of Medication: Non-Compliance and Adverse Drug Reactions in Hospitalizations of the Elderly," *Archives of Internal Medicine* 150 (1990): 841–45.

11. W. S. Rowe and Glenn Marcotte, "The Challenge of Risk Reduction Practices" in *Social Work and HIV: The Canadian Experience*, (Eds.) W. S. Rowe and W. Ryan, (Toronto: Oxford University Press, 1998). 316.

12. Erik H. Erikson, *Childhood and Society*; Erik H. Erikson, *The Life Cycle Completed: A Review.*

13. H. I. McCubbin and C.A. Figley, *Stress and the Family*, vols. I and H (New York: Brunner Mazel, 1983).

14. Sonya L. Rhodes, "Family Treatment," in *Social Work Treatment*, (Ed.) Francis Turner (New York: Free Press, 1986).

15. Ibid., 13.

16. Barbara Star, *Domestic Violence, Encyclopedia of Social Work* (18th ed.) (Silver Spring, MD: National Association of Social Workers, 1987).

17. Murray Strauss, "Wife Beating: How Common and Why?" in *The Social Causes of Husband-Wife Violence*, (Eds.) M. Strauss and 1. Holaling, (Minneapolis: University of Minnesota Press, 1980).

18. Alvin Toffler, *The Third Wave* (New York: Bantam Books, 1981).

19. Edward Sagarin, (Ed.) *The Other Minorities* (Watham, MA: Xerox College Publishers, 1971).

20. Marshall McLuhan, *War and Peace in the Global Village* (New York: McGraw-Hill, 1968).

21. Donald F. Krill, "Existential Social Work," in *Social Work Treatment*, (Ed.) Francis Turner (New York: Free Press, 1996).

chapter fourteen

Poverty and Declining Living Standards in a Changing Economy

Brigitte Kitchen

THE GROWING SOCIAL DIVIDE

At a time when the Canadian economy was putting on just about the best performance in the growth of GDP per person among OECD (Organisation for Economic Co-operation and Development) countries, including the United States (Jackson, 2003, 1), Canadians experienced a significant decline in their quality of life. The annual United Nations Human Development Index (HDI) downgraded Canada as the most desirable country in the world in which to live (Human Development Index, 1999, 1998, 1997, 1996), shifting it to third place in 2001 and 2002, and in its latest report to eighth place (Human Development Report, 2003).

HDI rankings are based on three aspects of human development: (1) opportunity for a long and healthy life in terms of life expectancy at birth, (2) educational attainment, through gauging adult literacy (two-thirds weight) and the combined gross enrolment ratio in primary, secondary, and tertiary education (one-third weight); and (3) standard of living by GDP (gross domestic product) per capita US$PPP (purchasing power parity) (Calculating HDI, Technical Note 1341). This final measure denotes the purchasing power of currencies. By averaging these three components we produce the final tabulation, or ranking, in the world.

The strength of the Canadian economy has been attributed largely to the Government of Canada's drastic slashing of social spending. This allowed it to turn an annual federal budget deficit of $38 billion within four years into a $2.1 surplus, the first surplus in 27 years. Indeed, by 1998, government spending had been so severely cut that the Minister of Finance could boast that his budget financed the lowest level of government activities in 50 years. Canada stood first among G-7 countries, the privileged club of the seven most powerful economies in the world, in solving its budget deficit problem and reducing its debt load (Canadian Centre for Policy Alternatives, 1999).

While the fiscal health of federal and provincial governments has been restored, the UN Committee on Economic, Social, and Cultural Rights rebuked Canada "for balancing its budget by bringing about a very harmful, a very inhumane social and economic revolution" (*Toronto Star*, 1998, A8). A privileged minority in the country saw a remarkable, perhaps unprecedented, increase in income and wealth, yet low-income households saw little improvement in their own circumstances. In fact, the gap between those with the most income and those with the least widened (Federation of Canadian Municipalities, 2001, 2).

On the UN Human Poverty Index (HPI), Canada ranked twelfth out of the 17 selected rich OECD countries with 12.8 percent of its people having incomes below 50 percent of average median income. This compares poorly with 6.6 percent in Sweden and 6.9 percent in Norway, which ranked first and second on the HPI. Immigrants of less than five years' residency are greatly overrepresented among Canada's poor. Their poverty rate was 2.5 times that of persons born in Canada (*Daily*, June 9, 2003). The share of income and consumption going to the poorest 20

percent of Canadians was a mere 7.3 percent, whereas that of the top 20 percent in the income hierarchy was 39.3 percent. In Sweden, the respective share of these two income groups was 9.1 percent and 34.5 percent. Despite a lower per capita GDP income than Canada's, Sweden is doing more to keep its people from living in income poverty.

Canada's commitment to education and health also languished. Public expenditure on education as a percentage of GDP fell by roughly 15 percent from 1990 to 1998–2000 and by 2.9 percent on health with its population growing at 1.1 percent a year. With less public spending for more people, Canada's standard of living has not kept pace with that of other industrialized countries. In the words of one concerned bank president, "We face challenges in the areas of critical importance to our social well-being such as healthcare, education and the infrastructures of our major cities" (Nixon, May 6, 2000).

The structural adjustments made in the competitive entrepreneurial and fast-moving and flexible climate of open trade and global integration have created new income needs that are met inadequately through market wages and government income policies. Among OECD countries Canada has the second-highest incidence of low-wage employment; 25.3 percent of Canadian workers were paid less than two-thirds of the national median hourly wage of $15.65 an hour in 2002 (Campaign 2000, Nov. 2003, 4). They are earning less than $10.42 an hour.

Corporate profits before taxes, on the other hand, increased by 54.0 percent between 1998 and 2002, and wages, salaries, and other supplementary income grew by 25 percent, less than half the corporate profit rate (Statistics Canada, 1998–2000). The weekly average industrial wage rose by a mere 14 percent from

$608.44 in November 1998 (*Daily*, Feb. 25, 1999) to $694.14 in the same month in 2003 (*Daily*, Jan. 29, 2004). This works out to a comparatively miserly 2.8 percent a year and does little to offset the 2.6 percent decline overall in average employment income from 1990 to 1995.

Corporations have frozen their wage bills for ordinary production workers while increasing the remuneration of their chief executive officers by unparalleled amounts. The CEOs of the top 68 publicly traded companies earned an average of $7.2 million in 2002. The average Canadian worker making $35 417 a year would have to work 203 years to earn what these CEOs made in just one year (Centre for Social Justice, 2003). The Toronto Board of Trade reported that average salaries of its CEO members averaged $291 000 in 2001 (Media release, Nov. 21, 2001). And these CEOs' base salaries do not include their often excessive benefits from cash bonuses and the stock options that drive up their overall compensation packages, even when the performances of the corporations they were leading were flat. A few examples are Lee Scott, CEO of Wal-Mart, who has been paid an average of $23 million in the last three years, Belinda Stronach, former CEO of Magna International, with about $12 million last year, and the CEO of the Bank of Montreal, who made a total of $11.2 million (Crane, 2004).

An executive officer of a big multinational corporation can now expect to earn at least 40 times more than an ordinary production worker. A gap of such magnitude runs counter to the sound advice Plato gave his pupil Aristotle—that within an organization nobody should earn more than five times what the lowest-paid worker earns. Neo-liberal economic logic insists on high rewards for entrepreneurs to legitimize their role in the economy and society (Loney, 1987). The employment opportunities and wealth they are expected to create are supposed to "trickle down" to all Canadians, improving their standard of living. This has not happened. Unemployment has remained high. It stood at 7.8 percent in March 1999 and at 7.4 percent in December 2003.

STRUCTURE OF THE LABOUR MARKET

The demands of capital have generally shaped the structure of the labour market. The restructuring of the way production is organized through the use of new technologies, replacing human labour, and downsizing operations to reduce production costs comes only at a human price. This upheaval has sharply divided Canadians, devastating the lives of those, including university graduates, who do not even have a chance to enter the labour market and others who are trapped in bad or low-paying jobs. Unemployment and underemployment, reflected in the increase in part-time, contract, and seasonal work with few or no benefits and low wage and salary levels, are a fact of life for too many Canadians. While almost a third (30.2 percent) of part-time workers reported doing so because they are going to school, another 27.0 percent cited business conditions and their inability to find full-time work as the reasons (Statistics Canada, 2002). Many young unskilled Canadians, aged 15 to 24, recent immigrants, lone mothers, and people with disabilities working part-time in non-unionized jobs have become painfully aware that jobs are no guarantee of income insecurity.

Nonetheless, recent developments offer some promise. The proportion of the working-age population holding jobs rose to an all-time high of 62.7 percent in December 2003 and the labour-force participation rate reached a record 67.7 percent (Statistics Canada, Jan. 9, 2004). Even though employment has been growing, most of the rise has been in part-time employment, which grew 10.5 percent compared to 7.8 percent in full-time jobs between 1999 and 2003 (calculations based on Statistics Canada, labour force characteristics). Again, a slight improvement is taking place. From 2002–2003, the growth rate in part-time jobs was only 0.5 percent compared to 1.8 percent for full-time jobs.

Less encouraging is the fact that organizational restructuring has limited the career ladders that once defined the paths of advancement for many people within both corporate hierarchies and state bureaucracies. Cuts in middle management positions have particularly affected younger age groups—those under the age of 30, whose chances for promotion and increased earnings have been blocked. Parents, facing the additional costs of raising their children and having to support them for longer periods of time in this economic climate, have been hit particularly hard by these changes in the labour market. If they want to maintain an adequate standard of living, they require two incomes. By working more hours and by women taking on paid work, families try to produce the income necessary to meet their consumption costs. In 1998, 15 percent of employees worked 50 or more hours each week (Statistics Canada, Historical Review, 1998, Table 16, VI). Five years later, in 2003, 13 percent carried such excessive workloads, the lowest such level in a decade (Canadian Labour Congress, 2003).

Lone-parent breadwinners, most of them women, lack this additional earning capacity. More than half of lone parents, 84 percent of them mothers raising children on their own, have incomes of less than $30 000. By contrast, the average income of lone fathers was $48 248 in 2001. Clearly the risk of poverty for lone parents is not so much the result of family breakups as it is the consequence of the persistent wage gap between men and women (Statistics Canada, 2001). The fact that women and their children make up the majority of the poor remains by itself politically significant. In one encouraging development the incidence of poverty for lone-mother families fell by 26.9 percent to 45.5 percent in 2001 from 61.6 percent in 1996. This decline can be seen as part of an overall trend. In 1996, the poverty rate was 18.5 percent and fell to 14.4 percent in 2001, a percentage change of 22.1 percent.

When the House of Commons unanimously agreed to eliminate child poverty by 2000 in 1989, one in seven children and their families were living in poverty (Campaign 2000, 1998). One in six children were still growing up poor in 2001 and every second poor child lives in a family with an employed parent.

Article 25 of the Universal Declaration of Human Rights in 1948, which Canada signed, gives everyone the right "to a standard of living adequate for the health and well-being of himself and his family, including food, clothing, housing and medical care and necessary social services." In 1776 Adam Smith suggested in his monumental work *An Inquiry into the Wealth of Nations* that everyone should share in the kind of comforts "the custom of the country renders indecent for creditable people, even of the lowest order, to be without." Governments clearly play a role in defining how this obligation will be met. In modern industrial nations like Canada, poverty links individuals and families to the state through cash benefits and social service provisions. Without these government income transfers, these people's economic circumstances would be far more precarious. These transfers through the social welfare system help protect the standard of living of Canadian families at the lower end of the income scale. Average transfer payments for economic families—

individuals related by blood, marriage, common-law relationships, or adoption who share accommodation—in the lowest 10 percent income group was $10 782 in 2001, which raised their income by 49.6 percent (Statistics Canada, 2001).

DIFFERENT SOCIAL WELFARE SYSTEMS

The Organisation for Economic Co-operation and Development (OECD) countries identify three major social welfare systems that define the different ways that governments provide income protection: a liberal-residual system, a corporatist statist regime, and a social-democratic solidaristic and universalistic system (Esping-Anderson, 1989).

The liberal-residual system focuses primarily on market-based provisions of individual welfare and on limiting the extent to which social programs replace or interfere with market forces and their impacts on individuals and families. Corporatist statist systems are less concerned with free-market dogmatism; their social welfare provisions concentrate on the preservation of status differences and families' responsibility to help their own members in financial need.

By contrast, social-democratic solidaristic and universalistic systems largely socialize the cost of "familyhood." They take "direct responsibility for children, the aged, and the helpless" (Esping-Anderson, 1989). With its emphasis on a fusion of social welfare and employment, this last model promotes the equality of adequate living standards. This goal differs from that of the two other social welfare systems. They aim to meet only the minimal consumption needs of those whom the market economy has failed and whose families are not able to support them (Olson, 2002).

Since the mid-1980s, the Canadian welfare state could be categorized as an example of the liberal-residual system. However, it did contain some features of the solidaristic-universalistic systems as Esping-Anderson defined them. Federal transfer payments to the provinces for health care, post-secondary education, the Canada Assistance Plan, and federal equalization payments provided roughly equivalent social programs and services across the country. Old Age Security benefits, the Canada Pension Plan/Quebec Pension Plan, and universal family allowances pointed toward socializing the costs of "familyhood." These programs assumed an intergenerational contract between the income needs of seniors and the financial responsibility of parents raising children.

The Neo-Liberal Social Welfare System

Trade integration and the greater international mobility of capital prompted the reconfiguration of Canada's "mixed" social welfare system along free market principles. The cost was the hollowing out of the solid foundation of the Canadian welfare state built on a compromise between business's profit interests and labour's concern for decent living standards. As long as the economy grew, its profits ensured that social welfare provisions did not seriously affect the accumulation of capital, and this compromise among the classes remained unchallenged. With the economic recessions of 1973 and 1981–82, however, fundamental cracks became visible in the compromise. Political neo-liberals and most professional economists claimed that "Canadians [were] supporting one of the world's most over-governed and foolishly generous welfare states" (Francis, 1991). Capital accumulation required a form of government that did not attempt to regulate market forces and mitigate their effects with social transfer programs (Boyer and Drache, 1996).

The shift away from universality and horizontal equity over the last two and a half decades marks the move towards individualizing those income needs closely associated with the neo-liberal social welfare system. Its three key principles—individual economic self-sufficiency, fiscal responsibility, and the ethic of paid work—have played a crucial role in squeezing money out of tax and social transfers that previously protected living standards. De-universalization of Old Age Security benefits and family allowances amounted to outright spending cuts. The partial de-indexation of tax credits and tax brackets (re-indexed in 2001) translated into an automatic tax hike. Combined with the tightening of eligibility criteria and cuts in benefit levels for such key income-support programs as Employment Insurance and social assistance, the neo-liberal restructuring of Canada's welfare system had been put in place (details to be discussed in a later section).

A mixture of market liberalism and moral authoritarianism concerned with the presumed behavioural dysfunctioning of poor people fuelled the new policy orientation. Employment Insurance and social assistance in particular were singled out as encouraging recipients to depend on social transfers rather than moving them into jobs. Social transfers were even questioned for jobless lone parents and persons with long-term disabilities, two groups that had up to that point had a special claim for public income support in the eyes of society. The realization that some individuals and particularly families were better off not being in the workforce gave rise to the notion of a "fairness gap" between those on welfare and the working poor. Accordingly, social transfer scales were slashed drastically to match minimum wage levels and to ensure that people were always better off holding down jobs.

The Canada Health and Social Transfer The Canada Health and Social Transfer (CHST) was proclaimed in the February 1995 federal budget. It characterized the neo-liberal approach to federal funding of social programs. It consolidated Bill C-60, Changes to Established Program Funding, which the previous Progressive Conservative government had introduced in 1991 without consulting the provinces. The CHST replaced specific cost-shared arrangements for social assistance, social services, health care, and post-secondary education with the provinces with a consolidated block fund. The provinces now receive a lump sum of cash transfers that gives them the flexibility to decide their own priorities in funding decisions. Most have chosen to spend the money on health care rather than social assistance and aid to students and universities, which are less popular with the general public.

The introduction of the CHST required repealing the Canada Assistance Plan (CAP) of 1966. This had far-reaching implications on the quality of life for low-income Canadians. The CAP had served these persons well as both an income support and a poverty prevention program. While the bulk of the CAP's costs (62 percent) covered income support for those in need, the remainder of the money had been applied to a wide range of poverty reduction and prevention services. It covered shelters for women and children who were victims of violence as well as subsidized child care so that low-income parents, mostly mothers, could participate in the workforce.

Without the influx of this federal money, the provinces generally decided to severely cut these programs, substantially reducing the social service sector at the same time. A shocking $7 billion in federal transfers were cut from this sector over a three-year period. The different economic strengths of individual provinces and territories meant that access to and equality of health care, social assistance levels, tuition fees at post-secondary institutions, and the quality of the personal social services soon began to vary across the country. In this way, the federal starving of funds for these programs has damaged the Canadian social fabric more than any other cost-cutting measures.

Health care, post-secondary education, and social assistance are now in crisis across the country. Steep increases in tuition fees, coupled with changes in financial aid to students, leave students without financial support from parents and frequently with hefty debt loads on graduation. Post-secondary education threatens to become once again the privilege of those who can pay for it. Young people from families at the lower end of the income scale participate to a considerably lesser degree in post-secondary education (Barr-Telford et al., 2003). The Millennium Scholarship begun in 2000 provides insufficient financial aid for students enrolled in post-secondary education.

THE SOCIAL UNION FRAMEWORK: NEW GROUND RULES FOR SOCIAL WELFARE POLICY

The federal and the territorial and provincial governments, with the exception of Quebec, signed a three-year agreement on February 4, 1999. It attempts to resolve the ongoing disagreements between Ottawa and the provinces that arise from the constitutional division of powers over social programs. The provinces are responsible for health care, education, and social assistance yet do not have the power of taxation to pay for them.

The Social Union Framework Agreement (SUFA) signalled the neo-liberal renewal and modernization of the Canadian social welfare system. It committed all governments to working more closely together to meet Canadians' needs. The agreement was to ensure, first, that Canadians did not face unreasonable residency-based barriers to crucial social services, whichever province or territory they moved to. This meant that residence requirements were lifted for student loans, social housing, youth training programs, basic education and skills development, health, and persons with disabilities programs (Federal/Provincial/Territorial Ministerial Council on Social Policy Renewal, 2003, 5). Certain barriers for non-residents considered reasonable and consistent with the SUFA principles were maintained, however. One example is the residency requirement for students enrolled in specialized post-secondary education programs.

Second, and most significantly, only a majority of the provinces, instead of the previous seven provinces representing 50 percent of the Canadian population, have to agree to the new federally initiated social programs. Ottawa agrees to give at least 12 months' notice before introducing new social policy initiatives and to consult with other governments to avoid duplication and overlap. Each province or territorial government can adjust the details of any new programs to fit its own interests as long as it meets the agreed objectives.

Third, the SUFA marked the re-entry of the federal government into the social policy arena and confirmed its essential role in ensuring the funding of that sector.

While media and social-policy sector responses to the Social Union Framework have generally been positive, critics have voiced dissatisfaction over its dispute resolution mechanisms. They point to issues concerning interprovincial mobility, intergovernmental transfers, any new joint initiative, and most significantly the interpretation of the Canada Health Act. Disagreements over the Canada Health Act are to be referred to a third party panel consisting of one federal-government appointee and another from the province or territory involved in addition to a chairperson approved by each government. The panel hands down non-binding recommendations or advice that must be made public, and the final decision rests with the federal Minister of Health (Health Canada, 2002).

The Canada Child Tax Benefit

Another important outcome of the SUFA was the consensus all the governments reached regarding children in poverty. They agreed that this should be one of the first priorities of the Social Union initiatives.

In January 1993, the three then existing child benefits, the non-refundable and refundable child tax credits, and universal family allowance were integrated into one income-tested program, the Canada Child Tax Benefit (CCTB). It was restructured again in 1998 as the Canadian Child Tax Benefit (CCTB), consisting of a basic benefit and a supplement for working families. The supplement was to specifically address the fairness gap between parents in and out of work. It was just as likely, however, a response to the fastest growth in the labour market in the low-paid sector of the economy and the need to fill those jobs.

Families with net employment incomes below $21 529 in 2002 qualified for the maximum base benefit of the CCTB and the maximum NCB Supplement for 2003–2004. With net incomes between $21 529 and $33 487 in 2002, families received the maximum base benefit of the CCTB and part of the NCB Supplement. Those with net incomes of more than $33 487 collected a part of the base benefit of the CCTB.

In 2003–2004, each applicant received an additional supplement of $232 for each child less than seven years of age for whom no child care expenses were claimed. The CCTB base is reduced by 2.5 percent for every $1000 of additional net income of more than $33 487 for families with one child; with two or more children, the benefit has been cut back 5 percent, giving rise to speculation that the government is encouraging one-child families. In 2001–2002, the CCTB's base benefit was paid to 3.2 million families with 5.8 million children—approximately 82 percent of Canada's families with children. The NCB Supplement pays low-income working families additional child benefits on top of the base benefit. The NCB Supplement went to 1.5 million families with 2.7 million children, or 40 percent of all Canadian families with children. Children whose families are on social assistance receive the federal government benefit only to have it clawed back from their share of the provincial/territorial welfare cheque. The National Council of Welfare, a citizen body that advises the Minister of Human Resources Development, estimated that about 64 percent of the nation's poor children and 83 percent of its poor single parent children receive no increased income support from the child benefit (1998).

Over the years, Canada' most vulnerable children, those whose parents are on social assistance, have paid dearly for the policy reorientation that links income support to paid work. The proof lies in the shameful fact that child poverty persists. The NCB supplement denotes a reversal of traditional Canadian social welfare objectives. The

Personal Income Tax Act of 1917 first recognized the incompatibility of the economic wage based on the market value of individual productivity and the consumption costs of families of different sizes in the form of a tax deduction. The revolutionary concept of universal Family Allowances in 1945 broke the link between income support and employment, which had brought such incredible hardship to unemployed Canadians in the 1930s Depression. At that time the municipalities had paid out public relief to the heads of families no matter how many dependants they had. The tax exemption for children and Family Allowances recognized the extra costs of children to parents, and the latter did so regardless of whether the parents were in the paid workforce and whatever their income levels.

The NCB Supplement for parents with low earnings in the workforce has transformed the CCTB from a child benefit into a parental work-incentive program. This is unfortunate. Work incentives have no place in child benefit programs. Canada is the only country of the OECD countries to have such a provision, and this country is also unique in having abdicated the principle of horizontal equity between individuals with children to support and those without this responsibility.

The C. D. Howe Institute (1999) concluded that current Canadian tax policy treated children in middle- and high-income families as if they were items of discretionary spending. It does not seem to matter to neo-liberal tax policy-makers how taxpayers spend their after-tax income. Children should have a claim on society's resources not only when their parents find themselves in economically vulnerable circumstances. Children are a benefit to society and not a personal extravagance of their parents. As an expression of society's support for and investment in the upbringing of children, a child should be available to all (British government, 1998). The Labour government in Great Britain increased its universal Child Tax benefit by 20 percent in addition to its normal inflationary updating by reducing the value of the marital tax allowance. In Canada, we continue to support marriage through the tax system but reduce the value of the child benefit as parents' incomes increase.

The latest transmogrification of the child benefit is the integration of the federal program and the child portion of the provinces' social assistance programs. The governments intend to remove children from welfare in acknowledgement of the psychological damage done to the self-esteem of those children who are raised on welfare. While this is undoubtedly a laudable objective, it seems hardly plausible when the significant adults in the children's lives still have to rely on social assistance. Ample empirical evidence suggests that low-income families pool their income to pay for the necessities of life. Are the children even aware that their share of family income comes from a non-stigmatizing income-support program? It seems unlikely that splitting the income support for children and for their parents will convince the children that they have escaped the embarrassment of provincial social assistance and that their shattered self-esteem has been miraculously restored.

Employment Insurance

We must examine the restructuring of unemployment insurance as consistent with the political abdication of the responsibility for job creation. Its represents the most fundamental change of the program in 25 years.

Coverage for those pushed out of the labour market was steadily expanded following the program's inception in 1941 to include more and more vulnerable workers—those most likely to lose their jobs. Eventually nearly all workers and employees were covered. In 1990, 87 percent of those out of work were still eligible for Unemployment Insurance for a maximum period of one year. After renaming the program Employment Insurance (EI) in 1996, the federal government drastically reduced its coverage. In 1996 only 42 percent of those out of work were eligible for a maximum of 32 weeks. Once these families exhaust the EI coverage and they are unable to find re-employment, they lose more than their EI benefits; they find they qualify only for the child benefit as social assistance recipients.

While EI benefits have been cut, taxpayers' contributions to the program have been substantially increased, from 5 percent in the 1970s to 14 percent in 1996. Now the fund is showing a healthy surplus. Even those who can find work for only a couple of hours a week and who were exempted previously from making contributions are now required to pay into the fund. Yet they do not qualify for Employment Insurance benefits themselves when they fail to accumulate enough working hours.

EI benefits were once meant to protect those temporarily out of work from suffering too sharp a drop in their standard of living. This is no longer the case. Benefit levels have been reduced from 57 percent of insurable earnings based on previous earnings to 55 percent. In the 1980s, the replacement level was still 60 percent. To soften the impact of this reduction in income replacement for families with dependent children, Ottawa brought back a family supplement—Section 16 of the EI Act—that it had abolished in 1976. At that time the government had declared such a supplement inappropriate for a program based on individual contributions. The new

Family Supplement is limited to families with one or more dependent children who qualify for the Canada Child Tax Benefit (CCTB) and the NCB Supplement. The full Family Supplement is scaled back at a net income level of $20 921 and peters out at $25 921. The supplement takes the form of a top-up of individual insurable earnings, taking family income into account. In 2001 the top-up could reach a maximum of 80 percent (55 percent basis rate plus a 25 percent top-up) of average insurable earnings (HRDC, EI website).

The introduction of the Family Supplement raised considerable concern. Critics worried that it would open the door to making eligibility for Employment Insurance benefits dependent on total family income. If this had indeed happened, it would have hurt mainly women, who continue to be overrepresented in the 25 lowest-paying occupations with little job security. Those with spouses or partners with higher incomes would have lost the economic independence the EI cheques still give them when they lose their own paycheques. Increasingly, men are becoming economically dependent on their wives or partners. Low-wage labour markets offer more employment opportunities for women than for men. The proportion of families in which both spouses or partners reported employment earnings decreased from 62 percent to 59 percent from 1990 to 1995 (Statistics Canada, 1998a). Significantly, men's employment rates are rising again after almost two decades of decline, although their growth rate remains somewhat slower than that of their female counterparts.

Most Canadians, regardless of their political ideologies, have repeatedly expressed support for social welfare policies that support families. Their governments are slowly recognizing the social importance of such policies. A welcome change in this direction was the reduction from 700 hours to 600 hours of the insurable hours one needs to qualify for maternity, parental, and sickness benefits under Employment Insurance. The overall number of claims for these benefits rose by 17.7 percent in 2001—a jump from the early 1990s when considerably fewer eligible mothers and fathers made claims. Mothers continue to be the primary childcare providers; they took an average of 29.9 weeks out of the available 35 weeks of parental leave benefits, and men averaged 15 weeks. This represented an increase of almost 80 percent in the claims men made and may be a promising sign that they are beginning to share more in child care responsibilities (HRDC, 2003,18). With improvements in maternity benefits, too, a growing number of mothers can afford to forgo 45 percent of their regular earnings to stay with their newborns or newly adopted children in this crucial period of mother–child bonding.

As of January 2004, Employment Insurance has been expanded to include a Compassionate Care Benefit. This allows people to take a leave of as long as six weeks to care for a family member who is likely to die within 26 weeks. Even so, this important new policy initiative does not address the plight of some families. These exempt families are taking care of severely incapacitated persons who are unable to live independently and who are not terminally ill. Compassionate care benefits should be extended to these families as well for as long as they are needed.

PROVINCIAL SOCIAL ASSISTANCE REFORM

Among the million or so people on social assistance throughout the 1990s were those who had exhausted their Employment Insurance coverage. Many unable to find re-employment were hard-working individuals who had never expected to end up on social assistance. As these individuals and families with no other sources of income increased their demands, the provinces began to limit applicants' eligibility and reduce the benefit levels. The exceptions were Saskatchewan and New Brunswick. The latter already had one of the lowest assistance rates in the country for most categories of recipients and therefore no room for further cuts.

Ontario, claiming its social assistance rates were overly generous, cut them by 21.6 percent in October 1995. The province has not increased them since then. The loss of one of every five assistance dollars means that a sole-support parent with two children now receives a basic needs allowance of $532 and a maximum shelter allowance of $707 for a total of $1239 a month; one adult and two children have to get by on $5.91 a day per person (Kitchen, 1997).

The impact of these cuts has been disastrous, particularly in metropolitan Toronto. There the costs of rented housing are some of the highest in the country. Parents forced to choose between feeding their children and paying their rent generally opt for the former. Once behind in their rent payments, many face eviction orders and end up homeless. The Daily Bread Food Bank reports that 37 percent of those households that rely on food banks in the Greater Toronto Area include at least one child and that 32 percent of the children in such households go hungry at least once a month (Daily Bread Food Bank, 2002).

Ontario's re-introduction of the "spouse-in-the-house" rule, once described as the most sexist discriminatory piece of welfare legislation, amounted to a bitter attack on poor mothers (Kitchen, 1997). Those applicants for and recipients of social assistance who live with unrelated members of the opposite sex are once again found ineligible for benefits if they are in spousal relationships with men or women who live in the same houses with them.

Previously, eligibility for social assistance followed the definition of a spousal relationship as stipulated by family law. A man or a woman on assistance, moving in with a partner of the opposite sex, now must immediately assume support obligations for that partner. However, family law requires such an obligation only after the couple has been living together for a period of three years. The intimate lives of poor people are once again open to welfare bureaucrats' inspection and harassment regarding chastity. Provincial savings from the enforcement of this discriminatory rule have added up to a substantial $45 million a year, far surpassing government expectations (Constante, 1996).

Four courageous women have challenged the rule under the Ontario Social Assistance Review Board and won. The board decided that they had entered spousal relationships with the expectation that they would remain financially independent from their partners for the three-year period stipulated under family law. The provincial government immediately appealed the decision to the Ontario Court of Appeal and lost. Mr. Justice Laskin, writing for the court, held that the rule discriminated on the grounds of sex and family status as it disproportionately affected sole-support mothers on social assistance.

WORK ACTIVATION POLICIES

A prominent myth in Canada holds that people on social assistance prefer to receive welfare cheques over paycheques. There is no factual basis to this myth. One's inability to find a job is the single most often cited reason a person gives for being on welfare, followed by having a disability.

Throughout the 1990s, concern about social assistance recipients' motivation for finding employment among those considered "employable" dominated the policy agenda. The idea of active labour-market measures continues to serve as a key concept in social assistance reform. These measures are intended to encourage recipients to make themselves self-sufficient through unpaid work. In Ontario the introduction of mandatory workfare, euphemistically dubbed "Community Participation," went furthest in moving people into the job market. Workfare is the obligation to engage in a minimum of 17 hours of unpaid work a week in return for a welfare cheque. It adds the requirement that the recipient seek paid work while living on assistance.

In 1992, Human Resources Development Canada developed two test projects, one in New Brunswick and the other in British Columbia. The department used temporary earnings supplements to encourage single parents to get off social assistance and find full-time employment. The Self-Sufficiency Projects began in New Brunswick in November 1992 and in British Columbia in February 1993 and continued until 2000. Eventually more than 9000 single parents participated. The participants had to have been on provincial social assistance for at least one year to be eligible for an earnings supplement for up to three years, provided they could find full-time paid work for 30 hours a week or more. The supplement used an income reference level of $30 000 in New Brunswick and $37 000 in British Columbia and a tax-back rate of 50 percent—that is, for every dollar of income above these levels the parents could keep half (HRDC, Applied Research Bulletin, 1998).

Only 29 percent of these welfare recipients found full-time work and were eligible to participate in the project. Among those who failed to meet the participation criteria, 42 percent could not find enough hours of work, 15 percent had personal or family responsibilities that interfered with their efforts, and another 14 percent had disabilities or suffered from health problems. These reasons for non-participation clearly reveal that the barriers for paid employment remain, above all, the lack of jobs, the lack of child care, and poor health rather than people's unwillingness to work. Governments' efforts to move poor parents off social assistance, most of them women, whether with the carrot of an earnings supplement or the workfare stick, fail to address why these people tend to have such precarious attachments to the labour market.

Making mothers with very young children enter the job market characterizes the neo-liberal policy shift, reversing a tradition that dates back to the 1920s. At that time, lone mothers were considered unemployable. They already had a job; they were mothers. Today, in Alberta, for instance, even mothers with babies as young as six months of age are expected to be in the labour market. The new eligibility criteria are rooted in suspicions that women in their reproductive years might use their children to avoid their personal responsibility of earning a living through paid work. In the United States, this concern has taken the most extreme form in the "right-to-work" states, which have cut off women who give birth to children while on public assistance and introduced a five-year lifetime limit on assistance.

In Canada, the change in direction regarding the treatment of lone mothers has been prompted largely by the recognition of a fairness gap between parents caring for their children on public income support and parents in the workforce caught in "the time bind." The American sociologist Arlie Hochschild defines the scarcity of family time that lone-parent-earner and two-earner families face as the Taylorization of family life, making the same demands for efficiency in family life that the workplace does: "Parents are becoming supervisors with stopwatches, monitoring meals and bedtimes and putting real effort into eliminating wasted time" (Hochschild, 1997, 218). The more time parents have to spend in their workplaces, the more family time they have to devote to the demands of those workplaces. This imbalance in the availability of time has led to the often bitter resentment parents in the workforce show to those parents outside the paid workforce. They envy them their family time.

Governments use the time gap in their own ways; they compel parents on social assistance to take up employment. Making the time gap a policy issue, they claim it would not be fair to exempt lone parents on assistance from having to seek employment while other parents, who would also love to be at home with their preschool children, work and help support the unemployed parents with their taxes (Freiler and Cerny, 1998, 68).

Supplementing low wage levels is by no means a policy panacea to encourage work. However, these levels are currently governments' and the business sector's preferred policy instrument for containing public expenditures and stabilizing the low-wage labour market. Balancing low earnings with wage supplementation programs does not produce self-sufficiency in recipients. These measures actually keep wages down and discourage business investments in productivity-enhancing technologies. Besides, their cost-savings are modest. In the Self-Sufficiency Projects, for example, taxpayers saved $2600 on every participant.

A number of European countries have avoided the political pitfall of both social assistance and wage supplementation policies. They base their social programs on the family rather than the individual. Their family policies recognize that wage levels are based on the market value of individual productivity so they do not reflect family consumption needs. Equalizing the differences in families' financial burdens is a crucial aspect of family-oriented social welfare systems. The preferred policy mix combines direct cash benefits, including universal family allowances, income-tested housing allowances, and tax-free minimum subsistence levels, as in Germany, for example, where a court ruling compelled the government to do so (Leisering and Leibfried, 2001, 208).

In addition, parents of either sex can use the extended parental-leave programs, for as long as two and three years in some countries, to care personally for their children. For women in the workforce and their husbands, this option becomes available after the women have used up their maternity benefits. The policy tries to prevent as many families as possible from ending up on social assistance, which is considered a social program of last resort. The programs expect the mothers of young children and not only the lone parents to enter the labour market once their children are old enough for public child care.

Children's age levels regarding this deadline differ among countries of the European Community. In France, which offers the longest period of parental leave, over 70 percent of children are in full-time day care after the age of 3. In Canada child care discussions still spark high emotions and plenty of controversy over the ideological preference some vociferous lobby groups give to mothers who stay at home. We still do not have a national child care program in place although the Royal Commission on the Status of Women identified a child care crisis back in 1970.

Given the policy push toward encouraging parents with limited earning capacities to take up paid work, governments' reluctance to support parents to do so by making affordable child care available seems surprising. Parents working in low-wage jobs cannot afford to hire sitters, and many have been known to leave their children at home alone after school hours. If parents have to pay for their child care arrangements out of their earnings, wage levels will have to be increased considerably. Such an alternative would not be popular with employers who already claim that their share of the financing of payroll taxes (compulsory social insurance) is too high. Employers, however, carry the costs for social insurance programs in the short run only. Workers assume the real costs in the form of their reduced wages and the higher prices we pay for the goods and services we buy.

Besides the child care crisis, families today are facing a time crisis, as already mentioned. For the sake of our children, our society must begin the crucial debate on how to give parents more time to spend with their children. Overworked parents affected by the time deficit could find a common cause in the interests of their children with those other parents who have more time but no earnings. As in many European countries, we could substantially increase parental leave policies. Also, we could reduce the workweek from 40 to 30 hours to take care of the time problem for overextended families and also free up existing jobs for those currently forced to live on social assistance.

The United Nations Declaration on the Rights of the Child in 1989 stipulated that children have the first claim on the social wealth of their societies. It is about time that Canadian parents demanded family and child-friendly social policies and programs from their different levels of government.

CONCLUSION

Interventionist governments in the 1950s to the mid-1970s created the welfare state that gave Canadians a sense of income security. The first decade of the twenty-first century looks set to be a time when governments beholden to business interests neglect the well-being of their citizens. The labour market in Canada remains structurally frozen with high levels of unemployment, underemployment, and a substantial low-wage sector. At the same time, cuts in social program and services spending and their rationing through stricter eligibility regulations and lower benefits, fail to compensate individuals and families adequately for market inequities.

The Speech From the Throne of February 2, 2004, confirmed the neo-liberal social welfare system that dominates the political agenda: "To ensure that the hard-won gains of the past decade are never squandered, the Government of Canada is unalterably committed to fiscal prudence, as evidenced by balanced budgets and a steady reduction in the debt relative to the size of the economy. This Government will not spend itself into deficit." No unalterable commitment was pronounced to improve the declining living standards of Canadians.

Many social critics have observed that cooperation and concern for others decline with the rise in inequalities of income and wealth. These factors produce what John Kenneth Galbraith (1992) has called an ebbing away of the habits of the heart. There cannot be much sense in a government agenda that places debt reduction ahead of income support programs and services that allow people to lead the kinds of lives they value. New democratic strategies have to be found to push for a social agenda of human rights that make life worthwhile.

The quest for human advancement through material well-being has pressed on despite the centuries of blatant inequalities and physical hardships. The Swedish economist Gunnar Myrdal (1969) credits the motivation for this quest to what he calls the shining light of equality. Left to itself the market will extinguish that light. Yet the goal remains the same for those who believe in human well-being, full freedom, and material security for all.

REFERENCES

Arundel, C. & Associates in association with Henson Consulting Ltd. 2001. *Falling behind: Our growing income gap.* Federation of Canadian Municipalities **www.fcm.ca/english/communications/igfull.pdf**

Barr-Telford, L., Cartwright, F., Prasil, S., & Shimmons, K. 2003. *Access, persistence and financing: First results from the post-secondary education participation survey.* Ottawa: Statistics Canada, Cat. # 81-595-MIE-No. OO7.

Boyer, Robert, & Drache, Daniel (Eds.). 1996. *States against markets: The limits of globalization.* London: Routledge.

Canadian Centre for Policy Alternatives. *Alternative federal budget, 1999.* Ottawa.

Canadian Labour Congress, 2003 Annual Report. *Is work working for you in 2003?* **www.cbc.ca/news/background/cdngovernment/thronespeechtext.html**

Campaign 2000. 2003 Report Card on Child Poverty. *Honouring our promises: Meeting the challenge to end child and family poverty.* Toronto: c/o Family Services Association.

CBC News Online. February 2, 2004. Text of *Throne Speech.* **www.cbc.ca/news/background/cdngovernment/thronespeechtext.html**

C. D. Howe Institute. 1999. *It takes two: The family in law and finance*, D. W. Allen and J. R. Richards (Eds.). Ottawa: Renouf Publishing Company.

Centre for Social Justice. 2003. Exposing the face of corporate power. **www.socialjustice. org/poster.php**

Constante, K. 1996. Affidavit. Ontario Court (General Division). Divisional Court File No. 810/95 in the Matter of Judicial Review Procedure Act, R.S.O. 1990, c.J.l.

Crane, David. 2004. *Toronto Star* (January 28), p. C2.

Daily Bread Food Bank. *Who's hungry now?: The demographics of hunger, 1995, 2001, 2002.* **www.dailybread.ca/forms/Who.pdf**

Esping-Anderson, Gosta. 1989. The three political economies of the welfare state. *Canadian Review of Sociology and Anthropology*. 26.1.

Federal/Provincial/Territorial Ministerial Council on Social Policy Renewal, June 2003. *Three year review of Social Union Framework Agreement (SUFA)*. **www.gov.bc. ca/igrs/down/FPT_SUFA_E.pdf**

Francis, Diane. 1991. Quoted in Mel Hurtig. *The betrayal of Canada*. Toronto: Stoddart Publishing.

Freiler, Christa, & Cerny, Judy. 1998. *Benefiting Canada's children: Perspectives on gender and social responsibility*. Ottawa: Status of Women Canada.

Galbraith, John, Kenneth. 1992. *The culture of discontent*. Boston: Houghton Mifflin.

Government of Great Britain. 1998. *White paper on better financial support for families*. London: Her Majesty's Social Security Office.

Health Canada. 2002. *Dispute avoidance and resolution process under the Canada Health Act*. **www.hc-sc.gc.ca/medicare/ DAR.htm**

Hochschild, Arlie Russel. 1997. *The time bind: When work becomes home and home becomes work*. New York: Metropolitan Books.

Human Resources Development Canada. Summer–Fall 1998. Making work pay for welfare recipients. *Applied Research Bulletin*. 4.2.

Human Resources Development Canada. October 9, 1998a. *Workload reports*. **http://worldchat.com.public/tab/ocbcc/ ccnr15.htm**

Human Resources Development Canada, EI website. 2002. *Employment Insurance and the Family Supplement*. **www.hrdc-drhc.gc.ca/ae-ei/pubs/219017.shtml**

Human Resources Development Canada, Employment Insurance. March 31, 2003. *Employment Insurance 2002: Monitoring and assessment report*. **www.hrdcdrhc. gc.ca/ae-ei/loi-law/2002/eimar_ complete_2002.shtml**

Jackson, Andrew. December 10, 2003. *Paul Martin's economic record: Living standards of working families and prospects for future prosperity*. Alternative Federal Budget 2004, Technical Paper #2. Ottawa: Canadian Centre for Policy Alternatives.

Kitchen, Brigitte, 1987. Common sense assaults on families, in Diana Ralph, Andre Regimbald & Neree St-Amand (Eds.), *Mike Harris' Ontario: Open for business— closed to people*. Halifax: Fernwood.

Leisering, L., & Leibfried, S., 2001. "Path out of poverty," in Anthony Giddens (Ed.), *The global third way debate*. Oxford: Blackwell.

Loney, Martin. 1987. A war on poverty on the poor? In A. Walker and C. Walker (Eds.), *The growing divide: A social audit, 1979–1987*. London: Child Poverty Action Group.

Myrdal, Gunnar. 1969. Social values and their universality. *International Social Work*. XII.

National Child Benefit. Progress Report, 2002. Ottawa: Her Majesty the Queen in Right of Canada, 2003. **www.nationalchildbenefit. ca/ncb/NCB-2003/toc_e.html**

National Council of Welfare, 1998. Poverty profile. **www.statcan.ca/english/Subjects/ Labour/LFS/lfs-en.htm**

Nixon, Gordon. May 6, 2000. *Building Canada's prosperity in a new century*, Speech to the Canadian Club of Montreal.

Olson, G. 2002. *The politics of the welfare state: Canada, Sweden and the United States.* Don Mills, ON: 0xford University Press.

Statistics Canada. 1998. Income distribution by size. Cat. no. 13-207-XPB. **www.statscan.ca/ english/Pgdb/People/Families/famil4l.htm**

Statistics Canada. 1998. The Labour Force. *Historical review.*

Statistics Canada. 1998–2002. Gross domestic product, income based. **www.statcan.ca/ english/Pgdb/econ03.htm**

Statistics Canada. 1999–2003. Labour force characteristics. **www.statcan.ca/english/ Pgdb/econ10.htm**

Statistics Canada. 2001. Families, households and housing: Government transfers and income tax. **www.statcan.ca/english/ Pgdb/famil88a.htm**

Statistics Canada. 2001. Average total income by economic family types. **www.statcan. ca/english/Pgdb/famil05a.htm**

Statistics Canada. 2002. Labour, employment and unemployment: Reasons for part-time work. **www.statcan.ca/english/Pgdb/labor63a.htm**

Statistics Canada. May 2003. Women in the workplace in *Women in Canada*. Work Chapter Updates. Cat. No. 89F0133XIE. **www.statcan.ca/english/freepub/89F013 3XIE/89F0133XIE02001.pdf**

Statistics Canada. January 9, 2004. Latest release from the labour force survey. **www.statcan.ca/english/Subjects/Labour/ LFS/lfs-en.htm**

The Daily. February 25, 1999. Payroll employment, earnings & hours **www.statcan.ca/ Daily/English/990225/d990225.htm**

The Daily, June 19, 2003. Low Income rates among immigrants. **www.statscan.ca/Daily/ English/030619/d030619a.htm**

The Daily. January 29, 2004. Payroll employment, earnings & hours. **www.statcan.ca/Daily/ English/040129/d040129b.htm**

Toronto Star. November 27, 1998. *United Nations call Canada "inhumane."* A8.

Toronto Board of Trade. November 21, 2001. CEOs averaging $291,000 in GTA. Media release. **www.bot.com/contentislands/ publicpages/floatingpages/press_11_21_ 2001.asp**

United Nations. 2003 Human Development Indicators. **www.undp.org/hdr2003/ indicator/index.html**

chapter fifteen

Social Agencies and Human Service Organizations

Rose Marie Jaco

Barbara Decker Pierce

INTRODUCTION

Social agencies and human service organizations exist so that the services and resources our social welfare system provide can be delivered to people in need. They are the contact points between governments' social policies and targeted populations, between a community's charitable aims and its members in need. Social-service agencies and organizations must therefore have a physical presence, clearly defined purposes, and a set of characteristics that make up their unique identities.

In this chapter we examine some aspects of social agencies and human service organizations, acknowledging that while they all have some common elements they are also varied and diverse in their natures. They differ in regard to their histories, the needs they address, the clients they serve and the programs they deliver, the communities in which they are located, the philosophies of helping that their professionals and volunteers have adopted, and the availability of their funds. As a result, all social agencies and human service organizations share a common core of features; each also has a unique set of traits that sets it apart from the others, even those in the same field of service.

DEFINITIONS

A *social agency* is a formally structured unit, sanctioned by society, whose goals and activities focus on meeting human needs. Agencies vary in size from one-employee operations to those with hundreds of workers. The majority are considered *primary* social work settings with staffs consisting mainly of professional social workers. Agencies have locations, purposes set out in the form of mission and policy statements, and programs designed to provide services to defined groups of clients.

Alternatively, *human service organizations* are likely to be *secondary* settings for social work practice; social work is only one of several professions that provide such services. One type of human service organization sponsors a network of social agencies to deliver their specific services—for example, the Canadian National Institute for the Blind, which operates out of both a central office and many smaller locations in communities across the country. Other such organizations, such as hospitals, schools, government departments, or social planning bodies, may be local or regional in nature, and "have as their stated purpose enhancement of the social, emotional, physical and/or intellectual well-being of some component of the population."[1]

THREE TYPES OF SPONSORSHIP AND FUNDING

Answering the question of who is responsible for establishing and funding social agencies requires that we reflect on the nature of Canadian society from historical, political, and social perspectives. The mandate to create social agencies and human service organizations rests with three major sectors of Canadian society—*government, voluntary*, and *commercial*—in what has been termed "a mixed economy of welfare."[2]

We find reasons for this mix of service providers in the history of social welfare development in Canada. From the nation's beginning all levels of government have attempted to meet the social and health care needs of both citizens and immigrants. Governments were strongly supported in this work by religious groups. Eventually many voluntary bodies interested in particular groups or social problems emerged to take their places in the network of service providers. Despite an increasing role for governments in meeting basic human need, volunteers and church groups still maintain a presence in the social service field, often entering into financial partnerships with some levels of government to establish particular services needed. The commercial sector is a relative newcomer to the field, filling gaps left by the government and the voluntary social service network with profit-making organizations.[3]

The Canadian pattern of social service delivery offers many examples of funding partnerships among the three sectors, of agencies that obtain funds from one or several sources—through charitable donations, government grants, or fees for service. This section will examine the major characteristics of the government, voluntary, and commercial sectors and discuss the types of agencies each sponsors.

The Government or Public Sector

Because the constitutional obligation to provide social welfare and health care services is divided between the federal and provincial governments—which in turn assign some of their responsibilities to municipal and local bodies; all three levels of government have agencies or organizations through which these services are delivered. Government agencies are often termed ministries, offices, bureaus, or departments. Many social services are seen as rights that accompany citizenship and are provided by legislation and funded by means of taxation.

Government agencies traditionally have had a larger presence than those in the other two sectors; this may be changing in the current debate in governments at all levels between those who support neo-conservative approaches, with a focus on curbing government expenditures on health and social welfare, and those who advocate strong government roles in social policy-setting and providing services.[4]

The final shape the government sector will take can be known only with the passage of time. What is clear now is that in the past 15 years billions of dollars have been drained from the social security system, ending programs, closing agencies, curtailing services, and losing jobs.[5] This shift in governments' funding priorities demands that the voluntary sector play a new role, one that Browne predicts will reflect the fact that the "non-profit organizations, especially those that mobilize volunteers, are being touted either as substitutes for the welfare state or as agents for a new, leaner government."[6]

Areas of Government Responsibility

The Constitution has allocated the following welfare measures to either the federal or provincial jurisdiction: income support, health care, child welfare, employment insurance, vocational rehabilitation, housing, corrections, and services to veterans and First Nations citizens. Clearly, our society requires many types of agencies and organizations to deliver such a wide variety of services. These range from the computerized, information-processing environment of the federal department of Human Resources Development Canada to the more informal setting of a municipal social service office where people come in person to apply for welfare benefits.

While federal departments with health and welfare responsibilities base their central offices in Ottawa, they also run a network of provincial, regional, and local agencies to ensure that people have relatively easy access to their services. For example, because Employment Insurance legislation demands their staff make direct contact with recipients to confirm that they meet eligibility and job-search requirements, a network of Human Resources Centres has been created across the country. Similarly, although Old Age Security and Canada Pension Plan benefits are administered by means of a computer-based operation in Ottawa, local area offices have also been established to provide direct access to people who need particular information about their situations.

The Constitution also assigns the provincial governments and territories responsibility for specific health and welfare services that affect many Canadians' lives. These include physical and mental health care, institutions for the aged and those with disabilities, child welfare, aspects of corrections, and short-term and emergency income support. Each of these governments locates its central health and social welfare offices in its capital city, which is connected to a system of regional and branch offices. Each also funds human service organizations such as hospitals and residential treatment centres.

The provincial governments often delegate some of their responsibilities to municipal and local governments on the grounds that these bodies are closer in touch with their communities' needs and can therefore respond more quickly and effectively than a distant office could. Typical of these kinds of responsibilities are emergency income support, homes for the aged, daycare, homemakers, home nursing, public health, and accommodation and food for transients and the homeless.

While the federal government covers the entire cost of its services and agencies from the country's tax base, it also shares the cost of selected provincial social services by transferring funds to the provincial governments. Provincial governments must raise the balance of the funds they need through their own means of taxation. In turn, municipal services and agencies receive a large portion of their funding from their province—occasionally with some added federal money—but they must supplement this money with local property taxes and other measures of revenue generation. One additional source of funds consists of client user-fees, which are becoming an increasingly common feature.

Through these complicated funding arrangements, social agencies often have their costs divided among several or all levels of government, according to a variety of formulas, and they obtain further funds in a variety of ways. To add to the complexity of the Canadian system, each province presents a slightly different picture of the ways it mixes the public, voluntary, and commercial sponsorship of its social agencies and organizations. Studying the ways social services are delivered in Canada involves an understanding of the national picture as well as some knowledge of the pattern a specific province or region has adopted.

The federal and provincial governments took a positive step in 1999 by signing the agreement *A Framework to Improve the Social Union for Canadians* (SUFA). The federal, provincial, and territorial governments (excepting Quebec) promised to work together to ensure that all Canadians have access to essential social programs, receive assistance when in need, have adequate health care facilities available to them, are able to participate in Canadian society, and have the opportunity to submit meaningful input into designing social policies and programs. (See **www.socialunion.gc.ca** for more information on this initiative.)

The Voluntary, Private, or Charitable Sector

Thousands of private agencies and organizations exist in Canada, sponsored by an array of charitable, philanthropic, or religious bodies, national organizations, special interest groups, and individual citizens.

Some statistics illustrate the size of the voluntary sector. It is estimated that there are approximately 180 000 voluntary organizations in Canada, with slightly half registered as charities. These organizations employ more than 1.3 million people in communities across Canada, and the entire sector has annual revenues of more than $90 billion and assets of $109 billion in total.[7] In 2000, Canadians made direct financial donations to charitable organizations totalling $4.94 billion, of which $503 million was channelled to social service organizations.[8]

Organizations in the voluntary sector provide both direct and indirect social services. One example of a *direct* service provider is Big Brothers. Its services include matching children who lack adult role models with volunteers who offer friendship, social support, and recreation through character-building activities. *Indirect* service organizations in the voluntary sector usually operate from a central location, as the services they provide do not require face-to-face interaction with their clients. These organizations, of which the Canadian Council on Social Development, the Arthritis Society, and the Kidney Foundation are examples, carry out a variety of activities. They raise funds, research, advocate for certain causes, and sponsor education or training endeavours, all to create a supportive environment for people suffering from health or psychosocial problems and prevent the growth of the problems they target.

Describing the Voluntary Agency

Every voluntary agency begins as a response to an unmet human need. Need arises when the resources or conditions of life required to lead a fully human existence are lacking. When others in a community recognize a human need, their natural response is often to help. Their efforts become a collective effort to lessen the damaging effect of that specific deprivation on people. Helping consists of providing resources to those in need and developing strategies to prevent others from experiencing similar needs.

Efforts to help often begin with a needs assessment. This is a structured process through which attempts are made to measure unmet need. Research is carried out to identify the incidence of a problem and its impact on people, what service responses are already available, and the cost of setting up effective programs to deal with it.[9] The assessment determines the capacity of a community to meet its own needs, emphasizing people's ability to solve their own problems within that community.

The voluntary sector is characterized by a flexible response to emerging social needs and problems. Chiefly it does not work through a cumbersome legislative process to develop a service or change a policy. In large measure the efforts of voluntary social service organizations have traditionally supplemented the more substantial and basic provisions governments have made. However, they also offer a sort of experimental social laboratory in which various approaches to meeting human needs can be tried and tested before society decides whether they should be incorporated into legislated services and government agencies.

Voluntary agencies and organizations vary according to such factors as the degree of public support for them, sources of funding, and the involvement of the target population in designing the program and running the agency. Agencies in the private sector offer services to answer a broad range of human needs. These may include counselling for individuals, families, and couples; children's mental health facilities; psychological and social supports for clients suffering mental and physical health problems; social services designed for the special needs of women, children, the aged, those with disabilities, the bereaved, the poor, young offenders, and immigrants; recreational and socialization facilities for certain groups, such as children from impoverished families, the aged, and persons with disabilities; crisis intervention services in cases of family violence, child abuse, suicide, sexual assault, and incest; community information; debt counselling; job readiness; social planning; and fundraising.

Various levels of government and the voluntary sector form partnerships in areas such as child welfare, recreation, residential care for the elderly and persons with disabilities, children's mental health, employment programs, and corrections. These funding and policy-setting partnerships enable governments to deliver services sensitive to local values and standards and to foster the mutual care ethic the voluntary presence provides. Nonetheless, many voluntary organizations do not seek government sanction, particularly those based on the self-help model or whose purpose is to advocate for a special cause or group that may lead to a conflict of interest with the government.

Creating a New Social Agency

In creating a new agency today the first requirement remains the same: a group of people must share a common concern about some unmet human need. Group awareness does not have to arise spontaneously; it may need to be encouraged through education and leadership or the sharing of an ideology whose expression demands action. For example, the increase in services to abused women and their children grew out of the demands for justice feminist groups made, yet many citizens have supported it who would not describe themselves as feminists—including the governments that now fund women's shelters and counselling services. Groups with differing philosophies develop a collaborative approach out of the greater public awareness of the frequency of spousal abuse and its devastating consequences on the abused women and children.

Whatever the origins of their concern, the founders of a voluntary social agency must all carry out a set of tasks that include the following, although not necessarily in this order: assembling a board of directors to represent the community; establishing a mission, goals, and objectives for the agency; seeking a reliable source of funding; possibly searching for a suitable partner in government or the voluntary sector; observing relevant government regulations; developing a constitution, bylaws, and policies; designing programs; setting a budget; finding quarters for the agency; hiring an executive director who must then employ staff; and publicizing the service. This process can take many months or years (more often the latter), but most of the voluntary social service agencies and organizations in Canada today have had to follow similar steps in creating themselves, whether sponsored by small local groups or by more powerful national bodies.

One common feature of the voluntary agency is its board of directors. To assure public accountability and the agency's close connection to the community, citizens are elected or appointed to a board. The board generally oversees the agency's operations, assuring the community it is achieving its stated goals, that its programs

are relevant and effective, and that it is spending funds responsibly. The board of directors legitimizes the agency's activities in the eyes of the community. In the same way, politicians and public servants legitimize the work of government agencies through accountability to the public. Board members may serve in advisory capacities only or they may form working committees that design policies, evaluate programs, or work more directly with clients.

Funding Challenges Funding is a constant concern to voluntary agencies. Although these organizations receive increasingly more government funds for specific programs, much of the money that supports their services comes from a very uncertain source—charitable donations. Charitable dollars express the donors' concern for the well-being of strangers, and the collection of money is often based on cleverly orchestrated appeals to both the heart and the head, to the emotions of both pity and fear. People may pity those in need and have great sympathy for them; they may fear that adversity will befall them as well or those whom they love. A mixture of motives, including the "good citizen" approach, which corporate donors employ, produces donations of substantial sums to voluntary agencies each year. Foundations are playing a more and more important role in supporting agency-based programs and initiatives. These may be community foundations, endowments sponsored by specific families, or money collected as an expression of concern about a particular social problem or illness.

Governments like to encourage the growth and strength of the voluntary sector. Obviously every activity supported by the charitable dollar means less demand placed on the tax dollar. So important is this component of the social welfare system that the government of Canada supports the

Voluntary Sector Initiative (**www.vsi-isbc.ca**). Specifically, the VSI is a five-year government-funded project that began in June 2000. It focuses on strengthening relations between the voluntary sector and the federal government and enhancing the capacity of the voluntary sector. It aims to improve the quality of life in Canada through joint research and collaboration.

Charitable campaigns are extremely vulnerable to any public perception that funds being collected are not being used wisely or are being applied to a controversial service. Voluntary agencies will often avoid taking a stand on contentious issues or offering services that might attract public criticism. This does not mean that the voluntary sector never addresses "unpopular causes." However, these causes must be presented to the public in such a way as to elicit the maximum amount of understanding, empathy, and acceptance for the client group affected in order to attract those charitable dollars.

As well as giving to charitable causes many Canadians volunteer their own time and effort to help others. It is estimated that more than one in four (27 percent) of all citizens over the age of 15 volunteered a total of slightly more than one billion hours of service in 2000.[10] These hours represent a significant contribution in dollar value, and one perhaps even more significant in the social connections forged among people when they invest in mutual aid activities with fellow community members.

The Commercial Sector

A lack of services in some areas of human need has encouraged entrepreneurs to move into the area of social service in the hope of realizing profits—an objective that they may well combine with more altruistic motives. The commercial or profit-making sector is a small and gradually increasing part of the social welfare system. It provides services in areas where neither the government nor voluntary groups wish to assume responsibility, usually because the cost of fully meeting the particular need over time would be substantial.

The recent policy objectives of fiscal restraint and privatization have made the purchase of services from commercial providers attractive to governments. There are other reasons for their support of for-profit operations as well. Private service delivery includes such advantages of increased efficiency through competition; more clearly defined and flexible services; fewer fixed costs than established government services would incur; and the possibility of changing providers if one provider's service proves unsatisfactory. Disadvantages consist of uncertainties related to program design and objectives, quality control, and potential disruption for clients if contracts are terminated.[11]

Concerns about For-Profit Social Services There are additional objections to for-profit providers involved in social welfare.

Philosophically, the money-making objectives of the commercial sector conflict with the mutual support ethic of social welfare and social work.[12] Some cite realistic fears that if the commercial sector becomes too large a part of social welfare or obtains a monopoly in any one field of service, the poor may not be served at all because they will not be able to afford the fees. Quality control is difficult for governments to exert at a distance, and in some areas there are very minimal regulations to establish standards of care and protect clients.

Commercial providers are always caught between their contract to provide service and their need to show a profit. There may be times when these agencies curtail services in the interest of financial gain, resulting in inadequate service to clients. On the other hand, some critics take the position that the provincial governments should get out of the business of providing social services directly in favour of contracting them from the voluntary and commercial sectors; the governments could always retain the right to set policies, budgets, and standards. Issues related to ideology, efficiency, quality of service, cost, and accountability continue to be hotly debated while the commercial sector grows and thrives.[13]

Developments in the Commercial Sector Many forces encourage this growth. They include both the current economic policies of all levels of government and the increasing demand for service in certain areas. Commercial agencies and organizations seem to respond faster than the government or the voluntary sectors in such areas as residential care for emotionally disturbed children; group homes for discharged psychiatric patients; facilities for youth in conflict with the law; chronic care, nursing homes, and residential care for the aged; and operating support services such as home nursing and homemaking.

Employee Assistance Programs are one example of a growth area in the commercial field. Employers establish EAPs by purchasing a block of counselling time from an organization, which employees can use anonymously and without charge. EAPs treat such problems as couples' and families' conflicts, addictions, child management, and bereavement. Employers provide these services as an employee benefit to maintain their employees' work performance at acceptable levels, despite the disturbing situations the employees may be facing in their home lives.[14]

The private practice of social work is also an expanding area of commercial social services. Professionals, singly or in groups, offer therapy and counselling services for a fee, while others consult with government and voluntary agencies on program planning and evaluation or agency management.

On balance, this mix of agency sponsorship, which has been referred to as a "blurring of the sector boundaries,"[15] appears to work fairly well, although inadequacies can found in the social services that all three sectors provide.[16] Answers to the question of what an ideal service delivery model should be are elusive. One aspect of the issue with particular significance for Canada is the challenge of providing services in isolated and sparsely populated areas, such as rural and northern communities. Government intervention here is clearly necessary as neither the voluntary nor the commercial sector is able or willing to offer adequate social services to these small, scattered populations. In these areas the voluntary sector could find too few dollars and volunteer resources, and the commercial sector would find it difficult to realize sufficient profits outside relatively large-scale operations.

INTERNAL MANAGEMENT AND THE BUREAUCRATIC STRUCTURE

Like most modern institutions, the social welfare system operates through a bureaucratic structure and processes. This framework enables its agencies to carry out their complex tasks. Bureaucratic rules and regulations allow an even-handed distribution of social welfare goods and services to clients according to agency policy. Benefits do not depend on the workers' personal preferences, except when the regulations state that the provider can exercise its own judgment in providing or withholding a benefit in individual cases.

Nevertheless, the bureaucratic model and the objectives of social welfare and social work fit together only imperfectly. The very formality and regulation that organizations need to run efficiently also make for a rigidity that hinders their adapting easily to the unique nature of the human beings who come to them with their different needs.

Issues Affecting Bureaucratic Organizations

Bureaucracies present problems for both workers and clients of different kinds. Clients may find the intricate nature of the bureaucracy hard to deal with because they do not fully understand the rules or how best to interpret the regulations in order to qualify for service. Applying for a benefit demands that clients put forward the most convincing case possible on their own behalf and that they advocate for themselves with some skill. Unfortunately, they run into this expectation when they are most under stress because of the specific problems for which they are applying for help. They may find going through the necessary steps to obtain this help from a social agency discouraging or even intimidating; the agency may request that they share personal information with strangers or fill out extensive application forms. These expectations combined with the possibility of rejection and the reality of waiting lists or possible referrals to other service providers cause stress for prospective clients. (The problems workers experience will be discussed later in this section.)

The sponsorship and size of the agency determine the extent to which the same agency follows the bureaucratic model. Large government organizations rank highest on the scale of most bureaucratic characteristics and the small voluntary agencies, the lowest.

Despite differences in degree some of the following bureaucratic features are found in almost all human service agencies and organizations. Each is guided by mission and policy statements that state the agency's goals and objectives. From these the agency develops a strategic plan that outlines the tasks necessary to carry out its mission. This plan then becomes the blueprint for structuring the agency into specialized work units or departments.

Managing the Agency

This structure makes the agency's management possible. Qualified staff can then be assigned to specialized departments and their activities coordinated efficiently. Arranging positions in a hierarchy and allocating work to assigned units eliminates confusion about who should be doing which tasks and in what sequence.

Managers frequently supervise performance. They monitor and coordinate the work of the staff. It is their responsibility to see that standards of performance are adequate and that the overall organizational plan is being implemented. Recent cutbacks in social services and health care funding have resulted in fewer managers and supervisors of social work in practice settings. A whole layer of middle management seems to have been stripped out of the agency structures in many fields. Consequently, social workers are expected to practise far more independently and they have fewer opportunities in terms of support, consultation, and guidance from colleagues than was the case in earlier decades.

The number of levels within which staff is organized varies from agency to agency. Small agencies may have only two levels: front-line workers who serve clients face to face and a director who oversees the operation. Larger agencies need internal structures to manage a variety of staff: front-line workers, department heads, middle management, coordinators, consultants, and an executive director. Organizational charts for complex agencies can be drawn to indicate reporting responsibilities and to specify the correct channels through which to send information.

Social Work within a Bureaucracy

The bureaucratic structure causes much tension for social workers, especially when "individualization is sacrificed to proceduralism; when efficiency becomes more important than quality of service; and when administrative accountability serves to stifle practitioner creativity and constrain the exercise of professional judgment."[17]

However, steps can be taken to modify the negative impact of rigid bureaucracy both on social workers and on service to clients. Resnick and Patti suggest a dynamic organizational model with the following characteristics:

(1) a division of labour and tasks based on the flexible use of staff knowledge and skills

(2) hierarchical authority, with supervisors who manage the quality and flow of work, but who rely heavily on independent action and sound judgment among their staff

(3) a decision-making process that allows wide participation by those affected by the decisions

(4) rules and procedures that offer workers guidelines but allow them to adapt their behaviour as situations require

(5) communication processes that permit information to flow in many directions—up and down the hierarchy, and diagonally, among departments

(6) an understanding of and commitment to the organization's goals as a replacement of blind compliance to the rules

(7) a climate that supports professional growth and is free of worker exploitation

(8) a consultative style of leadership.[18]

While the bureaucratic structure presents problems for delivering human services, this form of organization in the social services is considered the one most likely to deliver services effectively, to respond to communities' needs, and to keep employees satisfied and productive.

Besides the formal structure of an agency there exists a hidden, powerful substructure that cannot be drawn on a flow chart. Nonetheless it contributes greatly to high or low morale among staff members. This is the network of peers who develop their own relationships through their daily interaction and shared perspectives. The informal network can strengthen or weaken the agency, depending on whether or not the members agree with the directions the agency is taking and the administration's methods to settle differences and allocate resources.[19] The informal network functions in many ways: it gives emotional support to its members, allows them to complain without confronting the administration, controls aspects related to the quality and amount of work expected of workers, and corrects errors administration makes through the many decisions and adjustments that front-line workers can make.

Power within the Bureaucracy

Power influences much of what occurs in an organization. Those possessing the power can carry out their wishes despite opposition and exercise command over resources. Power attaches to position.

Those at the top of an organization have more and those at the bottom less, at least theoretically. A major factor determining the amount of power a person actually has in the workplace is his or her personal power—the individual's natural ability to influence and lead others. It sometimes happens, because of a lack of personal power, that those highly placed in a hierarchy are unable to exercise the full measure of their authority while workers lower in the hierarchy, those with a good measure of personal power, exercise more power and influence than their jobs warrant. Ideally, the workers in a social agency should command enough power to carry out their own duties, but not enough to allow them to interfere in other workers' appropriate use of their own power.

Staff members need to believe that the people who control the organization—the administrators, board members, civil servants, or commercial operators—are exercising their power legitimately, with the ultimate well-being of clients, staff, and organization uppermost in mind rather than their own personal benefit. Without this belief it is difficult for workers to remain committed to the organization, to adhere to regulations, and to work under constraints. Most social agencies make provisions for workers to share a part of organizational power through their participation in decision-making. Membership on planning committees, representation on the board of directors, and a consultative approach to developing internal policies are some of the ways staff may share power. Unionization has given some social service workers an additional power base from which to exert influence on their agencies and control some of the conditions of their work.[20]

Changing the Agency from Within

At times the professionals involved in the provision of social services may wish their agencies or organizations would change in some way. Often they are frustrated by the unresponsive nature of their own bureaucracies. Social workers promise in their code of ethics to seek change when they believe that their clients' well-being is in jeopardy because of circumstances in their organizations' workplaces.[21]

What circumstances could motivate social workers to confront management and possibly risk losing their jobs to protect clients? Mullaly identifies these conditions within social agencies. Policies and programs that force clients to accept roles or engage in behaviours that sustain and sanction oppressive relationships are clear targets for front-line action. As well, overbearing supervision, reward systems that favour administrative convenience over client service, and caseloads far too large for individual workers to manage can lead social workers to demand change.[22]

One difficulty in ensuring that client rights are uniformly respected arises when non-professionals whose work is not guided by a code of ethics are delivering the services. In some settings untrained personnel are hired to provide services that professionals should provide as the priority becomes that of saving money.

Social workers can adopt one of three positions in their efforts to bring about agency change. The first calls for the social worker to exercise some skill within agency regulations. Here the professionals act as advocates on their clients' behalf while fulfilling the role of "good bureaucrats," those who can function effectively within their organizations without compromising larger social work values.

As organizational change takes time, Pruger counsels workers to develop a philosophy, lifestyle, and set of skills that will make them competent, active participants in shaping the life of the organization as it develops. A social worker with patience, high energy, and the ability to think independently can enlarge his areas of discretionary judgment, and so earn the power to interpret rules and regulations as liberally as possible, in his clients' interests.[23] This is an appropriate use of personal power and influence.

Working within the system can be an effective process but circumstances may persuade the professionals involved that they must act directly and openly to bring about some kind of change in their organizations. In this second approach, several strategies are available. Resnick and Patti outline both collaborative and adversarial methods for altering agency patterns and policies.[24] Change is as difficult for social agencies as it is for human beings, and in attempting to initiate change the authors caution workers to try collaborative methods first. Adversarial approaches often polarize an issue and harden the agencies' resistance to change. When social workers elect to collaborate in order to change some aspect of their agencies' operations, they are applying a problem-solving model to their agencies' processes. Workers provide information, present alternative approaches, ask permission to try innovative or experimental practices, produce statistical data to support the need for change, and point out the negative impacts that current rules have for clients.

If the agencies resist this slow-moving, incremental process or it is otherwise ineffective, the final method available to workers is confrontation. Being adversarial in seeking agency change is stressful and can be hazardous for workers, Workers who actively oppose their employer's methods of operating inevitably provoke anger and conflict. Nevertheless, putting the well-being of clients first may make this choice necessary. Adversarial tactics on an ascending scale of intensity include the submission of petitions, encouraging staff not to comply with a disputed regulation, open conflicts at meetings, using the media to publicize the problem with all the attendant threats of loss of public support and funding, instituting work stoppages or strikes, and finally litigation. Social workers participate actively in shaping their agencies' responses to meeting clients' needs. They need to be skilled, knowledgeable, and courageous in playing their parts well.

Management Practices and Agency Costs

In an attempt to answer the question of how best to manage the inner workings of the social agency so that staff members perform well and deliver the most cost-effective services to clients, a large body of literature and an active consultation business for management experts has developed. Both structure and flexibility seem to be fundamental. Social workers are more likely to work well in an orderly milieu where they and their colleagues accept organized work patterns and can see that the values of the profession are being observed.

As social agencies deal with human problems on a case-by-case basis, every person who requests service must be assessed for eligibility, her situation documented and kept on file, and outcomes of the intervention evaluated before closing her case. Dealing with requests for service is termed "intake" and the responsibility is often assigned to specialists who assess whether the client's need falls within the agency's mandate and resources. These specialists then recommend acceptance of the client or her referral to another source of help.

In providing social work services to clients, workers are guided by their agencies' policy. Where these are in place, agencies also operate according to written protocols. The latter are detailed lists of steps for staff to take in specific types of cases. For example, in a child welfare agency, workers always follow certain procedures in investigating and dealing with a complaint of child abuse. Although the use of protocols tends to standardize procedures in a somewhat rigid way, it also ensures a uniform quality of service delivery in that the workers carry out all the essential steps and minimizes their possible oversight or incompetence.

All agencies maintain client records. They may take a brief form, which summarizes the nature of the problem, describes the interventions made, and notes the outcomes achieved. Records usually contain short case histories and periodic notes about a client's progress as well as a closing summary of all that occurred during the agency's contact with him. More comprehensive recordings are of particular importance in cases involving child abuse or custody disputes when there may be legal proceedings, and they are invaluable should a social worker be accused of malpractice. Contents of the record are confidential and cannot be used outside the agency without the client's permission or a court order.

Most workers also develop their own systems of personal information that allow them to keep track of their work commitments with appointment books, day sheets, and working notes. Workers need to keep careful records of their daily activities because they must periodically provide their agencies with statistical breakdowns of how they spend their time. Computers are an increasingly important feature in this aspect of agency life, to manage case records, perform statistical analysis, and communicate among workers and other agencies.[25]

Workers often see reporting on their statistics as tedious, but the statistical analysis of agency data is an important management tool. Statistical data yield information about the characteristics of the people the agency serves, changing needs in the community, referral sources to the agency, outcomes of interventions used, case conferences held, and education or training sessions attended. The administration uses this information to demonstrate accountability for agency costs to its board of directors, funders, government regulators, and the larger community. Administrators can also discern trends in requests for service, as the profile of human need changes over time, with some needs increasing as others diminish in importance. As well, administrators and managers can compare workers' productivity, information that can lead to performance improvement, better allocations of talents, or additional training.

COST-EFFECTIVENESS IN THE HUMAN SERVICES

The cost of providing services varies considerably among agencies, even among those offering similar programs. Costs depend on many factors, including the educational qualifications of the staff, how extensive and labour-intensive the programs are, whether the organization offers group or individual treatment, whether volunteers provide some services, and the expenses of housing and running the agency.

At all times, but perhaps especially in times of fiscal restraint, agencies must justify their expenditures. They do this in part by measuring the impact their programs have in helping their clients deal with their problems or in alleviating the social problems the agencies target. For example, if an agency offers education and training to youth who have dropped out of school prematurely, they could measure their program's effectiveness by keeping track of the percentage of clients who find employment or who go on to higher education following their agency's intervention compared with the employment of a similar group the agency does not serve. It is reasonable to expect that over time a network of such services would lower the number of youth who are unemployed, which would affect local unemployment rates.

Deciding what to choose as valid indicators of successful outcomes is a problem for those who evaluate the success or failure of social programs. Numbers alone are not enough nor is an emphasis on how many dollars have been saved. Somehow an agency evaluating its own performance over time must identify variables that measure the impact of a service in terms of personal growth, family harmony, community strength, or other specific goals that the agency has expressed.

Costs also affect an agency's physical surroundings, of course. Notable differences are often found when social agencies are compared according to how attractive, adequate, and well maintained their facilities are. Sometimes a justified complaint is made that the poor are offered services in inadequate surroundings, usually the result of operating a program on too meagre a budget, often in a deteriorated location. For the agency's clients such appearances can create a negative experience, demonstrating both deprivation and lack of respect. Physical settings send strong messages to clients, and an environment that is uncomfortable, dirty, lacking in privacy, and generally unattractive may tell clients that they are not valued, that the agency overlooks their rights to dignity and privacy, and that they do not merit an attractive environment as they seek help.

COMMON PROBLEMS

An overall planned design has never been established to guide the development of the social welfare system in Canada. Despite this, we lack an accepted process for interaction among agencies and organizations in the government, the voluntary, and the commercial sectors. Three major problems result from this absence of a blueprint.

The first issue is *gaps in service.* Certain human needs appeal more strongly to the public than others and these attract more support and money from all sources. Those agencies that serve children with disabilities or the aged tend to appeal more to the public than services for those whose troubles are often seen as partly self-inflicted, such as people with addictions, AIDS patients, never-married mothers, or the mentally ill.

In contrast to gaps in service, a second problem, *duplication of service*, also exists between and within sectors. This problem can be interpreted in two ways. Some may see having several agencies provide virtually the same service as a waste of scarce funds; others may consider that more than one form of service is desirable because it suggests diversity and could give clients more choice when they seek help.

The third problem is *discontinuity of service*. Clients often find it difficult to move smoothly from one agency to another as their needs change. For example, an elderly person might encounter this problem if he has to move from home to hospital, and then back to supported living at home with help from various social and health care services along the way. Poor communication and coordination among these different services could make the transitions very complicated for him. A new emphasis on the professional skills of case management is emerging, especially in the field of health care of the elderly and the chronically ill to ease these transitions for them and to coordinate the simultaneous use of many services.

Correcting the Problems

Other efforts have been made to solve these problems. Strategies are available to communities to enable them to create a more comprehensive and well-coordinated network of services. These include forming a social planning council to organize local services; developing coordinating committees to plan around specific problems, such as difficult-to-serve children; hiring more case managers experienced in dealing with complex service systems; and giving the users themselves the power to choose among services by providing information and establishing citizens' advisory groups. The lack of easy-to-access information about available services often prevents prospective users from acting effectively to meet their own needs.

Sometimes social planners suggest that two or more agencies whose programs seem to overlap should amalgamate as a cost-saving measure. Staff and volunteers often resist such proposals strongly, and if forced through, such measures can actually decrease efficiency or even lead to the dissolution of the agency.

NEW AND EMERGING NEEDS

We live in an age of rapid social change and rising expectations for personal happiness. These forces converge to make our society more aware of the variety and extent of human need than ever before possible. Not only do we recognize new needs, but we have the capability and often the will to try and relieve them by taking action. Hence we continually create new agencies and organizations with special programs designed to correct contemporary problems in living.

We speak of "new" needs, but the term actually has two meanings: some needs that have always existed but are newly uncovered because they can now be discussed and dealt with openly, or alternatively, some needs we have never before experienced that have arisen as a result of some change in society or the environment.

For example, violence in the family, especially against women, is not new. What is new is society's powerful response against it. In collaboration with strong legislation, a variety of services for abused women and their children have been developed—legal advice clinics, shelters, and transition houses.

With the advent of HIV and AIDS in the early 1980s, an entirely new and unanticipated area of human need appeared. Agencies and services of many types, such as hostels, hospices, and counselling programs, are being established to respond to the needs of these patients and those related to them. Here we have an opportunity to study the many human reactions to a tragic social problem. Many segments of the voluntary community have reacted with generous support while governments have often operated at arm's length, perhaps because of the political risks they would run in seeming to endorse people with stigmatized illnesses.

New agencies sometimes appear as our society finds innovative ways to cope with "old" needs. Bereavement services are one such instance. People have always had to deal with death, and recent advances in therapeutic counselling and the use of mutual support groups offer the possibility of relieving human suffering and preventing family breakdowns after the deaths of loved ones.

Self-help is a long-established method of helping others. The strengths to be found through mutual aid are being applied to current problems caused by changing social forces. For example, mutual support groups are being developed to assist farmers whose livelihoods are threatened by poor economic times; to help the victims of incest and rape; to encourage widowed people to live more fully; and to allow the adult children of alcoholic parents to overcome negative influences from their past. Self-help and professionally directed services developed for First Nations clients both on and off the reserves help them deal with problems of cultural adjustment, work readiness, addictions, and personal development. The government and the private sectors unite to help the elderly through a variety of community-based agencies that offer recreation, retirement counselling, home support, and nursing services. As a country that encourages the immigration of people from many other cultures, Canada supports a network of services to assist the newcomers in their adjustment or "settlement" in their new country. Professionals in health and social welfare today see using cultural interpreters as necessary so that they can provide their services in a culturally and linguistically sensitive manner.

In this era of information overload, many clients discover that finding out the correct facts regarding an appropriate service is difficult. One type of agency has been created to guide clients through the maze of resources available. Information centres collect and categorize vast amounts of data on legislation, social, health, and community agencies, and human rights. As well as giving clients clear facts relevant to their situations, information centres also refer them directly to specific services.

The creation of the multi-service centre represents another step toward simplifying help-seeking. Several agencies staff this organization, from both the government and the voluntary sectors, so that clients with complex problems can find the many resources they need there. Rural settings are finding the multi-service concept particularly useful.

CONCLUSION

From the information contained in this chapter it is apparent that the safety net that covers Canada in support of the needy and the vulnerable among us is woven of strong fibres. Social agencies, human service organizations, social workers, health care professionals, volunteers, social policies, and funding sources constitute the strands.

Like all human institutions, agencies and organizations have problems. Yet flawed as these organizations might be, their mere existence offers concrete evidence of that aspect of the human spirit that moves us to care for strangers' well-being. It would be difficult to visualize Canadian society without them.

NOTES

1. Brager, G., & Holloway, S. (1978), *Changing human service organizations: Politics and practice.* New York: Collier Macmillan, p. 2.

2. Lightman, E. (2003), *Social policy in Canada.* Don Mills, ON: Oxford University Press, p. 86.

3. Armitage, A. (1996), *Social welfare in Canada revisited: Facing up to the future*

(3rd ed.). Don Mills: Oxford University Press, pp. 118–119.

4. Browne, P. (1996), *Love in a cold world: The voluntary sector in an age of cuts.* Ottawa: Canadian Centre for Policy Alternatives.

5. Graham, J. R., Swift, K. J., & Delaney, R. (2003), *Canadian social policy: An introduction.* Toronto: Prentice Hall, pp. 40–41.

6. Armitage, A. (1996), *Social welfare in Canada revisited*. p. 81.

7. Voluntary Sector Initiative (n.d.). Retrieved May 20, 2004, from **www.vsi-isbc.ca/eng/about/voluntary_sector.cfm**

8. Canadian Centre for Philanthropy (2000), *Charitable giving in Canada*. Retrieved May 20, 2004, from **www.givingand volunteering.ca/factsheets.asp**

9. Reviere, R., Berkowitz, S., Carter, C. C., & Ferguson, C. G. (1996), *Needs assessment: A creative and practical guide for social scientists*. Washington: Taylor & Francis.

10. Canadian Centre for Philanthropy (2000), *Volunteering in Canada*. Retrieved May 20, 2004, from **www.givingandvolunteering.ca/factsheets.asp**

11. Armitage, A. (1988), *Social welfare in Canada: Ideals, realities and future paths* (2nd ed.). Toronto: McClelland & Stewart, p. 226.

12. Wilensky, H., & Lebeaux, C. (1965), Conceptions of social welfare. In H. Wilensky and C. Lebeaux (Eds.), *Industrial society and social welfare*. New York: Free Press.

13. Lightman, E. (2003), *Social policy in Canada*, pp. 93–99.

14. Brothers, C., & Brothers, J. (2001), Industries and the provision of social services. In J. C. Turner, and F. J. Turner (Eds.), *Canadian social welfare* (4th ed.). Toronto: Pearson Education.

15. Chappell, R. (2001), *Social welfare in Canadian society*. Scarborough, ON: Nelson Thomson Learning, p. 119.

16. Davies, L., & Schragge, E. (1990), *Bureaucracy and community*. Montreal: Black Rose Books.

17. Patti, R. J. (1980), Internal advocacy and human service practitioners: An exploratory study. In H. Resnick and R.J. Patti (Eds.), *Change from within: Humanizing social welfare organizations*. Philadelphia: Temple University Press, p. 287.

18. Resnick, H., & Patti, R. J. (Eds.), (1980), *Change from within: Humanizing social welfare organizations*. Philadelphia: Temple University Press, pp. 6–7.

19. Gibelman, M. (2003), *Navigating human service organizations*. Chicago: Lyceum Books, p. 115.

20. Foley, J. (1999), Professional associations in Canada. In F. J. Turner (Ed.), *Social work practice: A Canadian perspective*. Scarborough: Prentice-Hall.

21. Canadian Association of Social Workers (1983), *Code of ethics*. Ottawa.

22. Mullaly, B. (1997), *Structural social work: Ideology, theory and practice* (2d ed.). Don Mills, ON: Oxford University Press, p. 181.

23. Pruger, R. (1973), The good bureaucrat. *Social Work, 18*, 26–32.

24. Resnick, H., & Patti, R. J. (1980), *Change from within*.

25. Perlmutter, F. D., Bailey, D., & Netting, F. E. (2001), *Managing human resources in the human services: Supervisory challenges*. New York: Oxford University Press, ch. 4.

chapter sixteen

Informal Helping and Mutual Aid

John Cossom

INTRODUCTION

This chapter focuses on various kinds of informal help that people use outside the boundaries of formal social service agencies with employed, professional helpers. It has several objectives.

First, the chapter intends to draw attention to the wide continuum of formal and informal helping resources that people use to deal with personal problems. Second, we examine why informal care and support are now a subject of renewed importance for professional helpers, social science research, and social policy. Third, we consider the concepts of natural helping and social support, the important roles they play in the ecology of helping, and why professional helpers need to understand them. We look at mutual aid groups and, in particular, self-help groups. We deal with the latter at some length because of their ubiquity, their phenomenal growth, and their increasing significance as a source of support and empowerment for so many people. Then we draw a contrast between lay, informal helping and the kinds of help that social service professionals offer.

Because we can look at informal helping according to distinct ideological perspectives, we examine its social policy and political significance. The chapter concludes with a discussion of how professional helpers can understand, establish links with, and champion informal help and mutual aid in their practices.

THE LEXICON OF INFORMAL HELPING

As various kinds of informal helping have attracted a burgeoning interest, a plethora of terms and definitions has sprung up to describe what is a complex and diverse phenomenon. A reader is likely to encounter, among others, terms such as:

- informal or natural helping
- natural helping network
- natural or lay helper
- caregiver or natural caregiver
- social network
- social support network
- informal support system
- support group
- mutual aid
- self-help

These concepts interest many different academics and professionals in the fields of social work, sociology, psychology, nursing, anthropology, psychiatry, the clergy, and so on. As often happens in social science, there is far from universal agreement on the meaning of these terms, and a great deal of overlap and variation in their use. As this chapter progresses, we will offer definitions of some of these terms.

MUTUAL AID, INFORMAL, AND PROFESSIONAL HELP

Mutual aid is a generic term. Historically it refers to the many ways that human beings care for one another. People sharing resources and taking common action to deal with shared problems are the essence of society (Kropotkin). Throughout recorded time, people in differing cultures have developed their own, natural ways to deal with inevitable but unpredictable personal troubles, social problems, and environmental catastrophes. Humankind's very survival has often depended on social cooperation in, for example, food gathering, mutual protection against invaders, child care, and agriculture. Families, neighbours, and clan members were the significant sources of mutual assistance.

Over time, other, more structured approaches to mutual aid arose.

An important twentieth-century Canadian example is the Antigonish Movement. This liberal, Catholic, social and economic community-development movement began in the 1920s and ultimately led to the establishment of credit unions and fishing, agricultural, and consumer cooperatives that dotted the Atlantic provinces in the 1930s and 1940s (MacPherson).

With the emergence of faster moving, urbanizing industrial societies, professional, paid helpers and state social welfare interventions increasingly became a feature of the social structure. In Canada, this was primarily a twentieth-century development, a response to human need that surfaced in increasingly formal, specialized ways. In part, public social welfare programs and professional helpers were necessary to deal with the inordinate demands placed on informal helping systems in a rapidly changing world. Geographic population mobility and the transition to a nuclear family made the support of the extended family system much less viable.

An industrially driven economy disrupted the long-standing natural support systems for many people. When economies crashed, family and friends usually did not have the resources needed to help one other survive the ravages of mass unemployment. Their support could not generate jobs that no longer existed. Also, local churches, charities, or benevolent associations could not cope with the tremendous human need this large-scale dislocation produced. In response to widespread social, health, and economic problems, an increasingly complex social welfare system slowly assumed greater responsibility for broad public needs. Specialized professional disciplines evolved to address people's personal troubles. Sometimes grassroots volunteer helping evolved into formal social services organizations that employed professional staff. Many social service agencies emerged from such voluntary services and caring.

In complex situations, society accepts the importance of specialized professional help in assisting individuals and groups deal effectively with their troubles. We also better understand today that both informal and professional kinds of assistance perform important, legitimate, if different, functions and that we usually need them to work together to people's advantage.

Not surprisingly, though, in our age of expanding professional specializations, status, control of turf, and the rapid growth of knowledge and helping technologies, paid helpers often overlook the significance of mutual aid and natural forms of help. Indeed, professionals are quite capable of treating informal helping as of lesser importance or, worse, as irrelevant to a specialized helping process. Still other professionals may consider mutual aid an "adjunct" or "aftercare" to their clinical work and see it as secondary to the "real" work that they do as experts (Humphreys).

It is tempting to assume that with the development of public assistance, social insurance, universal transfer payments, and a wide array of public and voluntary personal social services, the more informal natural helping roles have greatly diminished in importance. Such is not the case. These contrasting cultures of care continue to exist side by side in our communities. All manner of informal, everyday helping continues to play a crucial role in people's lives. Even though we claim to understand these natural and informal kinds of help better now, we still have much to learn about them.

Helping takes multiple forms. It can range from individual self-reliance—think of the glut of self-improvement and self-healing books on the market today—to sophisticated professional therapies and national social security schemes. The continuum in Figure 16.1 illustrates the range of helping models.

These different helping systems interact with and affect one another, whether or not this mutual influence is recognized. Unfortunately, they too often operate in rigid isolation from, ignorance or suspicion of, or competition with one another.

RENEWED AWARENESS OF INFORMAL HELPING

Nowadays, professional helpers are becoming much more knowledgeable about the extent and significance of natural

| FIGURE 16.1 | A Continuum of Helping Resources |

INFORMAL ◄─●──────●──────────●────────────●──────────●────●► FORMAL

| Personal resources and self-reliance | Natural helping networks and social support groups | Self-help groups | Mutual aid membership societies | Social services and professional therapies | Social security programs |

helpers and support systems in people's lives. One simple but striking example comes from research into the care of older people (Brody; Kane, & Penrod).

This is an important issue, given Canada's significant and growing population of elderly people. Many in our society think that the public and private institutional health care and social services personnel constitute all the services available for our elderly. The reality is very different: "In Canada, as in comparable western economic systems, it is estimated that 85 to 90 per cent of the care of old people is provided informally, largely in the context of families. The rest, only 10 or 15 per cent, is supplied by the formal health and social services" (Aronson).

Informal family care roles are of huge significance. Women provide most of this "family" care. This is true not only in the case of the elderly, but in other areas too, such as the care of disabled children and adults. Knowing such facts aids our understanding of these crucial informal helping patterns.

Support as Social Buffering

There are a number of reasons why professionals are now less likely to see informal kinds of helping as insignificant, antagonistic, or competitive. The first is that social science and health researchers are paying more attention to informal helping. Patterns of lay help are becoming more visible and society therefore takes them less taken for granted as a feature of people's social ecology. A body of knowledge, concepts, and theory is growing about the forms that natural help takes, and how people use these various informal resources. As we appreciate more and more the nature and extent of informal help in society, we also learn what positive effects these social connections have on people's individual health and general well-being and how this kind of help is an integral part of a community's health care: "The conclusion that supportive interactions among people are important is hardly new. What is new is the assembling of hard evidence that adequate social support can protect people in crisis from a wide variety of pathological states: from low birth weight to death, from arthritis through tuberculosis to depression, alcoholism, and other psychiatric illness. Furthermore, social support can reduce the amount of medication required and accelerate recovery and facilitate compliance with required regimes" (Cobb, p. 310).

Evidence is mounting strongly in many quarters about the many ways that people benefit from their everyday relationships with family, friends, or neighbours; how these social relationships support them; and how people's participation in mutual aid groups can help them solve problems and live with challenges.

The social-buffering hypothesis posits that people with strong natural support systems are better able to deal with major life changes and challenges. The corollary is that those with little or no social support are at a greater disadvantage in coping with the demands of everyday living (Cameron & Vanderwoerd; Cohen & Syme; Cohen & Wills; Gottlieb, 1981, 1983). Generally, then, people in stressful situations are likely to suffer less physical, emotional, or social dysfunction if they have good connections to supportive social networks, compared to those who do not have the advantage of these connections. This research directs practitioners to pay attention to support networks as important health-promoting and -preserving features in people's lives.

THE LIMITATIONS OF FORMAL HELPING SYSTEMS

A second reason for increased attention to informal helping is that professional helpers realize there will never be sufficient formal helping systems to answer society's growing demands for health and social services. This realization has deepened with compounding cutbacks to health and welfare services, leading to even scarcer resources and more competition for those that are already limited. These factors have pushed many professionals toward a greater appreciation of, alliance with, and dependence on natural helping systems.

For example, in contemporary practice, patients are discharged from hospital at breathtaking speed after having major medical interventions. It is true that medical knowledge and technology allows many patients to spend far less treatment time in hospital than they did in the past. However, these early discharges also demonstrate the extreme scarcity of hospital and medical resources, and the enormous pressures on health personnel to free up hospital beds. A major implication of such discharge practices is that family and friends are expected or pressured to assume caregiving roles, with or without adequate community health and social services support.

Recently we have heard debate regarding the exorbitant human and economic costs of residential care as they compare to community living arrangements. This issue surfaces particularly when the economy is weak. In many provinces large numbers of sick, elderly, and physically and mentally disabled people previously housed in institutions have been returned to live in their communities. At the same time, all people are admitted to acute care and long-term health care institutions less frequently and discharged more quickly from them.

These policy shifts force public attention on community-based services and supports for people who would otherwise be institutionalized. (Some policy issues related to this development will be discussed later in the chapter.)

This policy moves informal helpers to the forefront of caregiving and support and into more prominent roles alongside professionals. However, government savings through deinstitutionalization are rarely reallocated in kind to support the informal helpers and community services that now exert heavy emotional and physical effort in caregiving (Bullock, p. 74).

NEW PARADIGMS OF PRACTICE AND POLICY

A third reason for embracing lay helping is that, despite explosions of knowledge and theories about human problems, professionals are humbler about the limits of their own expertise to solve them. Major social problems such as poverty, addictions, child abuse and neglect, and violence toward women are not being resolved and diminishing. Professionals and society in general are becoming painfully aware of the limits of professional interventions and social policy.

All these factors point to the need for new models for practitioners. We need ways that shine a spotlight on natural helping systems. Social work has always focused on helping people in their own social environments. In its early days caring emphasized intuitively seeing people in this context and understanding the importance of their family, friends, and neighbours. In later decades, however, this central feature of social work did not receive the attention it warranted. Now, new ways of thinking about helping reassert the importance of this understanding and of working with people and their social situations.

A social–ecological paradigm of practice places renewed emphasis on the interaction and relations between people in their social networks and shows a renewed appreciation of and interest in natural helping systems. Social and emotional loneliness and isolation can lead to people's feeling especially vulnerability. Accordingly, practitioners must think about informal support and helping relationships as critical environmental factors in helping their clients cope with stress (Germain & Gitterman, p. 491). In current thinking, then, social work takes the whole of their clients' social landscapes into account and concentrates on working with their own social ecology. This entails understanding their social support networks and relationships, or their absence, depletion, or exhaustion.

In fact, what often brings people to the doors of the social agencies is their lack of natural supportive relationships, or relationships that are frayed, broken, or dysfunctional. Intervention efforts may link these people with new support systems or rebuild and sustain existing ones.

SOCIAL SUPPORT AND NATURAL HELPING NETWORKS

People belong to *social networks* (Abrams; Attneave; Israel; Maguire; Mitchell). The concept conjures up the image of a "net" and what it is—a set of connections or relationships between people (Collins & Pancoast, p. 18). A network is a set of relationships among family members, friends, co-workers, members of a religious, ethnic, or political group, self-help group, sports or recreational club, or any other interest group.

The term "network" has become a buzzword. Despite the term's everyday use, social networks are relatively invisible to us and are easily taken for granted. To social workers especially, however, the concept of network is very useful for understanding people's social functioning. Social workers can focus more on people's helping and social support networks as key resources in dealing with life and developmental tasks and particular problems of living.

The generic concept of social network has given rise to subsidiary concepts of the helping network and the social support network. These social science terms describe the natural relationships to which people turn for help with their physical care, emotional support, advice, and material assistance. Whittaker and Garbarino define a *social support network* as "a set of interconnected relationships among a group of people that provides enduring patterns of nurturance (in any or all forms) and provides contingent reinforcement for efforts to cope with life on a day-to-day basis" (p. 5).

Like professionals, informal helpers can listen, empathize, help clarify problems, make referrals to other helpers, and give advice. Lay support is more likely "to involve practical help, reciprocity, friendship-based relationships, altruism, experiential knowledge, solicited and unsolicited advice, self-disclosure on the part of the helper, reassurance, alternative interpretations, minimization of the importance of problems, consensual validation, and self-deprecation" (Ayers, p. 217). On the other hand, professional, consultative relationships "focus on such elements as communication and listening skills … confrontation, goal-directed problem solving, and behavior change" (Ayers, p. 217).

We see various patterns of natural helping in Canada's social and cultural mosaic. People in different classes, cultural, ethnic, age, and religious groups have different attitudes and norms about seeking and giving help. Professionals are slowly becoming aware of these factors affecting the patterns of informal help in various First Nations cultures, for example, and how the majority culture's disregard of these has led to untold misery for First Nations people.

Similarly, those who speak the same language and understand an immigrant's culture may be the most important initial resource for newcomers to Canada. The notion of formal services may actually be anathema to someone not familiar with turning to a professional stranger to deal with a life problem.

People select other forms of help differently. At the same time we must not forget that some people use neither professional help nor informal networks in times of stress, for a variety of reasons (Brown; Veroff, Douvan, & Kulka). When they are in difficulty, most people turn first and most frequently to their family members, friends, co-workers, neighbours, and even acquaintances (Gottlieb, 1980, 1982; Cowan).

People often seek assistance from *natural helpers*. These people have intuitive helping skills and they use them to assist others in their everyday lives. They can be people with sound reputations for wisdom, concern, or empathy in a family, group, or neighbourhood. People who fill this role may be experienced foster parents to whom other surrogate parents turn at times of special need; teachers with whom students can talk comfortably; or neighbours who just have a natural ability to understand. Natural helpers are found in all kinds of social niches. A number of researchers have studied natural helpers and the informal roles they play (Cowan; Eddy, Paap & Glad; Gottlieb, 1982; Turner, Kimbrough, & Traynhan). Also, projects

have been undertaken to train people in key contact roles with the public—such as taxi drivers, bartenders, and hairdressers— to recognize and help others in crisis.

People in need are likely to contact professionals much later as problems develop, if at all. When a problem has resisted other attempts at resolution, or when the stress it produces becomes intolerable, a person is more prepared to seek out and accept professional help (Gourash). Then clergy, teachers, and physicians are often among the first consulted.

Ironically, people are likely to rank the formal social services quite low on the list of resources to which they turn. This is unfortunate, given the special resources, information, and expertise available to them in this sector. All this research reinforces the importance of professionals' understanding the sociology of help-seeking and how people approach it.

SELF-HELP AND MUTUAL AID GROUPS

A multiplicity of mutual aid groups exists in our society. These groups form whenever people face common problems and join to tackle them, for reciprocal support or common action. Such groups can take form spontaneously, as when students discover a difficulty they share and get together to help each other learn the challenging material. Groups can also be created deliberately for quite specific purposes. For example, a social worker sets up group sessions at a clinic for people coping with a diagnosis of cancer; or single parents in a housing complex organize a cooperative child care pool. Increasingly the formal social service sector uses these sorts of created mutual aid groups to bring together clients who face similar problems. They represent a blend of professional and informal approaches to support.

Gitterman and Shulman (1994) provide an excellent array of examples of formed mutual aid groups that social workers mediate for a wide range of vulnerable populations at all stages of life. Created mutual aid groups demonstrate how child welfare practitioners can reach out to economically disadvantaged, isolated families to deal with distressed family relationships. In this instance, previously disconnected families with vulnerable children engaged in a mutual aid process and helped to join and create new social support networks for themselves. (See more on this successful Canadian example later in the chapter.)

The *self-help group* is one particular form of mutual aid occupying an increasingly prominent place among the means of helping people. According to Katz and Bender,

> Self-help groups are voluntary, small group structures for mutual aid and the accomplishment of a special purpose. They are usually formed by peers who have come together for mutual assistance in satisfying a common need, overcoming a common handicap or life-disrupting problem, or attempting desired social and/or personal change. The initiators and members of such groups perceive that their needs are not, or cannot be, met by or through existing social institutions. Self-help groups emphasize face-to-face social interactions and the assumption of personal responsibility by members. They often provide material assistance as well as emotional support; they are frequently "cause"-oriented, and promulgate an ideology or values through which members may attain an enhanced sense of personal identity (p. 9).

Self-help groups have become extraordinarily numerous in recent times (Reissman, 1982; Katz & Bender). Metropolitan areas such as Toronto, Montreal, or Vancouver boast hundreds of self-help groups. While proportionately fewer exist in smaller communities, some self-help groups exist virtually everywhere in Canada these days. And new groups are constantly emerging to help people cope with common problems that they feel are not addressed properly elsewhere, or in response to perceived deficiencies in professional care.

Not surprisingly in an electronic age, all kinds of computer-based self-help groups are also flourishing, made possible by the explosive growth of computers in the home and the workplace (Madara; Finn, 1999). Ready availability and cheap access to commercial and private computer-based e-mail, chat, and bulletin board systems have attracted all kinds of self-help groups to them. For example, a person can now attend an Alcoholics Anonymous meeting in cyberspace at any time, from any location (Finn, 1996).

A number of different explanations are offered to explain the popularity of self-help groups (Adams). According to one, the growth of self-help extends traditional forms of natural helping in a contemporary way. A functional perspective suggests that self help fills gaps left by formal services and the state's and professionals' inability or unwillingness to help in certain circumstances. Others see the self-help movement as a natural developmental reaction to the professional view of what people need. A more radical interpretation attributes self-help's popularity to people's alienation from technological development, their communities, dehumanizing institutions, and from the increasing professionalization and impersonalization of social welfare services. Gartner and Reissman (1977, p. 3) concur with this latter view and point out that self-help values emphasize "concern for personal autonomy, participation, quality of life, human potential, consumer rights, deprofessionalisation and decentralization."

Whatever the explanations for their existence, self-help groups undoubtedly deal with a wide range of human problems and they play a significant part in many people's lives. The groups offer individuals a strategy for recovery from all manner of addictions; therapy; self-fulfillment and personal growth; an avenue to tackle social issues by pursuing social action; raising consciousness and engaging in social and self-advocacy; help dealing with stigma; assistance for the friends, relatives, or care-givers of those facing special problems; support for survivors of traumatic events; and so on. Some groups come into being to protest the inadequacy of the state's provision of care for a particular group—such as Canadian hepatitis C victims.

Probably the best-known type of self-help group is one that offers an anonymous help to those recovering from all kinds of addictions. More than 200 different programs base themselves on the original Alcoholics Anonymous 12-step model—Overspenders, Emotions, Co-dependents, Sexaholics, and even Clutterers Anonymous (Powell; Canadian Broadcasting Corporation).

Self-help groups can offer short-term help to people undergoing a crisis, such as a bereavement support group, or long-term support for lifestyle change—Overeaters or Gamblers Anonymous. They can focus on their members' inner well-being, as Al Anon does, or on some external point in order to change some feature of the social environment, such as a welfare rights group (Katz & Bender, p. 39). This classification is not watertight, as some groups combine these functions. For example, a gay liberation group may seek to support individual members as well as actively espouse its larger causes.

Given the tremendous variations in form and substantive concern of these groups, generalizing about their features is hazardous. Nevertheless, themes culled from the extensive literature and research

about them help explain how these lay group-helping approaches differ from professionally led groups and what qualities they share:

1. The help provided is not a commodity that is bought and sold. It is a free, shared resource and a voluntary activity. Self-help draws on the often-unfulfilled need of people to be helpful, concerned, and involved (Banks; Reissman, 1982; Romeder).

2. The "helper-therapy" principle seems to be important for participants, through which people are themselves greatly helped through assisting others (Reissman, 1965, 1977).

3. Self-help groups are usually small and quite informal and function on a face-to-face basis. The ties between members are horizontal, not vertical or authoritarian. They develop spontaneously and avoid size and bureaucracy (Adams; Banks; Reissman, 1982; Katz & Bender); however, some do develop national and international organizations through their success (Silverman).

4. They are populist in nature and anti-expert. Self-helpers are likely to be critical of professional methods. However, not all groups reject such help, and some develop working relationships with professionals (Adams; Reissman, 1982).

5. Empowerment of self is an important theme. Self-helpers seek to control their own lives. People are seen as experts in their own situations rather than as "cases with problems" (Adams; Froland, Pancoast, Chapman & Kimboko; Reissman, 1982).

6. Self-help groups usually have fluid structures, unlike bureaucratic or professional organizations. Often leadership is shared and shifts easily, or can be

diffuse. The groups emphasize democracy, equality of status, and cooperation in decision-making (Adams; Reissman, 1982; Romeder; Silverman).

7. The knowledge base is experiential, indigenous, and rooted in wisdom. Groups build on the strengths and common experiences of members, are based in reality, and look for results (Borkman; Froland, Pancoast, Chapman & Kimboko; Reissman, 1982).

8. Organization is usually from the bottom-up, not top-down. Ideology holds a self-help group together, not bureaucracy (Reissman, 1982; Silverman).

Self-help groups serve multiple functions for their members. They serve as information sources about problems and offer practical help and advice. Often a framework is presented to help cope with a difficult situation and specific strategies may be offered to deal with a problem. Members feel cared about and wanted, and learn that others very much like themselves share a particular problem, concern, or disability. A new social network can readily emerge for the member offering supportive peer relationships (Silverman).

One fact is very clear. Many people belong to such groups and find solace, help, and satisfaction in them. It has been estimated that more than 400 distinct types of mutual aid groups exist, comprising 500 000 groups in the United States (Finn, 1996). Wuthnow (1994) notes that, in 1994, four out of every 10 Americans belonged to a rapidly growing small-group movement, while Kessler (1994) shows through his research that the number of self-help and mutual aid groups and the frequency of their members' meetings are expanding.

Self-help groups are important helping networks, so helping professionals can ill afford to ignore the power of this trend.

The trend represents a potential resource for those they serve. At the very least, practitioners need to inform themselves of the range of self-help resources in their communities so that they can apprise consumers of these services, help them decide whether to use them, and make effective referral suggestions.

Beyond this, professionals can serve in advisory or consultative roles to self-help groups when asked. Several books have been written to help professional practitioners in understanding these groups and knowing how to offer appropriate support when invited (Gartner & Reissman, 1980; Kurtz; Powell; Silverman, 1980; Hill). Some groups such as La Leche League and the Ostomy Society maintain professional advisory committees to keep on top of new information that members can use to advantage (Silverman, p. 174).

Practitioners can also play facilitative roles in helping to establish new self-help groups where unmet client needs can be addressed. They have to do this without co-opting or colonizing the group, and they also have to know how to get out at the right time. Perhaps the most important quality a professional can cultivate is an open-minded philosophy regarding the benefits of both informal and professional helping, and a readiness to lend support to whatever means help people to find strength in themselves.

A Child Welfare Mutual Aid Example

When appropriate, social workers can play an active role in the formation, maintenance, and programming of mutual aid groups. A three-year Ontario child welfare demonstration project provides an excellent example of the innovative professional use of mutual aid groups (Cameron; Cameron, Hayward, & Mamatis).

Researchers have found that informal helping strategies and mutual aid programs, despite their known potential, are seldom used in child welfare practice. So the project investigators set out to discover "whether mutual aid organizations could be designed that would bring informal helping resources within the reach of professional helpers and the high risk families they are trying to help" (Cameron, Hayward, & Mamatis, p. 26).

Families were referred to the Parent Mutual Aid Organizations (PMAO) project from the open-protection caseloads of three Southern Ontario Children's Aid Societies (CAS). Comparison cases were selected randomly from the same caseloads and not referred to the mutual aid groups, but continued to receive standard child welfare protection services. The families in both groups were similar in that they all faced problems of very limited income, social isolation, family conflict, parenting difficulties, and managing a home. The children in both samples were at risk of neglect, and emotional and possible physical abuse (Cameron, p. 40).

The three CAS hosted the PMAOs. Approximately half the parents who were referred participated. The staff offered scheduled as well as informal contact for the participants, a range of supportive and educational activities, and a chance for the members to build their own peer social-support network and friendships. In short, they gave the participants the opportunity to benefit from all the known advantages of involvement in mutual aid/self-help groups.

The results showed that the PMAO sample felt significant benefits of social integration and social support, in both making and maintaining friendships. They found the same benefits in the members' more concrete exchanges of help among themselves—babysitting, transportation, clothing, and emergency shelter (Cameron, p. 46).

PMAO members also showed considerably more improvement in self-esteem than the comparison group. Like many self-help group members, they felt the power of helping others (helper-therapy principle) and being helped by peers, rather than receiving assistance from a professional child welfare worker. Many PMAO members described themselves as better equipped to deal with stress and cope with daily challenges and the research findings supported these conclusions. More mutual-aid group sample members reported positive changes in their parenting than the comparison group did, although the extent of the positive changes in this area was not as great as the changes in social support, self-esteem, and perceived stress measures (Cameron, p. 51). The data from this study showed that about half the referrals to the PMAOs enjoyed the rich and intense involvements the project model anticipated (Cameron, p. 53).

During the study period the PMAO sample were significantly less involved with child protection workers than the comparison group was. They also made significantly less use statistically of child placements than their counterparts (Cameron, pp. 49, 51). A basic cost analysis for the study showed that families involved in the PMAOs demonstrated a lower per-case cost than the comparison families and that this model of service produced cost savings for the host agencies (Cameron, p. 52).

As one might expect, this mutual aid group model did not suit all child welfare families, just as it would not satisfy everyone facing other life problems. Creating and supporting this model of self-help is difficult, time-consuming work that makes big demands of child welfare personnel. It calls for strong agency commitment and talented personnel to dramatically shift their child protection patterns (Cameron, p. 53).

Nevertheless, the project also proved that created networks could be a "powerful vehicle for support and healing... that it is both positive and practical to create mutual aid organizations for families coming to child welfare agencies [and that such networks] should be common and respected parts of what is available to protect children and support families" (Cameron, p. 54).

THE DIFFERENT STRENGTHS OF FORMAL AND INFORMAL SERVICE SYSTEMS

A number of authors have analyzed the respective advantages and disadvantages of informal approaches to helping and mutual aid as opposed to those services the formal social welfare sector provides (Froland; Froland, Pancoast, Chapman & Kimboko; Lauffer; Litwak). Informal services may be an effective, non-intrusive first line of defence for those in need but "voluntarism is no substitute for services that can best be delivered by government, particularly if coverage, equity and entitlement are valued" (Kramer).

The strengths of the informal sector are considerable. Help is usually available quickly and without complicated qualifying criteria. Often it comes at a time when it can prevent further problems, is highly personalized, and suited to the recipients' particular needs. Natural help is non-stigmatizing, and it is offered in the context of relationships that are natural and familiar to the people accepting it. It is a far less costly intervention (Humphreys).

We must avoid romanticizing the capacities of informal helping networks. All too often the familiar story applies of the rich getting richer and the poor poorer. As already pointed out, those with supportive networks are well served. However, many people are isolated, alone, and vulnerable. Those in the greatest need are often those with the fewest natural helping resources at their disposal—people who do not have informal helping networks that they can mobilize for support and care.

For others, the family network is the very reason they need help; they are abused, neglected, abandoned by their kith and kin, or caught up in a web of difficult relationships that complicate their problems. Just as social networks can be a source of support, so they can be sources of conflict. No cure-all necessarily exists in a natural system of relationships, just as professional helpers cannot guarantee help in every instance. Some people are no more comfortable accepting informal help than formal help.

It is simply not possible to supply enough informal care and support to people in many circumstances. Continuity of care may be a problem, and specialized knowledge and resources are often necessary to support people in community care. The burdens of care can be great for informal helpers. Caregivers frequently need respite themselves, lest they too become casualties and end up needing the same formal services that they provide (Montgomery).

The formal service sector can offer greater equity, breadth of coverage, continuity of care, diffusion of risk, and public accountability. It can respond to catastrophes and supply wherever care is required to address chronic and complicated needs. It can also marshal specialized and technical resources that lay people do not have and which most individuals cannot afford.

The weaknesses of formal service systems are well understood. They can be costly and may develop inefficiencies and methods of operation that in large bureaucracies are hard to change. Broad-based services may not respond readily to local, idiosyncratic needs. Large formal services tend to develop "red tape" in standardizing their services, which makes accessing them frustrating for consumers. The stigma attached to seeking their help can act as a significant deterrent or side effect for service recipients, too.

POLITICS, SOCIAL POLICY, AND THE RESPONSIBILITY FOR CARE

Considerable debate continues about the preferred relationship of state services to more informal approaches to care and support in society. Competing ideologies underlie these discussions about the means through which health and social services should be delivered and by whom.

National and provincial economic problems have led governments to severely curtail their social services. As far back as 1991, the passage of Canada's Bill C-69 reduced the amount of transfer payments from the federal to the provincial governments for health, education, and social services. It cut monies available for social assistance, child care subsidies, homemaking programs, and child welfare. The spiralling costs of health care have forced us to scrutinize cost-saving alternatives and consider some shift in emphasis to community-based health services. As previously noted, these factors mean that our society pays much more attention now to the role of informal helping services. A common assumption and policy stance has been that the other forms of "community care" would automatically take up the slack in the state's reduction in its services.

The political right calls for a greater reliance on community, family, volunteers, and natural helping. "Pro-family/informal help" advocates interpret state intervention in the social services as a force eroding family life and people's taking responsibil-

ity for their loved ones. Returning care to "community and family ownership" is heralded as a reinstatement of "traditional values" and a strengthening of informal ties. The powerful underlying economic rationale is that this shift would save costs and relieve the pressure on formal services.

Those on the political left see these rationales as thin rhetoric that disguises a wish to reduce health and social services further rather than a genuine commitment to strengthen the informal and voluntary sector and the community social infrastructure. They interpret the call for more community care as a way of off-loading expensive services from the state to a volunteer, predominantly female constituency that is ill supported to take on such draining assignments. Critics point out that rarely are fiscal resources or support services available to sustain these unpaid helpers in the demanding roles that they are expected to assume.

Jill Pitkeathly, director of the British Carers National Association, speaking at a British Columbia caregivers' conference, cited the example of one overextended caregiver. An 85-year-old woman looked after her 50-year-old daughter who suffered from Down syndrome and her double-amputee husband. Only after she broke her own wrist and was unable to lift her husband did she call the association about getting some temporary help (Helm, p. A7)!

An extreme case? Perhaps, but many caregivers are older women, and like this woman they desperately need help themselves at times.

A strong feminist criticism of the relationship of organized versus communal and family care has been expressed (Baines, Evans, & Neysmith; Bullock; Hooyman & Gonyea). In this society, women carry out and are assumed to carry out most of the caring roles—as wives, mothers, sisters, and daughters. Aronson

(p. 189) points out that women do indeed provide most of the care for older people, especially in Britain, and that this is well documented. "Community care" there tends to mean the unpaid care of female family members. Similarly, much of the care of the sick and the severely disabled is likely to fall to women. At the same time, the shrinking of the contemporary family, women's greatly increased participation in the labour force, people's geographic mobility, and high divorce rates all raise the question of what happens to this major source of informal care and what resources women do have left to give to their demanding caregiving roles. Public policy statements that assert that the family is the best kind of support leave unanswered such key questions as "How do we provide for the needs of all, and not at the expense of women?" (Segal, p. 242).

Two worlds of care exist today: the organized and the communal, "the public world of the bureaucrat and the private world of mothers" (Abrams, 1978). These two worlds now seem to be operating in greater proximity to each other and in more complex relations, with neither fully understanding the other or working with the other to their mutual advantage. Yet each of these systems of care is insufficient to meet contemporary human needs in our society by itself. Each can perform successfully only with the other. Our expanding expectation of the informal helping services means that we face many policy questions and will find no simple directions in that quarter.

Beginning in 2004, the Canadian government took a small but significant step to recognize and support informal caregivers by enacting a new compassionate leave program (**www.hrdc-drhc.gc.ca/ ei-ae/pubs/compassionate_care.shtml**). Compassionate care benefits can now be paid to people who need to be away from their paid work temporarily to care for or support immediate family members who are dying or gravely ill and very near death. Care or support in this regard is broadly defined as psychological or emotional support, arranging for care by a third party, or directly providing or participating in that care.

This benefit is now part of the national Employment Insurance (EI) program and available to workers with established eligibility through their employment contributions to this social insurance scheme. A maximum of six weeks of compassionate care benefits are payable within a 26-week period. An employee can share the six weeks of benefits with other family members who also qualify for them. The administrative demands of applicants appear to be reasonable and kept to a minimum. When requesting compassionate care benefits, the applicant provides a medical certificate as proof that the ill family member needs his or her care or support and is at risk of dying within 26 weeks.

This is a social policy breakthrough that recognizes the demands and stress placed on family members when a close relative is gravely ill with a probable life-ending condition. The outcomes from this national new program will be important in assessing informal family caregiving. They may also provide important data for other approaches to support informal caregivers in future.

PROFESSIONALS AND INFORMAL HELPING SYSTEMS

Clearly, formal and informal services are two different cultures operating on different sets of assumptions, values, rules, and norms. Can these cultures co-exist and collaborate, or are they doomed to remain worlds apart?

Besides the larger policy questions already posed, stronger interplay between these two sectors will require that professionals be prepared to adjust their practice paradigms to bridge the gaps. Most professionals who wish to work with the informal sector are likely to find that their training has not sufficiently emphasized this focus of practice. They are more prepared for and skilled in dealing with the organizational culture of the social welfare system, offering expert forms of help, and serving clients on professional turf. Working with informal helping networks is a much more uncertain and unpredictable form of practice than the planned, methodical work of professional intervention.

What are the implications for a practice that actively seeks to relate to natural helping systems rather than ignore or compete with them? Perhaps the single most important factor is the mindset of the individual practitioner. To work with natural helping systems, she has to be able to live with and accept the differences between the two helping cultures and leave behind the baggage of professional imperialism. Natural helping is spontaneous, based on mutual sharing and unspoken rules of operation. These qualities contrast with an agency's emphasis on planned change, efficiency, effectiveness, accountability and monitoring of costs, and its formal rules and procedures.

Despite advances in our knowledge about natural helping systems, there are no standard rules, no finely tuned models to apply. This is practice artistry, not science. It is guided as much by the philosophy of the practitioner as by the techniques of practice. Informal relationships are by their very nature unpredictable and lack formality compared to professional ones. An interested practitioner must be prepared to deal with uncertainty and fluidity in working with this other culture of social work, then. It is also true that if the social worker is to collaborate with natural helping networks, then he has carry out his practice more in the community than in his office.

Such practice demands sensitivity toward informal helpers. One of the great dangers in attempting to work with a natural, unpolished, spontaneous entity is the urge to change it, improve it, and make it look like the professional version. As a student of mine from the Northwest Territories once said, "The trouble with social workers is that they often try to improve people off the face of the earth!" Part of what he was saying, I think, is that sometimes the art of practice entails accepting something for what it is and letting it work in its own sweet way.

Working with informal helpers can mean just this. Avoiding attempts to co-opt and colonize natural helpers is an important professional objective. Our professional goal is to support, strengthen, and facilitate what exists, not change it into something else. This fits well with the fundamental philosophy of social work aiming to empower individuals, groups, and communities to take ownership of their own lives.

Sometimes working collaboratively with clients' natural support systems is easier said than done! Conflicts can emerge quickly. For example, suppose you work with a woman who is the victim of assault by her partner. Your priority may be to ensure her safety from further assaults. Her friends and family may urge her to maintain the relationship, despite its high costs. The challenge to creative practice may be to find some common ground between the two: for example, developing a sound safety plan with your client if *she* chooses to reconcile; involving her friends and family in a plan to prevent a further assault; or providing crisis support, if the worst happens.

A number of practitioner roles can be useful in relating to informal helping systems. Acting as a referral agent, broker, and link between networks is significant. One must be able to ask good questions and listen with an open mind to what people say about their support systems and helpers. Giving people clear information about mutual aid and self-help groups is another important step. Not everyone will find a self-help group helpful or to their liking. However, the risks of referring clients to this source of help are slight, but the potential benefits to them are considerable (Humphreys).

There are ways that professional education programs can better prepare prospective practitioners for these roles. First, the curriculum must include relevant content about the sociology of natural helping networks and how to recognize, understand, enhance, and support them. This education could include content on mutual aid, self-help groups, and the diverse roles that natural helping relationships play in supporting people. Informal helping can fill an important function at many different levels, from working with an individual client to bringing together groups of people who can support one another (building new support systems) to encouraging neighbourhoods and community leadership to take charge in identifying community issues and ways to respond to them.

But disseminating knowledge about informal helping systems is not enough. Students must be encouraged to interact with and use these resources. An undue emphasis on professional methods in a training program may actually prevent beginning practitioners from reaching out to informal helpers. Professional endorsement and support are important in ensuring that action follows knowledge (Davenport & Davenport). In the world of practice many formal organizations are not set up on the assumption that working with natural helping networks is an appropriate strategy. This can mean the practitioners who

consider this aspect of social work important must negotiate their own paths within their agencies to support this cooperation.

CONCLUSION

Relatives, friends, and neighbours cannot provide the basic safety net of security against events that produce great individual vulnerability, illness, accident, unemployment, and loss of income. And informal helping cannot replace the public provision and support for basic human needs. Natural support was all that was available to people who needed help in less complicated times. However, by itself, it is inappropriate, unacceptable, and unworkable in our modern, complex, capitalist society.

Nevertheless, people's helping people continues to be an integral part of everyday life, even in post-industrial societies. Informal helping takes many forms. It is an important first line of defence and antidote for most of us when we face inevitable troubles and catastrophes in our lives. Although a huge chasm often yawns between natural and formal systems of help, one of our challenges is to find ways to bridge that gap to the advantage of both individuals "and our society." It is not a question of which is better. They are different and both essential for our well-being (Humphreys).

Informal helping can work within a partnership and exist within the fabric of formal public and voluntary supports. The natural concern and involvement of individuals, groups, and communities must be supported as an indispensable part of human caring and cannot be replicated by formal mechanisms. It is essential to the health and lives of people, a vital ingredient in our social well-being. Our great challenge is to find new ways for formal and informal social support systems to co-exist, collaborate, and support each other in responding to human need.

REFERENCES

Abrams, P. (1978). Community care: Some research problems and priorities. In J. Barnes & N. Connelly (Eds.), *Social care research* (pp. 18–99). London: Bedford Square Press.

Adams, R. (1990). *Self-help, social work and empowerment*. London: Macmillan.

Aronson, J. (1991). Dutiful daughters and undemanding mothers: Contrasting images of giving and receiving care in middle and later life. In C. T. Baines, P. T. Evans, & S. M. Neysmith (Eds.), *Women's caring: Feminist perspectives on social welfare* (pp. 138–168). Toronto: McClelland & Stewart.

Attneave, C. L. (1976). Social networks as the unit of intervention. In P. J. Guerin, Jr. (Ed.), *Family therapy, theory and practice* (pp. 220–231). New York: Gardner Press.

Ayers, T. D. (1989). Dimensions and characteristics of lay helping. *American Journal of Orthopsychiatry. 59*, 215–225.

Baines, C. T., Evans, P. T., & Neysmith, S. M. (Eds.). (1991). *Women's caring: Feminist perspectives on social welfare*. Toronto: McClelland & Stewart.

Banks, E. (Fall 1997). The social capital of self-help groups. *Social Policy, 28*, 30–38.

Borkman, T. (1976). Experiential knowledge: A new concept for the analysis of self-help groups. *Social Service Review, 50*, 445–456.

Borman, L. (1982). Introduction: Helping people to help themselves: Self-help and prevention. *Prevention in Human Services, 1*, 3–15.

Brown, B. B. (1978). Social and psychological correlates of help-seeking behavior among urban adults. *American Journal of Community Psychology, 6*, 425–439.

Brody, E. M. (1995). Prospects for family caregiving: Response to change, continuity, and diversity. In R. A. Kane & J. D. Penrod, (Eds.), *Family caregiving in an aging society: Policy perspectives* (pp. 15–28). Thousand Oaks: CA: Sage.

Bullock, A. (1990). Community care: Ideology and lived experience. In R. Ng, G. Walker, & J. Muller, (Eds.), *Community organization and the Canadian state* (pp. 65–82). Toronto: Garamond Press.

Cameron, G. (2002). Motivation to join and benefits from participation in parent mutual aid organizations. *Child Welfare, 81.1*, 33–57.

Cameron, G., Hayward, K., & Mamatis, D. (1992). *Mutual aid and child welfare: The parent mutual aid organizations in child welfare demonstration project*. Waterloo, ON: Wilfrid Laurier Press.

Cameron, G., & Vanderwoerd, J. (1997). *Protecting children and supporting families: Promising programs and institutional realities*. New York: Aldine de Gruyter.

Canadian Broadcasting Corporation. (April 29, 1991). *Addicted to addiction*. Transcript of radio program "*Ideas*". Toronto: CBC Ideas Transcripts.

Cobb, S. (1976). Social support as a moderator of life stress. *Psychosomatic Medicine, 38*, 300–314.

Cohen, S., & Syme, L. (1985). *Social support and health*. New York: Academic Press.

Cohen, S., & Wills, T. A. (1985). Stress, social support and the buffering hypothesis. *Psychological Bulletin, 98.2*, 310–357.

Collins, A. H., & Pancoast, D. L. (1976). *Natural helping networks*. Washington, DC: National Association of Social Workers.

Cowan, E. L. (1982). Help is where you find it: Four informal helping groups. *American Psychologist, 37*, 385–395.

Davenport, J., & Davenport III, J. (1982). Utilizing the social network in rural communities. *Social Casework, 63*, 106–113.

Eddy, W., Paap, S., & Glad, D. (1970). Solving problems of living: The citizen's viewpoint. *Mental Hygiene, 54*, 64–72.

Finn, J. (1996). Computer-based self-help groups: On-line recovery for addictions. *Computers in Human Services, 13.1,* 21–41.

Finn, J. (1999). An exploration of helping processes in an online self-help group focusing on issues of disability. *Health and Social Work, 24.3,* 220–231.

Froland, C. (1980). Formal and informal care: Discontinuities on a continuum. *Social Service Review, 54,* 572–587.

Froland, C., Pancoast, D. L., Chapman, N., & Kimboko, P. (1981). *Helping networks and human services.* Beverly Hills, CA: Sage Publications.

Gartner, A., & Reissman, F. (1977). *Self-help in the human services.* San Francisco: Jossey-Bass.

Gartner, A., & Reissman, F. (1980). *A working guide to self-help groups.* New York: Franklin Watts.

Germain, C. B., & Gitterman, A. (1987). Ecological perspective. In *Encyclopedia of social work* (pp. 488–499). Silver Spring, MD: National Association of Social Workers.

Gitterman, A., & Shulman, L. (Eds.). (1994). *Mutual aid groups, vulnerable populations, and the life cycle* (2d ed.). New York: Columbia University Press.

Gottlieb, B. H. (1980). The role of individual and social support in preventing child maltreatment. In J. Garbarino, H. Stocking and Associates, (Eds.), *Protecting children from abuse and neglect* (pp. 37–60). San Francisco: Jossey-Bass.

Gottlieb, B. H. (1981). *Social networks and social support.* Beverly Hills, CA: Sage.

Gottlieb, B. H. (June 1982). Social networks and the gestalt of help-seeking. Keynote address presented at the national conference of the Canadian Counselling and Guidance Association. Victoria, B.C.

Gottlieb, B. H. (1983). Social support strategies. Beverly Hills, CA: Sage.

Gourash, N. (1978). Help seeking: A review of the literature. *American Journal of Community Psychology, 6,* 413–425. **www.hrdc-drhc.gc.ca/ei-ae/pubs/ compassionate_care.shtml**

Helm, D. (November 13, 1991). Caregivers need recognition, says director of British group. *Victoria Times-Colonist,* p. A7.

Hill, K. (1987). *Helping you helps me: A guide for self-help groups* (H. Balthazar (Rev. & updated). Ottawa: Canadian Council on Social Development.

Hooyman, N. R., & Gonyea, J. G. (1995). *Feminist perspectives on family care: Policies for gender justice.* Thousand Oaks, CA: Sage.

Humphreys, K. (Winter 1998). Can addiction-related self-help/mutual aid groups lower demand for professional substance abuse treatment? *Social Policy, 29.2,* 13–17.

Israel, B. A. (1982). Social networks and health status: Linking theory, research and practice. *Patient Counselling and Health Education, 4.2,* 65–79.

Kane, R. A. & Penrod, J. D., (Eds.). (1995). *Family caregiving in an aging society: Policy perspectives.* Thousand Oaks, CA: Sage.

Katz, A. H., & Bender, E. I. (Eds.). (1976). *The strength in us.* New York: Franklin Watts.

Kessler, R., et al. (1994). *Midlife development inventory (MIDI).* Chicago: John D. and Catherine T. MacArthur Foundation.

Kramer, R. (1981). *Voluntary agencies in the welfare state.* Berkeley: University of California Press.

Kropotkin, P. (1955). *Mutual aid: A factor of evolution.* Boston: Extending Horizons Books.

Kurtz, L. F. (1997). *Self-help and support groups: A handbook for practitioners.* Thousand Oaks, CA: Sage.

Lauffer, A. (1978). Natural and "extra-professional" helping systems. In A. Lauffer (Ed.), *Social planning at the community level* (pp. 241–258). Englewood Cliffs, NJ: Prentice-Hall.

Litwak, E. (1978). Organizational constructs and mega bureaucracy. In R. Sarri & Y. Hasenfeld (Eds.), *The management of human services* (pp. 123–162). New York: Columbia University Press.

MacPherson, I. (1987). Antigonish movement. In *Canadian encyclopedia*. (2d ed., p. 84). Edmonton: Hurtig Publishers.

Madara, E.J. (Spring 1997). Computer-mediated communication: Internet self-help groups. *Social Policy, 27,* 20–26.

Maguire, L. (1983). *Understanding social networks.* Beverly Hills, CA: Sage Publications.

Mitchell, J. C. (1969). The concept and use of social networks. In J. C. Mitchell, (Ed.), *Social networks in urban situations* (pp. 1–50). Manchester: University of Manchester Press.

Montgomery, R. J. V. (1995). Examining respite care. In R. A. Kane & J. D. Penrod, (Eds.), *Family caregiving in an aging society: Policy perspectives* (pp. 29–45). Thousand Oaks, CA: Sage.

Powell, T. J. (Ed.). (1990). *Working with self-help.* Silver Spring, MD: NASW Press.

Reissman, F. (1965). The "helper" therapy principle. *Social Work, 10,* 27–32.

Reissman, F. (1977). The helper-therapy principle. In A. Gartner & F. Reissman, *Self-help in the human services* (pp. 99–103). San Francisco: Jossey-Bass.

Reissman, F. (1982). The self-help ethos. *Social Policy, 13,* 42–43.

Romeder, J. (1990). *The self-help way: Mutual aid and health.* Ottawa: Canadian Council on Social Development.

Segal, L. (1987). *Is the future female? Troubled thoughts on contemporary feminism.* London: Virago Press.

Silverman, P. R. (1987). Mutual help groups. In *Encyclopedia of social work* (pp. 171–176). Silver Spring, MD: National Association of Social Workers.

Turner, J. T., Kimbrough, W. W., & Traynhan, R. N. (1977). A survey of community perceptions of critical life situations and community helping sources as a tool for mental health development. *Journal of Community Psychology, 5,* 225–230.

Veroff, J., Douvan, E., & Kulka, R. A. (1981). *The inner American: A self-portrait.* New York: Basic Books.

Whittaker, J. K., & Garbarino, J. (Eds.). (1983). *Social support networks: Informal helping in the human services.* Hawthorne, NY: Aldine Publishing Co.

Wuthnow, R. (1994). *Sharing the journey: Support groups and America's new quest for community.* New York: Basic Books.

chapter seventeen

Industries and the Provision of Social Services

Catherine Brothers

John Brothers

INTRODUCTION

Until the 1980s Canadian social workers might have expected to spend their entire careers employed within not-for-profit agencies funded through government and charitable sources. Until that point, many Canadians viewed fully funded social work services as the responsibility of the state, religious groups, and philanthropic individuals and organizations.

Before this time "user fees" had existed for 75 years in some social agencies, particularly the family service agencies, out of a belief that those who were able to afford their services ought to contribute their fair share towards their cost. In reality, the notion of social work services fully funded through the "customers," or clients, had never been completely accepted. Over the past 40 years, another "payer"—funding source—and a new area of social work practice has emerged across Canada—namely, social work within industry. Increasingly, employers are viewing social work as a positive, relevant, and meaningful resource in the workplace. And social workers are aggressively marketing their services to workplaces that they consider prospective customers.

This chapter explores issues related to the current practice of social work in industry. The goals of social work practice are to help individuals reach their maximum potential and to work with community members to ensure that all have equal opportunity to reach that maximum potential. This distinct and unique orientation within the profession towards building both strong individuals and healthy communities inspires the practice of social work in workplaces. The social worker's knowledge and skills in the areas of both clinical practice and community development provide the framework for delivering social work services within industry. The social worker's values and training are most relevant to understanding the perspectives of both the employee and the employer and to facilitating mutually beneficial interactions.

HISTORICAL CONTEXT

A brief overview of history relevant to the practice of social work within industry is helpful. Although the practice of social work within industry tends to be viewed as a development of the past 40 years, industrial social work, in fact, was one of the first areas of social work activity.

In the late 1800s, the social worker, initially known as a "welfare secretary," played a key role in American industry's social welfare movement. (Significantly, the New York School of Social Work and the Bryn Mawr School of Social Work offered specialized courses in industrial social work in the first quarter of the twentieth century.) The welfare secretary was the initiative of beneficent owners and management, and that person's general, role was to improve the social well-being and morale of employees, especially those of female employees and minority groups. The welfare secretary organized recreational activities and supported means of meeting employees' basic living needs, such as housing. Most historians view the welfare secretary's form of social work as the origin of the human resources profession. Originally a popular position, the welfare secretary came to be viewed with mistrust and eventually fell from grace as

the union movement emerged, which perceived this position as employers' paternalism and manipulation.

The present practice of social work within industry began with concerns about the impact of alcohol abuse within the workplace. High absenteeism rates and accidents on the job, both personal and in the manufacturing process, were adding to labour and production costs.

Over the past 150 years, with the exception of the Prohibition years, the use of alcohol was freely condoned, and even encouraged, in many workplaces. As recently as 20 years ago, the employees of Canadian breweries and distilleries were often rewarded with servings of alcohol during their working hours. Everywhere, however, a person endured a great stigma as a "drunk" or an "alcoholic." Until the introduction of Alcoholics Anonymous in 1935, alcohol abuse was considered a symptom of moral degeneration and personal failure. Counselling services for substance abusers, rather than discipline, were assumed to lessen such costs and to improve employee morale and performance.

In 1992, the Conference Board of Canada published a report by Shahid Alvi, *Corporate Responses to Substance Abuse in the Workplace*. Alvi reported that the founding of Alcoholics Anonymous in 1935 led to employer-sponsored rehabilitation programs in organizations like DuPont and Eastman Kodak in the United States. He also identified Canada's first occupational alcohol-abuse program, created at Bell Canada in 1947. Throughout Canada and the United States from the 1940s to the 1970s, recovered alcohol abusers who had positive affiliations as peers within the workplace and strong ties with Alcoholics Anonymous tended to provide workplace-counselling programs.

In Ontario, over the past 50 years, the Addiction Research Foundation (ARF)—

now the Centre for Addiction and Mental Health—an agent of the province, played a major role in helping workplaces to care for the social, emotional, and psychological well-being of their employees. The Addiction Research Foundation strongly promoted policies and workplace interventions related to alcohol and drug abuse. The foundation advocated strongly for rehabilitation rather than discipline and dismissal. During the 1970s, the ARF placed more than 50 consultants throughout Ontario, helping hundreds of corporations to recognize and deal with employees with problems related to substance abuse. The ARF emphasized helping workplaces to identify problem employees and then constructively manipulating them into treatment. Since the mid-1970s, the foundation shifted from a narrow focus on substance abuse to organizational interventions, encouraging workplaces to adopt more holistic and "broad brush" approaches.

In 1998, the ARF merged with three other major providers of addiction and mental health services in Ontario to form the Centre for Addiction and Mental Health. As in the general practice of social work in industry, this merger acknowledges the complexity of psychosocial issues and the need for collaborative relationships in finding solutions.

Using the language of the marketplace, social work practice in industry is often referred to as Employee Assistance Programs (EAPs) or Employee and Family Assistance Programs (EFAPs). Generally, EAPs aim to help employees find solutions to a broad range of personal and family problems. Prevention and reduction of workplace problems remains a constant goal of these programs.

Many non-profit and family service agencies began providing social work services in industry in the late 1970s and early 1980s. At that time, family service agencies provided most of the social work services within industry, and they were optimistic that these services, paid for by the employers, would provide profit margins sufficient to enable the non-profit agencies to enhance their services to poor and marginalized persons. As more private practitioners and national and international for-profit EAP providers entered the field, however, the profit margins shrank and competition intensified. It is impossible to determine how many workplaces in Canada use social work services today, but we know that the number is growing weekly. Most medium- and large-sized industries offer some form of professional counselling services to their employees.

The organizational trend in this area throughout the 1990s was to merge local social work providers and large national and international providers, with outsourcing to affiliates that can provide services to work sites throughout North America. Some observers speculate that the baby boomers have fuelled the growth of social work in industry. Born between 1946 and 1964, this group, now also known as the "sandwich generation," faces great challenges as single parents and dual-career parents, simultaneously caring for their young children and their aging parents. As they struggle to balance the stresses of their work and family lives, the boomers put enormous expectations and demands on industry to provide high-quality, accessible services.

During the 1990s the trend in social work services to industry expanded from a focus on reducing workplace problems to a wider perspective that included prevention and promotion of health and wellness. There was gradually less emphasis on the identification of workplace problems by supervisors, and an increasing emphasis on the importance of employee-initiated self-referrals. The present EAP strategy offers a range of social work services from which the employee may choose, rather than the mandated or involuntary referrals of the past.

A study by MacDonald and Dooley (1999a) found that, at the end of the 1980s in Ontario, 90 percent of industries with EAPs were using outside resources for treatment, and 75 percent were using public service community agencies to provide employee assistance services.

TARGET POPULATION OF SOCIAL WORKERS IN INDUSTRY

Social workers in workplaces are helping people in a variety of workplaces: hospital, university, school, and government employees, firms of professional engineers and architects, factory workers, financial institutions such as banks and credit unions, chartered accountancy firms, bus and aviation companies, police and fire departments, and gas bar and convenience store workers. It is hard to imagine a workplace that would not benefit from access to these services.

Social workers help both the employee and his or her family members, either individually or together. For social workers in industry the target population encompasses all levels of employees, including members of boards of directors, owners, senior management, supervisors, and front-line workers.

Types of Problems and Issues

Employees can seek assistance for almost any kind of problem. Social workers within industry continue to treat problems associated with drug and alcohol abuse. It is estimated that between 5 percent and 10 percent of the workforce suffer from problems associated with substance abuse.

The starting point for an EAP may be one employee with a substance abuse problem. This was the case for a North American company with its head office in Ontario. The company sought social work consultation from the Catholic Family Counselling Centre in Kitchener, Ontario, when a highly valued professional employee, J., began to deteriorate with a serious, but hidden, cocaine addiction. With the employer's support, the social worker successfully engaged J. in an intensive in-patient rehabilitation program, follow-up, and financial counselling. As J.'s addiction, suffering, and painful recovery unfolded to their full extent, the employer became increasingly convinced about the importance of early detection of such problems. The company created a comprehensive employee assistance program with the Catholic Family Counselling Centre in a sincere effort to offer support and prevention services for all its employees and their family members. For many companies, an individual's distress like J.'s signals the need of all employees for access to professional counselling services.

In 1991, the Alberta Alcohol and Drug Abuse Commission reaffirmed that substance use in Canadian workplaces remains a significant concern. Although excessive use of alcohol and drugs seems to be declining in Canadian society, we cannot overstate the enormous threat that these forms of substance use pose to the workplace. We have worked in several industries devastated by the deaths of several employees in alcohol-related workplace accidents.

Depression has become the number one reason that employees seek EAP counselling. Statistics Canada estimates that nearly one in five Canadian workers suffers from stress owing to home or work issues. Much has been said about the challenges of balancing work and family expectations. Depression is responsible for the greatest percentage of lost productive work time, and about one-third of all disability claims are related to depression and stress. The World Health Organization (2001) has estimated that depression will be the second-leading cause of disability worldwide by the year 2020.

Industries grappling with high rates of absenteeism often look to social work to play a role in solving the problem. This is certainly one problem area that calls on social workers to understand the circumstances of both the individual and the workplace. One manufacturing industry approached a social worker about this problem throughout the workplace. Most employees had boring, repetitive, exhausting jobs that required considerable physical exertion. The workplace itself was physically unattractive, and there was strife among employees and between employees and supervisors. In such an industry, the social worker would be hard-pressed to try to help an individual employee who is often away from the job without working with the industry to address environmental and general workplace matters at the same time.

In working with individual employees, the social worker understands that conflicting stresses related to work and family responsibilities may lead to absenteeism. Appreciating the stresses that families face, many social workers have advocated flexible hours in industry. They will often help employees to locate and arrange for resources for child care and elder care.

Social workers have successfully helped industries improve their policies regarding time off for family responsibilities. One human resources manager with no children of his own reminded a concerned social worker quite firmly that "either these people want to work, or they don't. A job is a job!" Three years later, the same manager, with a working wife and two young children of his own, introduced a policy into his own workplace that permitted employees to use their "sick days" to fulfill family responsibilities, such as caring for a child too ill to be brought to the child care provider.

Certainly, absenteeism is one of the issues the social worker in industry frequently addresses, and it is a complex issue and a symptom of forces both in the workplace and in the employee's personal and family life. The social worker hears from industry about the high costs associated with absenteeism, and hears from the individual employee who is genuinely distressed about his or her inability to be on the job.

Most frequently, social workers are treating a broad range of marital and family problems in industry. Many employees have stress-related problems that are often related to the conflicting demands of work and family life. Conflicts among employees and difficult people in the workplace are common concerns. Other problems include sexual harassment, workplace violence, living with shift work, feelings of being wronged in the workplace, financial worries, problem gambling, illness, and long-term disabilities. Employees seek out social workers' help in coping with the pressures of mergers, downsizing, early retirement, and employers' expectations that they accomplish more and more work with less job security and fewer resources. Employees often feel they have very little control over the major decisions that affect their whole lives. Working within boards of education, for example, social workers help teachers and principals cope after they have been transferred or reassigned with little or no consultation. Social workers in industry also address tensions in the workplace related to ethnicity, culture, or sexual orientation.

During the 1990s, social workers across Canada became increasingly involved in interventions related to sudden critical incidents and traumatic accidents. These could be workplace violence, industrial accidents, suicide, murder, robberies, rescue attempts, car, bus, and plane accidents, and fires. When such tragic events happen, social workers can respond immediately with well-defined strategies of stress management, debriefing, defusing, and damage control.

"Where the Client Is At"

The presence of social work within industry reflects major changes within the Canadian family. During the 1994 International Year of the Family, the Vanier Institute of the Family in Ottawa published an excellent document in partnership with the Conference Board of Canada, *The Work and Family Challenge: Issues and Options* (Alvi 1992). According to Alvi, its author, almost 60 percent of Canadian women are in the labour force and they account for more than 40 percent of the whole labour force. Further, in the last 30 years the dual-income family has replaced the "traditional" family unit of a mother at home, a working father, and two children. More than half of our society's women with children younger than six years of age are in the labour force. The Vanier document goes on to describe the high stress levels plaguing so many men and women under constant pressure to juggle their work and family priorities. Given the challenges today's families face, it makes good sense that social workers be "where the client is at"—that is, in the workplace.

Workplace clients may ask for specific help that social workers do not consider appropriate. Such might be the case in matters of family violence, for example. Similarly, a separated employee may demand that the social worker prepare a report for the court in support of his desire for child custody or access. As in other social work settings, the professional social worker may have to confront a client regarding the consequences of her own behaviour. This is a sensitive challenge within industry, where the employer expects to be pleased with the social worker's efforts and, at the same time, the social worker must act according to professional knowledge or maintaining standards. To begin "where the client is at," the social worker in industry must also sort out when social work treatment is appropriate and when a client simply needs information and access to other resources. Negotiating these differences with clients can be difficult.

ATTITUDES TOWARDS SOCIAL WORK SERVICES IN INDUSTRY

Not very long ago, considerable stigma attached to a person's receiving professional social work services, many of which were involuntary. The decision to seek social work services was a personal and private matter, and a course that women followed more frequently than men. Today, access to social work services is viewed as a standard workplace benefit and a matter that definitely involves employers. More employees are looking to their workplaces for benefit packages that include access to counselling from professional social workers. Rather than the old stigma attached to seeking professional mental health services, employees now expect that they or co-workers with problems will "get some help and deal with it."

Thirty years ago employers looked to EAPs as a means of changing employees whose troubles were affecting the workplace in the form of absenteeism, poor work quality, inadequate productivity, industrial accidents, or generally difficult behaviour on the job. Today's employer is far more likely to support those employees in balancing their work and family lives. Industry leaders consider it "good business" to form partnerships with social workers in promoting individual and family well-being and they consider such partnerships essential in promoting their organization's financial viability and the community.

Larger social factors in Canada have also contributed to the growing role of social work in industry: the rise of social movements, such as consumerism, environmental protection, and the rights of the individual as reaffirmed in the repatriation of the Constitution of Canada. We hear more people in industry discussing the importance of both "high tech" and "high touch." Twenty years ago, open dialogues on compassion and spirituality in the workplace would have been highly unusual. Today such conversations are held more and more frequently in many workplaces.

Employers appreciate the value of loyal and healthy employees and a positive community perception that they care about their employees and are building a better community. Society increasingly recognizes the importance of the relationship between a healthy economy and healthy individuals and families. For example, in 1999, it was remarkable to witness the Vancouver Board of Trade presenting a solid business plan to the federal minister of finance as to why early childhood supports and interventions are the core of a strong economy.

In the workplace social workers are recognized for their profound belief in the worth and dignity of each person and in the community's role in sustaining and enhancing this approach. These beliefs make an excellent starting point for helping both the employee and the employer pursue mutually beneficial goals.

A business making a real and visible commitment to supporting social work practice within its enterprise is generally a business that thrives. It enjoys positive workplace morale and is valued as a "good" employer in the community. An industry demonstrates this commitment to social work practice through lots of communications with its employees about readily available social work services, frequent and regularly scheduled training and orientation sessions conducted by social workers, and articles in business newsletters about the value of social work services in the workplace.

Not surprisingly, a company with an employee assistance contract and whose employees rarely use the services is usually a company with low morale and lots of mistrust. These companies often impose extra barriers to their people in their accessing social work services, such as imposing user fees or requiring that any employee's access to the service be approved internally. Top management in such companies does little to convey its belief in the importance of the social work program. It restricts distribution of education and promotion materials. Either the owners or the union members may have pressured top management into providing the social work services, while management's attitude toward social work value was skeptical. "Buy-in" at the top is essential!

THE ROLE OF LABOUR UNIONS

Union counsellors and union peers play very significant roles in encouraging employees to use social work services. The social worker in industry appreciates the importance of understanding the corporate culture and recognizing who employees normally seek out for their information, support, and referral. The social worker will build links with existing support networks within the industry, especially with labour leaders and union counsellors.

Unions have been both supportive and proactive in promoting these social work services. Union leaders, however, remain vigilant about warnings about placing too much emphasis on services to individuals in distress; this focus may perpetuate the notion that the employees' "personal" problems lie at the bottom of their work-related stress. As much as they support EAPs, unions are concerned about letting employers off the hook in addressing organizational issues that affect the health and well-being of their employees. Some union leaders see social work in industry as a Band-Aid approach to problem solving that detracts from the employers' responsibility to establish positive environments and proper working conditions.

Labour unions have led the way in sponsoring many EAPs across Canada. In reporting on the state of these in Canada in 1991, the Alberta Alcohol and Drug Abuse Commission (Wnek 1991) discovered that most unionized companies in Canada provide these programs under the joint sponsorship of labour and management. In both Ontario and Saskatchewan, almost two-thirds of those organizations with unions have both union and management representation (Macdonald and Dooley 1989a; SADAC 1990), as do more than half of the federally regulated transportation companies (Macdonald and Dooley 1989b).

The Canadian Labour Congress has developed union counselling programs across Canada to train union counsellors within industry. Social workers participate in delivering these programs, which focus on training union counsellors to help their peers access the supports and services they need.

CONFIDENTIALITY

Confidentiality, integrity, and honesty are cornerstones of the social work profession.

Employers and employees quickly size up social workers and decide whether they can trust them. While the social workers might be helping both management and line employees, it must be absolutely clear to everyone that they will not convey any information about clients to anyone else in the workplace. All social work reports that are sent to the workplace contain only non-identifying information—number of clients, number of units of service, lists of presenting problems, and clinical outcomes—none of which jeopardizes the identity of any individual employee.

For social workers employed in industry, it is critical to sort out with the industry or the "payer" the question of who "owns" the social work records. When industry contracts with off-site social work providers, the provider will find it easier to establish ownership and confidentiality of client records. The matter becomes more complex when the social worker is an actual employee of the workplace, working within the industry. The social worker with an off-site provider must anticipate that the funding organization will want to verify that the services it is paying for have, in fact, been provided. Such verification may include an audit of client records. The social worker needs to plan for this eventuality with the employer in advance, agreeing on procedures that do not disclose to the employer any names or identifying information about the employees. Privacy legislation introduced in 2004 across Canada further protects the employee confidentiality.

Social workers will want to clarify with the workplace beforehand how they are going to deal with requests for service from the children of employees and how they will deal with employees or family members who threaten to harm themselves or others.

EDUCATION ABOUT AND PROMOTION OF SOCIAL WORK SERVICES WITHIN INDUSTRY

The use of social work services within industry depends directly on the success of educating employees about the services available. While social workers provide most individual, couples', and family treatment outside the workplace, the social worker working with employees must be visible and present within that workplace. He does this through training and orientation sessions related to the EAP, wellness seminars, and presentations on topics of broad general interest, which are relevant to the employees' well-being. He has to nurture the workplace and communicate frequently with its members, all of which builds up trust and credibility. Communication tools may include brochures, general letters about services available to employees and their families, newsletters, information flyers, bulletin board displays, and promotional attention-grabbers such as pens, fridge magnets, wallet cards, and calendars.

When a social work program is new to an industry, the social worker will want to have numerous face-to-face sessions with all levels of staff, accommodating various work shifts. As the social work program becomes more established, her most important communication tool becomes word of mouth. Employees who have been helped will readily advise their friends and colleagues of the service. Equally important, if employees have any suspicion whatever that they cannot trust the social worker, word of that will also spread quickly. The emphasis for the social worker in industry is on delivering excellent customer service. After she has made the sale to industry, she puts just as much energy into maintaining the contract.

TIME

There are very specific time requirements related to providing social work in industry. When social work services are attached to benefits in the workplace, employees will expect immediate access to those services. Consequently, social workers are keeping pace with the most up-to-date developments in technology and communication devices. Most contracts between the social worker and the workplace establish that the employee will have access to a social work session within 24 to 48 hours from the time of referral and that critical incidents and emergencies will be treated immediately. More than one social worker has lost a contract with industry to a competitor who was better able to meet the customer's expectations of immediate and timely intervention.

The emphasis on accessible social work services within industry has introduced a whole new dimension to the concept of "time." Employee assistance providers compete with one another, and this has raised the standards regarding time expectations. Twenty-four-hour accessibility, wide-area dialling, evening hours, weekend appointments, telephone counselling services, and interactive Internet communications have all become common tools of social work practice.

Time presents another major challenge, too. Contracts between the social worker and the industry must define the number of social work sessions to which an employee and family members are entitled, generally on an annual basis. Many contracts in Canada limit the employee to between six and 12 sessions per year, to be paid for by the employer. Sometimes the employer will "cap" the amount to be paid to the social worker rather than "cap" the number of sessions. For example, both parties will negotiate the maximum payment to the social worker in one year, and the social worker will agree to provide the service to all employees within that fixed amount. Occasionally, an employer will agree to pay for an unlimited number of sessions for all employees and their family members. More commonly, however, the social worker and the employer negotiate the total amount of eligible services between them.

When an employer agrees in the contract to pay for only one to three sessions, the social worker faces an ethical dilemma. These are becoming an increasingly familiar for Canadian social workers as the American practice of "managed care" enters the Canadian workplace. An American EAP provider may coordinate the employee assistance program for the Canadian employees working within American-owned industries. Typically the "managed care" model emphasizes the information and referral role of the social worker and restricts the number of eligible sessions. Some social workers have declined requests to provide services that are capped at one to three sessions, on the basis that agreeing to enter into such a limited treatment relationship is impractical, imprudent, and unethical. Others take the position that some social work intervention is better than none, and they focus on helping their employee clients sort out what they can within the limited time frame.

PRICING, AND WHO PAYS?

Unless the industry employs the social worker directly as an "internal" provider, the social worker negotiates directly with the employer to set the costs of his services. As noted, the market is increasingly competitive and, like all businesses, social workers offer value-added services such as education, promotion, training, and wellness seminars when they are quoting their fees for their counselling services. In Canada in 2004, one hour of social work services to industry cost between $50 and $150. The sole practitioner, with little or no overhead costs and who deals directly with a single workplace, will have significantly lower costs than a large social work organization with a wide range of activities and services. Likewise, a single provider will be limited in the range of services that he or she can offer.

It has been demonstrated repeatedly that social work services are used much more within an industry that pays for the whole service and in which employees can approach the social worker directly. Sometimes the employee is expected to pay in part for the social work service. Third-party funding organizations such as insurance companies and workers' compensation programs may also cover these services. In some industries the employee must pay for the initial service, and then be reimbursed on submission of claims for subsequent services. Some plans require that she have a referral from an occupational health nurse, a physician, or a human resources professional before payment to her will be authorized. The employee and the social worker must understand the payment requirements before they enter into the social work treatment. They must also agree on how to handle issues related to confidentiality and access to records in advance of delivery of the services.

STRATEGIC ALLIANCES IN PROVIDING SOCIAL WORK SERVICES TO INDUSTRY

More and more industries, large and small, operate from multiple sites. Today a company often does business in different cities and provinces across Canada, across North America, and internationally. Head office generally expects that the employees at all work sites will have equitable access to benefits.

The social worker negotiating the provision of social work services with head office needs to have a plan to provide those services for all of the company's employees throughout Canada and the United States. Accordingly, social worker organizations have developed strategic alliances and joint ventures similar to those that businesses enter throughout the world.

Since the late 1970s family service agencies have allied themselves as member agencies of Family Service Canada to organize access to EAPs across the country. Typically, one family service agency will hold the "master contract" for the social work in a particular industry, and employees across Canada may access this help through their local family service agency. These agencies also belong to international associations of employee assistance providers that offer a network of experienced and qualified social workers who deliver such services throughout North America.

On a typical work day, a family service agency in Kitchener, Ontario, arranges for social work services for the employees of a Canadian-owned company at work sites in Phoenix and Chicago and receives calls from Detroit and Houston, requesting the same services for the local employees of the client's American-owned companies. Services provided at this Kitchener agency within a short time frame include critical incident debriefing services; social workers treat local bus drivers when they suffer the emotional impact of a fatal bus accident across the American border, for example. The agency conducted another debriefing for the executives of a local company who had been traumatized by a frightening nonfatal crash of their small plane on a business trip to the United States. The agency also arranged services in Minnesota for a Kitchener truck driver after he was victimized in an armed robbery.

Strategic alliances are evident in the collaborative networks social workers are building to ensure industries access to a range of social work and health promotion activities. More individual social workers are providing services that emphasize wellness and holistic health. While expectations of the generic social worker remain high, he could well focus on providing individual, couples', and family treatment, while seeking partnerships with other professionals to complement the core business of the social work provider.

QUALIFICATIONS OF THE SOCIAL WORKER IN INDUSTRY

There has been considerable discussion as to whether the social worker's provision of services to industry can be described as distinct. This question becomes especially relevant to a multi-service agency providing a range of services that include EAPs.

The contract with the industry defines the qualifications and experience required of the social worker. Within industry social workers must be self-directed and autonomous as they frequently work with little or no professional supervision. At a minimum, he will have a master's degree in social work and five years of clinical experience in treating individuals, couples, and families. Some contracts call for more specialization in areas such as substance abuse. Questions as to whether the social worker providing employee assistance services ought to be paid at a different salary rate have led to important debates regarding the pitfalls of first- and second-class social work practitioners in the same setting; these are reminiscent of the old conflicts related to the status of "medical" and "psychiatric" social workers working in the same hospital.

In some settings social workers assigned to industry or EAPs work in different locations away from other agency services. Accordingly, these may adopt a more "corporate" or business appearance. Their offices may look different, more polished, and their attire may take on a more formal or professional style. Some have used their need for more expensive wardrobes as the basis for a demand for higher salaries.

Truly, however, the clients of these social workers reflect the great diversity in the workforce. Many clients would not be comfortable in social work offices that mirrored corporate headquarters. As in all areas of practice, a social worker in industry needs practical judgment and should treat all clients, whether they are clients of an EAP or not, with dignity, respect, and hospitality.

IMPACT ON THE SOCIAL WORKER'S OWN WORKPLACE

One would not expect someone who does not own life insurance herself to be able to sell life insurance to others. Similarly, to provide congruent social work services in industry, practices within the social workers' own workplaces become more significant.

As social workers become more involved in industry, they pay more attention within their own workplaces to the importance of continuous quality improvement, staff training and development, positive working environments, strong employee morale, access to their own EAP benefits—for themselves—employee rewards, and employee incentives. To promote family-friendly practices within industry, social workers have renewed their emphasis on family-friendly policies within their own workplaces. As they support other employees during times of rapid technological growth, so they too need the same support within their own workplaces. As social workers support

those in industry who pursue values clarification and spirituality, so social workers now express interest in the same matters in their own places of employment. As they encourage other workplaces to make sure that working parents can receive the reassuring "I'm home! What's to eat?" phone call at work every afternoon, so the values of such family practices and accessibility have become topics of more open dialogue in the social workers' workplaces, too.

INTERNAL VERSUS EXTERNAL SOCIAL WORK SERVICES WITHIN INDUSTRY

The social worker who provides services to industry may be visible and present within the workplace. More frequently, the employee goes off-site to see the social worker. Some industries, such as BC Tel in British Columbia and the Oshawa Food Group, employ their own social workers with offices at corporate headquarters. These workers may offer a range of education, wellness, and recreational activities for staff and serve as information and referral resources to a wide array of community, legal, child care, and elder care resources. Other companies employ their own internal social workers, and to maintain privacy and confidentiality the social workers are located off-site and tend to specialize in more in-depth social work treatment services.

Social workers within internal EAPs have the opportunity to interact with employees and management on a regular basis. They may provide a more personal approach towards helping. They are able to build trust and healthy working relationships on a continuous basis and have the advantage of day-to-day informal interactions within the workplace. A good social worker in industry earns credibility as someone who can contribute to the organization. In sudden crises, the internal social worker responds quickly and has enough background information to plan an immediate and relevant response. On the negative side, the same social worker may easily be viewed as connected to top management and may have trouble earning employees' trust. While the value of relationships between the internal social worker and the industry is obvious, social workers deal with very significant challenges in maintaining professional social work relationships with clients who are also colleagues.

When a company or an industry enters into a contract with an external social work provider, the provider may supply the services on-site, but the vast majority of these are offered off-site. One food manufacturing company, with primarily female workers and a number of problems related to absenteeism, wanted on-site services both to control costs and to ensure employees' accessibility to information about child care resources. The social worker from the family service agency began with an office beside the human resources department—not the ideal position in terms of privacy or confidentiality. But it was a start and it did raise company awareness about the availability of social work help. Before long, employees were calling the family service agency and asking the social worker if they could meet off-site, to deal with private family matters.

By starting where the customer was "at," this particular social worker successfully established trust and credibility with the human resources manager, and that EAP has now moved to an off-site service location. One of the ways the social worker built the positive relationship with the human resources manager was by participating in a golf game! Social workers are finding that this kind of marketing technique, long

familiar in business, has become applicable to their seeking to build their own relationships at all levels within industry

Many employers prefer to sign contracts with external social work providers. Once these contracts are established, the industry has little bureaucracy to manage. Employees have access to a full range of social work services with minimal involvement on the part of the employer. Through strategic alliances and partnerships, the social worker takes on the responsibility of ensuring that all the industry's employees have access to service, regardless of the work-site location. To many, the services of an external social worker seem more objective. The external social worker can tailor a specific approach to service provision to suit the specific issues of individual workplaces.

OUTCOME MEASUREMENT

To be taken seriously within industry, social workers must demonstrate their accountability and their commitment to continuous quality improvement. Until recently, they measured the impact of their services by reporting on utilization rates, changes in absenteeism, accident rates, and, most frequently, employee or client satisfaction. Attempts to describe the changes taking place in the lives of those who have used social work services were limited to inferences drawn from rates of utilization, lists of presenting problems, and client satisfaction surveys.

Recently social workers have done a great deal of work to develop tools that measure in concrete, observable terms the major personal and family changes in the persons who use social work services. Family Service Canada has taken the first steps in helping family service agencies implement an outcomes measurement system that assesses the amount of change in at least 25 different areas, including levels of distress and ability to function at home and work.

Prudent social workers will involve a variety of stakeholders within their industry directly in determining the outcomes to be measured. The workers who try to present evaluation reports that do not measure changes of value to the workplace will be defeating themselves. Most frequently, clients, the funding organization, and social workers all agree on the areas where change is most valuable, but the quality of the communication that goes into determining the areas of shared belief is just as critical.

Increasingly, industries will expect social workers to produce solid evaluation methods by which to analyze both client outcomes and program benefits. These social workers must recognize the common sense behind the paying customers' expectations of specific services with demonstrated outcomes.

CONCLUSION

In the late 1800s, social workers began working in industry as "welfare secretaries." In the twenty-first century, a different and strong role has evolved for social work practice in the workplace. While no statistics are available to confirm the extent of the practice within industry, it is increasingly apparent that employees in most large workforces in Canada have access to social work services, and the profession is making constant progress in reaching small and medium-sized businesses. The profession of social work has become an essential element in the workplace.

REFERENCES

Alvi, S. 1992. *Corporate responses to substance abuse in the workplace*. Ottawa: Conference Board of Canada.

Alvi, S. 1994. *The work and family challenge: Issues and options*. Canada Committee for the International Year of the Family 1994, Ottawa: Conference Board of Canada.

Bilsker, D., et al. 2004. *Depression & work function: Bridging the gap between mental health care and the workplace*. Retrieved from **www.mheccu.ubc.ca/publications/**

Canadian Labour Congress 1986. *Joint employee assistance programme guidelines* (revised). Ottawa: CLC Educational Services.

Coshan, M. 1992. An EAP can be part of the solution. *Canadian Business Review*.

Fleming, C. W. 1979. Does social work have a future in industry? *Social Work, 24.5.* 183–85.

Foster, Z., Hirsch, S., and Zaske, K. 1991. Social work role in developing and managing employee assistance programs in health care settings. *Social Work in Health Care, 16.2.* 81–95.

Hartwell, T. D., Steele, P., et al. 1996. Aiding troubled employees: The prevalence, cost, and characteristics of employee assistance programs in the United States. *American Journal of Public Health, 86.6.* 804–08.

Hockley, D. 1992. Assisting employees at B.C. Tel. *Canadian Business Review*. Ottawa: The Conference Board of Canada.

Labour Canada and Health and Welfare Canada. 1990. *Discussion paper on employee assistance programs in the federally regulated private sector*. Ottawa: Government of Canada.

Loo, R., and Watts, T. 1993. A survey of employee assistance programs in medium and large Canadian organizations. *Employee Assistance Quarterly, 8.3.* 65–71.

Loo, R. 1992. Organizational actions to manage workplace stress: The Canadian experience. *Journal of Health and Human Resources Administration 15.1.* 90–109.

Macdonald, S., and Dooley, S. 1989a. *Ontario worksites with 50 or more employees: The nature and extent of EAPs, programs and worksite characteristics.* Toronto: Addiction Research Foundation.

Macdonald, S., and Dooley, S. 1990. A survey of employee assistance programs and health promotion programs at Ontario worksites. *Employee Assistance Quarterly, 6.1.* 1–16.

McKibbon, D. 1993. EAPs in Canada: A panacea without definition. *Employee Assistance Quarterly, 8.3.* 11–29.

Massey, M. and Csiernik, R. 1997. Community development in EAP: The employee assistance program council of Hamilton-Wentworth. *Employee Assistance Quarterly, 12.3.* 35–46.

Mercer, W. 1990. *A survey of CEO views on substance abuse and its impact in the workplace.* Vancouver: William M. Mercer.

Ontario Ministry of Labour. 1990. *Report of the advisory committee on employee assistance programs to the minister of labour.* Toronto: Government of Ontario.

Ozawa, M. N. 1980. Development of social services in industry: Why and how? *Social Work, 25.9.* 464–470.

Popple, P. R. June 1981. Social work practice in business and industry, 1875–1930. *Social Service Review,* 257–69.

Ramanathan, C. S. 1992. EAP's response to personal stress and productivity: Implications for occupational social work. *Social Work, 37.3,* 234–39.

Reina, Dennis S., & Reina, Michelle Reina. March/April 2004. Rebuilding employee trust during change. *Behavioural Health Management, 24.2.*

Shain, M. 1996. Employee assistance and organizational change: New evidence, new challenges, new standards? *Employee Assistance Quarterly, 12.1.* 1–13.

Shain, M. 2000. *Best advice on stress risk management in the workplace.* Health Canada.

Shain, M., & Groeneveld, J. 1980. *Employee assistance programs: Philosophy, theory, and practice.* Toronto: Lexington Books.

Solomon, R. M., & Usprich, S. 1993. *Consent, negligence and confidentiality: A legal primer for Canadian employee assistance programs.* Ottawa: Canadian Centre on Substance Abuse.

Stimson, J. 1990. *Employee and family assistance program and the assessment and referral service: "A successful model."* Canada: MacMillan Bloedel.

Warley, Raquel. 1st Quarter, 2004. Assessment in an EAP setting. *Journal of Employee Assistance, 34.1* (Arlington, VA).

Wnek, I. 1991. *Employee assistance programs in Canada.* Alberta: Alberta Alcohol and Drug Abuse Commission.

WEBSITES

Catholic Family Counselling Centre, Kitchener, Ontario:
www.cfcchelps.ca

Employee Assistance Professionals Association:
www.eap-association.org

Family Services Employee Assistance Programs:
www.familyserviceseap.com

Global Business and Economic Roundtable on Addiction and Mental Health:
www.mentalhealthroundtable.ca

Mental Health Evaluation and Community Consultation Unit:
www.mheccu.ubc.ca

Mental Health Works:
www.mentalhealthworks.ca

National Institute of Mental Health:
www.nimh.nih.gov

chapter eighteen

Canadian Approaches to Income Security

John R. Graham

INTRODUCTION

Many people reading this textbook are considering careers in the helping professions. Of these, a substantial proportion probably hopes to provide direct services to clients. This chapter will be especially relevant to these readers, as well as to students interested in social policy analysis.

Economic need is one of the most pervasive issues that arises out of any helping encounter between a social worker and client. As Chapter 6 elaborates, before the development of a comprehensive welfare state in the 1940s and 1950s, Canadians who lived in poverty had few places to turn for help. They were expected to be self-reliant. If, however, they had to seek help from others, ordinarily they would go first to

family, then to friends, and then to community institutions such as the church or a charity (Graham, 1992; Splane, 1965). When these resources were exhausted, the poor accessed "unemployment relief"—the precursor to contemporary social assistance (Graham, 1996; Struthers, 1983).

In today's world, a far more elaborate system of income security exists, encompassing all three levels of government in Canada—and hence different offices with which a social worker might be in contact—and applying to a wide spectrum of categories. Different income security programs have been designed for

- single parent families (Social Assistance—the exact name varies by province);

- single individuals who have been unemployed for a long time (Social Assistance— the exact name varies by province);
- individuals who have recently lost their jobs (Employment Insurance);
- youth who do not live with parents or guardians (Social Assistance—the exact name varies by province);
- individuals who are injured in the workplace (Workers' Compensation);
- people with disabilities (Social Assistance—the exact name varies by province);
- the elderly (Canada Pension Plan, Old Age Security, and Guaranteed Income Supplement; some provinces have top-up programs for the elderly poor);
- government-assisted refugees new to Canada (Resettlement Assistance Programme);
- veterans of wars (War Veterans' Allowance); and
- other categories.

Social workers need comprehensive familiarity with this system in order to help their clients identify particular program(s) for which they are eligible and ensure their prompt and full access to these programs. Social workers' success in this task may prove crucially important to a client. It may make the difference, for example, between clients' going hungry or having food, being homeless or being able to find accommodation, feeling desperate or feeling hopeful, being trapped in poverty or having the means to improve their standard of living.

POVERTY IN CANADA

Poverty is defined as having insufficient means of subsistence. There are two ways of thinking about poverty: in absolute and in relative terms. *Absolute poverty* denotes a standard of living so low that a person cannot obtain adequate nutrition or shelter. Many homeless people in Canada may be described as living this way. One lives in *relative poverty*, in contrast, if one has insufficient means in relation to prevailing community standards. So, for example, individuals who have food to eat and a roof over their heads may still be defined as poor in relative terms (Graham, Swift, & Delaney, 2003). Notions of poverty in that sense necessarily vary from place to place and over time. In Northern Canada, as an example, possessing a warm winter coat is essential to survival and the lack of it aptly indicates poverty, whereas in a tropical climate a warm winter coat is not essential.

Measures of Poverty

Measures of poverty are a systematic tool that enables determination of the level of income below which an individual or family is said to be living in poverty. One of the most frequently cited measures of poverty derives from the federal government's Statistics Canada: the "low income cut-off," or LICO.

The LICO is based on the share of income an average Canadian family devotes to food, clothing, and shelter—and hence assesses relative poverty by applying community standards to the prevailing benchmark—and then adds 20 percent to this amount. Any family that must spend more than this share of its income on such basic necessities is described as living in poverty (Ross, Scott, & Smith, 2000). Other organizations have come up with measures of poverty that differ from the LICO—either higher or lower; a number of reference sources delve into poverty-line distinctions in greater detail (National Council of Welfare, 1999; Ross, Shillington, & Lochhead, 1994). All discussion in this chapter, however, will refer to the LICO.

Four points are essential in any discussion of measures of poverty:

1. All measures of poverty are relative.

2. All measures of poverty are arbitrary.

3. Measures of poverty measure the incomes of *groups* of people and not individual need.

4. Any poverty line may be called into question because of points 1 to 3 above (National Council of Welfare, 1999).

Who Is Poor?

Social programs in the post–World War II period gradually began to make progress against poverty, but over the past 30 years few new inroads have been made. Indeed, in 2002—the most recent year for which statistics are available —13.7 percent of Canadians fell into a low-income category (Statistics Canada, 2002) compared to 14.2 percent in 1975 (Battle, 1999).

What factors contribute to poverty in Canada? One is the growing inability of provincial minimum wage levels to keep pace with inflation (Battle, 2003). Other issues, as other chapters in this book point out, are associated with poverty—ideology, patriarchy, racism, and other structural matters. Overall, the rate of household poverty rose in the 1990s from levels in the 1980s and 1970s.

But the point cannot be overstated: different age cohorts are affected quite differently. Seventeen percent of seniors are thought to be poor today as opposed to rates of 30 percent in the 1980s (Hick, 2004). Shocking to many readers, and certainly to me, is the fact that many young Canadian families are likely to be poor. According to the 2001 census, the poverty rate of lone-parent families with children passed the 50 percent mark for the first time in at least 20 years—a rate that most readers will agree is deeply troubling (Hick, 2004).

Child poverty rates continue to be a great concern; in 2002, the most recent date for which there are data, 702 000 children under the age of 18 were living in poverty. This represents 10.2 percent of all Canadian children, an improvement over the past 22 years but a figure that still falls short of many advocates' demands for a total end to childhood poverty. Lone-parent families, particularly female-headed families, continue to be most vulnerable to poverty; in 2002, of the 500 000 lone-parent families headed by women in Canada, statistics showed a shocking 35 percent with this low income.

Aboriginal peoples, minority peoples, and peoples with disabilities are also vulnerable to poverty. According to the 1996 census, 43.4 percent of Aboriginal people, 35.9 percent of visible minorities, and 30.8 percent of persons with disabilities were poor in 1995. These rates are significantly higher than the national average (Ross, Scott, & Smith, 2000; Statistics Canada, 2002).

People's abilities to climb out of poorly paying jobs are limited; fewer than half of those Canadians with low-paying jobs in 1996 had jobs that were not low-paying five years later (Janz, 2004). At the same time, income inequality has increased in Canada, as it has in many other advanced industrialized countries (Morisette, Zhangi, & Drolet, 2002). According to one report, the wealthiest 10 percent of Canadian families held 53 percent of the country's wealth in 1999, while the poorest 10 percent had average wealth in negative figures, or more debts than assets (Kerstetter, 2002).

Chronological age (how old one is) and age cohort status (in what decade one was born) are among the myriad of possible factors that affect these figures. Between 1984 and 1999, among families whose major income recipient was 25 to 34 years old, median wealth fell by 36 percent; in

FIGURE 18.1 | Percentage of Canadians with Low Incomes

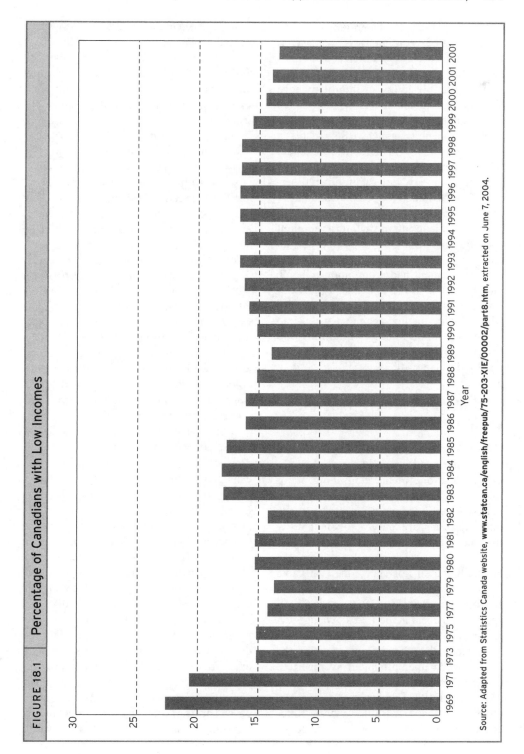

Source: Adapted from Statistics Canada website, **www.statcan.ca/english/freepub/75-203-XIE/00002/part8.htm**, extracted on June 7, 2004.

contrast, among those families whose major income recipient was at least 65 years old, median wealth increased 56 percent (Morisette, Zhangi, & Drolet, 2002). In 1999, people living in families whose main income recipient was 25 to 54 years of age and had no income earner were most likely to have no financial wealth (such as a house as equity—44 percent). Canadian families headed by female lone parents (43 percent), and very young families (40 percent) followed this group in the findings.

Poverty is especially acute among families whose main income recipient was aged between 25 and 34 and had no university education, families whose major income recipient had a limitation of some kind regarding work, unattached individuals less than 65 years of age, couples whose major income recipient was 25 to 34 years old, and immigrant families who had been living in Canada for less than 10 years (Morisette, 2002).

UNEMPLOYMENT IN CANADA

Unemployment remains a key cause of poverty in Canada. And the threat of unemployment is one of the continuing major risks of modern life. Many couples have both spouses in the workforce, while many other families are only a job loss away from poverty.

National jobless rates have increased gradually from 3.1 percent in the 1940s, to 5 percent in the 1960s, 6.7 percent in the 1970s, 9.3 percent in the 1980s, and an average of 9.8 percent in the 1990s. Average levels in the 1990s were the highest they had been since the Great Depression of the 1930s, when unemployment averaged 13 percent throughout that decade, peaking at 25 percent in 1933 (Graham, 1995; Torjman, 1998a; Torjman & Battle, 1999). Rates appear to have fallen modestly since then—

from 11.3 percent in 1992 to 7.3 percent in April 2004 (Statistics Canada, 2004b).

Yet we cannot take these numbers at face value, for official unemployment rates do not include those unemployed Canadians so discouraged that they have given up searching for jobs. Nor do official numbers count the underemployed. Those who would like to work longer hours and can find only part-time employment, known as "involuntary part-timers," increased threefold in number between 1976 and 1995. Having a wage is no guarantee one will avoid poverty. Indeed, the number of working-poor households, those in which one or more income earners were employed for at least 49 weeks of a year, increased substantially between 1981 and 1997 (Ross, Scott, & Smith, 2000). And the proportion of part-time workers in the labour force (voluntary and involuntary) has risen by 33 percent, so that it now constitutes nearly 20 percent of today's workforce. The number of people holding multiple jobs has also risen significantly; one in 20 Canadians can be so categorized (Torjman & Battle, 1999).

Unemployment varies significantly by region. Levels are much higher in the Atlantic provinces and Quebec. In March 2004, as one example, unemployment in Newfoundland stood at 15.5 percent, in Prince Edward Island at 12 percent, in New Brunswick at 9.9 percent, in Nova Scotia at 9.2 percent, and in Quebec at 8.6 percent; Ontario, on the other hand, had levels of 7.1 percent, British Columbia had 7.9 percent, Manitoba and Alberta had 5 percent, and Saskatchewan had 6.1 percent (Statistics Canada, 2004a).

This chapter discusses income security programs, which are defined as social programs that provide cash payments to recipients. Income security programs provide individuals, or families, with money in a variety of circumstances. Some programs cover various social risks that preclude or limit employment, such as disability, poverty,

FIGURE 18.2	Gender Equality Index for Total Income, 1986, 1991, 1995, and 2002

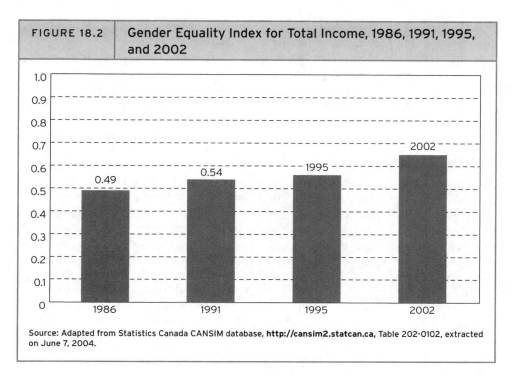

Source: Adapted from Statistics Canada CANSIM database, **http://cansim2.statcan.ca,** Table 202-0102, extracted on June 7, 2004.

sickness, or unemployment. Other programs provide money to individuals in various stages of life: for example, to the elderly, or to sole parents whose child-rearing responsibilities preclude their full employment.

Selective Programs

There are two major forms of income security programs: selective and universal. Each carries its own assumptions. Selective programs have a long history, stretching back to Elizabethan poor relief in England, and were brought to Canada with European colonizers. "Unemployment relief" was a selective program, as is its contemporary successor, general welfare assistance, also called "social assistance" or "a social allowance." A selective payment usually involves a transfer of money from a level of government to an individual.

Eligibility for selective programs is based on a means test. Social workers carry out means tests to evaluate, first, a person's financial resources—income, assets, debts and other obligations—and, second, other criteria such as the applicant's number of dependants or level of health.

Selective programs are subject to several criticisms. They may personalize problems of poverty rather than focus attention on broader societal structures beyond an individual's control that may create the conditions for poverty. One such economic change would be the closing of a pulp-and-paper mill in a one-industry town, leading to loss of employment for the man applying to a selective program. Selective programs, likewise, may stigmatize people who through factors outside their own immediate control face a temporary or permanent loss of income.

These programs devote considerable administrative resources to monitoring the lives of individual clients rather than focusing on broader community and societal changes that might improve the clients' opportunities in life. Proponents, on the other hand, believe that selective programs are the most efficient means of targeting money to those in need. As well, means tests, some believe, may motivate—to others, coerce—recipients to return to the workforce.

Universal Programs

Universal programs provide cash benefits to *all* the individuals in a society who fall into a certain category. They differ from selective programs in that eligibility to them is a right of citizenship, rather than a requirement that one prove personal eligibility through a means test.

The implications are many. A recipient's level of specific needs, or economic status, is not taken into account when determining eligibility. Where selective programs focus on an individual claimant's worthiness to receive benefits, universal programs operate under manifestly different assumptions. The state expresses a responsibility to provide income security for all citizens, and society implicitly recognizes the existence of conditions beyond an individual's control and that might impede her economic well-being. Stigma has little place in a universal program, since all people, regardless of their levels of need, may have access to benefits as long as they fulfil eligibility conditions—such as being the required age in the case of Old Age Security.

While universal programs may target a greater amount of money to a greater number of people, including the well-to-do, many argue that the income tax system should counterbalance payments to the rich—and not the social program itself. In a progressive income tax system, the proportion of taxes one pays increases with earnings; those with a greater ability to pay more do so. In a regressive tax system, in contrast, taxes are not collected on an ability-to-pay basis.

Regressive and progressive are relative terms, and the most extreme instance of a regressive tax—such as a sales tax—is one levied equally on all.

How so? Whether a person paying a sales tax is below the poverty line or is the president of a major bank, the sales tax charged remains the same percentage for each. Canada's tax system is somewhat—although far from completely—progressive. Thus, higher income earners pay a greater proportion of their money on income tax than do those in the lower income categories. The argument may be made that universal programs do not wrongfully direct monies to the better-off, given the existence (or potential existence) of a progressive income tax system (Muszynski, 1987). What is more, with everyone receiving benefits from a universal program, some argue that the middle and upper classes are politically co-opted into supporting the program, and so the benefits are less likely to be reduced in scope or eligibility than they would be in a selective program geared only towards the less politically powerful poor (Titmuss, 1958, 1987).

Universal programs came to the fore during World War II. But their presence has been systematically eroded over the past 35 years as selective programs have found new favour. The reasons for this erosion are complex, and at least part of the explanation rests with the emergence of neo-conservative ideology.

Demogrant, Social Assistance, Social Insurance

Several other terms are used to describe income security programs, so knowledge of them and their effective use is essential to social work practice.

A demogrant is a cash payment to an individual or family based on a demographic characteristic (usually age) as opposed to need; one example, as will be seen, is Old Age Security. Social assistance refers to selective income-security programs that apply a means or needs test to determine eligibility; these are often administered at the provincial or local government level, depending on the province.

Social insurance refers to income security programs in which eligibility for benefits is determined by a person's previous record of contribution and in the event of a particular contingency, such as unemployment, retirement, injury, or widowhood. Examples of these include the Canada Pension Plan and Employment Insurance (Armitage, 1996).

Government Jurisdiction

Sections 91 and 92 of the Canadian Constitution, which define federal and provincial government jurisdictions, allocate responsibility for social welfare to the provinces. Hence, many income security programs are administered at this level of government. But federal government participation has been equally important, since this jurisdiction has the greatest capacity to generate revenue, through income tax, tariffs, and corporate taxes.

Ottawa provides funding for the cost-sharing of major social programs, which the provinces deliver under the Canada Assistance Plan (1966–1996) and its successors, the Canadian Health and Social Transfer (1996–2004), which has been split into the Canada Health Transfer (CHT, 2004) and the Canada Social Transfer (CST, 2004). Other social programs, as will be elaborated, have also emerged at the federal government level, some, such as Employment Insurance, through constitutional changes.

Municipal governments, considered "creatures of the provinces," have limited constitutional jurisdiction and can be created or disbanded at the will of a provincial government. For centuries, social welfare in England, and then in Canada, came under the jurisdiction of local government. This explains why, in some provinces, programs such as general welfare assistance (a specific example of social assistance) have continued to be partially funded and entirely administered by local governments.

The Canada Health and Social Transfers (CHT and CST, 2004)

Perhaps the apex of the creation of a universal welfare state in Canada was the Canada Assistance Plan introduced in 1966 (CAP, 1966–1996). The CAP was a funding agreement that enabled the federal government to cost-share with the provinces those constitutionally prescribed provincial responsibilities for the delivery of education, health, and social service commitments. The CAP was a landmark social policy, allowing the federal government to ensure minimum standards of service delivery, relatively equal standards of services across the provinces, and a reliable funding base to achieve these ends.

The CAP started to unravel in the mid-1970s as changes in cost-sharing arrangements eroded the amount of money transferred to provinces. By 1992–1993, the federal share of CAP transfers to the country's three wealthiest provinces was down to 28 percent in Ontario and 36 percent in British Columbia and Alberta (National Council of Welfare, 1995). The CAP had ceased to be a 50–50 cost-shared relationship. And many provinces, in turn, downloaded significant financial responsibilities of their own onto local governments for funding and delivering social service programs such as social assistance, supported housing, home care, day care, and other services.

Those who know this history appreciate that local governments were responsible for funding and delivering most Canadian social programs until the end of the 1930s. During the Great Depression of that decade, many local governments went bankrupt and most could no longer afford the costs of delivering the programs, a significant precedent set in the wartime creation of a comprehensive welfare state.

Ironically, few proponents of municipal downloading appreciate why service funding and delivery were uploaded to higher levels of government some 75 years ago. As part of this downloading process, none considers expanding municipal fiscal capacity, which is based entirely on the property tax and hence is very limited and restrictive (Graham, 1995).

The CHST, which replaced the CAP in 1996, resulted in a 15 percent decrease in federal transfers to provinces intended for health, post-secondary education, and social services over the previous two years (Scott, 1998). The provinces, for their part, reduced benefit rates for social assistance and other programs. The CHST has also removed enforceable federal government standards, so the provinces are now free to allocate the money they receive in whatever ways they wish—even if this means substantially reducing program entitlements and restricting eligibility and access.

One of the country's foremost social policy think-tanks, the Caledon Institute of Social Policy (CISP), contends that this change in enforceability "constitutes one of the worst mistakes in the history of our social security system." It turns back "the social policy clock" to a period of minimal standards and far greater risks for society's most vulnerable (Torjman & Battle, 1995a, p. 5). "There will be no guarantee of a safety net in the country," a second CISP document points out (Torjman & Battle, 1995b, p. 2). This one piece of legisla-

tion—that passed in the federal House of Commons in 1995 and that created the CHST—highlights the profound significance of social policy in directing social work practice and affecting the lives of many social work clients.

The 2004 split of the CHST created two new entities: the Canada Health Transfer (CHT) and the Canada Social Transfer (CST). The CST is a federal block transfer to the provinces and territories in support of post-secondary education, social assistance, and social services, including early childhood development and early learning and child care. The CHT is the primary federal transfer to the provinces and territories in support of health care.

At the time of writing this chapter, the full effects of the 2004 split of the CHST were not yet assessed. Progressive social-policy research organizations such as the Canadian Council on Social Development are concerned that the CST will perpetuate the underfunding of social and education programs in Canada. It proposes improved federal government funding, mechanisms to evaluate outcomes, and to that end the further splitting of the CST, into programs for social welfare and post-secondary education, respectively (CCSD, 2004).

MAJOR INCOME SECURITY PROGRAMS IN CANADA

Several levels of government deliver income security programs. They constitute part, but not the whole, of transfers to persons and transfers to the governments, as shown in Table 18.1. The following program descriptions are deliberately succinct and simplified, covering major aspects of eligibility and benefits while omitting minor details that are too numerous to discuss here. More comprehensive analyses can be found in other sources (see Durst, 1999; Guest, 1997; McGilly, 1998).

TABLE 18.1	Federal Government Select Expenditures, 1996–1998		
Expenditures ($billions)	Actual 1996–1997	Actual 1997–1998	Budget 98 Estimate 1998–1999
Transfers to persons	34.0	35.8	35.5
Transfers to governments	22.6	19.8	19.5
Direct program spending	48.2	53.2	49.5
Sub-total program spending	104.8	108.8	104.5

Source: Adapted from Michael Mendelson, *To Everything (Even Fiscal Policy) There Is a Time: A Time to Restrain and a Time to Spend.* Ottawa: Caledon Institute of Social Policy, 1999, p. 3.

Michael Mendelson is a senior scholar at the Caledon Institute of Social Policy in Ottawa.

Federal Government Programs

Employment Insurance (EI, 1996–)

This was previously known as Unemployment Insurance (1940–1996). There are three ways to obtain EI: loss of job through termination, temporary disruption of work because of illness, and application for maternity/parental benefits. EI is based now on the number of hours, rather than weeks, worked—which is a fairer practice for part-time workers and those holding several jobs.

The entrance requirements have become more stringent over the past 15 years but continue to vary depending on the job type and the rate of unemployment in the region where the claimant lives. For example, in areas with high unemployment (above 13 percent), a claimant must prove work for a minimum of 420 hours, whereas in places of low unemployment (less than 6 percent), he or she must prove 700 hours of work to be eligible to apply (Human Resources and Skills Development Canada, HRSDC, 2004).

A May 2004 report indicates that only 42 percent of Canada's jobless received benefits the previous year, owing to increasingly severe restrictions on eligibility (HRSDC, 2004). Most recipients receive up to 55 percent of their average weekly insured earnings, the result of incremental drops in entitlement from as high as 64 percent of working wages in the 1970s (Battle, 2002). EI recipients receive lower proportions of average weekly insured earnings than they did previously. And the program itself now covers only roughly half of all unemployed individuals; many fall through the cracks because, for example, they were not in the workforce long enough to be eligible for the program, did not work enough hours, or their EI benefits ran out (HRSDC, 2002).

As of May 2004 the maximum benefits payment is $413 per week. The program used to be funded by the federal government, the employer, and the employee; now it is funded only by employer and employee contributions.

Canada Pension Plan/Quebec Pension Plan (CPP/QPP, 1966–)

The Canada Pension Plan and the Quebec Pension Plan are insurance plans to which people must contribute during their working years. Both were created the same year and are similar in design; the QPP is administered by the Quebec provincial government and is solely for those working in that province, and the CPP is administered by the federal government and is for those in all provinces other than Quebec. CPP and QPP also comprise survivors' pensions for the spouses of deceased pensioners, disability pensions, and children's and death benefits. Eligibility is based on past contributions to the plan.

In instances of retirement (as distinct from disability or a spouse's death), it is paid to contributing claimants older than age 60 and is intended to replace about 25 percent of the income the claimant paid into the plans. As of May 2004, maximum benefits are $814.17 per month for retirement payment, $992.80 for disability payments, $488.50 for spousal survivor payments (ages 65 or older), and $192.68 for children's survivor payments.

Employer and employee contributions fund the programs. These contribution rates were low and level from 1966 to 1986, and have risen gradually since that time. Over the next two decades, they are expected to nearly double (Battle, 1997). The plans are considered social insurance.

Old Age Security (OAS, 1952-)

The Old Age Security pension is a monthly benefit for people 65 years of age or older. It originated in 1927 as a selective, means-tested program and was transformed into a universal program in 1952. As a universal program, employment history does not play a part in eligibility, and a claimant need not be retired to be eligible.

Those on OAS pensions are subject to federal and provincial income tax on their incomes. Those with higher incomes also repay part or all of their benefits through the tax system (Government of Canada, 1999).

Some argue that OAS ceases to be a universal program owing to this so-called clawback of the benefits of higher income–earning Canadians through the income tax system. It precludes many people from full entitlement and a substantial number from ever receiving any compensation. Moreover, clawback amounts have systematically increased since the late 1980s.

As of May 2004, the maximum benefits are $463.39 per month. The program is

financed from federal government general tax revenues and is considered a demogrant.

Guaranteed Income Supplement (GIS, 1967-)

The GIS was established to supplement the earnings of low-income OAS recipients. It is administered under the OAS program. Eligibility is determined by need and may increase or decrease according to the claimant's overall yearly income.

As of May 2004, maximum benefits are $550.73 per month for a single applicant, and $358.73 for the spouse of an applicant. The federal government's general tax revenues fund the program and it is considered social insurance.

Spouse's Allowance (SPA, 1976-)

The Spouse's Allowance was established to provide income to the spouse of an OAS pensioner, either a widow or a widower. Like the GIS, eligibility is based on need, and the allowance is provided only to those within certain income limits. The SPA stops when the recipient turns 65 and becomes eligible for the OAS, or when the recipient moves out of the country or dies.

Maximum benefits as of May 2004 are $822.12 per month for a beneficiary married to an OAS pensioner and $907.64 for those widowed from a former OAS pensioner. The federal government's general tax revenues fund the program and it is considered social insurance.

Veterans' Pensions (VP, 1919-)

Those members of the armed forces who incur disabilities during wartime (Active Force), peacetime (Special Duty Area), or other forces service are eligible for the VP. The amount of pension is determined by degree of disability, and varies accordingly; maximum rates as of May 2004 are $1993.22 for single and $2491.53 for married recipients per month. The program is funded from federal government general tax revenues and is considered a demogrant.

War Veterans' Allowances (WVA, 1930-, with origins in World War I)

This income-related program ensures a minimum annual income for wartime service veterans who served in World War I, World War II, or the Korean War. Eligibility is based on financial and service eligibility and age, with a minimum qualifying age of 60 for a man and 55 for a woman. Survivors' allowances are also available.

June 2004 maximum benefits are $1107.73 per month for single claimants and $1681.86 for those living with a spouse and/or with one child. This program is funded from federal government general tax revenues and is considered a form of social assistance.

Resettlement Assistance Programme (RAP, 1998–)

Administered by the Ministry of Citizenship and Immigration (MCI), the Resettlement Assistance Programme (RAP) provides various supportive services as well as financial assistance for up to one year after the recipient's arrival, to government-assisted refugees arriving to Canada. In many instances funding may also be provided via cost-sharing sponsorship agreements between MCI and sponsorship agreement holders at the local, regional, and national levels.

As Chapters 11 and 12 explain, almost all newcomers to Canada are independent-class immigrants or sponsored by others, such as Canadian family members. A small proportion are convention refugees, defined as having "a well founded fear of persecution in his or her country of origin because of race, religion, nationality, membership in a social group or political opinion" (Government of Canada, 2004). The RAP program is only for refugee-class immigrants.

Benefit levels are usually identical to provincial social-assistance rates and are intended to provide necessary resources for food, shelter, and clothing, and to pro-

vide an opportunity for the immigrant to enrol in language classes and obtain a job.

The RAP emerged out of what used to be called the Adjustment Assistance Programme, which originated during World War II. It parallels the Immigrant Loans Programme, also intended to assist recipients in their resettlement process. Local, regional, and national immigration-service organizations provide hands-on transition assistance in a refugee's attainment of housing, education, employment, and other services; the RAP program is delivered in collaboration with these organizations. The program is funded from federal government general tax revenues and is considered a form of social assistance.

National Child Benefit (CCTB, 1998–)

This tax benefit is made up of two parts: the Canada Child Tax Benefit (CCTB), a tax-free monthly payment made to eligible families to assist with the cost of rearing children under the age of 18; and the National Child Benefit Supplement (NCBS), a monthly benefit for low-income families with children (National Council of Welfare, 2004). The benefits are usually paid to the mother of the child if the child lives with her.

The amount differs according to family income, number of children, and their ages. The CCTB is tax-free, and in all provinces except for Alberta may be as much as $1104 per child per year (in Alberta payments are less when the children are younger and more when they are older, but are intended to average out over 18 years to be equivalent to payments in other provinces). As of July 2000, the supplement annually provides $977 for the first child and $771 for the second in families whose yearly income is less than $21 214 (National Council of Welfare, 2004).

The CCTB and its predecessor, the Child Benefit, replaced the following three things: the Family Allowance

(1944–1992), a universal demogrant form of income security provided to all mothers of children under the age of 18; and refundable and non-refundable tax credits. The CCTB is considered a form of social assistance. It is an excellent example of a formerly universal program (the Family Allowance) that has been replaced by a selective/income tested program (the CCTB). Many commentators criticize the program for providing inadequate benefits in light of pervasive child poverty (Freiler & Cerny, 1998).

Provincial Government Programs

Workers' Compensation (WC, 1914–)

Workers' Compensation is designed to make payments and cover rehabilitation and medical costs for those workers who have been injured on the job. In the case of workplace death, it also provides payments to an employee's survivors.

It was first introduced in Ontario and subsequently spread to other provinces. Assistance levels vary from province to province. Eligibility criteria are stricter now than in the past, and benefits have been reduced in scope.

In Alberta benefits as of May 2004 are 90 percent of net income up to $58 800, (Government of Alberta, 2004) and in Ontario 85 percent of net income up to $74 439.52 (Government of Ontario, 2004a). In other provinces benefits may be as low as 75 percent, but the maximum net may be larger than the case of, say, Ontario's (McGilly, 1998). The program is funded by worker and employee contributions and is considered a form of social insurance.

Social Assistance (SA, Various Years)

Social Assistance, often called welfare or public assistance, helps people in need who are not eligible for other benefits, and is one of the most important income security programs with which a social worker

should be familiar. It is typically delivered to three broad categories of people: families with dependent children in need (often long-term need), individuals with disabilities (often long-term need), and individuals or families in short-term need. These three programs may have different names and may be administered out of different offices. The last category mentioned—intended for short-term assistance—is seen as an income program of last resort. Benefit payments help pay for food, shelter, fuel, clothing, prescription drugs, and other health services.

Eligibility rules and the amounts of payment differ from province to province, and where, in some provinces, the municipalities continue to administer and/or partially fund programs. Especially in short-term need assistance, means tests tend to prevail. Applicants must be of a certain age, usually between 18 and 65, but some provinces have provisions for minors under the age of 18 and not living with a legal parent or guardian. Full-time students of post-secondary education, under certain circumstances, may be eligible for assistance in some provinces but not in others. Single parents must try to secure court-ordered maintenance support to which they are entitled. Those on strike are usually not eligible for assistance, nor are sponsored refugees or sponsored family-class immigrants during their period of sponsorship.

In general, welfare is granted if a household's net assets are less than the cost of regularly recurring basic needs for food, shelter, and other necessities. Fixed and liquid assets are usually examined, and most provinces exempt the value of a car, a principal residence, furniture, and clothing. In most provinces, other assets—cash, bonds, securities that are readily convertible to cash, the value of life insurance—are limited by household size and employability. Applicants are usually required to convert non-exempt fixed

TABLE 18.2	Social Assistance Benefits for Select Provinces, 2003			
Family Type	Total Income	Poverty Line	Poverty Gap	Total Welfare Income as % of Poverty Line
Newfoundland & Labrador				
Single Employable	3298	16 516	−13 218	20%
Person with a Disability	8925	16 516	−7590	54%
Single Parent, One Child	14 903	20 644	−5741	72%
Couple, Two Children	17 886	31 080	−13 194	58%
Quebec				
Single Employable	6654	19 256	−12 602	35%
Person with a Disability	9565	19 256	−9691	50%
Single Parent, One Child	13 800	24 069	−10 269	57%
Couple, Two Children	17 642	36 235	−18 593	49%
Ontario				
Single Employable	6833	19 256	−12 422	36%
Person with a Disability	11 763	19 256	−7492	61%
Single Parent, One Child	13 871	24 069	−10 198	58%
Couple, Two Children	18 400	36 235	−17 835	51%
Alberta				
Single Employable	5034	19 256	−14 222	26%
Person with a Disability	7601	19 256	−11 654	39%
Single Parent, One Child	11 634	24 069	−12 435	48%
Couple, Two Children	18 412	36 235	−17 823	51%
British Columbia				
Single Employable	6461	19 256	−12 795	34%
Person with a Disability	9784	19 256	9471	51%
Single Parent, One Child	13 706	24 069	10 363	57%
Couple, Two Children	18 227	36 235	18 008	50%

Source: National Council of Welfare, 2003.

assets into liquid assets and deplete those assets before qualifying for welfare (National Council of Welfare, 1997–1998).

Benefit rates fall well below LICO measures of poverty, as indicated in Table 18.2. Definitions of eligibility, and benefit rates, have also tightened in recent years (National Council of Welfare, 2004). During its first term in administration, for example, Ontario's Progressive Conservative government in 1995 slashed Social Assistance by a remarkable 21 percent. Workfare has also been introduced in some instances—where recipients are expected to undergo training programs and/or other forms of work-related activities in return for benefits; and some provinces are exploring the introduction of a lifetime maximum for which people may receive some forms of social assistance.

The program is funded by federal and provincial monies under the CST, and in some instances partially by municipal governments. It should also be noted that funding arrangements with the federal Department of Indian and Northern Affairs pay for the delivery of Social Assistance programs in Aboriginal reserves; benefit rates and eligibility criteria are almost always identical to the prevailing provincial rates and criteria.

As the Caledon Institute of Social Policy points out, it may be wiser to approach Social Assistance as a human resource strategy issue rather than as workfare (Torjman, 1996a). Workfare implies compulsory labour and mandatory participation in designated activities. A human resource strategy, in contrast to workfare, is voluntary. Ideally, numerous stakeholders can collaborate in both—industries, educators, social welfare, and justice. Both also are supposed to provide a range of options including job search, academic upgrading and skills training, and employment creation, but some argue that workfare emphasizes these less. And a human resource strategy "also ensures" more explicitly "that appropriate supports are in place—notably, high-quality, affordable child care and transportation subsidies—so that recipients can move off welfare" (Torjman, 1996a, p. 1). Finally, and perhaps most importantly, a human resource strategy promotes, rather than destroys, human dignity and well-being.

Some provincial governments have sought to revise their Social Assistance programs previously targeted for children and families and align these with the federal CCTB. British Columbia was the first to consider a federally–provincially integrated child benefits system payable to low-income families with children, and other provinces such as Saskatchewan, Quebec, and New Brunswick are doing the same (Battle & Mendelson, 1997). Earnings supplement programs for working-poor families are also available in several provinces.

Provincial Top-Ups for the Elderly (Various Years)

The combined OAS and GIS supplements are low enough to qualify most elderly couples in most provinces for Social Assistance. To avoid having elderly SA recipients, some provincially administered income-supplement programs have been introduced.

Benefit rates vary from province to province, and are intended to raise incomes of recipients to roughly the income levels of public assistance recipients. For example, the Saskatchewan Income Plan provides a maximum of $90 per month to a single claimant and $72.50 to one who is married (Government of Saskatchewan, 2004). The Ontario Guaranteed Annual Income System (GAINS) provides a maximum of $83 per month (Government of Ontario, 2004b). Some other provinces have no such equivalent programs. Provincial top-ups for the elderly are selective social assistance programs, funded jointly by federal and provincial monies under the CST.

CONCLUSION: DIRECTIONS FOR TOMORROW

Income security policies work best when they are applied collaboratively with other social and economic policies, and when they are successful at addressing categories of people who are most in need.

The disgraceful incidences of poverty among Aboriginal peoples, children, peoples with disabilities, and women, among other social groups, ought to compel more comprehensive and successful policy responses. Disability pensions within the CPP, for example, have been criticized for not allowing beneficiaries who can work irregularly or part-time to do so—unless they are willing to forfeit all their benefits (Torjman, 1997). Some likewise argue that Social Assistance programs should be designed to provide income top-ups to low-income labourers, and that social programs should provide special transportation, child care, and other supports necessary to full and vital functioning in and beyond the workplace (Torjman, 1996a, 1996b, 1997, 1998a, 1998b, 1999).

So too might policies be delivered in ways that more sensitively appreciate people's diverse positions in terms of the basis of age, ethnicity, gender, geography, race, religion, and range of ability, among other parameters. High instances of poverty have been demonstrated among the 35.8 percent of persons who have recently immigrated to Canada versus the 14.3 percent who were native-born in this country (Statistics Canada, 2003); these statistics beg for further replication based on different data sets (Beiser, Hou, Human, & Tousignant, 1998). The implications are considerable. People new to Canada may have little appreciation of, or experience with, a welfare state and may require especially skilful and competent social work assistance to help them gain access to its income security programs.

More generally, income security policies are thought to reflect the national will. On the surface, this appears to be self-evident, and certainly plausible, yet as a growing policy literature points out, the forces of globalization are calling into question the limits of the state (Graham, Swift, & Delaney, 2003). As companies compete in an increasingly international marketplace, the demands on national governments to restrict their welfare states may grow. Some corporate leaders seek minimalist tax structures and minimal corporate contributions to income security, health insurance, and other forms of publicly administered programs. We in Canada are also prone to the assumption of American values in virtually all we think and do (Grant, 1965, 1969). Given the growing presence of American political culture in Canada, in part reinforced by the North American Free Trade Agreement, Canadian politicians have looked south of the forty-ninth parallel for political precedents. Many analysts are struck by the strongly American influences in contemporary Canadian social welfare retrenchment and workfare (Torjman, 1997, 1998b).

By virtue of its geography, Canadians have always appreciated the necessities of survival and of caring for one another to that end. The state has been an important instrument in Canadian history, expressed in the pragmatic conservativism of Sir John A. Macdonald's nineteenth-century National Policy of tariffs and westward settlement, in the Tory and social democratic ideologies that have distinguished our political life from that of the United States, and in the welfare state of the twentieth century. The choices we make in the twenty-first century cannot help but refer to what has come before. These choices could also reflect what we agree as a society should be our destiny. But will they?

REFERENCES

Battle, K. (1997). *Targeted tax relief.* Ottawa: Caledon Institute of Social Policy.

Battle, K. (1999). *Poverty eases slightly.* Ottawa: Caledon Institute of Social Policy.

Battle, K. (2002). *Social policy that works: An agenda.* Ottawa: Caledon Instiute of Social Policy.

Battle, K. (2003). *Minimum wages in Canada: A statistical portrait with policy implications.* Ottawa: Caledon Institute of Social Policy.

Battle, K., & Mendelson, M. (1997). *Child benefit reform in Canada: An evaluative framework and future directions.* Ottawa: Caledon Institute of Social Policy.

Beiser, M., Hou, F., Human, I., & Tousignant, M. (1998). *Growing up Canadian: A study of new immigrant children.* Ottawa: Human Resources Canada.

Caledon Institute of Social Policy. (1996). *Roundtable on Canada's aging society and retirement income system.* Ottawa: Caledon Institute of Social Policy.

Canadian Council on Social Development. (2001). *Canadian welfare incomes as a percentage of the poverty line by family type and province, 2001.* Accessed at **www.ccsd.ca/factsheets/fs_newpl01.htm**

Canadian Council on Social Development. (2004). *What kind of Canada? A call for a national debate on the Canada Social Transfer.* Ottawa: CCSD.

Durst, D. (Ed.). (1999). *Canada's national child benefit: Phoenix or fizzle?* Halifax: Fernwood.

Freiler, C., & Cerny, J. (1998). *Benefiting Canada's children: Perspectives on gender and social responsibility.* Ottawa: Status of Women Canada.

Government of Alberta. (2004). *Alberta Workers' Compensation Board.* Accessed at **www.wcb.ab.ca/home/**

Government of Canada. (1999). Human Resources and Development Canada website. Accessed at **www.hrdc-drhc.gc.ca**

Government of Canada (2004). Citizenship and Immigration Canada website. Accessed at **www.cic.gc.ca/english/refugees/resettle-3. html**

Government of Ontario. (2004a). Ontario workplace safety and insurance board. Accessed at **www.wsib.on.ca/wsib/wsibsite.nsf/ public/home_e**

Government of Ontario. (2004b). *Ontario guaranteed annual income system (GAINS).* Accessed at **www.trd.fin.gov.on.ca/userfiles/ HTML/cma_3_2441_1.html**

Government of Saskatchewan. (2004). *Saskatchewan income plan.* Accessed at **www.dcre.gov.sk.ca/financial/SIPoverview. html**

Graham, J. R. (1992). The Haven, 1878–1930: A Toronto charity's transition from a religious to a professional ethos. *Histoire Sociale/Social History, 25.50.* 283–306.

Graham, J. R. (1995). Lessons for today: Canadian municipalities and unemployment relief during the 1930s great depression. *Canadian Review of Social Policy, 35,* 1–18.

Graham, J. R. (1996). An analysis of Canadian social welfare historical writing. *Social Service Review, 70.1.* 140–158.

Graham, J. R., Swift, K., & Delaney, R. (2003). *Canadian social policy: An introduction.* (2d edn.). Toronto: Allyn and Bacon.

Grant, G. (1965). *Lament for a nation: The defeat of Canadian nationalism.* Toronto: Anansi.

Grant, G. (1969). *Technology and empire: Perspectives on North America.* Toronto: Anansi.

Guest, D. (1997). *The emergence of social security in Canada* (3d edn.). Vancouver: University of British Columbia Press.

Hick, S. (2004). *Social welfare in Canada: Understanding income security.* Toronto: Thompson Educational Publishing.

Human Resources and Skills Development Canada (2002). *The employment insurance coverage survey.* Ottawa: Human Resources Development Canada.

Human Resources and Skills Development Canada. (2004). *Employment insurance and regular benefits.* Accessed at **www.hrsdc.gc. ca/asp/gateway.asp?hr=en/ei/types/regu-lar.shtml&hs=tyt**

Janz, T. (2004). *Low paid employment and moving up.* Ottawa: Statistics Canada.

Kerstetter, S. (2002). *Rags and riches: Wealth inequality in Canada.* Ottawa: Canadian Centre for Policy Alternatives.

McGilly, F. (1998). *An introduction to Canada's public social services.* Don Mills, ON: Oxford University Press.

Mendelson, M. (1999). *To everything (even fiscal policy) there is a time: A time to restrain and a time to spend.* Ottawa: Caledon Institute of Social Policy.

Morisette, R. (2002). On the edge: Financially vulnerable families. *Canadian Social Trends, 67,* 13–17.

Morisette, R., Zhangi, X., & Drolet, M. (2002). Are families getting richer? *Canadian Social Trends, 66,* 15–19.

Muszynski, L. (1987). *Is it fair? What tax reform will do to you.* Ottawa: Canadian Centre for Policy Alternatives.

National Council of Welfare. (1995). *The 1995 budget and block funding*. Ottawa: National Council of Welfare.

National Council of Welfare. (1997–1998). *Welfare incomes 1996*. Ottawa: National Council of Welfare.

National Council of Welfare. (1999). *A new poverty line: Yes, no, or maybe?* Ottawa: National Council of Welfare.

National Council of Welfare. (2003). *Welfare incomes 2002*. Vol 119. Ottawa: National Council of Welfare. Accessed at **www.ncwcnbes.net/htmdocument/report welfinc02/WelfareIncomes.pdf**

National Council of Welfare. (2004). *Income for living?* Vol. 120. Ottawa: National Council of Welfare.

Ross, D. P., & Lochhead, C. (1998). Poverty. In *1998 Canadian Encyclopedia CD ROM*. Toronto: McClelland & Stewart.

Ross, D. P., Shillington, R. E., & Lochead, C. (1994). *The Canadian fact book on poverty, 1994*. Ottawa: Canadian Council on Social Development.

Scott, K. (1998). *Women and the CHST: A profile of women receiving social assistance in 1994*. Ottawa: Status of Women, Canada.

Splane, R. B. (1965). *Social welfare in Ontario, 1791–1893: A study of public welfare administration*. Toronto: University of Toronto Press.

Statistics Canada. (2002). *Analysis of income in Canada*. Ottawa: Statistics Canada. Accessed at **www.statcan.ca/english/ freepub/75-203-XIE/00002/part8.htm**

Statistics Canada. (2003). *Low-income rates among immigrants*. Ottawa: Statistics Canada. Accessed at **www.statcan.ca/Daily/English/ 030619/d030619a.htm**

Statistics Canada. (2004a). *CANSIM Table 202-0102—Average earnings by sex and work pattern*. Ottawa: Statistics Canada.

Statistics Canada. (2004b). *CANSIM Table 282-008—Labour force survey estimates (LFS), by sex and age group, seasonally adjusted and unadjusted, monthly*. Ottawa: Statistics Canada.

Struthers, J. (1983). *No fault of their own: Unemployment and the Canadian welfare state, 1914–1941*. Toronto: University of Toronto Press.

Titmuss, R. M. (1958). *Essays on the welfare state*. London: George Allen and Unwin.

Titmuss, R M. (1987). *Selected writings of Richard M. Titmuss: The philosophy of welfare*. London: Allen and Unwin.

Torjman, S. (1996a). *Workfare: A poor law*. Ottawa: Caledon Institute of Social Policy.

Torjman, S. (1996b). *History/hysteria*. Ottawa: Caledon Institute of Social Policy.

Torjman, S. (1997). *Welfare warfare*. Ottawa: Caledon Institute of Social Policy.

Torjman, S. (1998a). *Community-based poverty reduction*. Ottawa: Caledon Institute of Social Policy.

Torjman, S. (1998b). *Welfare reform through tailor-made training*. Ottawa: Caledon Institute of Social Policy.

Torjman, S. (1999). *Dumb and dumber governments*. Ottawa: Caledon Institute of Social Policy.

Torjman, S., & Battle, K. (1995a). *Can we have national standards?* Ottawa: Caledon Institute of Social Policy.

Torjman, S., & Battle, K. (1995b). *The dangers of block funding*. Ottawa: Caledon Institute of Social Policy.

Torjman, S. & Battle, K. (1999). *Good work: Getting it and keeping it*. Ottawa: Caledon Institute of Social Policy.

Veterans Affairs Canada. (2004). *Veterans affairs disability pension program*. Accessed at **www.vacacc.gc.ca/clients/sub.cfm? source=services/pensions**

chapter nineteen

Health Care in Canada: Under Stress

Patricia Taylor

INTRODUCTION: CANADIAN TRENDS LEADING TO THE TWENTY-FIRST CENTURY

The history of Canada is replete with stories of the rugged individualism of the earlier settlers. Mostly immigrants from Western Europe, they populated the land and tilled the soil in the hopes of creating for themselves and their families a life free from the tyranny of class distinctions and servitude. It was therefore not surprising that they looked after their own health care needs and those of their neighbours with a cooperative and energetic spirit fuelled by a strong will to survive.

As physicians were scarce, women were the traditional caregivers. They tended births and monitored the progress of life-threatening diseases in the community. Indeed, it was often their collective concern behind the trend in rural areas to band with neighbours to support bringing a physician into that community. Physicians came to identify strongly with the communities they served and often lived off the produce as well as the financial support the farmers could offer them.

As rural life gave way to developing urban communities, and family physicians evolved into medical specialists who required hospitals and technologies to support their services, the delivery of health care became complicated, costly, and discriminatory. The days of the personal physician who knew his or her patients and cared for their various concerns gave way to the impersonal physician, whose specialty might or might not fit the patients' symptoms or pocketbook. Money was the great leveller. Affording care, let alone the best care, was a serious problem. While the community reeled at the price tag on health care, the government felt the rumblings of dissatisfaction and the need to respond to the survival concerns of its citizens. Provincial politicians of the 1940s and federal politicians of the 1960s believed that a physically healthy citizenry constituted a socially healthy nation.

The concept of universal health care coverage was introduced in 1919 by William Lyon Mackenzie King. However, the enactment of universal coverage became a reality in 1946, when Tommy Douglas, premier of Saskatchewan, introduced the first insurance to cover hospital stays for all citizens of his province. Soon, organizing health care became as important an issue for the survival of the provincial and federal governments as building new roads was.

Government was listening to the people and counting votes. The correlation between a nation that was able-bodied and working and one that was prosperous and influential was obvious to all.

The battle for health care in Saskatchewan set the stage for the national scene. In the industrialized urban centres, the escalating costs of medical care were beyond the resources of many. Physicians were running their practices in a business-like fashion; each patient represented a certain amount of money, which added up to a substantial annual income. The fact that not everyone could afford to pay, however, limited access to the system, particularly for the poor. If the physician did not donate services, or if patients objected to being used for teaching purposes (as most indigent patients were), the system virtually excluded them.

The solution was clear; marry the health care needs of Canadians to governments' access to large amounts of money through taxes. The union worked, and universal health care was born. Stated simply, it meant that all Canadians—regardless of class, income, or health status—could visit physicians or be admitted to hospital without having to pay out of their pockets. With the passage of this universal legislation, Canada as a nation placed the welfare of its citizens before the profits of capitalism. The quality of life for all was of greater importance than the economic superiority of a few.

Frank McGilly notes details of the historic evolution: "The framework for nationwide public coverage of the costs of hospital care came into being in 1957, embodied in the Hospital Insurance and Diagnostic Services Act of that year. A similar system covering costs of medical care did not take shape until 10 contentious years later. Both the Hospital Insurance and Diagnostic Services Act and the Medical Care Insurance Act were ultimately merged in the Canada Health Act of 1984, which is now the authority for federal cost-sharing in both kinds of provincial programs."[1]

The new legislation meant that the federal government would share in the cost of the services provided and controlled by the provinces, provided the plan included

- uniformity of coverage for necessary services;
- free access for all;
- universal coverage for all residents of Canada on an equal basis regardless of age, sex, financial, or present health status;
- portability from province to province; and
- public accountability.[2]

In addition to the basic agreement, many provincial plans included additional benefits under certain conditions, such as

TABLE 19.1	Health Expenditures, by Type				
$ millions	1999	2000	2001	2002p	2003p
Health Expenditures	90 066.6	97 696.5	105 953.6	113 396.0	121 430.8
Hospitals	28 301.7	30 638.6	32 396.7	34 171.5	36 392.0
Other institutions	8524.1	9222.0	9979.0	10 681.7	11 557.7
Physicians	12 223.8	12 977.3	13 978.4	14 964.4	15 640.2
Other professionals	10 845.9	11 585.3	12 575.5	13 441.3	14 476.8
Drugs–prescribed and non-prescribed	13 520.0	15 093.2	16 669.7	18 140.8	19 619.1
Other expenditures	16 651.1	18 180.1	20 354.3	21 996.3	23 745.0
% of Gross Domestic Product					
Health expenditures	9.2	9.1	9.6	9.8	10

Note: Health expenditures include spending by federal, provincial/territorial, and local governments, Workers' Compensation Boards, and the private sector.

Source: Statistics Canada, website, **www.statcan.ca/english/Pgdb/health13.htm**, extracted on May 31, 2004.

the services of dentists, optometrists, psychologists, chiropractors, and pediatricians, as well as home-care services, prescription drugs, and general medical prevention. Also, federal contributions were made toward the cost of certain extended health care services such as nursing homes and adult residential, ambulatory, and home-care services. Most physicians were paid on a fee-for-service basis.[3]

For the poor, the Canada Assistance Plan ensured that disadvantaged Canadians received adequate health care. Indeed, the federal government paid up to 50 percent of the costs the provincially run programs did not cover. The plan's coverage varied by province and could include eyeglasses, prosthetic appliances, dental services, prescribed drugs, home-care services, and nursing home care.[4] Social work services generally have not been included.

THE CHANGING SYSTEM

The battle over universal health care coverage in Canada was won, but the war was

hardly over. The illusion that the coffers of the federal government were bottomless at last gave way to unprecedented increases in the costs of a health care delivery system that was ever more driven by high-technology and specialists. Hospital costs and physicians' bills were consuming the largest portion of the national health care budget, and these costs were growing. *Canada Yearbook 1997* reported that in 1991, Canada spent $66.8 billion on health care—$2474 per Canadian. One of every 10 dollars in the Canadian economy paid for health care costs, one-third of provincial budgets, and an increasing share of employer expenses went to health care.[5]

In 1999, the Canadian federal and provincial governments spent $86 billion on health care, an increase of 5 percent, or approximately $100 per person over 1998. Canada ranks fourth among the G7 nations in public spending on health care.[6]

In the 1970s, 1980s, and 1990s, community-based health care services with a holistic approach to patient care, including disease prevention, were expanding. A community approach directed at special needs led to the creation of gerontology centres, women's health care services, and community-based emergency services and clinics, all of which were part of the new wave delivery system.

Recently, the trend by government has been to decrease the percentages of Gross Domestic Product spent on health care. While Canadians worry about the implications of this trend in health care delivery, a brief comparison between the public Canadian system and the largely private system in the United States reveals a difference in outcomes in Canada's favour. Present data show that the percentage of Canadian GDP designated for health care is less than the percentage of US GDP (10.1 percent versus 14.4 percent in 1993), and that Canadian expenditures are growing more slowly (*Canada Yearbook 1997*). However, the health statistics of the two countries suggest that money does not always buy positive results. In 1991, the United States spent 13.2 percent of its GDP on health care yet its infant mortality rate (8.3 deaths per 1000 births in 1993) was higher than that of Canada.[7] This trend continues in the 2002 data from the Organisation for Economic Co-operation and Development (OECD) Health Data, where the Canadian infant mortality rate is reported as 5.3 per thousand live births, while the United States has a mortality rate of 7.1 per thousand live births.[8]

Other recent research has described the Canadian health care system in positive terms. Gorey et al. completed an international study comparing cancer survival rates between Canada and the United States. The study concluded that the consistent pattern of a survival advantage in Canada observed across various cancer sites and follow-up periods suggests that Canada's more equitable access to preventive and therapeutic health care services is responsible for the difference.[9]

All indicators suggest that although the system is in financial flux, it is working. Few Canadians today recall a time when they had to pay for a visit to a physician or a stay in hospital. The merits of universal coverage are obvious to the Canadian public and most consider such coverage a right. However, this sense of "right of access" to unlimited health care also parallels the public's overuse of physicians, particularly for other than purely medical reasons. Helen Rehr describes the trend that has produced our present crisis as follows: "the majority of visits to doctors are by the 'worried well' for minor illnesses or by the 'stabilized sick' who seek help with anxiety, depression, and stress [and the problem is that] medicalizing these problems does not achieve social-health solutions."[10]

Today, the national health care budget and the national debt continue to run out of control. Drastic measures have to be taken to restore economic stability to the nation. A new order is emerging in health care: governments are capping physicians' incomes and whittling away at the system itself. Closings of hospital beds, restrictions on hospital stays, limits on highly specialized services such as cardiovascular or spare-parts surgery to teaching or research centres, and the growth of day surgery all point toward a more refined definition of the old order.

Life Expectancy and Diseases Trends

In 1900, the major causes of death were infectious and contagious diseases. By the 1930s, the discovery of penicillin and improvements in living conditions brought about by a growing concern for public health practically eradicated those diseases. Today, health concerns are more likely to focus on chronic illnesses and a vast array of psychologically and socially

TABLE 19.2	Mortality Rates[1] by Causes							
Number of deaths	Age-standardized mortality rates		Both sexes		Males		Females	
	1996	1997	1996	1997	1996	1997	1996	1997
Deaths per 100 000 population								
All causes	212 880	215 669	668.6	645.5	860.6	822.3	526.6	479.1
All cancers	59 240	58 703	187.8	181.5	236.6	229.7	155.0	148.5
Lung	15 708	15 439	50.2	48.2	72.9	69.8	33.6	32.3
Colorectal	6158	6102	19.4	18.8	24.4	23.5	15.7	15.2
Breast[2]	5074	4946	...	...	...	...	28.9	27.4
Prostate[3]	3588	3622	...	...	29.2	28.6	...	...
Cardiovascular diseases	79 450	79 457	246.3	238.8	316.8	307.0	193.1	187.7
Heart diseases	57 926	57 417	179.9	173.0	239.9	230.8	134.7	129.7
Acute myocardial infarction (heart attack)	22 211	21 962	69.4	66.6	96.8	93.0	48.4	46.4
Cerebrovascular diseases[4]	15 593	16 051	48.0	47.8	52.9	52.8	44.1	43.9
Chronic obstructive pulmonary diseases (COPD)[5]	9346	9618	29.1	29.0	44.9	44.5	19.8	20.1
Unintentional injuries	8663	8626	28.2	27.6	39.2	37.8	18.1	17.9

[1] The rates, which are standardized to the 1991 Canadian population, were calculated using 1996 and 1997 population estimates (December 2, 1998, revision).

[2] Per 100 000 women.

[3] Per 100 000 men.

[4] Stroke is the major component.

[5] Include emphysema, chronic bronchitis and asthma. Not applicable.

Source: Adapted from Statistics Canada, *Health statistics at a glance*, Catalogue 82F0075, April 7, 2000.

related diseases, with stress playing an undeniable role in many of these.

As shown in Table 19.2 from Statistics Canada, the most common causes of death today are heart disease, cancer, and accidents.

As Canadians' quality of life improves, so does their life expectancy. A higher standard of living, more attention to public hygiene, and advances in medical care have all steadily increased their life expectancy.

Table 19.3 identifies life expectancy at birth by gender in Canada in 1997.

The major trends in health care problems as Helen Rehr singled them out in 1984 continue today. They are:

- chronic illnesses and their sequelae in the elderly, infants, and children, and the mentally and developmentally disabled;

TABLE 19.3	Life Expectancy at Birth		
Location	Both Sexes	Males	Females
Canada	78.5	75.7	81.3
Newfoundland and Labrador	77.3	74.6	80.0
Prince Edward Island	77.9	74.9	80.9
Nova Scotia	77.7	74.9	80.4
New Brunswick	78.0	75.0	81.1
Quebec	78.0	74.9	81.1
Ontario	78.8	76.2	81.4
Manitoba	77.9	75.3	80.6
Saskatchewan	78.5	75.6	81.4
Alberta	78.0	75.1	80.9
British Columbia	79.2	76.5	81.9
Yukon	76.7	73.4	80.1
Northwest Territories	76.6	73.9	79.2
Nunavut	68.3	66.0	70.6

Source: Adapted from Statistics Canada, *Vital Statistics Compendium*, Catalogue 84-214, November 25, 1999.

- social–psychological–emotional disorders, including family disequilibrium and interrelationship problems;
- social diseases resulting from lifestyle and environmental factors such as cirrhosis, emphysema, hypertension, coronary disorders, and, more recently, herpes and AIDS;
- social disorders such as violence, substance abuse, promiscuity, and excesses;
- stress, anxiety, and fear in the "worried well" and the "stabilized sick";
- minor ailments such as self-limiting illnesses and conditions.

Rehr adds that in the future people's lifestyles, behaviour, and environment will affect their health status more than anything else.[11]

THE CORPORATE MODEL: 1990 AND BEYOND

The general downsizing of the North American economy as well as advances in research and technology are changing the delivery of health care. From the starting point of a production model that linked increasing profits with infinite growth, the realities of excessive costs, foreign competition, new technology, and concern for the environment have forced cutbacks in the workforce without cutting productivity.

Health care has felt the impact of this general economic trend as much as any other sector. Indeed, most hospitals' trend to a business or corporate administrative model relates directly to cost containment and consumer satisfaction. Dr. Gail Siler-Wells, as quoted by Crichton, Hsu, and

Tsang, reviewed the trends internationally and noted that "If trends continue, we will move beyond the patient role into a more egalitarian and empowered partnership role with professionals in the treatment process."

Consumers expect to be partners and to share in the planning and decision-making process of the health care system. They are also broadening and redefining their role as both providers and self-care agents through their own efforts to maintain their own health or treat certain unhealthy conditions. In addition, the public is evolving its own health role. Accordingly, behavioural changes associated with heightened personal responsibility in chronic disease management and health maintenance involve a shift from the role of the passive sick to that of the more active empowered.[12]

In other words, the hospital as a corporate organization has as its goal lowering costs and cutting the workforce while still satisfying the demands of the consumer/patient. As a result, the traditional approach to health care that stressed the personalized application of an intuitive approach to medicine has given way to the notion of a technologically driven, scientifically informed approach in which fewer, but more highly trained workers will more efficiently and effectively treat their patients.

Taking its lead from business, the new model suggests not only an upgrading of expertise but a downgrading of the old bureaucracy that defined physicians as the leaders and administrators as the controllers of the system, with other health care personnel and patients fitting in as needed on various levels of the structure.

In line with the 1990s corporate model, the contemporary health care system is reducing both the size of hospitals and the absolute authority of the physician and the administrator. Instead the model promotes a sharing of power and control, with the new more highly educated health care team and also with the consumer, whose demands for responsive, effective, and flexible services are forcing such changes. The role of the physician as gatekeeper of the health care system is weakening.

The halcyon days of free spending are over. In their place, efficiency and problem-solving skills are needed. Ministers of health and hospital administrators are frantically scrambling for some kind of national standard that will save Canada's reputation as a provider of excellent health care. Costs are out of control; more than $250 000 is required to graduate one general practitioner. As a result, health care delivery is on the examining table. The government is looking at frequency of visits to physicians, frequency of diagnostic tests, number of diagnostic tests, hospitalization rates, length of stays, referral rates, physicians' salaries, demands for special services, the physician/patient ratio, the distribution of services (large cities have too many specialists; smaller communities have none), and the proliferation of costly high-tech equipment. Anything that contributes to the cost of health care is under the microscope.

Recently, Ontario enacted a plan to contain costs that has emphasized closing hospitals, cutting back on hospital beds, and reducing professional staff. The results have met with mixed reviews. Overcrowded emergency rooms, long waiting lists for some surgeries and treatments, and early discharges from hospital have proven very upsetting to a public that wants and expects more. At the same time, in a recent survey, Canadians reported satisfaction with the health care services they did receive.[13]

IMPLICATIONS FOR THE FUTURE

Government administrators and health care professionals can join forces and battle valiantly to reduce costs and save Canada's health care system, but the patients must also be enlisted to join the fight. Patients consume those health care services, and they have to be taught to be responsible consumers as part of being good citizens. The prime personal responsibility of a good citizen is to maintain good health, and it is the responsibility of good government and good health care professionals to teach everyone how to stay healthy. While some may suggest that this attitude tends to blame the victim for the problem, it also has the potential of reorienting the public to the new reality of limited health care services and health care consumers' role in the restructuring.

Health care in the twenty-first century will cease to grow exponentially because of the finite tax base that supports it. The new universal system, based on equal access and individual responsibility for all, will highlight an economy of scale or a system the government can afford, while aiming at increased efficiency and effectiveness in solving future health care problems. An overriding concern in the new high-tech health care industry is the preservation of the "caring" approach, which on the surface may appear labour-intensive and costly yet remains a critical element in responding to the human vulnerability of every "sick person."

Dramatic changes particularly in the field of biotechnology predict a total revolution in health care in twenty-first century. Genetic engineering has the potential to cure cancer, produce new blood vessels in the heart, and grow new organs from stem cells. The whole context of health care treatment in the future holds out the hope of eliminating the surgery, treatment, and drugs that we rely on today. However, such a brave new future is not the reality that we must cope with in our existing health care system.

Wellness: Caring for the Healthy

One of the most promising and pervasive trends in health care today lies in the concept of prevention. Government funding as well as service delivery is focusing on maintaining health instead of treating disease. National campaigns aimed at eliminating smoking and promoting early detection of cancer promise a reduction in both the incidence and costs of serious illnesses such as heart disease and cancer.

However, the concept of wellness encompasses more than the prevention of disease. The notion of maintaining a healthy lifestyle in the social and spiritual as well as biological aspects of one's life is defined by more than the simple presence or absence of disease. Rather, the promotion of health relates to the prevention of disease. This view of living is long term. By quitting smoking and drinking, cutting down on saturated fats, and exercising we will increase our chances of living more productive and satisfying lives as well as be more likely to survive longer.

Moderation and a lifestyle that stresses personal control in balancing the big three items in one's life (work, rest, and play) promise benefits for the individual, the employer, and the government-funded health care system. At the same time, government bears an additional burden of promoting policies that support the conditions for personal health. Clean water, clean air, and access for all to the necessities of life assume new importance.

A definition of health that is not centred on the presence or absence of disease bears consideration in this discussion. As Herbert Weiner, professor of psychiatry at the Neuropsychiatric Institute, School of Medicine, University of California in Los Angeles, suggests, two models define health in the Western world: the traditional and the reductionist. The traditional model defines health as the absence of disease. In this model disease is also the sole cause of illness. According to Dr. Weiner, the reductionist model is integrative. It attempts to explain the apparent paradox of a person's having a disease without being ill or being ill without having a disease. The model explains the obvious—that many elements play a role in the predisposition to ill health, its initiation, maintenance, and the effects of disease.[14]

Health in this definition refers to the whole person interacting with the environment. Consequently everything, including age, personal lifestyle, psychosocial factors, nutrition, genetic makeup, even the larger environment, especially water and air, affect an individual's health. As opposed to the traditional medical approach, which flooded health care services with patients and shot up government health care costs to unprecedented levels, the integrative definition of health as Dr. Weiner defines it offers a way to contain costs, control demands for services, and ultimately make the best possible use of limited health care dollars.[15]

Somewhat related to the wellness approach is the current concern about limiting access to the system for those people who ignore their health. These are the people who continue to smoke, drink, or eat to excess. Certainly access to high-tech and costly services such as organ transplants and/or cardiovascular surgery are already being questioned in terms of society's "return on investment" principle. In Canada, where most citizens have grown up with universal health care, the general perception that health care is a right long ago supplanted the more historic experience that defined it as a privilege.

Current attempts to change these values and perceptions to allow the government to produce a system we can afford will not be easy. Limiting access to the system in order to contain its costs clearly threatens universality and suggests that

money could again become the arbiter of access to service. Echoes of the old two-tiered system, one level for the rich, one for the poor, filter through the rhetoric.

The Elderly: A Group with Special Needs

One growing area of concern in health care is the elderly. Even prevention of illness and a concerted effort to remain well cannot stem inevitable physical decline. Persons older than 65 years of age represent a rapidly growing segment of the population whose susceptibility to heart disease, cancer, and arthritis puts more and more pressure on health care services and a further drain on government funds. The cost of their health care is an issue that demands consideration. One cannot ignore the potential for age discrimination in such a discussion. The fact that people over 65 tend to have more health problems and use health facilities more must be viewed as a major consumer trend that the system must confront with the same vigour with which it addresses the education demands of those younger than 25.

When addressing the cost of health care services for the elderly, the more important fact is that patients over 65 tend to take longer to get well. Frequently they suffer extended and costly stays in system facilities. The new thinking in response to this problem highlights the developmental as opposed to the medical context of aging. It also suggests an increase in community-based support services to keep the elderly out of institutions and in their own homes.

An offshoot of this approach is demonstrated in the current trend by gerontologists toward restricting and refining the elderly's use of medications. Because the federal government pays for most prescriptions for those on Old Age Security, the savings that are predicted in this area alone are expected to be substantial, not to mention the resulting improvement in quality of life for the elderly. Job opportunities will open up in the personal service industry for social workers, nurses, health aides, and visiting homemakers as our society tries to answer the needs of the elderly in our communities. The aging of the Canadian population will influence the cost and direction of health care. Services that are sensible and sensitive to their needs will be more and more in demand.

Multicultural Health Care

Canada is a country of great racial and cultural diversity. There is no single cultural group that constitutes a majority of the Canadian population. More than anything else this fact contributes to the image of Canada as a mosaic. Indeed, the diversity of the Canadian culture was given the highest legal recognition in the 1982 Constitution's Charter of Rights and Freedoms, Article 27, which states that "The Charter shall be interpreted in a manner consistent with the preservation and enhancement of the multicultural heritage of Canadians." That people of other cultures have had an impact on Canada goes without saying. That people of other cultures have had an impact on the Canadian health care system is not as clear. Theoretically, the health care system under the auspices of universal access discriminates against no one. However, on a practical level for people of cultures and races other than those of British and French background this is less true.

Until the last few decades, health care in English-speaking Canada has been typical of the middle-class, Anglo-Saxon, white majority. Efficiency, order, hygiene, scientific methodology, and objectivity have been the hallmarks of Canadian medical schools and medical practice. The physician dictated the treatment, the nurse carried out the physician's dictates, and the patient submitted in a spirit of complete trust to the care given.

The patient who did not conform to this system was considered either delinquent, neurotic, or at the very least "a problem." In all its rigidity, the system tended to deny cultural differences. A Mediterranean worker confined to a hospital bed and provided with homemade wine by his loving wife was considered delinquent and negatively disposed towards his own treatment and those treating him. A Middle Eastern woman describing her symptoms in graphic language, as is the custom in her homeland, could be seen in Canada as a hysterical neurotic, or as someone who was "not too bright." A First Nations man, by nature taciturn and stoic, could well be misunderstood and labelled uncooperative. The cold scientific atmosphere of the hospital, with its emphasis on precision, accurate timing, and clear-cut authority, is daunting enough for an Anglo-Saxon, but patients from a vastly different culture could be terrified by the seriousness of it all.

Canada today is a multicultural society, and medical care has to respond to this new and varied culture. Physicians from other countries have augmented Canada's own force of physicians. Patients often seek out physicians from the same cultures. This is frequently a great help, but it is not always possible. It is not uncommon for an Anglo-Saxon patient to be referred to a physician from a vastly different culture, or even one for whom English is not always clearly comprehensible. There must be adjustments and flexibility on all sides.

Today there is a far more integrated view of disease and health. Greater importance is given to the emotional, spiritual, and social aspects of the patient's functioning. Mainstream health care delivery has to respond to the individual and all that makes him unique; specifically, it must take into account the cultural background of the patient. Old family remedies, herbal treatments, large families in attendance, and even drum-beating may be necessary in part for the sake of the patient's security and well-being.

No one would deny that patients who feel comforted and supported by their cultural traditions are more likely to improve than patients who are abandoned to the sterility and coldness characteristic of many of our hospitals. Likewise, the highly guarded territory of who may deliver health care, and where and when it may be delivered, is being challenged to include a broader spectrum of more culturally acceptable healers. Midwives, chiropractors, and acupuncturists offer alternative services that the medical establishment no longer rejects out of hand. The goal of universal access, which in theory is non-discriminatory, is changing. Attaining this goal means developing sensitivities to the multicultural needs of the Canadian population. Not only are forms, directions, and advertising beginning to respond to these needs and differences in customs and language, but health care professionals and administrators are also beginning to identify cultural cues as important to treating their patients.

Understanding different value systems according to cultural expectations and norms is imperative to the delivery of culturally responsive health care. The importance of this approach is beginning to have an impact on service delivery.

The present downsizing and restructuring of health care along more cost-effective and efficient lines constitutes a serious threat to the multicultural nature of the community. Suggestions about restricting access and charging user fees, while cost-effective, could be counterproductive to the multicultural health care goals of availability, accessibility, and acceptability of services to all. It could recreate a two-tiered system of health care in which culture may no longer be a major variable.

There is controversy over how we define the problems in health care today.

Many politicians and health care administrators are suggesting that the critical issues focus solely on the exponential growth in costs and the overuse of the system by a population that demands to see a physician for every illness no matter how "minor." However, discrimination within the system as well as exclusion on cultural and racial grounds is also a problem.

COMMUNITY-BASED DELIVERY SYSTEM: IMPLICATIONS FOR SOCIAL WORK

The universal health care plan that lies at the heart of our present system is changing direction. It has to. Costs must be reined in. Misuse, abuse, and overuse in every part of the system have to be stopped and yet, all are agreed, universal access must be maintained. One of the principal changes slowly getting under way is a shift from the institution that provides all the care to the community that supplements that care.

Efforts to slow down the growth of health budgets will be frustrated unless we find new funding incentives and organizational arrangements to make more effective use of existing resources. The new approaches should improve the links among various levels of health services and related social services and should place greater emphasis on care in ambulatory and community settings. The implications of such a move are clear.

Medical services today command a broad range of high technology and refined skills that very effectively reduce the length of a hospital stay. Day surgery is on the increase. Community-based emergency treatment centres are multiplying. Although this approach directly reduces costs, it also promotes a more personal and caring family-based system that creates its own new problems. Shorter hospital stays suggest that patients will be returning to the community with greater physical and emotional needs. It also suggests a more time-consuming hands-on role for their families in an economy in which, in more than half the families, both parents work outside the home. When the families' needs are not addressed, the care of sick relatives often represents the one additional ingredient that squeezes the "sandwich generation" too thin.

In the face of limited hospital stays, the role of the health care team takes on dramatic importance as well. The social and emotional needs of the patients as well as the gravity of their illnesses will have to be carefully scrutinized and clearly identified before they are admitted to hospital. Identifying degrees of risk in the psychosocial area of patients' lifestyles is critical to the functioning of an integrated treatment team, both before admission and upon discharge. It can save time and money and it can also help reduce stress for patients and their families, who are often wary of taking ill relatives out of well-equipped and professional clinical surroundings. Even greater upset follows if the family members find themselves confronted with community arrangements that appear hasty, slipshod, or even unprofessional.

On the other hand, early discharge and cooperative team care could provide the impetus for augmenting the present community-based services so that families can be supported in their new responsibilities without losing privacy, control, or hard-earned wages. Options are important for the patient and the family when considering the consequences of medical treatment. While physicians are willing to discuss the results of surgery and the options for successful recovery, the health care team takes on dramatic importance in the face of limited hospital stays. A cooperative

community-support plan that promotes family care given in a realistic and sensitive way can enhance and even accelerate patients' rehabilitation in the more familiar surroundings of their homes. Certainly the new patients/consumers will demand a system that does not leave them stranded.

In a well-integrated community-based health care service, the social worker is the bridge between the institution and the community. Coordinating care will take on a new meaning. Greater involvement and closer monitoring will be required to achieve the desired goal of complete patient care.

Advocacy, empowerment, self-determination, and respect are critical to social work practice. They must be incorporated into the total health care plan. Social workers bring broadly based educational backgrounds and social sensitivities that would suggest that they have a great opportunity to assume a leadership role in the emerging new health care delivery system.

CONCLUSION

The most serious problem to be solved in the Canadian health care system in the twenty-first century is cost-containment. One solution politicians are proposing is privatization, which works on the basic business principle of selling goods and services for profit.

However, health care is a unique service. Everyone lives with the possibility of becoming sick. While this fact alone may incite more than one business to try and corner this market for profit, the pursuit is inconsistent with the democratic goals of a caring society. It smacks of making profits from human suffering. The elderly, in particular, are vulnerable in this delivery model because they are at a stage in their lives when their physical decline and medical interventions are more likely.

In Canada, the federal and the provincial governments continue to wrangle over who pays for the spiralling costs of drugs, technical services, and salaries. Some politicians would like to wash their hands of the problem by turning over health care to private industry. The government would be expected to pay or co-pay with patients or with patients' private insurance. This plan contains the inherent weakness that would ultimately destroy Canada's time-honoured universal health care. Instead of leaving our health care at the mercy of privatization, a better solution would promote all governments' working together to rein in excessive costs whether they are for drugs, salaries, or monument-building.

The ultimate goal of a caring society is to promote a health care system that is medically effective, financially efficient, and universally accessible to all the population.

NOTES

1. Frank McGilly, *Canada's Public Social Services: Understanding Income and Health Programs* (Toronto: McClelland & Stewart, 1990), 238.

2. Ibid., 238.

3. *Canada Year Book 1988*, Catalogue No. 11-402 (Ottawa: Statistics Canada, 1989), 102.

4. Ibid., 100.

5. *Canada Year Book 1997*, Catalogue No. 11-402-XPE/1997 (Ottawa: Statistics Canada, 1997), 94.

6. *Canada Year Book 2001*, Catalogue No. 11-402-XPE (Ottawa: Statistics Canada, 2003).

7. *Canada Year Book 1997*, Catalogue No. 11-402-XPE/1997 (Ottawa: Statistics Canada, 1997), 95.

8. *Healthy Canadians: A Federal Report on Comparable Health Indicators, 2002* (Ottawa: Health Canada, 2002).

9. Kevin Gorey, Eric Holowaty, Gordon Fehringer, Ethan Loukkanen, Agnes Moskowitz, David Webster, and Nancy Richter, "An International Comparison of Cancer Survival: Toronto, Ontario and Detroit, Michigan, Metropolitan Areas," *American Journal of Public Health* 87 (July 1997): 1156–63.

10. Helen Rehr, "Health Care and Social Work Services: Present Concerns and Future Directions," *Social Work in Health Care* 10, 73 (Fall 1984).

11. Ibid. at 71.

12. Anne Crichton, David Hsu, and Stella Tsang, *Canada's Health Care System*: *Its Funding and Organization* (Ottawa: Canadian Hospital Association Press, 1989), 242.

13. *Canada Year Book 1996*, 95.

14. Herbert Weiner, "An Integrative Model of Health Illness and Disease," *Health and Social Work* 9 (1984): 253–59.

15. Ibid., 253–59.

chapter twenty

Evaluation in
Social Welfare

Grant Macdonald

INTRODUCTION

Social welfare in Canada is entering a new era of accountability, in which everyone, including politicians, planners, program managers, and front-line social workers, is being held accountable and responsible for their actions. The public is asking whether a reasonable return on its investment of monies spent on social welfare programs is being achieved. Also, fundamental questions are being asked: Are those who need these programs the ones actually using them? Are they run efficiently? Perhaps most important, do the programs achieve their intended objectives and, if not, how can those programs be improved? Are they having unanticipated negative impacts? These

kinds of critical questions about the value of our social programs are addressed through the process of evaluation.

Simply stated, *evaluation* in social welfare can be defined as the process in which services and programs are examined to determine whether they are needed and used, how well they are run, whether they meet their stated objectives, and whether they are worth their costs. Evaluations serve a variety of target audiences, each with its own stake in the service or program being examined. Some of these stakeholders include governments at all levels, actual and potential funders, the general public, the media, policy-makers, planners, academics, professional program staff, and clients. Each target audience has different information needs and its own reasons for wanting evidence of effective and efficient service delivery. No single evaluation could possibly serve the needs of all these constituencies.

We can examine the elements and context of evaluation using a schematic overview of social welfare activities. Figure 20.1 illustrates the RSO cycle (Resources–Services–Outcomes) or the key elements in the development and delivery of social welfare programs. While social welfare programs are often talked about as important in enriching a society's or a community's quality of life, or that of a specific subgroup of individuals, in reality, most if not all programs evolve from a general perception of a "social problem" and a belief that something should be done to either alleviate or prevent the problem. Unemployment insurance was developed as a response to the plight of unemployed individuals and the problems their families experienced. Addiction treatment programs have been established across Canada and have grown out of a concern for the millions of dollars lost to business and industry through alcohol and drug abuse. Of course these programs arise as well from the untold misery of the families of those addicted. Similarly, children's aid societies developed to protect children at risk, programs for unwed mothers are intended to help resolve their problems and support them, and specialized programs are planned to help new immigrants adjust to Canadian society.

Social welfare programs and services evolve from a collective sense that there is a social problem that must be dealt with. Figure 20.1 illustrates that, in response to this perception of a social problem, funds collected either through our tax system or

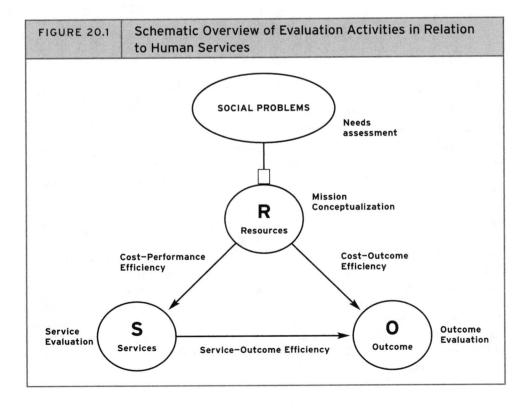

| FIGURE 20.1 | Schematic Overview of Evaluation Activities in Relation to Human Services |

through voluntary donations are dedicated toward social programs designed to deal with those perceived problems. These financial "resources" are managed ideally in accordance with the programs' stated mandates or purposes. Typically controlled by boards, executive directors, managers, and/or planners, this sector makes decisions about how to allocate these resources responsibly to achieve the programs' stated objectives.

Frequently, most of these funds support "services" delivered to clients, often by social workers or other helping professionals as in the case of a social agency. These social workers, governed in part by their professional codes of ethics, seek to achieve specific "outcomes" with their clients. They monitor these outcomes either routinely or as part of a formal evaluation to determine the degree to which the agency has achieved its mandate for the service. Is the service doing what it is supposed to do? Finally, based on the results of these assessments, the boards, managers, or planners complete the cycle by refining future allocations of resources either to improve the delivery of their services or attain the intended outcomes. This process of allocating resources to services to achieve desired outcomes will be referred to as the RSO cycle.

At various points in the RSO cycle, different types of evaluation activities can be carried out. These activities and their relation to the stages of the RSO cycle are also illustrated in Figure 20.1. The major categories of evaluation activities are (1) needs assessment, (2) mission conceptualization, (3) service evaluation, (4) outcome evaluation, and (5) cost–outcome efficiency.

Needs Assessment

The first level of analysis is a *needs assessment*. This level explores the need for a potential or already existing program

within a community. In the case of such an assessment conducted before the establishment of a proposed program, one would want to conduct it to confirm that a social problem that needs to be addressed does indeed exist and that existing community resources are inadequate to meet that need. This type of needs assessment might involve a survey to determine the extent and seriousness of the perceived problem, as well as a review of the community resources that might deal with various aspects of the problem. When examining the delivery of services, it is often helpful to examine the degree to which services are integrated, continuous, accessible, and accountable (Gilbert and Terrell 2002).

In examining an existing program, a needs assessment should consider who the proposed clients are, compared to who is really being served by the program. Are services offered in any way discriminatory based on age, disability, gender, race, ethnicity, religion, sexual orientation, or socioeconomic background? Sometimes a program developed to help one group in need ends up serving another. Those in need may not be aware of the program, or perhaps the service lacks accessibility owing to its location, hours of operation, lack of wheelchair access, and so on. Other factors might include other agencies' or services' reluctance to refer their clients or possibly the reluctance of a "gatekeeper" of the service to admit these clients for whatever reason.

For example, in the early 1970s in Ontario, a network of detoxification centres was set up to serve the needs of "skid-row" alcoholics. It was felt that these programs would serve as an alternative to jail and would be a more humane and treatment-oriented way of dealing with "revolving-door skid-row" alcoholics. However, an evaluation study found that in fact only two out of every five admissions to the detoxification centres were made by police, and almost half of the clients had not been arrested for public drunkenness in the past year (Annis, Giesbrecht, Ogborne and Smart 1979). Many of the clients had intact marriages and nearly half had stable accommodation and steady employment records. In short, the detoxification centres were not serving their intended clients.

Thus, needs assessments are helpful in establishing whether existing programs are indeed meeting the needs of those people they are intended to serve. They are also used to determine whether there is an appropriate blend of human services for a given community and to identify important areas where there are gaps in services. Needs assessments are central elements of program planning and are frequently used to justify requests for new funding or continued funding of programs.

Mission Conceptualization

The activities associated with resource allocation are guided by one's perception of the "mission" or goals of a given human service program. Goals are simply a statement, usually in quite general terms, about the desired qualities that a program seeks to achieve in the welfare of the individuals it serves (Rossi, Freeman, & Lipsey 1999).

For example, one of a child welfare agency's goals might be to protect children from physical, emotional, and sexual abuse, and neglect. Having stated goals is important since they help to begin to answer the question "What is this program or service supposed to do?" (Chambers 1999). All aspects of any program, including its personnel, structure, process, and outcome, can be examined and evaluated to determine whether these elements serve the program's goals. However, while goals are necessary and helpful in articulating desired ends, they are inadequate in evaluating whether or not these ends have been achieved.

Program objectives must be used in conjunction with program goals. Objectives differ from goals in that they constitute specific statements about desired outcomes expressed in measurable terms (Chambers 1999). Ideally, objectives relate to goals and are stated in such a manner that efforts made to implement them can be measured objectively. For example, a school program might have as an objective "to reduce the incidence of reported pregnancy of students in west-end schools."

Chambers (1999) recommends four criteria that might be useful in assessing the merits of objectives: (1) clarity; (2) measurability; (3) manipulability; and (4) concern with ends, not means to ends.

By *clarity* he means that there is consensus about the meaning of the terms used in the stated objectives. Terms such as child abuse, family violence, or racism can be defined in dozens of ways, and they mean different things to different people. Thus terms used in statements of objectives must be clearly defined.

Objectives must also be *measurable*. They enable evaluators and administrators to know when in fact they are achieving objectives.

Manipulability refers to the achievability of objectives. Objectives should be expressed in ways that convey the belief that they can be achieved.

Finally, according to Chambers, objectives should be conceived in terms of *ends, rather than means to ends*. Here is an objective expressed in terms of means, rather than ends: "The objective of the program is to provide 10 sessions of supportive counselling to single adolescent mothers." Compare this with this objective expressed in terms of ends: "The objective of the program is to increase the self-esteem of single adolescent mothers who have been identified as 'high risk' by Children's Aid and increase the parenting skills of these mothers."

In summary, the process of allocating resources to programs and services is done in order to achieve or meet certain goals and objectives. But how well are these goals and more specific program objectives articulated? Is the mission of the organization or social program conceived clearly enough and operationalized so that the program itself can be evaluated? Part of any evaluator's responsibility is to analyze how the mission of the service is conceptualized. Evaluators first need to know what results an organization is trying to achieve, if they are going to try to determine how well the organization has achieved them. As part of this mission evaluation, an evaluator will want to examine the program's objectives to assess their clarity, measurability, manipulability, and their concern with ends, rather than means.

Service Evaluation

Service evaluation involves the monitoring, measurement, and evaluation of services delivered to the intended targets of social programs. It is an examination of the service delivery process as distinct from its outcome, or as an examination of the means as opposed to the ends. Essentially service evaluation examines three things: What services were delivered by whom to whom? How well were those services delivered? Were the services delivered consistently in a standardized manner and according to predetermined standards and procedures?

Evaluators often examine records in order to establish a profile of who receives services. This may involve obtaining a picture of the types of clients a program or service serves in terms of sociodemographic characteristics and the nature of presenting problems. Typical variables that would be of interest are age, sex, marital status, ethnocultural background, and the nature and severity of problems. An

analysis of these variables regarding the distribution of these characteristics among the general population in the catchment area of the service will help identify who receives service and who does not.

Workload analysis can be part of service evaluation. It evaluates the allocation of workers' time to various activities. These analyses help program administrators monitor and assess the proportion of time devoted to the different categories of work, such as direct service, indirect service, community work, and operations/administration. These types of analyses can then lead to the development of standards or guidelines to help the workers allocate their time to best serve the organization's goals and objectives.

The monitoring of exactly what services are being delivered is increasingly done with the aid of computerized information systems. New software programs permit an analysis of staff workloads to help their managers have a better picture of how employees' time is being used.

The question of how well services are delivered is often dealt with by formal means that are articulated in a quality assurance program. *Quality assurance* is the process by which quality can be demonstrated through the development and articulation of desired, obtainable, and measurable standards; the assessment of the degree to which these standards have been achieved; and plans of action that are designed to correct any situations found to be substandard. A quality assurance committee generally oversees this process, composed of different stakeholders within the program.

One of the common methods of assessing the quality of interventions is *peer review* or *case review*. When the evaluation focuses on how well a service is delivered and the evaluation is conducted by other members of the same profession, it is generally referred to as a peer review process

(Osman and Shueman 1988). Typically it includes designating standards or criteria for the evaluation of workers' performance, monitoring on a regular or occasional basis the degree to which program workers adhere to standards, and delineating some set of procedures to remedy substandard performance. When the quality review focuses on cases as opposed to workers, it is generally called a case review.

Another important data source for assessing services delivery is client feedback. Clients can provide helpful information about which therapeutic techniques they believe enhance or hinder their progress so that practitioners can refine and improve their techniques. This kind of feedback can be obtained either informally as part of the client/worker therapeutic relationship or formally through the systematic administration of client feedback questionnaires. Client feedback should look at both the clients' perceptions of the service itself and their personal subjective assessments of how interventions have helped them. These kinds of feedback help practitioners evaluate their own behaviours, attitudes, and attributes as their clients see them.

Outcome Evaluation

Outcome evaluation involves a large variety of research activities that address the question "Does the program produce its intended outcome?" So outcome evaluations focus on the clients and on the impact services have on them.

There is a vast array of methods for assessing outcomes, and three general approaches are typical. The first compares those who receive services with those who do not. Here, of course, one hopes to find that those who received services are "better off" than those who did not. This *comparison method* may involve using a comparison group that may be waiting for help or may be receiving a different intervention or no intervention at all.

The second general approach is a *group method*, which involves monitoring only those who receive service. Most often this would involve gathering information before and after interventions. This broad approach uses a group of clients as their own controls and monitors changes in key indicators that the interventions target. Often data are collected at a number of points in the process, such as just before treatment, sometime during an intervention, at the completion of an intervention, and ideally at one or more follow-up occasions.

The third approach monitors treatment evaluation as an integral part of the intervention itself. Referred to as *case-level evaluations*, these obtain continuous feedback on the effects of interventions over time, through the repeated application of assessment measures (Grinnell, Williams, & Tutty 1997). The feedback gained from these assessments in turn helps shape the intervention strategy itself. Software programs have been developed that increase the efficiency, convenience, and accuracy of this kind of practitioner/researcher evaluation (Nurius & Hudson 1999).

Regardless of the broad approach one takes in conducting outcome evaluations, a number of alternative factors can account for the observed changes. Evaluations are not highly controlled experiments and they cannot be conducted in a laboratory. The severity of a problem that an intervention aims to address is influenced by many other factors besides the program itself.

Evaluators must concern themselves with a number of possible confounding variables or possible alternative explanations for the changes they observe. Simply because one group of clients improves does not necessarily mean evaluators can conclude that the program works or is effective. Other explanations for improvement or confounding factors are said to be threats to the internal validity of evaluations. By *internal validity* we mean the degree to which an evaluation design allows us to make causal conclusions about the impact of a program or intervention on client outcome. Possible threats to this internal validity come from many sources, and almost any social work research textbook discusses these in detail, as in Grinnell's (2000) *Social Work Research and Evaluation: Quantitative and Qualitative Approaches*.

Cost–Outcome Evaluation

Funders are not only concerned with the effectiveness of programs but also with their efficiency. Efficiency in the human services may be broadly defined as a program's ability to produce desired services or outcomes at the minimum cost or effort, according to a *cost–outcome evaluation*. In short, programs seek to achieve desired benefits for minimal costs. Evaluators therefore are concerned as much with efficiency as with effectiveness.

Cost–benefit evaluations can address three kinds of efficiency: cost–performance efficiency, service–outcome efficiency, and cost–outcome efficiency. These types of efficiency involve different sectors of the RSO cycle depicted in Figure 20.1. Cost–performance efficiency concerns the relation between resources and services; it focuses on those costs associated with producing the services. Cost–performance measures might include the average cost per interview or the per diem cost of services to clients. Analysis of the costs across a range of services can lead to a better understanding of the factors that influence unit costs of services.

Service–outcome efficiency deals with the relations between the amounts and the types of services in relation to the outcomes. This kind of evaluation allows for comparisons of amounts of service to achieve outcome objectives. For example, such an evaluation might look at the average number of interviews required to treat a drug addict successfully or the optimum length of time unemployed people use a program designed to help them develop skills to find work. Thus, service–outcome efficiency analysis involves examining service activities as they relate to outcome.

Finally, cost–outcome efficiency examines various kinds of costs in relation to outcomes. For example, how much does it cost to treat a cocaine abuser successfully on an in-patient basis compared to the cost to treat a similar case on an out-patient basis?

Cost–benefit analysis, then, allows the evaluator to examine the degree to which a program or service achieves its desired ends and at what cost.

QUALITATIVE VERSUS QUANTITATIVE APPROACHES TO EVALUATIONS

While it is important to determine whether or not programs are achieving their desired results, evaluation should go beyond simple verification and include elements of exploration and discovery. Programs may have unanticipated side effects that could have powerful negative impacts on clients or other stakeholders. Qualitative approaches to evaluation help to uncover the unexpected, unplanned factors that the more formal structured quantitative methods that focused on verification of desired outcomes can miss. While there has been a vigorous debate on the pros and cons of quantitative versus qualitative methods of evaluation, it is clear that each plays a distinctive role (Macdonald 2002).

Quantitative approaches are generally most appropriate when we want to determine whether a particular program achieves a clearly specified outcome. The approach focuses on key variables and typically watches for changes that can be attributed to the intervention. As noted earlier, internal validity is a strong concern here. Careful measurement is also critical. Standardized tests that can be used to measure changes in the attributes associated with positive and negative outcomes are often employed. In any event, quantitative approaches, although sometimes criticized for being used inappropriately, are valuable methods for establishing both the effectiveness and efficiencies of programs.

Evaluations should not be limited to examining outcomes but should also embrace process. Process evaluations examine the internal dynamics of a program and determine whether it is operating on schedule and doing what it is supposed to do (Yegidis & Weinbach 2002). They explore the "sequence of activities that a program undertakes to achieve its objectives, including all the decisions made, who made them, and on what criteria were they based" (Gabor & Grinnell 1994, 24). Process evaluations get at how and why interventions work or do not work. These evaluations examine how well programs actually conform to their plans or designs and help point the way to adjustments. The focus is on how an outcome is achieved or how a program gets the results it does. This type of evaluation is far more flexible, developmental, and inductive than the more formal structured-outcome evaluations. These kinds of evaluation can explore the complex dynamics of how a program operates day to day and seek an understanding of how the program works, its strengths, and its weaknesses.

Process evaluations typically call for the use of qualitative methodologies that can respond to the complex internal dynamics of an operating program. This approach calls for the researcher to get close to the issues at hand. Sometimes this includes face-to-face interviews with clients (past, present, or potential), program administrators and staff, board members, and even funders. The evaluator seeks to understand how the people and the situations influence the ways decisions are made and how the program operates. Sometimes participant observation is employed. Observational data can also help complement or confirm the conclusions obtained through the analysis of interview data.

Thus, both quantitative and qualitative approaches are important to successful evaluations. Each offers its own strengths and limitations, and each helps answer the questions "Does the program work?" and "How does the program work?"

CONCLUSION

The field of evaluation, as we have seen here, encompasses many kinds of activities and involves a wide range of stakeholders. It is a rapidly expanding field today, fuelled by new computer technologies that manage information and driven by demands for increased accountability in a time of fiscal restraint. The time has come when social welfare programs must produce evidence that their services are needed and used, that they are effective, that they are well run, that they achieve their stated objectives, and that they are worth their costs. These are the challenges that confront the evaluators of social welfare programs.

REFERENCES

Annis, H., Giesbrecht, N., Ogborne, A., & Smart, R. 1979. *The Ontario detoxification system*. Toronto: Addiction Research Foundation of Ontario.

Chambers, D. E. 1999. *Social policy and social programs: A method for the practical public policy analyst* (3d edn.). Needham Heights, MA: Allyn and Bacon.

Gabor, P. A., & Grinnell, R. M. 1994. *Evaluation and quality improvement in the human services*. Needham Heights, MA: Allyn and Bacon.

Gilbert, N., & Terrell, P. 2002. *Dimensions of social welfare policy*. Boston: Allyn and Bacon.

Grinnell, R. M. 2000. *Social work research and evaluation: Quantitative and qualitative approaches*. Itasca, IL: F. E. Peacock.

Grinnell, R. M., Williams, M., & Tutty, L. M. 1997. Case-level evaluations. In R. M. Grinnell (Ed.), *Social work research and evaluation: Quantitative and qualitative approaches* (pp. 529–559). Itasca, IL: F. E. Peacock.

Macdonald, J. G. 2002. The practitioner as researcher. In F. J. Turner (Ed.), *Social work practice: A Canadian perspective* (pp. 579–587). Scarborough, ON: Prentice-Hall of Canada.

Nurius, P. S., & Hudson, W. W. 1999. *Human services: Practice, evaluation and computers: A practical guide for today and beyond*. Pacific Grove, CA: Brooks/Cole Publishing.

Osman, S., & Shueman, S. A. July–August 1988. A guide to the peer review process for clinicians. *Social work*, 345–348.

Rossi, P., Freeman, H. E., & Lipsey, M. W. 1999. *Evaluation: A systematic approach* (6th edn.). Newbury Park, CA: Sage Publishing.

Yegidis, B. L., & Weinbach, R. W. 2002. *Research methods for social workers*. Toronto: Allyn and Bacon.

chapter twenty-one

Re-Conceptualizing Services for the Protection of Children

Ken Barter

INTRODUCTION

Child protection literature, research, and experience provide ample evidence that current child protection systems are struggling and fraught with difficulties and crises (Wharf, 2002; Barter, 2002, 2001a, 2001b, 2000; Berg & Kelly, 2000; Prilleltensky, Nelson & Peirson, 2001; Schorr, 1998; Waldfogel, 1998). Public inquiries into the abuse, neglect, and deaths of children in Canada (Office of the Chief Coroner for Ontario, 1997; Gove Inquiry, 1995; Aboriginal Committee Report, 1992) have alerted the public to two very important facts: one, that children are being maltreated and dying, and two, that serious flaws exist in the public children's protection systems. Such public inquiries tend to be put in place out of "moral panic" on society's part.

The public reaction creates the impression that something is being done to find out what went wrong and by whom. The focus tends to be narrow, dealing with specific events, and usually concludes with promising messages that conditions will be different with this or that change in the social system, or with this or that social policy put in place. The emphasis on risk assessment and risk management, concomitant with the maze of bureaucratic red tape, inflexible policies, and rigid procedures and protocols surrounding roles, responsibilities, and paperwork all seem set up to minimize the likelihood of scandal rather than out of genuine concern for the best interests of children and their families. Yet the maltreatment continues. As pointed out by Conway (2001) hardly a week goes by in Canada without some gruesome report of children's maltreatment.

What is happening that, despite research, public inquiries, literature, and feedback from parents and child protection authorities, leads to child protection systems' continuing to struggle and, in the opinion of some, totter on the verge of collapse? Does our society put more emphasis on trying to fix the system while skirting other fundamental issues such as poverty, discrimination, and other social injustices? Do we need to invest more in refining dominant thinking and practices as opposed to identifying alternatives? Should we concentrate on making changes within current rules and procedures rather than changing those rules and procedures? Are we facing a problem of resources or a problem of thinking and practising differently? Or are we making changes and improvements without addressing the system's underlying values and beliefs about what it really takes to promote and protect the health and well-being of our children?

With respect to these and other questions, one certainty stands out: everyone has opinions about child welfare, and about child protection in particular. However, despite consensus that something must be done, as poignantly pointed out by Berg and Kelly (2000), most people have no comprehensive ideas on what to do, and any discussion on the subject generally deteriorates into complaints about everybody else. This supports Meyer's (1984) comments that despite new legislation, programs, staffing arrangements, and practices, the child welfare field does not seem to be catching up with current knowledge, political awareness, and social change.

This chapter suggests that we re-conceptualize child welfare. This re-conceptualization would be based on the premise that before we change or abandon old concepts, we first develop new ones. New concepts would challenge our thinking, facilitate dialogue, create opportunities to address the protection of children, and form a basis on which we could establish programs and services. This chapter lays out the context for why this re-conceptualization is necessary and suggests changes to begin the process of re-conceptualizing our practice.

THE CONTEXT

Barter (2002) suggests that "If we in Canada were assigned the task to deliberately design systems that would frustrate the professionals/para-professionals who staff it, anger the public who finance it, alienate those who require or need its services and programs, that would invest in reactive responses to cope with symptoms of problems as opposed to being proactive, systems whose mandate is not shared and embraced by other public child serving organizations, and systems that would serve to be the scapegoat and bear the brunt of public criticisms should a child be harmed in any way, we could not do a better job than our present children's protection systems" (p. 28).

This statement, albeit harsh, reflects reality, despite the dedication and commitment of the workers, supervisors, and administrators working within these systems. They are assigned responsibility for legislative services and programs to promote and protect children's health and safety, yet they lack the necessary public finances and support to do so. They work in systems that endeavour to cope with multi-dimensional crisis (Barter 2000) in a reactive fashion and with little investment in prevention and early intervention (Prilleltensky et al., 2001).

Currently society emphasizes risk assessment and risk management in trying to make the future predictable in terms of abuse and neglect. This approach attempts to bring about consistency in investigations and decision-making in order to defend interventions with children and families rather than actually justifying the interventions that are deemed necessary (Wharf 2002, Barter 2002). This consistency and defensiveness have created organizational climates that are driven more by rules and procedures than by clinical and professional concerns. What is really taking place in the lives of the majority of families who come to the attention of child protection systems is being skirted—injustices associated with poverty, violence, isolation, discrimination, homelessness, and loss of hope and opportunities. In Canada, "Child welfare policy represents a reflection of the consequences of a society that has consistently shrunk from the task of distributing power and income between men and women, between races, and between classes in a fair and equitable fashion" (Wharf, 1993, p. 211).

These injustices and policies reflect contempt for poor people, undervaluing and not investing in caring and parenting, the state's unwillingness to provide adequate support services to compensate for family breakdowns, and attitudes that encourage ongoing racism, ageism, ableism, and ethnocentrism. Children and families who need protective intervention services, as well as those public child welfare systems that are delegated the responsibility to provide the same, are seriously affected by these attitudes. In many respects both the service provider and the service recipients are in comparable positions, both feeling the same sense of alienation and powerlessness. As Callahan (1993) suggests: "Child welfare organizations and practitioners are treated much like the children and families they serve. On one hand, they are often pilloried in the press and public forums when something goes amiss: a child under their care is abused or killed, or parents accuse workers of acting precipitously in apprehending their children. On the other hand, they are chronically neglected most of the time. The daily work of child welfare takes place without notice but often under trying conditions with limited resources" (p. 64).

For families, alienation and powerlessness create climates in which affection withers into hostility, discipline turns into abuse, stability dissolves into chaos, and love becomes neglect (Schorr, 1998). These settings are common in those families who come to the attention of child protection authorities. They are families struggling with the many difficulties associated with poverty and oppression. They are families who need assistance as much as, if not more than, their children need protection. Within child welfare organizations, such conditions create settings in which creativity withers into conformity, idealism turns into cynicism, collective sharing dissolves into turf protection, and critical questions, challenges, and new ideas are often feared and avoided (Barter, 2003). Critical dimensions develop out of such circumstances—low worker morale, fears of liability and prosecution, the lack of experienced and trained social workers, inadequate financial and human resources to respond to demand, the adversarial process of investigation, a constituency of children's protection colleagues who cling to traditional approaches, and the overall residual approach to children's protection. Many of these elements surfaced in the child welfare project conducted by the Canadian Association of Social Workers (CASW, 2003).

There is a consensus for change. Evidence suggests that public child welfare agencies can no longer carry out their mandate of protection and services without an investment in prevention and early intervention. Nor can they assume responsibility for the care and custody of children any longer in a foster care system where resources are limited or not available. They can no longer provide counselling and supportive services in a framework of poverty, and they can no longer present an image to the community and the children and families they serve that they are in a position of power and influence to adequately fulfill a protection mandate alone (Schene, 1996; Hooper-Briar, 1996).

These agencies find themselves in a difficult bind. Public expectations regarding children and their families are high. The statutory duties to prevent and detect child abuse, to investigate allegations of such abuse and neglect, to work in assisting and supporting families in order to prevent further abuse and neglect, and to assume responsibility for parenting children who have been removed from their families because of the severity of their abuse and neglect take place at the expense of any of the others listed. This leaves the agencies and the workers vulnerable. They are then criticized for either intervening too soon, or, in the event of a child's being hurt, for not intervening soon enough.

There has to be a better way.

We can assume several certainties when it comes to finding a better way. For one thing, we do not lack knowledge. The needs of children are widely known and accepted in our society. Those needs begin before birth, with a healthy, knowledgeable mother who has the personal and environmental resources that facilitate caring, love, support, encouragement, and health. Following birth, children need the basics of attachment, love, continuity of care, acceptance, relationships, safe environments, education, health care, and resources. All of

these contribute significantly to their maximum physical, emotional, social, and psychological development.

We also know in Canada that, despite efforts on the part of the federal, provincial, and municipal governments to restructure themselves in response to a global economy, demographics, political uncertainty, and technological advances, many Canadian children and their families are struggling to maintain their health and well-being. Child and family poverty continues to be a critical problem; child abuse and neglect statistics are astounding; the number of children coming into the care of the state is increasing in significant numbers; substitute care resources are limited and in crisis; children and families are relying on food banks in growing numbers; there continues to be little investment in prevention and early intervention; violence in families, schools and communities is a real concern; power imbalances that hurt women, children, youth, and minority groups continue; and pervasive negative public attitudes continue towards poor and disadvantaged citizens. These social injustices and the absence of political will and leadership to invest in Canada's children in ways that affect them meaningfully are well documented in the literature (Trocmé, et al., 2001; Conway, 2001; Prilleltensky, et al., 2001; Pulkingham & Ternowetsky, 1997; Campaign 2000, 1998, Ross, Shillington & Lochhead, 1994).

We also know for certain what makes for successful programs and services in working with children and families. For example, Schorr (1998) identifies several attributes of successful programs. She states: "Practitioners know that effective programs are characterized by flexibility, comprehensiveness, responsiveness, front-line discretion, high standards of quality and good management, a family focus, community rootedness, a clear mission, and respectful, trusting relationships" (p. 18). These attributes are very much a part of Family Resource Programs Canada's operating principles in its community and family resource centres throughout the country. However, the same principles underlying family resource programs, which we know to be effective in working with families, create tensions within child welfare systems (MacAulay, 2002; Barter, 2002, 2003).

These tensions are well known. The paradox is that even though research supports the attributes and principles underpinning the effective programs, child protection systems are unfortunately organized and structured in such a way as not to take them into account in providing protective intervention services. Workers within these systems often find themselves in positions of doing more judging than helping, more investigation than relationship-building. They are busier following rules and protocols than creatively intervening and taking risks, relying more on tools and instruments than on professional integrity and assessments, attending more to the needs of the organization than to families and children's needs, and reacting more often after family breakdowns than intervening to prevent those breakdowns. It is important to find a common ground (MacAulay, 2003).

Another well-known certainty affects child welfare services and it is very much a women's issue (Hutchison, 1992). Some observers estimate that some 70 percent (Swift, 1995) of direct service work in Canadian child welfare is provided by women. The caring, stress, and responsibility attached to child protection work carry considerable implications for these women, given that the caring functions are not necessarily valued in a patriarchal society. Under this certainty, child welfare work has not been afforded the recognition and status it so justly deserves. Child welfare is also a women's issue in that mothers comprise most child protection caseloads. They are the persons ultimately held accountable for the protection of their children. Even when men are the perpetrators of maltreatment, women are held accountable for controlling the maltreating behaviour.

These mothers and their children also rank the highest in terms of poverty. Many are single and alone and are members of racial minorities (especially First Nations and black in origin), and the majority lack sufficient resources and support to care for themselves and their children. These mothers find themselves in situations where they not only neglect, abuse, and fail to protect themselves but they have to make choices about what to neglect. As a result of some of these tough choices, their children end up neglected and abused.

There is also certainty and knowledge that the community's or public's role with respect to social injustices and the protection of children seems to end with their funding public child welfare systems and employing professionals and paraprofessionals to provide the mandated services. The community tends to abdicate its responsibility to formal, public child-serving systems and professionals. In so doing, organizational and professional responses to social problems have tended to focus more on problem-solving personal troubles without devoting the necessary attention to public issues. Abdicating responsibility to service organizations and professionals enhances their authority and power and leaves citizens and their communities in the background. The power of the community to act is weakened as a result (Barter, 2001a).

These known certainties suggest the importance of shifting paradigms. Knowledge well grounded in research, literature, and experience not only suggests there has to be a better way but also raises critical questions. For example, is the status quo with respect to child protection services and organizations acceptable? Is it important that child-serving organizations collaborate with respect to their child protection? Do primary prevention and early intervention and outreach services use most of the resources within child protection organizations? Is the general community informed and involved in child protection organizations? Are structural dimensions such as poverty, discrimination, violence, and social injustices important aspects of the work being done in child protection? Is child welfare sufficiently defined?

Responding to these and other critical questions will help identify what we know as well as tease out those assumptions on which we can agree in order to re-conceptualize child protection.

RE-CONCEPTUALIZATION

We know that the protection of children must move beyond mere protection in their own families to include their protection from the social, economic, and political forces that affect families and communities (Gil, 1998). To this end, the following definition of child welfare is proposed: "Child welfare is a collaborative process between community, families, and child-serving organizations and professionals. That process aims to reclaim these parties' strengths and capacities to develop the necessary preventative, supportive, supplementary substitute and advocacy services that respect children's rights to health and well-being and to actively seek to influence and change the social, economic, and political policies that affect children and their families."

Re-conceptualizing child welfare according to this definition elicits several critical ideas. First, services to children who require or need protective interven-

tion demand that many stakeholders collaborate in their approaches. Schools, mental health clinics, and correctional services are public child welfare systems. Similar to child protection agencies, they are financed by the public purse and are mandated to serve children in accordance with legislation.

However, there remains a perception that child protection is the sole responsibility of the child protection agencies. For example, many claim that child protection is the central function of the practice of child welfare (Kamerman & Kahn, 1990). This claim stems from the fact that child protection absorbs the bulk of agency resources, leaving little for prevention, early intervention, and family support services (Callahan & Wharf, 1993). It is important to shift from a primary emphasis on risk assessment and risk management (Wharf, 2002) as the driving forces for child welfare services. Although both are important, these concentrations should be a part of a full continuum of services designed to meet the needs of all children, families, and communities.

Suggesting that child welfare is a collaborative approach implies doing things differently and is usually based on a need to change the delivery and configuration of services (Graham & Barter, 1999; Barter, 1996). Current child protection caseloads involve crisis intervention, counselling, protection services, foster care, residential treatment, and court intervention, all geared to preventing further abuse and neglect.

Doing things differently would mean moving into prevention, early intervention, and outreach. That would mean working at the community-based level to promote collaborative initiatives in providing comprehensive emergency services, establishing drop-in centres, heightening community awareness, involving volunteers, promoting family resource centres, and creating opportunities for parent and family involvement. Primary prevention initiatives would include legislative advocacy, parent education, public school education, community service networks, parent advocacy groups, and life and family planning.

Second, the willingness to work differently suggests not only collaborative partnerships but innovation. The concepts within the proposed definition promote what Smale (1998) calls second order change. This implies innovation. It suggests introducing new practices, designing new methods of service delivery, approaching social problems differently, and developing models of best practice. Change on the other hand, "first order change," refers to changes within current rules, current organizational climates, and existing patterns of working relationships. Innovation means changing the rules, changing the system, and changing the nature of the relationship. We emphasize opportunities rather than problems when we are innovative; use collective intelligence; build on diversity and strengths; act upon knowledge, experiences, and research; and support the emergence of new systems that promote growth.

According to Hansenfeld (1983), innovation suggests an organization's adoption of a direction, service, or method of service delivery that is considered new. He further suggests that innovation "becomes radical when its implementation requires changes in the allocations of resources, the distribution of power, and the internal structure of an organization" (p. 220).

Change, on the other hand, refers to alterations in the allocation of resources to accommodate any shifts or adjustments within the organization. Change is not associated with doing business differently based on a rethinking of tasks, values, and priorities. Change identifies with the "fix-it" approach. There may be a program change or an adjustment in the method of delivery; however, the values underpinning the change are seldom challenged. In the case of innovation, values, roles, and expectations are critically challenged. Innovation means deviating from traditional ways of doing things and embracing new approaches. The context and knowledge base with respect to current child protection services, as well as the proposed definition of child welfare, suggest the appropriateness of radical innovation.

Radical innovation promotes moving the protection of children to the macro level (Barter, 2003; Baines, Evans, & Neysmith, 1993). Interventions at this level represent a shift in focus. This implies that the community must become a primary-client system. The social work profession will have to engage with the community this way to introduce change that will positively influence the lives of children and families who require protective interventions. Recognizing children in the context of the family and the family in the context of the larger social, economic, and political spheres highlights the importance of understanding "that many of the most critical problems that face families and their children are beyond individual control and reflect external conditions under which families live" (Goffin, 1983, p. 284). Making this shift is radical in that it is a direction that deals with the roots of many issues underpinning child protection work.

Issues of poverty, oppression, distribution of power and income, and social injustices tend to remain in the background in child protection interventions. Moving them into the macro arena demonstrates the importance of connecting personal troubles and public issues. It is no longer acceptable to deal with symptoms only (Carniol, 1995): hence the significance of advocacy as a third critical concept in the re-conceptualization of child welfare.

Advocacy activity is necessary to promote organizational changes, community development, and education to ensure programs and services are conducive to meeting the needs of children and their families (Herbert & Mould, 1992). Children have little power in society and they have a limited political voice. Action does not often follow the rhetoric about their best interests. An active advocacy role collaboratively driven by all stakeholders will provide children with a much needed voice in the political and policy arenas.

A fourth concept is the recognition and acknowledgment that services for vulnerable children must recognize their rights as well as their needs. Until we accept that children are equal persons under the law, society will continue to have no obligation to provide for their needs. Economic, social, and cultural rights include the right to education, to social supports, to having basic needs met, and to a sense of continuity and belonging in significant relationships. Endorsement of these rights is necessary to guide services, policy decisions, and child protection practices. Such support would mean agreement with a common base of values and beliefs about vulnerable children as well as an acknowledgment that children are persons with distinctive developmental needs and interests (Goffin, 1983; Ife, 1997).

Current practices do not necessarily reflect this agreement. Nor does the United Nations Convention on the Rights of the Child stand front and centre in child protection practice and policy. Mitchell (2003) puts forth a valid argument in writing that the convention is a framework from which to base theory and practice in working with children.

Talking about needs and rights in terms of children's health and well-being promotes their determinants of health. Protection is one key determinant in con-

junction with three others: relationships, opportunity and hope, and community (Guy, 1997). Referring to the determinants of health suggests the importance in child protection work of expanding interventions beyond the four walls of parenting to include advocacy, innovation, collaboration, early intervention and prevention, and community. It means taking both an ecological and a social justice perspective to child protection. Where the ecological perspective is based on principles of holism, sustainability, diversity, and equilibrium, the social justice perspective recognizes structural disadvantage, empowerment, needs, rights, and participation (Ife, 1995). All of these principles connect personal difficulties and public issues, assuming a dual response to working with children, parents, and citizens.

A dual response furthers wellness: "Family wellness is more than the absence of discord: it is the presence of supportive, affectionate, and gratifying relationships that serve to promote the personal development of family members and the collective well-being of the family as a whole" (Prilleltensky et al., 2001, p. 8). Wellness is an ecological concept and suggests the importance of social and economic supports. Thinking wellness means that poverty and oppression, the two fundamental barriers that interfere with the healthy development of individuals, must not remain hidden in terms of policies, practices, and planning. Wellness promotes the importance of ensuring interventions at the child and family level, the professional and organizational levels, and the community level.

Finally, the re-conceptualization does not define child welfare too narrowly. The proposed definition provides for a new vision for child protection services that gives priority to family-centred practice and building on community capacities.

Family-centred interventions bring in parents as collaborative partners where they are perceived as having strengths and capabilities and as they live in the context of their families, neighbours, and communities. Such practice brings with it a sensitivity to culture, coping mechanisms, the importance of parent-to-parent support, and involvement of parents in processes that affect them. A family-centred approach supports child-centred interventions.

Hooper-Briar and Lawson (1994) suggest that family-centred interventions connect children, parents, families, neighbours and communities. They put forth the premise that if interventions try to do things to, and for, children and youth, things that parents could do themselves if they had the necessary supports and resources, then those interventions are child-centred. By comparison, the family-centred approach offers a framework that assumes a greater ecological and social justice perspective in working with children, families, and communities.

Building community capacity to protect children is a people-centred approach. It emphasizes building capacity "of" people, "by" people, and "for" people (Barter, 2001c). "Of people" suggests enhancing, strengthening, and renewing people's capabilities, personal skills, self-knowledge, and self-awareness. This heightens their capacity for self-determination in identifying needs and interests that are important for them based on their own experiences. "By people" denotes commitment, engagement, application of enhanced capabilities, skills and knowledge, participation, collaboration, self-governance, and ownership. "For people" implies mobilization of capacities to take action and work toward change, equal opportunities, and access to resources that are sustained in order to promote collective good. Building capacities of people, by people, and for

people essentially means mutual investment and commitment by all the stakeholders to collaboratively work together. This partnership is paramount.

Community capacity building concentrates on bringing services to children and families out of the professional/bureaucratic model into the citizen/family/community model. The professional/bureaucratic environment is not necessarily the right environment for creating opportunities for caring, investment, and compassion to take place. Instead, this environment is governed by rigid policies and procedures, and the power remains with high-level bureaucrats who are isolated from the grassroots. The thinking at that level is compartmentalized and often reactive in its attempts to fix things. Here there is unwarranted political involvement, the system is closed and not necessarily user- or family-friendly, professional autonomy is stifled, and those who seek services or provide services are not seen as equal partners in the decisions.

In these environments the traditional top-down, programmatic, fix-it approach dominates—what is referred to as a knowing-in-action approach (Fabricant & Burghardt, 1992). This approach fails to acknowledge that many of the issues facing children and their families, as well as their communities, elude hierarchical and bureaucratic approaches. It is no longer appropriate to just throw money at problems that are only growing worse (Schorr, 1988). The evidence shows that "pouring money on the problem" has not helped, and our society can no longer blame citizens who require or need services for the iatrogenic practices of human service professionals and their organizations.

The citizen/family/community model suggests that public services and programs be more community-based. Communities would assume responsibility for this governance based on the goals and priorities they consider important for the well-being of their citizens. Expectations associated with community capacity-building include partnerships, interprofessional team work, client participation and involvement, staff empowerment, user-friendly services, primary prevention and promotion, community development, seamless systems of delivery, integrated programs and services, and community decision-making and governance.

Community capacity-building is about caring, respect, acceptance, and personal and social power. Instead of a knowing-in-action approach, community capacity-building is a reflection-in-action approach (Fabricant & Burghardt, 1992). Reflection is a process of dialogue, analysis, and consciousness-raising. This process creates opportunities to challenge thinking, develop relationships, revisit assumptions and beliefs, and consider new approaches to service delivery.

SUGGESTIONS FOR PRACTICE

The concepts associated with the proposed vision of child welfare suggest that services to children and families requiring or needing protective intervention services must embrace both the family-centred and the community capacity-building approaches. To do so, stakeholders must agree to embark on a journey to solicit the investment and commitment of all. Child welfare research, literature, and past experiences provide the knowledge base that indicates strongly that going it alone in this important and complex field of child protection is no longer acceptable (Barter, 1997).

This is a particularly important realization for the social work profession. The community recognizes and sanctions social work as responsible for child welfare services (Kadushin & Martin, 1988) and as a primary discipline in child welfare

(Meyer, 1984). As Callahan points out (1993), "Social work has little identity or authority as a profession apart from child welfare. It is the only field of practice consistently recognized as the domain of social work" (p. 66).

Social work defines itself according to its "strong commitment to values and justice" (Hoffman and Sallee, 1994, p. 38), its being a "value-driven profession" (Saleebey, 1994, p. 357) that is "founded on humanitarian and egalitarian ideals" (Canadian Association of Social Workers, 1994), with its primary purposes being "the enhancement of human well being and the alleviation of poverty and oppression" (Schriver 1998, p. 3). These ingredients commit the profession to making a difference in the lives of children and families requiring or needing protective intervention services. Social workers in public child welfare systems throughout Canada display their strength and resilience by continuing to persevere in the face of very difficult circumstances. As the Canadian Association of Social Workers child welfare research project indicates, these circumstances include poor morale, lack of organizational support, a shortage of qualified social workers, low pay, a high attrition rate, unmanageable workloads, and a major image problem in many communities. These are just a few of the many difficult challenges identified by the 1113 social workers across Canada who participated in the project. That the Canadian Association is involved in such research speaks to its dedication to working with child welfare authorities to bring about change in practices.

Social work is in a position to lead the way in creating opportunities for innovation. Re-conceptualizing child welfare is one dimension in facilitating such innovation. Several suggestions for social work practice stem from this re-conceptualization.

First, society's ongoing tolerance for major social injustices must become the focus of any work related to children's protection. We must accept and realize that children are a community responsibility. Their protection must be a collective concern. It is vital for child welfare work to embrace community capacity-building as a framework for practice. Families, public child-serving organizations and their professionals, as well as citizens, are each communities of individuals connected by relationships, difficulties, common challenges and vulnerabilities, and interdependence. A commitment to capacity-building requires that we rethink current practices to appreciate the significance of integrating individual and community practices—in other words, connecting personal difficulties and public issues. In making this connection we convey a particular response to personal troubles, with support, counselling, and membership and a response to a public issue that will build community capacity.

Integrating these two concepts suggests that social work should centre on a generalist rather than a specialist approach to practice (Ife, 1997). We must grasp a broader domain in which many institutions and professions invest in dealing with social problems and their solutions, only a small portion of which will be by the social workers already involved in child protection. Expanding to this broader domain supports in turn the importance of embracing an emancipatory approach to working with people (Dominelli, 2002). It moves beyond the traditional therapeutic and maintenance approaches. An emancipatory approach recognizes the critical reality that the protection of children touches on issues related to poverty, violence, diversity, health, justice, gender, and the community.

Second, collaboration and innovation require a willingness to relinquish power and control. We do this by operating on the understanding that individuals, families, and communities understand their own needs. Extending them the trust, respect, autonomy, and opportunity to develop this understanding is essential in child protection work. Parents and citizens are essential resources and partners. Public child welfare organizations must welcome them in a way that not only focuses on their problems or issues but taps into their creative talents and strengths. For example, are parents who require or need protective interventions today invited to participate in the policy and management decisions that affect them? Are they invited to act in advisory or evaluative capacities in terms of services delivered to them? Are interested citizens and volunteers asked to participate? Are child protection workers and agencies making such participation possible? We can create these opportunities for active participation only through a willingness to cross traditional professional and bureaucratic boundaries. Professionals, systems, and the people themselves need to be flexible so they serve can work collaboratively on their common issues of concern. This willingness means challenging traditional practices and assuming new roles and expectations. It means venturing away from familiar practices and moving toward non-traditional settings and hours of work.

Third, complexity, unpredictability, and uncertainty permeate much of the terrain of child protection work. The emphasis on evidence-based and competence-based approaches to practice do not necessarily encourage engaging and creating opportunities for change, particularly with citizens who are marginalized and excluded. Although the emphasis on evidence-based practice may have obvious attractions in terms of improving accountability and effectiveness of services, as well as having the potential to be cost-efficient, its contribution to tackling poverty and oppression and other social injustices is less clear (Stepney, 2000).

Evidence is not new to child protection work. Yet, despite efforts to address this evidence, for example, the child deaths and increases in child maltreatment, the situations for children and families and for workers in child protection systems have not dramatically changed. What has changed however is the current emphasis on rules, tools, techniques, and conformity to procedures and mechanisms for obtaining and measuring competencies. This emphasis seems to attempt to reduce the complex personal, professional, and social issues associated with child protection work to problems of bureaucratic administration. This approach reflects many of the criticisms and shortcomings of competency-based practice (Adams, 2002; Stepney, 2002, Rossiter, 2002).

Another suggestion for practice regarding a re-conceptualizing of child welfare is that we understand that, in the uncertain and complex work of child protection, relationships are what bring about change. Creating opportunities to build these relationships between professionals, organizations, citizens, and families who require protective intervention services is paramount. Accordingly, professionalism, reflective inquiry, creativity, and process are integral dimensions to practice. These priorities promote partnerships, capacity-building, empowerment, and collaboration.

A fourth suggestion for practice concerns the use of language. Child-protection families are most commonly referred to as "cases"; "Treating people as cases dehumanizes them" (Wharf, 2000, p. 132). Workers use the term to classify and categorize their practices for purposes of management control and administration. However, such language does little to treat children, parents, and families as citizens who have rights to services and basic needs. Labelling children and parents as cases demonstrates the same disrespect for them that using the term "clients" does. "Client," similar to "patient" and "customer," implies that the labelled person has less knowledge, information, expertise, or resources than the professional. Rather than being seen as an equal, a "client" denotes someone of concern who requires professional attention rather than someone who can make an individual contribution.

The re-conceptualization of child welfare advocates a change in approach that recognizes the people requiring or needing services, as well as the people providing services, as citizens, all with their own skills, resources, strengths, and vulnerabilities. The term "citizen" supports emancipatory practice. The person is seen in the context of the broader domain and individual and public issues. All these aspects are to be understood and connected, each doing its part in bringing about innovation. Many initiatives associated with the Community Action Program for Children (CAPC) use the term "participant" rather than "client." The term denotes equality among all those involved, both professionals and those being served.

Another language issue arises through use of the term "at risk." Swadener and Lubeck (1995) promote the alternative term "at promise." The notion of children and families being "at risk" perpetuates deficit-model assumptions and discourse that tend to locate problems or pathologies in individuals and families rather than in the institutions that create and maintain inequality. "At promise" conveys the importance of identifying many problems that parents and children face outside their families. It takes into account the larger contexts within which families struggle and where change is required both individually and structurally. Viewing children and families as "at promise" enhances the possibilities of constructing authentic relations in which all parties listen actively and learn from one another (Muluccio & Anderson, 2000; Waldfogel, 1998).

Abandoning "clinical" labels is equally important. Terms such as "behaviour disorder," "dysfunctional," "disruptive," and "disturbed" remain a part of practice language. According to Seita (2000), "These terms border on the derisive, are disrespectful of our children, focus on so-called weaknesses, fail to recognize the social context; and may contribute to negative, judgmental, and punitive practices by those in the child welfare field and by society in general" (p. 80).

A fifth suggestion for practice is that we place emphasis on the four key determinants of health: protection, relationships, hope and opportunity, and community. Interventions in child protection must be more holistic and wellness-oriented. A protective plan endeavours to prevent further abuse and neglect. Albeit this is critically important, it is equally important to ensure that this protective plan respects the children and their parents in their relationships, their opportunities and hopes, and their communities. These determinants require as much care in assessment as does the assessment of the risks, whether the intervention plan is either to remove risks or to remove the children. Current risk-assessment procedures and tools tend not to stress environmental influences and the critical dimensions associated with the four key determinants of health. These dimensions include income and social status, social support networks, education, employment/working conditions, social environments, physical environments, personal health practices and coping skills, health services, gender, and culture. The four key determinants of health are consistent with Seita's (2000) suggestion that a major shift in child welfare practices would result following the adoption of four key principles—connectedness (promoting close, positive relationships), dignity (courtesy, respect, and safety), continuity (ongoing belonging to a group, family, community), and opportunity (capitalizing on one's strengths and forming a personal vision). A reconceptualized child welfare would build practice principles to support the four key determinants of health for the health and well-being of children.

A final suggestion for practice is understanding that interventions to prevent further child neglect and abuse in families and communities, or stop it ever taking place, are interventions to curtail violence. Violence is a public health issue and should be defined as such. For example, the World Health Organization (2002) defines violence as "the intentional use of physical force or power, threatened or actual, against oneself, another person, or against a group or community, that either results in or has a high likelihood of resulting in injury, death, psychological harm, maldevelopment or deprivation" (p. 4). Si Kahn (1994) supports the idea of expanding the definition of violence when he suggests that society must appreciate that poverty is violent, oppression is violent, and most violent of all is the loss of hope. Categorizing violence in this way is appropriate for child protection given that the majority of parents and families who require or need protective intervention services live in poverty, are isolated, and struggle to find hope and meaning in their lives and those of their children.

The Canadian Incidence Study of Reported Child Abuse and Neglect (Trocmé et al., 2001) found that 58 percent of the substantiated cases of emotional maltreatment of children resulted from the children's exposure to family violence. Emotional maltreatment in this study was defined as acts or omissions by parents or caregivers that cause or could cause serious behavioural, cognitive, emotional, or mental disorders. Maltreatment of children through their exposure to family violence has increased dramatically in recent years and it presents a significant challenge to child protection agencies in their policies and practices as protective intervention services (Trocmé et al., 2001). Linking child protection and violence as concerns regarding the health and well-being of children and their families supports more than the significance of connecting personal troubles and public issues; it supports both family-centred and community capacity-building approaches to child protection work just as strongly. Making these fundamental connections is paramount in re-conceptualizing child welfare.

CONCLUSION

The re-conceptualization of child welfare proposed in this chapter recognizes that the protection of children must move beyond social workers. It should include parents, teachers, law enforcement officials, courts, mental health workers, public health workers, and other citizens. All have an important role to play. It is important to act upon the knowledge base we gain through research and experiences. This knowledge supports the concepts that pertain to the proposed re-conceptualization of child welfare and produces suggestions for innovations in practice. The challenge for social workers is to act on the knowledge that "there is a better way."

REFERENCES

Aboriginal Committee Report. (1992, October). *Liberating our children: Liberating our nations*. Report of the Aboriginal Committee, Community Panel, Family and Children's Legislation Review, British Columbia.

Adams, R. (2002). Social work processes. In R. Adams, L. Dominelli & M. Payne (Eds.), *Social work: Themes, issues and critical debates* (2d edn., pp. 249–266). New York: Palgrave.

Baines, C., Evans, P., & Neysmith, S. (Eds.). (1993). *Women's caring: Feminist perspectives on social welfare*. Toronto: McClelland & Stewart.

Barter, K. A. (1996). Collaboration: A framework for northern social work practice. In R. Delaney, K. Brownlee, & K. Zapf, (Eds.), *Issues in northern social work practice* (pp. 70–94). Thunder Bay: Centre for Northern Studies, Lakehead University.

Barter, K. (1997). Rethinking values and beliefs in child protection: A challenge for social work. *Child & Family: A Journal of the Notre Dame and Family Institute, 1.2*. 6–15.

Barter, K. (2000, Summer). Renegotiating relationships in child protection. *Canada's children*. Ottawa: Child Welfare League of Canada, 35–38.

Barter, K. (2001a, July–August). Building community: A conceptual framework for child protection. *Child Abuse Review: Journal of British Association for the Study and Prevention of Child Abuse and Neglect, 10.4.* 262–278.

Barter, K. (2001b). Services for vulnerable children: A conceptualization. In J. C. Turner &. F. J Turner (Eds.), *Canadian Social Welfare*. (4th edn., pp. 250–264). Toronto: Pearson Education Canada.

Barter, K. (2001c). *Capacity building as a core element of evaluation: A literature review.* Paper prepared for Population and Public Health, Atlantic Regional Office, Health Canada.

Barter, K. (2002, Spring). Enough is enough: Renegotiating relationships to create a conceptual revolution in community and children's protection. In *Canada's children*. Ottawa: Child Welfare League of Canada. 28–29.

Barter, K. (2003, Spring). Strengthening community capacity: Expanding the vision. *Relational Child and Youth Care Journal, 16.2.* 24–32.

Berg, I. K., & Kelly, S. (2000). *Building solutions in child protective services.* New York: W. W. Norton.

Callahan, M.. (1993). Feminist approaches: Women recreate child welfare. In B. Wharf (Ed.), *Rethinking child welfare in Canada* (pp. 172–209). Toronto: McClelland & Stewart.

Callahan, M., & Wharf, B. (1993). The case for removing child abuse and neglect investigations from the mandate of child welfare. In *Rethinking social welfare: People, policy, and practice* (pp. 87–108). Sixth Biennial Social Welfare Policy Conference, St. John's, NF.

Campaign 2000 (1998). *Child poverty in Canada: Report card 1998.* Toronto: Child Poverty Action Group.

Canadian Association of Social Workers (1994). *The code of ethics.* Ottawa: Canadian Association of Social Workers.

Canadian Association of Social Workers. (2003). *Child welfare project: Creating conditions for good practice.* Ottawa: CASW.

Carniol, B. (1995). *Case critical: Challenging social services in Canada.* Toronto: Between the Lines.

Conway, J. F. (2001). *The Canadian family in crisis.* (4th edn.). Toronto: James Lorimer & Co.

Dominelli, L. (2002). Anti-oppressive practice in context. In R. Adams, L. Dominelli, & M. Payne (Eds.), *Social work: Themes, issues and critical debates* (2d edn., pp. 3–19). New York: Palgrave.

Fabricant, M. B., & Burghardt, S. (1992). *The welfare state crisis and the transformation of social service work.* New York: M. E. Sharpe.

Graham J., & Barter, K. (1999). Collaboration: A social work practice method. *Families in Society: The Journal of Contemporary Human Services, 80.1.* 6–13.

Gil, D. G. (1998). *Confronting injustice and oppression: Concepts and strategies for social workers.* New York: Columbia University Press.

Goffin, S. G. (1983, April). A framework for conceptualizing children's services. *American Journal of Orthopsychiatry, 53.2.* 282–290.

Gove Inquiry (1995). *Matthew's story.* Ministry of Social Services, Victoria, B.C.

Guy, K. A. (Ed.). (1997). *Our promise to our children.* Ottawa: Canadian Institute of Child Health.

Hansenfeld, Y. (1983). *Human service organizations.* Englewood Cliffs, NJ: Prentice-Hall.

Herbert, M. D., & Mould, J. W. (1992, March–April). The advocacy role in public child welfare. *Child Welfare, LXXI.2.* 114–130.

Hoffman, K. S., & Sallee, A. L. (1994). *Social work practice: Bridges to change.* Toronto: Allyn & Bacon.

Hooper-Briar, K. (1996). Building new capacities for work with vulnerable children, youth, and families. In K. Hooper-Briar & H. A. Lawson (Eds.), *Expanding partnerships for vulnerable children, youth, and families* (pp. 352–361). Alexandria, VA: Council on Social Work Education.

Hooper-Briar, K., & Lawson, H. A. (1994). *Serving children, youth and families through interprofessional collaboration and service integration: A framework for action.* Oxford, OH: The Danforth Foundation and The Institute for Educational Renewal at Miami University.

Hutchison, E. D. (1992, February). Child welfare as a woman's issue. *Families in Society: The Journal of Contemporary Human Relations,* 67–78.

Ife, J. (1995). *Community development: Creating community alternatives: Vision, analysis and practice*. Melbourne, Australia: Longman.

Ife, J. (1997). *Rethinking social work practice: Towards critical practice*. Melbourne, Australia: Longman.

Kahn, Si. (1994). *How people get power*. Washington, DC: NASW Press.

Kamerman, S. B., & Kahn, A. J. (1990, Winter). If CPS is driving child welfare, where do we go from here? *Public Welfare*, 9–21.

Kadushin A., & Martin, J. A. (1988). *Child welfare services* (4th edn.). New York: Macmillan.

MacAulay, J. (2002). *Tensions and possibilities: Forging better links between family resource programs and child welfare*. Ottawa: Family Resource Programs Canada.

MacAulay, J. (2003). Searching for common ground: Family resource programs and child welfare. In B. Wharf (Ed.), *Community work approaches to child welfare* (pp. 163–180). Peterborough, ON: Broadview Press.

Meyer, C. H. (1984). Can foster care be saved? *Social Work, 29*. 499.

Mitchell, R. C. (2003). *Ideological reflections on the DSM IV-R*. Paper presented at the 7th International Child and Youth Conference, University of Victoria, B.C., August 20–23.

Muluccio, A. N., & Anderson, G. R. (Eds.). (2000, January–February) Future challenges and opportunities in child welfare. *Child Welfare, LXXIX.1.*

Office of the Chief Coroner for Ontario (1997). *The child mortality task force*. Toronto: Ontario Association of Children's Aid Societies.

Prilleltensky, I., Nelson G., & Peirson L. (2001). *Promoting family wellness and preventing child maltreatment: Fundamentals for thinking and action*. Toronto: University of Toronto Press.

Pulkingham, J., & Ternowetsky, G. (1997). The changing context of child and family policies. In J. Pulkingham & G. Ternowetsky (Eds.), *Child and family policies: Struggles, strategies, and options* (pp. 14–38). Halifax: Fernwood.

Ross, D. P., Shillington, R. E., & Lochhead, C. (1994). *The Canadian fact book on poverty*. Ottawa: Canadian Council on Social Development.

Rossiter, A. (2002). The social work sector study: A response. *Canadian Social Work Review, 19.2*. 341–348.

Saleebey, D. (1994, July). Culture, theory, and narrative: The intersection of meaning in practice. *Social Work, 39.4*. 351–359.

Schene, P. (1996). Innovative directions in child welfare. In K. Hooper-Briar & H. A. Lawson (Eds.), *Expanding partnerships for vulnerable children, youth, and families* (pp. 25–30). Alexandria, VA: Council on Social Work Education.

Schorr, L. B. (1988). *Within our reach: Breaking the cycle of disadvantage*. Toronto: Doubleday.

Schorr, L. B. (1998). *Common purpose: Strengthening families and neighborhoods to rebuild America*. New York: Anchor Books.

Schriver, J. (1998). *Human behaviour and the social environment: Shifting paradigms in essential knowledge for social work practice*. Toronto: Allyn & Bacon.

Seita, J. R. (2000). In our best interest: Three necessary shifts for child welfare workers and children. *Child Welfare, LXXIX.1*. 77–92.

Smale, G. G. (1998). *Managing change through innovation*. London: National Institute for Social Work.

Stepney, P. (2000). Implications for social work in the new millennium. In P. Stepney & D. Ford (Eds.), *Social work models, methods and theories* (pp. 9–19). Dorset: Russell House Publishing.

Swadener, B. B., & Lubeck, S. (1995). *Children and families "at promise."* Albany: State University of New York Press.

Swift, K. (1995, May/June). Missing persons: Women in child welfare. In S. Scarth, B. Wharf, & E. Tyrwhitt (Eds.), Changing the child welfare agenda: Contributions from Canada (pp. 486–502). *Child Welfare, LXXIV.3.* Washington, DC: Child Welfare League of America.

Trocmé, N., MacLaurin, B., Fallon, B., Daciuk, J., Billingsley, D., Tourigny, M., et al. (2001). *Canadian incidence study of reported child abuse and neglect.* Ottawa: Health Canada, Government of Canada.

Waldfogel, J. (1998). *The future of child protection: How to break the cycle of abuse and neglect.* Cambridge, MA: Harvard University Press.

Wharf, B. (1993). Rethinking child welfare. In B. Wharf (Ed.), *Rethinking child welfare in Canada* (pp. 210–230). Toronto: McClelland & Stewart.

Wharf, B. (2000). Cases or citizens? Viewing child welfare through a different lens. *Canadian Social Work, 2.2.* 132–139.

Wharf, B. (Ed.). (2002). *Community work approaches to child welfare.* Peterborough, ON: Broadview Press.

World Health Organization. (2002). Violence: A universal challenge. *World Report on Violence and Health.* Geneva, Switzerland. 1–11.

chapter twenty-two

Youth and
Youth Services

Teri Kay

Melanie Cohen

INTRODUCTION

Adolescence is one of the most chaotic stages of life. It is marked by rapid body changes both anatomically and physiologically (Borhek 1988). According to Erik Erikson (1963), identity formation is the most important developmental task of adolescence.

Included in the general framework of adolescence is the development of complex problem-solving skills and values that are learned in part, through peer group interaction (Hartup 1983). More and more youth rely on their peers for support that the family previously provided (Douvan and Adelson 1966). It is a time of exploration for friends who will be trustworthy and loyal. It is also a time of conformity as the young people search for acceptance as members of the group. Interests, use of language, hairstyle, and dress are among the characteristics teens share and learn from one other. Peer groups also provide the opportunity to experiment with new behaviours and assuming adult roles in a context that facilitates their individual development of self-identities and sense of self-worth (Erikson 1963).

Peer relationships and the support they provide can enhance self-esteem and well-being. Conversely, rejection by friends can create adjustment problems, anxiety, or involvement in socially inappropriate or deviant activities. Although inconclusive, studies show that teens who smoke cigarettes, or use alcohol and other drugs, usually have friends who engage in the same activities (Dingis and Oetting 1993).

So peer groups can influence both positive and negative behaviours. Families, too, play a major role in influencing teenagers' behaviour both positively and negatively. We see many "troubling trends" in our society regarding marriage and family life. In general, the number of divorces, remarriages, single-parent families, teenage pregnancies, poor families, families affected in some way by AIDS (Acquired Immune Deficiency Syndrome), and families reporting family violence have all increased. These statistics indicate a decline in the quality of family life, affecting our children and youths most profoundly.

Complex family structures are emerging to challenge our traditional definition of family and test our ability to search for the strengths, the necessary supports, and the areas of prevention to enable us to treat some of these problematic issues. What are some of the issues facing youth today?

THE CHANGING FAMILY

Each year a growing number of parents face what may be the greatest test of their parenthood—helping their children deal with the breakup of the family unit. The parents of teens know the unique challenge of parenting this age group, and breakup can have a powerful impact on teenage children. The effects can include periods of mourning and sadness, tiredness, lack of concentration and poor school performance, angry outbursts, and challenges to parental authority.

As with a child of any age, it is important not to involve the teenager in the parental dispute. To do so invites the teenager's resentment and bitterness toward both parents. What is clear from the research (Wallerstein and Blakeslee 1989) is that the post-divorce relationship

between the parents becomes the most important feature in shaping the emerging identity of the adolescent. Children of all ages fare much better when their parents can set aside their spousal differences and cooperate around the children. Allowing teens to make choices about visitation, holidays, primary residences, and meeting new mates improves the chances of building a new and viable family structure.

In most communities across Canada, family service agencies offer programs for the changing family. They range from education and information about the process, alternative-dispute resolution, and the impacts on children and youth, to counselling programs for parents and children, grandparents, and step-parents. What to Tell the Kids, Successful Step-Parenting, Shared Parenting, Adolescence: A Trying Time for Teens, The Importance of Grandparents, and Single Again are examples of the programs these agencies offer. Family Service Canada generally accredits service agencies and they provide their services on a sliding-fee scale.

Inquiries about discussion groups with other teens should also be made at schools, religious institutions, and community associations. If they do not exist, parents could request that they be created.

LIFESTYLE CHOICES

During this time of rapid change and growth, teens are also balancing a number of their own lifestyle choices. These choices can have direct impacts on their futures and on their present lives.

For many teens, adolescence is a time of exploration and a healthy search for identity and a future career path. But those living in marginalized environments often find it a time marked by vulnerability and destructive behaviour. Too many teenagers live in environments characterized by poverty, abuse, and family breakdown. Any one of these factors can lure teens to abuse drugs and/or alcohol. The substance abuse is a problem not only for marginalized youth but also for youth in general. According to *U.N. Chronicle* (1998), which quotes from the *Report of the International Narcotics Control Board* for 1997, "Drug abuse is now emerging as a part of a youth subculture that is quickly spreading around the globe a benign image of drugs. Drugs such as methamphetamine, 'ecstasy' and other amphetamine-type stimulants—drugs closely associated with the 'rave' or dance scene are growing in popularity."

The false comfort of drugs can have disastrous results not only psychologically and physically but also through the users' increased exposure to major health risks such as AIDS.

In April 1998 the United Nations International Drug Control Program (UNIDCP) sponsored a five-day get-together for youth in Banff, Alberta. More than 150 young people from 33 countries met and discussed their experiences and shared their ideas about drug prevention. While some focused on the problem of marginalized youth, others saw drugs as part of current youth culture, an image aided by music, television, and movies.

One of the major outcomes of this conference is a developing global network made possible through the proliferation of computers and the worldwide internet. Equally important is the notion that youth need to be heard and empowered to become part of the solution rather than simply the problem.

Schools are the obvious venue for drug and alcohol prevention programs. While many schools across the country have such programs, others need to be supported and encouraged. Family Life Education programming is perceived as one of the most effective means of prevention. While some schools offer such courses, parents and youth are encouraged to advocate for changes to the curriculum that would also include mandatory drug and alcohol prevention programs.

Excellent films have been created. One of these is an animated cartoon, *Goldtooth*, produced by the Canadian non-governmental organization Street Kid International (SKI). It is an action-adventure film about substance abuse. *The Karate Kid*, another SKI film, deals with health issues such as HIV/AIDS. These two cartoons help both youth workers and teens work together.

In a similar vein, increasing numbers of youth are involved in gambling. Based on the South Oaks Gambling Screen (SOGS), 4 percent of adolescents between the ages of 12 and 19 in Ontario are probable pathological gamblers and another 33 percent have some gambling problems. In a study of 702 adolescents between the ages of 15 and 18 years, correlates of problem gambling include school difficulties, regular drug use, delinquency, parental gambling, and being male (Insight Canada Research Survey 1993). Casino gambling is restricted to people over the age of 18 years, making it an adult activity; however, this fact has not deterred or prevented teens from gaining access to gambling establishments. Many young people report they can enter casinos with relative ease, and 79 percent reported that their parents knew about their gambling (Acuri et al. 1985). Adults in general do not consider gambling a dangerous activity for adolescents, and the very fact that our society views gambling as a pleasurable adult activity adds to its attraction for many young people. Some gambling activities such as sports pools and raffles do not even attempt to restrict young people.

The level of involvement of adolescents in gambling, the growth of gambling activities in Canada, and the lessons learned from the literature all support the need for education and prevention programs in schools. Adults who work with young people are aware that gambling does not have the recognition that alcohol or drug abuse do, yet the incidence of cross-addiction has been documented as high; substance abusers are about six times as likely to be addicted to gambling as the general population (Gambino, Fitzgerald, Shaffer, and Renner 1993).

Addressing substance abuse and gambling problems in adolescence requires partnerships. Schools have neither the time nor the skill to develop effective experiential programs. By virtue of their training social service providers can bring such an approach into classroom learning and could usefully bridge the two systems. The Toronto District School Board (TDSB) and the Jewish Family and Child Service (JF and CS) have formed such a partnership. Classroom presentations are jointly created from input from the teachers and the students and facilitated by an outreach social worker from the TDSB or JF and CS.

Schools throughout the country have developed peer-mentoring programs with social service agencies. These programs recognize the importance of youth's talking with youth and help identify young people at risk. Programs such as conflict resolution are gaining momentum, too, as schools struggle to curb violence on school grounds and in the classrooms. Youth involvement is essential to the success of these programs.

Most communities offer community information services. The Kids Help Phone, for example, can be reached through 1-800-668-6868 or **http://kidshelp.sympatico.ca/** and is available across Canada.

Most communities also offer 12-step programs for teens and parents through Alcoholics Anonymous and Gamblers Anonymous.

LEAVING HOME

Leaving home is often associated with obtaining higher education, training, or job enhancement; however, some young people leave home because their parents can no longer care for them or because their family situations are intolerable. Many teens cannot live independently, and the need for substitute care is obvious. Their issues require a variety of support systems, including specialized foster homes, group homes, children's mental health centres, hostels, and maternity homes.

Most communities have some of these services, and some communities have set up a point of centralized access to these resources through children's mental health centres. Other services can be accessed through the Children's Aid Societies and family service organizations. Unfortunately, more and more youths are finding their way to the streets and becoming part of Canada's growing number of homeless. These adolescents are without the benefit of adult guidance and must make decisions on their own at a time when they are ill-equipped to do so. These young people face severe challenges, including exploitation and abuse. While overall statistics are scant, it is believed that a disproportionate number of gay and lesbian youth are part of the army of street youth. These teens are homeless because they are no longer welcome at home, not by choice.

Street youth usually rely on the public for their day-to-day subsistence. They beg, scrounge, wash car windows, and perform other "services" that consumers generally do not appreciate. Street youth are quite likely at the highest risk of being abused, developing health problems, using drugs, and becoming involved in criminal activities.

Services for street youth are mainly non-traditional. Youth organizations often reach out to this population by placing youth workers on the streets. As street youth are primarily a problem of urban centres, cities such as Toronto, Calgary, Edmonton, and Vancouver have specialized programs that work in conjunction with hostels and youth police.

The Protection of Children Involved in Prostitution Act, introduced in Alberta on February 1, 1999, is the first attempt to allow police and social workers to remove girls younger than age 18 from the streets for 72 hours with or without their consent. In addition, the law allows for fines of up to $25 000 and jail terms of two years less a day for pimps caught with juvenile prostitutes.

In the first 10 weeks of the law's enforcement, the number of juvenile prostitutes on the streets of Calgary dropped dramatically. Other provinces are watching the results very closely, and similar laws may be enacted in Ontario and British Columbia (*Toronto Star* 1999).

Teens involved in criminal behaviour are dealt with under the Young Offenders Act (R.S.C. 1985). The Act covers children from ages 12 to 17 who commit offences and allows for youth to be treated and rehabilitated in specialized institutions called training schools. Specialized Juvenile Courts hear the offences and determine their outcomes. Unlike adult courts, Juvenile Courts emphasize rehabilitation. The Act is a federal statute but the provincial governments administer and operate the facilities required to assist in the process. Although programs may vary, all are designed to meet the education, recreation, and counselling needs of youth.

NEWCOMERS

In 1998, the Department of Citizenship and Immigration Canada, Settlement Directorate, Ontario Region, conducted a province-wide consultation on the needs of newcomers to the country. The consultation concluded that families and children need greater access to settlement services. The consultation has since resulted in a pilot project in Toronto, which began in mid-1999 and concluded in mid–2000, a partnership between the Toronto District School Board and the community settlement agencies, which are funded by the federal government.

The project intended to expand access to traditional settlement services by moving them into the elementary and secondary schools, which acknowledge that newcomer families require outreach services. Many of these families do not access traditional agencies.

Most communities in Canada today have a definite multicultural flavour. One principal in Toronto recently remarked that 77 different languages are spoken in his school. The related challenge for families, schools, and social workers is enormous, particularly when prevention programs are being eliminated.

In addition to issues of normal adolescent development, students from other countries face language and cultural differences, and perhaps unfamiliar vocation and education choices. Some may have learning difficulties; others may be traumatized by coming from countries where they or their families endured discrimination and/or terror.

In addition to learning new language skills and finding employment, families often find their children adjust more quickly and easily to Canadian daily life than the adults do. Family conflicts can arise as the adolescent opts for the norms and values of the prevailing youth culture rather than that of the family's traditions. Teens' language skills often develop beyond those of their parents and can complicate family matters even further. Frequently, the teens are asked to take on the role of translator to help the family acquire needed services. Neither their parents nor the teens themselves always welcome this role reversal. Teachers struggle to understand issues affecting these students, but the influx of so many different cultures makes their job overwhelming.

The initiative of the Ministry of Culture and Immigration, therefore, holds great promise. It is a model that can be repeated in other communities. It also recognizes that reaching out to families and teens in schools is a more accessible and more comfortable route for parents to accept.

EATING DISORDERS

In Western society, chronic dieting has become very common. Not only is dieting, as Rodin et al. (1985) suggest, a way of life for many, but it often starts in early adolescence. Rodin et al. (1986), using a random sample of male and female undergraduates, discovered that weight and body shape were the central determinants of a female's self-perception of her attractiveness much more than they were for the males.

Dieting often precipitates eating disorders. *Woman's Health Weekly* (1995) reported the following definitions by Dr. Donald Durham, a leading authority on eating disorders and the keynote speaker at a symposium at Texas Christian University:

- Anorexia nervosa, characterized by a body weight of 15 percent or more below normal, refusal to gain or maintain normal weight, and a phobic fear of weight gain that takes on irrational proportions.
- Bulimia nervosa, characterized by episodes of binge eating and purging, is more prevalent than anorexia. Secret binges, in which the patient might consume 20 000 calories at once, are followed by self-induced vomiting, use of laxatives and diuretics, fasting, and compulsive exercise.

- Compulsive overeating, also known as binge-eating disorder, is characterized by binge eating without extreme weight-control measures.

Eating disorders are about more than an obsession with food; they are a reflection of a person's body image, self-esteem, sense of belonging, and societal and peer pressure. Eating disorders kill if left untreated. Treatment often involves hospitalization, antidepressants, nutritional planning, counselling, 12-step programs, support groups, and family therapy.

While eating disorders are considered a major problem among adolescents, the problem continues to be surrounded by a strange silence/secrecy. As a society our focus continues to be on appearance and the notion that "thin is in."

In school girls often form cliques and, within these groups, members struggle to be cool or to be perceived as leaders. A girl may have more status if she diets, takes appetite suppressants, and exercises feverishly. Some girls watch each other at lunchtime and focus more on what is on their plates than what is in their books. How many brilliant minds are we losing to these diseases?

Parents and youth are encouraged to become informed about eating disorders and their devastating effects. Only one-half of all persons diagnosed with anorexia recover fully, and one out of every 30 dies as a result (Patton 1989).

Here are some recommended self-help books:

Bruch, H. 1998. *The gold cage: The enigma of anorexia nervosa.* Cambridge, MA: Harvard University Press, 1998.

Cash, T. 1995. *What do you see when you look in the mirror? Helping yourself to a positive body image.* New York: Bantam Books.

Cooper, P. 1995. *Bulimia nervosa and binge eating: A guide to recovery.* New York: University Press.

DATING VIOLENCE

Definitions and Facts about Dating Violence from the National Clearing House on Family Violence—Canada (1995)

Dating violence is defined as any intentional sexual, physical, or psychological attack on one partner by the other in a dating relationship. The definition takes all abuse seriously. It acknowledges that although both women and men may act abusively, the abuse of women by men is more pervasive and usually more severe.

Dating violence is a serious problem in Canada, but there are still only limited statistics to assess its extent. However, between 16 percent and 30 percent of women surveyed say they have experienced at least one physical assault by a male dating partner. Studies on sexual violence are less clear-cut because of the low reporting rate. Surveys suggest that 45 percent of the women surveyed state that they had been victimized since leaving high school.

Canadian, British, and US studies indicate that women are at far greater risk of being assaulted by men they know.

In order to work with youth involved in violent dating relationships it is important to understand their social context. Developmentally, adolescence is a time of confusion and vulnerability. This is especially true for a young woman in love. Young women may absorb the romantic fantasies featured in movies, on television, and in magazines in addition to the covert pressure of family and friends asking "Do you have a boyfriend?" Having a boyfriend certainly may increase one's status among peers. Having a boyfriend may also increase one's value in a couple-oriented society. These pressures, and the other challenges of adolescence, can create a needy young woman searching for acceptance. In her interviews with 11 dating-violence survivors, Rosen (1994) found that the interviewees were all experiencing difficult times when they met their boyfriends. They saw their boyfriends unrealistically and allowed themselves to be swept away by men who they thought would make their lives easier.

Not only is there pressure to be in a relationship, but there is pressure to stay in the relationship as well. Many young women believe that staying in a relationship is so important that they think a violent relationship is better than no relationship at all.

Work on this issue is necessary on both a formal level and an informal one. The formal level refers to sending public messages about non-violence through institutions such as schools and universities. Informal work involves the work of individual social workers who meet with adolescents and the parents of adolescent children.

The most obvious place to start to work on preventing dating violence is in the schools. Educational institutions have a tremendous responsibility to address violence and take an active stand against it. Again, policies need to be backed up with education. Hird (1995) reported that most Canadian provinces have produced at least one course for students that includes information on family violence. The next step is to expand the definition of family violence to include dating violence and then to make such courses mandatory.

Parents, teachers, school nurses, principals, and janitors all need to be educated about dating violence. At the university level this training includes security personnel, residence staff, and health services. Also, students must be educated to identify the signs of dating violence in friends. It is critical that all youth be informed.

It is especially important at the university level, for three reasons. First, Carlson

(1987) points out that men who attend higher education are more receptive to "talking" interventions. Second, it is at university age that many people enter their first serious relationships. Last, many students are away from home for the first time and may be more anxious to be in relationships.

Part of the work that can be done on a more informal level is for parents, teachers, and social workers to be more open when discussing sex and relationships. Developmentally, youth not only tend to disengage from their parents at this age but they also view adult help as a complicating factor (Litch Mercer 1998). Parents and teachers can play a part in making themselves more accessible to adolescents. Through better communication a youth may feel more comfortable approaching an adult. As well, with more information about safe, consensual sex and reciprocal relationships, young people may recognize violence in their relationships faster. Litch Mercer (1988) supports open discussions, especially given that sexuality is transmitted through society as pornography, rape, seduction, and romanticism. When we do not engage in discussions about sexuality and relationships with teens, the young people have no evidence or information to counter those particular images.

Routinely, parents need to ask their daughters (and sons) about their dating relationships. Sometimes simply asking shows youth that their parents care. Parents need to learn how to recognize the signs associated with abusive relationships. Also, they need to know the steps to take if they suspect violence. Rosen (1994) describes interviews conducted with young women in which their parents reportedly saw the violence without really perceiving it. Ignoring such signs not only puts a daughter at risk but also sends her a message that the violence is acceptable.

Social workers as well can play an important part in protecting youth from violent dating relationships. Like parents, we can be more open to discussing sexuality and relationships. Obviously, we must do this when we work directly with survivors of dating violence. In fact, questions about violence need to be a part of the assessment interviews in all contexts (Bergman 1992). School social workers must try to monitor sudden changes in students' behaviours and attitudes. Exploring the changes and asking questions may bring a problem to the worker's attention. Often this is a key step that health professionals and social workers overlook when they work with abused women. For example, an emergency room physician may treat a young woman's broken arm, but does not treat her by pressing for details of how the injury happened.

When working with youth who are involved in violent dating relationships, it is very important that the social worker send a strong message against violence. At all stages of a relationship, women need information about violence that dispels myths, explores sex-role socialization, and helps them identify dangerous situations (Mills and Granoff 1992).

In her article, Rosen (1994) discusses the treatment goals when working with survivors of violence. Assuring the safety of the client is paramount. This requires creating a safety plan, informing the woman about available resources, and possibly informing her guardians and the police about the situation. The therapist must refuse to minimize the violence and emphasize that violence is a crime. The second step is to help the client expand her perspective by reading literature on the cycle of violence and the common characteristics of abused women. This will help her see the abuse from a more detached point of view and help her realize she is not alone. The last step is to empower her to establish more appropriate boundaries between herself and her partner, and to strengthen her connections to friends and family.

Male youth need resources on the issue as well. Research has suggested that young men often turn to other male friends for support (DeKeseredy and Hinch 1991). With the help of these friends, a young man may minimize and accept the violence. Offering alternatives for men therefore is essential. This can be accomplished through peer counselling, university-run groups, and late-night hotlines.

IMPACT OF THE INTERNET ON YOUTH

The internet has been referred to most often as "the information highway." It serves people's business, shopping, and banking needs, is used for research purposes, and much more. In today's society, one has to ponder the question: Is the internet a friend or a foe to the youth of today? Youth Culture, Inc., a publisher and market research company that targets teens, conducted the Canadian Teen Landmark Study on the Internet, which is supported by a survey done by Northern Research Partners. The survey questioned 1000 young net surfers between the ages of 12 to 17 and 450 parents. It estimated that 85 percent of Canada's 2.4 million teens use the internet, connecting for an average of 9.3 hours per week (Newsbytes, 2000).

Since such a large number of teens use the internet, the next question is "How useful is the time spent while surfing the information highway?" The Young Canadians in a Wired World survey canvassed 5682 students between the ages of 9 and 17 in schools across Canada. According to this survey, 57 percent spend their time downloading and playing music, 56 percent send and receive email, 50 percent surf for fun, 48 percent play and download

games, 40 percent send instant messages, 39 percent use chat rooms, and only 38 percent spend their time doing homework (Media Awareness Network, 2001).

An alarming finding from the Young Canadians in a Wired World survey is that more and more youth are entering private and adults-only chat rooms. Children lack supervision and rules regarding internet use at home. Youth most commonly enter these chat room sites when they are alone, whether that is at home, in internet cafes, or elsewhere. What is even more alarming is that not only do teens enter inappropriate chat rooms; they often also meet in person people they have previously spoken with only on the internet. According to the survey, 73 percent of males and 27 percent of females were likely to put themselves at risk in this way (Young Canadians in a Wired World: The Student's View, 2004).

GAY AND LESBIAN YOUTH

Growing up can be an extremely trying and complex time for adolescents. A large part of growing up revolves around the formation of one's sexual identity. It is quite normal and healthy for children and teenagers to explore and experiment with their sexuality. They may do this with same-sex partners or with partners of the opposite sex. For those who have thought about and/or actively experimented with same-sex partners, anxiety may persist. "Homosexuality" is "the persistent sexual and emotional attraction to someone of the same sex" (American Academy of Child and Adolescent Psychiatry, 2002).

Misperceptions, myths, and stigmas regarding sexual orientation can complicate the social, emotional, and physical processes of teenage development (Vare and Norton, 1998). A previously misconceived notion is that homosexuality is a mental illness or disorder. Parents and loved ones should understand that "homosexuality" is not a mental illness and that the causes of "homosexuality" are not fully understood. Sexual orientation is not a matter of choice.

Another misconception according to Remafedi and Blum (1986) is that only those with homosexual identities engage in sexual activity with people of the same sex. In reality, adolescence can be a time of experimentation with partners of both sexes. "Sexual activity alone does not necessarily indicate sexual orientation."

The stigma surrounding homosexual behaviour hinders the ability of gay and lesbian youth to confront the confusion they may be experiencing regarding their emerging identities. Because of this, many teens may opt to engage in avoidance strategies, such as the denial of their homosexuality. These avoidance strategies can be manifested as specific behaviours, such as limited interaction with the opposite sex to prevent being "found out" and the refusal to explore the subject of homosexuality.

Health and psychosocial difficulties often surface with youth who identify themselves as homosexual. Some of these difficulties include deteriorating school performance, truancy, running away from home, substance abuse, the need to consult mental health professionals, juvenile prostitution, and psychiatric hospitalization (Vare and Norton 1998).

In spite of the fact that as a society our knowledge about being gay and lesbian has increased, our youth still worry about various related concerns. These range from feeling different from their peers, feelings of guilt or anxiety provoked by loved ones' reactions, and fears about being teased and ridiculed, sexually transmitted diseases, discrimination, rejection, and exposure to harassment by others around them.

Social isolation and low self-esteem are common in gay and lesbian teens.

Depression is also common among gay and lesbian youth, and it frequently is a factor leading to suicide. According to the AACAP, recent studies have shown that gay and lesbian youth account for a significant number of deaths by suicide (2002). In conjunction with this, there is a blatant lack of "emotional support" for gay and lesbian youth. Rejection can originate from parents, family members, educators, and peers. It is vital that we help youth, whether heterosexual or homosexual, to feel wanted, worthy, and able to express their identities. "Acceptance" must be our future.

Parents may have difficulty accepting their teens' homosexuality; therefore they may find organizations such as Parents Families and Friends of Lesbians and Gays (PFLAG) useful. Parents may turn to counselling for gay and lesbian youth; however, no one should expect counselling to change people's homosexual orientation. Doing this can confuse teens and only perpetuate their anxiety by reinforcing negative thoughts and emotions that they have already been dealing with (AACAP, 2002). The purpose of counselling should be to help youths feel free and able to address their feelings openly and in an environment in which they feel safe.

YOUTH SUICIDE

Rates of depression are below 1 percent before puberty but shoot up to 8 percent to 10 percent following puberty (Cooper, 2004). A large percentage of Canadian teens suffer from depression, which is one of the main causes of suicide among youth. Suicidal teens often have feelings of overwhelming hopelessness, which stem in turn from feeling unloved, unworthy, and not good enough (Ibid.). Teen suicide is the second leading cause of death among youth, after motor vehicle accidents, according to

Health Canada sources (UBC Public Affairs, 2001 and the Canadian Psychiatric Association, 1995). According to the Psychology Association's Professor Paul Hewitt, about 700 children and teens die every year in Canada by suicide (UBC Public Affairs, 2001).

Why do young people commit suicide? There is a general agreement that young people kill themselves when they feel hopeless about a situation and believe that it will never change. Suicide appears to be a response to "intolerable pain."

Several other factors can also contribute to teen suicide. "Biological factors" are among them. A person may succumb to clinical depression owing to a chemical imbalance, physical fitness, a physical disability, a learning disability, the chemical changes of puberty, or a physical dependency on drugs or alcohol. "Emotional issues" can also lead to suicide among youth—sadness, stress, impulsive behaviour, feelings of powerlessness, loss, grief, low self-esteem, anger or rage, guilt, hopelessness, feeling overwhelmed, anxious, confused about sexual identity/orientation, and an emotional dependency on chemical substances

"Intellectually," youth may find it difficult to communicate their feelings. They may feel pressure to achieve or perform; criticize themselves very harshly; view death unrealistically; want to exact revenge; and may exaggerate their own faults, any or all of which may also contribute to suicide.

Finally, there are also "social" reasons behind young people's committing suicide. They may suffer isolation, withdrawal, friendlessness, and a lack of social skills; they may be unpopular, feel they do not belong, feel embarrassed before their peers, or be labelled "crazy," "stupid," or just "different." They may have troubles at home, at school, or with

the law and may be runaways (The Acadia Hospital, 2003a).

Knowing the suicide warning signs is the first step in helping a child or teen in need. It is important to remember that no single sign can be taken as a concrete indicator of suicide. Look for a pattern. Look for direct statements: for example, "I want to die" or "Life sucks and I want to get out." Observe behaviour, such as a lack of energy, boredom or disinterest, teariness and sadness, and anger or destructive behaviour. For environmental warning signs, look for previous suicide attempts by a family member or friend, problems at school, family violence, sexual abuse, and major family change (The Acadia Hospital, 2003b).

There are many ways to help when a person admits to having suicidal feelings. It is very important to listen to young people, to talk openly with them about suicide, remain calm, be positive, realize your own limits, emphasize alternatives, and know what resources are available to help. It is crucial to find professional help following your initial interaction with the youth in question. Notify the primary-care physician, local hospital, mental health agency, school guidance counsellor, or another trusted professional in your community. Two specific organizations that may be useful are The Acadia Hospital–Access Centre and the Youth Crisis Stabilization Program, a program run by Community Health and Counselling Services.

In cities across Canada, there are emergency mental health–assessment and crisis counselling teams. In Halifax, Nova Scotia, the IWK Children's Health Centre's Intervention Facility is open 24 hours a day, seven days a week. Some other helpful resources are the Suicide Information and Education Centre—**www.suicideinfo.ca**, The Kids' Help Phone—**www.kidshelp. sympatico.ca/en**—and the Canadian

Mental Health Association for Suicide Prevention—**www.suicideprevention.ca**.

CONCLUSION

Working with adolescents is complex and it requires the expertise of a variety of professionals, including social workers, teachers, physicians, police officers, parents, and teens themselves. Social workers bring to the mix an ability to work with a variety of systems and organizations to encourage partnerships and inclusivity. Social work methods range from prevention and education to group and classroom participation, from advocacy and outreach to individual group and family counselling.

Youth issues present social workers with a formidable set of challenges and tasks. Social workers, however, must remember what it was like to be a young adult. This means keeping in mind the importance of "fitting in," the profound influence of the media on values and styles, and simply how scary it can be to grow up.

REFERENCES

The Acadia Hospital. (2003a). *Why do youth commit suicide?* Retrieved Sept. 16, 2004, from **http://acadiahospital.org/Youth+ Suicide+Prevention/Why+Do+Youth +Commit +Suicide%3f.htm**

The Acadia Hospital. (2003b). *Warning Signs.* Retrieved Sept. 16, 2004, from **http://acadia hospital.org/Youth+Suicide+Prevention/ Warning+Signs.htm**

Acuri, A. F., Lester, D., and Smith, R. D. 1985. Shaping adolescent behaviour, *Adolescence, 20.* 935–938.

Addiction Research Foundation. 1995. *Insight Canada research survey 1993.*

American Academy of Child and Adolescent Psychiatry. (2002). *Gay and Lesbian Adolescents.* Retrieved Sept. 16, 2004 from **www.aacap.org/publications/factsfam/ 63. htm**

Bergman, Libby. 1992. Dating violence among high school students. *Social Work, 37.1.* 21–27.

Borhek, M. 1988. Helping gay and lesbian adolescents and their families. *Journal of Adolescent Health Care, 9.* 123–128.

Canadian Psychiatric Association. (1995). *Youth and mental illness.* Retrieved Sept. 16, 2004, from **www.mentalhealth.com/book/ p43-yout.html**

Carlson, Bonnie E. January 1987. Dating violence: A research review and comparison with spouse abuse. *Social Casework: The Journal of Contemporary Social Work.* 16–23.

Cooper, Jen. (2004). *Teen Suicide: What causes it, and how do we prevent it?* Retrieved Sept. 16, 2004, **www.mindful-things.com/ Features/features_TeenSuicide.html**

DeKeserdey, Walter, and Hinch, R. 1991. Premarital woman abuse. In *Woman abuse: Sociological perspectives.* Toronto: Thompson Educational Publishing.

Dingis, M. M., and Oetting, E. R. 1993. Similarity in drug use patterns between adolescents and their peers. *Adolescence, 28.110.* 253–266.

Douvan, E., and Adelson, J., 1966. *The adolescent experience.* New York: Wiley.

Erikson, E. 1963. *Childhood and society* (2d edn.). New York: W. W. Norton.

Gambino, B., Fitzgerald, R., Shaffer, H. J., and Renner, J. Perceived family history of problem gambling and scores on SOGS. *Journal of Gambling Studies, 9.2.* 169–184.

Hartup, W. W. 1983. Peer relations. In E. M. Hetherington (Ed.), *Handbook of child psychology; Socialization, personality and social development* (Vol. 4). New York: Wiley.

Hird, Myra Jean. 1995. Adolescent dating violence: An empirical study. *Intervention, 100*. 60–69.

Litch Mercer, Shirley. 1988. Not a pretty picture: An exploratory study of violence in high school dating relationships. *New Feminist Research, 17.2*. 15–23.

Media Awareness Network. (2001). Retrieved Sept. 16, 2004, from **www.media-awareness. ca/english/index.cfm**

Mills, C. S., and Granoff, B. J. November 1992. Date and acquaintance rape among a sample of college students, *Social Work, 37.6*. 504–509.

Newsbytes. (2000). *Teens cut back on TV to surf the Net*. Retrieved Sept. 16, 2004, from **http://jimbo.canadacomputes.com/ story_3365_24**

Newsweek. 1993. Boy meets girl, boy beats girl. December 13.

Patton, G. 1989. The course of anorexia nervosa. *British Medical Journal, 299*. 39–140.

Rodin, J., Silberstein, L. R., and Striegel-Moore, R. H. 1985. Women and weight: A normative discontent. In E. M. Hetherington (Ed.), *Nebraska Symposium on Motivation, 32*. Psychology and gender. 267–307.

Rodin, J., Silberstein, L. R., Striegel-Moore, R. H. 1986. Toward an understanding of risk factors for bulimia. *American Psychologist, 41*. 246–263.

Rosen, Karen H. August 1994. Empowering young women in violent date relationships. *Family Therapy News*.

Silverstein, Shel. 1981. *A Light in the Attic*. New York: Harper and Row.

Toronto Star. 1992. New law allows police and youth workers the authority to get juvenile prostitutes off the street for 72 hours. April 18.

UBC Public Affairs (2001). *UBC researcher probes perfectionism as suicide predictor in youth*. Retrieved Sept. 16, 2004, from **www.publicaffairs.ubc.ca/media/releases/ 2001/mr-01-47.html**

U.N. Chronicle. 1998. *35.2*. 14.

Wallerstein, Judith S., and Blakeslee, Sandra. 1989. *Second Chances*. New York: Ticknor and Fields.

Women's Health Weekly. 1995. Eating disorders. December 4.

Young Canadians in a Wired World: The Student's View. (2004). Retrieved Sept. 16, 2004, from **www.mediaawareness.ca/ english/special_initiatives/surveys/phase _one/ students_survey.cfm**

chapter twenty-three

Services for Families

Jack Spence

INTRODUCTION

This chapter is based entirely on the ideological premise that the family is at root the source of basic well-being, or the lack of it, for the individual, the community, and society as a whole. Hence, for good reason, the family should be given special status and attention in the life of a society. Certainly, it should receive considerably more than it does today in Canada.

If a family does not contribute to such "basic well-being" in one way or another, then the reasons why not should be determined since there is virtually no family that does not want "to do well for its members." The adult(s) who created the family may be "fragile" and "vulnerable" and therefore less than ready or able to assume the socially ascribed role and function and responsibilities associated with a family unit.

Society is responsible for ensuring that these persons are ready and able to assume these duties. The environment in which the family lives may also hinder its doing well. Society must ensure such adversity is mitigated or removed. With respect to such responsibility the contemporary multi-faceted service and resource delivery system for families in Canada is woefully inadequate. It lacks a synergistic, family-centred character to focus its efforts. The system contains overlap, duplication, inaccessibility, and huge gaps in funding. The services and resources that are available are provided without the enriching and energizing direction that would be produced if the providers were to collectively embrace the shared vision, commitment, and ownership for such an agenda.

This chapter intends to stimulate the discussion of philosophical, ideological, sociological, policy, resources, service planning, and delivery issues relating to the well-being of Canadian families with dependent children. In this, the chapter advocates for the family's well-being. To some degree the chapter may be slightly prescriptive in character. Whatever points are put forth are made with a degree of hesitation since I could not lay claim to the full substantial and credible knowledge base required to do so responsibly and effectively.

DEFINITION OF THE FAMILY

The definition of the "family" used by Family Service Canada provides the broad frame of reference for this chapter. Its definition embraces all who choose to call themselves "family" as desirable in principle and in practice. It reads: "As a matter of policy and practice Family Service Canada considers defining the family in the broader and most inclusive way. In practice, Family Service Canada supports families as being self-defining and promotes that all types of families be respected and supported."

For the purposes of this chapter we narrow the definition of family as "a constellation consisting of one or more adults living with children under the age of 18 years for whom they consider themselves responsible for their essential well-being."

STATISTICS ON THE FAMILY

This chapter will not attempt the gargantuan task of providing a demographic profile of Canadian families according to the above definition. Instead, should the reader be interested, here are three primary, reliable sources of that demographic information. All are located in Ottawa, Ontario:

(1) *Statistics Canada.* This resource has a multitude of publications related to family. The most recent is *Growing Up in Canada, 0–11 Years*. While this was published a couple of years ago, the data were gathered in 1994. Much more is available at the website **www.statcan.ca** under "Children."

One heading is "Size of Canadian Families." There we find the following types of interesting information: Just over one million children live in low income families; 750 000 children live with common-law parents; 78 percent of families with dependent children have two parents in their home while the remainder live with one parent in charge; the typical number of children in two-parent families is 1.9 while in one-parent families it is 1.6; in the year 2000 there were 8 194 300 children living in Canadian families; the average size of those families was three people.

(2) *The Vanier Institute of the Family.* This institute has many family-related publications available from its website, **www.vifamily.ca**. For example, under "Virtual Library Publications" you will find "Same Sex Parent Families," "Aboriginal Families," and "Profiling Canada's Families II, 2000."

(3) *The Canadian Council on Social Development.* At its website, **www.ccsd.ca**, under "CCSD Publications" we find a number of family-related publications, such as "Family Security in Insecure Times," "Poverty Among Young Families," "A Statistical Profile of Urban Poverty," and "Progress of Canada's Children, 2002."

INDIVIDUAL AND COUPLE DYSFUNCTIONING

While the vast majority of people living in Canadian homes, neighbourhoods, and communities are doing quite well with their lives, there are a great many people who are not. These are not finding happiness and fulfillment and/or they behave in ways that hurt other people; they inappropriately require social maintenance services and resources to meet their basic needs; require social remedial and/or security services to keep them from harming themselves and/or other people.

Examples of such dysfunctioning[1] are well known and quite endemic to Canadian communities—underachievement and maladaptive behaviour at school and at work, substance abuse and addiction, mental illness, domestic violence, child neglect, abuse and deprivation, marriage/couple-relationship breakdown, delinquency and crime, sexual assault/rape, underemployment and unemployment, prostitution, and sexual deviancy. Those who present these problems are all human beings who are not able to realize their inherent potential for personal and social well-being. Consequently, they can experience associated debilitating anger, depression, stress, alienation, social isolation, and other conditions in ways that maintain and even exacerbate their life-adjustment problems.

IS ALL OF THIS A MANIFESTATION OF FAMILY DYSFUNCTIONING?

Yes, it is. Such dysfunction that many individual members of Canada's families exhibit is antithetical to either their own basic needs or to those of their significant others, their neighbourhoods, their communities, and the societies in which they live. It clearly indicates that families have failed, for whatever reasons, to effectively discharge their primary responsibilities to provide effectively for the basic bio-psychosocial needs, to humanize and socialize those members. This affirmative position is based on the introductory premise of this chapter—that when the family functions well, then generally its individual members, its community, and society will function well too.

"Functioning well" is thought to mean living with a general sense of well-being and fulfillment. So people's readiness to establish a family and the family's environment are variables that will play critical roles in determining how well the family is able to function in that respect. Hence, the question is, "How will our society come to constructively address and manage these etiological variables?"

It seems that those who recognize the problem and care about it must seek to influence those with the resources, power, and authority to do so—to prepare adults for their family life responsibilities and to shape a supportive environment with family well-being, individual and collective, as its primary focus. The most important of the principal players who hold the "power and resources" must be all levels of government since they have the relevant socially assigned responsibility and financial capacity to make that significant impact. Their colleagues in these efforts would be business and industry, voluntary-sector united funding bodies, faith organizations, charitable organizations, and foundations among others. Publicly proclaimed and jointly developed philosophical and ideological vision and mission statements, statements of goals and objectives, facilitating legislation, regulations and policies must unequivocally reflect this understanding and commitment. These parties must recognize that they bear broader responsibilities for the well-being of their communities and society as a whole that this agenda will enhance. They must present as a "common front" with shared vision, mission, goals, commitment, and ownership as the essential characteristics of their endeavours.

Only by creating this ethos can society in the broadest sense give primacy to the provision of the type and amount of services and resources that will maximize the well-being of its member families. As a positive sequel to this reasoning, it follows that those families will work together to create neighbourhoods, communities, and society that will serve the best interests of all families, individually and collectively, and all individuals. Social capital[2] is the principal, dynamic ingredient that emerges from this process. In turn, it would engender the production of the physical, economic, and human capital required to provide for overall family well-being.

CANADA TODAY

Somewhat paradoxically, in Canada today, while we have a plethora of services and resources "available" for dysfunctional people, these people do not seem to be as successful in resolving their problems as is hoped. Many programs that were designed to serve families have lost touch with how the family and family life have changed in the past decade.

Consequently, we find far too many examples of fragmented, uncoordinated, overlapping, competitive, and under-productive services for the family and its members. For example, today's workplace does not appear to be adequately geared to being "contemporary family-friendly" in its personnel policies and practices. Today, there are compelling social reasons for greater workplace flexibility when it comes to the needs of parents and adult caregivers. Another example is the large number of jurisdictions and organizations that offer services to families and their members that

are simply not provided in a functional, synergistic manner that works well—for example, mental health, physical health, education, employment, income support, child welfare, justice, immigration, housing, credit/debt counselling, and individual/marriage/family counselling.

Rarely, it seems, do communities, within a framework of shared vision, commitment, and ownership seek to provide services and resources for families (individually and collectively) and their members in a truly synergistic way. Consequently, many of those with problems must seek to access services in ways that subject them to somewhat counterproductive conditions—such as dealing with a variety of different geographical locations, a variety of eligibility and service provision conditions, and delivery by representatives of many different disciplines—any one of which may actually prevent another element from being effective. Many people are not accessing available services and resources because they are not even aware they exist.

Unfortunately, in Canada today those with the "resource power and authority" required to meaningfully pursue a credible family-focused synergized agenda do not share the necessary vision and commitment. Without publicly proclaiming they subscribe to the premise for this chapter, these entities ensure that this "cornerstone" underlying meaningful endeavours to enhance family, individual, community, and society well-being will not exist. If those in power and authority do not share such a vision, a commitment to collaborative partnering, commonly agreed-upon values, goals, objectives, and standards, and ownership in this regard, there can be no relevant substance, integrity, or sustainability to their endeavours to realize family well-being.

A search for ideological, philosophical, vision, mission and/or goal statements to this effect on the part of virtually all levels of government, major corporations, human service organizations, commercial enterprises, united fundraising organizations, and major Canadian foundations discloses very little even closely related to this premise.[3] If this is indeed the case, it will likely be a long time before truly meaningful family-centred legislation, policies, resources, and services will emerge in Canada. The fact that the federal government does not have a Minister of the Family among its 39 cabinet ministers speaks volumes. So we can readily deduce that the federal government does not endorse the premise for this chapter. Without effective advocacy on the part of those who understand and care, no such measures are likely to come about. It appears that one can legitimately say the same thing about all provincial and territorial governments in Canada, with the apparent exception of Quebec. In the same context, we note the existence of a review of information available on Canadian Foundations in the year 2002[4] that contains some encouraging evidence of such vision and commitment on their part. Of the nearly 3000 foundations this publication cites, only 75 or 80 make specific reference to support for the family. Those associated with the Roman Catholic Church make the strongest statements in that regard. Since many do not offer websites it was not conveniently possible to determine whether or not those who cite a family focus also provide a rationale even remotely related to the main premise of this chapter.

Many organizations in Canada cite the family as one focus among many in their helping agendas. Federal, provincial, regional, and municipal levels of government do so in various contexts. For example, Ontario's premier Mike Harris in two open letters to Ontario residents on November 17, 1998, and January 14, 1999, wrote, "We want Ontario to be the best place in the world in which to live, work, and raise a family."

At a meeting of first ministers in September 2000, the government of Canada and the provincial and territorial governments (with the exception of Quebec) announced an Early Childhood Development Agreement that stated: "The best way to help children reach their full potential is to provide programs and services that make a real difference in the lives of Canadian families and their young children."[5] The same document does not say why or how the various governments intend to go about giving tangible expression to such statements.

Similarly, united funding organizations such as the United Way, Catholic and Jewish charities and foundations under the aegis of major corporations such as Canadian Tire, Zellers, Labatt, and Safeway cite the family as their focus in various contexts. Direct-service organizations such as Family Service Agencies, children's aid societies, mental health clinics, and Boys and Girls Clubs commonly claim the family is a prospective beneficiary of their services. Obviously, they all provide valuable services that families and family members use.

Again, while it seems relatively certain that most do approach the issue of supporting the family this way, few if any include in their mission or vision statements any meaningful public expression of this priority. No group appears to have committed itself to pursuing the well-being of the family as its goal through working partnerships and collaborative ownership arrangements with other principals who share the same commitment. These major limitations will almost certainly guarantee that they do not serve the Canadian family as well as it should be served.

The following graphically illustrates this point with excerpts from various organizations' vision/mission statements that contain "family service" in their names:

• Family Service Canada's mission statement: "Our mission is to promote families as the primary source of nurture and development of individuals, to promote quality services which strengthen families and communities and to advocate policies and legislation which advance family well-being in Canada."[6]

- Catholic Family Service Calgary: "Our mission is strengthening people and communities in the pursuit of wellness." Its vision statement states: "It is our vision that in our relentless pursuit of enhancing the quality of life Catholic Family Service delivers premiere services that help build caring communities."[7]

- Catholic Family Counselling Centre (Region of Waterloo) "sees its work as an expression of Christian charity by promoting well-being for individuals, families and the community."[8]

While all the above are commendable goals, all lack preambles for these mission and vision statements that declare a strong unequivocal philosophical or ideological objective to the effect that families who function well are an absolute prerequisite for individuals, communities, and society who also function "well."

It seems imperative that these organizations in particular should provide direction and leadership in this regard. To do so would help to bring all sectors of the community together in the cooperative, collaborative, and complementary pursuit of a shared family-centred agenda.

Some contemporary examples of agendas that appear to illustrate recognition of the primacy of the family in terms of the essential well-being of the individual, the community, and the society do exist:

(1) The Vanier Institute of the Family makes the following declarations in its vision/mission statement: "the Vanier Institute is... dedicated to promoting the well-being of Canadian families."

"A strong family is the one indispensable element that can assure a child's good health as she or he grows to adulthood."

"Families are the key building block of society."

"The Vanier will identify and respond to social challenges from a family perspective."

"The Vanier sees the family as the centre of the lives we all live, at home, at work, and in our communities."

"The Vanier's vision is to make families as important to the life of Canadian society as they are to the lives of individual Canadians."[9]

(2) Family Service Ontario states: "Vision: Strong People, Strong Families, Strong Communities." In a philosophical statement accompanying its vision statement the organization adds: "Family Service Ontario believes that people who actively participate and contribute in their communities, and attend to their own essential well-being and that of others, come from healthy families who are able to effectively meet their members' basic human needs—i.e., biological, mental, emotional, socialization, and spiritual. Hence, the corollary, strong families produce strong people and together they constitute strong communities that effectively and efficiently ensure that the basic needs of all their members are known, attended and met in just, caring and humanitarian ways."

"FSO believes that strong families make for a stronger and safer society for us all to enjoy. Family is crucial to all of our well-being. The strengthening of family life is a priority of Family Service Ontario agencies in helping us all cope in today's world."[10]

(3) The George W. Bush administration in the United States has recently taken an initiative that illustrates how the public sector could make a valuable contribution toward such an end. In keeping

with their stated ideological commitment to support the family they have promised legislation with commensurate funding designed to provide public-sector sponsorship for marriage counselling and classes. Their stated principal goal is to prepare couples for married life that is happy and fulfilling.[11]

(4) The Families and Schools Together program, which is widely available in Canada under the aegis of Family Service Agencies, is based on an explicitly stated premise that the well-being of children relates directly to the capacity of their families (not the "professional") to generally "protect them" and enhance their overall well-being more effectively than anyone or anything else could. In the case of elementary- and middle-school children, this goal focuses completely on how the family can play the principal role in resolving their life-adjustment problems and preventing more serious problems in their future—school failure, substance abuse, anti-social behavior. In the case of babies, it focuses totally on building their parents' capacity to parent by nurturing normal healthy growth and development patterns for them.

(5) Quebec[12] is the only Canadian province in which family policy appears to be organized into a complete set of coherent measures designed to enable the government to "think and act family" (Quebec, 1987, 13). Those measures aim specifically at the well-being of families. They seem exemplary in many respects. To achieve its goal, in the 1980s the Quebec government adopted a family policy for the province and set in place an administrative structure and mechanisms that called on the services of numerous participants in a myriad of government sectors of activity. All

shared one goal: improving the well-being of the family. The root of these changes at that time was the public's deep concern about a major change in a variety of socio-demographic indicators regarding family life—for example, a drop in the province's birth rate, a decline in legal marriage, and a dramatic rise in the number of working mothers, what the government articulated as a framework for their approach to pursuing the well-being of families deserves serious thought in other parts of the country today.

Accordingly, Quebec named a Minister of State for Family Policy who would be responsible to a Family Secretariat directly attached to that government's cabinet. A National Family Policy Council was created at the same time. The Quebec cabinet issued a "Statement on the Approach and the Administrative Process for Family Policy." The basic principles of the statement call for:

- recognition of the family as a fundamental value;
- willingness to make the family more stable and cohesive;
- willingness to support parents, the primary caretakers of children, while protecting the interests of the child;
- coordination between government agencies and the families themselves in order to formulate a policy whose general objective would be to "recognize the importance of the family as an institution and as a living environment... in particular, to support the parent–child relationship, which is the nucleus common to all forms of families."

The Secretariat à la famille was established to provide the minister with the resources required to implement the multi-sectoral family policy within government; among its roles the secretariat was to analyze the socio-economic development of families and their needs and study the impact of the government's actions on the family.

Finally, the Quebec government created an agency with the sole mandate of studying family matters. The members of the Advisory Council on the Family, appointed by the government after consultation with family associations, were given a dual mandate to receive and to transmit to the government requests and suggestions submitted to them, and to issue public statements on matters relating to family policy. The council was to function as a watchdog over family-related policy, its mission being to formulate constructive criticism of the measures proposed by the government and the actions that the various ministries took that affected families, to ensure implementation of the action plan named "Families First," and to develop future plans.

The action plan would implement Quebec's family policy. The government intended that the plan would extend itself to the involvement and coordination of some 20 of its ministries and agencies. One major oversight was the government's failure to provide for a functional evaluation system as well.

The Family Secretariat issued a second action plan (1992–1994) with which it changed focus considerably. Instead of the "pronatalist" aim it introduced initially, it now expressed a desire to see the whole of society become family-oriented.

The group put considerable emphasis on addressing five major areas— "prevention, reconciling family and work, economic support for the family,

improving the family living environment, and pursuing a family focus." It stressed the need for measures designed to promote the family-agenda idea to families, all levels of the provincial government, municipalities, business, labour, and other community actors in the hopes that all would become more involved in responding to the needs of families.

"Information and promotion" became one of the principal components in this second action plan. The secretariat was demonstrating a clear willingness to decentralize initiatives to a more local level with the secretariat and the council designated as playing the principal role of animation, consultation, and coordination. However, a definite limitation in the plan seems to have been that the secretariat did not directly involve those whom it hoped would become involved in family-serving roles in its process of developing shared visions and planning. In effect, the second action plan did not create real community ownership and commitment.

In contrast to Quebec's initiative, with its forward-looking plans for a progressive and coherent set of public policies, programs, and related administrative infrastructure to better support families, there does not seem to be anything comparable in the rest of Canada. Elsewhere in the country, support is still delivered through sectoral, piecemeal measures in response to single issues such as child care, domestic violence, childhood poverty, mental health, delinquency and crime, misbehaviour in schools, income support, etc. All of these measures, then, fall under the aegis of such circumscribed administrative entities as social welfare, health, education, and employment, structures designed for the most part to respond to the problems of families and individuals in difficulty. Typically, each such pressing issue has been approached as though it were discrete from the others and dealt with by government bureaucracies more oriented to the differentiated functions of public administration than to the integrated functioning of families. This whole approach represents a myopic, "reactive" one rather than the inclusive, "proactive" role that the Quebec government prescribes.

RELATED CONCERNS ABOUT THE CONTEMPORARY CANADIAN SOCIAL WELFARE SYSTEM

It is very interesting to note that several of the learned contributors to the previous, fourth edition of *Canadian Social Welfare* have expressed similar, albeit more universal, concerns about the contemporary social-service delivery system in Canada. Presumably, that "system" would include those organizations that provide services to families as well. Some of their profound prescriptions for change seem especially noteworthy in a chapter that looks at the service system for Canadian families.

Norene Pupo writes about "Complex Networks, Costly Gaps: Connecting Social Welfare and Other Major Systems" in Chapter 14 of the fourth edition of *Canadian Social Welfare*: "Within the social services it is very common to encounter individuals [and, as I propose, "families"] who 'fall between the cracks,' whose particular problems are not dealt with by the existing realm of social agencies, whose problems are defined as belonging to another jurisdiction, or whose problems are as yet undefined by the sys-

tem of social welfare, and therefore are not serviced. There are also individuals [again, "families"] who at once require assistance from a variety of agencies—medical care, mental health, family and employment counselling, educational, and financial advice. These individuals must not only travel from one agency to the next to seek 'parcels' of service for particular aspects of their problems, but also sometimes receive conflicting advice on the best course available" (p. 210).

She goes on: "The tendency toward specialization within institutions or subsystems may exacerbate the difficulty of unravelling the maze of institutions and their interconnected functions and sometimes contributes to the need for altering other spheres" (p. 211). And finally: "Establishing interdisciplinary networks and linkages among service institutions is crucial to their overall efficiency" (p. 211).

In Chapter 17 of the fourth edition of *Canadian Social Welfare* (2001), "Services for Vulnerable Children: A Conceptualization" (pp. 250–262), Ken Barter writes: "Current programs and services, albeit individually helpful in certain circumstances, do not adequately address barriers associated with poverty, discrimination, alienation, oppression, hopelessness, and inequality" (p. 257).[13]

He defines "child welfare" as "a process of inter-professional collaboration and service integration for purposes of reclaiming capacities in communities, families, professionals, and organizations." Accordingly, child welfare services "should be part of a full continuum of services designed to meet the needs of all children, families, and communities" (p. 258).

He states that the importance of "promoting social change to deal with economic and social issues adds necessary dimensions to child welfare. Recognizing children in the context of the family and the family in the context of the larger social, economic, and political spheres highlights the importance of understanding 'that many of the most critical problems that face families and their children are beyond individual control and reflect external conditions under which families live' (Goffin, 1983, 284). With this recognition comes the realization of society assuming more responsibility to support families" (p. 259).

Finally, he declares that "the definition provides for a new vision for services for vulnerable children that reflects the importance of family-centred practice that involves interprofessional collaboration and service integration.... The emphasis on community suggests the importance of best practice models to facilitate interprofessional collaboration and service integration. These models are family resource centres that are geared to respond to the needs of parents and communities based on their definitions and participation; community-based systems that are accessible and available in a number of settings such as health clinics and shopping malls; and school-based systems where the school becomes the hub of activity for children and families in the neighbourhood" (p. 260).[14]

He drives home his message: "The emphasis on interprofessional collaboration and service integration for purposes of building community capacities to protect and provide services for vulnerable children moves away from the primary focus just being child welfare. Building community capacities expands the focus to be equally concerned about family and community welfare. Involving the entire community in identifying and resolving social, educational, health, and economic issues establishes a collective response in providing services to vulnerable children. It also suggests that these services are too important to be left to any one organization or profession" (p. 260).

It is abundantly clear that Barter gives primacy to the family when it comes to principles, policies, and practices deemed essential for children's welfare.

Rose Marie Jaco, in Chapter 25 of the same edition of *Canadian Social Welfare*, "Social Agencies and Human Service Organizations," writes: "Because an overall, planned design has never been established to guide the development of the social welfare system in Canada, we lack an accepted process for interaction among agencies and organizations in the governmental, voluntary, and commercial [I would use the term "corporate" here] sectors. There are three major problems resulting from this *absence of a blueprint*. The first issue is that there are *gaps in service* because certain human needs appeal more strongly to the public than others, and these receive more support and money from all sources.... [A] second problem of duplication of services also exists between and within sectors.... The third problem involves the discontinuity of service. This common feature of the service delivery system refers to the fact that clients find it difficult to make a smooth transition from one agency to another as their needs change" (pp. 379–380; emphases mine).

Jaco makes the point that "strategies are available to communities to enable them to create a more comprehensive and well-coordinated network of services. These include forming a social planning council to organize local services; developing coordinating committees to plan around specific problems...; hiring more case managers who are expert in dealing with complex service systems;... and establishing citizens' advisory groups. The lack of easy-to-access information about available services often prevents users from acting effectively to meet their own needs" (p. 380).

Somewhat paradoxically, it is interesting that while the community has generally not given the family primacy with respect to the well-being of individuals, communities, and societies, nor has the profession of social work always been exemplary in that area. Again, in this regard, we can look at two of the contributors to the previous edition of this book.

One is M. Dennis Kimberley, who wrote Chapter 30, "The Profession of Social Work: An Integrative Perspective." He does not cite the family as the principal resource to be recognized and facilitated by the profession. He speaks of a helping role for the profession in serving families but does not position it as a transcending goal in realizing the well-being of individuals, communities and societies. His principal focus is on the individual and "collectives" (without defining what these are).

Conversely, Rose Blackmore in Chapter 31, "Models of Social Work Practice," places considerable emphasis on the importance of the family in various practice situations for the professional social worker. For example, she writes, "Social work has always emphasized the importance of working with families (Hollis 1981). For social workers, families were and are crucial for the nurturance of children and a major source of support for the individual" (p. 471). "In family therapy, the problem belongs to all family members. When a child is identified with a problem because of disruptive behaviour in school, all the family members share in owning the problem. Family system theory suggests that the child's disruptive behaviour affects all members and that they can help to resolve it. In some situations, family members contribute to the problem" (p. 471). She does not particularly recognize a pivotal role for the family with respect to community and social well-being.

CANADA TOMORROW: WHAT DIRECTION SHOULD CHANGE TAKE?

Certainly, Norene Pupo, Ken Barter, and Rose Marie Jaco all provide valuable direction toward the future. If we accept that those with the power and authority to effect change must "buy in" to the original premise for this chapter, then how should we proceed to address it?

First, we would require a constituency of the concerned who believe that this must happen. This constituency might be made up of politicians, bureaucrats, clergy, academics, health and social service professionals, representatives from business and industry, united funding bodies, family serving agencies/organizations, and family members, among others. Theoretically, they will be seen by those with the requisite power and authority as a constituency of some political/economic/social/cultural significance and be influenced accordingly. This group of like-minded people must be prepared to offer a family-centred service and resource delivery-system model to those among the powerful with the authority to act.

What might this model look like? Certainly many European nations, notably Scandinavian, have systems that could be studied for adaptation to the Canadian venue. However, closer to home we have the Quebec experience in system paradigm-building and implementation. In the 1970s, Quebec established locally based "community service centres." Their goal was to provide an integrated system to deliver publicly funded health and social services

Rose Marie Jaco offers a more detailed perspective on their role and function and their place in the broader social welfare system (*Canadian Social Welfare*, 4th edn., p. 381). Then in the 1980s and the 1990s the Quebec government pursued the much broader family agenda described earlier in this chapter.

Many years ago, the Regional Municipality of Ottawa-Carleton varied its human-services system paradigm with the introduction of an entity called *community health and resource centres* that were "neighbourhood-based." They were designed to integrate health and social services within their jurisdiction with a view to blending their delivery at the neighbourhood level in the best interests of their citizens.

They were not a focused attempt to enhance family well-being as such. They were open to hosting services that other jurisdictions offered, such as family service agencies, in order to integrate their total community services as much as possible. Providing essential information with respect to services and resources not located in their particular centre was deemed an important function. Today, there are about 11 of these community health and resource centres but their focus has shifted primarily to health services. Perhaps that is easy to understand since apparently approximately 90 percent of their funding comes from the Ontario Ministry of Health. As the saying goes, "The piper calls the tune."

In her chapter in *Canadian Social Welfare*, fourth edition, Rose Marie Jaco provides a broad overview of other attempts at the integration of health and social services in several Canadian provinces.

WHAT MIGHT A FAMILY-CENTRED SERVICE SYSTEM LOOK LIKE?

In the future, how could we design a service system model to recognize this primacy of the family? Presumably, its focus on the family's well-being would be readily apparent in its name.

First, there must be a governance component that might simply be called the *family council*. It would provide the philosophical and ideological framework for such an initiative.

Next, there would have to be an administration or service-implementation entity that could be called the *family centre*. It would bear responsibility for the operationalization of the vision, mission, and goals set out by the governing body. The latter term is closely related to Ken Barter's idea of the family resource centre in his chapter of the previous edition of this book.

The conceptual framework for family councils and family centres could be very much as the province of Quebec envisioned them 20 years ago. Presumably, there would be family councils established to match the jurisdictions at each level of the Canadian family-services infrastructure. Certainly, there would have to be one at the federal and the provincial levels of government. From those levels the preponderance of authority and resources for a family-serving organization would presumably emanate. Should it provide for other levels of government to have complementary roles and functions, like regional, county, and municipal, then they too might wish to create family councils that would play a role in their particular jurisdictions' endeavours.

A facsimile of what the Quebec government has developed could be a very good beginning for a philosophical and ideological framework to be adapted elsewhere. In addition, the Vanier Institute of the Family presents the following view of itself that could also be useful.[15]

The institute expresses its vision: "To make families as important to the life of Canadian society as they are to the lives of individual Canadians." Its mission is "to create awareness of, and to provide leadership on, the importance and strengths of families in Canada and the challenges they face in their structural, demographic, economic, cultural and social diversity."

To give operational expression to these vision and mission statements, the Vanier articulates a series of "goals," the essence of which a *Family Council of Canada* might also appropriately consider for itself. The institute addresses such matters as building national awareness of the critical importance of health and of well-functioning families to society as a whole; the identification of family needs and the means by which they can best be addressed by families themselves, by various levels of government, by employers, and by community institutions; advocacy with those components of Canadian society that can complement their efforts to provide resources essential for the well-being of all families. As Vanier expresses expresses its own goal, "Through the Institute's activities, cooperation among all organizations—charitable, religious, educational, welfare, culture and other—is encouraged, and the range of groups in Canadian society committed to supporting and improving the lives of Canada's families is enlarged."

Generically, it is conceivable there would be a close parallel between the roles and the functions articulated for the new Canada Health Council and the Canada Family Council.

Whatever the jurisdiction in which the Family Council might be established, one would want it to serve as an independent organization that could be trusted and respected for policy advice and guidance in such matters as legislation, regulations, goals, policies, priorities, services, and resources. Somehow it would seek to constructively mediate the customary rhetorical avalanche of intergovernmental, inter-agency, inter-organizational, and interdisciplinary conflict. It would provide representatives from the council's commu-

nity with an annual report on the performance of the family-care system. That community could be broad enough to include cabinets at the federal and the provincial levels of government, local funding bodies, or generally the citizens in the community it serves.

It is important to recognize that the council could not solve all the problems confronting the family-care system. However, it would be in a strong position to play a critical role in putting pressure on the power and authority centres in the community (sources of essential mandates and funding) such as politicians, corporations, and united funding bodies. It would be hoped that the council would be able to help to generate public pressure that would build sufficient political will to force the pace of change.

Role and Functions for a Family Centre

Since the range of services families in any community require would be very wide—multiple disciplines and programs would be required—the primary services a family centre would provide would probably be reception, assessment, links and referrals to appropriate community resources in many areas, including social welfare, health, education, justice, and housing. Assessment would simply involve hearing about an expressed need and collecting information on the services and resources that seem relevant. Referral would entail ensuring the family was appropriately directed, received, and served by the designated resource or service-providing agency ororganization(s).

In these respects the centre would function like the HMOs (health management organizations) that are so widespread in the United States,, although the American organizations are more extensively involved in "professionally based diagnoses" than would seem appropriate for the proposed family centre for the Canadian scene.

Related media promotion, marketing, and public relations would constitute a major budgetary item since the existence, role, and function of the family centres would have to be well publicized in the larger community. Individual members of families, couples, and families as a whole would be encouraged to use their services. They would provide only information and support regarding the availability of and means of access to community resources that appeared relevant to the needs and problems presented to them. In doing so, they would be "engineering" access to a full continuum of services within a complex service system including specialized, para-professional and professional expertise.

Where Would a Family Council and a Family Centre Find Leadership and Governance?

Since the public sector must inevitably play the principal role in funding family services, much of the responsibility for putting the family centres' infrastructure in place must rest with it. One would hope that guidelines for creating family councils at the community level would stress the importance of meaningful involvement for the private and the voluntary sectors of each community as well as, for example, service delivery organizations and agencies, ethnic, cultural and faith-focused groups, united funding bodies, business and industry, labour, foundations, and professions.

Perhaps as important or even more important would be the families from the communities to be served. Collectively their perspectives on family life and well-being would contribute greatly to the council's overall knowledge of the conditions for each community's families. One would like to think that the voluntary and private sector services and resources that are essential and complementary to those that the public sector funds would fit synergistically into the overall services for the families paradigm.

How Would the Council and Centre Manage Information and Evaluate Performance?

Certainly this model would require the best possible information management and performance evaluation systems. It appears that to its detriment Quebec neglected to provide adequately for these, so we should learn from that province's experience.

Essentially, this system would monitor family well-being or the lack of it. With the best systems and technology available for accomplishing its task, it would endeavour to study family functioning with a view to determining the incidence, prevalence and etiology of family dysfunctioning that leads to the dysfunctioning by its individual members. Ideally that information would lead to the development and provision of those services and resources required to prevent or reduce the incidence, through appropriate preventive and remedial measures.

It will be imperative that the implementation of family centres take into account the capacity for them to be rigorously evaluated for their efficiency and effectiveness. Society must be able to assess their predetermined goals, objectives, and service standards. The centres should also be able to demonstrate a financial return on the investment made in them, to prove that the cost of running the centres and providing their services is less than the costs involved in serving families and individual members once they have become seriously dysfunctional. All this is possible. The conceptual frameworks and technology required are available now.

An evaluation schemata would be rather straightforward. There would have to be clear documentation of three key dimensions to the role and function of these centres: the presenting need or problem accepted for service, related links and/or referrals, and related outcomes achieved by the service or resource providers. Families and family members using the centres' services would have to formally agree to the necessary exchange of information. We would hope that the analysis of information collected from this service/resource delivery configuration would demonstrate how the family has emerged as a primary resource. This in turn would lead to the amelioration and/or resolution of the needs and problems the families brought to the family centre in the first place.

The Families and Schools Together Program mentioned earlier is quite widely provided by family service agencies all across Canada and the United States. It employs an exemplary evaluation component that could be replicated in some respects. At least it could offer a demonstration program design with which to study the efficacy of the proposed family centre.

Again, this program uses the family rather than the professional and/or para-professional service provider as its principal preventive, developmental, and remedial resource for children who are underachieving at school and are presenting serious behavioural problems both at school and at home. The program has found that generally the families of these children have been somewhat dysfunctional in relation to recognizing and meeting their children's basic needs. The nature of these dysfunctions and the reasons for them are many. In general, the families were found to be highly stressed, socially alienated, and isolated. They had virtually no meaningful neighbourhood or community to which they should normally be able to turn for help or other supporting resources. Any kind of relationship with the child's school was generally non-existent. In other words, these families had no working "social capital."

The program helps families build much more normal roles and functions for themselves. Parents are empowered to take responsibility for their families' lives. Parents and school work as partners in enabling the children to achieve and function normally in school. Neighbourhood and community become real, hence the source of essential services, resources, and support for the parents and their entire families. Social capital would become a working resource for them.

All of this would be rigorously evaluated with tools with scientific validity and reliability. Parents and teachers would evaluate the children's school performance and behaviour both before and after their experience in the program.

This type of evaluation could conceivably find a place for itself in conjunction with the introduction of family centres. When this happened, it would then be possible to demonstrate to the mandating and funding bodies that the return on their investment would be very positive in every respect.

Who Would Staff the Centres?

Clearly, the family centres would not employ the conventional direct service providers for families—physicians, nurses, psychologists, psychiatrists, social workers, credit counsellors, employment counsellors, family life educators, lawyers, income maintenance workers, vocational rehabilitation counsellors, guidance counsellors, domestic violence workers, legal aid lawyers, or paralegal workers. At least the centres would not engage these particular professionals to function in their conventional capacities.

As individuals they might present other engaging and facilitating capacities and qualities for "helping" that would make them candidates for case-manager roles in family centres. They would have to be people of genuine warmth, caring, empathy, and understanding that were readily apparent. They would have to be very knowledgeable about the broad spectrum of community services and resources available and relevant to an even broader spectrum of family needs and problems. They would have to be effective communicators. They would have to be knowledgeable about services and resources that would enable them to act as appropriate links and referrals for families and family members in need. They might have to help with transportation and/or child care costs. They might even have to arrange to have the person(s) in need accompanied to the actual locations of those resources.

How Would the Family Council and Family Centres Be Funded?

This would not readily materialize in a rational, coherent manner. The contemporary pattern for funding the services/resources that families and family members require is rigidly vested in a number of budgetary "envelopes" or categories—such as education, mental health, physical health, alcohol and drug treatment, child welfare, legal aid, woman abuse, income support, social housing, early childhood education, and individual, marriage, and family counselling. The current sources of funding and practices tend to be traditional and vested—public, private, voluntary/charitable, and commercial.

Some services are funded predominantly by only one source while others depend on a number of sources. For exam-

ple, Family Service Agencies generally have funding from all sources and sometimes the funding is fairly equal between them. Some groups would resist change since it would affect existing patterns of power and authority.

We would expect that the amount of funding from any one sector should relate directly to the proportion of the total amount of that sector's services and resources that the families and family members referred or steered to it by the community's family centres actually used. Initially, to get these centres established, funding sources would have to develop a formula based on a reasonable approximation of what those proportions might be. With working experience, reliable, valid data regarding utilization would base these costs in reality.

Preferably, monies from the public, voluntary (United Way, Catholic and Jewish Charities), and foundation sectors of the funding spectrum would be characterized formally by joint statements of philosophy, ideology, vision, and mission citing the family as pivotal for the well-being of the individual, the community, and society. The public sector would require facilitating legislation to that effect. It would also need related regulations and policies. While other sectors would not involve the use of legislation and regulations, they would need related policy statements.

How Would the Centres Deal with Implementation Difficulties?

Unquestionably there will be many since changes in infrastructure and practice involving interprofessional collaboration, and service integration in any field of endeavour does not come easily. Traditionally, the public sector has assumed full responsibility for providing certain services and resources that families and family members use—income maintenance, child welfare, physical and mental health, vocational rehabilitation, education, social housing, justice, employment.

While the nature of that responsibility would not change as family centres entered the scene, all the sectors involved to date would have to accept a new access dimension for the services and resources that would be new. Convincing the powerful with authority that this reform is essential and its related costs would be a necessary improvement would not be easy.

Similarly, the voluntary-sector mandating and funding bodies in particular would have to be convinced that such a new investment in the current service and resource delivery infrastructure is important and will pay long-term dividends in terms of their communities' well-being through the related vision, mission, and goal statements. All mandating and funding bodies would fear a loss of their own visibility and status through this proposed blending of their contributions.

CONCLUSION

This chapter has focused primarily on the importance of having those with the power and authority to provide essential services and resources to families recognize the wisdom of seeing the family as central in human, community, and societal well-being. It also postulates that, should we as a society recognize this as true, then we will have taken an initial step in moving toward optimal levels of family well-being in our communities and society. We see the possibility of achieving this vision through the creation of a network of family councils and family centres. Associated with this framework would be an information management system to provide reliable, credible information about the real needs of families and family members. With this information in hand, we would hope that the essential shaping of a genuinely relevant portfolio of services and resources system for families would materialize.

One must not think of a family centre as a conventional social-service entity. It would have to be much more than that. It would have to seek to provide any family and any individual family member with meaningful access to all essential services and resources. These would come from all of the areas for service and resourcing in any community, and would include physical and mental health, education, employment, justice, housing, and others.

NOTES

1. *The Canadian Oxford Dictionary* (1998) defines *dysfunctioning* as "an abnormality or impairment of function."

2. *Social capital* is the term sociologists commonly use to describe the social connections a person, couple, or family has with other people in his/her/their community that produce networks, norms, social trust, altruism, coordination, and reciprocal cooperation for their mutual benefit. Social capital helps more than the individual and his/her family; it affects the entire community. Communities with high social capital are said to work better.

For example, education researchers have conducted a number of studies that show that, when parents are actively involved with their children's education, those children do better in school, and the schools they attend generally do better, too. In high social-capital areas the public spaces tend to be cleaner, the people are friendlier, and the streets safer. High-risk children in single-parent families seem to succeed in life when their mothers have enough social capital.

3. The Vanier Institute of the Family, the government of Quebec, and Family Service Ontario are noteworthy exceptions. I would hope

there are others. Related information will be provided later.

4. From the Canadian Learning Agency website: **www.canadianfoundations.ca**

5. From a Government of Canada news release, 2001-126, November 20, 2001. Available at **http://media.health-canada.net**

6. Available from Family Service Canada's website: **www.familyservicecanada.org**

7. From Catholic Family Service Calgary's website: **www.cfs-ab.org/whoweare.php? section=whoweare**

8. From the Catholic Family Counselling Centre (Region of Waterloo)'s website: **www.counselling-cfcc.ca**

9. From the Vanier Institute of the Family's website: **www.vifamily.ca**.

10. From Family Service Ontario's website: **www.familyserviceontario.org**

11. *Globe and Mail*. Toronto (November 6, 2003).

12. Credit for all of the information pertaining to the Quebec scene is given to Celine Le Bourdais and Nicole Marcil-Gratton with the collaboration of Daniele Bélanger. Please see their 1994 article, "Quebec's Pro-Active Approach to Family Policy: 'Thinking and Acting Family,'" in *Canada's Changing Families: Challenges to Public Policy* (Ottawa: Vanier Institute of the Family).

13. Largely "environmental" in nature.

14. For example, the school serves this function in the Families and Schools Together Program that family service agencies make available across Canada and the United States.

15. This information is available at the Vanier Institute's website, **www.vifamily.ca**. To serve a particular purpose, a province's or a community's name could replace "Canada" wherever it appears in this statement.

REFERENCES

Goffin, S. G. 1983. A framework for conceptualizing children's services. *American Journal of Orthopsychiatry, 53(2)* (April): 282–290.

Hollis, F., and Woods, M. E. 1981. *Casework: A psychosocial therapy*. New York: Random House.

Mathews, R. *Canadian foundations 2002*. Ottawa: Canadian Learning Agency; **www.canadianfoundations.ca**

Quebec. 1987. *La politique familiale. Enonce des orientations et de la dynamique administrative*. Quebec: Gouvernement du Québec.

Turner, J. C., and Turner, F. J. 2001. *Canadian social welfare*. 4th edn. Toronto. Prentice-Hall.

The Vanier Institute of the Family. Maureen Baker, Guest Ed., 1994. *Canada's changing families: Challenges to public policy*. Ottawa.

chapter twenty-four

Services for Older Adults

James Gladstone

Kerri-Ann Fitzgerald

INTRODUCTION

Older people are beginning to represent a large proportion of the general population. There are currently more than 2.7 million Canadians aged 65 or older, and, by 2021, when the baby boom generation reaches an average of 65 years of age, this number will increase to more than 6 million people. Over the next 45 years, the older population is expected to triple in size (Denton and Spencer 1980).

An increasing number of older people will mean that a greater number of persons will experience one or several of the major life events often associated with aging: namely, caregiving, retirement, widowhood, and relocation to a long-term care institution. These major life events

represent the focus for the rest of the chapter because of their significance for social work practice.[1] Historically, social work has long been concerned with people in the context of their own environments, and each of these major life events—caregiving, retirement, widowhood, and relocation—represents change in people's environments, be it the physical, family, or work situation. These transitions also demand the attention of social work practitioners and policy-makers, who work to reduce the stress often associated with these experiences.

Because these events are often perceived as stressful, we will describe and analyze them in terms of a stress model. Stress is mediated by coping behaviours, which in turn may involve the utilization of resources, including formal services[2] (Pearlin et al. 1990). Before a person employs coping strategies, however, the stressor will be appraised, in the course of which the person affected attaches a subjective meaning or significance to the stressful event (Lazarus and Folkman 1984; Yates, Tennstedt, and Chang 1999).

This process also takes place within the contexts of gender and ethnicity. These contextual factors are important since men and women, and members of different ethnic and racial groups, may have different access to the resources they need to cope successfully (Pearlin et al. 1990).

MAJOR LIFE EVENTS

Caregiving

It is generally acknowledged that providing ongoing care for an older person is stressful. Research shows that family members, especially spouses, are most likely to be primary caregivers. If a spouse is unavailable or unable to provide care, then adult children, followed by other family members such as siblings, nephews, and nieces, will usually take on this role (Horowitz 1985a; Johnson 1983). Primary caregivers are also likely to be female (Guberman, Maheu, and Maille 1992; Canadian Study of Health and Aging 1994). While men also perform caregiving tasks, they usually provide types of care that differ from that of women; the latter are more likely to provide personal or "hands-on" assistance (Horowitz 1985b; Miller and Cafasso 1992). Some findings suggest that structural and familial factors interact with feelings of filial obligation to shape the caregiving behaviour of sons (Campbell and Martin Matthews 2000). In Western societies, family members in general, and women in particular, are expected to care for older relatives. The strength of these societal values has led some scholars (Aronson

1990; Walker 1991) to question whether the state is shifting the burden of caring for families onto women.

Stress While there is consensus in the literature that caregiving is a stressful experience, there is controversy over the sources of the greatest stress. Some researchers point to specific tasks that caregivers perform as especially stressful. These usually include personal care tasks such as bathing, lifting and transferring, and toileting and managing incontinence (Horowitz 1985a; Jutras arid Veilleux 1991). Other researchers (Fengler and Goodrich 1979; Marcus and Jaeger 1984) suggest that the need to always be available is a central stressor in caregivers' lives.

Some researchers report a positive correlation between caregiver stress and the degree of functional or cognitive impairment the older person experiences (Horowitz 1985a; Moritz, Kasl, and Berkman 1989). Others, however, find no relation between stress or burden and the severity of the older person's illness (George and Gwyther 1986; Zarit, Reever, and Bach-Peterson 1980).

Horowitz (1985a) has suggested that caring for a person with a cognitive impairment may be more stressful than caring for someone with a physical impairment. Cattanach and Tebbes (1991) however, find no significant differences between caregivers of relatives with cognitive, as compared to physical, impairments in terms of depression or psychological problems. More recently, Pinquart and Sorensen (2003) conducted a meta-analysis of caregiving studies and found that caregivers experienced greater burden when their relatives displayed behaviour problems, as compared to physical or cognitive limitations. Similar findings have been reported by Gaugher et al. (2000).

Researchers have also cited some contextual factors related to caregiving stress, including the caregiver's relationship to the person receiving the care, his or her co-residency, and gender. According to Horowitz (1985a), many studies show that spouses report higher levels of stress than other caregivers. Jutras and Veilleux (1991) and Young and Kahana (1989), on the other hand, find that spouses experience less stress than adult child caregivers do.[3] Kosberg, Cairl, and Keller (1990) find that caregivers who lived in the same homes as care recipients reported higher burden scores, possibly because they experienced greater restrictions in their personal lives. And, although there are exceptions (for example, Jutras and Veilleux 1991), most studies have indicated that women perceive higher levels of caregiving stress than men (Barusch and Spaid 1989; Miller and Cafasso 1992). Possibly men receive greater support from others in their caregiving roles (Noelker and Wallace 1985; Pruchno and Resch 1989). A study by Carpenter (2001) suggests that daughters who are more attached to their older mothers may experience less burden and may provide more emotional support than those who are less attached. Feelings of attachment, however, are not necessarily related to the instrumental care that is provided.

Aside from the primary sources of stress, secondary sources of stress may emanate from the primary stressors. One such example is the family conflict that can result from tensions associated with caregiving that are experienced by other family members as well as the primary caregiver. Horowitz (1985a), for instance, has suggested that conflict may develop between primary caregivers and their spouses regarding tasks in their own household that either perceives as neglected or emotional needs that are perceived as unmet. Conflict may develop between adult child caregivers

and their siblings, too, especially when the caregivers believe their siblings are not providing them or their older parents with additional support. Conflict may also emerge between the primary caregiver and the older care recipient, especially concerning day-to-day issues.

The demands associated with working outside the home may also become a secondary stressor. Caregivers who devote a lot of time and energy to a dependent older person may find it difficult to maintain outside employment, and this in turn can represent an additional stressor in their lives. Scharlach, Sobel, and Roberts (1991), however, suggest that the critical factors associated with occupational stress may not be working outside the home as such, but the degree of job flexibility inherent in their outside work, and the support provided by co-workers and supervisors regarding their caregiving.

A further point bears mentioning. While the amount of research related to caregiver stress has grown in the past number of years, very little is known about the perceptions or experiences of the older person receiving such care. In one of the few studies addressing this issue, Aronson (1991) found that older mothers felt ambivalent about receiving care from their daughters. The older women wanted to retain their independence, yet were concerned about their own deteriorating health and need for security.

Appraisal The meanings that caregivers attach to their caregiving experiences influence the coping strategies they employ to manage stress. Hasselkus (1988) finds that caregivers may eventually feel that their caregiving responsibilities do not allow them to attend to their own needs. They may question their personal capabilities, feeling that someone else could perform the caregiving role better than themselves. Or they may take responsibility for somehow causing the situation, feeling that if they had recognized their older relative's symptoms earlier, that care recipient's health might not have deteriorated so far.

A study by Wadley and Haley (2001) suggests that adult children may be more compassionate and more willing to provide assistance if their parents have been diagnosed with a condition such as Alzheimer disease. Otherwise, children may interpret their parents' behaviour as intentionally difficult and may feel less committed to offering them support.

Farran et al. (1991) have pointed to the loss and powerlessness caregivers feel. Some caregivers mourn the loss of their relationships with older impaired relatives. At the same time they feel powerless in their choices to become caregivers and feel incapable of rebalancing their lives once they have done so.

Some studies, however, suggest that some caregivers may attach more positive interpretations to their caregiving experiences. Motenko (1989) finds that wives who feel that caregiving allows them to reciprocate to their spouses support and affection that they themselves have received in the past derived greater satisfaction from their new roles than those who provided caregiving out of a sense of duty. Taking an existential approach, Farran (1997) refers to caregivers who feel fulfilled by their ability to "rise to the occasion" or who may feel "transformed" by their caregiving experience.

Coping   Several researchers have discussed strategies for coping with caregiving stress. Miller (1987) has referred to a number of problem-solving strategies they employ, such as establishing daily routines or pursuing specific activities for oneself or for one's dependent spouse. Farran et al.

(1991) notes a variety of cognitive strategies caregivers use successfully, including focusing on choices they feel they have concerning their caregiving, placing importance on certain aspects of caregiving, such as appreciating their older relatives' positive responses to their care, and looking for positive meanings in their caregiving activities. Pratt et al. (1985) finds that caregivers who avoided stressful experiences and who had confidence in their problem-solving abilities showed lower burden scores than those who did otherwise. Barusch and Spaid (1989) have found that women used significantly more coping styles than men.

In the stress model, effective coping is often associated with the use of social supports. Several studies have suggested that caregiving spouses are more likely than other caregivers to provide support alone (Baum and Page 1991; Tennstedt, McKinlay, and Sullivan 1989), although this might not be true for all cultural groups (Miller and McFall 1991). Studies conducted by Birkel and Jones (1989), Miller (1987), and Montgomery and Borgatta (1989) suggest that caregivers may be especially reluctant to draw on social support when their relatives are suffering cognitive impairment. Caregivers may be self-conscious about their care recipients' public behaviour or may perceive a social stigma attached to that impairment. Montgomery and Borgatta (1989) have identified a point of irony here: spending time with friends may represent a form of respite for caregivers who are overtaxed by their caregiving responsibilities. However, going out with friends also requires of the caregivers an expense of energy that they may not have because of their commitments to their caregiving roles.

When secondary caregivers do help support a care recipient, that help appears to supplement, rather than complement, the assistance the primary caregivers supply. Central caregiving responsibilities remain the primary caregiver's responsibility (Horowitz 1985a; Tennstedt, McKinlay, and Sullivan 1989). Horowitz (1985a), however, has suggested that it is not the actual support secondary caregivers provide to the care recipient or to the primary caregivers that alleviates the latter's sense of stress, but the perception that others are available and willing to help.

Globerman (1995) finds that particular members of some families, whom she refers to as the "unencumbered children," are excused from caregiving responsibilities and are not even expected to become involved in that care.

Services Numerous studies have shown that caregivers are reluctant to use formal services. They usually request such services only when they have reached a period of crisis (Montgomery and Borgatta 1989). This is especially true of those caregivers caring for persons with dementia (Canadian Study of Health and Aging 1994). Horowitz (1985a) has stated that family caregivers usually ask for fewer services than professionals would recommend. Spouses in particular are likely to try and provide care on their own (Johnson 1983; Tennstedt, McKinlay, and Sullivan 1989), particularly when their husbands or wives have dementia (Canadian Study of Health and Aging 1994).

There may also be differences in the extent to which caregivers access formal services, depending on race. Miller and Guo (2000), for example, find that white caregivers were more likely than African Americans to use formal resources. Janevic and Connell (2001), however, point out that minority groups' using less formal care may reflect structural and social inequalities that place such groups in disadvantaged positions within society.

Aneshensel et al. (1995) suggest that different types of services might be needed at different points of the "caregiving career." They posit that education is of greatest importance when caregivers first begin to assume their role. They need information about their relatives' diseases, their causes, what lies ahead, and what practical issues relate to the relatives' care.

At later stages, the caregivers may benefit more from interventions directed at stress management. These services can be offered through self-help and mutual aid groups (Colantonio, Cohen, and Corlett 1998; Toseland and Rossiter 1989) or through respite services (Gaugher et al. 2000; Kosloski and Montgomery 1995). Individual or family counselling may also be helpful, especially when addressing secondary stressors such as depression (Mittelman et al. 1995). Greater service options may also present themselves as communication technologies, involving more sophisticated telephone systems and the internet, continue to be developed (Schulz et al., 2002).

Retirement

Recent studies suggest that retirement is not an event defined by a uniform style of adaptation (Hanson and Wapner 1994). Rather, there are variations in the ways that individuals adjust to this life stage transition (Clifford and Taylor 1996; Hanson and Wapner 1994; Maule, Hershey and Mowen 2000; McDonald and Wanner 1990; Price 2002; Szinovacz and DeViney 2002). Factors that contribute to the complexity of the issue include the decision-making process (Maule, Clifford, and Taylor 1996), the timing of retirement (Szinovacz and DeViney 2000), people's self-perceptions throughout this phase (Hershey and Mowen 2000; Mutran, Reitzes and Fernandez 1997) as well as physical, economic, social, gender, and ethnic differences (Hanson and Wapner 1994; Kulik 2001). This transition is not problematic for everyone—studies in Canada and the United States indicate that a sizeable proportion of the older workforce wants to retire early (Fames 1981; McDonald and Wanner 1990)—though some may find the adaptation process may be difficult (Martin Matthews and Brown 1987).

Stress Health and income have been studied as two significant factors related to retirement satisfaction (Maule, Clifford, and Taylor 1996; Secombe and Lee 1986; Szinovocz and DeViney 2000). More specifically, Martin Matthews and Brown (1987) have identified occupation and lifestyle as critical to men's retirement satisfaction, and to women's health and attitude. Mutran, Reitzes, and Fernandez (1997) have also investigated gender differences and find that men and women contend with different types of stress throughout the retirement phase as each gender tends to experience different diseases, faces different financial situations, and lives in different interpersonal environments.

Previous studies indicate that people's concern about financial security is often associated with the level of stress they feel in retirement (Dorfman, Secombe, and Lee 1986; Kohout and Heckert 1985; Maule, Clifford, and Taylor 1996). While workers with relatively lower incomes may experience greater financial stress in retirement, those who anticipate declines in their incomes may become even more negative in their attitudes toward retirement (Mutran, Reitzes, and Fernandez 1997).

We can analyze these issues on a more macro level. Political and economic influences may determine income levels, and therefore have a bearing on people's adjustment to retirement (McDonald and Wanner 1990; Wanner and McDonald 1986). The adequacy of public and private pension funds as well as tax legislation, for example, affect the income levels of retirees. Pension policies, moreover, may have differing effects depending on a person's marital status, race, or gender. Women are more likely to be interrupted in the time they spend in the paid labour force (Ginn and Arber 1996; Marshall, Clarke, and Ballantyne 2001; Simmons and Betschild 2001) while blacks are particularly disadvantaged in retirement because of previous lower wages and poor pension plans (Markides and Mindel 1987). Loss of a work-related social network may be an additional source of stress in the transition to retirement.

Appraisal Not only might retirement be accompanied by external sources of stress, but the subjective meanings a person attaches to this life transition may also generate stress. Mutran, Reitzes, and Fernandez (1997) report that attitudes toward retirement are formed by one's perception of oneself; high self-esteem correlated with a positive attitude, and low self-esteem with a more negative attitude

In light of the several stresses associated with retirement, Maule, Clifford, and Taylor (1996) identify the decision-making process as complex and varied among individuals. Rather than viewing the decision as dominated by a single attribute, such as health or finances, they view decision-making surrounding retirement as a "multi-attribute problem" in which the potential advantages of making certain decisions need to be balanced against the disadvantages of others. Zimmerman et. al. (2000) conclude that the timing of a person's retirement may be contingent on family caregiving duties.

Hanson and Wapner (1994) refer to earlier work conducted by Wapner and Gail A. Hornstein, who focused on the influence of cognition, effect, and values during the transitional period of retirement. They identified four ways of a person's making the transition to retirement: taking the time to rest and reflect upon individual past experiences; viewing retirement as a revitalizing new phase of life; looking at retirement as an opportunity to continue the pleasures of life with less demands; or associating retirement with a severe loss of personal identity.

Experiencing a loss of self or identity is a common theme in the literature on retirement. Emphasis on the "worker role" may create confidence in retirement or make the individual cope with the loss of a valued identity (Mutran, Reitzes, and Fernandez 1997). Karp (1988) notes that women are less likely than men to feel positively about retirement, possibly because they enter the paid labour force later and have not reached their occupational goals. Conversely, Hanson and Wapner (1994) refer to a study by Walker MacRae, who found that Caucasian women maintain a sense of continuity in retirement by continuing to derive their identities from informal and interpersonal roles. Likewise, Simmons and Betschild (2001) find that paid and unpaid contributions to social life correlate positively with women's perceived identities.

Markides and Mindel (1987) point out that subjective meanings associated with retirement may vary according to cultural or racial groups. Among the First Nations, for example, retirement is a nebulous concept since old age is defined in terms of a person's continued ability to contribute to the community.

Coping Very little is known about the ways that people cope with stress associated with poor health or lowered income that might have precipitated or accompanied retirement (McDonald and Wanner 1990). Studies have generally suggested that the presence of social support contributes to retirement satisfaction. Findings from other studies (Mutran, Reitzes, and Fernandez 1997; Secombe and Lee 1986) have suggested that the presence of a spouse might mediate stress associated with retirement, though Kulik (2001) identifies differences in marital satisfaction according to gender. Price (2002) identifies women's coping patterns as influenced by previous work in professional versus non-professional positions, and that they tended to structure their time differently once retired.

Services Drawing on formal support services such as pre-retirement counselling has been found to have a positive impact on a person's retirement experience (Hanson and Wapner 1994; Mutran, Reitzes, and Fernandez et al. 1997). Accordingly, pre-retirement counselling has been found to increase the quality of life in retirement slightly but significantly (Maule, Clifford, and Taylor 1996). Pre-retirement counselling may address financial-planning, role-adjustment, and time-management skills as well as identify and access leisure activities. Service workers should be especially tuned in to the needs of those who are not married, who are rapidly approaching retirement, and who do not view themselves as competent workers since these groups have been identified as a vulnerable population (Mutran, Reitzes, and Fernandez et al. 1997). Hershey and Mowen (2000) also recommend that education forums be held to address retirees' different personality constructs and related savings habits.

Widowhood

Losing a spouse is one of the most traumatic experiences associated with aging. The grief associated with such a loss can manifest itself through physical or psychological symptoms and can affect every aspect of the survivor's life (Kastenbaum 1986). Women tend to experience widowhood more than men owing to their longer life expectancy and the Western social norm for men to remarry in their later years because they have a greater choice of potential mates (Lopata 1996).

Stress There is extensive research on the relationship between stress and widowhood. In describing the stressful impact of bereavement, Kastenbaum (1986) states that the most intense period of grief usually persists from one to six months and is characterized by numbness and despair, followed by physical symptoms of dizziness, headaches, body aches, loss of appetite, and sleep disturbances. As the physical reactions subside in intensity, the bereaved person may feel anger, confusion, and anxiety. Throughout the first year the survivor continues to move away from a complete focus on the loss, yet may continue the grieving process for a minimum of two years.

Several studies have shown that the most severe problem perceived by both widows and widowers is loneliness (Clark, Siviski, and Weiner 1986; Lopata 1996; Martin Matthews 1987). Widows employ three strategies to combat loneliness— keeping busy, developing new roles and relations, and focusing on their social roles such as mother or friend (Lopata 1996). Experiencing loneliness in widowhood appears to be a Western phenomenon since it is not as evident in non-Western communities where there is a high degree of interaction between extended families and neighbours (Lopata 1996).

Long-standing relationships with a spouse may be associated with the level of stress the surviving spouse experiences in widowhood. Women who have had close relationships with their husbands may experience stress following the death of their partners because they lack social and emotional support. Other women may feel a sense of relief at the passing of their husband who had been a demanding or unpleasant part of their lives (Lopata 1996). Financial insecurity is another common stressor, particularly for widows, as women in general are less likely to have private pensions or personal sources of income (Martin Matthews 1987).

Additional factors that influence stress in widowhood are age, gender, and race. Different support services exist depending on the age of the consumer; men tend to be less accustomed than women to developing and accessing social support (Lopata 1996); and because of its having a narrower social support network, the white population has more short- and long-term difficulty with the loss of a spouse than the black population does (Wortman, Silver, and Kessler 1993).

Appraisal Little has been written about the subjective meanings that are attached to grief or bereavement. In one of the few references made to this subject, Martin Matthews (1987) refers to "anticipatory socialization" and states that women are more likely than men to think about widowhood as a possible event in their lives. While a person may engage in this thought pattern, other research (Hill, Thompson, and Gallagher 1988) suggests that it does not necessarily reduce the intensity of the survivor's grief reaction after the spouse's death. Lopata (1996) states that in appraising the experience of widowhood, one must construct a self-concept that distinguishes between past and present attachments and sentiments. The ability to embark on this process depends on the person's individual desire, ability, and opportunities. There also appears to be a positive correlation between a person's level of education and his or her ability to perceive change in the self (Lopata 1996).

Coping

To manage the stress of widowhood, the survivor may draw on internal as well as external resources. One internal resource is developing feelings of competence through learning new skills and making decisions in new situations (Lopata 1996). Educated and middle-class women tend to have more personal resources to help them cope, including finances, health, knowledge, and self-confidence (Lopata 1996). Overall, persons with previous emotional stability appear to cope best (Stroebe and Stroebe 1993).

Several studies identify external resources in coping with widowhood. Maintaining frequent contact with significant others is associated with a lower incidence of depression (Dimond, Lund, and Caserta 1987). As already mentioned, women tend to have more extensive social support networks to draw on than their male counterparts (Lopata 1996; Wister and Strain 1986). Relationships with friends are subject to change following the death of a spouse, while relationships with family members are likely to remain relatively stable (Connidis 1989). However, Morgan (1989) has shown that widows do not always interpret supportive gestures by friends and family as support. Research highlights the importance of demonstrated social support before relatives are deceased (Bass, Bowman, and Noelker 1991). Sankar (1991) has found that the meaning that caregivers associate with support they receive during the caregiving period has implications for their relationships with others following their relatives' deaths. Other positive means of coping include church involvement, religious faith, pets, humour, and expression of painful sentiments to others (Lopata 1996).

Services

Western society has developed economic, emotional, and social support resources to respond to the stresses associated with widowhood (Lopata 1996). Social security benefits and supplementary grants are available to widows aged 65 and older; however, recipients commonly use the monies for the basic necessities of life (Lopata 1996). Community and religious programs also exist (Lopata 1996). The most effective means of attaining social support is in self-help groups, which emphasize a process of mutual support (Lieberman and Videka-Sherman 1986; Lopata 1996; Silverman 1986).

Widows vary in the extent to which they access social support (Lopata 1996; Utz 2002). Constraints affecting this access include lack of transportation, poor health, and language or literacy barriers. Furthermore, Lopata points out that the women least likely to access social support are socially isolated, of working-class backgrounds with limited education, are sporadically employed, and are not connected with a religious community.

Since few social programs are specifically designed for older widowed persons, older adults in general may need access to such programs (Lopata 1996). Another consideration in delivering services for widows is education on nutrition and self-efficacy as these skills tend to decrease at the onset of widowhood (Fry 2001; Quandt 2000). These skills may be influenced by rural, gender, and economic variables.

Relocation to Long-Term Care Facilities

Elderly people generally view their relocation to long-term care facilities as stressful experiences (Forbes, Jackson, and Kraus 1987) and as experiences that they postpone for as long as possible (Chenoweth and Spencer 1986). While the percentage of elderly Canadians living in such facilities at any one point may approximate only 8 percent to 9 percent (Schwenger and Gross 1980), 20 percent to 25 percent of elderly people can be expected to spend at least some time in these facilities before they die (Chappell, Strain, and Blandford 1986).

A combination of various risk factors has been associated with institutionalization. These include a person's being older than 85, being unmarried, living alone, having been recently in hospital, having difficulties with activities of daily living, and having some kind of cognitive impairment (Pearlman and Crown 1992; Shapiro and Tate 1988). Carriere and Pelletier (1995) find that the rate of institutionalization in Canada differs by region, the likelihood of living in facilities being greater in Quebec, Ontario, and the Prairies and less so in British Columbia and the Maritimes. This possibly owes to differences in the way that provincial policies influence the distribution of services to the elderly. Some American studies (for example, Mui and Burnette 1994; Wallace et al. 1998) have suggested that rates of relocation might also differ according to race and culture.

Stress The anticipation of moving away from home to a long-term care institution, as well as the move itself, can be a stressful experience for elderly people and their families (Rutman and Freedman 1988). Whether an elderly person chooses to relocate to a long-term care facility or whether someone else makes that decision, such as a physician or a discharge planner at a hospital, the thought of moving to a long-term care facility can produce feelings of loss, depression, and a sense of helplessness in the person moving.

As Solomon (1982) has pointed out, relocation represents a public acknowledgment of one's diminished capacity to care for oneself. Family members may also find the anticipated move stressful. Even primary caregivers who have spent years attending to relatives and who may be "near the breaking point," may feel guilty about "abandoning" their relatives (Rosenthal and Dawson 1991). In Zarit and Whitlach's (1992) study, caregivers were especially concerned about the quality of the facilities, their relatives' safety, and whether their relatives would be upset living in the facilities.

At the point of admission to a long-term care facility, elderly people may feel angry, rejected, or abandoned. They may also worry about losing their autonomy and becoming increasingly dependent on others (Solomon 1982). Studies have shown that relocation stress is most intense for the three to six months following the move (Borup 1981; Tobin and Lieberman 1976) and may be especially difficult for ethnic minorities moving into long-term care facilities where most of the residents are of a different culture. Elderly people from ethnic minorities, who speak a different language, may also receive less attention from staff (MacLean and Bonar 1983).

While family caregivers may experience a reduced role overload following their relatives' moves (Aneshensel et al.1995), the emotional strain of their caregiving often continues after the relocations. A recent study by Tornatore and Grant (2002), for example, suggests that ongoing caregiving is particularly difficult for those who are older, have spent a shorter period of time in the caregiver role before the relocation, and are currently more involved in providing hands-on care. Another study by Whitlach et al. (2001) finds an association between caregivers' depression and the extent to which they perceived that their relatives adjusted to their long-term care environment.

Appraisal Some researchers have suggested that an older person's attitude towards relocation mediates the potential stress associated with the move. In research conducted by Borup (1981) and Mirotznik and Ruskin (1985), people who felt more positively about entering long-term care facilities were more satisfied with their moves than those who felt otherwise. Interestingly, both Borup (1981) and Mirotznik and Ruskin (1985) also find that differences in satisfaction between those who felt more and less positively about their relocation disappeared three to six months following the moves.

In Gladstone's (1995a; 1995b) study of elderly married couples, spouses felt positively about moving to long-term care facilities for several reasons. Some spouses felt that they would no longer be burdens on their husbands or wives who had cared for them when they lived in the community. Some felt overwhelmed by the amount of caregiving that they had to perform and looked forward to the assistance offered to them and their partners by the facilities. Others felt relief that they would no longer have to worry about their husbands' or wives' security and safety. Bowers, Fibich, and Jacobson (2001) examined the quality of care that older persons received in a long-term care facility. Satisfaction with the care was found to be associated with the way that the residents viewed themselves in relation to the staff. Older persons appeared to rate their care differently, depending on whether they saw themselves as consumers of service or as friends with the staff.

Coping Elderly people and their families manage the stress associated with relocation in various ways. Elderly people who are frightened and unsure about their future may deal with their stress by complaining, withdrawing, or becoming self-absorbed (Solomon 1982). Similarly, family members may cope with their ambivalent feelings about the need for their relatives' moves to facilities by becoming demanding and critical of the staff (Smith and Bengston 1979). Farkas (1980) finds that spouses may cope with their feelings of guilt or anger by becoming over-attentive towards their relatives or by directing their feelings inward, resulting in depression or anxiety.

On the other hand, elderly persons may take part in new activities and social relationships in their facilities (Gladstone 1991). Research also shows that family members continue to visit their relatives in long-term care facilities regularly (Port et al. 2001; Yamamoto-Mitani, Aneshensel, and Levy-Storms 2002) and are often involved in their care (Bowers 1998; Ross, Rosenthal, and Dawson 1997). Family members may also consolidate their position within the facilities by carefully negotiating their relationships with staff (Gladstone and Wexler, 2002a, 2002b).[4] This may be beneficial to older residents, in terms of alleviating any fears of abandonment or even drawing them closer to their families (Smith and Bengtson 1979). By visiting and continuing to provide assistance to their relatives after relocation, family members may also feel that they are able to demonstrate their commitment and sense of closeness towards their relatives in long-term care facilities.

Moreover, the importance of cultural differences should not be overlooked. Lee, Woo, and Mackenzie (2002), for example, have pointed out the role that socio-cultural values play in elders' adjustment to life in long-term care facilities.

Services Services to the elderly living in long-term care facilities include activity programs that give them opportunities for social contact as well as sensory stimulation (Forbes, Jackson, and Kraus 1987). These activities include outings, visits from groups in the external community, recreation activities, residents' councils, and reminiscence groups (Forbes, Jackson, and Kraus 1987). Social workers can offer counselling that helps ease the entry of residents and their families to life in the facilities or that addresses the psychosocial needs that residents and families have after relocation. Social workers can also consult with nursing staff to facilitate optimal communication between these parties and enhance the quality of the services delivered (Edelson and Lyons 1985). Kayser-Jones (2002) points out the importance of attending to the psychosocial, spiritual, and cultural needs of residents and families, especially as the end of their lives approaches.

CONCLUSION

A review of the literature on caregiving, retirement, widowhood, and relocation to long-term care facilities elucidates some themes common to these transitions. First, each of these major transitions is potentially stressful, although the impact of the stress can be mediated by the appraisal of the event and the coping strategies employed to manage the event.

While the focus of this chapter has been the stressful aspects of these life transitions, it should be remembered that older adults are a heterogeneous group, characterized by individual differences, as are members of every age cohort. Consequently these transitions are not necessarily experienced as stressful by everybody. Horowitz (1985a) and Cohen et al. (1994), for example, have stated that caregivers may derive a sense of satisfaction if they feel that they are successfully able to handle the situation, meet a perceived obligation, or act as role models for their own children.

McDonald and Wanner (1990) have pointed out that many persons nearing retirement look forward to the experience.

Kastenbaum (1986) has distinguished between the concepts of "bereavement" and "grief," adding that persons may be in a bereaved state, yet not grieve over or feel sorrow for their loss. Stein et al.'s research (1985) showed that older persons are not always worried about moving to long-term care facilities or concerned about autonomy and dependency.

Each of these major transitions is a process, rather than a discrete event that takes place at any one moment in time. Aneshensel et al. (1995), for example, have referred to the "careers of caregivers." McDonald and Wanner (1990) have conceptualized retirement as a process that may include a decision-making stage as well as the actual termination of employment. Lopata (1973) has described the various emotional, psychological, and social changes associated with widowhood. Solomon (1982) has identified the four stages associated with relocation to a long-term care facility.

This conclusion has implications for practice and policy. If each of these transitions unfolds as a process, then older adults and their families may have different types of needs at different stages that can be placed within the context of gender and ethnicity.

Several Canadian social programs are currently undergoing restructuring, adjustment, and adaptation phases that may lead to fragmented and uncoordinated services in an unstable array of public, voluntary, and private services (Aronson 1999). Wallace (1990) refers to gaps in the continuum of services as "no-care zones" whereby the services provided are not appropriate to meet elders' needs. In order to avoid the "no-care zone" he stresses availability, accessibility, and acceptability in service delivery. Availability determines whether a service is provided on the basis of a particular need. Once provided, it should be accessible to the population that needs it in terms of transportation, physical mobility, finances, and knowledge of its existence. Furthermore, it must be acceptable in the sense that clients who need the service are willing to access it. In order to reduce fragmented service delivery, Keating et al. (1997; 2001) stress that partnerships between informal and formal care in the community are essential.

NOTES

1. There are a number of fine Canadian texts that discuss other issues related to social gerontology. Examples include B. D. McPherson, *Aging as a Social Process* (Toronto: Butterworths, 1983); V. W. Marshall, *Aging in Canada* (Markham, ON, 1980; 1987); and M. Novak, *Successful Aging* (Markham, ON, 1985).

2. While this article focuses on formal services, resources in one's informal social network are also important mediators of stress. See, for example, L A. Connidis, *Family Ties and Aging* (Toronto: Butterworths, 1989), and J. E. Norris and J. A. Tindale, *Among Generations: The Cycle of Adult Relationships* (New York: W. H. Freeman, 1994).

3. Several good studies have compared the contributions of daughters and sons to the care of elderly parents. For example, Brody, Hoffman, Kleban, and Schoonover (1989) and Crawford, Bond, and Balshaw (1994) found different degrees of caregiving involvement between daughters and sons. Matthews (1995) has pointed out why sisters are perceived to contribute more than brothers, and in a later study (Matthews and Heidorn 1988) he suggests that brothers place different meanings on their filial obligations. Harris (1998) has identified four types of caregiving sons, while Globerman (1996) has described the various patterns of helping displayed by sons- and daughters-in-law.

4. Dupuis and Norris (1997) have developed a very useful conceptual model of family–resident–staff relationships.

REFERENCES

Aneshensel, C. S., Pearlin, L. I., Mullan, J. T., Zarit, S. H., & Whitlatch, C. J. 1995. *Profiles in caregiving: The unexpected career.* San Diego: Academic Press.

Aronson, J. 1990. Old women's experiences of needing care: Choice or compulsion? *Canadian Journal on Aging, 9.* 234–247.

Aronson, J. 1991. Dutiful daughters and undemanding mothers: Constraining images of giving and receiving care in middle and late life. In C. Baines, P. Evans, & S. Neysmith (Eds.), *Women's caring: Feminist perspectives on social welfare* (pp. 138–168). Toronto: McClelland & Stewart.

Aronson, J. 1999. Conflicting images of older people receiving care: Challenges for reflexive practice and research. In S. Neysmith (Ed.), *Critical issues for future social work practice with aging persons* (pp. 47–69). New York: Columbia University Press.

Atchley, R. C., & Miller, S. J. 1983. Types of elderly couples. In T. H. Brubaker, *Family relationships in later life* (pp. 77–90). Beverly Hills, CA: Sage.

Barusch, A. S., & Spaid, W. M. 1989. Gender differences in caregiving: Why do wives report greater burden? *The Gerontologist,* 29. 667–676.

Bass, D. M., Bowman, K., & Noelker, L. S. 1991. The influence of caregiving and bereavement support on adjusting to an older relative's death. *The Gerontologist, 31.* 32–42.

Baum, M., & Page, M. 1991. Caring and multigenerational families. *The Gerontologist, 31.* 762–769.

Birkel, R. C., & Jones, C. J. 1989. A comparison of the caregiving networks of dependent elderly individuals who are lucid and those who are demented. *The Gerontologist, 29.* 114–119.

Borup, J. H. 1981. Relocation: Attitudes, information network and problems encountered. *The Gerontologist, 21.* 501–511.

Bowers, B. J. 1988. Family perceptions of care in a nursing home. *The Gerontologist, 28.* 361–368.

Bowers, B. J., Fibich, B., & Jacobson, N. 2001. Care-as-service, care-as-relating, care-as-comfort: Understanding nursing home residents' definitions of quality. *The Gerontologist, 41.* 539–545.

Brody, E. M., Hoffman, C., Kleban, M. H., & Schoonover, C. B. 1989. Caregiving daughters and their local siblings: perceptions, strains and interactions. *The Gerontologist, 29.* 529–538.

Campbell, L.D., & Martin Matthews, A. 2000. Exploring men's involvement in filial care. *Canadian Journal on Aging, 19.* 57–79.

Canadian Study on Health and Aging. 1994. Patterns of caring for people with dementia in Canada. *Canadian Journal on Aging, 13.* 470–487.

Carpenter, B.D. 2001. Attachment bonds between adult daughters and their older mothers: associations with contemporary caregiving. *Journal of Gerontology: Psychological Sciences, 56B.* P257–P266.

Carriere, Y., & Pelletier, L. 1995. Factors underlying the institutionalization of elderly persons in Canada. *Journal of Gerontology: Social Sciences, SOB,* S164–SI72.

Cattanach, L., & Tebes, J.K. 1991. The nature of elder impairment and its impact on family and caregivers' health and psychosocial functioning. *The Gerontologist, 31.* 246–255.

Chappell, N. L., Strain, L. A., & Blandford, A. A. 1986. *Aging and health care: A social perspective.* Toronto: Holt, Rinehart and Winston.

Chenoweth, B., & Spencer, B. 1986. Dementia: The experience of family caregivers. *The Gerontologist, 26.* 267–272.

Clark, P.O., Siviski, R.W., & Weiner, R. 1986. Coping strategies of widowers in the first year. *Family Relations, 35.* 425–430.

Cohen, C. A., Pushkar Gold, D., Shulman, K. I., & Zucchero, C. A. 1994. Positive aspects in caregiving: An overlooked variable in research. *Canadian Journal on Aging, 13.* 378–391.

Colantonio, A., Cohen, C., & Corlett, S. 1998. Support needs of elderly caregivers of persons with dementia. *Canadian Journal on Aging, 17.* 330–345.

Connidis, I. A. 1989. *Family ties and aging.* Toronto: Butterworths.

Crawford, L. M., Bond, J. B., Jr., & Balshaw, R. F. 1994. Factors affecting sons' and daughters' caregiving to older parents. *Canadian Journal on Aging, 13.* 454–469.

Denton, F., & Spencer, E. G. 1980. Canada's population and labour force. In V. W. Marshall (Ed.), *Aging in Canada.* Toronto: Fitzhenry and Whiteside.

Dimond, M., Lund, D. A., & Caserta, M. S. 1987. The role of social support in the first two years of bereavement in an elderly sample. *The Gerontologist, 27.* 599–604.

Dorfman, L. T., Kohout, F. J., & Heckert, D. A. 1985. Retirement satisfaction in the rural elderly. *Research on Aging, 1.* 577–599.

Dupuis, S. L., & Norris, J. E. 1997. A multidimensional and contextual framework for understanding diverse family members' roles in long-term care facilities. *Journal of Aging Studies, 11.* 297–325.

Edelson, J. S., & Lyons, W. H. 1985. *Institutional care of the mentally impaired elderly.* New York, Van Nostrand Reinholt.

Farkas, S. W. 1980. Impact of chronic illness on the patient's spouse. *Health and social work*. 39–46.

Farran, C. J. 1997. Theoretical perspectives concerning positive aspects of caring for elderly persons with dementia: Stress/adaptation and existentialism. *The Gerontologist, 37*. 250–256.

Farran, C. J., Keane-Hagerty, E., Salloway, S., Kupferer, S., & Wilken, C. S. 1991. Finding meaning: An alternative paradigm for Alzheimer's disease family caregivers. *The Gerontologist, 31*. 483–489.

Fengler, A. P., & Goodrich, N. 1979. Wives of elderly disabled men: The hidden patients. *The Gerontologist, 19*. 175–183.

Forbes, W. F., Jackson, A., & Kraus, A. S. 1987. *Institutionalization of the elderly in Canada*. Toronto: Butterworths.

Fry, P. S. 2001. Predictors of health-related quality of life perspectives, self-esteem, and life satisfactions of older adults following spousal loss: An 18-month follow-up study of widows and widowers. *The Gerontologist, 41*. 787–798.

Gaugher, J. E., Edwards, A. B., Femia, E. E., Zarit, S. H., Parris Stephens, M-A., Townsend, A., & Greene, R. 2000. Predictors of institutionalization of cognitively impaired elders: Family help and the timing of placement. *Journal of Gerontology: Psychological Sciences, 55B*. P247–P255.

George, L. K., & Gwyther, L. P. 1986. Caregiver well-being: A multidimensional examination of family caregivers of demented adults. *The Gerontologist, 26*. 253–259.

Ginn, J., & Arber, S. 1996. Gender, age and attitudes to retirement in mid-life. *Ageing and Society, 16*. 27–55.

Gladstone, J. W. 1991. Elderly married persons relocating to institutions: Implications for mutual caregiving. Paper presented at the International Conference on Care of the Elderly, Hong Kong.

Gladstone, J. W. 1995a. The marital perceptions of elderly persons living or having a spouse living in a long-term care institution in Canada. *The Gerontologist, 35*. 52–60.

Gladstone, J. W. 1995b. Elderly married persons living in long term care institutions: A qualitative analysis of feelings. *Ageing and Society, 15*. 493–513.

Gladstone, J. W., & Wexler, E. January/February 2000. A family perspective of family-staff interaction in long-term care facilities. *Geriatric Nursing*. 16–19.

Gladstone, J., & Wexler, E. 2002a. Exploring the relationships between families and staff caring for residents in long-term care facilities: Family members' perspectives. *Canadian Journal on Aging, 21*. 39–46.

Gladstone, J., & Wexler, E. 2002b. The development of relationships between families and staff in long-term care facilities: Nurses' perspectives. *Canadian Journal on Aging, 21*. 217–228.

Globerman, J. 1995. The unencumbered child: Family reputations and responsibilities in the care of relatives with Alzheimer's disease. *Family Process, 34*. 87–99.

Globerman, J. 1996. Motivations to care: Daughters- and sons-in-law caring for relatives with Alzheimer's disease. *Family Relations, 45*. 37–45.

Guberman, N., Maheu, P., & Maille, C. 1992. Women as family caregivers: Why do they care? *The Gerontologist, 32*. 607–617.

Hanson, K., & Wapner, S. 1994. Transition to retirement: Gender differences. *International Journal of Aging and Human Development, 39*. 189–208.

Harris, P. B. 1998. Listening to caregiving sons: Misunderstood realities. *The Gerontologist, 38*. 342–352.

Hasselkus, B. R. 1988. Meaning in family caregiving: Perspectives on caregiver/professional relationships. *The Gerontologist, 28*: 792–796.

Hershey, D. A., & Mowen, J. C. 2000. Psychological determinants of financial preparedness for retirement. *The Gerontologist, 40.* 687–697.

Hill, C. D., Thompson, L. W., & Gallagher, D. 1988. The role of anticipatory bereavement in older women's adjustment to widowhood. *The Gerontologist, 28.* 792–796.

Horowitz, A. 1985a. Family caregiving to the frail elderly. In P. Lawton & G. Maddox (Eds.), *Annual Review of Gerontology and Geriatrics, Vol. S* (pp. 194–246). New York: Springer.

Horowitz, A. 1985b. Sons and daughters as caregivers to older parents: Differences in role performance and consequences. *The Gerontologist, 25.* 612–617.

Janevic, M. R., & Connell, C. M. 2001. Racial, ethnic, and cultural differences in the dementia caregiving experience: Recent findings. *The Gerontologist, 41.* 334–347.

Johnson, C. L. 1983. Dyadic family relations and social support. *The Gerontologist, 23.* 377–383.

Jutras, S., & Veilleux, F. 1991. Informal caregiving: Correlates of perceived burden. *Canadian Journal on Aging, 10.* 40–55.

Karp, D. A. 1988. A decade of reminders: changing age consciousness between fifty and sixty years old. *The Gerontologist, 28.* 727–738.

Kastenbaum, R. J. 1986. *Death, society, and human experience.* Columbus, OH: Charles E. Merrill.

Kayser-Jones, J. 2002. The experience of dying: An ethnographic nursing home study. *The Gerontologist, Special Issue 3.42.* 11–19.

Keating, N., Fast, J., Dosman, D., & Eales, J. 2001. Services provided by informal and formal caregivers to seniors in residential continuing care. *Canadian Journal on Aging, 20.* 23–45.

Keating, N. C., Fast, J. E., Connidis, I. A., Penning, M., & Keefe, J. 1997. Bridging policy and research in eldercare. *Canadian Journal on Aging,* Special issue supplement:, 22–41.

Kosberg, J. I., Cairl, R. E., & Keller, D. M. 1990. Components of burden: Interventive implications. *The Gerontologist, 30.* 236–242.

Kosloski, K., & Montgomery, R. J. V. 1995. The impact of respite use on nursing home placement. *The Gerontologist, 35:* 67–74.

Kulik, L. 2001. The impact of men's and women's retirement on marital relations: A comparative analysis. *Journal of Women and Aging, 13.* 21–37.

Lazarus, R. S., & Folkman, S. 1984. *Stress, appraisal, and coping.* New York: Springer.

Lee, D. T. F., Woo, J., & Mackenzie, A. E. 2002. The cultural context of adjusting to nursing home life: Chinese elders' perspectives. *The Gerontologist, 42.* 667–675.

Lieberman, M. A., & Videka-Sherman, L. 1986. The impact of self-help groups on the mental health of widows and widowers. *American Journal of Orthopsychiatry, 56.* 435–449.

Lopata, H. Z. 1973. *Widowhood in an American city.* Cambridge, MA: Shenkman.

Lopata, H.Z. 1996. *Current widowhood: Myths and realities.* Thousand Oaks, CA: Sage Publications.

MacLean, M., & Bonar, R. 1986. Ethnic elderly people in long-term care facilities of the dominant culture: Implication for social work practice and education. *International Social Work, 29.* 227–236.

Marcus, L., & Jaeger, V. 1984. The elderly as family caregivers. *Canadian Journal on Aging, 3.* 33–42.

Markides, K. S., & Mindel, C. H. 1987. *Aging and ethnicity.* Newbury Park, CA: Sage.

Marshall, V. W., Clarke, P. J., & Ballantyne, P. J. 2001. Instability in the retirement transition. *Research on Aging, 23.* 379–409.

Marshall, V. W. 1987. *Aging in Canada: Social perspectives.* 2d ed. Markham, ON: Fitzhenry and Whiteside.

Marshall, V. W. 1980. *Aging in Canada.* Markham, ON: Fitzhenry and Whiteside.

Martin Matthews, A. 1980. Women and widowhood. In V. W. Marshall (Ed.), *Aging in Canada* (pp. 145–153). Markham, ON: Fitzhenry and Whiteside,

Martin Matthews, A., & Brown, K. 1987. Retirement as a critical life event: The differential experiences of women and men. *Research on Aging, 9.* 548–571.

Matthews, S. H. 1995. Gender and the division of filial responsibility between lone sisters and their brothers. *Journal of Gerontology: Social Sciences, SOB.* S312–S320.

Matthews, S. H., & Heidorn, J. 1998. Meeting filial responsibilities in brothers-only sibling groups. *Journal of Gerontology: Social Sciences, 53B.* S278–S286.

Maule, A. J., Clifford, D. R., & Taylor, R. 1996. Factors that influence aging and how they affect later quality of life. *Ageing and Society, 16.* 177–204.

McDonald, P. L., & Wanner, R. A. 1990. *Retirement in Canada.* Toronto: Butterworths.

McPherson, B. D. 1983. *Aging as a social process.* Toronto: Butterworths.

Miller, B. 1987. Gender and control among spouses of the cognitively impaired: A research note. *The Gerontologist, 27.* 447–453.

Miller, B., & Cafasso, L. 1992. Gender differences in caregiving: Fact or artifact? *The Gerontologist, 32.* 498–507.

Miller, B., & Guo, S. 2000. Social support for spouse caregivers of persons with dementia. *Journal of Gerontology: Social Sciences, 55B.* S163–S172.

Miller, B., & McFall, S. 1991. Stability and change in the informal task support network of frail older persons. *The Gerontologist, 31.* 735–745.

Mirotznik, J., & Ruskin, A. P. 1985. Interinstitutional relocation and its effect on psychosocial status. *The Gerontologist, 30.* 583–594.

Mittelman, M. S., Ferris, S. H., Shulman, E., Steinberg, G., Ambinder, A., Mackell, J. A., & Cohen, J. 1995. A comprehensive support program: Effect on depression in spousecaregiver of AD patients. *The Gerontologist, 35.* 792–802.

Montgomery, R. J. V., & Borgatta, E. F. 1989. The effects of alternative support strategies on family caregiving. *The Gerontologist, 29.* 457–464.

Morgan, D.. 1989. Adjusting to widowhood: Do social networks really make it easier? *The Gerontologist, 29.* 101–107.

Moritz, D. J., Kasl, S. V., & Berkman, L. F. 1989. The health impact of living with a cognitively impaired elderly spouse: Depressive symptoms and social functioning. *Journal of Gerontology, 44.* SI 7–27.

Motenko, A. K. 1989. The frustrations, gratifications, and well-being of dementia caregivers. *The Gerontologist, 29.* 166–172.

Mui, A. C., & Burnette, D. 1994. Long-term care service use by frail elders: Is ethnicity a factor? *The Gerontologist, 34.* 190–198.

Mutran, E., Reitzes, D., & Fernandez, M. 1997. Factors that influence attitudes toward retirement. *Research on Aging, 19.* 251–273.

Noelker, L. S., & Wallace, R. W. 1985. The organization of family care for impaired elderly. *Journal of Family Issues, 6.* 23–44.

Norris, J. E., & Tindale, J. A. 1994. *Among generations: The cycle of adult relationships.* San Francisco: W. H. Freeman.

Novak, M. 1985. *Successful aging.* Markham, ON: Penguin.

Parnes, H. S. 1981. From the middle to the later years: Longitudinal studies of the pre- and postretirement experiences of men. *Research on Aging, 3.* 387–402.

Pearlin, L I., Mullan, J. T., Semple, S. J., & Skaff, M. M. 1990. Caregiving and the stress process: An overview of concepts and their measures. *The Gerontologist, 30.* 583–594.

Pearlman, D. N., & Crown, W. H. 1992. Alternative sources of social support and their impacts on institutional risk. *The Gerontologist, 32.* 527–535.

Pinquart, M., & Sorensen, S. 2003. Associations of stressors and uplifts of caregiving with caregiver burden and depressive mood: A meta-analysis. *Journal of Gerontology: Psychological Sciences, 58B.* P112–P128.

Port, C. L., Gruber-Baldini, A.L., Burton, L., Baumgarten, M., Hebel, J. R., Zimmerman, S. I., & Magaziner, J. 2001. Resident contact with family and friends following nursing home admission. *The Gerontologist, 41.* 589–596.

Pratt, C. C., Schmall, V. L., Wright, S., & Cleland, M. 1985. Burden and coping strategies of caregivers to Alzheimer's patients. *Family Relations, 34.* 27–33.

Price, C. 2002. Retirement for women: The impact of employment. *Journal of Women and Aging, 14.* 3–4.

Quandt, S. A., McDonald, J., Arcury, T. A., Bell, R. A., & Vitolins, M. Z. 2000. Nutritional self-management of elderly widows in rural communities. *The Gerontologist, 40.* 86–96.

Pruchno, R. A., & Resch, N. L. 1989. Husbands and wives as caregivers: Antecedents of depression and burden. *The Gerontologist, 29.* 159–165.

Rosenthal, C. J., & Dawson, P. 1991. Wives of institutionalized elderly men: The first stage of the transition to quasi-widowhood. *Journal of Aging and Health, 3.* 315–334.

Ross, M. M., Rosenthal, C. J., & Dawson, P. O. 1997. Spousal caregiving in the institutional setting: Task performance. *Canadian Journal on Aging, 16.* 51–69.

Rutman, D. L., & Freedman, J. L. 1988. Anticipating relocation: Coping strategies and the meaning of home for older people. *Canadian Journal on Aging, 7.* 17–31.

Sankar, A. 1991. Ritual and dying: A cultural analysis of social support for caregivers. *The Gerontologist, 31.* 43–50.

Scharlach, A. E., Sobel, E. L., & Roberts, R. E. L. 1991. Employment and caregiver strain: An integrative model. *The Gerontologist, 31.* 778–787.

Schulz, R., O'Brien, A., Czaja, S., Ory, M., Norris, R., Martire, L.M., Bele, S.H., Burgio, L., Gitlin, L., Coon, D., Burns, R., Gallagher-Thompson, D., & Stevens, A. 2002. Dementia caregiver intervention research: In search of clinical significance. *The Gerontologist, 42.* 589–602.

Schwenger, C., & Gross, J. 1980. Institutional care and institutionalization of the elderly in Canada. In V. W. Marshall (Ed.), *Aging in Canada* (pp. 248–256). Markham, ON: Fitzhenry and Whiteside.

Secombe, K., & Lee, G. R. 1986. Gender differences in retirement satisfaction and its antecedents. *Research on Aging, 8.* 426–440.

Shapiro, E., & Tate, R. 1988. Who is really at risk of institutionalization? *The Gerontologist, 28:* 237–245.

Silverman, P. R. 1986. *Widow to widow.* New York: Springer.

Simmons, B. A., & Betschild, M. J. 2001. Women's retirement, work and life paths: Changes, disruptions and discontinuities. *Journal of Women and Aging, 13.* 53–70.

Smith, K. F., & Bengtson, V. L. 1979. Positive consequences of institutionalization: Solidarity between elderly parents and their middle-aged children. *The Gerontologist, 19.* 438–447.

Solomon, R. 1982. Serving families of the institutionalized aged: The four crises. *Journal of Gerontological Social Work, 5.* 83–96.

Stein, S., Linn, M. W., & Stein, E. M. 1985. Patients' anticipation of stress in nursing home care. *The Gerontologist, 25:* 88–94.

Stroebe, W., & Stroebe, M.S. 1993. Determinants of adjustment to bereavement in younger widows and widowers. In M. S. Stroebe, W. Stroebe, & R. O. Hansson (Eds.), *Handbook of bereavement: Theory, research and intervention,* (pp. 208–226). New York: Cambridge University Press.

Szinovacz, M. E., & DeVinvey, S. 2000. Marital characteristics and retirement decisions. *Research on Aging, 22.* 470–498.

Tennstedt, S. L., McKinlay, J. B., & Sullivan, L. M. 1989. Informal care for frail elders: The role of secondary caregivers. *The Gerontologist, 29.* 677–683.

Tobin, S. S., & Lieberman, M. A. 1976. *Last home for the aged.* San Francisco: Jossey-Bass.

Tornatore, J. B., & Grant, L. A. 2002. Burden among family caregivers of persons with Alzheimer's Disease in nursing homes. *The Gerontologist, 42.* 497–506.

Toseland, R. W., & Rossiter, C. M. 1989. Group interventions to support family caregivers: A review and analysis. *The Gerontologist, 29.* 438–448.

Utz, R. L., Carr, D., Nesse, R., & Wortman, C. B. 2002. The effect of widowhood on older adults' social participation: An evaluation of activity, disengagement, and continuity theories. *The Gerontologist, 42.* 522–533.

Wadley, V. G., & Haley, W. E. 2001. Diagnostic attributions versus labeling: Impact of Alzheimer's Disease and major depression diagnoses on emotions, beliefs, and helping intentions of family members. *Journal of Gerontology: Psychological Sciences, 56B.* P244–P252.

Walker, A. 1991. The relationship between the family and the state in the care of older people. *Canadian Journal on Aging, 10.* 94–112.

Wallace, S. P. 1990. The no-care zone: Availability, accessibility, and acceptability in community-based long-term care. *The Gerontologist, 30,* 254–261.

Wallace, S. P., Levy-Storms, L., Kington, R. S., & Andersen, R. M. 1998. The persistence of race and ethnicity in the use of long-term care. *Journal of Gerontology: Social Sciences, 53B.* S104–S112.

Wanner, R. A., & McDonald, P. L. 1986. The vertical mosaic in later life: Ethnicity and retirement in Canada. *Journal of Gerontology, 41.* 662–671.

Whitlach, C. J., Schur, D., Noelker, L. S., Ejaz, F. K., & Looman, W. J. 2001. The stress process of family caregiving in institutional settings. *The Gerontologist, 32.* 665–672.

Wister, A. V., & Strain, L. 1986. Social support and well-being: A comparison of older widows and widowers. *Canadian Journal on Aging, 5.* 205–219.

Wortman, C. B., Silver, R. C., & Kessler, R. C. 1993. The meaning of loss and adjustment to bereavement. In M. S. Stroebe, W. Stroebe, & R. O. Hansson (Eds.), *Handbook of bereavement: Theory, research and intervention* (pp. 349–366). New York: Cambridge University Press.

Yamamoto-Mitani, N., Aneshensel, C. S., & Levy-Storms, L. 2002. Patterns of family visiting with institutionalized elders: The case of dementia. *Journal of Gerontology: Social Sciences, 57B.* S234–S246.

Yates, M. E., Tennstedt, S., & Chang, B-H. 1999. Contributors to and mediators of psychological well-being for informal caregivers. *Journal of Gerontology: Psychological Sciences, 548.* 12–22.

Young, R. F., & Kahana, E. 1989. Specifying caregiver outcomes: Gender and relationship aspects of caregiving strain. *The Gerontologist, 20.* 649–655.

Zarit, S. H., Reever, K. E., & Bach-Peterson, J. 1980. Relatives of the impaired elderly: Correlates of feelings of burden. *The Gerontologist, 20.* 649–655.

Zarit, S. H., & Whitlach, C. J. 1992. Institutional placement: Phases of the transition. *The Gerontologist, 32.* 665–672.

Zimmerman, L., Mitchell, B., Wister, A., & Gutman, G. 2000. Unanticipated consequences: A comparison of expected and actual retirement timing among older women. *Journal of Women and Aging, 12.* 1–2.

chapter twenty-five

Services for the Physically Disabled

Mel Basbaum

INTRODUCTION

Statistics on the numbers of disabled persons in Canada depend very much on how one defines disability. Yet certain facts suggest the numbers are increasing and will likely continue to do so.

Among these facts are the following:

- Our population is aging and therefore more likely to incur disabilities.

- Medical technology continues to improve, which means a high survival rate for trauma victims (such as the spinal cord– or brain-injured).

- Increasing numbers of low-birth-weight infants are surviving into childhood and beyond, often with significant chronic impairments.

Before World War II, services to the disabled in Canada were available primarily from hospitals or provincial institutions only, often far from the disabled person's home community. Since then there has been a slow evolution of community-based services, which expanded rapidly between the 1960s and the late 1980s. Initially programs continued to be characterized by the segregation of the disabled and their families, and only in the latter part of that period did many of these services become part of the broader system of services provided to all Canadians.

Central to the changes are the beliefs that:

- people with disabilities have to be full participating members of their communities;

- it is possible to create responsive communities concerned with justice for the disabled;
- programs for the disabled should not be segregated from other services; and
- integration should not mean denial of appropriate supports.[1]

Despite these ideals, the Ontario Advisory Council in its 1988 discussion paper *Independent Living: The Time Is Now* still had to identify the following philosophical guidelines in its recommendations to government:

- Community living should be recognized as a fundamental right for all citizens of Ontario.
- Accessible services should be created and expanded to meet the needs and expectations of active and participating people living independently in communities across the province.
- Consumers should have the most control possible over the design and provision of their own assistance with independent living.[2]

And as recently as 1996 the Federal Task Force on Disability Issues had the following to say in the introduction to its report to Parliament: "Members of Parliament produced a series of reports and recommendations that started in the early 1980s with the *Obstacles* report and finished with... *Pathways to Integration* in 1993. But implementation... has left a lot to be desired."[3]

The period since the Task Force report has been one of mixed reviews for disabled Canadians. On the one hand, they have suffered many of the problems facing vulnerable groups as a result of increasing fiscal conservatism by all levels of government. On the other hand, they have at times been either exempted from the new rules and regulations or an important part of efforts to improve service delivery systems. We discuss both elements of this sometimes paradoxical situation in greater detail below.

Before attempting to consider how successful or unsuccessful we have been as a society, it is also important to understand the distinction between "disability" and "handicap." The World Health Organization identifies four elements in a continuum of illness and disability: disease, impairment, disability, and handicap. For the purposes of this paper we need to define only the last two.

A *disability* is "any restriction or lack of ability to perform in a manner considered normal." Disabilities are the consequence of impairment representing a disturbance at the level of the individual, such as a loss or reduction of the individual's ability to perform certain physical functions. A *handicap,* on the other hand, is a disadvantage that prevents the individual from fulfilling a role or conforming to the expectations or norms of society. Thus, a handicap may be the consequence of a disability—not being able to get into a building that has no wheelchair access or being passed over for a job on the basis of disability.[4]

This distinction is important since the ensuing discussion will, for the most part, focus on the concept of handicap as defined above. The issues facing someone with a disability do not result purely because of a physical or mental disability; rather, they concern the fit of such disabilities with the person's social, attitudinal, architectural, medical, economic, and political environment. While there exists a wide variety of disabilities, each with its own unique features and needs, it should be obvious by the end of this chapter that many of the problems confronting the disabled owe at least as much, and probably more, to issues of public will and attitudes as they do to an individual's or group's specific impairment and disability.

LEGISLATION

Legislation may be of two types: that which addresses the civil rights of the individual and that which is intended, as enabling legislation, to provide for the needs of particular groups.

Civil Rights Legislation

Though not originally included amongst the protected groups under Section 15 of the federal Charter of Rights and Freedoms, the charter now provides, with only rare exceptions, for equality rights of the disabled, and requires that government not ignore the handicapped in any "legislative, administrative or judicial" decision-making that extends rights, benefits, or privileges to Canadians in general.[5]

Provincial governments have, in most cases, enacted legislation designed to reinforce and even strengthen the intentions of the charter. The Ontario Human Rights Code, for example, identifies the "handicapped" as one of approximately 15 groups of people that have the right to freedom from discrimination in the areas of services, goods and facilities, accommodation, contracts, employment, and membership in vocational associations and trade unions.[6]

Enabling or Social Legislation

As noted, the 1990s were a time of mixed experiences for Canada's disabled. In an era of cutbacks they benefited from special status, which saw services to this population exempted from many of these changes. As well, there were significant changes in the philosophical basis for services to the disabled that can be considered significant improvements.

Though most governments have consciously avoided including the disabled in their efforts to restrain public spending, the disabled have been affected by a number of broader based reductions. Two of the most significant federal acts affecting services to the disabled were the Vocational Rehabilitation of Disabled Persons Act (VDRP) of 1961 and the Canada Assistance Plan (CAP) of 1966.

Under the provisions of the former, the federal government contributed 50 percent of the provincial costs of providing vocational rehabilitation services to physically and mentally disabled persons. Under CAP, the provinces were reimbursed 50 percent of the cost of assistance to persons in need and/or for the improvement or extension of services designed to prevent their dependence. While not a guarantee that the provinces would create and provide such services, it did control the provincial governments' access to and use of their federal transfer payments. The repeal of CAP in 1996, coupled with ever-increasing reductions in transfer payments, has meant significant hardships for all vulnerable populations in Canada. (The VDRP is discussed further under the first of the "Employment" sections of this chapter.)

Some significant legislative improvements have been made, however. Traditionally, disability has been defined in terms of a person's inability to work, a major work disincentive. More recently, some provinces, led by British Columbia in 1996, shifted the focus from employability to a "condition that requires either that the person have significant extra disability-related costs or requires significant assistance or supervision in activities of daily living."[7]

Similarly, we are beginning to see a shift in attitude toward the "duration" and "status" of the disability. Rather than defining *duration* strictly in terms of a particular time frame within which to qualify for services, both British Columbia and Ontario now allow for recurrent rather than continuous disabilities. Also, there are intimations of an allowance for different *status* (for those with permanent rather than shorter-term disabilities). The advantage of this is that those with permanent disabilities will no longer risk delays in their reinstatement should they make unsuccessful attempts to gain employment.[8]

The National Building Code While having no legislative or jurisdictional authority, the code provides a model for the provinces and the municipalities to follow and help them develop their own standards and procedures. As part of the code, the federal Department of Public Works has developed accessibility guidelines that it applies to new and existing federal buildings.[9]

Canada Mortgage and Housing (CMHC) Established as a Crown corporation in 1964, CMHC was active in the 1980s and early 1990s in promoting barrier-free design and modification of various programs. The latter allowed for the construction of a wide variety of accessible dwellings. Among these initiatives was the provision of financial assistance to groups interested in establishing non-profit housing programs.

Until the early 1990s, Canada Rental Supply Plan grants were made available to developers to stimulate their construction of rental units in areas with low vacancy rates. A portion of all the units built had to include accessibility modifications. However, in 1995 the Ontario government canceled all its support for non-profit housing. Next, the federal government transferred its responsibility to the private sector in 1996. Nevertheless, British Columbia, as recently as 1999, announced additional funding for 2400 new units, a portion of which was to be devoted to supportive housing.

These differences are just one example of the inconsistencies in social policy across the country. For residents in many parts of the country the result has not only been an increase in the numbers of homeless persons but also a reduction in available accessible, affordable housing for disabled persons.

The Housing Technology Incentives Program was created to stimulate research and development in innovative housing-related products or systems, including those that make housing more habitable for the disabled. Finally, the Residential Rehabilitation Assistance Program (RRAP) makes available loans for altering and repairing existing housing. Additional funds are also available if the renovations include necessary interior changes to bring buildings' standards up to current codes. As many as one-half of these loans could be forgivable, depending on the homeowners' incomes.[10] Unfortunately, this program, which could never meet demand, has suffered from fiscal restraints and has been reduced, thus further limiting access.

Implementing Legislation

As noted, when the CAP was in force it required that the provinces provide services. As a result, disparity existed in the nature and extent of such programs, and which programs were implemented often depended more on the financial resources available to a province than its positive intentions. This is especially true now with the repeal of the CAP, and programs are affected further by the more recent efforts of the federal government to download its own program costs through capping its federal transfer payments to the provinces. The result is a further limiting of the provinces' abilities to develop or in some cases even maintain existing services. It remains to be seen whether current surplus budgets will result in the restoration of and perhaps even improvements to services.

It is beyond the scope of this chapter to compare all programs within each province. However, some general principles do prevail, and what follows is a description of how these most commonly apply to various service-delivery systems.

Housing Housing options available to the disabled range from totally segregated to totally integrated and consist of the following:

- **Institutional care.** Usually hospital-based and intended for, but unfortunately not always limited to, those individuals who require medical, nursing, or health-related care as well as support services.

- **Group homes.** These would include both larger homes that are fully staffed on a 24-hour basis and smaller homes where a paid live-in helper provides physical aid.

- **Attendant care apartments.** These are adapted apartment units, within larger apartment buildings, for which personal attendant-care services are provided on a 24-hour, on-call basis by a small staff. These programs are most often provided as part of a non-profit housing project or an apartment complex.

- **Parental care.** Parents or a foster family may be paid to provide room, board, and often other forms of care.

- **Independent living.** Some individuals are able to live independently but require certain forms of support such as a homemaker, partial attendant care, assistance with the costs of rent, or accessibility modifications.[11]

Funding support for these alternatives will range from the provincial ministry of health and hospital-based services to the provincial ministry responsible for social services and other programs and services. Programs involving subsidized rents also require the involvement of the ministry of housing. Eligibility also varies and may depend on a disabled person's individual health status, as in the case of hospital-based services; his or her income level, as in the case of subsidized housing; or simply his or her having a disability that limits self-care, as in the case of most attendant care services.

Education The Charter of Rights and Freedoms has had a profound effect on the provincial legislation governing elementary and secondary education. Whereas the education of children with disabilities traditionally was provided through segregated, and at times second-class, programs, there have been dramatic changes.

For example, Ontario's Education Amendment Act of 1980 requires every school board to provide appropriate education for disabled children in regular programs with peers of their own age as possible or through more individualized special programs within the regular school system. Services under this program include assessments, transportation. teacher aides, and any necessary individualized equipment.[12] A major difficulty still centres around children who become disabled after having started their schooling and have major requirements in terms of physical accessibility. Normally school boards are required to provide accessibility only within their own jurisdictions, and not necessarily within all their schools. This means that these children frequently are confronted with long bus rides and also, more significantly, they are separated from peers and teachers and their previously established relationships with them. A second, more recent, and in many ways more significant, difficulty—at least as demonstrated in Ontario—has been the reduction in special education services as school boards have had to deal with declining financial resources.

There have been similar improvements in the level of colleges' and universities' awareness of disabled students' special needs. Most campuses now have on-site advocates for disabled students.

Employment Having a job is an important part of participating in and contributing fully to society. Yet people with disabilities often face obstacles that keep them from participating in the labour force. Numerous efforts have been or are under way to improve what until now has been an extremely poor record in this area. While estimates of the number of unemployed disabled people vary, all studies demonstrate figures of at least 50 percent. Of course, the recession of the late 1980s and the early 1990s, with generally high unemployment, only made matters more difficult.

Numerous groups, such as the Canadian Committee on Employment and Disabilities, have been formed to come up with an overall strategy for improving service in this area. To provide better services to Canadians with disabilities, awareness-training programs have been developed for front-line staff in Canada Employment Centres. Attempts are ongoing to make the centres' offices totally barrier-free. At the same time, the Canadian Job Strategy attempts to link persons with disabilities with potential employers. Outreach projects at both the federal and provincial levels seek out persons with disabilities and make them aware of services at the community level.[13]

Until 1997, federal/provincial vocational rehabilitation programs cost-shared under the Vocational Rehabilitation for Disabled Persons Act (VRDP). While the two levels of government shared costs on a 50-50 basis, the programs were administered at the provincial level and might include assessment, counselling, training/education, and the provision of assistive devices necessary for a disabled person to undertake employment.[14]

In 1997 the 35-year-old VRDP was replaced by the Employability Assistance for People with Disabilities Act (EAPD) in an effort to recognize more contemporary needs and expectations. Under bilateral agreements, the Government of Canada contributes 50 percent of the cost, up to a maximum amount, of eligible provincial/territorial programs and services. EAPD supports a range of programs and services, from taking the initial steps towards gaining employment through to skills development, and finally ensuring a person can continue to work.[15] The actual provision of services continues to be discretionary, and it remains to be seen whether the new act will have a positive impact or serves merely as window dressing.

Additional employment services are available to individuals who qualify under Workers' Compensation, Veterans Affairs, or through insurance plans such as no-fault motor vehicle insurance, or Canada Pension and private disability plans.

Transportation Lack of accessibility to transportation services not only creates a handicapping environment but it also perpetuates systemic discrimination and segregation. A 1987 report presented to the Ontario government identifies the following principles:

- Transportation is an essential service for everyone.

- An integrated system of transportation requires a range of accessible vehicles and facilities that meet community needs in a dignified and equal manner.

- Development of fully accessible, integrated transportation requires the allocation of funds for research and development.[16]

The 1980s saw a growing recognition on the part of governments of the need to make transportation services available to the disabled. Many municipalities, with the support of the provinces, developed local accessible transportation systems, some integrated, but still others as stand-alone, segregated systems. At the federal level the Canada Transportation Act created the Canadian Transportation Agency and empowered it to remove obstacles to travel by disabled persons. Legislation requires that major airports and railway stations be accessible, while interprovincial and even intercity bus-travel routes are becoming fully integrated. While the limited wheelchair space on each bus requires individuals to book in advance, the system is otherwise fully integrated, making what was considered the impossible possible.

Much remains to be improved in the area of transportation, particularly in rural communities. Not until this happens can the disabled, in a country as large—and therefore as dependent upon adequate transportation—as Canada, be truly integrated.

BARRIERS TO SOCIAL SERVICES FOR DISABLED PERSONS

The above descriptions, while on one hand attesting to the considerable gains our society has made, at the same time point out the reality of services that are often inadequate or inappropriate. The reasons for difficulties are multiple and are examined below.[17]

Fragmentation and Restrictive Criteria

Every kind of service has a different legislative base with its own eligibility criteria, and it is supported by a unique combination of funding sources. At times certain parts of what can become a confusing puzzle may be missing completely. Most programs are set up to deal with the needs of a particular population, and frequently services become inaccessible because the individual fails to meet specific criteria.[18]

Funding Barriers

The funding of disability-related services comes mainly from the following sources:

- voluntary private insurance plans purchased by individuals or their employers;
- Workers' Compensation;
- compulsory insurance programs, either publicly or privately managed, the most common example being motor-vehicle no-fault insurance plans;
- provincial government health and/or social service programs;
- personal finances.

Other resources that are available in very specific and usually relatively smaller numbers include Veterans Affairs programs, criminal injuries compensation, or Native Affairs programs.

The number of different resources creates a basic problem of inequity among disabled persons who require health and social services. Despite Canada's claims to universality in health and social services, the nature and amount of the service available to disabled individuals vary greatly depending on the source of their support. Beyond basic health care, what one is entitled to depends on either one's personal wealth or the nature of one's illness/disability.

For example, consider two individuals with significant respiratory problems, one acquired in the workplace environment and the second a disability with no specifically identified cause. In the case of the former individual, Workers' Compensation will cover the cost, not only of related health care but also of any assistive devices that person may require and of any attendant care services if his or her disability is serious enough to warrant them. All the while, this person would receive income replacement, based upon the degree of disability, as well.

The second individual would certainly be entitled to cost-free hospital and medical services. However, should he or she require medications and/or assistive devices, the degree of government assistance available would vary from province to province; in most cases it would not provide 100 percent coverage. The coverage of any outstanding balance would depend on the availability of a private, major medical policy, the person's own finances or, as a last resort, on means-tested Social Assistance. Income replacement, if the individual was forced to quit work, would depend on the existence of private long-term disability insurance or, if the individual had minimal assets, on municipal or provincial welfare.

Similar comparisons can be drawn between the person who becomes quadriplegic following a motor-vehicle accident and the person who becomes quadriplegic as the result of a fall in his or her own home.

Rigid Rule Barriers

If one uses group homes as an example, the rules of conduct and behaviour are often no less restrictive to their residents than those of institutions. Because options are limited, however, residents have no choice but to stay. Similarly, transportation services that may require 24-hour pre-booking (and sometimes longer) limit the choices available to many disabled. Ideally, the consumer, and not the program, should be the focal point around which the services adapt and adjust.

Most programs, residences, and services usually have long waiting lists. In some communities, especially those with smaller populations, certain services do not even exist. For example, numerous studies have identified the need for respite care to assist people in coping with the physical, psychological, and financial strains of caring for family members with severe disabilities. While funds are scarce to support such services, monies are available to support the disabled individual who lives away from family. Without individual control over the process, the rules, and/or the type of service provided, the client becomes a passive recipient.[19]

Linking Service to Income

One of the key eligibility characteristics for much of the current funding is poverty, but income tests do not take expenditures into account. Thus, some individuals with disabilities may have what appear to be high incomes but they incur high disability-related costs. Yet they would be disqualified under welfare service provisions.[20] At the same time, unlike the Canada Health Act, which provides universal health services, there is no cost-sharing for the types of services that are considered socially useful or that constitute a social infrastructure, such as independent living centres. A few provinces do provide certain services to the disabled on a universal basis, and these may ultimately serve as a model for others.[21]

Administrative Barriers

Many needs and the programs that address them cross lines between two or more provincial ministries, which means that the players and the funds from various sources must be assembled into a package that works for each disabled recipient. The onus is generally upon the consumer or the sponsoring agency to bring together the relevant parties.

Recently some changes have been made in this area, as demonstrated, for example, by the BC Ministry of Human Resources' becoming the Ministry of Social Services and Housing—thus facilitating, at least administratively, the development of social housing. Another hopeful sign is the creation of inter-ministerial departments, as in the case of Health and Community and Social Services in Ontario.[22]

Attitudinal Barriers

Finally, community opposition to programs designed to promote full integration still persists. Consider, for example, the difficulties experienced by some group homes in gaining zoning approval or the fears expressed by parents when disabled children are integrated in the classroom.[23] Legislation at all levels of government is helping to overcome these barriers, but education and experience must continue to be an important part of the process of integration.

FURTHER DEVELOPMENTS

It is barely three years since the fourth edition of this text was published, and it would be overly optimistic to expect that all of the outstanding difficulties identified at that time have since been resolved. The period 2001–2004 has in some ways been a paradoxical one. While some positive changes have occurred there have also been a number of retrograde steps, most often owing to overall political and economic decision-making and not necessarily specific to the disabled population.[24]

What follows are comments on only three significant areas of public policy, housing, employment, and health care. These are particularly relevant to the disabled community since to date they are the first among those overrepresented with low to moderate household incomes. Underrepresented within the Canadian labour force and by virtue of their various conditions, many disabled are heavier users of the health care system than others in society. It is important to recognize, however, that implementation of the policies discussed below would benefit all Canadians and not just the disabled.

Affordable Housing

In November 2001, the 10 provinces signed the Affordable Housing Framework Agreement in Quebec City. Under this agreement, the federal government promised to provide the provinces and territories with $680 million in matching funds over five years for new affordable housing. However, as of early 2004 the majority of the provinces have not signed bilateral deals. In addition, the current Liberal government under Prime Minister Paul Martin has eliminated the Secretary of State position for Housing (**www.creative resistance.ca/canada/2003-dec19-martin-continues-the-liberal-assault-on-affordable-housing-carol-goar-toron-tostar.htm**).

Employment

The Employability Assistance for People with Disabilities has been replaced by the Multilateral Framework for Labour Market Agreements for Persons with Disabilities (**http://socialunion.ca/pwd_e.html**). While this agreement reaffirms the federal government's commitment to "ensuring that people with disabilities can participate successfully in the labour market," I stated in a 1981 submission to the Year of the Disabled Obstacles Commission that the disabled have been studied to death and it was time for action.

The goal of the Multilateral Framework aims to improve the employment situation of people with disabilities, by enhancing their employability, increasing the employment opportunities available to them, and building on the existing knowledge base, and all this is certainly commendable. However, before any implementation of this framework in April 2004, a best practices study—the Promising Practices Project—was to be undertaken. At the time of writing it is not known how far this strategy has progressed but as the country prepared for a federal election, a great deal was on hold and many promises were being made by all the political parties.

Health Care

Health care has been identified as Canadians' first priority among all social programs. The governments' economic constraints of the 1990s at both the provincial and federal levels have resulted in the restructuring of health care, including the availability of fewer services overall and early discharges home for many patients from hospitals. At the same time rather than expanding home care services, some provinces have actually reduced such access, especially to support services such as homemaking. The absence of appropriate home care and support services directly affects the disabled population's ability to function independently in their communities.

As noted above, the disabled are overrepresented among the unemployed and therefore among the country's low income families. For many, however, the very nature of their disability or illness increases their need for prescription drugs. At present the availability of pharmacare services is by no means consistent among the provinces and territories, and these discrepancies create inequities, based on place of residence, in people's eligibility for assistance with medication costs.

During the recent federal election all parties promised improvements specifically in both home care and pharmacare services. It remains to be seen whether those electioneering promises will actually result in action. Also, even if the federal government does follow through on its promises, the division of constitutional powers will continue to cause ongoing concern since health care remains a provincial responsibility. Nothing will happen without the full cooperation of Canada's provinces.

NOTES

1. John Lord, "The Content of Human Services Planning," in *Dialogue on Disability: A Canadian Perspective,* ed. M. J. Marlett, R. S. Gall, and A. Wight-Felske (Calgary: University of Calgary Press, 1984), 8.

2. Ontario Advisory Council for Disabled Persons, *Independent Living: The Time Iis Now* (Toronto, OACD, 1988), 25.

3. Federal Task Force on Disability Issues, *Equal Citizenship for Canadians with Disabilities: The Will to Act* (Ottawa: Government of Canada, 1996).

4. Philip H. N. Wood, "Appreciating the Consequences of Disease: The International Classification Impairment, Disabilities and Handicaps," in *World Health Organization Chronicle,* 34 (1980): 377–78.

5. *The Constitution Act,* 1982, section 15.

6. Secretariat for Disabled Persons, *Inventory of Ontario Government Programs and Services for Disabled Persons* (Toronto: Queen's Printer for Ontario, 1986), 104.

7. Harry Beatty, *Consultation Report on Disability Income Supports and Services Project.* Prepared for Council of Canadians with Disabilities (Toronto: Advocacy Resource Centre for the Handicapped, 1998): 17–18.

8. Ibid., 18–19.

9. G. Clarke, A. Haworth, B. Hemens, C. Hallio, and S. Yuen, *Programs and Policies to Facilitate Accessibility for Physically Handicapped Persons* (Waterloo, ON: School of Urban and Regional Planning, University of Waterloo, 1984), 44–45.

10. Ibid., 45–47.

11. The G. Allan Roeher Institute, *Poor Places: Disability-Related Housing and Support Services,* (Toronto: York University Press, 1990), 55–62.

12. Secretariat for Disabled Persons, *Inventory of Services for Disabled Persons* (Toronto: Queen's Printer for Ontario, 1986), 61.

13. R. D. Cohen, In conversation with the Honourable Pauline Browes, *Abilities* V (Summer 1993): 88.

14. Secretariat for Disabled Persons, *Inventory of Services for Disabled Persons* (Toronto: Queen's Printer for Ontario, 1986), p. 24.

15. Human Resources Development Canada, *Internet publication,* **www.hrdc-drhc.gc.ca/dept/disab/0619.shtml**

16. Government of Ontario, *The Freedom to Move Is Life Itself: A Report on Transportation in Ontario* (Toronto: Ontario Advisory Council on the Physically Handicapped and Ontario Advisory Council on Senior Citizens, 1987), ii.

17. For a more detailed description of proposals for more appropriate and nationally consistent standards and programs, see the publications of the Council of Canadians with Disabilities and the Advocacy Resource Centre for the Handicapped (ARCH); Harry Beatty's three publications: *Income Assistance Case Studies*, 1998; *Consultation Report on Disability Income Supports and Services Project*, 1998; and *Tax Reform Positions*, each prepared for the Council of Canadians with Disabilities (Toronto: Advocacy Resource Centre for the Handicapped, 1998). See also A. Crichton and L. Jongbloed, *Disability and Social Policy in Canada* (Toronto: Captus Press, 1997).

18. The G. Allan Roeher Institute, *Poor Places: Disability-Related Housing and Support Services* (Toronto: York University Press, 1990), 68–69.

19. Ibid., 70–75.

20. Ibid., 78.

21. Ibid., 114.

22. Ibid., 81.

23. Ibid., 82.

24. For an extensive discussion of the improvements and remaining shortcomings in services for the disabled, see *In Unison: A Canadian Approach to Disability Issues* at **http://social union.ca/pwd/unison/unison_e.html**

chapter twenty-six

Adult Custodial and
Community Corrections

Donald G. Evans

INTRODUCTION

As we enter the twenty-first century the question of what to do with citizens who offend against the law continues to be a serious matter of public and political debate. The swings in ideological positions regarding the management of offenders have been dramatic in the past century. For example, in the last 55 years we have witnessed the shift from rehabilitation as a major focus for working with offenders to a greater emphasis on strict discipline and punitive approaches. The major focus has been selective incapacitation and in some instances a curtailing of conditional-release opportunities for incarcerated offenders. As a result, working in corrections today is a challenging experience.

Changes in community tolerance toward the management of offenders have put new pressures on correctional administrators to develop effective programs and to find ways to lessen the cost of administering correctional services. Although governments have passed legislation that increases the length of sentences, they have not increased significantly the budgets of correctional services.

The last 30 years have seen considerable reform in sentencing, which has led to an increase in the lengths of sentences for violent and sexual offenders and efforts to detain those offenders deemed at risk of reoffending. Accordingly these offenders are denied statutory release and they are incarcerated until the expiry of their sentences. There has also been a growth in legislative remedies that add to or supplement sentences such as those in recent sex offender legislation and the proposed sex offender registry.

This effort of getting tough on offenders has crowded the prison system and left the community programs woefully short of supervising capacity. As a result, there has been no substantive impact on recidivism, and the return rate of offenders to the system is unacceptably high. In recent years there has been some recognition that the answer to reducing crime is not to toughen the justice system or build more prisons, but to work toward prevention through social development. This effort to convince governments that crime prevention can be achieved by improving social conditions that contribute to criminality is in its infancy. It is one of the hopeful signs we see as we embark on the twenty-first century.

CORRECTIONAL SERVICES: A HISTORICAL OVERVIEW

The criminal justice system in Canada is composed of three major systems: the police, the courts, and correctional services. Most simply one can describe their functions as apprehension, adjudication, and containment.

The importance of each of the various elements of the criminal justice system was evident even in the earliest days of the emerging Canadian state. The Royal Canadian Mounted Police's contribution to providing law and order has been widely acclaimed and romanticized. Similarly, courts have been available from our earliest days to adjudicate disputes and to deal with the accused. Early settlers usually saw fit to construct a local jail to contain difficult citizens. In fact, to be recognized as a county, a community had to have a courthouse and a jail. Consequently, throughout the older parts of the country one often finds courthouses and jails, usually formidable structures, in the central part of the county towns.

We owe some of the most humanitarian features of the current prison system to the kind-heartedness of the Quakers (Society of Friends), who believed that capital punishment was being applied in too many cases and covering too many categories of offences. They urged the creation of an environment where offenders could repent of their deeds and could reform. The Walnut Street Jail in Philadelphia, opened in 1789, was the product of their efforts. This institution kept each inmate separate from the others, and each inmate was assigned his own cell with a small exercise yard. The Quakers felt that solitude was vital to allow the offender to listen to his own conscience and dwell on the errors he had committed. In 1829, the development of the Auburn system challenged the Pennsylvania system by allowing inmates to work in groups while continuing to provide the majority of the prisoners with solitude during their incarceration. This congregate style of managing offenders would eventually predominate in North America.

Kingston Penitentiary, modelled on the Auburn system, was built in the 1830s. It was only a few years later that Charles Dickens, in his visits to both Kingston and Auburn, recorded his opinion that, while well-intentioned, the isolation enforced in these institutions was causing mental illness in many of their inmates.

Penitentiaries developed rapidly across North America from the early 1800s on and, in Canada, reformatories—usually called industrial farms—for less serious offenders were established.

While local jails were usually comparatively small institutions, penitentiaries and reformatories tended to be considerably larger. The jails were originally designed to hold individuals during the process of their trials as well as those who were incarcerated for very short periods of time. The reformatories, on the other hand, held people for terms ranging from 30 days to two years, and the penitentiaries assumed responsibility for individuals serving terms of imprisonment that exceeded two years.

The jails built since the 1970s, often called detention centres, are more spacious and are usually capable of accommodating offenders for as long as three months, although many accused individuals who are remanded in custody sometimes spend far more than three months there while awaiting completion of their trials. The provision of legal aid in the latter part of the twentieth century has offered offenders the opportunity to provide formal defences, and, therefore, requires more time in processing them before judgment is rendered and sentencing commences.

Until the 1950s reformatories and penitentiaries had programs that involved inmates in mainly agricultural and industrial work. Just as with large psychiatric hospitals and institutions for the mentally handicapped, reformatories and penitentiaries were usually surrounded by large farm acreage, in which the inmates were the principal workers. Within the institutions, the inmates engaged in activities such as metal trades, licence-plate manufacturing, sewing mailbags, weaving baskets, and manufacturing shoes as well as performing basic maintenance and food services. Almost all of these activities related to goods and services the correctional system itself needed, and in many ways the system was self-sufficient.

The staff-to-inmate ratio in these institutions was quite low, and staff members had little training, let alone any professional consultation, to assist them in dealing with offenders in any manner other than direct supervision. Until the late 1950s some institutions still required that inmates maintain silence in dining rooms and other institutional areas. Since the 1970s more attention has been given to the number of staff required as well as to providing staff training and professional staff for consultation. These measures have allowed for a more efficient allocation of security and program space within the institutions.

The conditional release of offenders from prison evolved slowly over the years. Commencing in 1899 with the "ticket of leave" legislation, the gradual release was used sparingly. The legislators were interested in shifting the responsibility from the correctional authorities to the offender for earning an early release. The public voiced concerns at the time about separating what today we call high-risk offenders from those who present less of a safety risk to the community. The conditional release is designed to assist this latter group.

In those early days the released offender was required to report to the local police for supervision, but by 1905 the appointment of the first parole officer in Canada augmented this requirement. The duties of the parole officer were to include visiting inmates to assess whether they were ready for release and to provide supervision, in conjunction with the police, of released inmates.

For the next 50 years this approach continued to develop, and the system slowly took on a more systematic approach to managing the conditional releases that today's modern parole system resembles. The parole system as we know it began in 1959 when the "ticket-of-leave" legislation was repealed and the Parole Act came into force. This act established an independent National Parole Board with the authority to grant, deny, terminate, or revoke conditional releases. The board was to be guided in its decision-making by three criteria:

- Parole would be granted when the inmate had derived maximum benefit from incarceration.

- Parole would assist the inmates in their rehabilitation.
- The release of the inmate would not constitute a major risk to the community.

With minor amendments this act stood until 1992, when the Corrections and Conditional Release Act replaced it. Probation supervision, the most frequently used alternative to imprisonment, had its beginnings in England in 1841. From 1876, the English court missionaries provided a formal supervisory service in the courts. It is further evidence of how unevenly the corrections system developed across the world that Canada's earliest probation supervisory service began in Ontario in 1921 and was expanded into a province-wide service only in the 1950s.

With the development of probation and parole, we see the first recognition that offenders must be managed according to their individual needs. Between 1955 and 1975, Canada saw an exceptional expansion of options for incarcerated offenders. For a brief time therapeutic programming was in vogue; given the predisposition of the corrections system to move from one panacea to another, many people believed that all offenders could and should be treated and that all could be cured of whatever compelled them to offend. This, of course, was folly and led, in the 1970s, to the widespread notion that nothing works in the treating of offenders.

Since 1965, community program alternatives for offenders have expanded markedly. Specifically, there has been an expanded use of probation and associated specialized service programs, such as community service orders and victim–offender reconciliation projects involving the offenders paying some form of restitution to the victims of their crimes. Supervised community work programs and temporary absence programs for regular employment or school attendance have also been imple-mented. In the 1970s, correctional services became much more versatile and responsive to the needs of the offender, the victim, and the community.

MORE RECENT DEVELOPMENTS

To understand the Canadian correctional system one must first appreciate the developments in the current Canadian criminal justice system as a whole, including corrections, the police, the courts, and the government.

The correctional system in Canada underwent considerable review during the mid- to late 1970s. The review was based on an interest in developing an approach that balanced the need for punitive measures, which were viewed as often having limited impact on offenders, with the desire to reintegrate the offenders and assimilate them back into society as productive and contributing members. This led to the expansion of adult-offender skills training and therapeutic programs and a refinement of the probation and parole system with a focus on victim–offender reconciliation and community restitution.

The basic desire was to establish a correctional system that could be flexible and responsive to the needs of both the community and the offender. In fact, corrections was the first sector of the criminal justice system to successfully employ alternative tactics and move towards a community-based model of operations.

A similar examination of traditional police work took place in the late 1980s. This led to the development of community-based policing, a model of policing that balances law enforcement with crime prevention. Community policing identifies factors such as poverty, neglect, unemployment, and abuse as the contributing causes of crime and social order problems. In doing so, it recognizes that only through cooperative efforts on the part of the criminal justice system and the social welfare system are we likely to provide lasting solutions to the problem of crime.

Over the last decade of the twentieth century, public opinion about the criminal justice system shifted toward more concern for law and order. Social protest centred on the alleged leniency of the courts, particularly as they dealt with young offenders, and on the operations of the parole system in relation to cases of violent offenders.

In the field of corrections this shift has manifested itself in higher incarceration rates and longer sentences. This in turn has led to prison overcrowding at a time when the public funding needed to build additional long-term facilities is not readily available. The result has been that governments cut back on programs aimed at rehabilitation of offenders and provide stricter regimes in both institutional and community correctional programs. Development of boot camps, intensive supervision of probation, and super-max prisons are examples of this trend. The curtailment of conditional releases for serious offenders and the development of community notification programs for sex offenders who are released from prison at the ends of their sentences are further efforts by government officials to satisfy public opinion.

As a result of their inability to build new jails and prisons quickly, some governments in Canada are flirting with the idea of privatizing some of their prison capacity. This trend is especially noticeable in jurisdictions favouring incapacitative correctional strategies. Others are coming to a different conclusion, based on the growing awareness that crime and economic and social disadvantages may be linked. These people are reaffirming a commitment to rehabilitation in their prison programs and to expanding community programs. This renewed interest in rehabilitation has been fuelled by the desire to develop evidence-based programs, which are based on research and owe a great deal to the "what works" research that has been a major focus of the past decade. Governments and, as a consequence, correctional departments have had to look at other ways of doing business, including working closely with police and the courts in the areas of prevention, information-sharing, and offender supervision.

CUSTODIAL CORRECTIONS

Convicted offenders serve sentences of two years or more in federal penitentiaries while those sentenced to less than two years serve in provincial correctional centres. Besides the jurisdictional differences between federal and the provincial prisons, institutions are categorized differently according to their security classifications.

Institutional Levels of Security

Most prison systems tend to organize their accommodation into three major types of institutions, classified as maximum, medium, or minimum security.

Maximum-security institutions are for offenders who are considered a risk to the staff, to other offenders, or the community. Offenders' movements are restricted, as are their associations with others and other privileges. This classification of institution also includes psychiatric centres and special handling units (super-max facilities).

Medium-security institutions comprise the majority of prison accommodation in most jurisdictions and they are for offenders who pose a risk to the community. It is at these institutions that the majority of correctional programming takes place. Offenders' movements and associations are more flexible but are regulated and supervised.

Minimum-security institutions are for those offenders who pose little or no risk to the safety of the community. Offenders have minimal restriction on their movements, associations, and privileges, and minimal supervision is provided. Cottage-style facilities or camp-type structures usually indicate a minimum-level institution.

Industrial Programs

Industrial programs are considered an important part of the programming in adult institutions. In Ontario, for example, outside industries operate commercial ventures within the institutions. In the federal system a special agency, Corcan, provides industrial program opportunities for offenders. This agency expects to recover its costs through the sales of the products offenders make.

Agricultural programs are another mainstay of many prison systems. In the last couple of decades farming has seen a resurgence as institutions attempt to offset high food costs. This trend towards self-sufficiency is also seen in the manufacturing end of the programs, in that the institutions use some of the products internally.

In some of these programs, offenders are paid regular wages, while in others they are paid an amount that reflects the training aspect of the job. In some programs, an incentive allowance is provided; usually this is available for offenders serving longer sentences. The incentive allowance program allows the offender a spending allowance for use in the institution and provides a compulsory savings allowance. It is a graded system in which an offender's earning depends on his or her conduct, industry, and attitude. The introduction of regular industrial wages for offender employment in the federal system addresses the difficulty in creating work incentives in institutions, especially for long-term offenders. Regular industrial wages are based on the recognition that work training, with its demands and rewards, may be an effective means to prepare offenders for successful reintegration.

Education and Life Skills

A wide range of academic, vocational, and correspondence (distance-education) programs, as well as on-the-job training, are provided in many correctional facilities. Corrections either employs or contracts with local school boards for highly qualified teachers. Recently, courses available on computer are being used in some institutions and allow teachers to work with a larger number of students while still providing individual assistance when required.

Life-skills programs give offenders opportunities to develop skills that can assist them to function more effectively in the community. This type of training focuses on decision-making, family life, sex education, the world of work, consumer education, the use of leisure time, and human relations.

Programs for Special Needs

In recent years the public's attitude toward violent, sex, and drug offenders has led correctional authorities to develop specialized programs for these categories of offenders. Special emphasis has been devoted to developing programs that deal with substance abuse and anger management, as well as programs that deal with the offenders' own victimization—some offenders have been sexually and/or physically abused as children—and help the offenders work through the traumas associated with their victimization.

Women Offenders

The vast majority of incarcerated offenders are men. Consequently, there are few women's correctional centres in Canada. Until very recently, there was only one facility for federally sentenced women in Canada, and it was situated in Kingston, Ontario's Prison for Women. That facility is expected to close sometime in the next couple of years. This announced closing is the result of a series of events that include both positive—the task force recommendations of a women's advocate and correctional officials group in their report, *Creating Choices*—and negative—the Arbour Inquiry.

Creating Choices recommended an emphasis on women-centred programming and the establishment of five new institutions across Canada and the closing of the Prison for Women in Kingston. The Arbour Inquiry was established following a disturbance at the Prison for Women and the subsequent problem of strip searches conducted by male guards.

There are now five women's centres for federally sentenced women, one of which is located in each of the regions—Pacific, Western, Ontario, Quebec, and the Atlantic. These facilities are intended to address the special needs of women offenders. Programming for women offenders still lags behind the efforts expended on men, and because of limited resources women offenders' needs are not being adequately met. Efforts to define principles to guide the programming for women have been undertaken. The principles stress that programs should match women's needs rather than merely fit women into existing programs. The programs are more beneficial when they take into account issues of housing, employment, therapy, services, relationships, and the offenders' individual rights as citizens.

In terms of effective programming for women offenders it appears that the outcomes would be influenced by:

- attention to designing a continuum of care and support,
- clarity in the stated expectations of the interventions,
- clarity about the enforcement of rules and sanctions,
- consistent supervision,
- the coordination of resources in the community,
- the provision of social and emotional support, and
- a multifaceted approach that deals specifically with the issues in the lives of women offenders.

The current economic situation and the emphasis on law and order have negatively affected the availability of resources for women offenders. However, the majority of programming has been limited to monitoring and surveillance and has not addressed the women's specific needs. The result has been a failure to supply adequate employment and affordable housing opportunities that would assist their re-entry and reintegration into the community. This situation provides an opportunity and a challenge to community corrections.

First Nations Offenders

First Nations are overrepresented in the criminal justice system, especially in the institutional population. Also, First Nations offenders are less likely to receive full parole and have higher recidivism rates.

Efforts to address the needs of this population have centred on the development of specific programs geared to First Nations and enlist the assistance of traditional cultural and spiritual leaders. The participation of elders in the evaluation process in parole hearings is one effort to improve the parole grant rate for First Nations offenders. In Alberta, the Native Counselling Services created a minimum-security forestry camp as an alternative to incarceration and also manages the operation of a minimum-security correctional institution. As is the case with women offenders, more attention will be given to this segment of the population in the coming years, and a greater involvement of the First Nations community is anticipated.

Community Corrections

The approach to managing offenders in the community falls to probation, parole, and the voluntary sector. Probation is, after fines, the most frequently used court sanction and is administered by provincial probation services. In recent years probation workers have been dealing with increased workloads that have necessitated a number of innovations.

Given the interest in public safety, some probation services have introduced special programs for the high-risk offender. These include intensive supervision programs that closely monitor offenders and enforce probation conditions strictly. Also, specialized teams, working with the local police, have been formed to deal with violent and/or sexual offenders to supervise them more adequately. Probation continues to provide reports to the courts to assist in the latter's sentencing decisions and to institutions and parole boards to assist in their release planning. The development of improved risk/need assessments and specific programs that address substance abuse issues and violence prevention are also being undertaken. In the future, probation services will be called upon to develop outcome performance measures to justify the resources expended. This will be one of the service's greatest challenges.

Another community correctional approach is the use of parole. The National Parole Board has jurisdiction for all federally sentenced offenders and for those offenders serving time in provincial institutions, with the exception of British Columbia, Ontario, and Quebec, which have their own provincial parole boards.

Parole allows an offender to be released into the community under specified conditions and with supervision. There are generally two forms of parole:

- Day parole, which is used to prepare offenders for full parole or statutory release. The offender must either return to a penitentiary or to a community-based residential facility each night unless specific authorization in writing has been given.
- Full parole is given under the authority of the parole board to allow the offender to live in the community subject to conditions and supervision.

Volunteers back up the supervision of offenders on parole by providing residential facilities for day parole or temporary-absence programs. At a community residential facility, the offender has the opportunity to go out into the community every day to pursue employment or education programs. This training effort, combined with a supervised living experience, has proven effective. Individuals are able to pay rent and taxes and support their families in ways that are not possible in the traditional institutional programs. Another benefit of the voluntary sector's involvement has been the increased contact between the community, offenders, staff, and, in some specialized programs, victims. The John Howard, Elizabeth Fry, and St. Leonard's societies, as well as the Salvation Army, are the primary voluntary organizations in the correctional environment.

CAN CORRECTIONS BE EFFECTIVE?

Investment in programs for offenders needs to be accompanied by evaluation efforts to ensure that the resources are being used effectively. In the last number of years an emphasis on evidence-based programming has developed. Much of this emphasis results from the work of a number of Canadian researchers. They have suggested some basic factors to consider in the development of effective programs to reduce recidivism:

- Intensive programs that are behavioural, provided to higher-risk offenders, and targeting the offender's criminogenic needs (needs that increase the likelihood of reoffending) are essential.
- Effective programs ensure responsivity, carefully matching offender, therapist, and program.
- Effective programs involve program contingencies and/or behavioural strategies being enforced in a firm but fair way.
- In effective programs, staff relate to offenders in an interpersonally sensitive and constructive manner. The staff are well trained and supervised.
- Effective program structure and activities disrupt the criminal associations of offenders by placing them in situations of predominantly pro-social activities.
- Relapse prevention in the community is provided.
- Advocacy and brokerage are provided to community agencies that offer programs that adhere to the principles of effective intervention.

More programs in correctional environments are attempting to develop programs and interventions using this research, and the Correctional Services of Canada has become a leading advocate for this method of corrections. It is also evaluating programs and providing research to better inform its work with offenders. As we enter this next century of correctional service, it appears that rehabilitative programming, based on solid research, is poised to make a significant contribution to the management of offenders.

FUTURE TRENDS AND CHALLENGES

In the coming years corrections in Canada will be faced with a more complex population of offenders and can expect an impact owing to the following factors:

- Increasing numbers of young offenders are becoming adults and entering the adult system.
- The number of women offenders being sentenced to periods of incarceration has increased.
- With the decrease in resources to mental health services, a greater number of people with mental health problems will end up in the corrections system.
- The number of offenders with contagious diseases will increase.
- Owing to longer sentences and an increase in the number of admissions to prison for offences committed 15 to 20 years ago, the system will see an increase in its demands on health care services.
- With the increasing disclosure of sexual offences, the population of sex offenders in the prison population correspondingly rises.
- An increase in the growth of gangs and gang-related activities will present order problems for prison administrators.
- Correctional services will work more closely with police major crime units and criminal intelligence services to supervise sexual and violent offenders.

We will continue to see an emphasis on cost-containment in corrections, and some jurisdictions will entertain ideas of privatizing parts of the correctional system. The full impact of the private sector's involvement in delivering correctional services cannot be adequately measured at this time, but it is very likely that we will see some privatized efforts. The continued search for technological applications will also dominate the correctional scene, especially in efforts to more effectively manage the system's information requirements, as well as in providing supervision assistance through drug testing or electronic monitoring.

CONCLUSION

Correctional programming, whether at the custodial or the community level, is attempting to meet the public demand for public safety. By improving their own capacity to assess, classify, and offer appropriate programs to offenders, corrections services are contributing to community safety. Continual evaluation and research are required to continue to improve the system's capacity to manage effectively those who offend against the law.

REFERENCES

Andrews, D. A., & Bonta, James. 2003. *Psychology of criminal conduct*, 3d edn. Cincinnati, OH: Anderson Publishing.

Hannah-Moffat, Kelly. 2001. *Punishment in disguise: Penal governance and federal imprisonment of women in Canada*. Toronto: University of Toronto Press.

Jackson, Michael. 2002. *Justice behind the walls: Human rights in Canadian prisons*. Vancouver: Douglas & McIntyre.

chapter twenty-seven

The Profession:

An Integrative Perspective

M. Dennis Kimberley

M. Louise Osmond

INTEGRATION OF CONVERGING PHILOSOPHIES

The Mission

Social work is an action-oriented profession, with both its actions and the purposes of its actions guided by repeated philosophical themes.

Transcending any one of these themes, within the context of globalization of community (McLuhan & Powers, 1992) is a social work mission that may be summarized as: Within the context of a new global order, to promote, enable, and enhance the biopsychosocial well-being and functioning of individuals and social collectives, through mutual, reciprocal, cooperative, and interdependent action, guided by values that promote justice and that respect and enhance the dignity and worth of diverse individuals and social collectives, and transcend national interests. Social humanism, social justice, the application of science and art in undertaking social responsibility, and the needs and rights of women and children, appear as the most common themes in the development of social work within the context of social welfare (such as the welfare of children and youth) and social movements (such as women's movements).

Typically, philosophical orientations and ideologies have not been treated as mutually exclusive domains; they have been approached most often as if they converge and relate to one another. While the integration of ideologies may be imperfect, each orientation gives the social worker sets of conceptual and value frameworks for undertaking and evaluating professional responsibilities for helping consumers, be they individuals, couples, families, groups, organizations, communities, or societies (often termed "client systems"). The profession is committed to promoting and enabling both personal and social change with special attention to the social well-being and health of oppressed and marginalized persons and groups (for example, Csiernick & Rowe, 2003).

Social Humanism

Since its inception as identifiable sets of practices in the late 1800s, social work has undertaken to promote and enable change in social well-being and health (Richmond, 1917) and to support individual and collective strengths, human potential, and diversity. Assuming the dignity, potential, and freedom of each individual and culture, in terms of persons and collectives being fundamentally interdependent, the profession has promoted the value of trying to better understand (termed assessment or diagnosis) (Turner, 2002) and to mediate between clients and their social and physical environments (termed social work intervention). Social workers aim to change personal and collective problems, risks, and unmet fundamental needs.

Also consistent with the humanistic tradition and moving beyond human deficits, social work has emphasized building on people's strengths and abilities and enabling them to grow and develop normally as well as fulfill their human potential (Berg & Steiner; 2003; Funk, 1982; Rapp, 1997). Typically the humanist position has called for individual and collective social responsibility in the interests of promoting and enabling biopsychosocial well-being of both the individual and the collective as well as in preventing and ameliorating health and social problems, and controlling social forces.

This tradition presents a paradox in that individual freedom and dignity depend in part on collective support and sacrifice; the strength of the collective is enhanced by the cooperation and sacrifices that individuals make. The other paradox is that, while each individual and collective is unique and diverse, social work can address so many problems, needs, risks, and potentials because of much that is common in the human condition (Towle, 1945).

Social Justice

Since its inception, and especially since the early 1900s, social work has attempted to get beyond the limits of a social responsibility perspective and beyond the provision of social services. The profession promotes universal human rights and freedoms that transcend national constitutions. The profession has promoted:

- human rights (for example, the rights of children not to be exploited),

- entitlements and provision (for example, assistance to developmentally delayed persons and to groups who face barriers to independence),

- fairness and equality (for example. paternity-leave opportunities for fathers),

- equity (for example, special and extraordinary supports to women to overcome barriers in male-dominated work environments),

- social and intellectual freedoms (for example, freedom of gay persons to be treated as married couples),

- social inclusion of diverse, minority, and marginalized collectives (for example, social integration of physically disabled persons or Aboriginal persons)

The social justice perspective advocates for the inclusion of multiple stakeholders in collective decision-making. It promotes not only the active participation of those with less powerful voices, but defines social work's responsibility as that of enabling multiple voices to be heard—especially those of marginalized and oppressed persons (Carniol, 2002; Mullaly, 2002). Here the paradox at the same time is that the social justice perspective also promotes the collective social controls needed to support individual and collective rights and freedoms.

Science and Art

Recognizing the limitations of abstract and value-laden philosophies in guiding professional practice, the profession since the early 1900s has sought to account for the judgments and actions of its members through adopting a scientific orientation to inform its practice. The profession has promoted the application of scientific knowledge that reflects observable and predictable truths (for example, many abused women demonstrate predictable patterns labelled "battered woman's syndrome") and realities (for example, many return to abusive partners) in guiding professional observations, judgments, predictions and actions. In accountable practice, to the degree that it is feasible, the social worker is expected to be able to support her judgments and decisions and to account for her actions with a credible base of evidence (Roberts & Yeager, 2004).

The lack of complete knowledge, or the presence of incomplete information, has not been an accepted excuse for inaction (Gambrill, 1997), but the profession has defined part of the social worker's responsibilities as that of creating new knowledge through the practice wisdom that comes from case study (see for example, Hancock & Millar, 1994) or the aggregate information in studies with multiple

clients (for example, the seminal work on children of alcoholics by Cork, 1969).

Scientific knowledge is expected to be evaluated and applied with, and in the interests of, the client. But historically the profession has recognized the dynamic interplay between the relatively common, repeated, and predictable human experience uncovered by systematic inquiry (for example, persons who have been abused are overrepresented among violent offenders) and the personal subjective human experience of a particular person (such as Nin, 1932–1934).

While recognizing some similarities among clients who experience particular types of problems, risks, needs, and oppression, the profession has promoted the individualization of service, based on each client's unique experience of reality and unique personal life journey (for example, Rothman & Sager, 1998). Consistent with the latter is a strong commitment to the importance of social work as art, in the sense that it is based on a personal and interpersonal process that involves the effective use of self (Baldwin & Satir, 1987; Goldstein, Hilbert, & Hilbert, 1984).

The dialectic continues in a profession that promotes practice as both art and science. Paradoxically this dialectic incorporates the scientific approach that generates common knowledge that can be applied generally and it often provides the insight that enables the promotion and enhancement of individual differences and collective diversity.

Women's Movements

Since its inception, various women's movements have influenced social work as a female-dominated profession, from social action groups such as the women's temperance movement to the more modern feminist movement (for example, Dominelli, 2002). Social workers have actively promoted equality (such as equal pay for work of equal value), advocating for equity (for example, support for mothers to complete their education while undertaking custodial parenting), and challenging barriers and practices that oppress women (such as "mother blaming"). In addition, the profession has promoted values, services, and practices consistent with themes espoused by women's groups. Included among these have been rights to social assistance, rights to safe contraception, accessible and safe abortion as personal choice, access to affordable daycare, the control of sexual exploitation of children and youth, and freedom from fear of violence and assault. Those stakeholder groups that advocate for the rights, needs, and potential of women have formed partnerships with the profession in various ways, in part influenced by overlapping ideological orientations.

A MANDATE TO PROMOTE AND ENABLE PERSONAL AND SOCIAL CHANGE

The Changing Biopsychosocial Functioning of Collectives and Individuals

Informed by converging ideologies and knowledgeable about individuals and collectives, professional social workers operate in dynamic interaction. They have developed and clarified a focus on change in the biopsychosocial functioning of individuals and collectives. Ideology influences social workers' actions in the interests of personal and social change, the function of their agencies and the professional mandates supported by the clients, agencies, governments, and/or society. Since social workers began to organize into a profession in the early 1900s, with the development of university-based education and social work associations, they

have come to be treated as professionals by society, under the law, and within the context of private contracts.

The focus of change in professional practice has included individuals, dyadic relationships (commonly referred to as couples), families, social and therapeutic groups, local communities, formal organizations, societies, and "the global village"—the latter reflected in international commitments such as that of the International Council on Social Welfare (ICSW), the International Federation of Social Workers (IFSW), and the United Nations. The focus of the individual social worker or agency may vary, depending on the situation, between personal change and collective change. In either case, social work values the importance of interpersonal relationships in enabling and sustaining meaningful personal and social change.

Since its inception, the profession has concerned itself with biological well-being, psychological well-being, and social well-being, as well as the interaction among these fundamental life dimensions. In current practice, the professional social worker and the client(s) (sometimes referred to as client systems) may focus on the notion of changing and improving biopsychosocial well-being and of building client strengths and may therefore focus on one or more of the following (based on Kimberley & Bohm, 1999):

- changing the *behaviour and actions* of an individual (wife battering) or the collective (prejudicial actions by the police against Aboriginal people). (See, for example, Gambrill, 1997.)
- changing, or learning to adjust to, *intense effect or feelings of* an individual (such as depression and related suicide risk) or a collective (such as critical-incident stress-debriefing for families and communities). (For example, see Roberts, 2000.)

- changing the *beliefs, attitudes, values, expectations, and other knowledge or awareness dimensions* of an individual (challenging beliefs that physical "punishment" is evidence of "good" parenting) or the collective (confronting community beliefs that support female genital mutilation). (For example, see Hepworth, Rooney, & Larsen, 2002.)

- *changing or adjusting to a biophysical or biomedical condition or other such realities*, of an individual (fostering an "ability" orientation in persons with physical challenges) or the collective (advocating social policies and legislation to remove social barriers for those with mental disabilities). (For example, see Rapp, 1997.)

- changing the *person-to-environment transactions* of the individual (strengthening the parenting capacity of a parent with an addiction problem) or the collective (enabling the members of a group of survivors of sex abuse to trust mutually supportive relationships). (For an example of the social-group work tradition, see Lindsay, Turcotte, & Hopmeyer, 2003.)

- changing *social environment-to-person transactions* that are part of clients' social reality at the level of the individual (enabling a youth to assert her rights within a family), the level of the individual in a position of power (advocating to a financial assistance officer on behalf of a client), or the collective with political power (promoting policies to persuade a community to provide services that are more ethnically sensitive and culturally relevant) (Al-Krenawi & Graham, 2002).

- changing, or adjusting to, some aspect of *biopsychosocial development* for the individual (ensuring corrective action for a child suffering from a premature sexualization), or the collective (group support services for persons with

relatives with Alzheimer disease). (See, for example, Davies, 2004.)

- changing how any or all of the above *factors interact to affect the sense of identity* of an individual ("I am always the hopeless victim"), a couple ("We are deviant because we are gay") a family ("We are failing to adjust to having a developmentally delayed daughter/sister"), or a larger collective ("We are a dying and hopeless community"). (See, for example, Dansky, 1997.)

- intervening to *enable change in patterns of interaction of biopsychosocial dimensions and interpersonal relationships* that converge to affect individual and collective well-being and biopsychosocial functioning (the patterns of efforts by a partner to control a mate who is addicted to pornography). (See, for example, Stuart, 2003; Shulman, 1991.)

- helping client systems to *process existential issues* associated with the realities of their existence, spirituality concerns, and meaning in life issues. (See, for example, Martin & Martin, 2003.)

By focusing on multiple dimensions that require change to ensure their clients' biopsychosocial well-being and functioning, social workers take a holistic and integrated approach to helping in client systems; (consumers) meet their needs, solve problems, control risks, reduce harm, mobilize strengths, and actualize more of their individual and collective potential.

A Professional Mandate

In promoting social responsibility, social justice, evidence-based practice, biopsychosocial change, and the needs and rights of disadvantaged and oppressed or marginalized persons, social workers—often under the direction of professional associations, and/or professionalized service organizations—have been given the right and responsibility, under law, contract, or informal social mandate

- *to make informed professional observations* ("The incidence of alcohol abuse and spousal violence problems has increased since the closing of the town's plant");

- to formulate *informed professional judgments* ("The stress of added economic hardship has affected individual and collective coping in this family; without effective support, there is a risk of its dissolution");

- *to make relatively independent professional decisions or recommendations* ("In the interests of the woman's safety and the prevention of violence, it is best if her partner leaves the familial home until he demonstrates effective, sustained, and verifiable anger management; the community also needs increased education-awareness interventions to prevent or intervene early in partner violence");

- *to undertake relatively independent professional interventions and related practices that require specialized knowledge, skills, and competent action (from professional assessment to after-care)* in enabling individual and collective well-being (post-trauma counselling with a battered woman; anger management therapy with a battering male; family therapy with children exposed to violence; and community-development focus groups to raise community awareness and to prevent partner violence);

- *to undertake and to provide what society would clearly define as professional services, and specialized and expert consultation* (expert testimony to the court and case consultation to a community service, sometimes within independent private practice);

- *to form partnerships and teams* with other stakeholders (clients), professionals (public health nurses), administrators, or community leaders, in promoting well-being, social welfare, and social justice as well as needed supports and services.

Professional Ethics in Action

In acting on a professional mandate, social workers cannot be guided solely by law, organizational policy, government policy, or political expedience. Given that people, individually and collectively, make decisions—not organizations—one of the professionals' distinguishing features is that their observations, judgments, decisions, and actions are guided by a set of principles reflected in statements of mission, belief, values, ethical decision rules, and standards of practice. The social workers' professional responsibility may even transcend the wishes of their clients, the agency, the law, and societal or cultural practices, and be guided more by a set of values and code of ethics that reflect the collective wisdom of the profession (for example, the Canadian Association of Social Workers [CASW]).

Consider the following examples:

- If the client wishes to have a social worker assist her with a suicide plan, the social worker must not assist with the self-destruction and would normally have a professional mandate to act to protect the client against her expressed wishes.

- If the agency within which a social worker is employed demands that he disclose confidential client information beyond the ethical principles and standards that permit such a breach of confidentiality, then the social worker is justified in refusing and would be able to call on his professional association as an external arbiter.

- If a society systematically maltreats or systematically disadvantages some members, then social workers as individuals and the profession as a collective, often partnering with others, have a mandate to advocate for a change in those policies, the law, and/or the practices—as those social workers in the mid-1960s did who advocated to ensure women's legal right to access contraception.

PROFESSIONAL KNOWLEDGE

When society or the law attributes professional knowledge to an identified group, society assumes that that professional knowledge encompasses a range of uncommon knowledge in the form of specialized information (impacts of child abuse) and specialized skills knowledge (how to complete a parenting capacity and risk assessment). Within the context of complex societies with their complex problems, needs, and risks, the group with this specialized and sometimes expert knowledge is expected to derive it from a number of sources as well as from researchers and professional groups, including social work. Professions and professionals:

- borrow and apply knowledge from cognate academic disciplines (such as understanding the impacts of the political economy on poverty and labour markets may help social workers address policy and program issues as well as community patterns of blaming the unemployed for their situations).

- borrow and apply knowledge from other related professional disciplines (understanding the expected biomedical course of a disease such as AIDS that social workers may factor into their areas of expertise, such as permanency planning for children of parents with HIV).

- co-create, sometimes in conscious partnerships, knowledge associated with problems, risks, needs, harmful impacts, client potential, and best practices for intervention (social workers, psychiatrists and psychologists have contributed to the development of solution-focused therapy with addiction problems).

- create new knowledge (practices to assess and help children who are infected with HIV) and refine existing knowledge (strategies to empower economically depressed communities) out of practice wisdom from case experience, case and community studies, and larger systematic studies, which guide interventions. (For example, in her research on children of parents with alcohol problems, Margaret Cork (1969) confirmed that alcoholism was a family problem and that family problems continued after the individual family members achieved sobriety; her findings were instrumental in the creation of services for the children of alcoholics.)

- continually create, improve, and synthesize knowledge, in part to derive current recommended best known practices for social work (demonstration projects that support the attachment between birth parents and their child in care, in the best interests of the child).

- modify existing practices and construct innovative solutions for unique expressions of problems, needs, and potentials, for which there are no standard practices (social policies, community development interventions and consciousness-raising groups to address female genital mutilation associated with specific cultural–religious practices).

What is important to recognize is that what constitutes professional knowledge changes constantly. Under conditions of complexity and uncertainty, knowledge is imperfect and subject to challenge (see, for example, social work literature on indicators of childhood trauma and the challenge of "false memory theory," Coulborn-Faller, 1998). The fact that specialized and professional knowledge is imperfect and that expected personal and social change cannot be predicted with absolute assurance has not stopped social workers from constructing innovative solutions to meet the personal and social goals of a client and society.

Skills and Competence

One of the defining characteristics of the profession is that knowledge is created and adopted, not knowledge for the sake of knowledge, but knowledge that informs professional observations, judgments, predictions, decisions and recommendations, actions, and reflective evaluation. In professional practice, such applied knowledge must be translated into skills through the clarification of abstract theories and concepts, as well as into more concrete information that guides applied practices.

Additionally, professionals must be more than knowledgeable and skilled; they must blend both qualities to ensure their competent application in ways that respect the uniqueness of each situation and each client system. In addition, professionals do not simply apply information and techniques in a vacuum; they apply these knowledge and skills with due respect to their professional mission, values, and ethics and to the social political climate in which the client system lives. (See, for example, Shulman, 1998.)

Professional Independence and Partnerships

One of the defining characteristics of a professional social worker is that that person is individually accountable and liable for his or her judgments, decisions, and

actions. All of these presume that person's personal professional knowledge, skills, and competence. Social workers must make independent decisions and take independent actions that affect client systems. (A children's protection social worker may have less than one minute to observe, judge, predict, decide, and act in apprehending a child at imminent risk.) Typically the most independent of social work practitioners are those who undertake private practice.

While the agency that employs the social worker is liable for the actions of its employees, each social worker as a professional is also independently accountable and liable for his or her professional judgments and actions. This is one of the reasons that professional social workers must carry independent liability insurance (National Association of Social Workers [NASW]/CASW). But while social workers often make independent decisions, the level of complexity and uncertainty associated with typical client systems suggests that social workers should partner with others in refining their observations, judgments, predictions, decisions, and plans.

CLIENTS, CONSUMERS, AND OTHER PARTNERSHIPS

Clients as Consumers and as Partners

The first level of partnership is with the client, and a large part of social work practice involves arriving at judgments, decisions, and agreed-upon plans with clients who expect professional services. Within this context, client systems are therefore defined as experiential expertise applied to clients' needs, risks, problems, harmful impacts, strengths, and potential solutions.

Social workers are responsible for using their expertise in conjunction with their clients' expertise, in their client's interests and unique goals in achieving changes. The profession currently embraces the concept of empowerment in reference to client and person-centred practices that enable client systems to optimize their strengths, develop capacity, and participate actively in creating solutions. These inclusion and empowerment notions assume that individual clients are sufficiently developed biopsychosocially, are sufficiently reality-based, and are not at imminent personal risk. Relatively independent or more coercive action may be required of the social worker, as when clients express the intent to harm themselves or others. More restrictions apply to the partnership when the clients are not involved in working with the social worker on a voluntary basis. (See, for example, DuBois & Krogsrud Miley, 2005.)

Professional Supervision

Because of the complexity, uncertainty, and uniqueness of most client situations, the social work profession has tended to support the practice of a more experienced social worker's acting as a support, mentor, consultant, teacher, supervisor, and, at times, the arbiter of final decisions for more junior or otherwise less experienced practitioners. Supervision may be formalized or take the form of informal case consultation, but the profession often demands that the social worker's professional judgments and actions be supervised by another professional social worker (Munson, 2001, and Shulman, 1993). In the current climate of multidisciplinary practice and managerial expedience, a social worker may supervise another professional or another professional may supervise a social worker.

Professional and Interdisciplinary Case Consultation and Case Conferencing

Social work has a long history of promoting the consolidation and application of collective wisdom through peer and interdisciplinary groups for case consultation and case conferences. Often the aim is to refine observations, judgments, and case or service decisions. Collective wisdom helps when addressing complex issues under conditions of relative uncertainty, and it also encourages basing the service to the client on reflective practice rather than reactive responses. The guiding principles are often the best interests of the client system and the least harmful or least intrusive interventions. Consistent with a philosophy of inclusion and empowerment, the clients of social workers may participate in the case conferences and other collective consultations concerning their situations.

Professional Teams   The current trend in most of the Western world is toward the integration of human services. Strategic social planning often defines education, health, social, employment related services, and justice and corrections as part of a dynamic and interdependent system established to meet the needs of students–patients–clients–consumers in a holistic fashion.

The assumption behind professional teams, including multidisciplinary teams, is that team members have an active contribution—of information, specialized knowledge and skills—to make to the coordinated and effective delivery of services. In some cases, each discipline plays a clear and professionally differentiated role in the overall service plan. The social worker is likely to be called upon to provide service to the client according to needs with biosocial, psychosocial, socioeconomic, sociolegal, or sociopolitical components. The social worker is also likely to be called upon to act as case manager, especially in cases requiring advanced case management (Radol, Raiff, & Shore, 1993).

SOCIAL WORK IS WHAT SOCIAL WORK DOES: PARTNERSHIPS FOR CHANGE

General Goals for Individual and Collective Change

Many elements converge to support professional competence and to guide practice. These can include guiding philosophies, mission, professional mandate to enable personal and social change, concern with the disadvantaged and the oppressed, professional rights and responsibilities, ethics, knowledge, and skills, as well as agency mandate and partnerships.

While these dimensions all help define the profession, social work has such broad boundaries of fields of practice (such as genetic counselling), methods of practice (critical incident debriefing after the SwissAir disaster off the coast of Nova Scotia), and goals of intervention (health promotion and prevention) that it is difficult to articulate, in a simple statement, what constitutes professional social work practice. This problem of producing a clear and simple definition also holds true for other professions such as medicine, law, and engineering.

One way to address the problem is to rely on philosophy, mission, and mandate to set some boundaries for action and to conclude that, being an action-oriented profession, social work is what social work does within a temporal and sociopolitical context. This approach recognizes that identity, including professional identity, is not fixed;

it is fluid and ever-changing as the personal, social, economic, and political contexts of practice and social welfare evolve.

Other General Goals

Helping professions establish boundaries for their expertise that address personal and collective needs, problems, risks, harm. and potential. To these dimensions, social work adds human rights, in the profession's loose partnership with law. Social work has made a commitment to help with biopsychosocial change and the interaction among these three overlapping dimensions.

While the profession may formulate many *general goals in the best interests of client–consumer systems*, the most common themes in theory, concepts, and practice that guide social work include the following:

1. Social work professionals undertake to evaluate and enable *the meeting of basic biopsychosocial needs* common to most persons (shelter for the homeless) and to meet special human needs reflected in the life experiences of the those disadvantaged by personal or social–structural limitations (the physical disability and social exclusion of the physically challenged). As well as intervening at the very point of personal and social interaction, the profession supports action to prevent undue client hardships and to empower client systems to meet their own needs.

2. Social work professionals undertake to evaluate and enable *the formulation of solutions to personal and social problems* common to many persons (adjusting to age–stage life-cycle problems) and to help address special problems at the person's own level (loss of income security) and/or the collective's level (a challenge to a small community's economy). Individual and social problems

are often reflected in the life experiences of those disadvantaged by personal or social–structural limitations (low academic achievement and the exclusion of the illiterate in training programs, respectively). As well as intervening at the point where the personal and the social intersect, the profession supports action to prevent problems from developing or getting worse and to empower client systems to share in managing common problems (social and economic development).

3. Social work professionals undertake to evaluate and enable *the avoidance, reduction, and/or control of personal or social risks* associated with common life experiences (substance use becoming substance abuse) or risks that surface less frequently (sibling incest). These are often reflected in the life experiences of those disadvantaged by personal or social–structural limitations (sexually exploited street kids). As well as intervening exactly where the personal and the social meet, the profession supports action to prevent risks from developing or getting worse and to empower client systems to share in controlling any risks. Some social workers have the power to enforce risk control such as in children's protection.

4. Social work professionals undertake to evaluate and enable *the reduction and/or control of personal or collective harm* common in life experiences (individuals and families adjusting to family dissolution) or less frequent experiences of harm (post-trauma effects associated with sexual assault), which are often reflected in the life experiences of those disadvantaged by personal or social–structural limitations (those forced to live in inner-city public housing "ghettos"). As well as intervening where the personal and the social intersect, the profession supports action to prevent harm from turning into a cycle or from increasing and to empower client systems to control harm and its impact (self-help groups for survivors of sexual assault). Some social workers have the power to enforce actions to prevent harm and to ameliorate the consequences (sex-offenders' assessment and treatment).

5. Social work professionals undertake to evaluate and promote *the recognition, enhancement, and development of client strengths, capacities, and potential*, which are often overlooked when clients demonstrate individual or collective personal deficits (parenting-capacity limitations that put children at developmental risk) and experience individual or collective social and structural barriers (language and cultural differences that reduce personal and collective opportunities). As well as intervening at the point of intersection between the personal and the social, the profession supports actions that prevent strengths, capacities, and potential being actualized and to empower client systems to demonstrate strengths, develop new capacities, and fulfill their potentials through their own actions and/or self-help, social system support and mutual aid.

It is important to recognize that social workers, as do other professions, undertake both social-control functions (reducing the risk and harm of wife-battering) and helping–enabling functions (community and social development with an Aboriginal community trying to manage solvent abuse and fetal-alcohol-syndrome risks). The preference is to enable individual or collective action within a facilitative framework and in partnership with the client. Even when some part of the client system is dependent or vulnerable (aged persons at risk for abuse), the profession prefers to avoid or reduce more intensive, intrusive, or coercive interventions as quickly as possible. Consider the following exchange, which implies mild coercion and also reflects the beginning of a partnership between a single mother and a children's protection social worker:

Social Worker: "I feel relieved that you have agreed to end your relationship with your boyfriend who has been convicted of sex abuse of children; it is an effective way to control immediate risks to you and your children."

Client: "I am going to miss my boyfriend, but it is better to lose him than to take a chance with my kids."

Social Worker: "It takes a lot of strength to do what you are doing; I will support you through this transition."

Client: "Thanks! Me and my kids are going to need it; we have no one to be there for us (pause) in this big city."

Social Worker: "I hope that as we put more supports in place for you and your children, you will feel more sure of your decision."

It is also important to note that while the goals articulated above are general, and while the social worker may predict many dimensions of need, problem, risk, harm, and potential based on his or her understanding of the human condition and human growth and development, the profession is also committed to respecting the unique objective experiences of individuals ("I have a parent who is an alcoholic") or collectives ("We believed we had to take care of Dad to take the pressure off Mom") and their subjective experiences.

While professional social workers typically have specialized knowledge and experience that may be applied generally from one client to another, the workers normally apply that knowledge with a reasonable understanding of the clients' unique life experiences, personal life stories, and particular successes or failures with a range of coping strategies. While professionals may have the knowledge and the skills to predict likelihoods ("This child exhibits patterns consistent with sex abuse or early eroticization") or outcomes ("If you return to living together too soon, you increase your risk of resuming aggressive behaviour towards your wife"), the accuracy of social workers' predictions is increased if they understand their clients in depth and the social contexts in which the clients have lived. As well, culturally and ethnically sensitive practice is defined as a professional responsibility to ensure effective partnerships for change.

In the interests of addressing needs, problems, risk, harmful impacts, and potential or opportunities, social workers may frame their interventions within the context of:

- preferred ideologies (we must help individuals address their problems versus we must change the system).

- preferred definitions of problem or need (children need protection versus the problem is blaming the mother).

- preferred practices (solution-focused therapy versus radical community action).

- preferred units of observation, intervention, and change (individual, family, community, society).

- preferred goals (taking a child into care versus giving the parent sufficient supports to be a "good enough," safe, and effective parent).

In an integrative approach preferences need not be acted out as either/or conflicts that might ensure that the client is forced into acting on a particular ideology rather than receiving professional actions tailored to his or her specific needs.

A CONTINUUM OF SOCIAL WORK INTERVENTION

No matter what the ideology, definition of need or problem, preferred practice, preferred unit of intervention, or preferred goals, a *continuum of social work intervention* in current practice involves the following professional responsibility areas. These areas are not the exclusive domain of social work or any one helping profession; social work brings its own knowledge, skills, and base of competencies to each sphere of health, social welfare, social security, social justice, and education.

Professional social workers may take more leadership and have a higher profile in some fields of practice within various dimensions of the continuum of biopsychosocial intervention. It is also important to note that these activity dimensions are not mutually exclusive; in practice there is a great deal of interaction across dimensions. Also, the worker and client systems may enter at many points.

Assessment and Social Diagnosis

Social workers focus on one or more levels of client systems and they enter into partnerships to assess needs, problems, risks, harm, strengths, potentials, and biopsychosocial development.

The professional makes direct observations (observing parenting skills in action), engages in interviews (in an office or on a ward), applies standardized instruments (designed to assess some aspect of individual or collective biopsychosocial functioning), or consults with collateral parties (to integrate the observations and experiences of others), in formulating judgments and arriving at decisions with the client or in the best interests of the client.

Since social workers undertook case studies and community studies at the turn of the last century, the profession has assumed that a clear understanding of individuals and collectives in their social situations and contexts would guide social policies and action to improve people's well-being, social welfare, and social security. Social work has emphasized optimal inclusion of the client system in the assessment process, as both the client and the social worker have their own expertise to bring to the assessment (Jordan & Franklin, 2003). Some observations and judgments may be translated into social diagnoses (Turner, 2003).

Formulation and Analysis of Social Policy

Sometimes based on their assessments, social workers have led in promoting, formulating, and analyzing both formal and informal organizational policies and social policies. Some of these may be enacted in legislation.

Social workers make possible social and political actions in taking on social responsibility. Policies generally address issues of biopsychosocial well-being, health and social welfare, social security, and social justice. The policies may focus on personal health and social services (addictions assessment and counselling) or on more generalized social benefits (universal old-age-security benefits). The profession is actively involved in creating legislation, policies, and agreements, and in revising these—provincially, nationally, and internationally.

Social policies may be interpreted as being directed at goals of promotion of health, welfare, and capacity-building; prevention of problems and need; reducing individual and collective harm; providing material and social supports; ameliorating needs, problems, risks, and harmful impacts; protection of individuals, families, groups, and the public; and promoting social justice (Wharf, 2003).

Promotion of Biopsychosocial Health, Welfare, Capacity, and Social Security

Historically, social workers have promoted the well-being of individuals and collectives and encouraged collectives and individuals to take on social responsibilities. Through its history social work has aimed at social development, in which a society's or group's strengths are mobilized and their further capacity developed. Through increasing public awareness and information, as well as other professional actions, social workers promote the creation of these individual and collective strengths and capacities, as well as biopsychosocial well-being, health, social security, and social justice (Lymbery & Millward, 2001; Fides & Cooper, 2003).

Prevention

The profession has shown strong leadership in policy and program development. It has also developed intervention methods to prevent unnecessary hardships, loss of security, problems, risks, harmful impacts, and unmet basic needs.

Social workers have always been engaged in preventative activities such as education (addictions awareness), dissemination of information (contraceptive information), raising collective awareness (the risks of unprotected sexual intercourse), early brief intervention (school social workers who try to re-engage recent dropouts), and timely, concrete support (material and social help to an abandoned mother and her children). Prevention activities may be aimed at individuals or collectives and currently they involve the whole global village, as in distributing condoms to prevent HIV infection (Bloom, 1996).

Harm Reduction

The profession recognizes many differences in individuals, collectives, and their different circumstances. While respecting the many personal choices available to people, social workers also recognize the harmful impacts to individuals, families, and society that promotion, prevention, and other measures can have if they are not likely to be really effective.

As a result, social workers have moved quickly to promote harm-reduction policies and programs. Most notable among these programs historically were those implemented to control the impacts of prostitution and street drug use. More recently, social workers have encouraged activities such as needle exchanges to prevent the spread of HIV infection (Malowaniec & Rowe, 2003).

Provision of Economic and Material Support

When promotion and prevention are not effective and harm reduction is not sufficient, the situation of any person or group may result in their becoming dependent on extended family, society, and community groups for economic and material support. Other groups may be systematically disadvantaged and marginalized (those with physical challenges).

Social workers have been instrumental in promoting programs to provide economic and material assistance, managing such programs, and in delivering concrete services (McGilly, 1998).

Ensuring Protection and Safety

When promotion, prevention, harm reduction, and social provision are not sufficient to solve particular problems, social workers may have to take on major responsibilities to formulate policies, programs, and legislation to ensure the safety of persons and collectives whom they define as dependent or at significant and imminent risk.

Under the authority of the law, social workers undertake children's protection activities such as investigation, apprehension, foster placement, and adoption services. Under the mandate of private not-for-profit agencies, social workers may play a major role in activities such as providing shelter and support for abused women and protecting children exposed to violence (Kurst, Swanger, & Petcosky, 2003).

Intervening to Stabilize Individual or Collective Crises and Traumas

When promotion, prevention, harm reduction, and social provision are not sufficient to help their clients, social workers undertake more major responsibilities to manage and control crisis situations. They might take steps to stabilize the conditions for an individual or group experiencing a crisis and post-traumatic stress, to enable the client to resume self-control and return to a state of relative well-being with as little intrusive intervention as possible. Such ameliorative interventions may range from individually oriented rape crisis assistance to collective critical-incident debriefing after a collective trauma (Roberts, 2000).

Counselling, Therapy, and Psychosocial Education

For many clients—individuals, couples, families, and groups—some fundamental aspect of themselves and their bio-psychosocial life experiences presents a barrier blocking them from social supports such as promotion, prevention, harm reduction, or crisis intervention. Their levels of need, the particular problem, the risk, and harmful impacts are often so extensive and so complex that the clients need help to change themselves more substantially (feelings of depression), their social lives (being excluded from much of what society has to offer), or their social situations (being currently unemployed while having reasonable skills).

Clients may also suffer from the effects of developmental experiences and trauma that have not been resolved (being abandoned to die as a disabled child). As well, they may confront systemic disadvantages such as being excluded from employment opportunities for which they are qualified or being marginalized by finding only low-paying and temporary work for which they are overqualified.

Under such conditions and such complex and multiple problems social workers have provided counselling, therapy, and psychosocial education since the early 1900s (Hepworth, Rooney, & Larsen, 2002). In fact, the largest group of professional counsellors–therapists in North America are social workers. Their practices may overlap with those of psychology and psychiatry, but as can be seen from the sample case above, social workers have not abandoned the poor in order to work as middle-class psychotherapists.

So social workers provide counselling, therapy, and psychosocial education services by various methods expressly designed for intervention with individuals (solution-focused therapy and assertion training), families (systemic family therapy and anger management education), couples (sexuality counselling and communication skills), and groups (psychodrama and education in breaking the patterns of repeated victimization).

New directions in which social workers have made contributions include postmodern approaches to counselling and therapy. The goal is still people's individual and collective well-being. Most social work clients are not likely to find their needs are met through psychosocial education, counselling, and therapy alone; these methods are often part of a more complex case or service plan.

Promoting Self-Help and Mutual Aid

Social work as a profession has developed with a strong recognition of the importance of natural and informal mutual aid (such as extended family or common interest groups). As well, social workers helped create social networks that could provide more formal support for people's personal growth and development (a YWCA psycho-education group) or for problem solving (a person in an incest-survivor group). Social workers have also taken active roles in creating self-help and mutual aid opportunities for clients who may come together themselves for mutual support based on their common interests, needs, or life experiences (Kimberley & Osmond, 2003).

Advocacy for Systemic Social Change

Faced with barriers to individual and social welfare, and to cooperative action, social workers, on behalf of individuals and collectives, have been among the traditional leaders advocating for systemic and other social change. The target of those changes may be rights (the right to access contraception) or entitlements (such as material support for the disabled) or opportunity (social integration of persons with mental illnesses) or social support (the gradual release of offenders into society with a residential support program).

While social workers prefer to employ methods that enable a client to cooperate in making necessary change, they are also prepared to improve social situations and to remove barriers to individual and social welfare. Their methods include publicly challenging the status quo, constructive confrontation, and conflict resolution. In some political contexts, social workers have engaged in civil protests. From another perspective, social workers act to empower client systems to mobilize their own strengths and capacity for self-advocacy (See DuBois & Krogsrud Miley, 2005; and Carniol, 2002).

Collective Social Action

Social workers have a history of promoting group and community strength through relationship-building, group partnering, and community-building. Their emphasis is on empowering the collective and facilitating effective action to define problems and needs, decide on priorities, confirm group ownership, plan and commit to action, and promote or establish needed services.

Social workers also emphasize cooperation in change, though they may use conflict strategies to remove structural and systemic socioeconomic or sociopolitical barriers. They concentrate on community ownership of solutions by themselves acting as professional animators, facilitators, and advocates (Carniol, 2002).

Case Management, Referrals, and Liaisons

What is defined as *case management* in current practice was derived out of what social workers called "social casework" in the early 1900s (Richmond, 1917). The practice of managing cases grew out of concerns that clients would "fall through the cracks" and their needs would not be met; that community services would be provided in an uncoordinated or counter-productive manner; services would be duplicated; the clients' situations would change but plans would not be modified to reflect this; new opportunities for help would be overlooked; and connections with needed services would not be made (referral and liaison).

As a result social workers have undertaken to ensure such coordination, integration, and relevance as a profession. In advanced case management (a social work practice), counselling, therapy, and other activities are integrated with the case management function. (See Radol Raiff, & Shore, 1993; Rapp, 1997.) Whether the client is an individual, a family, a group, a community or an organization, service management activities, conducted by a case manager, are necessary to ensure continuous, integrated, and high-quality service.

After-Care and Follow-Up

Social work practice promotes the provision of after-care and follow-up services:

- to enable return to needed service, for those who have terminated service prematurely;
- to enable clients to return to service, for those who might need additional services to maintain the positive effects of earlier interventions;
- to monitor clients' maintenance of their gains and progress;
- to ensure that clients are satisfied with the results of the services they have received to date.

Sadly, after the decades of serious underfunding of health and social services that began in the 1980s, follow-up is often one of the services people require and do not receive or receive only superficially.

Development of Social, Community, Health, and Other Service Programs

While more social workers are entering private practice, social workers and the profession have been very instrumental in leading the development and implementation of health, social, justice, and other community services organizations and programs. Our society and our global village today have come to expect all of these.

The services may emphasize one or more of promotion, prevention, harm reduction, social provision, protection, crisis intervention, psychosocial education, counselling or therapy, case management and follow-up, advocacy, collective social action and social justice.

Among social work's contributions are:

- universal benefits such as the Canada Pension Plan and family allowances;
- targeted security benefits such as workers' compensation;
- personal community health services such as addictions programs;
- personal social services, such as family services;
- protection services, such as children's protection legislation and services;
- family preservation services such as support for single parents;
- permanency policies and services such as fostering and adoption;
- crisis and trauma services, such as rape crisis and women's shelters;
- community mental health and Canadian Mental Health Association services;
- community correctional services such as the John Howard Society;
- prevention of HIV and AIDS and offering support to their victims;
- prevention and support programs such as planned parenthood;

- early intervention services such as school social-worker services;
- home support and social centres for the aged and the disabled;
- policies and services for the blind and the visually impaired;
- national policies and programs supporting the rights of the physically challenged;
- promotion of self-help and mutual aid for victims and survivors groups;
- disaster and emergency services, including the International Red Cross;
- United Nations programs for health, education, and welfare; and
- the International Council on Social Welfare (ICSW), the International Federation of Social Workers (IFSW), and the International Association of Schools of Social Work (IASSW) programs.

Development of Team, Community, and Organizational Capacities

Historically, social work has been responsible for mobilizing collective strength and building the collective capacity of teams—including professional and multidisciplinary teams)—and communities.

As well, social workers have demonstrated leadership in creating human services (such as social centres for those with mental illnesses) and social development organizations (such as the Canadian Council on Social Development [CCSD]), and on improving the performance of existing organizations. The profession operates on the assumption that collective team, community, and organizational action will best enhance community health, social welfare, social justice, and social security. Social workers also believe that people make decisions and actions fundamentally through interpersonal trans-

actions, not organizations or "the system" (Ewalt, Freeman, & Poole, 1998).

Systematic Inquiry

In support of assessment, promotion, harm reduction, and other responsibilities, social workers have always conducted systematic inquiries using a variety of methods, to inform their professional practice and social development. Among these activities are systematically codifying practice wisdom based on case experience; conducting systematic case studies and community studies; evaluating community problems and needs; evaluating how services are implemented, clients' satisfaction, clients' progress, and outcomes; conducting demonstration studies; and studying larger samples of biopsychosocial problems, risks, harmful impacts, strengths, and potentials.

The subject of such inquiry may be an individual or a larger collective, such as a group of organizations that help international refugees. Social workers often conduct the applied research and other systematic inquiry to further well-being, health, social welfare, social security, and social justice (see, for example, Neuman & Kreuger, 2002). Other studies may explore such cutting-edge issues as the sexual exploitation of children on the internet (Kimberley & Osmond, 2000).

Providing Expert Consultation and Opinion

A social worker may develop such verified professional knowledge, skills, competence, and experience that she or he is called upon to give expert opinion and consultation.

Formal venues include the courts (a child protection case), judicial hearings (a provincial inquiry into the death of children while in foster care), case conferences (an addictions agency dealing with a case of sex addiction), or international advisory bodies (the United Nations).

This kind of expert consultation and opinion is defined as that of a professional person provided to the body that needs the opinion. Such requests confirm the professional status of social workers provincially, nationally, and internationally (Barker & Branson, 1998).

Education and Mentoring for New Social Workers and Other Professionals

The profession progresses in a cycle of renewal and dissemination of knowledge through university-based social work programs throughout Canada. The Canadian Association of Schools of Social Work (CASSW) normally accredits these programs. The association sets the standards for the knowledge, skills, and competence at the Bachelor of Social Work level and at the Master of Social Work level.

Given that social workers operate under conditions of great complexity and with ever shifting variables, most schools of social work also offer continuing education courses. The profession requires that professional social workers pursue lifelong learning. Some CE programs may offer specialty diplomas or certificates to social workers. As health and social services become more multidisciplinary in their approach, social workers may enrol in more courses with cognate disciplines (such as health education), and those in cognate disciplines may enrol in more courses in social work (such as family therapy). Specialized studies in Aboriginal social work have been at the forefront of the field of interest to other professions.

The spirit of CASSW education policies and accreditation standards may guide social work doctoral programs, but these programs are also subject to independent regulations and criteria set by graduate programs.

Professional Associations and Future-Building

In Canada, associations for professional social workers at the provincial level may be affiliated with the Canadian Association of Social Workers (CASW).

Their mandates include establishing and confirming a code of ethics and setting the profession's standards of knowledge and practice. Professional associations for social workers also promote specific issues related to social work mandates (third-party billing by professional social workers and liability insurance), as well as advocacy on social issues (juvenile prostitution and sexual exploitation of children) at the provincial and the national levels.

The professional associations also support research (such as a study of the conditions that support effective child welfare practice) and professional and scholarly production in the form of articles, reports, and monographs. Some associations have also participated with women's groups to work as partners on issues of common concern, such as wife abuse. The CASW has also joined various coalitions, such as the Community Alliance for Better Solutions, to promote social welfare and social justice.

The national association represents the profession internationally in the International Federation of Social Workers (IFSW), and nationally through related organizations such as the Canadian Council on Social Development and the Canadian Association of Schools of Social Work (CASSW), as well as other voluntary-association interest groups.

At the provincial and the national levels, the profession models independent advocacy, partnerships, client consultation (for example, some associations invite client representatives to sit on their boards), and teamwork. In most provinces, the law regulates the profession of social work and either the professional association or an independent social-work regulatory body controls the granting of the title "social worker" and/or practice (especially within the areas of assessment, counselling, and therapy).

In short, often persons who call themselves social workers when they are not or who practise social work when they are not registered or certified to do so may be charged and punished.

Some of the initiatives that social work organizations have undertaken recently include:

- developing of social work capacity among Aboriginal people;
- promoting culturally and ethnically sensitive social work practice;
- drafting a labour mobility agreement to permit social work graduates to move freely between the provinces to take on various social work positions;

- advocating for third-party billing privileges and exemption from the Goods and Services Tax for social work clinical services; and
- studying the impact of global economies and trade agreements on the profession and its practice.

CONCLUSION

As we advocate for clients, social workers must view the profession, our mission, and our goals as worthy of our continued advocacy. It is important that we assert our strengths as we adapt to changes in the future and create more opportunities for our voices and those of our clients to be heard. We must participate actively in the new global order. Social workers today carry the values and strengths of social workers who assumed social responsibilities and built a respected profession, in the interests of creating better futures for individuals, for society, and for the profession itself.

REFERENCES

Note to Readers: The case examples used in this chapter are based on the current work of Canadian social workers in practice.

Al-Krenawi, A., & Graham, J. R. (Eds.) (2002). *Multicultural social work in Canada.* Don Mills, ON: Oxford University Press.

Baldwin, M., & Satir, V. (1987). *The use of self in therapy.* New York: Haworth Press.

Barker, R. L., & Branson, D. M. (1998). *Forensic social work: Legal aspects of professional practice.* New York: Haworth Press.

Berg, I. K., & Steiner, T. (2003). *Children's solution work.* New York: W. W. Norton and Company.

Bloom, M. (1996). *Primary prevention practices.* Newbury Park, CA: Sage.

Carniol, B. (2002). *Case critical: Challenging social services in Canada.* 4th edn. Toronto: Between the Lines.

Cork, R. Margaret. (1969). *The forgotten children.* Toronto: PaperJacks, in association with the Addiction Research Foundation of Ontario.

Coulborn Faller, K. (1998). *Interviewing for child sex abuse: A forensic guide* (VHS video and manual). New York: Guilford Press.

Csiernik, R., & Rowe, W. S. (Eds.) (2003). *Responding to the oppression of addiction: Canadian social work perspectives.* Toronto: Canadian Scholars' Press.

Dansky, S. F. (1997). *Nobody's children: Orphans of the HIV epidemic.* New York: Haworth Press.

Davies, Douglas (2004). *Child development: A practitioner's guide.* 2d edn. New York: Guilford Press.

Dominelli, L. (2002). *Feminist social work theory and practice.* Hampshire, UK: Palgrave Macmillan.

Dubois, B., & Krogsrud Miley, K. (2005). *Social work: An empowering profession.* 5th edn. Boston: Allyn & Bacon.

Ewalt, P. L., Freeman, E. M., & Poole, D. L. (Eds.). (1998). *Community building, renewal, well-being and shared responsibility.* Washington, D.C.: NASW Press.

Fides, R., & Cooper, B. (October 17, 2003). *Preparing for change: Social work and primary health care.* Ottawa: CASW.

Funk, Rainer (1982). *Erich Fromm: The courage to be human.* New York: Continuum.

Gambrill, E. (1997). *Social work practice: A critical thinker's guide.* New York: Oxford University Press.

Goldstein, H., Hilbert, J. C., & Hilbert, H. C. (1984). *Creative change: A cognitive humanistic approach to social work practice.* New York: Viking/Penguin.

Hancock, Molly R.. & Millar, K. I. (1994). *Cases for intervention planning: A sourcebook.* Chicago: Nelson-Hall.

Hepworth, D. H., Rooney, R. H., & Larsen, J. A. (2002). *Direct social work practice: Theory and skills.* 6th edn. Pacific Grove, CA: Brooks/Cole.

Jordan, C., & Franklin, C. (2003). *Clinical assessment for social workers.* 2d edn. Chicago: Nelson-Hall.

Kimberley, D., & Bohm, P. (1999). Drug addiction: A BSPI model. In F. J. Turner (Ed.), *Adult psychopathology: A social work perspective.* 2d edn. New York: Free Press.

Kimberley, D., & Osmond, L. (2000). *Assessment and treatment of persons sexually addicted to child pornography and sex exploitation, within the context of internet addiction.* Edmonton: Answers in Action: Healing, Sexual Exploitation & Prostitution.

Kimberley, D., & Osmond, L. (2003). Night of the tortured souls: Integration of group therapy and mutual aid for treated male sex offenders. In Lindsay, J., Turcotte, D., & Hopmeyer, E. (Eds.), *Crossing boundaries and developing alliances through group work.* New York: Haworth Press. 75–98.

Kurst Swanger, K., & Petcosky, J. L. (2003). *Violence in the home: Multidisciplinary perspectives.* New York: Oxford University Press.

Lindsay, J., Turcotte, D., & Hopmeyer, E. (Eds.). (2003). *Crossing boundaries and developing alliances through group work.* New York: Haworth Press.

Lymbery, M., & Millward, A. (2001). Community care in practice: Social work in primary health care. *Social Work in Health Care, 34 (3/4).* 241–259.

Malowaniec, L., & Rowe, W. S. (2003). Social workers and safer injection rooms: "We accept them the way they are..." In R. Csiernik & W. S. Rowe (Eds.), *Responding to the oppression of addiction: Canadian social work perspectives.* Toronto: Canadian Scholars' Press. 37–54.

McGilly, F. (1998). *Canada's public social services: Understanding income and health programs.* Don Mills, ON: Oxford University Press.

McLuhan, M., & Powers, B. R. (1992). *Global village: Transformations in world life and media in the twenty-first century.* Don Mills, ON: Oxford University Press.

Martin, E. P., & Martin, J. M. (2003). *Spirituality and the black helping tradition in social work.* Washington, D.C.: NASW Press.

Mullaly, Robert. (2002). *Structural social work: Ideology, theory, and practice.* 2d edn. Don Mills, ON: Oxford University Press.

Munson, C. E. (2001). *Clinical social work supervision.* 3d edn. New York: Haworth Press.

Nin, Anais. (1932–1934). *Incest: From "A Journal of Love."* New York: Harcourt Brace & Co. [Published 1992.]

Neuman, W. L., & Kreuger, L. W. (2002). *Social work research methods: Qualitative and quantitative applications.* Boston: Allyn and Bacon.

Radol Raiff, N., & Shore, B. K. (1993). *Advanced case management.* Newbury Park, CA: Sage Publications.

Rapp, C. A. (1997). *The strengths model: Case management with people suffering from severe and persistent mental illness.* New York: Oxford University Press.

Richmond, M. E. (1917). *Social diagnosis.* New York: Russell Sage Foundation.

Roberts, A. R. (Ed.). (2000). *Crisis intervention handbook: Assessment, treatment and research.* New York: Oxford University Press.

Roberts, A. R., & Yeager, K. R. (2004). *Evidence-based practice manual: Research and outcome measures in health and human services.* New York: Oxford University Press.

Rothman, J., & Sager, J. S. (1998). *Case Management: Integrating individual and community practice* Boston: Allyn & Bacon.

Shulman, L. (1991). *Interactional social work practice: Toward and empirical theory.* Itasca, IL: F. E. Peacock Publishers.

Shulman, L. (1998) *The skills of helping individuals, families, groups and communities.* 4th edn. Itasca, IL: F. E. Peacock Publishers.

Shulman, L. (1999). *Interactional supervision.* Washington, D.C.: NASW Press.

Stuart, R. B. (2003). *Helping couples change: A social learning approach to marital therapy.* New York: Guilford Press.

Towle, C. (1945; 1987 revised). *Common human needs.* Washington, D.C.: NASW.

Turner, F. (2002). *Diagnosis in social work: New imperatives.* New York: Haworth Press.

Wharf, B. (2003). *Connecting policy to practice.* 2d edn. Don Mills, ON: Oxford University Press.

chapter twenty-eight

Models of Social Work Practice

Rose Blackmore

INTRODUCTION

Social work practitioners work with individuals, groups, families, and communities, as well as administrators, educators, and researchers. In the daily practice of social workers, their methods may overlap. For example, a social worker practising family therapy may also teach a course at a school of social work and participate in a research project. Likewise, a group worker with adolescents may be involved in a community development project related to housing and practise individual work with single parents of adolescents.

This chapter will address only practices with individuals, groups, families, communities, and administration. Research, education, and social policy are addressed elsewhere in this book.

The chapter will be divided into (1) an introduction that outlines theories and practice principles, (2) clinical practice, (3) community development, and (4) administration. Clinical practice includes work with individuals, groups, and families.

THEORIES

Social workers apply many models of practice in working with individuals, groups, families, and communities. The models contain social work principles, theories of individual and group behaviour, family systems and dynamics, and community development.

For social workers, theories are ways of organizing observations and phenomena. Out of these theories social workers formulate applicable skills so that they and their clients can diagnose and make decisions about treatment goals and the best methods of achieving them. Stated another way, "Theory emerges through the process of ordering facts in a meaningful way: that is, the relationship between facts is posited through observation, speculation, inspiration, and experience, and as these relationships are observed and verified, theory is developed" (Turner, 1986, p. 3).

Put yet another way, "Every practitioner should know that her observations are not simply casual scannings; they involve a conceptually ordered search for evidence. Her eyes and ears are trained to help her select evidence relative to some framework that will permit inferences to be drawn, order revealed, meanings surmised, and an explanatory guide for action planned. These organizing frameworks are theories. They provide the conceptual models that help the worker grasp the meaning of the relationship among phenomena that practice leads her to observe" (Lewis, 1982, p. 61).

Selecting a model of practice is largely a matter of choice. Personal attraction to a model or models, those taught at schools of social work and models practised in agencies, are some of the influences affecting choice.

PRACTICE PRINCIPLES

Before discussing models of social work practice, it is important to outline the practice principles that all models share. They are (1) acceptance of and respect for people, (2) appreciating the uniqueness of individuals, (3) non-judgmental attitude, (4) client self-determination, (5) confidentiality, and (6) knowledge and skills of practice.

(1) *Acceptance and respect:* Anyone seeking resolution to problems expects and needs to be believed and to be taken seriously. This consideration requires that the social worker genuinely express concerns. It creates a climate of comfort and trust for the client.

(2) *Appreciating the uniqueness of individuals:* Social workers know that all clients bring their own personal experiences and perspectives to their problems. For example, even though many people may be unemployed, each one thinks about and experiences the situation differently. Acknowledging these differences is a key to helping.

(3) *Non-judgmental attitude:* Clients do not want to be judged as worthy or unworthy of assistance. As well, social workers meet clients they like and those they do not. Clients also meet social workers they like and those they do not. As professionals, social workers recognize these attitudes in themselves and in clients and the reasons for them. Non-judgmental attitudes are, therefore, the ability to assess and practise without bias.

(4) *Client self-determination:* This principle is based on the client's ability to formulate solutions and make decisions. The individual, group, family, and community "own" the problem. Based on the joint diagnosis of the social worker and the client, the client has the ability to make decisions, however limited in some instances.

(5) *Confidentiality:* The relationship between social workers and clients is privileged. However, where legally or otherwise required clients are made aware of when, why, and to whom the information is given. In the non–legally required sharing of information, clients are asked to give written permission for the sharing of information.

(6) *Knowledge and skills:* Social workers have undergone academic and practice

studies to become competent practitioners. Following graduation, they are expected to continue learning theory and honing their practice. In many jurisdictions, social workers must be licensed or registered through a college. This informs the public that the social worker is competent.

CLINICAL PRACTICE

In clinical social work practice, it is not unusual to work primarily with one method and secondarily with the other two. For example, a social worker practising family therapy in which families present with "problem" adolescent children will lead a group of adolescents referred by their schools for truancy and meet with adolescents individually.

Social Work with Individuals

Social work with individuals has a long history extending more than a century (M. Bogo, in Turner, 1999: Blackmore, in Turner, 2000). In the late 1800s and early 1900s, religious, benevolent, and philanthropic organizations visited individuals and families who were in need. Those offering help were known as "friendly visitors" who would offer financial assistance, clothes, information, about resources and advice. Although some individuals and families were able to use these resources successfully, others could not. It became clear that some required more than the friendly visitors could offer.

Knowledge about human behaviour, social functioning, community resources, and social policy was gaining importance as a necessary tool. As a result, friendly visitors began to receive formal training, which eventually evolved into professional training at the university level. Social workers such as Hollis (1964), Richmond

(1922), and Hamilton (1951) were some of the pioneers in social work, which at that time was based predominantly on working with individuals.

In perusing the social work literature of several decades ago, the terms "casework" and "caseworker" are used. These terms were used to differentiate practice with individuals from group work. As social work became involved in further practice models such as family therapy, community development, and others, the terms "casework" and "caseworker" were dropped in favour of clinical practice, community development worker, and so on.

Practice with individuals is based on a set of three concepts. One is that the individual presenting the problem is able to participate in diagnosis and treatment. In other words the focus of change is on the individual. Any changes the individual client makes are expected to have a ripple effect on his environment.

The second concept is the importance of the client–worker relationship. This relationship is the medium in which the intervention process takes place. Regardless of which theoretical model the social worker uses, the client–worker relationship is the key to any progress. The client feels accepted, safe, and comfortable in this relationship.

The third concept is the person-in-situation developed by Hollis and her colleagues (1981). It recognizes that individuals live in a milieu of families, friends, work associates, schoolmates, and neighbours and they have contact with various organizations, such as hospitals, schools, courts, etc. In order to understand the functioning of the individual, the social worker takes into account the client's relationship with these various environments. The social worker further recognizes as part of her social work skills the ability to work with a client's environment through intervention and advocacy.

Social workers learn a number of practice theories in order to understand their clients' social functioning and the skills that flow from the theories. Several have influenced social work practice. In its early beginnings, social work practice used two approaches to understanding human behaviour. One was based on psychoanalytic theory. For social workers, it was the "diagnostic" approach.

Hollis (1981) used this approach to develop the psychosocial model. One aspect of this model postulated that in order to understand current behaviours, it is important to understand past behaviours. This way, the individual can make connections and progress towards resolution. Social histories were important diagnostic tools.

The other approach was "functional," based on examining only the client's current situation. The client was then offered the services that existed in the agency. One aspect of this theory was that it was not necessary to understand the client's past behaviour in order to help. Competition arose between the two schools, but as other models were developed or refined, the differences disappeared over time.

Ego psychology theory as a refinement of psychoanalytic theory has influenced social worker practice (Goldstein, 1984). Social workers have been attracted to ego psychology because it "comprises a related set of theoretical concepts about human behaviour that focus on origins, development, structure and functioning of the executive arm of the personality—the ego—and its relationship to other aspects of the personality and to the external environment."

Another influence on social work practice is social learning or behaviour theory that has its origins in psychology. The key concept is that behaviour is learned. Individuals respond to stimuli in two ways. Appropriate responses lead to socially acceptable behaviour and inappropriate responses lead to maladaptive behaviour.

A popular treatment model related to behaviour theory is cognitive therapy. The focus is to challenge negative thoughts by promoting positive thinking. The aim is to change one's self-perception and relationships this way.

Other forms of behaviour therapy are used to treat phobias. Another influence on social work practice has been the client-centred approach arising out of Carl Roger's work. Its key concept is that, by nature, people strive to better themselves. Accordingly, treatment focuses on self-awareness in both the client and the worker. Self-awareness provides the energy required to make changes. The client-centred approach is used in sensitivity training for board members of organizations, staff, and volunteers.

Social work has also developed unique practice models that arise out of the influential theories. Psychosocial and functional approaches are two examples that have already been discussed. Perlman (1986) developed problem solving as an approach that emphasizes the client's ability and responsibility for diagnosis and treatment. The client is actively involved along with the social worker in a defined process working towards diagnosis and treatment.

Reid and Epstein (1977) developed the task-centred approach. Laura Epstein, whose practice was in child welfare and education, observed that many clients had multiple needs that required immediate attention. The task-centred approach focuses on the present situation, partializing the needs and setting achievable goals. Partializing the client's many needs makes the situation less overwhelming for him or her. It also empowers the client to make decisions.

Crisis intervention is a treatment model based on ego psychology. Crises are identifies as developmental, transitional and hazardous, or traumatic. Developmental crises are those difficult periods through which a person must pass in the various stages of life. Transitional crises are the expected ones people encounter, such as entering school, employment, marriage, divorce, death of a family member, retirement, moving, and illness. In other words, individuals facing these events are expected to experience them as crises. Hazardous crises are those associated with such traumatic events as wars, fires, floods, major accidents, torture, and physical and sexual abuse.

A current addition to crisis theory is critical incidence. This concept arises out of a recognition that individuals in high-risk careers, such as the military, police, firefighting, emergency department of hospitals, or paramedics, react to traumatic events. Some develop post-traumatic stress syndrome.

Readers will be familiar with the use of crisis counsellors. Crisis theory is based on the concept that reaction to crises is normal, that individuals pass through several stages towards regaining their equilibrium in functioning. Crisis intervention aids in achieving that equilibrium.

Practice with individuals is indicated in situations in which clients feel comfortable with their one-on-one relationships with their social workers. Clients who are uncomfortable in groups or family therapy or whose relationships are maladaptive may find individual treatment a way of beginning positive relationships. For clients who have difficulty articulating their needs—children for example—techniques such as drawing, music, and play acting are used to enhance communication. Clients who feel uncomfortable in a one-on-one relationship would likely prefer a group setting.

Social Work with Groups

Social work with groups also has a history extending over a century. It had its begin-

nings in the settlement movements in England, the United States, and later in Canada. Toynbee Hall established in 1884 in London, England, and Hull House in 1889 in Chicago are considered pioneers in the settlement movement.

Some of the pioneering settlements in Canada were established in large cities (Mesbur in Turner, 1999) by the Presbyterian Church and YWCA. Examples of this movement are settlement houses such as St. Christopher House, University Settlement House, and Central Neighbourhood House in Toronto; Chalmers House in Montreal; Robertson Memorial House in Winnipeg; and the Vancouver Community House. Large numbers of people dislocated by the Industrial Revolution, who relocated from rural to urban centres, provided the impetus for the settlement movement. Many of these people were poor, unemployed, and lacked skills for the new industries.

The settlements encouraged people to view social problems such as poverty as not the fault of individuals, but of society. Citizens were encouraged to take responsibility to change their situations. To achieve this goal, the settlement movement provided opportunities through groups to learn skills such as literacy, acceptable social behaviours, community resources, and recreation. It can be assumed that some houses included advice on health and nutrition.

Since the early days of the settlement movement, group work has evolved into a social work modality that reflects changing types of group theory and practice. However, the major rationale for group work still is the recognition that groups are microcosms of a democratic society. Individuals form relationships with a wide variety of other individuals and groups in society. Productive interactions depend on people's ability to form these relationships. Otherwise, the individual will experience difficulties in daily life and either act out or become lonely.

Social work with groups can be defined as "an orientation and method of social intervention in which small numbers of people who share similar interests and common problems convene regularly and engage in activities designed to achieve certain objectives" (Barker 1995). Another definition, by Toesland and Rivas, states that group work is a "goal-directed activity with small groups of people aimed at meeting socio-emotional needs and accomplishing tasks" (1995).

- Mutual aid: Members experiencing similar problems derive support from each other.
- Socialization: Members learn adaptive social skills in a safe environment.
- Problem solving: Members learn new and socially acceptable ways of resolving issues.
- Rehabilitation and education: Members learn new ways of adaptation following crises such as traumas, disabilities, and illness.

Based on the functions cited, groups are categorized into types. Authors vary in the way they define the types of groups. This chapter presents two typologies. Northern (1988) categorizes groups as follows:

- Socialization: Groups provide information, support, and problem-solving strategies. Some groups may include recreation, art, music, etc. as adjunct activities.
- Therapy and counselling: The goal is the improvement of social functioning.
- Support and self-help: The goal is mutual aid and support.
- Task groups: This model of group is used in community development and organizations.

Another typology is that presented by Mesbur (1999). She classifies groups into the following models:

- Social goals: The main purpose is the encouragement of individual growth through participation in a group setting.
- Reciprocal: The group members learn strategies in mediating between themselves and others.
- Remedial: The purpose is remedial or corrective and applied in medical and psychiatric settings as part of the rehabilitation process.

Any reader who has led a group or participated as a member in a group will recognize that the purposes, categories, and models can overlap. However, on closer examination, it may become evident that one purpose and category predominate in each type.

Groups can be either closed or open-ended. *Closed-ended* implies that the group consists of an agreed-upon number of members and sessions. The usual number of members varies between four and eight. Eight is the preferred maximum, given that the leader and members will have to manage the dynamics of the group. A group of fewer than four people loses some momentum in terms of the interactions of a larger group and often does not "feel like a group." Groups generally meet weekly for about eight to 10 weeks. However, the duration and frequency of the meetings varies. For example, in hospital settings, groups of in-patients may meet daily. Where group members have not resolved their issues, they may agree to meet longer than the 10 weeks they agreed to earlier.

Open-ended groups imply that members come and go. The dynamics of such groups vary considerably from closed-ended groups. Open-ended groups attract a core of members who attend regularly while others may attend infrequently. The duration of this type of group tends to go on for months. I am aware, for example, of one open-ended support group for the families of residents at a long-term care facility that has been meeting regularly for years.

An interesting model of group work I have attended followed a three-step approach based on timing. This support group was organized for the spouses of Alzheimer patients. The closed-ended group of six met for 10 weeks when the spouses with Alzheimer were living at home. The second step involved the same members in a 10-week closed-ended group about seven months later. By that time, the conditions of the Alzheimer patients had worsened and the issues affecting their spouses differed from those that had concerned the group's members when they met the first time. In the second step, the members were discussing placement in long-term care facilities, homemaking services, day programs, and their feelings. The third step involved the same group that met once a month for one year. At this time, most of the spouses with Alzheimer had either passed away or were living in long-term care facilities. Again, the issues at that point differed from those of the earlier group meetings.

Social work group leaders have the responsibility to practise ethically and democratically. The groups are a safe and trusting place for the members regardless of the group's purpose. Social workers practising with groups, whether acting as solo leaders or as co-leaders, possess useful knowledge about group dynamics, the stages of a group's development, and the purpose of the group. They are skilled in working with this knowledge.

Social Work with Families

Social work has always emphasized the importance of working with families (Hollis 1981). Family members provide useful information, such as dates for diagnosis and treatment of the individual. However, early social work provided no theoretical way of thinking about families, even though social workers and other therapists observed that individuals' behaviours were affected substantially by their families' dynamics (Nichols and Schwartz 1998).

Early theories of families borrowed group dynamics from group work and role theory from sociology. Neither theory was very useful although each was a beginning. As well, the marriage counselling model did not provide the theory necessary to explain family functioning. Eventually, marriage counselling or marital therapy became part of family treatment.

Early pioneers in the development of theories of family began to emerge in the early 1960s. They were Gregory Bateson, Don Jackson, Jay Haley, and Virginia Satir. These pioneers were involved in research and practice with schizophrenic patients at the Mental Health Research Institute in Palo Alto, California (Foley 1974). They observed that the conditions of patients who responded to treatment while in hospital worsened when their families visited them or when the patients returned to hospital after a visit home with family. In Philadelphia, Salvador Minuchin and his colleagues observed similar dynamics in families of children who were in residential treatment programs.

From the many observations and hypotheses produced, the pioneers proposed that the most appropriate way to think about family is to consider it a system not unlike a physical system. Some of the associated terms, such as equilibrium, stasis, and boundaries, were adopted at the same time.

Thinking about the family as a system requires a shift in diagnosis and treatment. In individual and group treatment, the client owns the problem and is expected, albeit with much support, to change. In family treatment, all members own the problem and all are expected to change. In other words, if one member of the family is identified as "the problem," then he or she affects the other members. When one of the members begins to change behaviour, whether that person is the identified "problem" member or another one is, that change affects all members of the family. Therefore, diagnosis and treatment involves all the members of the family.

As in practice with individuals and groups there are many theories and models of family treatment. This chapter will not address them in any detail but will outline some of the key concepts common to them and necessary for social workers' repertoire of knowledge and skills. They are:

Membership: Individuals are expected to know who the members of their families are. However, in some situations, such as remarried families and families in which the children live in two homes, there may be a difference of opinion regarding what constitutes family.

Boundaries: A functioning system has definite but flexible boundaries. In families, members over time enter the family unit by birth or marriage and leave by moving away, separating, and dying. Families are expected to be flexible enough to accommodate these changes. In family treatment, language such as "closed," "open," and "diffuse" are used to describe boundaries. *Open boundaries* are those that allow family members to enter and leave at appropriate times. Families with *closed boundaries* resist their members' moving away, such as adult children going off to college, and they refuse entry to new members, such as children's spouses. *Diffuse boundaries* permit family members to enter and leave at will. The family environment is emotionally unsupportive and uncaring.

Equilibrium: The family maintains equilibrium much as a physical system does. A new member entering the family unit, such as a baby or an adult child moving back into the home, creates disequilibrium. The family will try to accommodate the new member until a new equilibrium is reached. When a family member leaves, that change also creates disequilibrium; and again the remaining members will attempt to compensate for that loss. Crises such as illnesses and disabilities also create disequilibrium as they change the roles of the members. Equilibrium is restored when the members redefine their roles.

Communication patterns: Healthy communications within families are open, direct, and respectful. Unhealthy patterns are indirect and stressful. In family treatment the social worker looks at who speaks to whom, about what, when, and how. Non-verbal communication such as gestures, facial expressions, and posture are essential components of communication patterns.

Rules: Rules in families can be explicit and flexible or vague, confusing, or rigid. Families may have rules about the language used in the home, types of food permitted, religious affiliation, school and career choices, residential area, etc.

Roles: Roles of members are defined by age, tradition, competence, and gender. Roles can be flexible or rigid.

Power: A family is not a democratic entity because of the various needs and abilities of the various members. Parents are at the top of the hierarchy and are more powerful than the children. Problems arise when a member abuses power, as in family violence, or when a member abdicates power, as in neglecting the children.

Intergenerational transmission: Values, expectations, beliefs, lifestyles, heroes, villains, etc. are transmitted through the generations. They define the family. Awareness of one's ancestors can contribute to understanding current issues.

In family treatment it is expected that all members will attend the sessions. When this is not possible, treatment can proceed with those who attend. At times it is necessary to see members individually if they have difficulty expressing their concerns in the family sessions.

Social Work with Communities

Social work practice with communities likewise has a long history. The early days of group work in settlement houses were a forerunner of community development. Later, the term "community organization" was applied to community planning and the term "community development" was applied to developing countries. Currently, the term "community development" has been adopted.

One of the early pioneers in community organization was Murray Ross. He cites a definition of community development by the United Nations: "The term 'community development' designates the utilization under one single programme of approaches and techniques which rely upon local communities as units of action and which attempt to combine outside assistance with organized local self-determination and effort, and which correspondingly seek to stimulate local initiative and leadership as the primary instrument of change.... In agricultural countries in economically under-developed areas, major emphasis is placed upon those activities which aim at promoting the improvement of the basic living conditions of the community, including the satisfaction of some of its non-material needs" (Ross, 1955).

Another definition is that of *community organization*: "Community organization... has been defined as the process of bringing about and maintaining a progressively more effective adjustment between social welfare resources and social welfare needs within a geographic area or functional field. Its goals are consistent with all social work goals in that its primary focus is upon needs of people and provision of means of meeting these needs in a manner consistent with the precepts of democratic living" (Ross, 1955). In this context, community development focuses on the coordination of the agencies providing social services. Where there were gaps and needs, the community organization worker's objective was to encourage those agencies to fill the unmet needs.

Combining the United Nations definition and Ross's definition, the current definition of *community development* can be stated as "collaborative, collective action taken by local people to enhance the long-term social, economic and environmental conditions of their community. The primary goal of community development is to create a better overall quality of life for everyone in the community" (Google search engine, 2004). *The Social Work Dictionary* defines social workers in community development as "facilitators of planned efforts to achieve specific goals in the development of a group, neighbourhood, constituency or other community" and community development as "efforts made by professionals and community residents to enhance bonds among members of the community, motivate the citizens for self-help and develop responsible leadership" (Barker 1995).

What is a community? As community development has evolved over the years, several types of communities have been identified. They are:

Neighbourhood: A neighbourhood is a geographic area. Its residents recognize a problem and band together to solve it. The process is generally task-oriented, in that the need and the goals are defined. The social worker assists the neighbourhood in the process of achieving the goals. Some examples are neighbours concerned about pollution from a nearby factory, a lack of recreation facilities, or a lack of public transportation.

Functional communities: Concerned individuals have common issues. Examples are the parents of autistic children, consumer groups, and individuals with disabilities.

Social planning: Social planning involves identifying issues, researching the issues, defining goals, and developing strategies to implement goals. Some examples are the United Way, district health councils, and social planning councils.

The knowledge and skills required for social work practice with communities are:

- the community and its members
- issues and problems
- assessment of the issues
- research into the issues
- developing strategies
- funding sources and fundraising if necessary
- leadership skills
- lobbying skills.

ADMINISTRATION

Administration in social work and the social services differs considerably from that in business. Although many of the administrative processes in both settings are similar, the one major difference is the financial base. Businesses derive their financial base from profits by selling goods or services. Social services do not "sell" their services. For some agencies, the financial base consists mainly of charitable donations from the public and government grants. For public social services the funding comes entirely from taxes.

In a profit-making business setting, the main objective is to sell the product, be it a car or advice about interior decorating. In social services, the main objective is to offer services to the public. Traditionally social services were offered free and this precedent continues to this day. It is a commitment to the poor. Even though some services such as individual, group, and family treatment have a fee, and even though people of every economic stratum use social work services, these fees are insufficient to cover the cost of administration, let alone produce a profit. The various social services offered by agencies depend on the funding sources.

In recent years, when social services suffered funding cutbacks by governments, the agencies faced having to reduce their level of services. Some agencies began to explore developing business enterprises that would turn profits, which would then be used to complement the social services funding.

Lutherwood, a children's residential and out-patient treatment facility, is one such successful venture, in Waterloo, Ontario. It also offers consultation to local schools and developed a program to assist adolescents and young adults with employment. As treatment of children and employment services became costlier and funding decreased, Lutherwood decided to embark on a business enterprise. It established a retirement village—Luther Village—consisting of bungalows, apartments, and an assisted-living building. Financially and socially it is a success (Kays

2003). Not only does Luther Village provide services to seniors, but its profits today complement the funding gaps of Lutherwood.

In social service administration, there are several levels of management. The first level is the front-line staff. They are responsible for providing services to the clients.

The second level is that of supervisor. As supervisor, the social worker performs three functions. The first is that of administrator. The task generally consists of establishing caseloads or projects, assisting in hiring, and conducting performance evaluations. The second role is that of educator. The supervisor ensures that the staff maintain professional competence. This may be accomplished by conference, individual or group consultation, providing professional literature to co-workers, or funds and opportunities for staff development.

The third function is that of support. The supervisor does not become the social worker's therapist. However, workplace or non-work-related stresses need to be acknowledged. The supervisor must encourage and make possible assistance to the social worker.

The role of the supervisor has changed considerably over the years. Earlier, the supervisor played a key role in the administrative and education functions. As the profession matured, it became clearer that practitioners were autonomous. In addition, resources for professional development increased by such avenues as courses, workshops, and conferences. The relationship between the supervisor and front-line social worker became one of consultation.

The executive director of a social service agency has several functions. The first is providing leadership in developing and promoting the current and future direction of the agency. The second is managing the resources, such as professional and support staff, and physical space. The third is communicating both within and outside the agency. The fourth is maintaining relationships. The executive director deals with the board, the staff, the funding sources, and the general public.

Generally social workers begin their careers in the front lines. After gaining some experience in dealing directly with clients, some social workers become more interested in and knowledgeable about the agency overall. Consequently, they may gravitate towards administration.

CONCLUSION

This chapter introduces the reader to several models of social work practice. Various models contain social work values and principles and theories of individual, group, family, and community behaviour, and administration. These are useful only if the social worker can apply them when working with clients. In other words, these models must make sense.

Theories are also useful when they are able to use new information. For example, early family theories assumed that the family unit consists of two parents and children. Such a theory does not explain single parent families or remarried families or gay/lesbian families.

Subsequent theories have revised their definition of family and also the skills required to work with them. In community development, some communities—whether they are actual neighbourhoods or otherwise functional as a collective—may have members without much experience in cooperative efforts or skills in collective behaviour. In these situations, the process guiding the community towards its desired goal differs considerably from those described in textbooks. The leader's first goal is to teach these skills before addressing other issues. Eventually the theory developed to understand this community will catch up with social work practice. We need to refine theories and practice constantly as we acquire new knowledge.

REFERENCES

Barker, R. L. 1995. *The social work dictionary.* 3d edn. Toronto: NASW Press.

Blackmore, R. 2001. Models of social work practice. In J. C. Turner & F. J. Turner (Eds.), *Canadian social welfare.* 4th edn. Scarborough, ON: Allyn & Bacon.

Foley, V. D. 1974. *An introduction to family therapy.* New York: Grune and Stratton.

Goldstein, E. 1986. Ego psychology. In F. J. Turner (Ed.), *Social work treatment: Interlocking theoretical approach.* 3d edn. New York: Free Press.

Hamilton, G. 1951. *Theory and practice of social casework.* 2d edn. New York: Columbia University Press.

Hollis, F., & Woods, M. E. 1981. *Casework: A psychosocial therapy.* 3d edn. New York: Random House.

Jaco, R. M. 1999. Social work with individuals. In F. J. Turner (Ed.), *Social work practice: A Canadian perspective.* Scarborough, ON. Prentice Hall.

Kays, D. Winter 2003. Social entrepreneurship: Changing the paradigm of caring. *Child and family.*

Lewis, H. 1982. *The intellectual base of social work practice.* New York: Haworth Press.

Mesbur, E. S. 1999. Social group work: The Canadian experience. In F. J. Turner (Ed.),

Social work practice: A Canadian perspective. Scarborough, ON: Prentice Hall.

Nichols, M. P., & Schwartz, R. C. 1998. *Family therapy: Concepts and methods.* 4th edn. Allyn & Bacon.

Northern, H. 1988. *Social work with groups.* 2d edn. New York: Columbia University Press.

Perlman, H. H. 1986. The problem-solving model. In F. J. Turner (Ed.), *Social work treatment: Interlocking theoretical approaches.* 3d edn. New York; Free Press.

Reid, W. J., & Epstein, L. 1977. *Task-centered practice.* New York: Columbia University Press.

Richmond, M. 1922. *What is social casework?* New York: Russell Sage Foundation.

Ross, M. 1955. *Community organization: Theory and principles.* New York: Harper and Harper.

Toesland, R. W., & Rivas, R. F. 1995. *An introduction to group work practice.* 2d edn. New York: Allyn & Bacon.

Turner, F. J. 1986. Theory in social work practice. In F. J. Turner (Ed.), *Social work treatment: Interlocking theoretical approaches.* 3d edn. New York: Free Press.

chapter twenty-nine

Regulation: A Key to Enhancing Professional Accountability

Dan Andreae

INTRODUCTION

Regulation marks an evolutionary step in the ongoing development of a profession, during which a government body sets out a code of conduct in law for that group. A group of trained and competent university-educated individuals may possess a body of knowledge, scope of practice, and specialized skills, but until the state legally sanctions the group's status through statutory legislation, the group's members are practising without being members of a recognized and defined profession.

The achievement of regulatory legislation confers upon a profession and its members accountability to their peers for their delivery of services. And more important, the members demonstrate

their obligation to the public at large, for whom the regulation is intended. Above all, the need for public protection gives rise to and legitimizes the enactment of a government-sponsored bill.

The vast majority of social workers are highly trained and university-educated, holding either a Bachelor's (BSW), a Master's (MSW), or a Doctoral (PhD) degree. Many have taken further specialized training in areas such as child welfare, mediation, crisis management, various methodologies of short-term and long-term therapy, gerontology, or hospital-based social work. They keep abreast of emerging developments by participating in continuing education programs, through conferences, seminars, and workshops. They adhere to a code of ethics that their profession endorses and are dedicated, responsible, and ethical practitioners.

Yet, as within any professional group, some abuse their power and privilege by occasionally committing breaches of professional conduct and need to be held to account. Regulation of a profession can provide the legally sanctioned structures, means, and processes that allow clients to redress any indiscretions or complaints in a formal and recognized manner. The process benefits all clients and especially those who may lack the means, access to funds, or expertise to engage in costly and time-consuming court challenges that could invade their privacy. Regulation recognizes members of the public who can and cannot call themselves social workers and gives clients the security of knowing that they are entitled to a certain level of service. They also know that social work practitioners are accountable to a legal body (a college) that is empowered to carry out actions, including:

- to establish and enforce professional and ethical standards
- to receive and investigate complaints against members
- to address discipline, professional misconduct, incompetence, or incapacity
- to promote high standards and quality assurance in the professions
- to communicate with the public on behalf of members
- to establish and maintain membership qualifications
- to approve professional education programs for purposes of registration
- to approve and provide ongoing professional development programs
- to issue certificates of registration
- to renew, amend, suspend, cancel, revoke, and reinstate certificates.[1]

Opponents to social work regulation have suggested that, at best, regulation may be appropriate for those who work directly with clients in clinically oriented settings in the field. They argue that those engaged in macro or systemic social work in areas such as community development, policy, education, or administration do not find such definition necessary or relevant.

The issue is complicated further by the fact that social work is, in some respects, so broad a field that some consider defining the glue that binds its diverse sectors together a problem. Indeed, a scope of practice is more easily defined in a profession such as nursing or medicine in which the practitioners perform actual physical interventions—say, the administration of a needle. These procedures are more amenable to the application of exacting, rigorous measurements and standards of practice.

Social workers practise in a plethora of settings—mental health clinics, counselling agencies, hospitals, not-for-profit organizations, children's aid societies, seniors' centres, non-profit housing, government, academic institutions, industry, think-tanks such as the Caledon Institute and the Canadian Centre for Policy Alternatives, and private practice. They work on such diverse issues as poverty, homelessness, environmental issues, custody and access, and competency assessment. They work with individuals and groups through every phase of life and development, employing a biopsychosocial approach to understanding human behaviour in its various individual contexts.

Social workers recognize the importance of the synergy of micro stresses and macro presses on people's behavioural and systemic functioning. Unique among the professions, social workers practise what Dr. Frank Turner has termed the "person in situation."[2] This truth stands as one of the bedrocks of social work theory and intervention. It encompasses all facets of professional practice, regardless of specialization or focus. This common denominator binds the profession together at its core and helps foster in its practitioners a professional cohesion and identity.

OBJECTIONS TO REGULATING SOCIAL WORK

Others have objected to regulation of social work because they see the concept as supporting an elitist philosophy. According to Globerman, "Carniol and Kitchen elucidate the arguments against legislation. They suggest that the profession is motivated by a desire for greater power and privilege." Turner counters this argument, pointing out that regulation is motivated by an interest in the public welfare, and particularly in "guaranteeing adequate protection for the public."[3]

Yet statutory regulation can also provide secondary benefits to the social work profession indirectly. One of its key tenets is its advocacy of social change to benefit clients at all levels, especially the most vulnerable. How can regulation possibly help social work reach this objective?

To be included in key pieces of government-sponsored legislation, an occupation such as social work must often be a profession regulated by an appropriate government ministry. While it is not impossible to be included or added to a list of professions authorized to provide specific services or to engage in particular tasks, regulation occasionally makes these services more difficult.

For example, in the province of Ontario, social workers are often responsible for carrying out capacity assessments that determine whether a person is compos mentis—in his or her right mind—and thus capable of making rational decisions. However, social work was originally excluded from a list of professions empowered to conduct these assessments. It was added only because social workers as a body made a concerted effort to educate government about their role in this regard. In fact, the provincial government was seriously contemplating professional regulation for social workers at the same time.

In terms of the social worker's role in hospital settings, it might be tempting for a physician leading a multidisciplinary team to delegate certain tasks and functions to the colleagues of a regulated profession. She might refer the patient to a psychologist for counselling and to a nurse for discharge planning, thus circumventing the social worker and depriving that patient of the social work approach that could prove potentially beneficial to the patient. As hospitals move more and more toward models of program management and away from operating through individual departments—medicine, nursing, occupational therapy, social work—it becomes increasingly vital that the profession be a regulated body. In order to participate as individual entities, departments are being phased out or closed down and programs are being staffed by allied multidisciplinary professionals.

In addition, when social workers interact with regulated colleagues, they find it advantageous to do so on an equal footing. They can rely on the greater professional credibility accorded them as a profession under the rule of law as well as the implicit self-respect and recognition they earn through their professional training.

According to Barbara Chisholm, a renowned child advocate and expert witness, being regulated greatly enhances a social worker's legitimacy when giving testimony before a judge. The fact of regulation, of course, will not change what the professional social worker may say or recount in, for example, a child custody case. Yet perception becomes reality, and an officially recognized profession is more likely to be respected and treated as professional. Whether this perception is fair or just, it is a reality that should be acknowledged. Being legally accountable to one's peers and the public through a statute-based body lends credibility to a social worker's individual assessment. Indeed, Chisholm argues that regulation represents a natural evolutionary step in the maturing of a profession.[4]

In Canada, the form and scope of regulation differs from province to province as such regulation falls under the varied jurisdictions of the provincial governments. However, regardless of the structure, McCorquodale outlines the key criteria that the regulated professions share. These include:

1. A governing body consisting of representatives of the public as well as the profession.

2. Registration that outlines the standards and procedures for evaluating applicants.

3. A complaints review process wherein structure and procedures are identified in terms of which complaints may be received and investigated and a review conducted.

4. Disciplinary procedures for hearing complaints. This stage of the complaints review process requires a more formal structure, legal representation of the parties, examination and cross-examination, witnesses and expert witnesses.

5. An appeals process by which the regulatory body's decisions may be appealed. The form of the appeals process depends on the legislation of the specific province regarding that regulatory body. Appeals procedures may differ for each of the regulatory decisions.

6. "Continuing competency," the element that requires professionals to maintain their professional knowledge and skills and to meet specified standards for maintaining the relevance of their professional knowledge.

7. "Standards," the responsibility to develop and publish guidelines and provisions for consultation with regard to the interpretation of those standards.[5]

McCorquodale provides the following table, an analysis of social work legislation throughout the country (Table 29.1[6]). Ontario can now be included with the Social Work and Social Service Work Act (Bill 76) (1998), under the jurisdiction of the Ministry of Community and Social Services, which established the Ontario College of Social Workers and Social Service Workers (OCSWSSW).

As McCorquodale points out, the goal of professional regulation is to advance the public interest and not the interests of the profession, although of course the profession may derive secondary benefits from regulation. As she states, "Regulation is aimed at advancing the public interest in four ways: (1) protecting the public to the extent possible from unqualified, incompetent and unfit social workers; (2) developing mechanisms to encourage the provision of high quality social work services; (3) permitting the public to exercise freedom of choice of a social work service provider within a range of options; (4) promoting evolution in the roles played by individual professionals and flexibility in how individual professionals can be utilized so that social work services are delivered with maximum efficiency."[7]

DIFFERENT REGULATIONS FOR DIFFERENT PROVINCES' REGULATIONS: ONTARIO AS EXAMPLE

The government in each provincial jurisdiction has the power of deciding whom to regulate and which ministry or system provides the most appropriate mechanisms for each profession's accountability, given

TABLE 29.1	Analysis of Social Work Legislation Throughout Canada[6]						
Province	Title of Act	Year	Jurisdiction	Title Protection	Licensing	Scope of Practice	Academic Requirement
Newfoundland & Labrador	An Act Respecting the Newfoundland and Labrador Association of Social Workers, S.N. 1993, c. S-18.1	1993	Department of Social Services	✚	✚	X	✚
Prince Edward Island	Social Work Act, S.P.E.I. 1988 (Bill 55)	1988	Health and Social Services	✚	✚	✚	✚
Nova Scotia	An Act to Regulate the Practice of Social Work, S.N.S. 1993, c. 12	1993	none	✚	✚	✚	✚
New Brunswick	An Act to Incorporate the New Brunswick Associations of Social Workers, S.N.B. 1988, c. 78	1988	none	✚	✚	✚	✚
Quebec	The Professional Code, R.R.Q. 1981, c. 26, r. 1, to c. 60, r. 12	1994	Offices des Professions du Québec	✚	X	✚	✚
Manitoba	An Act to Incorporate the Manitoba Institute of Registered Social Workers, S.M. 1966, c. 104	1966	Ministry of Family Services	✚	X	X	✚
Saskatchewan	An Act Respecting Social Workers 1993, c. S-52.1	1993	Social Services	✚	X	X	✚
Alberta	Social Work Profession Act, 1991, c. S-16.5	1991	Labour	✚	X	X	✚
British Columbia	The Social Workers Act, R.S.B.C. 1996, c. 389, amending R.S.B.C. 1979	First enacted 1968	Ministry of Children and Families	✚	X	X	✚

Source: *Social Work Practice: A Canadian Perspective*, ed. Francis J. Turner (1999), p. 466. Legislation may have changed since original publication. Reprinted with kind permission from Pearson Education Canada.

already existing structures and a particular jurisdiction's culture.

In Ontario, for example, the provincial government in 1998 made social work the first profession to be regulated under the Ministry of Community and Social Services. The government chose that ministry rather than the Ministry of Health, which oversees the Regulated Health Professions Act (RHPA) and sets out a framework for the self-regulation of 23 health professions. According to Robert England of the law firm Miller Thompson, "The statutory model employed for the regulated health professions is predicated upon all the regulated health professions being subject to two separate statutes: the RHPA and the individual statute that governs each such profession. The policy objectives sought to be achieved by this statutory regime include, in the public interest, definition of those potentially hazardous or intrusive acts performed by health care professionals and the allocation as amongst the health care professions of the authority to perform such acts. Thus, the RHPA defines 'controlled acts' and prohibits the performance of such acts save by those authorized to perform the controlled act."[8] As social work does not practise controlled acts in the manner of certain health professions and given that social work is a broadly based profession with an expertise in the psychosocial functioning of individuals, the government decided that the Ministry of Community and Social Services was a more appropriate fit for both. Thus social work regulation has become a template for other social service–based professions should the government decide to expand the scope of public protection into other domains by setting up similar incorporated bodies such as a college.

In Ontario's case, it is important for the public to recognize the separate functions of the college and the professional association. Table 29.2 delineates their responsibilities.

Ontario has chosen to establish a professional model that separates the profession from the college, which is responsible for protecting the public. Other provinces, such as Alberta, follow a different system that combines the college and the association into one body.

Should a client wish to lodge a complaint against a social work practitioner for professional misconduct or indeed if one practitioner wants to file a complaint against a colleague, the regulatory body outlines the appropriate channels and processes to follow. These involve specific committees, including a complaints committee. The Ontario College of Social Workers and Social Service Workers (OCSWSSW) lays out the mandate of the Complaints Committee as: "the College is required to have a formal complaints process, which gives anyone (clients, colleagues, other regulated professionals, etc.) the ability to have their complaint about a College member's conduct or actions submitted to the College's Complaints Committee. This complaints process is designed to identify and address concerns about professional misconduct, incompetence or incapacity of College members. The process is also designed to ensure fairness to both the individual making the complaint and the member who is the subject of the complaint."[10] According to the Ministry of Community and Social Services, "in response to a written complaint relating to professional misconduct, competence or incapacity, the Complaints Committee would take one of the following courses or action:

• Dismiss the complaint.

• Determine that the matter be referred to the Discipline Committee or the Fitness of Practice Committee.

• Caution the member.

• Refer the matter for alternative dispute resolution Take other action considered appropriate."[11]

TABLE 29.2	Distinct Mandates of Professional Membership Association and Regulatory College[9]	
Organization	**Professional Association (OASW)**	**Regulatory College (OCSWSSW)**
Mandate	To advocate for the interests and concerns of professional social workers and to contribute to social justice	To serve and protect the public interest as set out in the Social Work and Social Service Work Act
How fulfills mandate	1. Ensures a voice for social workers at the local, provincial, national, and international levels.	1. Regulates the practice of social work and the practice of social service work and governs its members.
	2. Advocates for social and professional issues.	2. Develops, establishes and maintains qualifications for membership in the College.
	3. Represents the interests and concerns of the social work profession.	3. Approves ongoing education programs for the purpose of continuing education for members of the College.
	4. Heightens the visibility and profile of social work and social workers.	4. Provides for the ongoing education of members of the College.
	5. Responds publicly to issues of interest to social workers and their clients.	5. Issues certificates of registration to members of the College and renews, amends, suspends, cancels, revokes and reinstates those certificates.
	6. Provides a wide range of tangible and intangible benefits to social workers, including discounts on insurance and other services.	6. Establishes and enforces professional standards and ethical standards applicable to members of the College.
	7. Publishes numerous publications, position papers, and resource materials.	7. Receives and investigates complaints against members of the College and deals with the issues of discipline, professional misconduct, incompetence and incapacity.
	8. Promotes the celebration of National Social Work Week annually.	8. Promotes high standards and quality assurance with respect to social work and social service work and communicates with the public on behalf of the members.

Source: Adapted from OASW and OCSWSSW documents. Reprinted with kind permission.

Another key committee in the process is the Discipline Committee, whose mandate in part is "to hear and determine allegations of professional misconduct or incompetence on the part of the member of the College directed or referred to it by the Complaints Committee, the Council, or the Executive Committee; and perform any other duties assigned to it by the Council. Hearings of the Discipline Committee are usually open to the public."[12]

According to the Ministry of Community and Social Services, "after hearing a matter, the Discipline Committee could:

- Dismiss the complaint
- Revoke a certificate
- Suspend a certificate
- Impose terms, conditions, or limitations on a certificate
- Postpone a penalty in certain circumstances."[13]

In cases of professional misconduct, the Discipline Committee could, in addition:

- Reprimand, admonish, or counsel the member.
- Impose a fine on the member payable to the Minister of Finance.
- Direct that the finding be published in the official publication of the college.
- Fix costs to be paid by the member.

It also states that "a member could appeal a decision of either the Discipline Committee or the Fitness to Practise Committee to [the Ontario] Divisional Court. The filing of an appeal would not stay an order of the committee."[14]

The Fitness to Practise Committee has a mandate "to hear and determine allegations of incapacity on the part of a College member and to perform other duties as assigned by Council. Hearings of this committee are usually closed to the public due to their confidential nature."[15]

According to McCorquodale, "social workers are asked to articulate reasons for the judgments they have made through demonstrating: (1) adherence to professional standards; (2) the ability to form judgments that adhere to those standards; and (3) the ability to defend the rationale for these judgments."[16]

Examples of the complaints regarding social work services that involve harm to clients include the following:

1. An error in judgment of leaving an infant in, or returning an infant to, a situation where abuse, both sexual and/or physical, might occur, leading to serious injury or death.

2. Placing a child in a foster home with persons unsuitable as foster parents with serious, long-term adjustment difficulties for the child.

3. Making an incorrect assessment of an adoptive home that leads to an adoption breakdown with permanent personality scars for the child involved.

4. Misdiagnosing the seriousness of an adolescent's depression that could lead to suicide.

5. Misdiagnosing the intensity of a young adult's suppressed rage that could lead to lethal acts.

6. Misdiagnosing a person's readiness for probation that leads to further anti-social and possibly injurious behaviour to self and others.

7. Underevaluating the potential of further assault by a violence-prone partner in supporting a person's decision to remain in a highly dangerous domestic situation.

8. Failing to recognize the intensity of a person's highly controlled crisis response to a situation of high stress that results in a failure to provide the needed intervention.

9. Failing to diagnose adequately the operative factors in a family system that are causing serious family disruption and thus lead to a situation of a total disintegration of a family that could have been helped.

10. The inadequacy of a home assessment that leads to a decision to leave a highly dysfunctional person in a situation in which he or she is at grave risk to himself or herself and others.

11. Employing a particular treatment where it is inappropriate and thereby causing further trauma to the client.

12. Further traumatization of a client when the social worker violates boundaries and breaches fiduciary duty, as in the case of breach of confidentiality or sexual abuse.[17]

The Social Work and Social Service Work Act incorporates the college as a legal entity and establishes a council to oversee its operations. An executive committee of the college is responsible for approving the college's strategic plan and also for striking additional task groups to assist in accomplishing the strategic priorities identified in the plan and monitoring their progress against projected timelines.[18]

The governing council consists of 21 persons, with equal representation from social workers, social service workers, and members of the public appointed by the government. There are seven representatives from each sector, making up the 21-member council. As self-regulation has conferred professional status on social work, the government considers it important to include significant public representation on the council to give it an added perspective to potentially augment professional accountability. The public members are appointed for a set term of office. These public appointees may accept their positions with no previous knowledge of social work practice or legislation and learn these specifics when they assume their duties.

The legislation identifies who is and who can and cannot call himself or herself a social worker. In Ontario a social worker must be a graduate from an accredited social work program and hold a Bachelor's (BSW), Master's (MSW), or Doctoral degree in social work to qualify for membership. People accepted as members are granted the designation of RSW (registered social worker).

Also included in the legislation are those social workers who have earned community college diplomas from accredited education institutions—usually a two-year program—and hold the designation RSSW (registered social service worker).

The regulation allows for title protection and does not cover other groups with similar educational backgrounds, such as development service workers.

Other provinces structure the profession differently and may allow both social workers and social service workers to hold the designation of social worker. There has been considerable discussion and debate across Canada as to who should be included in any legislation, proposed act or changes in existing acts. The differences often focus on the level of one's education, its perspective and complexity. Some believe that an education at the university level is based more in theory than a community college education, and they emphasize the applied focus of community colleges. Indeed, several universities now offer what are termed "articulation agreements" that allow a community college graduate to earn a certain number of credits toward a Bachelor of Social Work degree. Others argue, for example, that some community college graduates have completed clinical placements that BSW graduates might never have experienced, especially if they focus on specialization in policy and are not exposed to clinical training. However, there is generally consensus that there are discernible differences in the comprehensiveness and rigour of the methodologies employed in community colleges and those used in university-based programs.

As previously mentioned, the act in Ontario does not include a scope-of-practice provision that delineates certain acts as the exclusive or shared domain of social work. In other words, the legislation does not restrict social work practice and therefore it should not be confused with licensing, which the law is not. In addition, the act does not differentiate between university and community-college functions. Indeed, some have argued that one of the act's potential deficiencies is that individuals who do not wish to be accountable to the regulatory body, for whatever reason, may opt out and use another title for themselves, such as psychotherapist or addictions counsellor. Indeed, at the time the legislation was introduced, it was considered politically problematic and challenging to restrict such acts as counselling, which would affect an overlapping range of professions from social work to nursing to lay counsellors to the clergy. Yet the act does restrict use of the title "social worker" and offers clients and potential clients the assurance that social workers are accountable to the regulatory body and practise according to a code of ethics. The government has included a built-in review process of this act that will come into effect in 2005, at which time the structure and effectiveness of the legislation will be scrutinized.

The Campaign to Achieve Statutory Regulation in Ontario

Social work regulation in Ontario was achieved only with considerable struggle. Indeed, anecdotal evidence suggests that regulation was first attempted in the 1930s. If true, this means that it has taken more than 60 years to eventually bring into being an act governing social work in Ontario and make it a profession based on statute.

Indeed, Ontario was the last jurisdiction in North America to achieve some form of professional legislation of social work. All 50 American states and nine Canadian provinces had acts that defined the profession to some degree, some of the laws being stronger than others.

So why did it take Ontario so long to join the rest of Canada and indeed North America in recognizing social work as a distinct profession? There are many reasons. Ontario is a diverse province geographically, culturally, economically, and politically. As a body, social workers exerted considerable effort to engage the government in discussions leading to the implementation of appropriate legislation. Governments have enormous agendas and must deal with various crises that demand their attention on a regular basis. To stay on government's legislative radar screen is indeed difficult for any group in society. The Ministers of Finance in the province were also, one surmises, reluctant to endorse professional regulation since they believe that the change of status for a group's practitioners could lead to higher salaries that government and other institutions would have to pay.

Besides, the broad profession of social work was not completely united in its desire to achieve regulation. Many who chose not to endorse this initiative for various reasons, although the Ontario Association of Social Workers (OASW), the organized voice of social work in Ontario, supported it and so did the voluntary college at the time, the Ontario College of Certified Social Workers (OCCSW). Organized labour also did not support regulation and raised concerns about double jeopardy; they believed their members were already covered by the unions and did not need to be responsible to another outside authority or body.

Others were also convinced that organizations such as the Children's Aid Society, among others, already operated with elaborate accountability mechanisms in place. Some groups in society feared that the regulation of social work would restrict their own ability to practise, although this was not the case. Individuals who did not possess social work degrees were concerned that government regulation would restrict their ability to act in certain roles, such as counselling; they therefore opposed any move toward formalizing social work as a profession.

For these and myriad other reasons, it became incumbent on the profession and those involved in the voluntary college at the time to convince the government that the public needed its protection bolstered and that this could best be achieved through government regulation. The process involved several strategies, such as the building of extensive coalitions who agreed with the cause. In the early 1990s, this included organizations such as Jewish Child and Family Services, the Stroke Recovery Association, the Clarke Institute, the Baycrest Centre for Geriatric Care, the Sarnia General Hospital, the J. D. Griffin Adolescent Centre, Catholic Family Services in Windsor, the C. M. Hincks Treatment Centre, the London Geriatric Interest Group, the Ontario Coalition of Seniors, the Employee Assistance Program Association of Toronto, and the deans and directors of the schools of social work. Promoters held periodic press conferences to impress upon the government the necessity of bringing in the appropriate legislation. They cited sample cases of clients who would have benefited from such an act. They arranged meetings with media representatives across the province, including the editorial boards of newspapers such as the *Toronto Star* and the *London Free Press*, who produced editorials highlighting the issue. Local branches of the association met regularly with politicians from all three major parties to educate them about the need and the glaring gaps that could be bridged by the inclusion of social work as a regulated profession. They referred to more than the nature of the Canadian landscape but to the desirability of achieving parity with other allied health-oriented professions. Occasionally regulation advocates blitzed

the government with phone calls and faxes at particular junctures to illustrate the need for the legislation.

As part of the strategy, members of the opposition parties raised questions in the provincial Legislature that demanded of the government of the day why it had not yet acted on this particular issue. Hansard, the official record of the legislative debates, documented lengthy exchanges between MPPs, including petitions signed by social workers, colleagues, and the public, all of which were presented at Queen's Park in Toronto. The campaign pressed on steadily for 10 years, debated and argued back and forth and painstakingly hammered out with three different governments, the Liberal, the NDP, and the Conservative, as well as seven different Ministers of Community and Social Services. As well as liaising with elected officials, social worker representatives also met with senior public servants in the Ministry of Community and Social Services to provide any research, documentation, or cases that might strengthen their case for regulation.

Tenacity and perseverance characterized the continuous push to achieve regulation. Politicians will not always behave in the best interests of the electorate regarding an issue, as its proponents perceive; a lot of the time they rather wish that most difficult issues would simply drift away. In fact, the elected representatives tend to do whatever they believe they must to ensure that systemic changes do not come about easily.

One instructive lesson emerged from the whole endeavour: social work practitioners must continually educate various sectors in society, including politicians, about the work they do and the benefits that society derives from social work. On more than one occasion, it became evident that, although politicians were exposed to the issue through mailings, meetings, and ongoing dialogue, many still did not grasp the essence of the need for regulation. Indeed, one politician relatively close to the issue assumed that the voluntary college was a fine education institution and inquired how many students would be graduating that year. Yet advocates had made several past attempts to explain the college's role and the concept of regulation. The profession has recognized numerous benefits from its struggle to achieve regulation, and this knowledge has served it well as a template for how to deal with other issues that affect the welfare of those clients served by practitioners working outside regulation.

CONCLUSION

It is important to note that the self-regulation of social work, while representing an advance in professional maturity and accountability, does not solve all problems; it simply closes one door. One would be overly hasty to interpret regulation as an end unto itself and the answer to all the profession's concerns.

According to McCorquodale, it does protect the public in two main aspects: "(1) compensating for the client's lack of knowledge about the services they are receiving; and (2) providing equitable treatment by obliging all members of the profession to meet common standards."[19]

Indeed, potentially regulation can assist social workers in future quests to pass legislation to benefit their clients; but, in and of itself, regulation will not resolve long-standing societal problems that have long concerned the social work profession—the battle for justice, equality, fairness and tolerance in society.

Regulation has not meant improved salaries or compensation for social workers and it has never been intended in any way to accomplish such a goal. It has lifted the profession's profile in the public mind and highlighted the valuable work that social workers do to improve the quality of life and the social fabric of the community. Indeed, in the quest for legislation in Ontario, the Ontario Association of Social Workers commissioned a public opinion poll about the matter. The vast majority of respondents said they believed social work was already regulated. They were surprised to learn that no such regulation existed at the time.

Models of regulation are constantly being developed and refined. This represents a process that will continue well into the future. Social workers must remain vigilant about not allowing regulatory status in whatever form to create or exacerbate gaps between values and practice. Indeed, social work regulations should strengthen the bonds between ethical practice and the pursuit of a more just society.

NOTES

1. Compendium, *Social Work and Social Service Work Act*, 1998, p. 2.

2. Conversation with Dr. Frank Turner, 1998.

3. J. Globerman, "Regulating social work, illuminating motives," in *Canadian Social Work Review, 9.2* (Summer 1992), p. 230.

4. Conversation with Barbara Chisholm, 1992.

5. M. Samuels and E. Tanner (2003), *Managing a legal and ethical social work practice*, p. 20.

6. S. McCorquodale (1999), "The role of regulators in practice" in F. J. Turner (Ed.), *Social work practice: A Canadian perspective*, p. 466.

7. Ibid., p. 464.

8. Robert W. England, Miller Thompson, Barristers and Solicitors, correspondence to the Ontario Association of Social Workers (OASW), November 1998.

9. Adapted from OASW and OCSWSSW documents. Reprinted with kind permission.

10. Ontario College of Social Workers and Social Service Workers (OCSWSSW), *Annual report, 2003*, p. 5.

11. Compendium, p. 4.

12. OCSWSSW, *Annual report, 2003*, p. 6.

13. Compendium, p. 4.

14. Ibid., pp. 4–5.

15. OCSWSSW, p. 16.

16. S. McCorquodale, p. 472.

17. Ibid.

18. OCSWSSW, p. 4.

19. S. McCorquodale, p. 463.

REFERENCES

Compendium. *Social work and social service work act*, 1998.

Globerman, J. (Summer 1992). "Regulating social work, illuminating motives" in *Canadian Social Work Review, 9.2.*

McCorquodale, S. "The role of regulators in practice" in F. J. Turner (1999), *Social work practice: A Canadian perspective.* Scarborough, ON: Prentice Hall/Allyn and Bacon Canada.

Miller Thompson, Barristers and Solicitors. (1998, November). Correspondence to the Ontario Association of Social Workers from Robert W. England, Toronto, Ontario.

Ontario Association of Social Workers (OASW) (1998). Distinct mandates of professional membership association and regulatory college, Toronto.

OASW. (2003). *Annual report, 2003.* Toronto.

Samuels, M., and Tanner, E. (2003). *Managing a legal and ethical social work practice.* Toronto: Irwin Law.

chapter thirty

Research in Social Work

Ross A. Klein

INTRODUCTION

As you turn to this chapter, you may hesitate and think, "Why should I know anything about research in social work? After all, my primary interest is social work practice or social welfare policy. Research certainly has neither value nor interest to someone pursuing an education that will lead to practice as a professional social worker."

To the contrary, research is an integral part of social work. Much of what practitioners know and do is based on research.

In considering research in social work, this chapter is divided into four parts. First, it discusses what is meant by social work research. It defines what research is and considers different methods by which it is carried out. Second, the chapter looks at the value of research to social work practice. It considers how research is related to social work practice, how social work practitioners use it, and how it informs social welfare policy and programs. The third part of the chapter considers research methods that are commonly integrated into the practice of social work. Specifically, it looks at the use and value of single-subject design research in social work practice. The chapter then concludes with a discussion of ethics in research. This section identifies and discusses key ethical issues to be considered when undertaking research in social work settings.

WHAT DO WE MEAN BY "RESEARCH"?

When you read the word "research," you may think about a research paper you recently wrote for a course. Or you may recall a general science course in junior high school in which you were introduced to the scientific method and the importance of conducting research to gain scientific knowledge. Whether for a research paper or as part of scientific inquiry, we conduct research as a process through which we work, systematically, to uncover information and/or knowledge. In social work, research is often referred to as "systematic inquiry."

Systematic inquiry begins with a question or a problem. You might be interested in knowing why people would abuse or neglect children in their care. The first step in answering the question is to look at the literature—books, journals, and magazines—to determine what is known about child abuse and child neglect. By familiarizing yourself with the work others have done, you can learn about such things as the risk factors associated with child abuse, the personal characteristics common among those who commit abuse, and the social situations in which abuse is common or uncommon. You may be able to answer the question or problem through a systematic review of the literature.

Sometimes, past research does not provide the answer to a question or problem. You may undertake your own empirical study (research involving direct observation). In this case, the literature provides a guide for your pursuing the question or problem systematically. It provides a framework for understanding different ways of defining a concept and it tells us what is known (and what is not known) about the phenomenon. With insights and knowledge drawn from a critical analysis of the literature, you as a researcher can

then design a study that will contribute to the knowledge base of social work.

STEPS IN SYSTEMATIC INQUIRY

Once you have identified a question or problem, you proceed with your systematic inquiry generally by the following steps: (1) specifying a hypothesis or proposition; (2) developing a research design; (3) gathering data; (4) analyzing data; and (5) interpreting the data. A research report is a simple presentation of this information. Let us briefly consider each of these steps.

Specifying a Hypothesis or Proposition

Guided by the question, we as researchers look at the literature to better understand what is known about the topic of interest. The literature tells us how a phenomenon has been viewed and provides direction for us to define the concepts being used (child abuse, physical abuse, sexual abuse); to operationalize these concepts (that is, express what is meant by these concepts); and to arrive at some means to measure the concepts (determine what constitutes "child abuse" so that we recognize it when we see it). This process is important because it gives us a clear understanding of what we are studying and reduces the risk of measuring something other than what was intended.

For example, to measure child abuse we have to define first what constitutes abuse. Is corporal punishment—spanking a child—considered abuse? To some it may be; to others it may not be. Or is grounding a child considered abuse? It may appear that way to a child. We operationalize a concept so that what we will study is clearly defined. Both the researcher and those who read the research will know, in this case, what constitutes child abuse for this particular study.

Reading the literature is also important when we are formulating a hypothesis or a set of expectations for a study. Much of the research we are most familiar with begins with a hypothesis and we use the data to test the hypothesis. A hypothesis might state that "levels of parental stress are related to the incidence of child abuse." Some research, particularly exploratory or descriptive research, begins with a set of expectations. For example, a study may begin by stating that the research team "expects to determine the factors that are associated with the incidence of child abuse." Both hypotheses and expectations help guide and organize research. They give a clear direction and focus.

Developing a Research Design

A research design is a plan or a road map that the researcher follows in completing a study. A research design consists of four common elements. First, who or what is going to be studied? In other words, who will be the subjects or respondents in the study? They could be children in a school, clients in a treatment group, or social work practitioners. The design clearly identifies who will be studied.

And a second decision needs to be made: how will the subjects or respondents be selected? Will they be chosen at random or will they be selected based on other criteria? This decision has other implications: a random selection allows the researcher to use statistical tests that are not appropriate when a sample's selection is not random.

A third decision reflected in the design of research is how will subjects or respondents be contacted? Will the researcher use mail, the telephone, door-to-door soliciting, or some other method? And once these people are contacted, what will be done

with them? The study could employ interviews, direct observation, a survey, or other methods for gathering data. These need to be identified.

The last set of concerns relates to the nature of the data the research generates. A research design lays out how concepts and variables are to be measured, what instruments will be used to gather the data, and how the data will be analyzed.

All of these decisions are made before beginning a study. Formally laying out the design for a study allows the researcher to ensure that the methods used will answer the question(s) being asked.

Gathering Data

Following the direction provided by the research design, the researcher gathers the data. Subjects or respondents are found. Surveys, interviews, and/or observations are completed.

The sources and different types of data commonly used for research in social work will be discussed later.

Analyzing Data

Data analysis often conjures up an image of statistics and the presentation of numbers and tables. When working with surveys, this is often the way that responses to questions are summarized and understood. Researchers produce statistical analysis with this type of data. But not all data are appropriate for statistical analysis. Analysis of data from direct observations—children playing in the playground, perhaps—or from historical events often involve searching the data for patterns or for "meaning" in the interactions.

Interpreting the Data

In analyzing data, the researcher intends to arrive at an understanding of what has been observed and to identify the relations between different phenomena. For example, when looking at the path of alcoholism for men versus women, researchers are not concerned primarily with generating a single view of how alcoholism proceeds; they are interested in key differences between male and female patterns of alcoholism. Once these differences have been identified, the researchers try to interpret the differences—what accounts for male patterns of alcoholism differing from the patterns commonly seen in women? The interpretation aims to test the hypothesis on which the study was based or to provide answers to the expectations stated for the research at the outset. The researcher may also deduce generalizations from those data as they apply to the larger population.

Writing a Report

With these formal steps completed, the researcher writes a report that presents the research. A typical report, whether an article in a journal or a free-standing document, discusses each of the steps considered above. It will give the reader an overview of the literature on the subject being studied, a hypothesis or set of expectations, a clear statement of the research design and procedures used for data collection and data analysis, a clear description of the data, an analysis of the data, and interpretations of what the data mean and how they relate to what is already known.

By laying out each step, the researcher ensures readers can understand everything the researcher has done and can judge for themselves whether the methods used and the conclusions drawn fit the data.

SOURCES OF DATA

We typically think of social work research as the study of people. Indeed, people are the most common source of data. People are surveyed, interviewed, or observed.

Most of us have at some point been given a survey questionnaire to complete; we might also have been interviewed about something we have done or with which we have been involved. The survey or the interviewer asks a series of questions and we as the subjects or respondents give our answers. Surveys generally use closed-ended questions: several categories of responses are given to a question and we choose the one that reflects our opinion or view most closely. Interviews, by contrast, often use open-ended questions, questions that ask respondents for explanatory or descriptive answers. There are many different types of interviews; some solicit opinions, some seek an understanding of a person's life experiences, and others are used to document a person's life history or an organization's historical development. While surveys and questionnaires are the most common source of information for the social work researcher, interviews are used more and more.

We find two other common sources of data in social work research. One is the use of field research. Sometimes referred to as *participant observation* or as *naturalistic inquiry*, field research involves observing people in natural settings. One could study "kids' society" by observing children at play in the playground or in the classroom. One might observe the way that mothers relate to their newborn children to understand the steps in the bonding process between mother and child. Or one could study the way that death and dying are managed in a hospital (as in David Sudnow's *Passing On: The Social Organization of Death and Dying* [1967]) by observing health care workers in their daily routines with dying patients.

In field research, researchers take their places in particular settings and observe what goes on in those settings. Often researchers participate only to the extent that they must in order to observe the settings. Based on their observations, the researchers generate understanding and gain insights into the specific situations and about the dynamics that characterize them. One example is a study a young sociologist undertook who had been sentenced to one year in a maximum security penitentiary. He used his experience to observe prison life, from the inside, and to document how those in prison handled such concepts as "time," "relationship," and "self" (Schmid and Jones 1993).

Another type of data is referred to as *unobtrusive* or *non-reactive measures* (Webb et al. 1981). As the name suggests, unobtrusive measures are sources of data upon which researchers can draw but that the researchers do not influence or directly affect through their observations. In contrast to survey research, interviews, and field research where the presence of the researcher or the content of the survey may influence the nature of the information gathered, unobtrusive measures produce observations or findings that are not influenced by the fact of people's being observed. For example, the simple act of filling out a questionnaire or going through the process of an interview may influence the responses subjects give to questions. An interviewer who is immediately likeable may be given different answers than an interviewer whom an interviewee dislikes. In these cases, the questionnaire and the interviewer are potentially obtrusive. They therefore influence the data collected.

Webb (1981) gives some good examples of unobtrusive measures. If we wanted to determine which exhibit in a museum was the most popular, we could look at the floor and see in front of which exhibit it was most worn. Or to determine the most popular book in a high school library, one could search for the book whose cover and pages are most worn. Reviewing historical documents is another example of an unob-

trusive measure. The act of reading and observing historical documents does not change the documents' content or influence history. Some time ago, a colleague and I conducted a study of youth in care in Newfoundland and Labrador, between 1984 and 1995. Based on a review of a random sample of case files of children in care during those years, our study provided insights into how and when children enter care and about their experiences while in care. The data also showed patterns according to when reports of different types of abuse or neglect were most common. Spikes in the reporting of physical abuse appeared to coincide with the time that children's school report cards were issued. Reports of sexual abuse appeared to spike following the children's return to school immediately after summer vacation (Kufeldt and Klein 1998).

TYPES OF DATA

Researchers commonly distinguish between two types of data, the quantitative and the qualitative.

Quantitative Data

Quantitative data uses numbers to represent the data gathered. Some things we measure (ages, birth order, income, years of education) are themselves commonly measured in terms of numbers. But many of the things social scientists study are put into categories that are represented by numbers. When people are asked about their majors in college or about the nature of the communities in which they live (urban, suburban, semi-rural, rural), each category of their responses is converted to a number. For example, a survey question that asks about subjects' educational attainments may assign a number "1" to those who have graduated from Grade 8, a "2" to those graduated from Grade 12, a

"3" to those with university degrees, and a "4" to those with post-graduate education. By using numbers we allow the data to be easily analyzed by computer.

The use of numbers for response categories may be illustrated by a brief discussion of different *levels of measurement* used with quantitative data. The most basic level of measurement is nominal. A *nominal* measure is categorical. Religion, gender, and questions that yield "yes" or "no" answers are examples of nominal measures. These categories have no numerical relation to one another, but the numbers (1 = male; 2 = female) allow for statistical analysis.

A second level of measurement is *ordinal*. In this case, each response relates to the others in an order ranging from low to high, with no precise or equal distance between the categories. There are several good examples of an ordinal scale of measurement. (1) Educational attainment, when measured by categories such as "high-school graduate," "some university," "university graduate," and "graduate degree," reflects an increasing order of achievement but the distances between categories are not the same. The difference between a high-school graduate and a college graduate is not necessarily the same as the difference between a person with a university degree and one with a graduate degree. (2) A Likert scale, which gives the choice of "strongly agree," "agree," "undecided," "disagree," and "strongly disagree," presents an order, but we cannot assume that the difference between any two categories is the same magnitude or size as the difference between any other two categories. (3) The Richter scale used to measure earthquakes is an excellent example of an ordinal scale. Each step on the scale is exponentially greater than the step before it. Thus the difference between an earthquake of 6 versus 7 on the scale is considerably greater than the difference between an earthquake of 3 versus 4. As with a Likert scale and measures of educational attainment that specify the last degree a subject received, each point on the scale is in order, but the distance between points varies.

The other two levels of measurement, *interval* and *ratio*, are very similar. Each is a measurement in which there is an equal distance between numbers. In measuring a person's age in years, the distance between age 18 and 19 is the same as the distance between age 29 and 30. One year is one year. As well, if we compared weight when measuring in kilograms, each kilogram is the same regardless of whether we weigh 25 kilograms or 100 kilograms. The distinguishing characteristic between an interval measure and a ratio measure is that the ratio measure is represented on a scale by an absolute zero. For example, weight begins at zero and moves up, as does age. However, temperature, which can be positive or negative, does not have an absolute zero, so it is an interval measure rather than ratio.

Levels of measurement are not mentioned in order to cause confusion. They should help illustrate the distinction between quantitative data and qualitative data. Each level of measurement demonstrates how observations in the world are translated into a number that can then be analyzed. This analysis often includes statistical operations that seek to describe the relation between two or more variables. For example, if the researcher asks for opinions about corporal punishment, the analysis would describe differences in the attitudes of men versus women, and/or between parents, grandparents, and non-parents.

Qualitative Data

Qualitative data are also based on observations, but they are not coded in numerical form. We might observe the relationship between children and their parent(s) or, using the example above, observe life in a prison. In working with qualitative data, researchers attempt to uncover and describe patterns or trends.

In the study of life in prison, the researcher found that "time" was something inmates never discussed. They might make an occasional reference to time when particular inmates' time was "short"—when they were close to their release dates—but otherwise inmates avoided the topic. The reason for this taboo is simple. If you are serving a sentence of 25 years, thinking in terms of time makes "doing time" that much more difficult. Short-timers learn very quickly that it is not in their interests in terms of physical well-being to talk about time with others in prison (Schmid and Jones 1993). Field research is one means of gathering this type of data.

Research that is historical in nature can also produce qualitative research. This research aims to describe what has happened. For example, we might want to describe and analyze how social workers have influenced governments in gaining support for the former's registration as a profession. The study could also look at the political motivations for social work registration and the negotiations (and trade-offs) between government and the provincial association of social workers in developing systems of registration. In historical research, the data are viewed in their context and researchers derive their findings within that context.

Qualitative research has a long tradition in the social sciences and among social work practitioners. However, the political and social systems in which most social workers are employed prefer quantitative results. Governments and policymakers are more concerned with demonstrating reduced demand for a service than demonstrating that, despite equal or increased demand for a service, recipients of that service feel better about themselves. This does not argue against the use of qualitative research, but it does reflect a bias in favour of quantitative research.

Numbers and statistics are generally viewed as more "scientific." Professional journals also reflect this orientation, both in social work and in the social sciences generally. (A more in-depth discussion of types and sources of data can be found in Grinnell [1997], Wilkinson and McNeil [1996], Palys [1977], or Monette et al. [1998].)

RESEARCH AND SOCIAL WORK PRACTICE

We now turn our attention to the relationship between research and social work practice. Consideration will be given first to the relationship of research and social work practice. The discussion then shifts to the use of research by social work practitioners and at research and social welfare policy and programs.

THE RELATIONSHIP OF RESEARCH TO SOCIAL WORK PRACTICE

A distinction is generally made between research that is "pure" and research that is "applied." The former refers to research that is oriented toward building knowledge without practical application as its primary purpose.

Much of the knowledge that social work practitioners draw on in the fields of sociology, psychology, economics, political science, and education is the product of *pure research*. For example, pure research underlies Lawrence Kohlberg's (1984) work describing stages of moral development, Sigmund Freud's writing on psychosexual development (see Longres 1995), Erving Goffman's (1961) classic study of asylums, and Michel Foucault's (1980) work that asserts that knowledge is power. In the case of each author, research led to formal knowledge that informs social work practitioners. The knowledge provides a better understanding of the world in which social work practitioners work, of the people with whom they work, and of the dynamics in families and communities. Think back to what you read in Chapter 3, "The Knowledge Base of Canadian Social Welfare." Much of what was discussed there is based on pure research.

Applied research, by contrast, refers to systematic inquiry in which the knowledge generated is intended for use in direct practice. Beck's Depression Inventory (BDI), the Minnesota Multiphasic Inventory (MMPI), and Bovolek's Adult–Adolescent Parenting Inventory (AAPI) are examples of psychometric scales that social workers use in assessing the individuals with whom they work. These scales are the product of applied research. (See Bloom, Fischer and Orme [2002] for a number of scales used in clinical social work practice.)

Research that seeks to understand the "best" mode of treatment with sex offenders or the most effective intervention with alcoholics also has an applied orientation. Its purpose is to inform the practice of social workers to make their services as effective as possible.

The Use of Research by Social Work Practitioners

As we have seen, research is an integral part of social work practice. The knowledge that pure research provides serves as the foundation on which social workers base their practices. Applied research provides social workers with many of the tools used in practice and an understanding of how best to match social work skills and methods with the needs of those who receive those services.

In these ways, social work practitioners are consumers of research. They draw on the knowledge generated by others' research in order to inform and refine their individual practices. For example, a worker concerned with the discontinuities that children in foster care experience will find invaluable insights in the research done by Kufeldt et al. (2003), Fanshel et al. (1990), Kufeldt (1984), Thomlinson (1990), and others. In the absence of research about these and other topics, each individual social worker would provide intervention without the benefit of the knowledge and experience of others.

In addition to consuming research, social work practitioners often engage in research of their own and building on the body of social work knowledge. Those social workers who evaluate their practices and then report the results to their colleagues are contributing to the profession. They provide insights to others about what may work with a particular type of client and what may not work.

Several years ago a social worker was asked to design an innovative program for enhancing the employability of youth on social assistance. He used research in producing the design. First he developed a profile, based on computer data, concerning youth on social assistance. He augmented this by interviewing a sample of these youth by telephone to better understand the barriers to employment they faced and the reasons that prevented them from finding jobs. He also used the interviews to understand the expectations these young people had regarding their employment opportunities and income potential. With this knowledge, the social worker could design and implement a program that fitted the needs of the youth and that addressed many of the difficulties they had in availing of and succeeding in such programs. Had the program been designed without this advance research it would have been less effective; it would have overlooked or ignored concerns and factors that were fundamentally important for the youth the program was intended to serve.

Research and Social Welfare Policy and Programs

Chapter 29 addresses the evaluation of social welfare. Therefore, we will not discuss it here. It is sufficient to say that social welfare policy and programs could not be developed with any sense of confidence if we did not have research on which to base that evaluation. Research is an indispensable part of both social work practice and social welfare policies and programs.

SINGLE-SUBJECT DESIGN RESEARCH

Thus far, we have discussed research in social work in general terms. We have focused primarily on the way that research informs social work practice. Now we will look at the most common application of research in social work practice: the use of single-subject design research. Practitioners often use single-subject design research to evaluate their own effectiveness and/or the effectiveness of particular interventions. They may also use this kind of research as a method that provides direction for intervention.

In this section, we will first consider the key terms used in single-subject design research. Second, we will describe the main variations in the use of single-subject designs and will illustrate how a practitioner can use the research method. Finally, through a case illustration, we will demonstrate how single-subject design research can provide useful and meaningful results, both as a way of evaluating practice and of generating applied knowledge. (See Rubin and Babbie [2001] for a more complete description of single-subject design research.)

Key Concepts

One of the main reasons we use single-subject design research is to evaluate the effect of intervention. Two key elements exist in a single subject design: the *baseline* and the *intervention*.

Baseline   A baseline is a measure of the current state of a client. If we were working with a youth who has difficulty with acting-out behaviour, the baseline would reflect the frequency of this behaviour as measured each day over a specific period of time. Before the social worker intervenes with treatment, she would have to know the nature and frequency of the behaviour targeted for change. Only then could she measure the effect of any intervention. For example, if a social worker were attempting to determine his effectiveness in reducing conflict within a marital relationship, he would first have to have some idea of the level of conflict that existed before treatment. The baseline is the level or frequency of a behaviour or feeling before the intervention begins.

Creating a baseline is simple. The social worker, or the client, measures at predetermined intervals the frequency of a behaviour or a particular feeling. That which is measured depends on the client and/or the problem. As above, we might measure acting-out behaviour or conflict. Or we could focus on the frequency of a person's suicidal thoughts or on the number of times a parent uses corporal punishment to discipline a child. The main point is that the social worker and the client establish a baseline for the behaviour or ideation that is targeted for change. The effectiveness of the treatment is deduced as an improvement from the baseline.

Intervention   After a baseline is determined, intervention begins. At predetermined intervals (daily, weekly, biweekly) during the intervention, the behaviour targeted for change is measured again. The purpose is to see whether the undesirable behaviour is decreasing with the intervention—whether the intervention is having its intended effect.

Using the example of a token economy, the social worker would want to determine whether the token reward is affecting the client's goals positively. If the desired effect is not found, the social worker may find it necessary to alter the intervention. She may increase the value of the token reward. If that fails, she may introduce a different form of intervention.

Main Variations

There are four alternative single-subject designs worth mentioning: the basic single-subject design, the withdrawal/reversal design, the multiple-baseline design, and the multiple-component design. Each will be described briefly.

The Basic Single-Subject Design

We have already described the basic single-subject design. It is the simplest form of single-subject design. It includes a baseline phase in which the targeted behaviour/attitude is measured before intervention, followed by the intervention phase during which the behaviour/attitude is monitored while treatment is provided. The social worker and the client can then see whether or not the intervention is having its intended effect.

The Withdrawal/Reversal Design

The withdrawal/reversal design begins as the basic single-subject design does, then adds a second baseline and a second intervention. We establish the second baseline by withdrawing the intervention and measuring to see whether the targeted behaviour or attitude remains stable or reverts with the withdrawal of treatment. Once the second baseline identifies a stable trend, the intervention is reintroduced.

This design allows the social worker and the client to determine whether continued treatment is necessary to maintain the desired outcome. It also allows them to see whether resuming the intervention reverses any loss of effect experienced during withdrawal and whether the resumption of the intervention results in further improvement. An illustration may help. Let us assume that the social worker is working with a man who has emotional outbursts toward his partner. After the first baseline is established, the client and the social worker monitor the frequency of the man's emotional outbursts each week during a period of intervention—perhaps over three months. The intervention is then stopped, and the client is asked to continue to still monitor the frequency of his emotional outbursts. After a set period, the social worker and the client review the effects of his not receiving treatment and then reintroduce the intervention. The withdrawal/reversal design provides a measure of the client's ability to continue without treatment. The new baseline also allows the client and the worker to see whether additional treatment further improves the targeted behaviour.

The Multiple-Baseline Design

A multiple-baseline design involves a basic single-subject design, and it measures the same targeted behaviour either in more than one setting or with more than one client. In the first, measuring a targeted behaviour in more than one setting, we will return to the client who is receiving treatment for his emotional outbursts. The client and the social worker monitor his emotional outbursts toward his partner, toward his child(ren), and/or toward his friends. This establishes baselines and post-intervention levels for each type of relationship being monitored.

In the case of multiple clients, the social worker may intend to evaluate an intervention with different clients who have the same target for change. For example, a social worker may provide clinical intervention with four men who have difficulty controlling emotional outbursts toward their partners. A separate basic single-subject design study is done with each man, and the effectiveness of the intervention is assessed by looking at whether there are common results with each of the men. If the intervention produces similar results with all clients, then the social worker and clients can be more confident about the effectiveness of the intervention than they would be if some men showed improvement while others did not. The use of multiple subjects provides a fuller understanding about the intervention being used.

The Multiple-Component Design

We employ multiple-component designs when we consider it necessary to modify an intervention that does not appear to be helping a client or when the social worker wants to determine which element of an intervention package accounts for the change in the client's targeted attitude or behaviour.

Say, for example, that the social worker provides services in an Employee Assistance Program (EAP) and is working with a client who is frequently absent from work. In the course of the intervention, the social worker may first use an approach aimed at educating the client about the implications of her absenteeism and the support services that are available to her. We may follow this with a series of rewards for regular attendance at work. Or the EAP counsellor may advocate on behalf of the client to link her to a particular social support. The level of her absenteeism is monitored to determine which intervention, individually or in concert with the others, has the most beneficial impact on changing the client's behaviour.

An Illustration

Schuchts and Witkin's study (1989) of marital change during the transition to parenthood provides an effective illustration of the usefulness of a single-subject design study to the social work practitioner. In their article, they offer three figures that present a comparison of four different couples. We describe figures one and three briefly.

Figure one shows husbands' and wives' marital satisfaction before and after the birth of their children. For each couple, a baseline measure of marital satisfaction is shown for three to seven weeks before childbirth. Marital satisfaction continues to be monitored for nine months after the children's births. The figure shows that before childbirth marital satisfaction for the wives is generally higher than that for their husbands. In contrast, two of the four husbands after childbirth show a higher level of marital satisfaction than their wives do. As well, the figure reveals that, for two couples, the difference in satisfaction between husbands and wives increases with the ages of the infants. For all but one couple, marital satisfaction for both husband and wife is lower after childbirth than it is during the baseline period.

Schuchts and Witkin also present a figure showing the division of labour between husbands and wives. The figure illustrates that before childbirth, household chores are relatively balanced between husband and wife; following the birth of the child, responsibility for household work shifts heavily to the wives. Except for the single week following childbirth, when the husbands take greater responsibility for both household chores and household work, the pattern of wives bearing the heaviest responsibility for household work continues after the birth of the children. The figure also shows that wives have considerably more responsibility for parenting than do their husbands. As Schuchts and Witkin state, "Beginning either right before or after the birth... husbands assumed immediate responsibility for household chores, [while] wives' participation in housework tasks steadily increased over time. Conversely, husbands' housework and child care activities gradually decreased. These changes resulted in a greater division of labour according to gender stereotypes..." (p. 74).

It may be useful to review Schuchts and Witkin's article in order to see how the data are presented on graphs and to see how effectively a single-subject design study can trace relative changes over time. While Schuchts and Witkin focus on marital satisfaction and the division of labour, their method would also be effective for monitoring any type of change that may be the target of social work intervention.

SOCIAL WORK ETHICS AND RESEARCH ETHICS

Just as the social work practitioner subscribes to a code of ethics, so the researcher in social work is expected to maintain ethical standards. These standards are generally overseen by Institutional Review Boards (often called "Human Subjects Review Committees"), which give their permission for research to be done in their settings or under their sponsorship.

For example, most hospitals require a review committee's approval before allowing any research that would involve their patients or take place within their facilities. Similarly, all universities in Canada require review and approval of any research involving human subjects done by its faculty or under its sponsorship. These are governed by the *Tri-Council Policy Statement: Ethical Conduct for Research Involving Humans* (2003). In this context, "human subjects" refers to research that requires human beings' participation (through a questionnaire, observation, or interview).

Ethical Responsibilities to Human Subjects

Two of the fundamental elements of ethical treatment of human subjects are the subject's informed consent and voluntary participation. *Informed consent* refers to the requirement that all prospective participants in a study know the purpose of the study in advance. They must know the use to which their responses will be put and about all the researchers' expectations regarding the time and place of the interviews or meetings. And they must clearly understand any risks associated with their participation in the research. Potential subjects are also expected to be told how they were selected for the study, the name of the sponsor of the study, and where the results of the study will be reported or published.

Normally, subjects must sign an informed consent form before they participate in a study. The form lays out all information and expectations about the research and explicitly confirms the subject's right to withdraw from the study at any time. Only after the potential subjects have signed their consent forms and confirmed their understanding about the research can the researcher proceed to gather the data.

Voluntary participation refers to the requirement that prospective participants in research freely choose to be part of that study while reserving the right to withdraw from the research at any time. Subjects must not be pressured in any way to participate in a study. They cannot be put in such a position that participation or nonparticipation in a study will influence their individual standing at work, in the community, or their relationships with others.

Ethical research guarantees anonymity and confidentiality, and promises that respondents will not be harmed as a result of their participation. In his study of obedience to authority Stanley Milgram (1974) considered a specific concern for non-harm to research subjects to be paramount. Milgram wanted to determine how far a person would go in harming another, specifically when someone in authority assumes responsibility for that harm. The study was inspired by Milgram's curiosity about why individuals in Nazi Germany participated in the murder of so many in the concentration camps. Participants in Milgram's study were led to believe that they were physically harming another—even though they were not. On this basis, many participants demonstrated psychological and emotional distress. At the time, Milgram's research created no controversy. Today, because of the distress the study caused its subjects, it would not be allowed to proceed.

Anonymity and confidentiality are similar qualities, but they differ in significant ways. *Anonymity* is a guarantee that the individuals participating in a study will not be known or identified through any report of that research. Researchers must protect the identities of their subjects, even if doing so means not reporting some data. *Confidentiality* refers to the actual data gathered in the course of the study. Records produced through research, whether through a questionnaire, through an interview, or in notes taken during observations, must remain confidential. This means that no one, other than the researcher, is to be allowed access to these notes and that only the researcher holds any information regarding the identity of the study's participants.

Other guidelines surround research ethics, particularly when the research involves vulnerable populations—children, those who are institutionalized, and some ethnic or cultural groups—but these will not be addressed here. They are clearly spelled out in the *Tri-Council Policy Statement: Ethical Conduct for Research Involving Humans.* The social worker must be familiar with and follow the strict guidelines that protect human subjects used for research in social work.

Ethical Responsibilities to Other Researchers

Winston Jackson (2002) astutely points out that researchers also have an ethical responsibility to other researchers and to the scientific community. His points are simple, but they cannot be over-emphasized.

In particular, he warns the researcher: do not set out to prove a point; do not hunt through data to find pleasing findings; be aware of sources of bias; represent the scientific literature fairly; and acknowledge all literature and human resources. Jackson is reminding us that the researcher must remain objective. The purpose of research is not to prove a political or personal position; it is to discover answers to questions.

He also reminds us that researchers have an obligation to be fair in the way that they use and represent the work of others, and an obligation to acknowledge any help they receive from others. Researchers often add a footnote in an article or to the acknowledgments of a book that thanks specific individuals who helped them with their research or who provided editorial assistance in the writing or production of the work. Researchers should be conscientious about their ethical responsibility to their subjects, their peers, and to the scientific community at large.

CONCLUSION

This chapter provides an introduction to and an overview of research in social work. We discuss what is meant by research, consider the relationship between research and social work practice, and briefly consider single-subject designs and research ethics. The discussion is cursory, but will provide a better understanding and insight for those who will be the primary consumers of social work research.

REFERENCES

Bloom, M., Fischer, J., & Orme, J. G. 2002. *Evaluating practice: Guidelines for the accountable professional.* 4th edn. Boston: Allyn & Bacon.

Fanshel, D., Finch, S., & Grundy, J. 1990. *Foster families in a life course perspective.* New York: Columbia University Press.

Foucault, M. 1980. *Power/knowledge.* New York: Pantheon.

Goffman, E. 1961. *Asylums: Essays on the social situation of mental patients and other inmates.* Garden City, NY: Anchor Books.

Grinnell, R. M., 1997. *Social work research and evaluation: Quantitative and qualitative approaches.* 5th edn. Itasca, IL: F. E. Peacock.

Jackson, W. 2002. Methods: *Doing social research.* 3d edn. Toronto: Pearson Education Canada.

Kohlberg, L. 1984. *The psychology of moral development.* New York: Harper & Row.

Kufeldt, K. 1984. Listening to children—Who cares? *British Journal of Social Work, 14.3.* 257–264.

Kufeldt, K.. & Klein, R. 1998. *Review of children in care in Newfoundland and Labrador, 1984–1995.* St. John's: Government of Newfoundland and Labrador.

Kufeldt, K., Simard, M., Tite, R., & Vachon, J. 2003. The Looking After Children in Canada Project: Educational outcomes. In K. Kufeldt & B. McKenzie (Eds.), *Child welfare: Connecting research, policy and practice.* Waterloo, ON: Wilfrid Laurier Press. 177–190.

Longres, J. F. 1995. *Human behavior in the social environment.* 2d edn. Itasca, IL: F. E. Peacock.

Milgram, S. 1974. *Obedience to authority: An experimental view.* New York: Harper & Row.

Monette, D. R., Sullivan, T. J., & DeJong, C. R. 1998. *Applied social research.* Toronto: Harcourt Brace.

Palys, T. 1997. *Research decisions: Quantitative and qualitative perspectives.* 2d edn. Toronto: Harcourt Brace.

Rubin, A., & Babbie, E. 2001. *Research methods for social work.* 4th edn. Belmont, CA: Wadsworth.

Schmid, T. S., & Jones, R. S. 1993. Ambivalent actions: Prison adaptation strategies of first-time, short-term inmates. *Journal of Contemporary Ethnography, 21.* 439–463.

Schuchts, R. A., & Witkin, S. L. 1989. Assessing marital change during the transition to parenthood. *Social Casework: The Journal of Contemporary Social Work, 70.* 67–75.

Sudnow, D. 1967. *Passing on: The social organization of dying.* Englewood Cliffs, NJ: Prentice Hall.

Thomlison, B. 1990. Continuity of care: Family, development, and attachment needs of children in long term care. In B. Galaway, D. Maglajlic, J. Hudson, P. Harmon, & J. McLagan (Eds.), *International perspectives on specialist foster family care.* St. Paul, MN: Human Services Association. 131–160.

Tri-Council Policy Statement: Ethical conduct for research involving humans. 2003. Ottawa: Medical Research Council of Canada. **www.pre.ethics.gc.ca/english/pdf/TCPS%20June2003_E.pdf**

Webb, E. J., Campbell, D. T., Schwartz, R. D., Sechrest, L., & Grove, J. B. 1981. *Nonreactive measures in the social sciences.* 2d edn. Boston: Houghton Mifflin.

Wilkinson, W. K., & McNeil, K. 1996. *Research for the helping professions.* Pacific Grove, CA: Brooks/Cole.

chapter thirty-one

Distinguishing Features of Social Work Education in Canada

Roland Lecomte

INTRODUCTION

The education of social welfare personnel in Canada is characterized by a multiplicity of programs, ranging from on-the-job training to community college and university education, delivered in English, French, and First Nations languages. These programs share some common values and orientations and they also have some distinguishing features, which we will examine briefly in this chapter.

IN-SERVICE EDUCATION

In the 1930s and 1940s, social welfare institutions often hired people without professional education and trained them on the job to deliver the services that social workers normally provided. These were usually college graduates who were viewed as temporary substitutes for professionals with Bachelor's degrees in Social Work (BSW) or Master's degrees in Social Work (MSW), who were in short supply. This situation is less common today because of the large number of university- and community college–educated personnel now available for employment. But paraprofessionals still play a significant role in the social-service delivery system.

Indeed, some social service organizations, such as the Centres locaux de services sociaux du Québec (CLSC) and some family agencies in Ontario, Alberta, and British Columbia, officially seek the participation of such personnel. These persons are trained to assist in family-life education programs or to work with citizens' groups. These people's life experiences and their knowledge of the individuals or groups they will serve are the most important qualifications. They learn the rest on the job through what has been labelled the apprenticeship approach. Pre- or paraprofessionals trained through in-service education do not compete for jobs with community college- or university-trained professionals as they did in the 1950s. Today they are a welcome addition to the social service delivery system.

In-service training has evolved rapidly in the last decade and is now offered mostly to persons who already have an education in social work. For instance, the Ontario Child Welfare Training System was formed in 1994 in order to meet the complex exigencies of service delivery in Children's Aid Societies. The International Social Service of Canada and Career Source Centres of Quebec also give supplementary in-service training to their staff. University-trained practitioners often deliver these education programs, which are independent from the college and university programs in standards and accreditation.

COMMUNITY COLLEGE EDUCATION

The late 1960s saw community college programs introduced for the education of social welfare workers and heralded the arrival of new practitioners, the social service technicians, techniciens d'assistance sociale (TAS), and social service workers. All these different labels identify the graduates of this first level of formal education. A remarkable number of such programs have sprung up in the last 40 years. In fact, more than 56 community colleges in Canada now offer an education for practice in social welfare.

The educational programs for these graduates have not developed uniformly, yet for the most part they take a generalist approach to practice. They focus on preparing students to provide direct services in a variety of social agencies. Students in the programs in Quebec (CEGEP) take three years to complete them while those in the rest of Canada take two years. Students graduate from these diploma or certificate programs that feature extensive field experience. Community colleges owe their primary allegiance to vocational and job training, and the needs of the workforce system greatly influence their educational objectives.

Community college and CEGEP graduates have suffered a great deal of frustration over employers' and university-trained social workers' not recognizing their particular education qualifications. They are especially concerned about the ongoing discrepancies between the nature of the tasks they are assigned and those assigned to BSW and MSW graduates. If they wish to enter university, they also find the faculty there unwilling to recognize their previous studies.

However, several developments have taken place during the last decade to change these attitudes. One is the development of partnerships between colleges and universities in education in several provinces. Some universities are now formally recognizing the two-year diploma in social services with up to 30 credits' equivalence, which is comparable to a full year at university. This trend has been observed in Ontario, Quebec, and Alberta, and it represents a major departure from the earlier policy of giving equivalence only on the basis of individual courses. New partnerships between community colleges and universities in gerontology programs, for instance, also raise interesting implications for the future in the ways that they may affect social work education. Certain universities, such as Ottawa, St. Thomas, and York in Ontario, and Mount Saint Vincent in Halifax, among others, have developed programs in which the universities teach the theoretical and research components and the community colleges teach the practice components.

Second is the beginning of a rapprochement between the professional associations of community college graduates and university-trained social workers. In some instances, the two have even fused, which produces a clearer understanding of the role and function of each profession. In Ontario recently legal recognition was accorded an association that combines the two within one professional title, Social Worker and Social Service Worker. We observe other types of links in the rest of Canada.

While these efforts are commendable, the profession needs to clarify its different levels of education and levels of practice further. More often than not, decisions regarding the hiring or the performance of community college graduates are still quite arbitrary and are based on economic and regional factors.

UNIVERSITY EDUCATION

Bachelor's Degree in Social Work (BSW)

Education and practice at the Bachelor's level has been formally recognized and professional only since the late 1960s, although many universities have been offering a Bachelor's degree in arts with a major in social welfare since the 1950s.

Since 1967, we have witnessed the development of 32 undergraduate programs in social work in Canada. These are accredited through the Canadian Association of Schools of Social Work (CASSW). Along with CASSW's recognition, the BSW programs are now well accepted by the Canadian Association of Social Workers (CASW) and by the Corporation of Social Workers in Quebec. Job descriptions in turn acknowledge the

competence and abilities of those social workers who have completed these programs. Their salaries and work assignments differ from those of community college graduates and MSW graduates.

This first university degree in social work combines both a general liberal arts education and a professional education. While most BSW programs promote a general education, most graduates tend to work in direct practice—that is, they work with individuals, families, and groups. As well, some programs are more committed to educating community-oriented workers who can work with citizens' groups, associations, and unions, within a more policy-oriented framework. This is particularly true of those programs that require that collective as well as individual interventions be expressed within a framework oriented toward social change.

The undergraduate programs in Canada reveal a remarkable diversity. While the CASSW accredits all the programs and those programs should therefore meet strict professional exigencies, their emphases differ greatly according to their geographical locations and regional needs.

Of particular interest is the recent development of First Nations programs. The School of Indian Social Work in Saskatchewan is a First Nations–controlled school of social work, and its degree is accredited by CASSW. In 1993–1994, Yukon College began to offer a four-year program leading to the Bachelor of Social Work degree, in cooperation with the Yukon's First Nations, the University of Regina, and the Saskatchewan Federated College. Laurentian University in Sudbury, Ontario, also offers an autonomous undergraduate First Nations social work program. Similar developments can be observed in British Columbia and in Alberta. These programs are delivered in First Nations languages. The schools seek the assistance of elders and respected

Native people in delivering the programs, which is an original way to encourage community participation. Also, all these programs demonstrate a remarkable level of cooperation among themselves in spite of the great geographical distances often separating them.

Master's Degree in Social Work (MSW)

The Master's of Social Work degree (MSW), now offered by 21 social work graduate schools in Canada, was the first degree to be offered in social work. In Canada, the first school of social work was established at the University of Toronto in 1914. During this period these schools and others moved social work away from an apprenticeship, in-training approach toward more academic preparation. By the 1940s, the two-year MSW had become the minimum requirement for professional practice in the United States and in Canada.

Since the 1960s, there have been several significant developments in social work education in Canada at the graduate level. Up to that time, most graduate programs prepared generalists or experimented with a common-methods approach to social work practice, especially in the first year of graduate education. Since the establishment of the BSW, the MSW's objectives have been redefined.

Specialization has been a recurring theme in the curriculum objectives of most MSW programs. The schools are contemplating more specialization in the MSW degree, not only by those universities that use specialization to distinguish their MSW degree from their BSW degree, but also by a number of universities that do not intend to offer a BSW. Three such programs in Canada currently offer a two-year MSW program based on an undergraduate degree (BA). They are Ottawa, Toronto, and Wilfrid Laurier, in Waterloo, Ontario.

They attract students with a variety of backgrounds—sociology, psychology, political science, criminology, women's studies, for example, as well as medicine and law. The variety of specialization in these programs usually revolves around fields of practice such as health and child and family welfare and around methodologies of intervention and research.

However, the majority of graduate programs in social work in Canada follow the format of the one-year MSW program. The latter is based on a BSW and assumes that students have a reasonably standardized background for their Master's level studies. The one-year MSW is organized specifically around additional objectives. The one-year MSW programs encompass a variety of specializations ranging from policy, planning, and administrative roles to advanced practice. Each of these programs requires a strong research component.

And the popularity of the two-year MSW programs is growing dramatically, judging by the number of requests for admission. Ottawa's Carleton University, which abandoned its two-year program in favour of a one-year MSW, recently reinstated the two-year program and gives advanced standing to BSW students. In the last decade the relationship between the two-year and one-year MSW programs in Canada has changed in some interesting ways. Many universities are admitting BA students or social science undergraduates to their one-year MSW programs and offering qualifying courses at the graduate level as well, rather than requiring the usual BSW degree of those students who want to enrol. This situation has created some controversy among social work educators in Canada (Taylor & Brownlee 1995). The impact of BSW graduates on the traditional Master's program has yet to be evaluated systematically in Canada, so it is hard to predict whether this approach to graduate education will resist the ongoing pressures of the one-year program. In the meantime we can discern obvious accommodations between the one-year and the two-year programs.

A great deal of diversity also exists in MSW programs' content and structure. For instance, many Quebec programs offer students the opportunity to meet the practice and the research requirements differently. They can opt to acquire advanced practice and critical skills, with a specialized field practicum and a research essay rather than write a thesis; or they can choose to emphasize research, without a practicum but with a field research component, and write a thesis (Rondeau & Gommelin, 2003).

Another interesting feature of francophone programs compared to anglophone and First Nations programs is the former's reliance on French social sciences and research in their curricula. As we shall see later, in the 1960s and 1970s Quebec students who wished to pursue doctoral studies in social work had to go to Toronto or to the United States. This often led to a great deal of difficulty in translating and adapting knowledge to particular francophone contexts.

Since the 1990s, we have seen a large number of educators trained in French who are bringing a different outlook to social work education and social work practice, one based less on American and British literature than formerly. This phenomenon has led some observers to conclude that there are "social work solitudes" yet to be properly understood in Canada.

Other provinces offer programs with distinctive orientations, such as local development and the promotion of social networks. Others focus on policy analysis, social administration, program evaluation, or national and international development, for example. Students can enrol on a full-time or part-time basis and some schools are considering the possibility of offering their programs or some of their courses through the internet.

Another interesting feature of the Master's level of education in social work in Canada is the rise of combined programs such as the ones offered in Law and Social Work at McGill and Toronto, and soon to be offered in Ottawa. Graduates of these programs obtain two degrees upon graduation: one in Law (LLD) and one in Social Work (MSW). Other similar arrangements are currently being considered with programs such as the Master's of Business Administration (MBA) and the Master's of Health Administration (MHA). These combined programs have integrated curricula that allow the candidates to complete their studies in less time than they could if they took the programs separately.

Advanced Education

Advanced education at the doctoral level has become an essential qualification for appointment to university faculties of social work and to certain key administrative positions outside academia. Until the early 1980s, the only doctoral program in Social Work (PhD) in Canada was offered by the Faculty of Social Work at the University of Toronto. The 1980s have seen the rise of doctoral education at Wilfrid Laurier University and at Laval University. The latter is still the only doctoral program in Social Work offered uniquely in French in all of North America. In the 1990s the University of Calgary, University of Manitoba, and Memorial University developed doctoral programs. McGill University and the University of Montreal have offered a joint bilingual PhD program in social work since 1995. The University of Montreal and the University of British Columbia also offer a multidisciplinary doctoral program that attracts many social work graduate students.

All of these programs prepare students for teaching and research, and some focus more on advanced practice and policy analysis. They generally have a residency requirement varying from one to two years. But there is a wide range of flexible arrangements to allow students' completion of the program on a part-time basis and off campus.

The rise of so many doctoral programs in social work in the 1990s is a welcome phenomenon. For years, many MSW graduates had to pursue a doctoral education in the social sciences or go the United States to seek a doctoral education in social work. This situation was widely judged to be undesirable. It was even more unacceptable for francophones who, until the 1980s, had no doctoral education in social work available to them in French in all of North America. This fact led to raised recruitment problems for personnel in schools of social work in Canadian universities, which as a rule require a doctoral education. This scarcity of such programs led a larger number of individuals with MSWs and doctorates in psychology, sociology, and other disciplines entering the faculties. They have been characterized as "applied social scientists," with no education in social work as such but with definite interests in certain areas of practice and social policy. These people had and still have a significant impact on the development of social work knowledge and the nature of social work identity (Lecomte 2000, 2002). The current number of doctoral graduates in social work now available to teach and do research is already changing the nature of recruitment and will probably have a major impact on the future of social work education in Canada.

CONTEMPORARY ISSUES IN SOCIAL WORK EDUCATION IN CANADA

At the beginning of this new millennium, social work education and social work practice can be described as moving into a state of serious questioning regarding their purpose as well as their social recognition. The many changes that have occurred in the 1990s in social welfare and in the role of the state have had major implications for the development of the profession. A national research project (Stephensen et al. 2001) sponsored by the Deans and the Directors of Schools of Social Work (CCDDSSW), the Canadian Association of Social Workers (CASW), and the Canadian Association of Schools of Social Work (CASSW) with a financial grant from the Human Resources Canada presents a disquieting picture of the demands made of social workers in Canada following the many restructurings in all provinces in the fields of health and social welfare.

It is possible to speculate on some of the issues that the study has raised. The explosion in complexity and variety of the fields of practice, the impact of new technologies, the emergence of new social problems requiring rapid adjustments in knowledge, skills, and values (including AIDS, the aging of the population, and ethnic and First Nations needs and rights), and the changing organizational context in which social workers must work are among those that social work educators and social work practitioners currently identify as significant. Another concern is the growing interdisciplinary context of practice in social and health services, which is blurring professional boundaries (Lecomte 2003). New management approaches have challenged the taken-for-granted autonomy of professional social work practice. Partnerships with community college graduates and other professionals are inevitable but are yet to be articulated in an acceptable and effective manner. While this state of affairs was identified more than 10 years ago (Wien & Walsh 1992), significant shortcomings and unresolved issues still remain to be tackled to meet the education needs of social workers in Canada.

CONCLUSION

A great range of programs is currently offered to those who wish to enter the field of social welfare in Canada: in-training programs, community college programs, and university programs. As we have seen, each of these has specific distinguishing features.

However, this plethora of programs is not without its problems and issues. While the programs are tending toward a rapprochement among themselves, we still lack sufficient in-depth analysis of the substantive knowledge and analytical and intervention skills that are to be taught at each level of the education spectrum. We have witnessed some promising developments along these lines (Nutter & Zarf 1990; Taylor & Brownlee 1995). But educators and practitioners are still concerned about this situation.

We continue to struggle as individual social workers and collectively as a profession to resolve for ourselves the nature of our commitment to certain ideals, such as equality, non-sexism, non-racism, and social change, and to certain groups in our society, such as the oppressed (Carniol 1992; Groulx 1993; Lecomte 1990). Our commitment is forcefully expressed in the CASSW education policy on accreditation standards. The CASSW states that the social work schools provide education that enables its professional members to remove obstacles to social functioning and to eliminate all forms of inequality, including those based on ethnicity, culture, sexual orientation, and race.

REFERENCES

Carniol, B. 1992. *Case critical: Challenging social work in Canada.* 2d edn. Toronto: Between the Lines.

Groulx, L. 1993. *Le travail social: Analyse et évolution.* Québec City: Éditions agence d'Arc.

Lecomte, R. 1990. Connecting private troubles and public issues in social work education. In B. Wharf (Ed.), *Social work and social change in Canada.* Toronto: McClelland & Stewart, 31–51.

Lecomte, R. 2000. Fondements théoriques et identité professionnelle en service social. *Les politiques sociales,* Bruxelles, *nos. 1 et 2.* 31–44.

Lecomte, R. 2002. Do intellectuals exist? The question of intellectuals in social work: Beyond contradictions. *Canadian Social Work Review, 19.2.* 311–328.

Lecomte, R. 2003. La nature du travail social. In Y. Hurtubise & J. P. Deslauriers (Eds.), *Introduction au travail social: Méthodologies et pratiques nord-*américaines. Québec: Les presses de l'Université Laval. 23–36.

Nutter, R. W., & Zapf, M. K. 1990. Comparisons among community college graduates, university transfer and after-degree students in a BSW program. *Canadian Social Work Review, 7.2.* 260–282.

Rondeau, G., & Commelin, D. 2003. La formation en travail social. Tiré de *Introduction au travail social, op.cit.,* 229-224.

Stephensen, M., Rondeau, G., Michaud, J.-C., & Fiddler, S. 2000. *In critical demand: Social work in Canada.* Final report. Ottawa: Human Resource Canada.

Taylor, S., & Brownlee, K. 1995. Academic preparation of students admitted into the HBSW program. *Canadian Social Work Review, 12.1.* 28–35.

Wien, F., & Walsh, M. 1992. The national continuing education project: Some major findings and some issues for future consideration. *The Social Worker, 60.1.* 6–20.

chapter thirty-two

Globalization and Social Welfare

Glenn Drover

INTRODUCTION

In a recent book on globalization and social welfare, Vic George and Paul Wilding (2002) state that globalization is profoundly affecting the way we live in both positive and negative ways. In some parts of the globe (for example, East Asia), it has encouraged economic growth. In other parts of the world (Africa), there has been no growth or the economy has even declined.

In countries throughout the world (including Canada), globalization has been accompanied by a redistribution of income. Within and between countries (particularly between countries of the north and the south), we have seen a widening disparity in incomes. In

Northern Europe, market income has been distributed more and more unequally and governments have intervened to offset the disparities (Hyde & Dixon, 2002). North America has seen some increase in income inequality but it is not clear to what extent the inequality in our society is owing to globalization or to changing demographics and employment (Mishra, 2002). In East Asia, the degree of inequality varies from country to country, depending again upon the extent of government involvement in social welfare issues (Sze, 2002; Leong & Mok, 2002).

In some ways, the impact of globalization is similar to other major upheavals in social welfare in centuries past. Until the nineteenth century, Canadian social welfare practices were mainly a responsibility of the family, the church, and benevolent organizations; the state played a minor role in welfare during the French and British colonial periods except as it encouraged immigration and land settlement. By the time of Confederation in the late nineteenth century, the role of the state began to change in order to accommodate industrialization and emerging national markets. At the same time Canadian governments were pushed to expand basic civil and political rights, to build a sense of national identity, and to ensure an informed electorate. Universal education and public health became state obligations.

In the twentieth century, Canadian governments, under pressure from organized labour and radicalized politics, expanded public services to provide benefits for the disabled, the unemployed, the sick, and the elderly. In doing so, they extended the notion of entitlement to include social and economic rights as well as civil and political rights. Throughout the century, the welfare state gradually took root and flourished (Banting, 1982: Guest, 1997).

At the beginning of the twenty-first century, we are engaged once again in a transformation of social welfare provision. Massive changes around the globe challenge the foundations of the welfare state. The realities of global interdependence affect more than trade and labour markets, finance and communications; they influence the way the state functions and our public services are provided.

The state welfare services that developed in many countries during the twentieth century, including Canada, are increasingly being called into question for two fundamental reasons. Fiscally and monetarily, governments are restrained from expanding or even maintaining existing social services as global trade and development modify the role of the state. Politically and morally, services are being reconfigured to respond to identity claims

from increasingly diverse populations, minorities, and marginalized people. Globalization requires us to think beyond the welfare state, to develop new concepts of social welfare entitlement, and to identify new ways of meeting human need.

This chapter, therefore, describes five key trends and issues that arise from the globalization process; they include globalization's impact on the welfare state, the governance of welfare institutions, social movements, the uses of information technology, and rethinking welfare. Before turning to these five issues, however, we must clarify the term *globalization*.

GLOBALIZATION

George and Wilding (2002) suggest that our understanding of globalization depends on our way of looking at it. Technological enthusiasts emphasize the impact of technology. Nationalists focus on the driving logic of capitalism and the decline of the nation-state. Pluralists stress the multi-faceted nature of globalization. Internationalists acknowledge a trend toward greater trade and financial integration but reject the notion of a borderless world.

Anthony McGrew (Held & McGrew, 1992) defines *globalization* as a multiplicity of links and interconnections that transcends the nation-state. Anthony Giddens (1991), a highly respected social theorist, suggests that global forces are compacting the distinctions between time and space, interlocking the local and the universal. Overbeek (1993) claims that it represents a new world order in which a neo-liberalist ideology dominates. Sklair (1991), a sociologist, describes globalization as a system based on transnational practices. The Organisation for Economic Co-operation and Development (OECD) (1994) associates it with an expanded trading system.

Part of the difficulty in defining globalization is that the term is used in two different ways, as multilateralism and as regionalism. As multilateralism, it is primarily a global trading system fostered by four major determinants: technology, finance, production, and trade. As regionalism, it is a concerted effort by corporations and states to integrate regional economies that are bound by political alliances, geography, culture, and language. Both forces are at work and both challenge the nation-state.

In the Canadian context, multilateralism is manifested through a rapidly expanding information infrastructure and an international financial system that have essentially no national boundaries. Competition is international in its scope. Similarly, multilateralism forces changes in the Canadian labour market, creating greater flexibility in the face of international competition, challenging structural barriers, undermining commitments to full employment, substituting non-unionized labour for unionized labour, and fostering export markets (Workman, 2003; Scott, Salas, & Campbell, 2001).

But globalization is more than multilateralism. It is also a form of regionalism (Drover, Johnson, & Tao, 2001). The world is being divided into major regional trading blocs dominated by Europe, the Americas, and East Asia. Canada is profoundly influenced by developments within the Americas, particularly through free trade agreements and cross-border concerns about trade and security in a post-9/11 world. Hence, Canadian companies and labour markets are under pressure to meet international norms, and they are also being pressured to integrate within a continental economy. Since the introduction of the Canada–United States Free Trade Agreement (FTA) in 1989 and the North American Free Trade Agreement (NAFTA) in 1992, American ownership of the Canadian economy has intensified, public procurement is open to American competi-

tion (the purchase of goods by governments), Canadian culture is threatened, and Canadian environmental standards are challenged. Equally important, American corporate interests aim to extend their influence through a Free Trade Agreement of the Americas (FTAA) and possibly a multilateral agreement on investment (Clark & Barlow, 1997; Council of Canadians, 1999). To offset American dominance, Canada's governments are promoting multilateral and bilateral agreements with other countries more and more.

Welfare State

Thus far, the welfare state has responded in roughly three ways to globalization (UNRISD, 1995). In social democratic welfare states like Sweden, in which the majority of the population still shares a common set of welfare values, changes have been minor and cautious, promoted more by fiscal restraint than by any shift in political priorities (Timonen, 2003). In spite of minor restraints, however, observers express some concern about whether the model can be maintained, and unemployment persists at particular levels. In Germany, where there are insider–outsider problems with the country's large numbers of guest workers and where unemployment rates are also high, commentators identify the basic challenge as the existence of a two-tiered system of social insurance. In this system, insiders, mainly white non-immigrant males, enjoy comprehensive coverage and other workers are excluded entirely. Finally, in liberal welfare states like Canada, which contain a diverse population and equally diverse welfare values, a counter-reaction to the welfare state is building, fed in part by right-wing politics and in part by resistance from sectors of society who do not benefit, or benefit only marginally, from established social welfare benefits. The policy response to globalization has been to cut social welfare expenditures, to limit people's accessibility to some social services, to deregulate the labour market, and to stimulate economic growth through lower taxes.

One well-known political observer of the Western welfare state is scientist Bob Jessop (1993). He claims that global pressures are fundamentally changing the welfare state to a workfare state. The welfare state created a legal form of welfare provision associated with bureaucracy, standardization, clientelism, and an intensified personal dependency on the state that can no longer be sustained in a global economy. According to Jessop, the workfare state is replacing a state welfare provision based on national interests. In the original welfare state, social programs were closely aligned with the needs of a global labour market, the redistribution of income toward capital, a growing reliance on welfare technology, and an increasing surveillance of individuals to see how they perform.

To make national economies like Canada more competitive, social policy choices seem to be shrinking for two reasons. The general impression is that states must reduce taxes to become more competitive, and this in turn raises their capacity to spend money on a variety of social initiatives (Brawley, 2003, chapter 5). However, globalization is more than a change in taxes and services; it is also a shift in the way we are governed, introducing new notions of social rights and obligations.

Canadians have become acutely aware of this pressure through the debates surrounding the FTA and NAFTA. They have learned that the agreements redefine our cross-border trade in services and make virtually no mention of the need to protect public programs from market-oriented provisions. Some argue strongly that the impact of free trade has been anything but good for working people, public services, and the environment (Workman, 2002; Barlow, 2004). In addition, while the agreements do not require the re-alignment of social services and social security based on harmonization, critics of the deals argue that pressure toward harmonization will succeed over time once American interests dominate our economy. Furthermore, since the agreements require that professional standards be harmonized to eliminate cross-border barriers to trade in services and also open government procurement to American and Mexican companies, it is clear that NAFTA is about far more than trade in the conventional sense; it actually establishes a regulatory environment that safeguards corporate interests while constraining governments and social services as well as social benefits. Deep down, therefore, globalization and free trade raise fundamental questions not only about the future of the welfare state but also about welfare governance.

Welfare Governance

In the mid-1990s, Kenichi Ohmae (1995) wrote about a borderless world. Like other commentators of globalization, Ohmae attempts to highlight the importance of emerging forms of economic and political governance that transcend national boundaries and replace national governments. The term *governance* implies a shift from government to a variety of complex institutional arrangements by which nations are governed. Globalization's greatest implication regarding welfare is that no single form of governance, such as the welfare state, can prevail any longer. The reality of global interdependence is that welfare policies, like economic and foreign policies, are increasingly subject to multiple mechanisms and strategies of coordination that involve international, national, and sub-national institutions. Among the most influential of these are transnational corporations, which some writers view as being so powerful that they describe them as ruling the world (Greider, 1997; Korten,

1995). Certainly few would disagree that they are powerful, that they have contributed to a weakening of nation-states, and that international trade and investment agreements enhance their operational autonomy. The dominance of corporations, and various institutions that seem to be aligned with them, such as the World Trade Organization, the World Bank, and the International Monetary Fund, has led opponents of globalization to feel that the whole process must be reversed or at least slowed down (Pauly, 1997; Cox, 2000).

Other commentators, however, present an optimistic view of new governance mechanisms and their implications for social welfare. According to John Naisbitt (1994), one paradox of globalization is that the bigger the economy, the more welfare shifts into the hands of the small players. The breakdown of national boundaries liberates the forces of the free market. According to this perspective, the new information technology allows the small to compete with the large. The more one moves to a free-market democracy, the more each individual takes control of her or his own destiny.

On a similarly optimistic note, Robert Lawrence, Albert Brossard, and Takatoshi Ito (1996) claim that globalization is pushing us toward a world marked by openness, diversity, and cohesion, a world in which the wealthy nations can no longer use their domestic policies to exclude the products of poorer nations or gain unfair advantage. In addition, they suggest that globalization is leading to new forms of governance by which national governments remain players that assure minimum standards and the redistribution of resources while other players establish rights and duties for their members according to shared values and benefits.

While we must consider these differing views of world governance, pessimistic and optimistic, with caution, we can see that they emphasize the changing com-

plexity of a new world order and, within it, the growth of welfare pluralism and experimentation. Given challenges to established welfare provision within and without national boundaries, more and more observers agree that multiple bodies must meet basic welfare needs, not just the state. To equate welfare with the state, therefore, is to ignore other forms of protection and benefit, forms as diverse as the family, social networks, voluntary associations, and the market. Mishra (1990) notes one implication of welfare pluralism, that not only can there be state equivalents to welfare provision but also that human welfare entails more than state intervention.

In Canada, as in other countries throughout the world (Rieger & Leibfried, 2003; Timonen, 2003), there is a growing and contested trend toward experimentation with public-and-private partnerships. *Privatization* extends well beyond the sale of government assets or even Crown corporations. In its common usage, the term covers general efforts to reduce the scope of government. More restrictively, it includes "efforts to replace policies based on ownership or control by policies based on information or incentives" (Howlett & Ramesh, 1993, 19). It embraces denationalization, contracting out, de-monopolization, partnering, user fees, and mandatory private provision (Aulich & Reynolds, 1993).

An important area of public provision that is partially privatized in Canada is retirement income protection and Canada Pension Plan investments. Contracting out is common in the provision of personal social services and health care. User fees are pervasive in many social welfare programs. We see examples of partnering in such areas as community economic development.

Social Movements

New forms of governance also raise questions about the role of social movements in civil society; in the past, these movements played an important role in social welfare reform. A healthy civil society "sustains and enhances the capacity of all its members to build a caring and mutually responsible society" (Torjman, 1997, 2). Through this civil society, people come together in geographic, occupational, voluntary, and political communities to articulate their view of the good life and to persuade others of its merits. Through civil society, organizations are formed to address social concerns and social problems. Through civil society, citizenship is furthered through democratic means. Through civil society, people develop caring communities, promote economic security, and foster social investment. Our ability to make claims that are recognized in civil society, however, depends ultimately on the legitimacy of our representation (Jenson, 1993; Jenson & Phillips, 2002).

Not all the actors in civil society are equal. They represent different constellations of power. Nor are they necessarily making claims against the nation-state. In fact, their claims may transcend the state. Some struggle to maintain their place in society. Others want to change it.

In the twentieth century, the labour movement profoundly influenced the development of the Canadian welfare state. Our society based its construction of social services and social security on a pan-Canadian vision of welfare in which all citizens of the country were to have common provision. Quebec nationalist movements challenged the idea of pan-Canadian welfare by highlighting the right to a distinct society by making welfare claims and social provision without reference to the federal state. Recently, Alberta has also challenged federalist claims of dominance in the welfare field. In a similar fashion, Aboriginal movements have made identity claims that transcend the nation-state. As Canada continues to confront globalization pressures to restructure its economy, other sectors of society are increasing their own demands for change. The plight of women, visible minorities, disabled persons, environmentalists, prisoners, and children has reconfigured our thinking about welfare entitlement and citizenship rights. Social movements spotlight the fragility and the limits of the Canadian state to meet the growing insistence that our society accommodate differences.

In a sense, therefore, the central dilemma Canadian social movements face is whether they function simply to articulate welfare claims or whether they also serve to resolve them, whether they are simply a part of the civil society or whether they can transform state and economic relations. Based on studies of social movements in Montreal, Lustiger-Thaler and Shragge (1993) argue that two kinds of social movements exist: those that try to influence political processes by framing their demands in terms of basic rights and those that try to alter existing political and economic decision-making processes by articulating counter-rights. This distinction stresses that social movements not only make claims for resources; they also make demands that they be permitted to participate and exercise their own self-determination. Hence, in dealing with global realities, Canadian social movements play an important role in redefining our welfare expectations and basic rights. Community economic development is one way that they have done this (Shragge, 1993; Loizides, 1995).

Social movements have also stood at the forefront of the resistance to corporate globalization. Environmental groups like Greenpeace, Friends of the Earth, and the Green Party were among the first to sound the alarm about this growing force. Recently, however, a groundswell of reaction to international free trade agreements has united traditional social movements such as labour, women, and students with citizen organizations that represent the marginalized and the powerless. While this new loose alliance of social movements does not represent the kind of threat to established authority that the labour movement represented in the early part of the twentieth century, it nevertheless challenges the legitimacy of corporate-dominated globalization (Mitzman, 2003, 160). The new movements demand greater consideration of the rights of labour, women, children, and minorities. They also pose a challenge to those national governments that try to dismantle their welfare states.

Information Technology

Globalization has also shaped welfare through its increasing use of information technology (Carlson, 1998; Resnick & Anderson, 2002). Information technology has affected at least four aspects of social welfare: management, education, professional practice, and professional ethics. The debate regarding global development in these four areas covers more than concerns about the speed of information technology or the diffusion of technological applications. It deals fundamentally with whether information technology is transforming society, building on the technologies of the past, or transforming some aspects of society while retaining others.

Back in the 1980s, Peter Drucker (1989) claimed that the management structures of social agencies, hospitals, and symphony orchestras were closer even at that time to the information-based organizations of today or tomorrow. Because each department in a large social service organization or a hospital has its own specialty, knowledge, training, language, and values, it is in a strong position, according to Drucker, to maximize its use of complex information technology, to accommodate innovation and entrepreneurship, and to integrate people with shared values in common ventures. In spite of this potential power, though, social welfare organizations have been slow in

some respects to take advantage of information technology. In part they demonstrate a concern about technology's impact on human communication and interaction, in part as it translates into power struggles among staff and professionals (Neugeboren, 1995: Benbenishty & Oyserman, 1995).

Some authors also elaborate on how information technology can been employed to further social action and social change. Recently, non-governmental organizations (NGOs) in many countries used the internet to facilitate communication around the globe and to successfully oppose the implementation of the proposed Multilateral Agreement on Investment (MAI) (Jackson & Sanger, 1998). They were concerned that the agreement, if approved, would dramatically and negatively affect national governments' capacity to control multinational corporations operating within their borders and their power to raise revenues to pay for social welfare programs. The debate swirling around trade and investment agreements reflects a growing conviction among NGOs that Canada's federal and provincial governments are accommodating free trade, investment, and international financial transactions in the name of economic growth and at the price of a sense of community and solidarity. And this collective feeling forms the basis for facilitating society's participation in and commitment to public institutions. One strategy rapidly developing to meet the challenge, both in Canada and the United States, is using computer networks to link individuals around the globe as well as local organizations (Schuler, 1997). According to OneWorld.net, information communication technologies form the basis of development, giving people the opportunity to participate in even the most marginalized communities.

Perhaps the greatest future application of information technology, however, lies in education (Garrison & Anderson, 2003). Distance learning (on-line) is transforming university and college education. The virtual university and the virtual library are signs of the present, not the future. They offer choices never before available for linking work and study, for professional studies and continuing education. They encourage lifelong learning, and link the local and the global, the urban and the rural, the north and the south. In response to demands from students as well as faculties, university and college programs in Canada—including social work education programs—are turning to computers to test the benefits of interactive technology, assess the impact of cyberspace, communicate by e-mail and listserv, engage in WebBoard conferencing, and reframe pedagogic issues. Computers in professional education can be viewed from two perspectives (MacFadden, 1995). As a tool, they calculate as well as identify new tasks and needs. As a mechanism for developing knowledge, more and more they frame the way human service professionals learn and the way they practise.

Rethinking Welfare

Finally, it is important to realize that globalization makes us reconsider the very meaning of human welfare and future welfare provision. In a global society, how do groups and individuals articulate their welfare claims? How do they engage in making those claims? And how are institutions structured to respond to claims?

During the heyday of the welfare state, the answers to such questions seemed deceptively simple. For the greater part of the twentieth century, there was a consensus that the state should and could act to satisfy basic human needs. Human welfare, regardless of class, was maximized through the provision of a comprehensive services-and-income security. Professionals allocated scarce resources to those in need. Society came to view universal services as rights of citizenship, available to all who

qualified. As noted earlier, however, one major difficulty with this interpretation of welfare provision is that it excludes many in society (minorities in particular) and it also presupposes a highly centralized welfare state that is capable of responding to all human needs. In the globalized and regionalized world of today, neither assumption makes much sense.

Another view of future welfare provision is associated with neo-liberalism (Mitzman, 2003). Today we can give it credit as the driving ideological force in the opening up of global markets through international free trade agreements. But it is much more than a theory of markets. It is also a theory of well-being. Neo-liberalism affirms the primacy of individual choice as an arbiter of human worth. Each individual, not the state, not a collectivity, is in the best position to decide what is right for him- or herself. Each person should be free to maximize that right with only one restraint, respecting the capacity of others to do the same.

The maximization of human welfare, therefore, is the maximization of free choice. More than any other institution, the market is best able to respond to human need. Obeying the dictates of the market, however, does lead to a problem in that this leads to a society in which human values are wrapped around lifestyles. Through the commercialization of lifestyles, corporations help to shape the society of the future. They define appropriate forms of behaviour and codes of conduct. Among youth, they do this through taking over mass culture and sporting events—what Naomi Klein (2000) calls the branding of lifestyles. For other observers, the process may appear more gradual but people's emulation of consumption is no less pervasive as the values of consumerism are inculcated into all strata of society. As a vision of a welfare future, this is not one that many are willing to accept.

Another view that rejects the fundamentals of neo-liberalism while it accepts the multiplicity of human difference is post-structuralism or postmodernism. Post-structuralism is closely associated with those who reject the universalizing principles on which the welfare state or markets are built. They argue for an emancipatory project of welfare that frees people from the grand narratives of the past. Like Foucault, they problematize welfare assumptions and social practices that are taken for granted (Chambon, Irving, & Epstein, 1999).

For many who have reacted negatively to globalization, particularly the young, the liberating influence of post-structural or postmodern theories has helped to fire their rebellion. The theories have served as an intellectual force for minorities, the forgotten, and the neglected. They remind us of the stigmatizing ideas that shape our way of thinking, speaking, and acting. They challenge the idea that universal institutions can respond to the multiple needs of different people throughout the world. They affirm the need for the freedom to deconstruct 'dominant ideologies and phoney universalism' (Ferguson, Lavalette, & Mooney, 2002, 179). The difficulty with post-structuralism, and the identity politics that flow from it, is the negation, or downplaying, of people's commonalities that are integral to their own well-being. In addition, it contributes to a process of fragmentation between and within oppressed groups that, in turn, weakens their capacity to be heard in a global world (Ferguson, Lavalette, & Mooney, 2002, chapter 10).

Faced with a highly standardized notion of neo-liberal welfare and a fragmented notion of welfare inherent in post-structuralism, it is imperative to think about a way of balancing, or linking, the welfare bonds between the individual and the collectivity. In *A Theory of Human Need*, Doyal and Gough attempt to come to

terms with globalization according to a concept of basic needs. They claim that all people share two basic needs regardless of culture or background, autonomy and health. Without satisfying these two needs, Doyal and Gough point out, people cannot be fully human. Therefore needs are more than drives, goals, or strategies; they are fundamental to human functioning. They transcend class, race, gender, age, sexism, and other forms of oppression. Because of the nature of fundamental needs, however, their satisfaction requires four societal preconditions: production, reproduction, cultural transmission, and authority. Hence, at an institutional level, they fully recognize that we can satisfy needs through the market as well as the state and civil society.

There is at least one other element that is central to a concept of welfare in a global village, and that is the potential of people to participate in the process of making claims. None of us is fully autonomous. All of us are interdependent. Drover and Kerans (1993) argue that without the freedom of people to name their claims, and an institutional framework in which those claims can be legitimately recognized, a theory of need risks being either a subjective assessment grounded in individual experience or an objective assessment based on the judgment of experts. To avoid both extremes, they suggest that welfare has to be rooted in social action that presupposes a duality of claims-making; they perceive a tension between individual and community, agency and institution, identity and relationship. Welfare is a dynamic process, which they call "well-seeking" (rather than well-being), because it involves "increasing levels of personal and institutional complexity within which bonds of attachment and affection are integral parts of relationships" (Drover & Kerans, 1993, 7).

They focus on the dynamic nature of welfare in a global context for three reasons. First, welfare claims-making involves a creative use of language. Need may be universal, as Doyal and Gough suggest, yet its expression is culturally specific. Second, to have meaning and value, those claims must be acknowledged by others. Without others' encouragement, individuals rarely, if ever, find their claims are accepted. Third, claims-making is fundamentally moral as it requires the claims-makers to assume the perspective of others. In a global society, therefore, the claims of welfare that take into account only the needs of people within one nation-state are necessarily selective rather than universal. To move beyond particularism, we must reconstruct welfare provision on a global basis and think about global citizenship.

CONCLUSION

Throughout much of the twentieth century, it was largely assumed that welfare policy was determined by each nation. This chapter implies that such an assumption no longer holds true because of the dynamics of globalization. While we must be cautious about attributing too much to globalization, we would be equally imprudent to attribute too little to its forces. Whether we like it or not, globalization is an intractable and irreversible process that affects us all in some measure.

In welfare terms, the fundamental impact of the global process is the limitations it places on nation-states. Fiscal and monetary policies that governments once invoked to garner and redistribute resources are increasingly counteracted by the flexibility of international labour markets and the mobility of international capital. In addition, the welfare state frequently cannot satisfy the multiplicity and diversity of claims made on it at a national level. Faced with this dilemma, people look increasingly to other forms of governance to make certain that their voices are heard in the political process. While national governments are not forgotten, they have become only one source of legitimacy.

Other institutions are implicated in the welfare agenda. Deep down, globalization raises fundamental questions about that agenda. Since the global process concerns the compression of time and space, welfare too must bridge the local and the global, the particular and the universal, the individual and the collective. First and foremost welfare has to do with people's sense of themselves, their aspirations and their identity. At the same time, it also has to do with mutual respect and taking into account other people's welfare as well as institutional reliability and stability. Without mutual respect, there is little sense of self-worth. Without the latter two, there is little trust. Globalization's great advantage is that it makes us more aware of the interdependency of the three aspects of welfare. Its great disadvantage is that it challenges many of our assumptions.

REFERENCES

Aulich, C., & Reynolds, M. (1993). Competitive tendering and contracting out. *Australian Journal of Public Administration, 52.4.*

Banting, Keith. (1982). *The welfare state and Canadian federalism.* Kingston: McGill-Queen's University Press.

Barlow, Maude. (2004). *The free trade area of the Americas and the threat to social programs, environmental sustainability and social justice in Canada and the Americas.* **www.attac.org/fra/list/doc/barlow.htm**

Benbenishty, R., & Oyserman, D. (1995). Integrated information systems for human services: A conceptual framework, methodology and technology. In J. Rafferty, J. Steyaert, & D. Colombi (Eds.). *Human services in the information age.* New York: Haworth Press.

Brawley, Mark. (2003). *The politics of globalization: Gaining perspective, assessing consequences.* Peterborough, ON: Broadview Press.

Carlson, R. (1998). Using case-based reasoning to develop computerized guidance for effective practice. *Conference program and proceedings: Information technologies for social work education and practice.* Charleston: University of South Carolina College of Social Work.

Chambon, Adrienne, Irving, Alan, & Epstein, Laura. (1999). *Reading Foucault for social work.* New York: Columbia University Press.

Clark, Tony, & Barlow, Maude. (1997). *MAI: The Multilateral Agreement on Investment and the threat to Canadian sovereignty.* Toronto: Stoddart.

Council of Canadians. (1999). *The MAI inquiry: Confronting globalization and reclaiming democracy.* Ottawa.

Cox, Robert. (2000). Political economy and world governance: Problems of power and knowledge at the turn of the millennium. In Richard Stubbs & Geoffrey Underhill (Eds.), *Political economy and the changing global order.* Don Mills, ON: Oxford University Press.

Doyal, L., & Gough, I. (1991). *A theory of human need.* London: Macmillan.

Drover, G., & Kerans, P. (1993). *New approaches to welfare theory.* Aldershot: Edgar Elgar.

Drover, Glenn, Johnson, Graham, & Tao, Julia (Eds.). (2001). *Regionalism and subregionalism in East Asia: The dynamics of China.* Huntington, NY: Nova Science Publishers.

Drucker, P. (1989). *The new realities.* New York. Harper and Row.

Ferguson, Iain, Lavalette, Michael, & Mooney, Gerry. (2002). *Rethinking welfare: A critical perspective.* London: Sage Publications.

Garrison, D. R., & Anderson, T. (2003). E-learning in the 21st century: A framework for research and practice. London: Rutledge Falmer.

George, Vic, & Wilding, Paul. (2002). *Globalization and human welfare,* Basingstoke, Hampshire: Palgrave.

Giddens, A. (1991). *Modernity and self-identity.* Stanford: Stanford University Press.

Greider, W. (1997). *One world, ready or not.* New York: Simon & Schuster.

Guest, Dennis. (1997). *The emergence of social security in Canada,* Vancouver: University of British Columbia Press.

Hile, M. G. (1998). (Guest Ed.). The history and function of the target cities management information systems. *Computers in Human Services, 14.* 3–4.

Howlett, M., & Ramesh, M. (1993). Patterns of policy instrument choice: Policy styles, policy learning and the privatization experiences. *Policy Studies Review, 12.* 1–2.

Hyde, Mark, & Dixon, John. (2002). Globalization, poverty, ideology and the privatization of social protections in Western Europe. *New Global Development: Journal of International and Comparative Social Welfare, 18, 1 & 2.*

Jackson, Andrew, & Sanger, Matthew. (1998). *Dismantling democracy: The Multilateral Agreement on Investment,* Ottawa: Canadian Centre for Policy Alternatives.

Jenson, Jane. (1993). De-constructing dualities: Making rights claims in political institutions. In G. Drover & P. Kerans (Eds.), *New approaches to welfare theory.* Aldershot, UK: Edward Elgar. 113–126.

Jenson, Jane, & Phillips, Susan. (2002). Redesigning the Canadian citizenship regime: Remaking the institutions of representation. In C. Crouch, K. Eder & D. Tambini (Eds.), *Citizenship, markets and the state.* London, UK: Oxford University Press.

Jessop, B. (1993). Towards a Schumpeterian workfare state? Preliminary remarks on post-Fordist political economy. *Studies in Political Economy, 40.* 7–39.

Klein, Naomi. (2000). *No logo.* London, UK: Flamingo.

Korten, D. C. (1995). *When corporations rule the world.* West Hartford, CT: Kamarian Press.

Lawrence, R., Bressand, A., & Takatoshi, I. (1996). *A vision for the world economy: Openness, diversity, and cohesion.* Washington, D.C.: Brookings Institute.

Leong, Apo, & Mok, Henry. (2002). Complexity in linking poverty and globalization. *New Global Development: Journal of International and Comparative Social Welfare, 18. 1 & 2.*

Loizides, S. (1995). *Corporate involvement in community economic development: Options, benefits and key success factors.* Ottawa: Conference Board of Canada.

Lustiger-Thaler, H., & Shragge, E. (1993). Social movements and social welfare: The political problems of need. In G. Drover & P. Kerans (Eds.), *New approaches to welfare theory.* Aldershot, UK: Edward Elgar. 161–176.

MacFadden, R. J. (1995). IT and knowledge development in human services: Tool, paradigm and promise. In J. Rafferty, J. Steyaert & D. Colombi (Eds.), *Human services in the information age.* New York: Haworth Press.

Michael, J. (1994). *Privacy and human rights.* Dartmouth. NS: UNESCO.

Miles, I., Rush, H., Turner, K., & Bessant. J. (1998). *Information horizons: The long-term social implications of new information technologies.* Aldershot, UK: Edward Elgar.

Mishra. R. (1990). *The welfare state in capitalist society.* Toronto: University of Toronto Press.

Mishra, R. (2002). Globalization and poverty in the Americas, *New Global Development: Journal of International and Comparative Social Welfare, 18.1 & 2.*

Mitzman, Arthur. (2003). *Prometheus revisited: The quest for global justice in the twenty-first century.* Amherst, MA: University of Massachusetts Press.

Naisbitt, J. (1994). *Global paradox: The bigger the world economy, the more powerful its smaller players.* New York: William Morrow.

Neugeboren, B. (1995). Organizational influences on management information systems in the human services. In J. Rafferty, J. Steyaert, & D. Colombi (Eds.), *Human services in the information age.* New York: Haworth Press.

Organisation for Economic Co-operation and Development. (1994). *The new world trading system.* Paris: OECD.

Ohmae, K. (1995). *The end of the nation state: The rise of regional economics.* New York: Free Press.

Overbeek, H. (Ed.). (1993). *Restructuring hegemony in the global political economy: The rise of transnational neo-liberalism in the 1980s.* London, UK: Routledge.

Pauly, Louis. (1997). *Who elected the gankers?* Ithaca, NY: Cornell University Press.

Rieger, Elmar, & Leibried, Stephan. (2003). *Limits to globalization: Welfare states and the world economy.* Cambridge, UK: Polity Press.

Resnick, Hy, & Anderson, Phoebe Sadie (Eds.). (2002). Innovations in technology and human services: Practice and education. *Journal of Technology in Human Services, Special Issue, 20.*

Schuler, D. (1997). *The new community networks: Wired for change.* Reading, MA: Addison-Wesley.

Scott, A. (1993). On Lustiger-Thaler and Shragge. In G. Drover & P. Kerans (Eds.), *New approaches to welfare theory.* Aldershot, UK: Edward Elgar. 281–283.

Scott, Robert, Salas, Carlos, & Campbell, Bruce. (2001). *NAFTA at seven: Its impact on workers in all three nations.* Ottawa: Canadian Centre for Policy Alternatives.

Shragge, E. (1995). *Community economic development: In search of empowerment and alternatives.* Montreal: Black Rose Press.

Singh, N., & Titi, V. (1995). *Empowerment for sustainable development: Toward operational strategies.* Halifax: Fernwood.

Sklair, L. (1991). *Sociology of the global system.* Baltimore: Johns Hopkins University Press.

Strange, S. (1996). *The retreat of the state: The diffusion of power in the world economy.* Cambridge: Cambridge University Press.

Sze, Alan. (2002). Globalization and poverty in East Asia. *New Global Development: Journal of International and Comparative Social Welfare, 18.1 & 2.*

Timonen, Virpi. (2003). *Restructuring the welfare state: Globalization and social policy reform in Finland and Sweden.* Cheltenham, UK: Edward Elgar.

Torjman, S. (1997). *Civil society: Reclaiming our humanity.* Ottawa: Caledon Institute of Social Policy.

United Nations Research Institute for Social Development. (1995). *States of disarray: The social effects of globalization.* London: Banson Productions.

Workman, Thom. (2002). *Social torment: Globalization in Atlantic Canada*, Halifax: Fernwood Press.

chapter thirty-three

International
Social Welfare[1]

Gayle Gilchrist James

INTRODUCTION

"[The International Year of Peace] has served to remind us that peace without development is not peace, that peace without racial equality and harmony is not peace, that peace without a reasonable quality of life is not peace. It is, therefore, the fullness of Canada's programs—from development assistance and active support for human rights to the protection of the environment and the promotion of a better standard of living for people across the country and, indeed, around the world—that constitutes a meaningful contribution to peace."[2]

When he crafted these words nearly 20 years ago, Senator Douglas Roche was Canada's Ambassador for Disarmament.[3]

He was, by implication, gracefully reminding us of many things: that long-term peace is the by-product of economic and social development rather than the suppression of wars, the quelling of skirmishes, or the subjugation of any peoples; that it is rooted in the operationalization of the basic tenets of the major United Nations declarations and conventions; that peace involves making peace with the environment; and that we in Canada cannot act as though our own social development and social well-being are somehow separate from that of the other nations that inhabit this planet.

This last decade has seen a series of dramatic shifts both within Canada and in Canada's intricate relationship with the outside world, a world that in its shrinking has brought us face-to-face with forces over which we appear not to have much control. As globalization proceeds, several trends and apparent contradictions have emerged, many of them unsettling, and especially so to those who have spent the better part of the post-war period constructing Canada's internal social safety net, while also contributing to our country's important role in international social welfare.

The "fullness of Canada's programs" (Roche, 1985) diminished through the 1990s as Canada surrendered the principle of universality—in all but its national health care scheme—for a more residual approach to social welfare. Ironically, in this same period, from 1995 until the beginning of the new century, the United Nations Human Development Index (HDI), invented in 1990 to measure quality of life, consistently ranked Canada as the best place to live. The HDI "embellishes traditional income rankings with less quantifiable dimensions such as political freedom, environmental sustainability and racial and gender equality."[4]

However, the growing gap between the rich and the poor in Canada has mirrored the growing chasm between the rich and the poor in the world, and it is not possible to say which is cause and which is effect, or whether we Canadians are merely co-conspirators with fate. The growing emphasis on economic development, and the apparent acceptance of a predominantly economic agenda, often at the expense of social development, is evident in Canada.

Hence, a recent report from the Conference Board of Canada more accurately reflects the current realities of Canada's social welfare provisions, when viewed comparatively. The eighth annual "Performance and Potential Report" of the Conference Board of Canada (October 2003) "based on 100 economic and social and environmental indicators for 24 countries... is a benchmarking exercise that

goes well beyond the United Nations' better-known Human Development Index, which uses only four indicators for its research."[5] The Conference Board of Canada (CBC) Report indicates that "Canada's actual performance is not as strong as many Canadians think.... [And] there is this Canadian complacency.... It's hard to light a fire under people who don't think anything is wrong" (Charles Barrett, executive vice-president of the CBC).[6]

The CBC Report relies on the data from 24 developed nations who are members of the Organisation for Economic Co-operation and Development (OECD); the board's eighth Report undertook to analyze the top dozen more closely. While Canada ranked in third place in Economy Indicators—tied with Ireland and trailing South Korea and Norway—it placed only 16th in Environment Indicators. In Innovation Indicators, Canada ranked 5th; in Education and Skills, 5th; in Health Indicators, 9th; and in Society Indicators, only 10th. These facts are far removed from the assumptions most Canadians hold about their country's place among developed nations. (Only Sweden and Switzerland consistently "pulled off a top-12 placement in all six categories.... Canada was a top performer in only five.")[7] Because Canada is a member of the Group of Eight, we should note—again, using OECD data—that the "United States, Japan, France and Britain made it to the top 12 on only three categories, and Italy in only two."[8]

Canada committed itself to debt and deficit reduction throughout the 1990s, in concert with diminished federal funding to the provincial and territorial governments for health, education, justice and social services—who, in turn, devolved their losses to municipal governments. This trend has seriously affected not only the lives of Canada's citizens but also Canada's historical role on the international stage as a middle power with a reasonably advanced welfare state. That we are tied for third in Economy Indicators and lower in the other rankings—education, innovation, environment, health, and society—should convince us that we have broken the Canadian contract of the 1960s, that social and economic development must proceed hand in hand.

There is now a serious dichotomy between our social goals and our economic goals, and we see this division reflected in Canada's ambivalence about foreign policy and international aid.

The comparatively recent tendency of national governments in democratic and developed societies to withdraw from some of their traditional welfare state responsibilities in meeting common human needs has pushed non-governmental organizations (NGOs) into an expanded and more activist role, as well as a variety of professional organizations in the broad field of social welfare. This is the stuff of this chapter.

We will raise some matters of definition and focus on Canadians' mixed attitudes toward international social issues, the United Nations (UN) and its associated agencies, the ambivalent role the various governments in Canada play in international social development, and the increasingly vital role that NGOs play. Primarily we will emphasize the non-governmental sector in what are known colloquially as the three "sister organizations": the International Federation of Social Workers (IFSW), the International Association of Schools of Social Work (IASSW), and the International Council on Social Welfare (ICSW). Their functions are highly complementary, largely cooperative and, at times, competitive; all employ the same official languages—Spanish, French, and English—and they attempt, whenever feasible, to hold their widely attended biennial conferences and general meetings in tandem in the same location.

These three organizations, enjoying various degrees of consultative status with the UN, find their nationally sanctioned counterparts within Canada: the Canadian Association of Social Workers/Association Canadienne des travailleurs sociaux (CASW/ACTS) with the IFSW; the Canadian Association of Schools of Social Work/Association Canadienne des écoles de service social (CASSW/ACESS) with the IASSW; and the International Council on Social Welfare Canada/Conseil international de l'action sociale (ICSW-Canada-CIAS) with the ICSW. The Canadian ICSW-CIAS contingent has been inactive for the last several years, but ICSW has on its international board Marcel Lauziere, executive director of the Canadian Council on Social Development (CCSD), who represents the voice of Canada's progressive social welfare community. Because they have both a national presence and significant international ties of long duration—since 1928–1929—this triad of NGOs may be classified in UN language as "international non-governmental organizations" (INGOs).

It bears noting that many individuals are involved in more than one of these national organizations and/or their international equivalents. In general, participation is open to those in the broad field of social welfare who endorse a worldview that recognizes the connectedness of personal and political events and the interdependence of all peoples and all environments.

PROBLEMS OF DEFINITION

It is equally difficult for those new and old to the field of social welfare to make discrete distinctions among a plethora of linked terms such as "comparative social welfare," "international social welfare," "social development," and "international social work."

Barker (1999) defines *social welfare* as a "nation's system of programs, benefits, and services that help people meet those social, economic, educational and health needs that are fundamental to the maintenance of society," and he defines *comparative social welfare* as an "analysis of the alternatives for providing the social services, economic, educational, and health care needs of a nation or social group by reviewing how different societies have addressed the same objectives."[9] Likewise, Hokenstad (1992) confirms that "international social welfare (sometimes referred to as 'comparative social welfare' or 'comparative social policy') has been concerned largely with the social welfare policies and human services of different countries"[10]

In the international context, *social development* is linked with economic development, the latter dealing with the technological and material aspects of growth and the former with its human aspects. The two maintain a dynamic tension between them, in part because some people are ideologically committed to the idea that economic growth, including free trade, is a necessary antecedent to social growth. At the same time proponents of social development argue that there are limits to growth, and they point to environmental disasters as support for their position. It must be said that it relatively easier to "count" economic progress through such measurements as the Gross National Product or the Gross Domestic Product of nations, its citizens' per capita incomes, unemployment statistics, a nation's debt load, and other benchmarks that the International Monetary Fund (IMF), the World Bank (WB), and the Organisation of Economic Cooperation and Development (OECD) use. Likewise, those whose major interests lie in social development have been "counting," too, but their sums include human rights abuses, infant mortality rates, the incidence of child labour, numbers of refugees, genocides, and unequal distribution of the world's wealth. It is this constant tension about the nature of development that underpins most of the

ongoing Canadian controversy regarding the North American Free Trade Agreement (NAFTA) and the grassroots campaign against Canada's role in negotiating the Multilateral Agreement on Investment (MAI), in 1998–1999, which resulted in the latter's defeat, or will do in the near future. The protagonists in the development debates squared off in highly public ways in the Vancouver protests against the meeting of the Organization of Petroleum Exporting Countries (OPEC) in 1999, and in the international protests against the Seattle Round of the World Trade Organization (WTO) negotiations, also in 1999. One might observe that the same sophisticated technologies—notably, electronic mail and satellite television—that highly developed countries produced through research and development, were also the means by which thousands of citizens could mount a well-organized and visible international campaign against what they viewed as an overemphasis on economic development for "the few" at the expense of social development by and for "the many."

Claire Huene provides perhaps the shortest and most global working definition of *development*, both material and spiritual: "development is an improvement in the total human condition."[11] It is also a long hard process.

Consistent with Huene's definition, Barker describes *social development* as "planned comprehensive social change designed to improve people's general welfare" and points out that "the interrelatedness of major social problems requires the economic and cultural efforts of national and international government structures and society's institutions and all of its citizens."[12] As Splane has noted, national policy and the international agencies concerned with development should aim to ensure that such services are created and made accessible to all sectors of society.[13] However, in many developing countries, poverty, illiteracy, overpopulation, war, and the unequal distribution of wealth and power block their people's attaining the range and quality of the programs and services they need.

Historically, social work has been the predominant discipline within the social welfare field. Indeed, among themselves Canadian social workers have long been committed "to the development of resources to meet individual, group, national and international needs and aspirations; and to the achievement of social justice for all."[14] Defining *international social work* is not easy, and Barker describes it with good reason as a "term loosely applied to (1) international organizations using social work methods or personnel, (2) social work cooperation between countries, and (3) transfer between countries of methods or knowledge about social work."[15] Hokenstad (1992, p. 4) feels that international social work "should focus on the profession and practice in different parts of the world, especially the place of the organized profession in different countries, the different roles that social workers perform, the practice methods they use, the problems they deal with, and the many challenges they face," and ought to include "the practice of social work in international agencies and programs." Healy writes: "International social work is defined as international professional action and the capacity for international action by the social work profession and its members. International action has four dimensions: internationally related domestic practice and advocacy, professional exchange, international practice, and international policy development and advocacy."[16]

The problems in defining international social work represent far more than perverse intellectual enterprises by worldwide social work educational institutions and professional social work practitioners. Operationalizing the multiple definitions of international social work presents many challenges. (To pursue a comprehensive review of social work history, practice, policy, and education in an international perspective, see the recent work of Dr. Lynne M. Healy.)[17]

First, more and more Canadian social workers are registered members of fully self-governing professions, with the same professional rights and duties of care as the more traditional professions such as law and medicine. To what extent can a provincial or territorial association's disciplinary provisions be enforced in an offshore or foreign setting, particularly one that lacks comparable legal provisions? What are the risks of two-tiered practice? In other words, can or should Canadian social workers tolerate a standard of practice abroad that they would not accept in their own jurisdictions?

Most social workers in North America, while committed to a common base of practice that includes macro-oriented approaches, are in fact employed in settings that offer social work interventions to individuals, families, and groups. Both Canadian and American educators and practitioners have frequently questioned the relevance of these micro approaches with populations who are marginalized, poor, ill-housed, and ill-fed, unemployed or underemployed, migrant or stateless. But the volume level of these voices rises even higher as we contemplate exporting micro-level models of intervention to developing countries. Such wholesale export is a great risk, given the pre-eminence of North American education materials and, by implication, this continent's practices, on the world stage.

One artifact of teaching and practising social work in a developing country is the sheer economic incapacity of publishing and disseminating knowledge about culturally relevant, indigenous, and alternative models of intervention there. Furthermore, these dissenting voices have queried whether such interventions can be applied to those same populations living in our own nation.

After all, Canada is a country constructed from influxes of immigrants and refugees—with one notable exception. In this country, most schools and faculties of social work education, along with social agencies, have listened to these newcomers and modified their curricula and their client service practices so they could introduce or emphasize culturally competent practice, a respect for diversity, and inclusion. And, venturing outside Canada, the best of us have focused on local capacity-building as opposed to practising educational and micro-practice imperialism.[18]

Hokenstad, Khinduka, and Midgley also note the many arguments that a "macro-oriented developmental approach would be more appropriate" in developing countries, and that a "social development-oriented approach would stress social change, social policy, planning, social action and community development rather than individual counselling or casework."[19] They conclude (1992, p. 186) that, "because social work is a contextual profession, its strategies of intervention should be relevant to the environment in which they are applied." They add that the "defense of human rights, the empowerment of people, universal access to services, and a fair distribution of resources must remain priorities for social workers wherever they practice."

CANADIAN ATTITUDES TOWARD INTERNATIONAL ISSUES

Canada's attitudes and actions on international issues might best be described as ambivalent and variable, particularly in the last decade and a half. There is little parliamentary debate about international aid funds; emergency relief for countries that suffer natural disasters tends to be late and paltry, given the depth of Canada's resources, and when such crises are declared these funds often seem to be given grudgingly. Media coverage of these issues is erratic and frequently confined to hot-button issues such as illegal immigrants' arriving on our shores by boat or presenting themselves at our international airports with no personal documentation or to the violent behaviour of some members of our vaunted peacekeeping forces while abroad.

The terrorist attacks on the World Trade Towers in New York, September 11, 2001, and the subsequent "war on terror" declared by President George W. Bush of the United States led the governments of that country and Canada to pass legislation restricting some of the traditional freedoms their own citizens have enjoyed. Given that human rights stand at the centre of most United Nations declarations and conventions, these restrictions have caused internal dissent in both countries and dissent between the bulk of the world's developed countries and Canada's closest neighbour and trading partner, the United States, as well. In such a climate, international sharing is less likely.

In fact, Canada carries out much of its involvement on the world stage more quietly, through its active membership as a UN states party, and through the many links and affiliations that individual Canadians maintain around the globe. Canada is a multicultural country with ethnic roots in many parts of the world, and its citizens travel widely and warmly welcome visitors from abroad. Their international relationships encompass individual friendships and a variety of professional, religious, fraternal, educational, scientific, and business associations. Transnational corporations, only some of which have headquarters in Canada, employ thousands of Canadians at home and abroad. Canadian governments have consistently encouraged international investment and have frequently reiterated the need for Canadians to compete with the rest of the world.

THE UNITED NATIONS CONNECTION

The UN carries out its social development and social welfare mandate through a complex legislative and administrative structure, comprising various programs and organs—such as the UN International Children's Fund, popularly known as UNICEF, and the Office of the UN High Commissioner for Refugees—as well as specialized agencies and autonomous organizations within the UN system. The International Labour Organization (ILO), the World Health Organization (WHO), and the UN Educational, Scientific and Cultural Organization (UNESCO) would be familiar examples for Canadians.

The parliamentary forum of the UN is the General Assembly, which represents roughly 180 nations, known in the UN's arcane language as "states parties." Most of the state parties are from the developing world, and each party, large or small, exercises a single and equal vote. As a result, the General Assembly has increasingly become the voice promoting economic and social development in the developing world. In 1974, the General Assembly approved a plan known as the New International Economic Order (NIEO), intended, over time, to eliminate the vast inequalities between the developed industrial countries—largely Europe and the northern parts of Asia and the Americas—and the industrially underdeveloped countries—largely the southern hemisphere. Indeed, Canada's North–South Institute (NSI) continues to tackle this challenge.

The NIEO wished to end some forms of aid—notably, tied aid—and to work on the progressive elimination of tariffs and barriers to trade that had kept Third World countries out of First World markets. It also aimed to reduce the debt burdens of less developed countries, to increase aid to promote scientific and technological infrastructures, and to introduce measures to curb undesirable activities by transnational corporations.

Another principal organ of the UN in addition to its General Assembly is the Economic and Social Council, known as ECOSOC. This body carries out the UN's functions regarding international economic, social, cultural, education, health, and related matters. The NIEO exercises much of its influence through this group. ECOSOC and its specialized agencies also acknowledge the importance of the international non-governmental organizations (INGOs) that work in social and economic development, and it grants "consultative status" to those it deems to have made significant contributions toward meeting its objectives—for example, the International Federation of Social Workers (IFSW) and the International Council on Social Welfare (ICSW).

The pace of social and economic development is slow, and this has always concerned the UN and its specialized agencies. As an additional means of attracting attention to this problem, the UN has designated "years" in which to direct the world's attention toward the needs of particular populations, and it has sponsored a number of world conferences—often referred to as "summits"—on specific aspects of development. So we have seen the Year of the Child, in 1979; of the Disabled, in 1981; of Youth, in 1985; of the Homeless, in 1987; of Indigenous Peoples, in 1992; of the Family, in 1994; and of Older Persons, in 1999.

Significant world conferences and their ensuing declarations have included the UN Conference on the Human Environment in 1972, and its famous Stockholm Declaration, plus its offspring, Environment and Development in 1992 in

Rio de Janeiro—now known as the Earth Summit—and, subsequently, the Kyoto Conference on Climate Change in 1997, with the issuance of the Kyoto Protocol, to oversee planned reductions in greenhouse gas emissions around the world. Some of the other key UN Conferences include Human Settlements (Habitat), in 1976 in Vancouver; Forward-Looking Strategies for the Advancement of Women in 1985 in Nairobi, Kenya; Developmental Social Welfare Policies and Programmes for the Near Future in Vienna in 1987; the Human Rights Summit, in 1993, also in Vienna; and the 1995 World Summit for Social Development in Copenhagen.

While all of the UN "Years of " conferences and summits have contributed greatly to the quality of our life on planet Earth, one that deserves special recognition is the Brundtland Commission and its report, *Our Common Future* (1987). It led to the Montreal Protocol of 1987 to protect the ozone layer. The General Assembly had established the World Commission on Environment and Development (WCED) (1984) "to assess the extent of the damage, and propose new forms of co-operation that would break out of existing patterns and policies."[20] The WCED became known as the Brundtland Commission because of the competence of its outstanding chair, Gro Harlem Brundtland, then the prime minister of Norway. That commission gave meaning to the phrase "sustainable development." This report defined the concept as "development which meets the needs of the present without compromising the ability of future generations to meet their own needs" (*Development*, p. 29).

The social work profession within Canada and elsewhere has long focused on person-in-environment transactions and it found validation of its unique perspective in *Our Common Future*. The report clearly states that "establishing a sustainable relationship between people, resources, environment and development hinges upon several commitments, such as tackling poverty and the debt issue; planning the family; investing in people; achieving food security and preserving soils and forests; caring for biodiversity, water and oceans; [and] making sound energy choices" (*Development*, p. 31). The report produced an agenda the world can truly live with.

Many Canadians feel an attachment to the UN and its agencies that can be understood only symbolically. Like many other members of a developed world in which technology and the information culture flourish, Canadians have come to "exhaust ourselves in the pursuit of the immediate and the minor, to the neglect of the real dangers that lie ahead."[21] Our preference for competition over cooperation, about the widening gaps among the generations, the prevalent encouragement of self-interest to the exclusion of group well-being and the measurement of success by solely individual standards have all left us with reciprocal longings for affiliation, intergenerational continuity, social solidarity, and community achievement—which includes achieving a sense of community or at least a common cause. The UN and its agencies speak to this hunger for solidarity, meaning in life, connectedness, and the historical superiority of cooperative human efforts, even though we may often feel that emptiness is frequently at a symbolic level rather than a manifest one.

CANADIAN GOVERNMENTS AND INTERNATIONAL SOCIAL DEVELOPMENT

Canada has a creditable record in its support of most of the UN's major endeavours. Of singular but often forgotten importance is the fact that Canada has ratified and not only signed most of the UN Human Rights instruments, including the Convention on the Rights of the Child, the Convention Relating to the Status of Refugees, the Convention on the Prevention and Punishment of the Crime of Genocide, the International Covenant on Economic, Social and Cultural Rights, and the Convention on the Elimination of All Forms of Discrimination Against Women.

This may not seem so remarkable unless one notices that the United States has signed but not ratified the conventions on Economic, Social and Cultural Rights, the Elimination of All Forms of Discrimination Against Women, and the International Convention on the Elimination of All Forms of Racial Discrimination. The United States—along with Somalia—still has yet to ratify the Convention on the Rights of the Child, "the most widely accepted human-rights convention in history."[22]

Arguably, Canada's history of peace-keeping missions has garnered us the most acclaim for the most sustained period of time. The Canadian government began to make this contribution in 1947–1948 when it sent Canadian troops to observe and supervise free elections in South Korea, and Canada has continued to assist the UN Security Council in maintaining law and order in Cyprus, preventing violation of the Camp David Accords in Egypt/Sinai, and investigating human rights violations and setting up an elections process in El Salvador, among many other missions.

Perhaps the mission to the former Yugoslavia in 1992 marked Canada's shifted emphasis from peacekeeping to peacemaking, which simultaneously signalled a major shift in Canadian foreign policy. The country moved away from defending itself from conventional threats to its security to defending itself from unconventional threats. Knox describes this new priority as the "well-being of people rather than states," and what the then Foreign Affairs minister, the Honourable Lloyd Axworthy, called "human security."[23]

While this view challenges traditional views of the military's proper role, it does accord with the tone of *Our Common Future* and it has resonance for many in the Canadian social development community. We confront economic realities in these peacekeeping and peacemaking plans: what proportion of the Department of National Defence's budget—consistently shaved during the 1990s—can be allocated to these humanitarian efforts in deploying troops abroad, in postings where the missions are highly stressful, and perhaps more so than sending them into active combat?

Canada broke with a 50-year tradition when it acted on its North Atlantic Treaty Organization (NATO) membership by participating in the 1999 bombing of Kosovo, an action that the UN Security Council (the UN organization with primary responsibility for maintaining global peace and security) neither approved nor condemned.[24] The UN's Secretary-General at the time, Kofi Annan, "described as tragic the failure to gain Security Council approval...."[25]

CANADA AND OFFICIAL DEVELOPMENT ASSISTANCE

The area of external aid—Official Development Assistance (ODA)—generates the most controversy among Canadians. They remember Canada's own mini-recession in the early 1990s, the dismantling of the country's social safety net—chiefly, the 1996 cancellation of the Canada Assistance Plan and the substitution of its pale cousin, the Canada Health and Social Transfer—and the numbers of poor and homeless within our own borders. We might argue that not only have the numbers of the poor increased, but their social and economic distance from the well-off has also widened considerably, both at home and abroad.

Canada's policies on development have increasingly moved away from philanthropy toward cooperation, led by the Canadian International Development Agency (CIDA). The organization's massive review of Canada's development assistance policies resulted in the widely circulated report, *Sharing Our Future*, in 1987.[26] Included was an ODA Charter, which listed the principles and priorities of Official Development Assistance. Both *Sharing Our Future* and the ODA Charter received broad support from the Canadian social welfare community, particularly because of their decisiveness in "putting poverty first." Both documents promote the forward-looking concept of poverty as "lack of choice" and a "lack of access"—to education, jobs, income, services, and decision-making power—and both refer to "inequity in opportunities, in the distribution of the benefits of growth, and in social justice" and, finally, they observe the "underdevelopment of human potential" (*Sharing Our Future*, 1987). The UN recommends 0.7 percent of a nation's Gross National Product (GNP) as the standard by which to gauge a developed country's contribution to international development.

A Toronto *Globe and Mail* editorial is instructive: it refers to the commission, headed by then retired Prime Minister Lester Pearson (1969), to investigate foreign aid, and it concluded that "the widening gap between the developed and the developing countries has become the central problem of our times."[27] In Pearson's time, "the ratio of living standards among the world's richest countries was more than 40 to one.... Today, the same ratio is more than 70 to one... [and] the United Nations Human Development Report for 1999... stated that such inequalities 'have reached grotesque proportions'" (July 15, 1999). Pearson said, "We can no longer delude ourselves that the poverty and deprivation of the great majority of mankind can be

ignored without tragic consequences for all." Even the same *Globe and Mail* editorial concluded that "worsening poverty in much of the world is the root cause of the wars, terrorism and ecological catastrophes that affect us all. Migration will ensure that inequalities between nations become internalized within nations."

In 1980, Canada reiterated its determination to meet this UN target of contributing 0.7 percent of its GNP, by increasing its financial appropriations annually. The Progressive Conservative government elected in 1984 under Brian Mulroney declared its dedication to raising ODA but stated that it might not be able to reach its goal by 1990; actual expenditures in 1989–1990 amounted to 0.45 percent of our GNP.[28] At the 1992 Earth Summit, the Canadian Environment minister once again committed Canada to increasing this aid to 0.7 percent of its GNP, a reaffirmation met with skepticism bordering on disbelief, given that cuts to aid budgets were common knowledge. By 1998, our ODA assistance had fallen to 0.34 percent of GNP, and by 2002 that contribution had shrunk to 0.28 of Gross National Income, or about $3.15 billion dollars. (To be fair, it should be noted that, "due to inflation and changes in exchange rates, the value of that aid increased" over 2001.)[29]

Canadian Council for International Cooperation (CCIC) released a report in 2004, *The Reality of Aid*, on behalf of a consortium of aid agencies and development groups, that expressed this fear: "Current attempts to divert resources for poverty reduction to pay for donors' security interests are the most serious expression... of aid resources being hijacked to fund rich-country priorities."[30]

In 2002, world leaders vowed to cut the world's poverty rate in half by 2015, as part of the United Nations Millennium Development Goals. Clearly, the events of the "war on terror" have prompted many developed nations to consider using funds formerly devoted to aid in other countries for their own national security. For example, even Denmark, long a leader in international assistance, now "demands that aid to countries be dependent on their active involvement in the war on terror."[31]

Although it may be less true today, sometimes the phrase "the use of aid to promote domestic imports" creeps into nations' discussions of international aid. This is an oblique reference to "tied aid"— that is, aid that depends on the recipient country using aid monies to "purchase" products from the donor country. On moral grounds, such arrangements cannot be seen as anything but self-serving to the donor country and, therefore, quite beyond the concept of "gift" in the philanthropic sense. Such arrangements demonstrate even less a joint partnership in the sense outlined in *Sharing Our Future* (1987).

Cohen is vehement in asserting that "the challenge of the next century is to reform aid, not abandon it."[32] He believes that foreign aid is a moral society's duty and that we must give it with our eyes wide open: "aid is more than a balance sheet. It is an obligation, which ought to be in the self-interest of the moral society, even when its pecuniary return suggests otherwise" (Cohen, April 1999).

It appears that the goals of the ODA Charter (1987) are unlikely to be realized in the near future, Canada's unimpeachable rhetoric notwithstanding. We might wish that our share were commensurate with our uniquely privileged position.

Also, we cannot ignore the fact that Canada has now been reprimanded twice by ECOSOC, once in 1993 and again on December 4, 1998.[33] The UN Committee on Economic, Social and Cultural Rights castigated Canadian governments for the way Canada treats the poor, especially women and children; for failing to provide an adequate standard of living, and the provincial courts for not protecting that right. The committee also attacked our treatment of Aboriginal people; the successive restrictions made to Unemployment/Employment Insurance; the clawback of the National Child Benefit—so that the majority of families on welfare receive none of this federal money; the issue of homelessness and Canada's failure to provide adequate housing for the poor; minimum wage laws, the growth of food banks, and policies that do not support single mothers and persons with disabilities. And, finally, the committee criticized our immigration and our student loan policies (Edmonton Social Planning Council, 1999). These are matters of import on the world stage, as well as internally, but they seem unfamiliar to us.

When Canadian governments and INGOs do decide on an action plan, they tend to move decisively and successfully. Moving from making war to peacekeeping to peacemaking over a span of five decades is a remarkable achievement, in the light of a rather longer history of world conflict. Canada's membership in the Group of Seven (with the United States, Japan, Germany, France, Italy, and Britain), and in the Group of Eight (add Russia), gives us a voice at the table with the rest of the world's major industrial powers, who have been most recently concerned with the debt burden on poor countries and with the late 1990s financial crises in East Asia, Russia, and Brazil that "reversed, in a matter of months, the economic and social gains of many decades."[34] Speaking at the World Economic Forum in Davos, Switzerland, in January 2004, Prime Minister Paul Martin announced forgiveness of $750 million of the debt that Iraq incurred to Canada between 1987 and 1990.[35]

Likewise, a Canadian former Foreign Affairs minister, Lloyd Axworthy, won acclaim for Canada's principled leadership in human security, with the 1997 Land Mine Treaty, "banning the manufacture, transfer, use and stockpiling of anti-personnel land mines...."[36] The then Prime Minister, Jean Chrétien (March 1999), announced a debt-relief plan to support poverty reduction in the world's poorest countries. By December 1999, Bangladesh was the first country to have 100 percent of the $600 000 it owed to Canada erased.[37]

In so doing, Canada was supporting an initiative of both the World Bank Group's president James Wolfensohn and the Archbishop of Canterbury, George Carey—and also involving many secular groups in what is known as the Jubilee Project. While this may seem an uncommon liaison, both have written that "in reality, we share the same dream: to eliminate poverty."[38] The issue of world poverty is a difficult one for Canadians to grapple with, beset as they are with unsolved issues of income redistribution at home and child poverty in our own nation in a time of relative plenty. Cynics wonder whether we can change the world when we seem to have difficulty changing our own country, one in which charity and targeted programs have become substitutes for a comprehensive safety net.

The deep importance of international trade to Canada's economic success is also a subject of internal conflict. International trade with nations well known for their human rights abuses makes Canadians deeply suspicious. It was, after all, a Canadian, John Peters Humphrey, who as UN Secretariat human rights director from 1946 to 1966 wrote the original draft of the International Declaration of Human Rights, essentially proclaiming human rights as universal and indivisible.

Canada was also "the first nation in the world to introduce crucial legislation paving the way for membership in a permanent international court aimed at prosecuting war criminals."[39] Representatives from 160 countries met in Rome in 1998 and agreed to rules to establish such a court, but at least 60 countries had to adopt compliance legislation and ratify the Rome deal before the court could be established. Canada began this legislative process before any other country. It should be noted, here, that "although there are currently world criminal courts with jurisdiction over conflicts in Yugoslavia and Rwanda, the International Criminal Court (ICC) would be the first permanent body" (Laghi, December 10, 1999).

Canada has been honourably represented on the world stage by its former Supreme Court justice Louise Arbour, who took on "the arduous role of chief prosecutor at the UN war-crimes tribunal in The Hague and return[ed] to Canada in 1999 to serve on the Supreme Court."[40] Her resignation from that august body in June 2004 was occasioned by her nomination, by the UN's Secretary-General, Kofi Annan, to the post of United Nations High Commissioner for Human Rights, for the next four years. As Kirk Makin of the *Globe and Mail* notes, "Judge Arbour is the second Canadian named to an important human-rights post in the last twelve months. Former Canadian diplomat Philippe Kirsch was elected president—in effect the chief magistrate—of the new International Criminal Court last March (2003)."[41] Louise Frechette—also a Kofi Annan nominee and a former deputy minister of Defence—must also be acknowledged in her ongoing position as Deputy Secretary-General of the United Nations. Malone states she "has played a vital role in co-ordinating the UN's many agencies and programs, and in developing strategies to enhance the UN's role on development issues."[42]

THE SOCIAL WELFARE NGO

Globalization, and especially the flows of corporate capital, appears to be decreasing the degree of influence the federal and provincial governments in Canada once held, increasing city-state revival and leading to a rapid expansion of the non-profit and voluntary sectors.[43] Indeed, the Canadian International Development Agency (CIDA) focused its 1999 annual report on the relationship between civil society and global change, defining "civil society" as comprising "nonprofit agencies, service clubs, religious organizations, unions, professional associations, and other community groups."[44] CIDA's September 2000 report lists its development priorities as "a strengthening of resources devoted to basic education, health and nutrition, HIV/AIDS, and child protection, with gender equality as an integral part of all these priority areas."[45]

In this section, we will deal with three international social welfare NGOs, each with a history of more than 75 years, and each with a legacy of enduring Canadian involvement.

The first meeting of the International Conference of Social Work was held in Paris in 1928, with the outstanding social welfare leader and physician, Dr. Rene Sand of Belgium, as its chair. During a "social welfare fortnight," participants from 41 countries, and all the continents, laid the groundwork for what later became the International Council on Social Welfare (ICSW), the International Federation of Social Workers (IFSW), both around 1928, and the International Association of Schools of Social Work (IASSW), about 1929.[46] Plans were made at this historic 1928 meeting to hold periodic conferences, and two more were organized before World War II. At the post-war conference in 1948, attendees decided to meet biennially and this has been the practice ever since.

These three international organizations—governed by separate boards of directors and staffed by comparatively small secretariats—have developed programs to advance their interests and objectives. Simply stated, the IFSW serves the social work profession, the IASSW is the voice of social work education, and the ICSW is concerned with all aspects of social welfare.

THE IFSW AND THE CASW

IFSW is the successor to the International Permanent Secretariat of Social Workers, founded in Paris in 1928, and active until the outbreak of World War II. However, not until the 1950 International Conference of Social Work in Paris was a decision made to create the IFSW as the international organization of professional social workers, and to include seven national organizations as members. This decision was enacted at the time of the International Conference on Social Welfare in Munich in 1956, and the Canadian Association of Social Workers (CASW) was a founding member of the federation, whose member associations now number approximately 80 national professional social work associations.

The federation is entirely self-reliant. It receives no sustaining funding from any level of any national government, which permits it a remarkable degree of independence in social policy and human rights matters. The member associations have been diligent about paying dues revenues—individually and/or on behalf of other associations, in a gesture of solidarity—and non-dues revenues arising from service contracts—such as a three-year international HIV/AIDS project funded by the World Health Organization. While IFSW is not an individual-membership organization, individuals and groups with a particular interest in international social work may become involved through the Friends of Social Work program, instituted in 1990.

Consistent with its aims, IFSW promotes the profession internationally through a variety of programs and activities. Its member associations are united by a common Code of Ethics, as well as a Declaration of Ethical Principles, and maintain a Permanent Committee on Ethical Issues. The IFSW also insists on common minimum standards for social work education credentials from the professional association of any country applying for admission. It assists national associations of social workers seeking admittance to IFSW and has encouraged many mutually beneficial "twinning" partnerships both in terms of cash and in kind between associations in developed and developing countries. IFSW awards a number of small development grants annually from the accrued interest on the Jane Hoey Development Fund, while running auctions at biennial and regional IFSW symposia—often held in conjunction with IASSW congresses—to help delegates from developing nations attend subsequent symposia. A quality newsletter in the three official IFSW languages, Spanish, French, and English, plus study visits, the publication of policy papers to guide member bodies in effecting common international policies and practices among individual professional social workers, and an excellent webpage all contribute to forging a sense of identity and solidarity among the world's social workers.

Key to this sense of solidarity has been the IFSW Human Rights Commission. The Stockholm General Meeting mandated its creation in 1988, appointing a commissioner—and, often, an alternative commissioner—from each of the five IFSW regions. For a decade after the commission's inception, its secretary was Terry Bamford of the United Kingdom, who also served as social work's permanent representative to Amnesty International, with which the commission remains linked today. More recently, Dr. Jim Ife of Australia has served as the secretary of the Asia and Pacific Region (he is a senior academic who has also taught social work in Canada); he was followed by Elis Enval of Sweden, a former IFSW president.

Using an "emergency alert" system similar to Amnesty's, the commission lobbies for the rights of individual social workers and social work students who are imprisoned, often without benefit of formal charges, legal counsel, a trial, or any other acceptable form of "due process," and for the tortured and "the disappeared." More recently, activities have included monitoring elections in East Timor, followed by high-level consultations with the "new" government officials there, surrounding the contributions that social workers, world around, could make to their social redevelopment efforts.[47] It bears noting again, as earlier in this chapter, that the technological advances in communication have greatly enhanced the commission's ability to respond promptly to various events around the world. Also, the IFSW Human Rights Commission does not confine its activities solely to the less-developed parts of the world; currently, this body expresses considerable concern about the existence of the death penalty in the United States, arguably the most powerful nation in terms of influence.

One of the achievements of the IFSW Secretariat and the Human Rights Commission, working in concert with IASSW, has been their drafting of a human rights manual and curriculum for schools of social work and the social work profession, and there have been revisions of these since then.[48]

The UN's ECOSOC, UNICEF, and UNESCO have all granted the IFSW consultative status. IFSW is also on the International Labour Organization's Special List of NGOs. At the regional level, IFSW cooperates with the Council of Europe and with the European Community by means of formally established Liaison Committees—unheard of under the North American Free Trade Agreement. Additionally, IFSW is well served by its representatives at the UN/New York, the UN/Geneva, the

UN/Vienna, UNESCO/Paris, WHO/Europe, and Sage Publications, London, which publish the journal *International Social Work*.

The Canadian Association of Social Workers (CASW), a founding member of IFSW, has demonstrated its consistent commitment to IFSW, and "hosted the world" for the third time, in Montreal in 2000, in concert with IASSW. At this meeting the IASSW joined the IFSW as a partner in the latter's Human Rights Commission.

We note two historical peculiarities here: first, for a brief interval, in 1988, the presidents of IFSW, IASSW, and ICSW were all Canadians; second, only the Alberta Association of Registered Social Workers has consistently had one of its members on the IFSW executive, from 1978 to 2003.

Further, Eugenia Moreno, the fluently trilingual executive director of CASW, currently serves as chair of the IFSW Nominations Committee.

THE IASSW AND THE CASSW

The second of the three "sister organizations" is the International Association of Schools of Social Work, currently housed with the (US) Council on Social Work Education, Alexandria, Virginia, after a long period in Vienna (1978–1993) under the leadership of Secretary-General Dr. Vera Mehta and its Canadian president, Dr. Ralph Garber (its current president being a resident of England).

The IASSW membership comprises more than 400 schools and faculties of social work, of the 1700 affiliated schools. They are linked regionally, sub-regionally, and nationally in schools representing approximately 70 countries. The association has played a highly effective role in promoting professional social work education in both the developed and developing world. It offers consultation and other direct services to schools of social work, organizes workshops, seminars and conferences, advises governmental and nongovernmental bodies on social work personnel and training, and publishes books, documents, and teaching materials pertaining to social work education. Of particular note is the book *Reflections on Social Work Education 1950–1978*, which traces the intriguing story of social work education over a period of 50 years, belying its title.[49]

The IASSW has consultative status with the UN, including UNICEF and UNESCO, the Council of Europe, and the Organization of American States, and has been consulted extensively on training for community and social development. It has contributed to many UN seminars and expert groups and has submitted recommendations at meetings of the UN Commission for Social Development and to the World Bank.

The Canadian Association of Schools of Social Work (CASSW) is the Canadian member of IASSW, and Canadian social work educators have played an important part in the international body's global activities, serving on major committees as overseas consultants and collaborating in research and demonstration projects. Additionally, they have helped seek resources to promote social work education and social development training in developing countries, often with the assistance of CIDA, to give a specifically Canadian example, including training paraprofessionals for work in rural and urban communities. Of recent importance is Dr. Ralph Garber's *World Census of Social Work Education,* a state-of-the-art exposition presented to the Montreal 2000 Symposia to both IASSW and IFSW.

THE ICSW AND ICSW-CIAS-CANADA

The final agency to be given detailed consideration here is the International Council on Social Welfare. From 1928 until 1967, ICSW signified essentially the "International Conference on Social Work." The organization's goals were to provide an international forum for discussing social work, to promote the exchange of information and experience among social workers and social agencies, to facilitate and promote cooperation between international organizations related to social welfare, and to make the views of the social welfare field known to the UN.

With the implementation of a new constitution adopted in 1966 the council, while continuing to pursue its earlier objectives and to stage international and regional conferences, became a more action-oriented organization committed to fostering a developmental social welfare agenda.

The ICSW has strengthened its UN consultative status with ECOSOC, UNICEF, FAO, ILO, WHO, UNESCO, the Council of Europe, and the Organization of American States.

Although it has had continued success with its international conferences and has performed strongly in some regions, it has not achieved all of its objectives to the degree originally anticipated 30-plus years ago. The council approved a further restructuring plan of itself in 1979, and major changes were made between 1998 and 2000, under the leadership of Julian Disney, then the ICSW's president (from Australia). One of the changes meant moving the ICSW International offices from Montreal, where they had been for nearly a decade after their initial move from their long-term site in Vienna, to (chiefly) London, Uganda, and Kuala Lumpur. The North American Region/Committee, of which ICSW-Canada-CIAS was a part, has become comparatively less active and, within Canada, a great deal of the local work that ICSW might ordinarily have undertaken now falls to the Canadian Council on Social Development, with its own 75-plus year his-

tory of leadership in national social development and social welfare. Ironically, too, the council had first sponsored ICSW-Canada, many years earlier. CCSD's executive director sits on the ICSW board, and so maintains a strong Canadian presence within that body.

Currently, in 2004, ICSW is a federation of "national committees," or national associations, with three categories of membership. Category A National Committees include organizations that represent "a wide range of non-governmental organisations within their own country which seek to enhance social welfare and social development."[50] Category A includes such National Committees as the Australian Council of Social Services, the Finnish Federation for Social Welfare, the Hungary Alliance for Social Professionals, and the Consejo Uruguayo de Bienestar Social. ICSW's Category B International Member Organizations include "global and regional organisations [who] can become ICSW members if they are non-governmental organisations and seek to enhance social welfare and social development" (Web address, January 5, 2000). A partial list of these organizations includes the International Social Service, the International Council of Jewish Women, and the International Federation of Red Cross and Red Crescent Societies. Category C of ICSW membership includes those "organisations which seek to enhance social welfare and social welfare development but have not joined as National Committees or International Member Organisations [wherein] each member is registered as a member in relation to the ICSW region in which it is based" (Web address, January 5, 2000).

ICSW has focused its major programs on the recommendations of the UN World Summit on Social Development in Copenhagen in 1995, and on what ICSW calls Copenhagen +5, emphasizing the importance of regional consultations in contributing to ICSW's program priorities.

It is a matter of hope and dream that IFSW and IASSW can join, once more, with their sister organization in common cause in the international arena.

CONCLUSION

Canada's role in international social work and social welfare is a story of grand leadership and faltering visions. It is also a history of more than 75 years of partnership among three major Canadian social work, social work education, and social welfare organizations. Since their inception in 1928–1929, these bodies have had the courage and the foresight to believe that a relatively new country had a role and a responsibility to play on the world stage, and they believed in partnership rather than competition in the arena of international intervention.

For Canadian social work and social welfare activists, "privilege" has always meant assuming more responsibility for the world's condition, not less. They have taken seriously, and will continue to do so, the observation of former Czechoslovakian president Vaclav Havel in his book, *Summer Meditations*: "People need to hear that it makes sense to behave decently or to help others, to place common interests above their own, to respect the elementary rules of human coexistence."[51]

NOTES

1. Dr. Richard B. Splane, Professor Emeritus and internationally known Canadian policy expert and scholar, was solely responsible for the chapter "Canada's role in international social welfare" in the first and second editions of *Canadian Social Welfare* (1982 & 1986). He and I co-authored the chapter in the third edition (1995). I acknowledge with great gratitude the previous and present contributions of Dr. Splane to the current material, and his lifelong dedication to social work and social welfare, nationally and internationally.

2. Senator Douglas Roche, The real meaning of peace, *Globe and Mail* (April 29, 1985), p. A7.

3. Senator Roche retired from the Senate of Canada in June 2004.

4. The best and worst places to live, *Report on Business* Magazine, *Globe and Mail* (January 1996), pp.18–19.

5. B. Little, Canada's latest report card has disappointing marks, *Globe and Mail* (October 4, 2003), B1.

6. Ibid.

7. Ibid.

8. Ibid.

9. R. Barker (1999), *The Social Work Dictionary* (4th edn.) (Washington, DC: NASW Press), pp. 92, 455.

10. M. Hokenstad (1992), The world of international social work. In M. Hokenstad, S. Khinduka, & H. Midgley (Eds.), *Profiles in International Social Work* (Washington, DC: NASW Press), p. 4.

11. C. Huene (1991), Ama llulla, ama sua, ama kella. *Participatory Development Review, 2(1)*, p. 8,

12. Barker, p. 448.

13. R. Splane (1986), Canada's role in international social welfare. *Canadian Social Welfare* (2d edn.) (Don Mills, ON: Collier Macmillan).

14. CASW (1983) (R. Ramsay, Ed.), *Code of Ethics* (Ottawa: CASW), p. 2.

15. Barker, p. 250.

16. L. Healy (2001), International social work: Professional action in an interdependent world. (New York: Oxford University Press).

17. Ibid.

18. M. Wilson & E. Whitmore (2000), *Seeds of fire: Social development in the era of globalization* (Halifax: Fernwood Books).

19. J. S. Hokenstad, S. Khinduka, & J. Midgley (Eds.) (1992), *Profiles in international social work* (Washington, D.C.: NASW Press), p. 185.

20. Canadian International Development Agency. (1992). Environment and development: The crucial decade. *Development*, p.28.

21. Polanyi, J. (1993). Science helped us get into this mess; now it must help us get out. In P. Elliott (Ed.), *Rethinking the Future: Canada's Liveliest Minds Take on the Twenty-First Century.* Saskatoon: Fifth House, p. 58.

22. Stewart, M. Reform MP slams UNICEF vote on rights for children. *Calgary Herald* (July 27, 1999).

23. Knox. P. Future of the forces: At odds over Canada's fate. *Globe and Mail* (November 30, 1999), A12.

24. Gee, M. Canada's part in bombing violates 50-year tradition. *Globe and Mail* (March 30, 1999), A8.

25. Knox, P. UN's actions don't match its words on human rights. *Globe and Mail* (September 21, 1999), A15.

26. CIDA (1987), *Sharing our future: Canadian international development assistance* (Hull, PQ: Author), p. 23.

27. The aid imperative. *Globe and Mail* (July 15, 1999), A12.

28. CIDA (1990), *Annual Report 1989–90* (Hull, PQ: Author), p. 123.

29. E. Oziewicz, Shift of foreign aid funds to terror fight decried, *Globe and Mail*, (May 28, 2004), A10.

30. Ibid.

31. Ibid.

32. A. Cohen, No blank cheques. *Report on Business* Magazine (April, 1999), pp. 29–31,

33. National Anti-Poverty Organization, *NAPO News, 70* (July 1999); and Edmonton Social Planning Council, UN's message to Canada—You're failing to protect economic, social and cultural rights. *Edmonton Facts* (November 1999).

34. World's poor in danger, says UN chief. *Calgary Herald* (May 22, 1999).

35. D. Leblanc, Martin forgives Iraqi debt. *Globe and Mail* (January 24, 2004), A5.

36. P. Dalglish, Witness to war. *Globe and Mail* (February 18, 2000), A13.

37. Foreign aid: Canada forgives Bangladesh debt. *Globe and Mail* (December 10, 1999), A8.

38. C. Carey & J. Wolfensohn, How do you spell "debt relief"? *Globe and Mail* (June 17, 1999), A13.

39. B. Laghi, Ottawa prepares to blaze trail for world body. *Globe and Mail* (December 10, 1999), A4.

40. K. Makin, Supreme Court losing Arbour to UN post. *Globe and Mail* (February 21, 2004), A12.

41. Ibid.

42. D. Malone, A hero, not a saint. *Globe and Mail* (March 8, 2004), A11.

43. A. Picard, Citizens groups new agents of change: Researcher studies rapid worldwide growth of $90-billion non-profit sector. *Globe and Mail* (September 20, 1999), A2.

44. CIDA (1999), *Canadian development report 1999: Civil society and global change* (Hull, PQ: Author).

45. Canadian International Development Agency, *International Development Priorities: A Framework for Action* (September 2000) (Ottawa: CIDA).

46. A. Anciaux (1988), *Rene Sand and the culture of human values* (Ottawa: ICSW—Canada [English and French versions]). Published to mark the sixtieth anniversary of the First International Conference on Social Work.

47. J. Ife & E. Serrano, *The East Timor independence vote: Report of the IFSW observers* (September 10, 1999) (unpublished report, IFSW). Also, J. Ife, Report of assessment mission to East Timor (November 1999) (unpublished report, IFSW), pp. 13–22.

48. United Nations Centre for Human Rights, IFSW, IASSW (1992), *Human rights and social work: A manual for schools of social work and the social work profession* (Geneva and New York: Author, & T. Bamford, P. Dolan, E. Envall, G. Gilchrist-James, N. Hall, H. Jakobsson, V. Mehta, M. Molina-Molina, E. Mouravieff-Apostol, E. Balais-Serrano, & D. Van Soest).

49. K. Kendall (1978). *Reflections on social work education, 1950–1978* (New York and Vienna: International Association of Schools of Social Work).

50. ICSW (January 5, 2000):
www.icsw.org/structure_membership/mem bers_category/membersa.htm

51. M. Lisac, Havel's ideas apply to Alberta. *Edmonton Journal* (August 18, 1992), A6.

Index